Handbook

of TROPICAL AQUARIUM FISHES

Handbook

of TROPICAL

AQUARIUM FISHES

Dr. Herbert R. Axelrod
Editor, Tropical Fish Hobbyist Magazine

Dr. Leonard P. Schultz
Curator of Fishes, U.S.N.M., Smithsonian Institution,
Retired.

Distributed in the UNITED STATES by T.F.H. Publications, Inc., 211 West Sylvania Avenue, Neptune City, NJ 07753; in CANADA by H & L Pet Supplies Inc., 27 Kingston Crescent, Kitchener, Ontario N2B 2T6; Rolf C. Hagen Ltd., 3225 Sartelon Street, Montreal 382 Quebec; in ENGLAND by T.F.H. (Great Britain) Ltd., 11 Ormside Way, Holme-thorpe Industrial Estate, Redhill, Surrey RH1 2PX; in AUSTRALIA AND THE SOUTH PACIFIC by Pet Imports Pty. Ltd., Box 149, Brookvale 2100 N.S.W., Australia; in NEW ZEALAND by Ross Haines & Son, Ltd., 18 Monmouth Street, Grey Lynn, Auckland 2 New Zealand; in SINGAPORE AND MALAYSIA by MPH Distributors Pte., 71-77 Stamford Road, Singapore 0617; in the PHILIPPINES by Bio-Research, 5 Lippay Street, San Lorenzo Village, Makati, Rizal; in SOUTH AFRICA by Multipet Pty. Ltd., 30 Turners Avenue, Durban 4001. Published by T.F.H. Publications Inc., Ltd., the British Crown Colony of Hong Kong.

PREFACE

The phenomenal growth of interest in tropical fishes has for a long time indicated the need for a comprehensive handbook that would be useful to hobbyists and scientists alike. Both authors, independently, had contemplated writing a book of this kind: a book that would be practical and scientifically accurate; that would contain as much information as possible about every popular aquarium fish; that would illustrate every species with the best drawings, photographs, and color reproductions of fishes available today.

The story of how the authors met and overcame the tremendous problems involved is worth recounting. At first the great expense of obtaining illustrations and the physical problem of checking them against hundreds of species of fishes appeared to be an insurmountable barrier. Then, with the outbreak of the Korean War, Herbert R. Axelrod was recalled to service and was sent to Japan where he had the good fortune to meet Dr. Tokiharu Abe of the Japanese Fisheries Institute. Through Dr. Abe he met Mitsui Shirao, one of the world's leading fish artists, and commissioned him to illustrate some three hundred species of fresh-water tropical fishes.

Here at last was the key to this volume—the preparation of drawings. Still another problem remained—checking these illustrations against actual specimens and making accurate, positive identification of the species. This task could be done only at one of the largest museums where vast collections were stored. As Axelrod was leaving Japan, he was asked by Dr. Abe to take back some specimens of Japanese eels for Dr. Leonard P. Schultz, Curator of Fishes, United States National Museum, Smithsonian Institution, Washington, D.C. Thus the authors met and the last obstacle was overcome with access to the vast collections of fishes in the National Museum.

During the many months of research that went into the preparation of this book the authors obtained many additional illustrations including photographs in black and white and in color. Credit to the sources of all illustrations is given in the acknowledgments, though special thanks are due to Gerard J. M. Timmerman, whose photographs replaced many of Shirao's drawings because in some instances greater clarity could be achieved with photographic illustrations.

We believe that a few words about the organization and content of this book will help readers to make the best use of it both as a guide and as a reference book. The introductory chapters are devoted to a brief survey of ichthyology, the aquarium and its management, aquarium plants, and diseases of fishes. At the end of the book the reader will find a complete glossary and a list of selected references.

The larger part of the book—more than five hundred pages—is devoted to what we believe to be the most detailed and comprehensive descriptions of tropical fishes to be published in the world. Some five hundred fishes are illustrated and described from the point of view of identification, range, size, temperament, sex differences, breeding, temperature requirements, food, color patterns, etc. The numerous species discussed in this book are divided into categories called families; these are then arranged from the primitive or less specialized to the more complex. Under each family or subfamily the genera and species are listed. For the convenience of the hobbyist, all genera and species are arranged alphabetically within the family.

Every fish described here has been carefully checked for accurate identification. The illustration for each species has been compared with authentic specimens of that species; counts of scales and fin rays and close examinations of color patterns were made.

In the planning stage of this book we were faced with the problem of selecting those fishes which should be included in a handbook of this type. Our decision was to include every fish known to aquarists in America and offered for sale within the past ten years. The inclusion of many of these fishes presented certain problems in nomenclature, for we found that some of the scientific names used in other aquarium books were incorrect. Nearly every book published in the United States utilizes the incorrect generic name of *Barbus* for the genus *Puntius*. The genus *Corydoras* alone took many months of intensive research to clear up, to say nothing of the cichlids and egg-laying tooth carps. Since accuracy in identification was our paramount goal, we had no alternative but to introduce the scientifically correct names for all the aquarium fishes we included in the book.

In order to help the readers locate easily certain genera and species which they may have known under widely accepted but incorrect names, the index has been made as complete as possible. Not only are the fishes listed by their correct scientific names, but also by their popular names and by their incorrect, though familiar, scientific names. For example, suppose you know the fish *Barbus lateristriga*. The correct scientific name would be listed: *Puntius lateristriga* and *lateristriga, Puntius*. But also included in the index would be three other listings—*Barbus lateristriga* and the popular name spanner barb under the entries Spanner barb and Barb, spanner. Thus, by whatever name you know the fish, you will be able to find it easily in the index.

Most of the information in this book has been collected from firsthand experience and from research. The authors have checked this work many times but they realize that a book as complicated as this one may contain some errors or that some bit of information may have been overlooked. Should any reader come across an error or feel that important information has been omitted he is invited to convey his suggestions to the authors. There is no last word on fish behavior but the authors hope that this book will be a useful and worthwhile guide to everyone interested in tropical fishes.

HERBERT R. AXELROD

LEONARD P. SCHULTZ

PREFACE TO 1971 EDITION

When it was originally published in 1955 by McGraw-Hill Book Company, *Handbook of Tropical Aquarium Fishes* was an immediate hit because it so ably fulfilled its express purpose of being a handbook useful to both hobbyists and scientists alike.

Although the book remained popular for many years, going through a number of re-printings to satisfy the steady demand for it, it became somewhat replaced in the affections of hobbyists by books (such as the massive and extremely colorful looseleaf *Exotic Tropical Fishes*) that offered more in the way of color photographs and breeding information at a comparable price. But because the aquarium world would be the loser if such a truly excellent and comprehensive book as *Handbook of Tropical Aquarium Fishes* were allowed to go out of print completely, T.F.H. Publications decided to re-publish it at a competitive price. In today's world of spiraling publishing costs, the only way this could be done was to replace the color photographs and drawings with black and white illustrations and to cut down the page size of the book slightly.

This, the replacement of color photographs and drawings by black and white photographs and drawings, was accomplished in the 1969 edition, although in all other respects that edition of *Handbook of Tropical Aquarium Fishes* was almost exactly the same as the previous $15.00 editions; all of the information that gave the original its reputation for excellence was left intact.

When the 1969 edition, even without any color illustrations, sold out quickly, T.F.H. Publications decided to make the 1969 edition even bigger and better than it was by adding 32 pages of color, and this was accomplished in the present book, the 1971 edition, which contains numerous color photographs of fishes discussed in the text.

PREFACE TO THE 1983 EDITION

There are two wonderful things to be happy about as I write this new preface. First, with this new printing of 50,000 copies, the HANDBOOK OF TROPICAL AQUARIUM FISHES reaches over the million copy mark, making it an all-time best seller in the aquarium world. The second thing is that both Dr. Leonard Schultz and I are both still alive to enjoy this feat.

This new edition is made from completely new plates, new lithographs and new color photographs. It has still been kept to an economy edition to make its price as low as possible; it is still behind the times in some of the fish names that have become superseded; a number of the fish descriptions have been updated to show new nomenclature. But the quality of the printing, the paper and the binding have all been enhanced because with the larger printing (50,000 copies!) we are able to bring costs down substantially. This book is not, however, a substitute for the huge volume EXOTIC TROPICAL FISHES by Axelrod et al., with over 1,300 pages in the expanded edition, with almost every known aquarium fish illustrated in color.

This is, however, the best "buy" for the beginner. It is filled with good, solid information and for almost 20 years it was the best there was available at any price. I hope you find it rewarding.

It cannot be stressed too greatly that this book was historically correct 30 years ago. It has some advice which is not found in other books, such as the care of aquariums with metal frames, but there aren't many such aquariums to be found any more! Also, for example, in the 1950's an "all-glass" aquarium meant just that: one piece of glass glued together with silicone adhesive and rimmed top and bottom with a plastic molding. Keep this in mind when reading about the equipment recommended, too. The information contained herein is correct, even to this day, but the main value of this book is for its historical perspective.

Dr. Herbert R. Axelrod
March, 1983 Neptune, N.J.

ACKNOWLEDGMENTS

The authors wish to extend their thanks to all the aquarists and dealers who freely gave specimens and related their experiences. This group is so very large that an individual listing would be impossible.

To Dr. Tokiharu Abe and Mr. Mitsui Shirao of Tokyo, Japan, we express our special thanks for drawings in black and white and color. Mrs. Dorothea B. Schultz gave freely of her time in preparing 65 original drawings bearing her initials "DBS" and correcting in addition over 100 other illustrations. Most of her work was based upon specimens in the collections of the United States National Museum or elsewhere. Gerard J. M. Timmerman, through the courtesy of *Tropical Fish Hobbyist Magazine*, supplied many photographic illustrations, including all color photographs not otherwise credited below. Dr. Francesca LaMonte, American Museum of Natural History, was helpful in the loan and gift of specimens of *Corydoras*. Gene Wolfsheimer, a leading fish photographer and fish breeder, kindly permitted us to use pictures of plants and fishes (see pages ii; 104; 112–14; 117; 119; 121–2; 182; 264; 330; 344; 372; 381; 419; 423; 429; 434; 445; 448; 534–5; 544–8; 550; 561; 576; 584; 608; 641; 646; 652). Sam Dunton, New York Zoological Society, aided with photographs. Hermann Meinken generously aided us in completing obscure references on aquarium fishes. Dr. Ethelwynn Trewavas, British Museum, kindly sent fishes on loan and exchange for our use and helped with obscure references. And Dr. Werner Ladiges, Hamburg, Germany, generously sent aquarium literature and books and, through Gustav Wenzel and Sohn, Germany, gave us permission to copy color drawings from his books *Zierfischbilderbuch* and *Tropical Fishes* (see pages 164; 413; 524).

We are grateful for the generous help with nomenclature of the cyprinodont fishes by Dr. Robert R. Miller, University of Michigan; and for advice on diseases of fishes by Dr. Stanislas F. Snieszko, U.S. Fish and Wildlife Service. For advice on aquatic plants we thank Drs. Jason R. Swallen, Egbert H. Walker, and Conrad V. Morton, all of the Smithsonian Institution; Dr. William J. Dress, Bailey Hortorium, Cornell University; and Albert Greenberg, Tampa, Florida. We are grateful to the Secretary of the Smithsonian Institution and the Director of the National Museum for permission to use the collections, drawings, and photographs in their files, numbering about 50.

We express our thanks to the following individuals, publishers, and institutions who so generously gave us their permission to use illustrations published by them on the page numbers enclosed in parentheses: Academy of Natural Sciences of Philadelphia (607); Dr. L. F. de Beaufort and E. J. Brill Co., Leiden, publisher of *Fishes of Indo-Australian Archipelago* (338; 442); British Museum of Natural History (288; 296; 314; 338; 411; 427; 636; 644); Carnegie Museum of Pittsburgh (173; 195; 228; 259; 346; 357; 628); Chicago Natural History Museum (434; 454; 457; 461); General Biological Supply House, Chicago (65; 93); Albert Greenberg, Everglades Aquatic Nurseries (522); Dr. A. Fraser Brunner, British Museum (592); Dr. Carl L. Hubbs, Scripps Institution of Oceanography (504; 517; 627); Illinois Natural History Survey (278; 431; 518; 564); Wm. K. Innes, courtesy of Robert Dempster (86; 87; 88; 90); Le Cuziat (477; 478); Museum of Comparative Zoology, Harvard University (192; 194; 432); Life Magazine (659–661); New York Department of Conservation (568; 570; 571); New York Zoological Society (102–3; 162; 166–7; 184; 206; 231; 272; 352; 368; 378; 430; 452; 473; 493; 502–3; 506; 526; 538–40; 558; 563; 582; 585; 657; 667); Dr. Jacques Pellegrin, who wrote *The Fishes of Asia Minor* (386); Lawrence Perkins (103; 273–77; 623); Mervin F. Roberts (394; 410; 428; 446; 479–81); De Regenboog of Amsterdam (516; 555); Mr. G. Sennfft (192 and 233); Dr. J. L. B. Smith of South Africa (591); Taylor and Francis, Ltd., publisher of *Annals and Magazine of Natural History* (592); O. Tutwiler Tropical Fish Farms (536; 537); D. Van Nostrand Co. publishers of *The Ways of Fishes* by Schultz and Stern, 1948 (265); Zoological Society of London (205; 238; 367; 377; 470; 485; 500).

CONTENTS

Ichthyology

THE science of ichthyology comprises our knowledge of fishes. It represents the observations of men for more than 2,000 years, now organized in an orderly fashion, tested through innumerable human experiences by the scientific method, by use of precision instruments and by mathematical analysis, and checked and rechecked by modern experimental methods. Thus, this branch of zoology, derived from the Greek words *ichthys,* meaning a fish, and *logos,* a discourse, was established by thousands of sincere, devoted men and women who were seeking the truth about fishes, their structure, relationships, ways of life, distribution in space and time, history, and orderly arrangement.

Ichthyologists define fishes as those vertebrates adapted for an aquatic life, respiring by means of internal gills throughout adult life, propelling and balancing themselves by means of fins. This definition, however, excludes that great group of animals known as whales, porpoises, and other aquatic mammals which respire by means of lungs.

Formerly the word fish or "Pisces" included only the true fishes, but as our knowledge of ichthyology was extended, it included more kinds of fishlike vertebrates. Today, two great superclasses are known as fishes. One, the Agnatha, without jaws, includes the lampreys and hagfishes. The other, Gnathostomata, with jaws, has been divided into three classes: (1) the sharks, rays, and skates, known as the Elasmobranchii; (2) the elephant and ratfishes, the Holocephali; and (3) the largest group, the bony fishes, the Osteichthys. The primitive fishlike animals, the lancelets or Cephalochordata, are excluded from this definition because they lack vertebrae. They are chordates, and many ichthyologists claim them with the fishes; in the United States National Museum they are classified as fishes.

The word fish is both singular and plural, but when plural it refers to two or more specimens of the same species. The word fishes is plural and refers to two or more kinds of fishes.

As a result of economic trends and the application of research to the production of more fishes, the field of ichthyology has expanded and branched out into subfields of endeavor that may be classified as follows:

1. *Systematic ichthyology* deals with the classification, nomenclature, structure, development, life history, distribution, and relationships of fishes.

2. *Fisheries biology* deals with the economic aspects of fishes, especially their life history, migrations, abundance, and statistics of catch per unit of

fishing effort. Its aim is to regulate a fishery so that there will be a maximum yield from a minimum fishing effort.

3. Expert aquarists may be classified as bionomic ichthyologists, derived from the Greek words *bios,* meaning life or the act of living, and *nomos,* a pasture or an abode. *Bionomic ichthyology* may be defined as that branch of ichthyology that treats of the habits, care, propagation, and principles of living in an aquatic habitat or an abode such as an aquarium.

Many times the question is asked of ichthyologists, "How many species of fishes are there in the world?" This question has been answered in various ways. Carl L. Hubbs published an estimate in the scientific journal *Copeia* (1932, page 184), in which he estimated there were 500 families and subfamilies, 5,000 genera, and 40,000 species of fishes. By using check lists of the fishes of various faunal areas of the world, we have determined the figure of 40,000 species and subspecies to be a fairly good estimate.

REGION	ESTIMATED NUMBER OF SPECIES AND SUBSPECIES
Australia	1,500
North America	4,500
South America	6,500
Africa	6,500
Tropical Indo-Pacific marine	9,000
Deep-sea and pelagic species	2,500
Europe, Asia, India	6,500
Islands, island groups, and restricted faunal areas with endemic species	3,000
Total	40,000

HOW FISHES GET THEIR SCIENTIFIC NAMES

The number of species and subspecies of fishes is about equal to the number of all other species and subspecies of vertebrates, amphibians, reptiles, birds, and mammals in the world. With so many kinds of animals it was necessary to establish a system of naming. More than 200 years ago it was observed that common names referred to more than one kind of fish. Linnaeus, in 1758, in his tenth edition of *Systema naturae,* proposed the present system of zoological nomenclature. After this system was established there followed a long period of exploration in which many species were inadequately described, illustrated, and named.

This binomial system provides a generic and a specific name, usually based on Latin or Greek words, such as *Gambusia affinis* (Baird and Girard). The scientific names are followed by the name of the author who first described the species and named it according to the International Rules of Zoological Nomenclature. When the author's name is enclosed in parentheses, that means that the species was described in another genus and that recent authors have transferred it to the present genus, in this case *Gambusia,* since Baird and Girard in their original description named this species *Heterandria affinis.* It is not necessary for scientific names of animals to have a specific or significant meaning, although many do.

Both generic and specific names may be chosen in honor of the collector, a friend, or a colleague, as well as for a geographical locality, a ship, or almost anything. Species names must be latinized, however; and when named after a man they must end in *i,* for example, *hollandi,* or after a woman, in *ae,* for example, *aliceae.* Although the International Commission of Zoological Nomenclature has established many pages of rules governing the naming of animals, the basic theory of the system is that of priority—the oldest name established for a genus, species, or subspecies is the valid one, going back to the year 1758, the tenth edition of *Systema naturae* by Linnaeus.

Whenever an ichthyologist thinks he has a new species, he must search the ichthyological literature all the way back to 1758 to be certain that it is not already named. This is a difficult and time-consuming process, requiring the facilities of extensive libraries such as the Library of Congress at Washington and those in the largest universities which have specialized in ichthyological literature. Bibliographical indices are used, such as the three-volume work by Bashford Dean, *Bibliography of Fishes* (1916–1923), along with the Pisces section of the *Zoological Record,* to find papers on the group being studied. The *Zoological Record,* published in London since 1864, classifies natural history literature on an annual basis. Although these tools are useful, the experience of the ichthyologist is important, too. The more expert ichthyologists do not name new species of fish on hunches; instead they review all other species in the genus to which they assign their new one, and if they are able to construct a key that separates the new one from all other species in that genus, they then feel that much reliance may be placed on their claim that the species is actually new.

The expert ichthyologists of today are continually confronted with the inadequate descriptions and figures of fishes printed during the past 200 years. So many authors have named fishes that were already named that on the average each species has one or two synonyms, and some may have as many as a dozen or more. This troublesome affliction of systematic ichthyology could be greatly improved if novices in the field submitted their "new species" to ichthyologists in the larger museums of the world for expert opinion. These museums, with a million or more specimens distributed among 10,000 to 20,000 species, are in a fine position to make careful comparisons.

The International Rules of Zoological Nomenclature require that whenever a new species is described and named a specimen must be designated as the *holotype,* the specimen on which the species is based. Other specimens used in describing the new species become *paratypes,* and data from them are included in the description. It is the custom for ichthyologists to give the type specimens to museums for permanent preservation, such as the United States National Museum in Washington, which makes its research collections available for study to all qualified students and professional ichthyologists.

To illustrate how complicated the process of naming a species may become before the matter is finally settled, let us refer to one of our commonest aquarium fishes, the molly or sailfin.

The first author to publish a description and give a scientific name for the molly was the early American ichthyologist, LeSueur. In the year 1821, in volume 2, page 3, of the *Journal of the Academy of Natural Sciences of Philadelphia*, there appeared as a boldface center head the name *Mollinesia latipinna*. This generic and specific name as first published would be the valid scientific name under ordinary circumstances, but further study of the original article indicates that the generic name was intended to honor Monsieur Mollien. However, there was a great amount of carelessness in those days, and on the plate in this first printing the name is spelled *Molienisia Latipinua*, whereas in the reference to the plate on page 409 it is spelled *Molinesia Latipinna*. Thus the molly had its generic name spelled three ways and the specific name two ways when first published. For more than 100 years the generic name of the molly has been spelled in at least three ways. To settle this and similar controversies in nomenclature, rules were established more than half a century ago to pass on such matters. The commission that considers nomenclatorial problems acts as a sort of international "supreme court" and the rule of priority, or the rule of long established use, is followed.

Two recent papers have given the history of the name. Fowler in 1945 and Bailey and Miller in 1950 chose to emend the name to *Mollienesia*, which follows closely the name of the man LeSueur intended to honor, and they use the ending *-esia*, which appears twice in the article. Thus the best conclusion that can be reached, according to usage and rules, is that the common molly should carry the name *Mollienesia latipinna* LeSueur.

This is only one of many complicated cases that occur in the naming of fishes; in general, about 95 per cent are named with sufficient care and accuracy so that no controversies are involved.

By 1900 the number of fish species became so numerous that the trend was to revise or review fishes on the basis of genera or of families. During the past 25 years statistical methods of analysis have been applied to what were previously considered species. Carefully made counts and measurements now reveal that many of these early species can actually be differentiated into subspecies or into two or more species.

To make these statistical studies large series of specimens are needed from numerous localities. This trend has caused a change in the policies of research museums. Whereas in the early days a species was represented by a single specimen, now that species should be represented by 25 or more specimens per lot, and each lot from as many localities within the range of the species as is practical. Such large collections in museums open the way for the solution of innumerable problems in ichthyology and in racial investigations in the field of fisheries biology. These methods apply to fresh-water fishes as well as marine. Many fresh-water species differ from stream system to stream system, whereas in marine fishes the differences appear from island group to island group, or according to latitude.

At times the layman naturalist will argue about "lumpers" and "splitters." Lumpers have a tendency to throw "doubtful" species together as a single form, whereas splitters differentiate a species into its component populations and give these populations a subspecific scientific name.

Isaac Ginsburg has proposed a principle to guide him as to when it is mathematically sound to give a population a scientific name and when it is not. This "law" or yardstick proposes that two subspecies are distinct biological units in nature when the character showing the greatest divergence overlaps approximately 10 to 20 per cent. A full species may overlap in one character by not more than 10 per cent. The percentage is calculated on the total number of observations for both supposed species or subspecies combined.

In the recognition of species and subspecies there remain certain characters that cannot be measured or counted, for example, the basic color pattern. This may be defined as those colors which occur regularly on specific areas of the fish. The basic color pattern may not include quality, tone, or shade of colors.

Experience has demonstrated that in both fresh-water and marine fishes the importance of basic color patterns cannot be overemphasized. Once the variability has been determined for a series of specimens, it is of the utmost importance as a factor in the recognition of species and subspecies. This has been demonstrated in studies of the reef-inhabiting species of the Phoenix, Marshall, and Philippine Islands by the constancy with which basic color patterns of browns, blackish shades, and light areas, in the form of spots, bars, and streaks, occur in preserved specimens of certain species and subspecies. These patterns were observed first in live specimens and were recorded by means of color photographs and colored drawings. Their persistence after a few years of alcoholic preservation was later confirmed by comparison of the photographs and drawings with the preserved specimens. Thus as a result of careful observation the older idea of lumping species or combining species into one "catch-all" species was not the true picture in nature. Authors who disregard such details as the basic color pattern are guilty of lumping species and subspecies incorrectly.

The recognition of genera has never been placed on so definite a mathematical basis. Therefore, the splitters and lumpers have had a freer hand and sometimes the splitters actually have set up new generic and subgeneric units for nearly every species in a particular group. This has been especially noticeable in the poeciliid fishes.

The concept of a genus should be to group closely related species together so that these species represent a small natural phyletic line. These phyletic lines are not all of the same value or definiteness in any family of fishes; they represent to a considerable extent the personal opinion of the ichthyological researcher.

The characters by which genera are recognized are variable. In general, dentition and small constant differences in the bones, their shape and relationship to each other, are excellent guides. Fleshy characters such as barbels or their absence, development of glandular scales, specializations of the digestive tract, presence or absence of luminous glands or scales, specialized development of lips, fins, arrangement and size of scales are most useful in recognition of fish genera.

No particular character or set of characters can be named in advance to cover the recognition of genera because fishes are so variable in structure from one order to another and from one family to another that the ichthyologist must test the characters he uses for each family. Those that reveal constancy for large series of specimens among few to several species may be used as generic characters.

HISTORY OF ICHTHYOLOGY

The written history of ichthyology coincides in general with that of zoology, which takes its start with Aristotle (384–322 B.C.). He had a fairly accurate knowledge of the general structure of fishes, correctly distinguishing them from the aquatic mammals or cetaceans.

Aristotle's information on the habits of fishes, their special adaptations, method and time of propagation has proved to be surprisingly accurate. However, it is not easy to recognize the species with which he was dealing because his idea of a species was vague. He adopted the nomenclature of the local fishermen. It never occurred to Aristotle that local popular names change from generation to generation and from one locality to another. His world of ichthyology was limited to about 115 species, all living in the Aegean Sea.

The men who followed Aristotle for the next 1,800 years were content to copy his writings without any original observations or checking on his contributions. They followed him blindly and added fabulous tales. It was a period of regression.

The first sparks of original observation may be attributed to Pierre Belon

(1517–1575) in *De aquatilibus libri duo;* Hyppolyto Salviani (1514–1572) in *Aquatilium animalium historae . . . ;* and Gulielmus Rondelet (1507–1566) in *Libri de piscibus marinis,* whose works are almost entirely limited to fishes of the Mediterranean and Europe. During the next century, Guilielmus Piso (1611–1678) and George Marcgrav (1610–1644) accompanied Prince Moritz of Nassau (1604–1679) to Brazil in 1637–1644 and studied about 100 species of fishes. However, not until the work of John Ray (1628–1705) and Francis Willoughby (1635–1672) appeared did a new era in ichthyology occur. These two men, in their *Historia piscium libri quatuor,* recognized that throughout the animal kingdom there were many similar anatomical structures. Thus they made the first serious attempt to bring order out of chaos by arranging animals into groups on the basis of their structure. They abandoned speculation and stuck to facts. They recognized in nature the species as a biological unit and in their works catalogued about 420 species of fishes.

More important than any other early investigator's writings are those of Peter Artedi (1705–1735), who is justly called the father of ichthyology. He was born in Sweden and was educated at the University of Uppsala. In 1728, Carolus Linnaeus (1707–1778) visited this university; upon inquiring who was engaged in the study of natural history, he was referred to Artedi. They became close friends and made an agreement that in case of the death of one, the survivor would make every effort to publish his works.

When in Holland, Artedi was short of money. Linnaeus learned of his needs at Amsterdam and introduced him to a rich man, Albertus Seba (1665–1736), who had an extensive collection of zoological specimens. Seba immediately employed Artedi to work up the collections of fishes. Several months later, on September 27, 1735, Artedi went to dine with Seba and other guests. He stayed late, had a pleasant evening, and started home through dark, unfamiliar streets. It is believed he made a misstep and fell into a canal and was drowned. His body was found the next day. Linnaeus kept his vow. After great effort and with the assistance of George Clifford, an Englishman, he was able to publish, in 1738, Artedi's *Ichthyologia.*

Artedi's main contribution to the understanding of the relationships of species lies in his concepts of the groups above the species. He believed the genus to represent a group of species which agreed with each other in general but which differed in minor characters. To each genus he gave a separate name. Daniel Merriman of Yale University has stated, "Whereas before some 14 names had been used to designate the members of his herring genus, he combined them all under the name Clupea. . . . He was meticulous in his choice of names, choosing only those of Latin and Greek origin, and rejecting all those used also to designate different objects." Now having established the generic concept, he proceeded to group the genera into "maniples," the family concept of today. The maniples were then arranged in natural orders, and these into a class, representing the whole group of fishes. In all, Artedi recognized 47 genera and 230 species.

The chief weakness in the Artedi system of classification was below the genus. He retained the polynomial scheme of nomenclature. Historians agree that Artedi's system of classification greatly influenced the Linnaean system that was to follow. Linnaeus, in his tenth edition of *Systema naturae* in 1758, did little more to Artedi's system of classification than to apply our present-day binomial system of naming, furnishing a generic and specific scientific or trivial name.

This new system was the most important event of the century, but, as stated by Jordan, "No system of naming can go beyond the knowledge on which it rests. Ignorance of fact produces confusion in naming. . . . The earlier naturalists had no conception of the laws of geographical distribution." They had no idea of the geological past of species or of groups, nor of the evolutionary concept of animal origin so ably developed by Darwin a century later. Classification then was a system of pigeonholing of forms without application of blood relationships.

The period following the establishment of a system of naming of biological units in nature was one of exploration in foreign lands, such as those Otto Fabricus (1744–1822) described in *Fauna Groenlandica*. Petrus Forskål (1736–1763), based his work *Descriptiones animalium* chiefly on Red Sea fishes. Petrus Simon Pallas (1741–1811) in his *Zoographia Rosso-Asiatica* recorded fishes of Alaska and Siberia. Antoine Risso (1777–1845) published in 1810 his *Ichthyologie de Nice*. Thomas Pennant (1726–1798) wrote on British fishes and on arctic zoology. Wilhelm G. Tilesius (1769–1857) wrote on the fishes of the Bering Sea and Japan. Another great man, a pioneer of Alaskan natural history, was Georg Wilhelm Steller (1709–1746).

Constantine Samuel Rafinesque (1783–1840), who wrote on the ichthyology of Sicily, went to America in 1815, and in 1820 published his *Ichthyologia Ohiensis*. Although he had a wide knowledge of fishes for his time and possessed a keen taxonomic insight, he was somewhat irresponsible and had little regard for accuracy, with the result that later ichthyologists have had difficulty interpreting his observations. Rafinesque became professor of natural history and modern languages in Transylvania University at Lexington, Kentucky. One summer, while on a trip of exploration, he became acquainted with Audubon, who was then painting birds and keeping a little grocery store at Henderson, Kentucky. A letter of recommendation from a friend in the East introduced Rafinesque as an "odd fish, which might not be described in the published treatises." Audubon put him up for the night after a pleasant evening of conversation about natural history, which greatly impressed his host. Audubon wrote of this as follows: "That night, after we were all abed, I heard of a sudden a great uproar in the naturalist's room. I got up and opened the door, when to my astonishment I saw my guest running naked, holding the handle of my favourite Cremona [violin], the body of which had been battered to pieces in attempting to kill the bats which had entered the open window. I stood amazed but he continued jumping and running around and around until he was fairly exhausted, when he begged me to procure one of the animals for him. I took up the bow of my demolished violin, and giving a smart tip to each bat as it came up, we soon had specimens enough."

The part of this event which Audubon did not tell has been one of the most amusing in the annals of ichthyology. Audubon was a great artist, and possibly the spirit of revenge led him to paint more than a dozen pictures of fishes, all of a hypothetical nature, in which the head of one kind was painted on the body of another, along with other impossible anatomical features. About ten of these were duly copied by Rafinesque and published in his *Ichthyologia Ohiensis*. This indicates the gullibility of Rafinesque's enthusiasm.

Although there were numerous other explorers of the time, the most important works may be classified as compilations. Marc Elieser Bloch (1723–1799) began writing on fishes at the age of fifty-six. His chief works are *Oeconomische Naturgeschichte der Fische Deutschlands*, 1782, and *Naturgeschichte der Ausländischen Fische*, 1785; even today these fully illustrated folio publications are invaluable to ichthyologists. Another publication of merit is that by Bernhard G. E. Lacepède (1756–1825) in five volumes entitled *Histoire naturelle des poissons* (1798–1803). The next big compilation was that of Georges L. C. F. D. Cuvier (1769–1832) and Achille Valenciennes (1794–1865). Their *Histoire naturelle des poissons*, in 22 volumes from 1828 to 1849, contained 4,514 named species, the major part written by Valenciennes after Cuvier died in 1832. The work was left unfinished because of a disagreement with the publishers.

The last attempt to write a series of volumes on the fishes of the world was by Albert C. L. G. Günther (1830–1914), entitled *Catalogue of the Fishes of the British Museum*, in eight volumes from 1859 to 1870. This work contains 6,843 species and 1,682 doubtful ones. It is obvious that the job of writing a series of volumes on the known fishes of the world was too large and complicated a task and that knowledge was accumulating faster in local faunal areas than it could be worked into a treatise on the fishes of the world. The same holds true today.

Efforts for the next century were directed to the study of local faunas or groups of related fishes. Johann Baptist von Spix (1781–1826) and Louis Agassiz (1807–1873) wrote *Selecta genera et species piscium quos in itinere per Brasiliam annis 1817–20* (published in 1829–1831). Johannes Müller (1801–1858) and Friedrich G. J. Henle (1807–1885) produced the first au-

thoritative work on sharks, *Systematische Beschriebungen der Plagiosto-
men*, in 1841. Pieter Bleeker (1819–1878) published 500 separate contributions, chiefly on the fishes of the tropical Indo-Pacific. Most noteworthy is
his nine-volume beautifully illustrated *Atlas ichthyologique des Indes Ori-
entales Néerlandaises*, 1862–1877. Bleeker's figures are fully as accurate as
many of those of today and his insight into what constituted a species was
excellent, far better than some of our more recent fish workers.

In Cuba, Felipe Poey y Aloy (1799–1891) labored for half a century on
the local fish fauna and published *Memorias sobre la historia natural de la
isla de Cuba* and *Repertorio* and *Enumeratio.* Coenraad Jacob Temminck
(1770–1858) and Hermann Schlegel (1804–1844) gave the first excellent
account of the fishes of Japan in 1838–1841.

To list all the great workers in foreign areas would burden the reader,
but the following noted ichthyologists should be mentioned: Franz Steindachner (1834–1919), George Boulenger (1858–1937), Robert Collett
(1842–1913), Carlos Berg (1843–1902), Francis Day (1829–1889), and
Leon Louis Vaillant (1834–1915).

American ichthyology dates from the feeble beginnings of Rafinesque
and from Samuel Latham Mitchill's (1764–1831) treatise on the fishes of
New York. Shortly afterward Charles Alexandre LeSueur (1778–1846), who
was both artist and naturalist, reported on the fishes of the Great Lakes and
Ohio Basin. Others of that period were Jared Potter Kirtland (1793–1877),
on Ohio fishes; James Ellsworth Dekay (1792–1851), on the New York
fauna; John Richardson (1787–1865), who published in 1836 his *Fauna
boreali-Americana*. Early work by David Humphreys Storer (1804–1891)
on the fishes of Massachusetts, and that of John Edwards Holbrook (1796–
1871) on the ichthyology of South Carolina were important.

In the city of Washington, D.C., there was established in 1846 the Smithsonian Institution under the direction of the United States government. This
gave permanent status to the United States National Museum, where it was
planned to store the natural history specimens used by the men and women
who were studying and reporting on the fauna of North America and the
world.

The National Museum, Division of Fishes, at the present time has more
than 1,550,000 fish specimens stored in over 155,000 containers on 3½ miles
of steel shelves, so crowded that there is scarcely room to add more jars.
This vast collection belongs to the people of the United States and is available for research by qualified students of ichthyology. The collections serve
the same purpose as books in a library. Each lot is used for checking past
observations and recording new ones.

The United States National Museum, assisted by the U.S. Fish Commission, now the Fish and Wildlife Service, has had a century of leadership in
systematic ichthyological investigations. Especially noteworthy are the con-

tributions by G. Brown Goode (1851–1896), *Oceanic Ichthyology;* the collaboration of David Starr Jordan (1851–1931) with Charles Henry Gilbert (1859–1928) and Barton Warren Evermann (1853–1932) in the publication of more than 100 papers on American fishes. Henry W. Fowler (1878–   ), Academy of Natural Sciences of Philadelphia, worked up many of the Philippine collections of the *Albatross,* a ship operated by the U.S. Fish Commission in exploratory work around the world. These have been published in seven volumes in Bulletin 100 of the National Museum. Other noteworthy publications are the large series of papers on Japanese fishes by Jordan and his students, published in the *Proceedings* of the United States National Museum. Also may be mentioned the volume on the fishes of Peru by Samuel Frederick Hildebrand (1883–1949) and that on the fresh-water fishes of Siam (or Thailand) by Hugh McCormick Smith (1865–1941).

Louis Agassiz (1807–1873) in 1850 monographed the fishes of Lake Superior and trained one of his students, Charles Frederic Girard (1822–1895), in ichthyology. Thus, when the United States Pacific Railway surveys were made in 1858 and the Mexican boundary surveys in 1859, naturalists collected and preserved fishes captured along the routes explored and brought them back to Washington. Here Spencer Fullerton Baird (1823–1887), one of the secretaries of the Smithsonian Institution, with the assistance of Girard, published on the survey fauna, chiefly from the western United States. Engaged in this early exploration were James Wood Milner (1841–1879), Marshall McDonald (1835–1895), William O. Ayers (1817–1891), William Neale Lockington (1842?–1902), and George Suckley (1830–1869), among others.

Certain American educational institutions in the latter part of the nineteenth and early twentieth century developed into centers of leadership in the study and exploration of fishes. Harvard University had Samuel Garman (1843–1927), a student of Agassiz, who made valuable contributions on the sharks and the deep-sea fishes collected by the *Albatross.*

Indiana University became an important center of ichthyological research under David Starr Jordan during the 1880's, and later Carl H. Eigenmann (1863–1927) took over the work and became famous for his many valuable contributions on South American fishes.

Jordan left Indiana University to become the first president of Stanford University, California, where he set up a fisheries center that is strong even today. Jordan took with him from Indiana Charles Henry Gilbert (1859–1928). At Stanford he gathered two other important men, John Otterbein Snyder (1867–1943) and Edwin Chapin Starks (1867–1932). Under Jordan's leadership Stanford was for half a century the chief center of training for students in ichthyology. More than 100 men under Jordan's influence published noteworthy contributions on fishes.

Charles Henry Gilbert, who began his career in systematic ichthyology at Indiana University, was one of the most careful workers on American fishes. He began to study the life history of salmon and to apply statistical methods to fishery research and may be truly called the father of modern fisheries biological research in America. This type of research has been developed to a still higher degree of perfection by William Francis Thompson (1888–   ) at the University of Washington, Seattle, during the past 30 years.

Jordan and Evermann, the latter a former director of the California Academy of Sciences, published the well-known four-volume Bulletin 47, United States National Museum, *The Fishes of North and Middle America*, 1896–1900; also, *The Genera of Fishes* and many other important papers. Although Jordan's influence on American ichthyology was very great, he was not as careful a worker as some of his students, for example, Charles Henry Gilbert. Jordan did not use refined methods of measurement of fishes nor did he use statistical methods of analysis of groups of species. In the early part of his career, he "only looked at the largest specimen in a jar," and ichthyologists have found in hundreds of lots that some or all of the other specimens belonged to other species. Today the attitude is a more critical one and a greater degree of accuracy is attained in ichthyological research.

The Academy of Natural Sciences of Philadelphia under Henry W. Fowler has been a one-man center of ichthyological contributions on world fishes for over half a century. Fowler has written more papers and made more illustrations of fishes than any other ichthyologist in the history of the science.

The California Academy of Sciences at San Francisco has had a long career in ichthyology. Yale University at New Haven, Connecticut, and the American Museum of Natural History and the New York Zoological Society, both in New York, are centers of ichthyological research. They are noteworthy for their experimental ichthyology during the past two decades.

The Chicago Natural History Museum, with its publications by Seth Eugene Meek (1859–1914) and Samuel F. Hildebrand on *The Fishes of Panama*, has built a worthy place in the history of American ichthyology during the last 35 years.

Two important centers of study of the fresh-water fishes of North America have developed during the past 40 years—the University of Michigan and Cornell University. In the museums of these universities are stored vast series of fresh-water fishes which make it possible to study in detail the finer points among closely related groups of species. These two institutions have introduced new life and vitality into American fresh-water fishes research.

There has been a trend away from systematic ichthyology during the past 40 years into what is known as fisheries biology and experimental biology. Numerous organizations doing this type of research attempt to apply the results of their studies to the control of a fish population. This is similar to what aquarists attempt in their tanks and ponds, the propagation of fishes

The common-sense minnow seine used by Herbert R. Axelrod (right) for capturing sticklebacks, sheepshead minnows, and various *Fundulus*. The top of this seine is floated by means of cork floats. The bottom is weighted with lead strips.

on a controlled basis. In comparison with the study and control of great fisheries, the aquarists' problems are extremely simple, but the principles are much the same.

METHODS OF COLLECTING FISHES*

Methods of collecting fresh-water fishes vary considerably from those used in obtaining marine fishes. The equipment used in streams and lakes is much simpler and less expensive than that needed for working under oceanic conditions.

Seines and Nets

The seine is one of the most useful items of equipment. These may be obtained in various lengths and widths and with various meshes. Those advertised in catalogues by mail-order houses are of two kinds:

1. Common-sense minnow seines
2. Seines made of cotton twine tied at each intersection of the threads

* Before collecting fishes, permits must be obtained from state and local governments, and local game wardens should be consulted.

The common-sense seine varies in length from 4 to 50 feet, with a usual depth of 4 feet for the shorter ones. At lengths of 10 to 50 feet the depth may be 4 to 6 feet. The size of the mesh for this type of seine varies from ⅛ to ½ inch square. These seines are attached to a leaded line below and to a line above with floats which may be of cork, wood, or plastic. When using the seine, a 6-foot wooden pole called the brail is fastened to both lines at each end of the net. This is useful for spreading the net when it is hauled through the water.

The more sturdy cotton-twine seine should be treated with a net preservative, since this kind of seine is more expensive. The mesh may vary from ¼ inch square to much larger for the bigger seines. The depth of seines 50 feet and shorter is usually from 4 to 6 feet, whereas those from 100 to several hundred feet in length have a depth of 10 to 30 feet or more, depending on the purpose for which they are designed. The larger seines usually have a bag of finer mesh forming the central section. This bag traps the fish when the seine is hauled into shallow shore waters.

Seines up to 50 feet in length may be hauled by two men, one at either end. Small seines are most effective on smooth bottoms and in water not too deep for wading. When hauled along a shore line or in a stream, the net should be kept in the form of a C or J, with the man farthest from shore somewhat in front. To land the seine it is best to haul it gradually toward shore, keeping it U-shaped with the open end toward shore. By grasping both lead and cork lines at each end of the seine, both men should ease it along the bottom. The cork line should be folded over toward the center but not farther than the lead line.

Fishes that are wanted alive must be removed at once from the debris in the net and placed in suitable containers. Only a few fish may safely be placed in each bucket unless there is some means of artificial aeration.

In seining small creeks among rubble and thick vegetation, a small 6- to 8-foot seine is the most successful. The two men who pull this net should work upstream, kicking and stirring the bottom and the plant growths vigorously. This will drive the fishes out and some of them into the net. The seine should be lifted in such habitats every 2 or 3 yards.

Many species of fishes are very wary. They hide under banks, in vegetation, under logs, among and under stones. They can be driven out but may go at once to a new hiding spot. Sometimes it is advantageous to go upstream a short distance and muddy up the water by stirring the bottom so that the fishes cannot see where to go or see the collectors or net. Then as they are driven from their hiding places they often become trapped in the net.

In deep water all seines and nets must be set from a boat and hauled onto shore by means of long lines.

Minnow traps of conventional design, baited with suitable food, are of considerable value in collecting fishes in a healthy condition. These may be set in streams, lakes, or ponds. They should be visited each morning and evening for removal of fishes caught and for rebaiting.

Among tropical fishermen the throw net is a popular type of equipment. It is used from boats or along river banks, and in deep or shallow water. This net is 30 or 40 feet in diameter, with the outer circumference leaded. It is thrown from the shoulder of the fisherman by a rotating motion that spreads the net by centrifugal force. It then settles into the water, and the lead line is puckered together by means of drawstrings, enclosing the trapped fishes.

Fish Poisons

The late Carl H. Eigenmann, during field work in South America in 1908, probably was the first ichthyologist to use vegetable poisons, although aboriginal natives in nearly all parts of the world have used them for centuries. Since that time most American ichthyologists have used vegetable poisons to collect fishes for scientific purposes. The active and lethal agent in these poisons is rotenone. It is so powerful that 1 part of rotenone in 20 million parts of water is lethal to many kinds of fishes. Such a powerful poison is not very satisfactory for collecting fishes for aquarium purposes, and its use is illegal in most states.

Eigenmann and Allen (*The Fishes of Western South America*, 1942) state:

"Our interest in the [cube] root was of course its effectiveness as an agent for fish collecting. The supply which we obtained in the high Andes, far from its point of origin, was always well-dried, the roots gnarled, shrunken, yellowish in color. Later, in the interior, the roots which I obtained fresh, still in the sap, well rounded out, smooth, resembled the others much as new potatoes resemble last year's crop toward the end of winter. There was a general opinion that the old dry roots are the more potent. I am inclined to agree, but for the reason that the water-extraction of the powdery alkaloid is easier and more complete than from the juicy, fresh root.

"The manner of using the roots consists, first, of thoroughly crushing them, either in the open, or in a bag, improvised in our case, from our supply of cheesecloth; then of further crushing and kneading the bag with its contents under the water to be poisoned, washing out the alkaloid in a milky stream. Afterward, the thoroughly macerated residue may be broadcast into the water.

"During the preparation, either between rocks, or by use of a cudgel on a stump, a fine, yellow dust of the dried sap is liberated. The operator must work with much care, for the powder gets into the air and materially impedes respiration. In high elevations with reduced oxygen this proved to be serious indeed. We had a very fair demonstration upon ourselves of the effect which the extract has upon the fish, causing it to struggle to the surface where it may gasp air. If the dosage is high enough it results in death to the fishes, and the more active they are the more susceptible. If speedily washed downstream, the fishes have an opportunity to recover."

When working with fish poisons in streams, great care should be taken not to destroy more fishes than are needed for scientific purposes.

The speed of action of rotenone depends on the temperature of the water. In warm waters, above 75°F, it acts within a few minutes, whereas in cooler waters, 55°F or lower, it may take an hour (with the same concentration) before fishes become strongly affected. The rotenone remains active for several days or longer in enclosed bodies of water such as lakes and ponds.

In poisoning a stream the chief problem is how to recover the fishes. Leonard P. Schultz, in his extensive scientific collecting experience with the use of powdered cube root in Venezuela, and the Phoenix, Samoan, and Marshall Islands, has found that the following method of recovery is most successful in streams or in tidal sloughs.

Before the poison is distributed in the stream at least two seines or nets must be placed across the stream, one ¼ mile and the other about ½ mile below the point where the poison is to be used. Additional nets may be set above or in between these. The nets should be long enough to strain all the water that flows down the stream. Since leaves and debris will be washed into them, such seines must be anchored firmly by ropes at each end and the lead line weighted to the bottom with a few additional rocks distributed at intervals. This helps prevent specimens from passing under the net. The cork line may be propped up with sticks.

After all preparations are made the powdered root containing the rotenone should be mixed into a chocolate-malted-milk consistency. The amount to be used may be calculated on the volume of water to be poisoned. The dilutions for 5 per cent content of rotenone in derris or cube powder should be about 1 pound of the powder to about 20,000 cubic feet of water. If it takes 10 minutes for the treated water at 60°F to pass any one point, the fishes will definitely be affected. The mixture should be spread in the water at the head of a riffle or rapids; the latter ensures more complete mixing before entering the pool below. The fishes should show signs of lack of oxygen, such as coming to the surface, within 10 minutes. If they do not appear, however, wait at least another 10 minutes before attempting to strengthen the rotenone cloud in one of the lower pools or riffles. Fishes will continue to come out from under stones and from burrows for an hour or more.

Each seine should receive constant attention from an attendant. The best location for each seine is at the lower end of a riffle or rapids just before the water loses its rapid flow. The water must be moving rapidly enough to keep the fish against the net or they may escape. Better results are obtained if the fish are not killed. Should the nets become clogged with specimens the attendant should continuously remove the fish and preserve them. One or two men with dip nets should constantly patrol the stream, picking up all fishes that may have stranded themselves on the shore or on the bottom of the deeper, quieter pools. The time required to work a single poison station usually amounts to 4 to 8 hours, depending on the abundance of the fauna.

The location of the poison station in the stream is very important. Because rotenone is highly toxic to fishes, even in small amounts, if too much of the chemical is used fishes might be killed for a distance of 1 to 3 miles downstream. To avoid such accidents and mortality, the section of a stream selected should be about ½ mile above its mouth, and the stream should enter a larger one with at least three times the volume and flow. This will dilute the rotenone so that no bad effects will occur beyond the mouth of the creek selected.

Preservation of Fishes for Identification Purposes

After fishes have been collected or if they die in an aquarium and it is desired to identify them, immediate preservation is necessary. In general, formalin instead of alcoholic preservation is recommended. The specimens should be dropped into a solution of formalin made up by mixing 1 part of commercial formalin with 9 parts of water. This solution is of sufficient strength to preserve small fishes up to 5 inches in length in about 2 or 3 days. Larger specimens should be left in it for a greater length of time, depending upon their size. Fish which are allowed to die before being preserved are usually faded and distorted, hence of less value than those that retain their color patterns with normal intensity.

All specimens over 3 inches in length should be slit in the belly with a sharp knife or scissors so that the formalin solution may enter and preserve the viscera of the body cavity. In addition to this, large fish and especially those with soft bodies should be injected about every 2 inches with a formalin solution. If the intestinal tract is filled with a vegetable diet, this, too, should be injected with formalin. This is very important during tropical weather.

An ordinary hypodermic injection apparatus may be used for this purpose. Several needles of various lengths should be available, including some 6 inches long for larger fishes. The capacity of this apparatus should be about ½ to 1 pint.

Although formalin makes the best initial preservative for fishes, it is not so good for permanent preservation unless the acidity of the solution is neutralized. This may be done by adding about 1 heaping teaspoonful of borax to a gallon of the mixture. Since the fumes from formalin will irritate the eyes of those who may study the specimens, alcohol is recommended for permanent preservation.

After the specimens have been in formalin for a week, they may be transferred to water for 2 days, changing them to fresh water each night and morning. Upon completion of the process of washing in water, the specimen my be transferred to 70 per cent grain alcohol or 45 per cent isopropyl alcohol.

Fish specimens should never be crowded in containers like "sardines in a can," because this prevents proper preservation, especially at the start of the process.

Unlabeled specimens are of little or no scientific value. Labels giving all essential data should be placed on the jar with the fish when collected and preserved. Accurate information about the locality is as valuable as the fish. Each label should have the following information: exact locality (with reference to a town commonly appearing on maps), date, collector, and any other information that seems pertinent such as depth of water, method of capture, and ecological data.

Many individuals sending specimens to ichthyologists for identification do not realize that most paper used for identification tags falls apart like newsprint when wet and by the time the container reaches its destination the label is gone. Therefore, all label paper should consist of a pure linen ledger, which does not disintegrate in liquid preservatives. Always write on the label paper with a *soft lead pencil* or with a waterproof carbon ink. Do not use ordinary writing ink or an indelible pencil, which wash off in water and alcohol.

Sometimes it is desirable to tag specimens with numbers and enter, un-

Field Data Record
DIVISION OF FISHES, U.S. NATIONAL MUSEUM

Acc. No. . . . . Tag No. . . . . Sta. No. . . . .

State or Country: . . . .

County: . . . . City: . . . .

Locality: . . . .

. . . .

Drainage: . . . . Date: . . . .

Water: . . . .

Vegetation: . . . .

. . . . Time: . . . .

Bottom: . . . .

Shore: . . . . Current: . . . .

Distance from shore: . . . . Tide: . . . .

Depth of capture: . . . . Depth of water: . . . . . .

Method of capture: . . . .

Collected by: . . . .

Preservative: . . . . Temp: . . . . . . Air: . . . .

List of species or kinds, with tag numbers if drawn or discussed: . . . .

der the corresponding number in a notebook, the essential data concerning the specimens. Many collectors find it most useful to carry a set of colored crayons in the field so that the color patterns of living fishes may be recorded in a sketch in their field notebook. All such specimens should be tagged with a number so that the specimen may be later compared with the sketch.

Color photography has proved most useful in recording the colors of living fishes. This is especially important since the reds, blues, yellows, and greens soon fade. So far no one has found a preservative that will keep the lipoid pigments from fading and eventually disappearing. The brown and black pigments remain for years if not exposed to daylight.

The field data sheet opposite is used by the Division of Fishes, United States National Museum.

DISTRIBUTION OF FISHES

Animal life was present in the waters of the earth at least 400 million years ago. In the rocks are traces of that life which represent vanished forms. When they died, their bodies settled on the bottom and were covered with silt or mud, sand or sludge, which aided in the preservation of their hard parts, chiefly the skeleton. As time passed these hard skeletal parts were gradually converted by various processes of infiltration of chemical solutions which replaced their calcareous skeletons with mineral substances to form fossils.

The oldest fossils occur in the deepest rock strata and usually are the most distorted and difficult to read. There are many gaps in the record, especially concerning the ancestral history of the characins, minnows, carps, suckers, loaches, and catfishes. In some animal groups the record is sufficiently complete to trace the ancestry so far back as to leave little doubt of the origin of the descendant form. However, the fossil record for some fishes, such as carps and suckers, suddenly stops, making it appear that they were created in their present forms. Perhaps someday scientists will discover the fossil remains of ancestors of these ostariophysans, but now it is almost a closed book.

The fossil remains of early fishes occur in rock strata in the form of skeletons; usually fragments of skeletons, more often only teeth, spines, and scales remain. Few complete fossil skeletons are found and the soft parts of fishes are largely unknown. Yet experts who have worked for a lifetime on fossil animals and have a broad knowledge of living forms can visualize and reconstruct from the fossil skeleton a close replica of the once-living animal.

The key to the solution of the present-day distribution of fishes lies largely in fossil records. However, much can be learned from the living fishes about zoogeography or geographical distribution. This branch of science treats of the laws and history of the wanderings of animals and fishes.

The subject is complex and partly theoretical. There are several diverse opinions on how animals moved over the earth's surface during past geological ages. Chief among these are by means of land bridges and by continental drift. The knowledge accumulated comes from various fields of science, such as geology, paleontology, zoology, embryology, morphology, and oceanography.

The wanderings of animals for the extension of their range is termed dispersion. It conveys the idea that a species originated in a definite area and that its present range resulted from its movements during the process of acquiring new territory for living and reproducing its kind. The center of distribution is the point or area thought to be the focus from which the species of animal dispersed. Dispersion is a general type of movement which involves the idea of the conquest of new inhabitable territory. Migration, on the other hand, means any movement in a definite direction, usually for a definite purpose, such as spawning.

The dispersion of fishes involves the problems of space or area and time. The movements may be thought of as continuous but modified by barriers and other conditions of the environment. David Starr Jordan long ago summed up the laws governing the distribution of fishes as follows: Each species is found in every part of the earth having conditions suitable for it unless: (1) its individuals have been unable to reach this region because of barriers of some sort; or (2) having reached it, the species is unable to maintain itself because of lack of capacity for adaptation, severity of competition with other forms, or unfavorable conditions of the environment; or (3) having entered and maintained itself, it has become so altered through the process of adaptive and selective evolution as to become a species distinct from the original type.

The absence of American species from the Japanese and Asiatic faunas comes under (1); as an example, *Gambusia* never reached those areas, although recent introductions indicate the habitat is highly suitable. Among the species under (2) which may have crossed the seas or entered rivers and did not find lodgment, there is in the nature of things no record, but we have multitudes of evidence of strays or fish tourists that have traveled far from their usual habitat.

The species that changed under isolation, such as island faunas and the fauna of many river systems, form noteworthy examples. However, almost every species must fall in this category, for isolation is a source of the most potent elements in the initiation, intensification, and selection of the minor differences that make related species different. This factor must never be overlooked in the study of the origin of species.

In hosts of species the persistence of characters rests not so much on their particular usefulness but on the fact that they are not harmful for the existence of the species. Individuals possessing these characters sometime in the past invaded the area and populated it; new selections of new adaptations have occurred, although these now "useless" characters have been retained also.

Extinction of species has come about, theoretically at least, in five ways: (1) modification or progressive evolution through geological ages which transforms the species into a more advanced form; (2) changes in the environment which occur more rapidly than the progress of the power of adaptation; (3) competition with other species; (4) extreme specialization of the species which limits it to special conditions; (5) exhaustion of the vigor of the stock. Probably most species have become extinct because of lack of ability to adapt to changes of the environment.

The distribution of fishes is aided by certain factors summarized as follows: (1) ocean currents which transport the pelagic stages of fishes; (2) man, who in his wanderings has taken with him numerous species that have become established far and wide; aquarium fishes that have escaped down the drainpipe or have been willfully introduced into various bodies of water over many parts of the world; (3) winds and storms which scatter fishes by flooding; (4) changes in the earth's surface, such as the sinking and rising of land masses—for example, Isthmus of Panama, Isthmus of Suez, and the connection between Alaska and Siberia, as well as a possible one between Europe and North America; (5) changes in the courses of rivers and streams —for example, during the glacier periods the Great Lakes discharged their waters down the Mississippi River as they do now through the Chicago Sewage Canal; Two Ocean Pass in the vicinity of Yellowstone National Park permitted an interchange of mountain-fish species between the Atlantic and the Pacific drainage systems; (6) the possibility of continental drift.

Barriers prohibiting the distribution of fishes may be physical, chemical, or biological. These are, for example, mountain ranges, land bridges, deserts, ocean currents, salt water (seas), and temperature. The physiological requirements of a species as well as its overspecialization in some specific character may be a barrier to its distribution. Man with his industrialization and resultant pollution is causing barriers to fish distribution, and in some instances extinction of established species.

Fresh-water Fishes

Aquarists have wondered why the exotic fresh-water fishes occurring in their tanks do not occur naturally in the warm southern American waters. The answer to that question is simply that they could not get there. However, to find the reason why they could not is difficult. First, we must understand what is meant by true fresh-water fishes. Fresh-water fishes may be defined as those fishes which through eons of time have not possessed the physiological ability to survive in even small amounts of salt water. George S. Myers has recognized two groups of fresh-water fishes, a primary and a secondary group.

The primary group includes those true fresh-water fish families whose members cannot live in salt water. They are (1) lungfishes with living representatives in Australia, South America, and Africa; (2) paddlefishes with *Psephurus* in the Yangtze River of China and *Polydon* in the Mississippi River of North America; (3) the lobe-finned ganoids (Polypteridae) of Africa; (4) the bowfin *Amia* of eastern America; (5) herringlike fishes such as the mooneyes (Hiodontidae) of North America, Pantodontidae and Kneriidae of tropical Africa, and bony-tongued fishes (Osteoglossidae) of South America, Africa, and Indo-Australia; (6) Mormyridae of Africa; (7) pikes and pickerels (Esocidae), mud minnows, and Alaskan blackfish (Umbridae) of North America, Europe, and Asia; (8) cavefishes (Amblyopsidae) of North America; (9) pirate perches (Percopsidae) of North America; (10) sunfishes and basses (Centrarchidae) of North America; (11) labyrinthine fishes of the Old World; (12) the Ostariophysi, by far the largest group of fresh-water fishes, comprising more than three-quarters of the primary fresh-water fishes of the world, composed of characins, knifefishes, carps, gymnotid eels, suckers, loaches, and catfishes. Only two families of the latter, Plotosidae and Ariidae, typically live in the sea, and these were derived from fresh-water ancestors.

The secondary division of fresh-water fishes includes those with the ability to enter both fresh and salt waters and adapt themselves to the physiological change which makes it possible to survive for a considerable length of time. Some of these are anadromous and catadromous fishes. The secondary division includes such fishes as (1) gars (Lepisosteidae), (2) sturgeons (Acipenseridae), (3) fresh-water eels (Anguillidae), (4) salmon and trout (Salmonidae), (5) synbranchid eels (Synbranchidae), (6) cichlids (Cichlidae), (7) and most important, top minnows (Cyprinodontidae and Poeciliidae). This group of fishes is of no value in trying to trace the wanderings of the fresh-water fishes through geological ages. It is too easy for them to pass through salt water along the coastal regions.

Marine Fishes

Marine fishes are roughly classified by ichthyologists into three ecological habitats: shore, pelagic, and deep sea. Although these groupings are useful, the zones overlap considerably and their limits vary in different seas. Shore fishes are those which occur along coastal areas never far out to sea and usually in depths shallower than 600 to 800 feet. Pelagic fishes are those which are not confined to coastal areas but which occur far out to sea, usually living at depths above 800 feet. Deep-sea fishes are those that live below depths of 600 to 800 feet. Most of the deep-sea fishes live in the stratified subsurface layers of the sea; because of the uniformity of these areas they may have a world-wide distribution.

The marine shore-fish faunas of the world may be divided into two main regions: (1) tropical and (2) temperate. The important tropical shore faunas may be subdivided into (*a*) Indo-West-Pacific, (*b*) American Pacific, (*c*) West Indian, and (*d*) Eastern Atlantic. The important temperate faunas may be subdivided into (*a*) North Pacific, (*b*) North Atlantic, and (*c*) temperate Southern Hemisphere.

Tropical Indo-West-Pacific

The richest marine shore fauna of the world is that of the tropical Indo-West-Pacific, containing, with but few exceptions, representatives of all the known living families and most of the genera occurring in all the other three tropical regions. The geographical boundaries of the tropical Indo-West-Pacific shore fauna are in general the region from the head of the Red Sea southward along the African coast to Natal, thence eastward including island groups and coastal regions of southern Asia, northward to the Ryukyu Islands and southern Japan, southward to northern Australia, the Great Barrier Reef, and New Caledonia, thence eastward to the Tuamotu Islands and Easter Island, northward to include the Hawaiian Islands. Although the boundaries of this region are ill-defined, the fauna is chiefly restricted to coral reefs as in the other three tropical regions.

Within the tropical Indo-West-Pacific region, in spite of the homogeneity of the fauna, occur several other subfaunas. Although extensive professional ichthyological collecting is somewhat limited, enough has been accomplished during the last 50 years to indicate certain island groups and regions as containing distinctive endemic species. Roughly these regions are (1) East African, Red Sea, Madagascar, and Mauritius; (2) East Indies to northern Australia, the Great Barrier Reef, and the Philippines; (3) Ryukyu Islands; (4) Hawaiian Islands and Johnston Island; (5) Marianas, Marshalls, Gilberts, Line Islands, Phoenix, Samoan, and perhaps others; (6) Tuamotu Archipelago. Other island groups may be distinctive too, but proof requires more careful ichthyological analysis of species.

Tropical American Pacific

The tropical American Pacific faunal region extends from the southern part of the Gulf of California southward to Ecuador and northern Peru. This faunal region, though distinctive, has several species common to the tropical Indo-West-Pacific and the West Indian region. No doubt these species wandered eastward in the Pacific and others came from the West Indies when the present Isthmus of Panama was below sea level during past geological times. Nevertheless, the tropical American Pacific fish fauna is not as extensive as that of the tropical American Atlantic or West Indian.

Tropical American Atlantic or West Indian

The West Indian marine shore fauna forms the next richest faunal area. Its boundaries are roughly southern Florida, the West Indies to the Atlantic side of Panama, thence southward to Baía, Brazil. This area contains about three-fourths of the fish families found in the tropical Indo-West-Pacific.

Tropical Eastern Atlantic

The tropical Eastern Atlantic shore fauna, including that of the Mediterranean Sea, is not very extensive when compared with that of the West Indian and tropical Indo-West-Pacific. Many of the genera and species of these shore fishes are the same as in the tropical American Atlantic, but as in every faunal area, certain genera and species are endemic.

Temperate

In the temperate Northern Hemisphere the most important and richest faunal area is that of the North Pacific. It contains a very large number of endemic genera and species. The North Atlantic, though important, appears to have derived its fish fauna mostly from the North Pacific.

The temperate Southern Hemisphere as compared with that of the north is not a rich area. There are three subregions: (1) Australian–New Zealand; (2) South African; and (3) Southern South American or Patagonian. The fauna of these three regions is not very extensive but each region, as in nearly every other area of the world, contains genera and species that are distinct and unique.

ANATOMY AND FUNCTIONS

The characteristic form of a fish as seen in an aquarium is highly variable, but generally it is more or less streamlined, resembling the shape of a submarine minus some of the superstructure. This shape is not arbitrary but conforms to definite mechanical principles related to the displacement of liquids. The streamlined shape offers the least resistance when moved through water at the speeds at which fishes swim. Experiments have shown that a streamlined model will "roll over" in the water unless it is equipped with fins as stabilizers.

Fins and Locomotion

There can be no doubt that fishes have developed fins for three purposes at least, as organs of stability, of steering, and of propulsion or locomotion. The fins are of two basic kinds: median or unpaired and the paired fins. The median fins serve as keels and are of three kinds: The *dorsal fin* occurs along the back and varies from one to three parts. Usually in the spiny-rayed

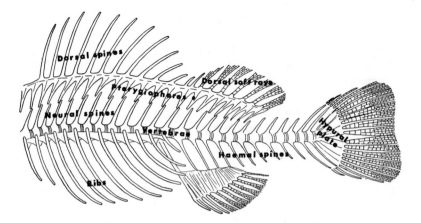

Skeleton of the body of a fish.

fishes the most anterior one is a spiny dorsal fin, whereas the second or posterior one is a soft dorsal fin. In codfishes, which have three dorsal fins, all of them are composed of soft rays and therefore are soft dorsal fins. The *anal fin*, along the midventral line, behind the vent on the belly, may be composed of one or two parts. Usually the first few rays are stiff spines in the spiny-rayed fishes.

The tail of the fish, composed of the *caudal* or *tail fin*, occurs at the rear end of the fish body. The tail fin assists in maintaining stability, acts as a rudder for steering, and probably most important, acts as the organ for forward propulsion. The caudal fin is modified in many ways to serve the best purposes for particular functions of different fishes. In the case of fast-swimming tuna, mackerel, and some jacks, for example, the caudal fin is crescent-shaped and is connected to the body by a narrow tubular-shaped

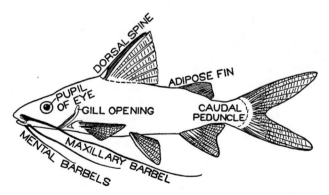

The nomenclature of the important external parts of a fish.

caudal peduncle, equipped with one or two sharp keels on the side of the peduncle. These characteristics are for the purpose of speedy propulsion in an aquatic medium.

The paired fins are of two kinds. The *pectoral fins* correspond to the forelimbs of land vertebrates, whereas the *pelvic* represent the hind limbs. The pectoral fins are very important in the locomotion of fishes, but the pelvics function chiefly as stabilizers. The former may be used exclusively for locomotion as in certain sea horses, or especially in skates and rays. Many slow-moving fishes use the pectorals for locomotion by means of a "flapping" or a "wavelike" movement. Other uses are for slowing down or braking the speed, steering, and for reverse locomotion. Backward propulsion may result from the reversal of movement of the caudal fin, the primary locomotor organ.

Another form of locomotion common in fishes is jet propulsion. Water is squirted out the gill openings in a backward direction, which forces the fish forward.

Speed of Locomotion

The speed of the swimming of fishes has been a subject of much discussion, but little accurate information has been recorded. Tagged salmon in Pacific Coast streams have been recorded as averaging about 7 to 10 miles per day upstream, but it is easy to observe that many fresh-water and oceanic fishes travel much faster for short distances. Experiments conducted during World War II in England and elsewhere indicate that the following speeds in miles per hour have been attained: Flying fishes 35, striped bass 12, black bass 12, mackerel 20.5, salmon 25, dolphin 37, tuna 44, bonito 50, albacore 50, and swordfish 60. It will be noted that the fishes making the greatest speed conform most closely to the true streamline form.

Other Types of Locomotion

Leaping

Other forms of locomotion besides swimming are characteristic of fishes such as leaping, burrowing, walking, and flying. Some fishes, such as mullet, tarpon, sailfishes, marlins, and devil rays, leap from the water. The leap is accomplished by rapid swimming upward through the water; as the body of the fish clears the surface, powerful flips of the tail give added momentum. This carries the fish several feet into the air. Some fish, such as tarpon and sailfishes, appear to leap for sport, whereas others do so to escape enemies.

Burrowing

Burrowing is accomplished in many ways among the various kinds of fishes. Some, such as the snake eels, have stiff tails that are used to burrow or actually swim backward in loose gravel or sand. The mud minnow, *Umbra limi,* when disturbed will dart into the mud and bury itself. Other fishes such as certain wrasses, the flatfishes, rays, and skates partially bury themselves by wriggling into soft sand or mud. The sand divers such as *Chalixodytes tauensis* and the lancelets, *Branchiostoma,* swim or dive into loose sand similar to the habit of larval lampreys, the ammocoetes.

Walking

Walking is another habit found in the various triglid fishes or gurnards. The lower rays of the pectoral fin are separate from each other and are controlled by muscles that cause these rays to propel the gurnard along the bottom similar to walking. *Periophthalmus* is a fine example, as is the walking perch.

Flying

Flying is one of the most highly developed skills of locomotion in fishes, especially in the family Exocoetidae, although it has been observed in one genus, *Euleptorhamphus,* of the halfbeak family Hemiramphidae, and in certain South American characids such as *Thoracocharax,* the hatchetfish.

The flying fish, *Cypselurus,* occurs in all tropical seas and its flight is of great interest and delight to travelers on ocean-going vessels. So many people have seen flying fishes sail through the air that a controversy developed over a century ago as to whether or not flying fishes flap their "wings" and use them for propulsion in the air as do bats and birds.

Anatomically, flying fishes do not possess muscles that could possibly cause the fins to flap like wings of birds. Instead, the fins are used as glider wings. Moving pictures of flying fishes in flight show that they sail.

When under water the fins of the flying fish are folded close to the body so that they offer the least resistance. As the fish approaches the surface and begins to emerge, the pectoral and pelvic fins are spread fully outward. There is increased speed as the body is free of the water and the fish enters into what is called a taxi. The lower lobe of the caudal fin remains in the water and is vibrated rapidly from side to side, causing the speed to increase to about 35 miles per hour. The movement of the caudal fin causes the rigid wings to move up and down a little; sometimes their tips alternately strike the surface causing little ripples. This up-and-down movement, mistaken for actual flapping of the fins, has been the chief cause of the controversy.

The flying fish, after several yards of taxiing, sails into the air and may remain aloft for several seconds. Sometimes it will strike the water and taxi again and again, as many as five times, resulting in a flight of 20 to 30 seconds. Most flights last only 1 to 3 seconds, but some single flights last 10 seconds or more. Observations of hundreds of flights by Leonard P. Schultz in the Marshall Islands indicated that usually the taxi occurred into the wind at some angle; only when the sea was calm did the flight occur with the wind. When the flying fish hits the water for another taxi it invariably turns again to taxi into the wind or at some angle to it. The flight appears to be longer in strong winds. Flying fishes almost always curve back with the wind as they sail along.

Specialization of Fins

Besides the alteration of fins for walking, leaping, and flying, there are several other modifications such as sucking disks, fishing rods, and various defensive and offensive weapons.

Sucking Disks

Certain bottom-inhabiting fishes living in turbulent water, such as swift streams and where wave action is strong, have developed sucking disks that enable them to maintain their position with little effort. The pelvic fin is always involved in this development, sometimes alone, and in certain fishes in connection with the pectoral fin.

The gobies (Gobiidae) have the pelvic fins modified into a cuplike disk, but this group of fishes is so variable in habitat that some of the members live in quiet waters and use their disk for clinging to vegetation and other objects.

The lumpsuckers (Cyclopteridae) and the sea snails (Lipariidae) are two other families of marine fishes with sucking disks modified from the pelvic fins. The clingfishes (Gobiesocidae) have the pelvic and pectoral fins joined under the rear of the head to form a complicated sucking disk. However, this disk is not as highly specialized as that of the *Remora*, whose dorsal fin is developed into an organ that resembles the sole of a rubber boot. Transverse ridges with tiny spines, in addition to a hydraulic suction, aid in clinging to the host. The little spines keep the *Remora* from slipping along the surface of its host, the shark, the barracuda, or other large fish.

In fishes such as the Homolopteridae of southeastern Asia and certain catfishes of South America, *Chaetostoma* and *Pseudancistrus*, the mouth, pelvic, and pectoral fins serve as sucking organs, enabling them to cling to stones in turbulent white-water streams. Such fishes are thin and waferlike in shape too, which adapts them to the stream bottom.

Fishing Rods

Among the highly specialized modifications of fins is the fishing rod on the anglers (Lophiidae) and the deep-sea anglers (Ceratiidae). The first dorsal spine and sometimes the second are modified into fishing rods with tentacle-like "worms" at their tips, used to attract prey. This bait is dangled in front of their big mouth, which opens quickly, sweeping the unsuspecting creature inside where it is held by long sharp teeth.

In some deep-sea anglers the tip of the fishing rod is illuminated, probably aiding in the attraction of crustaceans and other aquatic organisms in a medium of complete darkness.

Locking Mechanisms

The spines of fins have become modified in various groups of fishes as organs of defense. Noteworthy among such modifications are those dorsal spines which may be locked erect. This is a powerful defense apparatus for such fishes as the triggerfishes (Balistiidae), certain catfishes (Bagridae) and the sticklebacks (Gasterosteidae). In the latter both dorsal and pelvic spines lock erect. They may be depressed by rotating sidewise a little, whereas in the triggerfishes a second or third dorsal spine is the trigger in the locking and unlocking mechanism. If the second or third dorsal spine is depressed, the very large heavy first spine is unlocked at its base and is depressible. Otherwise it would break off before moving.

Spines locked into position serve as defense organs. When swallowed, the spines cause the victim to become stuck in the throat of the predator, resulting in the death of both fishes.

Poison Spines

The defense modifications of fins in several families of fishes are associated with poison glands. The sting rays, such as Dasyatidae, have a long sharp spine with toothed edges located near the middle of the length of the tail on the dorsal side. The poison glands lie along the bases of the side "teeth." The poison is highly toxic and some deaths are recorded as the result of injury by sting rays. Some sting rays occur in fresh waters, especially in South America. Other fresh-water fishes with poison spines in the New World are a few genera of catfishes: *Schilbeoides* and *Noturus* of North America and *Pimelodella* of South America. In these genera the pectoral spines are supplied with poison glands. The poison injected causes a reaction resembling that of a severe bee sting.

The most virulent poisons occur in certain families of marine fishes such as weavers, or Trachinidae, scorpionfishes of the family Scorpaenidae, as well as some of the toadfishes, family Batrachoididae. Others such as the butterflyfishes (Chaetodontidae) and the Siganidae have less powerful poisons. Poison glands are associated with the dorsal spines of the weavers and scorpionfishes, stonefishes, lionfishes, and toadfishes. The poison flows along a groove on the rear side of the spine of scorpionfishes, but in toadfishes the spines are like hypodermic needles. The pelvic spines deliver the poison in the siganid fishes.

Poisonous Fishes

The term poisonous fishes refers to those fishes whose flesh produces toxic symptoms when ingested by human beings, in contrast to venomous fishes, which produce their toxic effects by the injection of venom by means

of spines or stings, perhaps even teeth. Poisonous fishes have been recorded
in the literature for more than 200 years but the exact cause is not known
today although it is receiving research attention.

Fish poisoning has been called by such names as ciguatera in the Carib-
bean area and fugu in Japan. A more recent term classifies these and other
local names under *ichthyotoxism.*

Bruce Halstead[*] states that all fish poisons "are essentially the same, but
differ in the degree of virulence. *Tetradon* poisoning apparently is the most
virulent form because the victims usually die within 5 hours after ingesting
the fish." However, not all puffers (*Tetradon*) are poisonous; some are an
epicurean delight. Halstead has found over 300 species of tropical Indo-
Pacific marine fishes that have poisonous flesh at irregular intervals during
the year.

The symptoms appear within a few minutes or as long as 30 hours after
ingestion. A tingling sensation develops first about the lips and tongue, soon
spreading to the hands and feet, then gradually developing into general
numbness. Sometimes nausea, vomiting, and diarrhea occur with abdominal
pain. Later muscular weakness and paralysis may occur. One of the most
striking symptoms is the generalized paradoxical sensory disturbance in
which temperature sensations are reversed. Hot objects feel cold and cold
objects feel hot. Recovery is slow, taking several weeks.

To avoid fish poisoning in the tropics one should follow the advice of the
natives and not eat those fishes considered poisonous.

Skin and Scales of Fishes

The skin of fishes, like that of other vertebrates, is composed of two layers of tissue, the thin outer epidermis and the thicker inner dermis. The epidermal layer consists of epithelial cells. The innermost of these go through
cell division, multiply in number, and gradually crowd the older cells outward as they become flattened and wear away.

The dermal layer is made up of connective tissue intermingled with
nerves, blood vessels, and muscle fibers. Glands, when present, are located
in both dermal and epidermal layers but are chiefly composed of epidermal
cells. Mucous glands are abundant in the skin of fishes, especially in the region of the head. Their function is to produce the mucus or "slime" that
makes a fish slippery, enabling it to swim with a minimum of friction in water. The dermal layer of the skin produces the scales or exoskeleton so characteristic of fishes.

Kinds of Scales

There are four chief kinds of scales, placoid or odontoid, ganoid, cycloid,
and ctenoid, all of which have various modified forms. The placoid scale,

[*] *Med. Arts. Sci.,* 5(4):1–6, 1951.

characteristic of the elasmobranchs, is a minute unit with an ossified central dermal base, from which arises an enameled papilla-like projection. This type of scale has been modified into teeth on the jaws of sharks. It is thought that from this type of scale other kinds may have evolved.

The ganoid scale, found on primitive kinds of fishes such as the gar, *Lepisosteus,* is rhomboidal or diamond-shaped, without the enameled papilla. The surface is covered with a hard substance called ganoin, analogous to the ectodermal enamel of placoid scales but not homologous. As long as the epidermis took part in scale formation, enamel was present on the scale, but the tendency of scale evolution has been to reduce the part that the epidermis plays and to increase the importance of the dermal layer. The ganoid scale of the gars has ganoin with no enamel present; all that remains is the basal plate. In general, scales conform in number and arrangement to the segmental relationship of the subjacent myotomes of muscle segments. Scales occur roughly in proportion to or in multiples of the number of myotomes.

It is thought by some zoologists that the rhombic-shaped scales took that form because of the need for flexibility in swimming. However, the rhombic-shaped scale imposes restrictions on the fish by limiting lateral flexures of the body. Thus there arose a need for smaller scales that were more easily movable and caused less friction. The evolutionary process then produced cycloid and ctenoid scales.

The cycloid scale is disklike in shape and develops from the dermis. It lies within a pocket of the skin. There are no traces of enamel or of spines. The scale is set obliquely in the skin, like the shingles on a roof, the anterior end lying under the rear part of the forward scale, with few exceptions.

The ctenoid scale is a specialized form of cycloid scale with the posterior part of the scale supplied with minute teeth or ctenii. These aid in making the ctenoid scale more difficult to withdraw from the scale pocket. Cycloid scales of smelt, anchovies, round herring, and some minnows are easily shed, sometimes by a light touch, whereas ctenoid scales of bass, sunfishes, and numerous other kinds of spiny-rayed fishes are more firmly fixed. Both cycloid and ctenoid scales may occur on the same fish. In some flounders the scales on the eyed side may be ctenoid whereas those on the blind side are cycloid; or there may occur patches of ctenoid scales on a fish otherwise covered with cycloid scales. The posterior edges of scales may be smooth or crenulate.

Determining Age from Scales

During the development of cycloid and ctenoid scales, as well as other varieties, characteristic marks occur in the structure of the scales. These marks, or circuli, are laid down in a pattern that is proportional to the rate of growth. They are spaced more widely during rapid growth and much closer together during periods of slow growth, whereas in times of little or no growth the circuli do not form a regular pattern and a mark called the annulus, which may contrast sharply with the regular circuli formation, occurs all the way around the scale.

The annulus usually forms during the winter in fishes of the Temperate Zone, or it may form during the breeding season. If an annulus forms each winter, the age of the fish may be determined from its scales.

Fish scales are of value also in the identification of fishes since they grow in proportion to the increase in length of the fish. The number of scales for nearly all species of fish remains constant throughout life. Thus the number of scales, along with the number of fin rays and vertebrae, may be used in distinguishing closely related species.

Lateral Line

Another feature of scales is the lateral line, which consists of a series of modified scales, each provided with a mucous tube or pore, which connects below the scales with the lateral line canal. The lateral line canal usually runs parallel with the back in spiny-rayed fishes, whereas in soft-rayed fishes it often runs more or less parallel with the ventral outline of the body. No definite rule can be established since the lateral line is highly variable. It may be complete, interrupted, absent, or variously branched or arched. Some fishes, such as the greenlings (Hexagrammidae) have as many as five lateral lines on each side. In scaleless fishes, the lateral line lies in the skin.

Cephalic Canals

The lateral line canals extend forward on the head where they branch and are known as cephalic canals. On certain groups of fishes, such as darters and gobies, these cephalic canals form characteristic patterns of great value in distinguishing species.

The lateral line which connects with the ear functions as a sensory system in acquainting fishes with low-frequency vibrations in the water. Some fishes are able to detect the swimming movements of other aquatic animals.

Bony Plates

The scales of fishes in some groups have become specialized to form plates or a boxlike covering. Buckler plates occur in the sturgeons, *Acipenser,* and in the catfish family Doradidae of South America. The trunkfishes are encased in bony armor, whereas certain cottids have platelike spiny scales along the lateral line. The function of plates, bony armor, and spinous scales is for defense.

Skeleton

The skeleton of fishes may be composed of cartilage or bone. Whatever the substance, it serves the purpose of a supporting framework, to provide attachment for the muscles and tendons and protection to the delicate organs of the body. The skeleton of fishes, like that of man, is a complicated structure. It is divided into two parts, exoskeleton and endoskeleton. The former is composed of scales, scutes, and bony plates. The endoskeleton consists of three main divisions: (1) skull, (2) vertebral column, and (3) fin skeleton. The line of demarcation between exoskeleton and endoskeleton is not sharply defined in many groups of fishes since parts of the exoskeleton have become incorporated into the endoskeleton.

Skull

The skull, or syncranium, is composed of two contrasting divisions: (1) the neurocranium or brain case and (2) the splanchnocranium or branchiocranium. The neurocranium consists of an inner series of endosteal elements

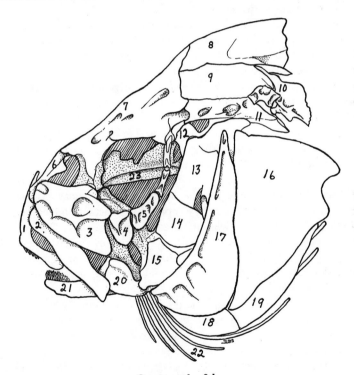

Cranium of a fish:

1. premaxillary	9. parietal	16. opercular
2. maxillary	10. posttemporal	17. preopercular
3. preorbital	11. pterotic	18. interopercular
4, 5. suborbitals	12. sphenotic	19. subopercular
6. ethmoid	13. hyomandibular	20. articular
7. frontal	14. metapterygoid	21. dentary
8. supraoccipital	15. quadrate	22. branchiostegal rays

protecting the olfactory, optic, and otic capsules and the anterior end of the notochord in primitive fishes. A series of superficial ectosteal or dermal bones, which were originally similar to ganoid scales in microscopic structure but which long ago lost their enamel-like surface, have become pitted, tunneled, and ossified. They have become modified and in the recent bony fishes the skin now covers them.

The skull or syncranium of fishes has had throughout its phylogenetic history the chief function of capture of living prey in connection with forward swimming. This is best accomplished by a bilaterally symmetrical apparatus protecting the sense organs, olfactory, optic, and otic lobes, which are always arranged in a fixed anteroposterior order in relation to the mouth and pharynx.

William K. Gregory considers the adult teleostean endocranium as a complex of four parts surrounding the orbits:

1. The ethnovomer block at the anterior end of the skull receives on its surfaces the forces resulting from forward swimming and transmits them to other parts of the cranium. Other functions are protection of the delicate olfactory capsule, formation of the anterior margin of the orbits by the lateral ethmoids, and reception of the forces resulting from the use of the jaws.

2. The interorbital bridge and septum and the orbitosphenoid bone brace the ethnovomerine block, transmit forces to the endocranial vault, supply channels for the olfactory nerves, and help support the orbits.

3. The cranial vault, according to Gregory, has eight functions: (a) receives forces of the vertebral column from the rear and thrusts of water from the front; (b) resists wrenching forces of the muscles of the back; (c) affords firm anchorage for the hyomandibular apparatus and resists forces created by jaw muscles; (d) supplies support and anchorage for the shoulder girdle and the muscles attached to those bones; (e) gives support to the muscles operating the opercular apparatus, branchial apparatus, and pharyngeals; (f) protects the brain and cranial nerves; (g) protects the semicircular canals and the inner ear; (h) protects the eye and furnishes support for eye muscles.

4. The keel bone or parasphenoid connects the ethnovomer block with the base of the cranial vault, forms the roof of the mouth and the floor of the interorbital septum, and supplies the support for attachment of eye and palatine muscles.

The branchiocranium consists of seven fundamental arches. The first or mandibular gave rise to the upper and lower jaw, the pterygoquadrate and hyomandibular bones. The second or hyoid arch gave rise to the opercular series. Gill arches 3 to 7 bear the gills of modern fishes.

Each gill arch is composed of five bones. Beginning at the ventral anterior end of the arch the parts are basibranchial, hypobranchial, ceratobranchial, epibranchial, and interbranchial.

Vertebral Skeleton

The vertebral skeleton is composed of bony units or vertebrae arranged in a linear series forming the vertebral column. In fishes the anterior vertebrae are known as abdominal vertebrae and are located chiefly over the coelomic or body cavity. Posteriorly the bony units are named the caudal vertebrae and may be recognized by the presence on their ventral side of the hemal arch, lacking on the abdominal vertebrae. Each vertebra is formed during embryological development from a number of parts, all of which fuse to form a single structure.

The central portion of the vertebrae is the centrum, dorsal to which is located the neural canal containing the nerve or spinal cord; ventrally the abdominal vertebrae bear the ribs; posteriorly the caudal vertebrae bear the hemal arch, which contains the hemal canal, the latter bearing blood vessels. Attached to the centrum laterally on abdominal vertebrae are the intermuscular ribs or epineurals, the latter very numerous in the clupeoid fishes.

Fin Skeleton

The fin skeleton is composed of median fins and paired fins. The latter are considered as homologous to the arms and legs of the higher vertebrates. Median fins are possessed by the lowest chordates but on such primitive forms as the lancelets (Branchiostomidae) and the lampreys (Petromyzonidae) paired fins are lacking.

The theories of the origin or evolution of fins of fishes forms an interesting chapter in ichthyology and vertebrate zoology. The trend in the evolution of paired and median fins has been considerably different. It is not difficult to trace the history of the median fins, but the evolutional history is vague and complex for paired fins. The median fins appear to be much older in geological time, whereas the paired fins occur only on the more highly developed vertebrates.

MEDIAN FINS

The median fins occur as a fold of skin or dermal fold in the most primitive forms, lancelets and lampreys, and are supported by very feeble rays, scarcely visible in lampreys. This fold of skin extends along the middorsal line of the back from head to tail and along the midventral line from near the anus to the tail. As time passed, the continuous fin broke up into separate units, dorsal, caudal, and anal fins. Some of our present-day fishes show this change as they pass through their embryological development to the adult stage, the continuous fin forming separate parts.

The bony supports of the median fins are of two kinds, spines and soft rays. The spines are called simple rays because they are not branched. Spines are usually pungent or sharp-pointed, but they may be long and flex-

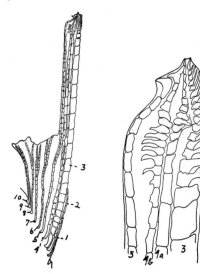

(Left) The anal fin of *Gambusia* showing the number of rays from anteropos-
teriorly. (Right) Distal tips of rays 3, 4,
and 5 showing details of the gonopodium
of *Heterandria*. (*After Hubbs.*)

(Below) Caudal skeleton of
the guppy, *Lebistes reticulatus*. (*Modified from Hollister,
Zool., vol. 25, no. 1, fig. 15,
1940.*)

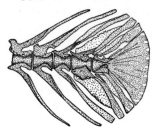

ible. They are never cross-striated. Soft rays are always cross-striated. They
are of two kinds, branched and unbranched. The soft ray is bilaterally symmetrical and is easily split into two parts, whereas spines cannot be split
easily.

Spines and soft rays usually are connected by a dermal membrane. However, in certain genera such as sticklebacks, *Gasterosteus*, the spines are isolated. Soft rays on the peduncular region of mackerels (Scombridae) and
related kinds of fishes may be isolated. These are called finlets, or little fins.

The rays of median fins, dorsal and anal, are supported basally by a series of spines, one each in close contact with the neural spine of each vertebra, or for the anal fin with the hemal spine. These interspinous bones or
pterygiophores have a small knob distally, to which the base of the fin ray is
joined by a small radial cartilage.

The bony structure of the caudal fin is more complicated than that of the
dorsal and anal fins. The most posterior vertebrae are reduced in number
and size, and the hemal spines become modified into the hypurals, the latter
forming the hypural plate. The tip of the vertebral column may remain as a
rudiment, called the urostyle. The caudal-fin rays are attached to the distal
edges of the hypurals.

PAIRED FINS

The paired fins, pectoral and pelvic, of bony fishes have a more complicated structure than the median fins. The pectoral fin is supported by fin
rays which are attached by means of pectoral radials to the shoulder girdle.
The latter is composed of a series of bones.

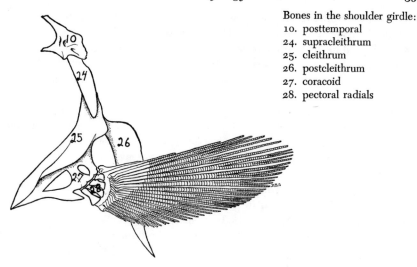

Bones in the shoulder girdle:
10. posttemporal
24. supracleithrum
25. cleithrum
26. postcleithrum
27. coracoid
28. pectoral radials

Among the theories of evolution of the paired fins, the fin-fold theory seems most plausible. As stated by Balfour, "The paired limbs are persisting and exaggerated portions of a fin fold, once continuous, which stretched along each side of the body and to which they bear an exactly similar phylogenetic relation as do the separate dorsal and anal fins to the once continuous median fin fold." Morphological and homological evidence for Balfour's theory is supported by certain extinct and living sharks.

Digestive System

Mouth and Teeth

The mouth forms the beginning of the digestive tract. The tongue of fishes is usually small. It may be free anteriorly or fused into the floor of the mouth. A protrusible tongue, common in amphibians, is absent in fishes, with the exception that a rudiment of that organ is present in some elasmobranchs.

The mouths of fishes are extremely variable in position and structure among the different fish families. The chief function of the mouth is for securing food and for aiding respiration. In general there are two types of mouths, those without opposing jaws, the Agnatha, lampreys and hagfishes, and those with jaws, the Gnathostomata, the sharks, rays, holocephalins, and bony fishes. The lamprey and hagfish mouth contains teeth that are used for rasping off flesh or making a hole so that they may suck blood or consume the flesh.

Those fishes with jaws, which include over 99 per cent of living fishes, have jaws adapted for ingesting, grasping, holding, or chewing prey or plant material. Associated with food getting, almost every fish has jaws and teeth well adapted for its particular habits. Carnivorous, predaceous fishes usually have long, sharp canine teeth suitable for holding captured prey, whereas vegetable or plant feeders have incisor-like teeth adapted to cutting algae off rocks or other objects.

Certain families, for example, the members of the Cyprinidae, lack jaw teeth, but in their throat is located a set of pharyngeal teeth for crushing their animal or plant food. The parrotfishes have jaw teeth resembling the beak of a parrot, and in their throat is an elaborate grinding mill formed by the pharyngeal teeth.

The position of the mouth is an indication of feeding habits. When the mouth is inferior or ventral in position, it is used to secure food from the bottom; for example, some sharks, rays, skates, paddlefishes, sturgeon, suckers, certain catfishes, and some bottom-dwelling minnows. The terminal mouth is used for grasping prey, usually during forward swimming or when at rest. This type of mouth, with some modifications, such as being oblique, occurs in the majority of bony fishes. The mouth that is vertical or nearly so is adapted for feeding at the surface, such as in *Anostomus*, and in the stargazers (Uranoscopidae) and their relatives. In *Trichodon* and *Astroscopus*, the sandfishes, the lips of the vertical mouth are supplied with numerous hairlike cirri or "teeth" used to keep the sand from entering their mouth, since they partially bury themselves in loose sand. Some kinds of fishes have both jaws greatly elongated, for example, the needlefishes, whereas their close relatives, the halfbeaks, have spearlike lower jaws and very short upper jaws. The halfbeaks contrast sharply with the swordfish, marlins, and sailfishes, whose snout is developed into a long spear and whose lower jaw is short. The most remarkable development of the snout or rostrum is that of the sawfishes, *Pristris*. On each side of the rostrum occur strongly set "teeth," projecting straight outward. This saw is used to flail a school of fish. They are stunned, then eaten. Tubular snouts occur, for example, in trumpetfishes, pipefishes, and *Mormyrops boulengeri* of Africa. Asymmetrical mouths are characteristic of the soles, tonguefishes, and other flatfishes, Heterosomata.

SHAPES OF TEETH

Fish teeth are of several kinds and shapes. The commonest is the conical tooth. This kind may be very minute, numerous, and close together, in patches or bands. They are called villiform teeth. Any conical tooth that is much longer than the adjoining teeth is called a canine tooth. Flat-topped teeth are molars, and chisel-like teeth are called incisors. Some teeth, called bifid teeth, have two tips; those with three tips are trifid. Long slender teeth resembling the bristles of a brush are called setiform. The piranha of South

America has triangular teeth with serrated edges, as do some of the sharks, e.g., the great white shark, or maneater.

Teeth are usually arranged in patches, bands, or one or more rows. The bones of the mouth bearing teeth are as follows: on the upper jaw, premaxillary and maxillary in certain fishes; on the lower jaw, dentary. The tongue may or may not be toothed. In the roof of the mouth, teeth may or may not occur on the vomer, palatine, and pterygoid bones.

Pharynx

The pharynx succeeds the mouth or oral cavity and is perforated by the branchial clefts between the branchial arches. The pharyngeal teeth occur on the branchial arches. In certain families the bones are highly modified and bear teeth in rows or patches. Especially notable are those of the Cyprinidae, Labridae, and Scaridae.

Among the various groups of fishes in general, the pharynx is followed in succession by the esophagus, stomach, and intestine, the latter terminating in the rectum or large intestine. The anus is the external posterior opening of the alimentary tract. The exact boundaries of these various organs are not always obvious but are indicated by a change in caliber or diameter, a change in the nature of the epithelial lining, valves formed by sphincter muscles, and the entrance of ducts from digestive glands.

Esophagus

The esophagus is occasionally separated from the stomach by a slight constriction, but the two may be distinguished more frequently by the squamous epithelium of the esophagus being replaced by the columnar epithelium of the stomach, along with the presence of gastric glands in the latter. Otherwise the two organs may be difficult to distinguish.

Intestine and Visceral Organs

The beginning of the intestine is usually indicated by the pyloric valve, a ringlike thickening of the circularly disposed muscle fibers of the terminal end of the stomach. Ducts or combined ducts from the pancreas and liver enter the digestive tract a little behind the pyloric valve. Associated with the pyloric part of the intestine are few to very numerous pyloric caeca. The small intestine is of various lengths in different kinds of fishes.

Predaceous bony fishes, living chiefly on an animal diet, usually have short intestines with one to three loops, whereas the vegetable feeders have long intestines with numerous loops; in some kinds the intestine is coiled around the air bladder or coiled upon itself many times. A black peritoneum frequently occurs in those fishes which are vegetable feeders.

Following the small intestine is the rectum or large intestine, which may be distinguished by its straight course, increase in diameter, and by a caecal diverticulum, the rectal gland. The large intestine is variously specialized. In such groups as the elasmobranchs, crossopterygians, dipnoans, and a few of the more primitive bony fishes, it contains the spiral valve, in which the tissues are arranged in layers like a spiral stairway. The function is to increase the digestive surfaces without increasing the length of the organ.

The rectum ends posteriorly in a cloaca in elasmobranchs and dipnoans, but in most bony fishes the cloaca is absent. The anus is the exterior opening of the digestive tract.

The alimentary canal from esophagus to rectum is covered externally by the visceral layer of the peritoneum, which consirts of an epithelial layer and a stratum of connective tissue. The peritoneum lines the body cavity and forms folds, the mesenteries, that support the digestive organs.

The tissues internal to the peritoneum of the alimentary tract consist of a succession of strata as follows: (1) longitudinal muscle fibers; (2) circularly arranged muscle fibers, (3) submucosa, and (4) epithelial mucous membrane. In the stomach an oblique layer of muscle fibers occurs between the longitudinal and circularly arranged muscle fibers.

The muscular layer varies greatly in thickness in different species. It is very thick in the gizzard shad and in mullets. Usually the intestinal muscles are of the smooth or nonstriated variety, but there are exceptions as in the case of the tench, which has striated fibers inside the smooth layer in both stomach and intestine.

The inner layer of epithelium differs in character in the various portions of the alimentary tract. It is squamous epithelial in the mouth, pharynx, and esophagus whereas in the lower esophagus, stomach, and intestine, it is columnar epithelial. In the rectum it is columnar or squamous. Goblet cells, interspersed among the superficial epithelial cells, may occur throughout the entire length of the alimentary canal.

The primitive ciliation of the chordate alimentary canal is retained in many groups of fishes, usually being associated with feeble musculature, as in the ammocoetes, the larval stage of lampreys. Bony fishes and the myxinoids (hagfishes) generally lack cilia except for the pyloric caecae, which are usually ciliated. In lungfishes the stomach and intestines are ciliated, whereas in elasmobranchs only the posterior portion of the esophagus and the edges of the spiral valve are ciliated. In the Holostei, esophagus, stomach, and intestine vary greatly but are usually ciliated.

The submucosa lies between the muscular layer and the mucous membrane internally. Histologically, the submucosa consists of a framework of connective tissue, enclosing lymphoid tissue with leukocytes, capillary blood vessels, lymph spaces or vessels, and sphincter muscles around certain arteries and veins.

The two inner layers of the intestine, submucosa and mucous membrane, are often developed into ingrowths in the space or lumen of the alimentary canal. These have the form of longitudinal or transverse ridges, or a combination of both, which serve the function of enlarging the secretive and absorptive area of the intestine and stomach. These folds may disappear on distention of the organs.

The folds are longitudinal in the branchiostomids. In the elasmobranchs, they are longitudinal or oblique to transverse, or they may be united to form depressions. Bony fishes, in addition to having longitudinal transverse folds, may have tubular crypts that appear to penetrate the intestinal wall.

The spiral valve is a remarkably beautiful specialization of the intestine found in most of the primitive fishes such as marsipobranchs, elasmobranchs, choanichthyans, chondrosterians, holosteins, and a few isospondylous fishes. The valve in its simplest form, as found in lampreys, is a longitudinal ridge of mucous membrane. Anteriorly it is dorsal in position, but as it proceeds backward it describes a partial spiral and terminates ventrally. A similar type of valve is found in some elasmobranch embryos, whereas in adult sharks it is complicated, consisting of nine or more turns. In general the holocephalians have about 3 to 3½ coils of this valve; lungfishes 5 to 9; sturgeons 7 to 8; gars and the bowfin about 2 to 3½, perhaps more; and in some isospondylous fishes it is rudimentary. The function of the valve is to increase the absorptive and digestive area of the intestine.

Gastric glands are embedded in the submucosa and open into the stomach through the mucous membrane. They do not appear to be differentiated into acid-secreting and pepsin-forming structures. In the pyloric end of the stomach, true gastric glands may be replaced by mucous glands. The formation of such digestive ferments as pepsin and trypsin is not limited to the stomach and pancreas, respectively, as in higher vertebrates, but may be present in stomach, intestine, pyloric caeca, and pancreas.

Phylogenetically the liver is the oldest gland in connection with the vertebrate alimentary canal, and by far the largest. It arises as a caecal outgrowth and through subsequent division and branchings becomes a compound tubular gland in adult fishes. It is of various shapes and sizes and of various degrees of lobulation, but anteriorly it takes the shape of the body cavity to which it is confined. It is usually bi- or trilobed and possesses a gall bladder, the duct from which opens into the commencement of the intestine.

The pancreas, although well-developed in the elasmobranchs, is a separate organ from the liver. In the bony fishes it is a diffuse gland, usually most or all of it being embedded in the substance of the liver, especially along ramifications of the hepatic artery, duct, and portal vein. The duct from the pancreas usually joins that from the liver before entering the intestine.

Pyloric caeca, although absent in lampreys, lungfishes, most or all elasmobranchs, and the bowfin, vary from few to hundreds in the bony fishes, with rare exceptions. Their function is thought to be digestive. The rectal gland, thought to be homologous with the appendix digitiformis in higher vertebrates, is a small organ of doubtful function that opens into the alimentary canal near the union of the small and large intestine.

Respiratory System

All aquatic animals without lungs depend on dissolved oxygen in the water for respiratory purposes. The oxygen in the air is not available to aquatic animals unless it is dissolved in the water. With few exceptions the gills are not able to take the gas directly from the air in correct amounts to be of use to fishes. Man is able to obtain oxygen for respiration by inhaling air. The oxygen is dissolved in the film of moisture on the lung tissues; then it is absorbed by the circulating blood as it passes through the capillaries.

Gills

Aquatic animals have two types of respiratory organs, external and internal gills, both of which are found among the various fishes, but external gills are more characteristic for amphibians. In larval lungfishes and crossopterygians external gills occur but are lost long before the adult stage is reached. All adult fishes have internal gills.

The internal gills consist of pairs of gill filaments supported by the branchial arches, between which are clefts or openings, the gill slits. The most anterior cleft occurs between the mandibulohyoid arches and is known as the *spiracle*, the latter a commonly observed pore in sharks, skates, and rays, with exceptions. The second or hyobranchial cleft, or hyoidean cleft, occurs between the hyoid and first branchial arches; the remaining clefts occur between the succeeding branchial arches.

The spiracle is a vestigial gill cleft. At an early stage of embryonic growth it differs little from its fellows, but later it degenerates until in the adult it is a small tubular passage between the oral cavity and the exterior. The anterior wall of the spiracle may retain a rudiment of a hemibranch in the form of a few to several vascular lamellae named pseudobranchs, because they are supplied with arterial and not with venous blood as are the ordinary gill filaments or lamellae.

The gills, vascular platelike filamentous tissues, occur on the anterior and posterior walls of the arches, with the exception of the first, second, and last. Filaments are absent on the first, and absent on the anterior wall of the second and posterior wall of the last.

The evolutionary tendency in fishes, in the direction of a reduction in the number of gill clefts, progresses from both ends, anterior and posterior. Along with the reduction in number of clefts is a reduction in the width of the gill septum, the membrane separating the pair of filaments on each branchial arch.

If we consider *Branchiostoma*, the lancelet, as a forerunner of fishes, we observe a very large number of clefts and gill bars covered over by the body walls to form the atrial cavity. The hagfishes possess from 6 to 14 gill clefts or gill sacs whereas the lampreys have 7. The pharynx of adult lampreys and of hagfishes is much modified. A small tube connects the gill sacs with the mouth, the former not opening directly into the pharynx but having external openings along each side of the head.

Elasmobranchs possess from 5 to 7 gill slits in addition to the spiracle, but there is no opercular cover. Holocephalians have 4 branchial clefts, the fifth is closed, and the gills are covered with a fleshy operculum. The lungfishes have 5 or 6 branchial clefts but the fifth arch lacks gill filaments. Bony fishes possess 4 or 5 clefts; usually a pseudobranch occurs on the inner wall of the operculum and the hyoidean arch is without a hemibranch, as is the last or fifth arch.

Nearly all fishes have either cartilaginous or bony tubercles, called gill rakers, attached to the inner side of the gill arches. Usually the anterior row of gill rakers interdigitates with the posterior row of the adjoining arch. The function of gill rakers may be twofold, to protect the delicate gill filaments from foreign particles or to strain out planktonic organisms used as food.

Aeration of the blood is caused by the rhythmical intake of water into the oral or mouth cavity and its expulsion through the gill clefts, thence past the gill filaments, which absorb the oxygen and give off as waste dissolved gases. Membranous oral valves in the mouth prohibit water from moving in the wrong direction. The rate of breathing differs in various species, but a deficiency of oxygen and too much carbon dioxide in the blood causes an acceleration of breathing movements.

The blood may be aerated to a small extent through the skin and the membranous fins. In certain families of fishes, such as the clariid and heteropneustid catfishes and the labyrinthine fishes (Anabantidae), an accessory respiratory apparatus is developed in addition to the gills. Hugh M. Smith states that in the Clariidae this organ occupies a chamber above each gill cavity and is an outgrowth of the fourth gill arch. It consists of an arborescent structure that provides a large surface for the absorption of the air reaching it through the mouth. In the Anabantidae a similar organ arising from the fourth gill arch is composed of a set of superimposed leaflike plates, which afford a large absorptive area for oxygen.

It has been observed through experimentation that in clariids and anabantids, even in well-aerated water, the gills may not provide enough oxygen to satisfy the requirements of the system, and death may ensue in as short a time as half an hour if the fishes are prevented from going to the surface to take in gulps of fresh air and to expel vitiated air.

In the Heteropneustidae an entirely different accessory breathing organ is found. "Extending from the pharynx," states Smith, "among the muscles of the back on each side of the vertebral column is a long cylindrical tube, richly supplied with blood vessels and serving as a primitive lung. These tubes, into which both water and air are forced by muscular action, enable the fish to obtain the requisite quantity of oxygen while living in hot, shallow, stagnant ditches and in other places where the water does not contain enough air to support life."

Although the Ophicephalidae, the serpent-head fishes, lack the elaborate air-breathing organs met with in the above-mentioned families, they have a large suprabranchial cavity lined with puckered vascular epithelium that serves the same purpose.

Air Bladder

The air bladder develops as a caecal outgrowth of the esophagus in the embryo and grows both posteriorly and anteriorly. The air bladder in lungfishes plays an important role in the aeration of the blood and is lunglike in many respects, but in the higher bony fishes this function is completely lost. The air bladder in the spiny-rayed bony fishes has no duct connecting it with the pharynx, and in many of the soft-rayed bony fishes this duct is highly degenerate. The walls of the air bladder seldom contain muscle fibers, although in certain sound-making fishes powerful extrinsic muscles are present which are used to produce sound.

The air bladder is absent in marsipobranchs and elasmobranchs, although in the latter it may be represented by a small caecal outgrowth in certain sharks. In crossopterygians it is a paired organ devoid of sacculations, the right sac being long and tubular, whereas the left one is smaller and more oval; anteriorly they join into a single chamber with two caecal outgrowths. The median chamber opens on the ventral side of the esophagus by means of the glottis, bounded by sphincter muscles.

The air bladder of sturgeons is nonsacculated, whereas in the gar pikes and the bowfin it is sacculated. In all three kinds of fishes it is connected to the dorsal side of the esophagus by a very short tube, the ductus pneumaticus.

Lungfishes may have a paired or unpaired air bladder. In the Australian lungfish, *Neoceratodus*, it is unpaired, whereas in the African lungfish, *Protopterus*, it is paired and the anterior median unpaired portion continues into a duct which opens on the ventral side of the esophagus by a glottis and an epiglottis. The posterior paired portions contain alveoli. Lungfishes have no "red glands."

The air bladder of bony fishes shows some remarkable specializations. It may be present or absent; it is usually present in soft-rayed fishes but is present or absent in spiny-rayed fishes. The shape of the air bladder in bony fishes conforms mostly to the shape of the body cavity, but in certain forms it bears outgrowths which extend into the transverse processes of the vertebrae, for example, arctic cod, *Eleginus*, or into the hemal arches of the vertebrae as in the silverside genus, *Atherina* of Europe. Probably the air bladder reaches its greatest complexity in the South American catfish family Doradidae and in the croaker of the drumfish family, Sciaenidae, and in such genera as *Corvina* and *Pogonias,* in which the air bladder is multiple-branched or "fringed." The complicated structures may be internally divided into compartments by means of longitudinal and transverse septa.

Red glands or red bodies, so far as known, occur only in bony fishes which do not have a functional ductus pneumaticus, the tube that connects the air bladder with the esophagus in more primitive fishes. The red glands, which occur at special points in the inner surface of the air bladder, are composed of tightly packed masses of blood capillaries and function to supply or absorb gases in the air bladder as an aid to equilibrium at various depths. This process is a slow one, the time needed to change the volume of gas taking from a few hours to several days, depending on the species of fish and the magnitude of depth involved.

The air bladder serves as a resonator for sound intensification, or it may produce sound. In certain drumfishes (Sciaenidae), extrinsic muscles, "musculus sonificus," are attached directly to the air bladder, or they run from the abdomen on each side to a central tendon situated above the air bladder. By a series of contractions, about 24 per second, "the rigid, gas-filled air bladder is set into vibration and resonant drumming results." The actual sound has also been variously described as humming, hissing, purring, croaking, and whistling. Drumming occurs especially during the breeding season, and the noise is audible at least 6 feet or more above the water surface.

In some of the South American catfishes the air bladder is divided into chambers by septa. Contraction of muscles causes the rapid movement of air from chamber to chamber over the septa edges, producing sound.

The air bladder of the Ostariophysi (catfishes, minnows, characins, and gymnotids) is connected to the auditory organs by means of a series of ossicles or bones, the Weberian apparatus. This complicated mechanism is formed from the first four vertebrae, just behind the skull. It was named after its discoverer, Ernst Heinrich Weber.

The *tripus* ossicle is inserted on the dorsal-anterior wall or end of the air bladder. It is a crescent-shaped bone that rotates on a projection from the concave side of the bone, which lies against one of the vertebrae. Its anterior end bears a ligament that connects with the most anterior ossicle, the *scaphium.* Sometimes a small ossicle, the *intercalarium,* is situated between the ligaments connecting the ends of the tripus and scaphium. The scaphium is a cup-shaped bone connecting with the perilymph surrounding the auditory organs and extending as a sinus to the base of the cranium. This complex mechanism probably functions to transmit vibrations from the air bladder to the ear. Although its function is not well-known, it must be an important organ since it occurs in every member of the most important families of fresh-water fishes in the entire world.

Nervous System

The nervous system of fishes consists of the same fundamental parts as in higher vertebrates, the central and peripheral nervous systems. The former is made up of the brain and spinal cord, the latter of afferent and efferent nerves. The brain of fishes lacks the gray matter so highly developed in man. The size of the fish brain is small, and varies considerably, being $\frac{1}{720}$ of the total weight in the turbot but only $\frac{1}{1305}$ in the pike, *Esox*, whereas man's brain is about $\frac{1}{50}$ of his weight.

The brain is divided into three parts, forebrain, midbrain, and hindbrain. The forebrain consists of the prosencephalon and diencephalon. The former usually is in the form of a pair of cerebral hemispheres, which give rise to the olfactory lobes; however, in some of the more primitive fishes they are unpaired. The diencephalon has its sides thickened to form the optic thalami. The roof gives rise to the pineal apparatus, at the anterior part of which is the parietal organ and posteriorly the pineal organ or epiphysis. These may be separate or joined to form a single organ. The floor grows downward into a funnel-like prolongation, the infundibulum, which gives rise to the pituitary body, or hypophysis, a ductless gland. The dorsal part of this organ is known as the saccus vasculosus.

The midbrain is called the mesencephalon, the dorsal walls of which form the optic lobes. The ventral wall is thickened into longitudinal bands named the crura cerebri. The hindbrain consists of the cerebellum or epencephalon and the medulla oblongata or metencephalon. The brain contains small cavities or ventricles. These chambers are in series which intercommunicate and are named after the lobe of the brain in which they occur.

Cranial Nerves

There are ten cranial nerves in the bony fishes. The first or olfactory nerve arises from the olfactory lobes at the anterior end of the brain and extends to the olfactory sacs. The second or paired optic nerves run outward from the optic chiasma, each to one of the orbits, perforating the sclerotic coat of the eye and terminating in the retina. The third or oculomotor nerve arises from the ventral region of the midbrain and supplies four of the six eye muscles—superior, inferior, and internal recti, and inferior oblique, as well as the ciliary muscles and iris.

The fourth or trochlear nerve arises from the dorsal surface of the brain at the junction of the midbrain with the medulla oblongata. It is a small motor nerve supplying only the superior oblique muscle of the eye. The fifth or trigeminal is a large nerve that arises in close contact with the seventh or facial nerve. As the fifth nerve passes into the orbit it swells into the Gasserian ganglion. There are three branches: (1) The superficial ophthalmic runs forward and ends in the snout, (2) the maxillary supplies the skin of the ventral part of the snout, and (3) the mandibular runs to the skin and muscles of the jaw.

The sixth or abducens is a small motor nerve arising from the ventral region of the medulla and supplying the external rectus muscle of the eye. Thus three out of ten cranial nerves control the muscles of the eye. The seventh or facial nerve, which is mixed with the fifth cranial nerve, arises from the side of the medulla. It has several branches. The ophthalmic runs through the orbit in close contact with the fifth, supplying the lateral line and ampullary canals of the snout region. The buccal branch runs forward with the maxillary branch of the fifth cranial nerve and supplies the sensory canals of the snout. The palatine branch supplies the roof of the mouth whereas the main branch, or hyomandibular nerve, supplies the lower jaw, spiracle, and muscles between the first branchial arch and spiracle, lateral line, and ampullar canals of the lower jaw.

The eighth or auditory nerve passes directly into the internal ear and innervates its internal parts. The ninth or glossopharyngeal nerve supplies the first branchial cleft. The tenth or vagus nerve is very large, giving off four branchial branches that supply the last four gill arches. The lateral nerve, a branch of the vagus, supplies the lateral line, and the cardiac innervates the heart. A gastric branch supplies the stomach.

Spinal or Nerve Cord

The spinal cord, a thick-walled tube containing a minute central canal, extends from the hindbrain posteriorly along the dorsal part of the vertebral column. The spinal cord is marked by two narrow deep fissures, the dorsal and ventral fissures. Spinal nerves arise in pairs with each myomere or vertebral segment. Each spinal nerve has two roots, dorsal and ventral. The former is an afferent nerve, distinguished by the ganglion, which conducts nerve impulses toward the spinal cord. The ventral root is an efferent nerve, not ganglioniated, conveying impulses from the neuron outward.

Sense Organs

Fishes are well equipped with special sense organs that acquaint them with their immediate environment. The simplest of these are the cutaneous sense organs. The touch cells have nerve endings in the dermis. End buds occur in nearly all fishes and are irregularly distributed on the surface of the head and body. They consist of a core of sensory cells with sensory "hairs" surrounded by mucus-secreting cells. Mucous pores located on the dorsal and ventral side of the head connect by a canal that terminates in a small bulb, the ampulla of Lorenzini. Nerve fibers are found in these bulbs from the fifth or trigeminal cranial nerve.

The lateral line is usually represented by an open groove or an embedded tube, extending along the sides. At intervals corresponding with the muscle segments a pore occurs in the skin, or usually a pore penetrates each scale and connects with the lateral line tube. In scaleless fishes, simple pores may open to the outside.

The lateral line is variable. It may be absent or there may be several lateral lines on each side of a fish. The lateral line continues forward on the head where the branching tubes are known as cephalic canals, which contain pits or give rise to short branching canals; some may end in hairlike processes. All such lateral line organs are innervated by the lateral nerve, whereas the cephalic canals are supplied by the seventh and ninth cranial nerves. The functioning of the lateral line system enables the fish to detect low-frequency vibrations in the water such as the swimming movements of other fishes. Sharks respond to wave vibrations set up by injured fishes with erratic swimming movements.

Olfactory Organs

The detection of blood and other animal juices in water is a well-established ability of fishes, especially in sharks and the piranha of South America. This is the sense of smell, and the ability to detect odors lies in the nasal or olfactory organs. The nostrils are pits or tubes, usually a pair on each side of the snout, leading to a chamber beneath the skin. The walls of this chamber are lined with the Schneiderian membrane, which is thrown into numerous folds. This epithelial lining consists of elongate sensory cells, often produced into hairlike processes. In bony fishes the nostrils do not connect with the mouth cavity. The external nasal apertures may be single, or they may be subdivided by a septum. Sometimes the aperture ends in a tube, or a flap of skin, or it may be a highly specialized elongate dermal structure, as in certain muraenid eels.

The sense of smell is very acute in the piranha of South America. Fresh blood quickly attracts large schools of these ferocious fishes and a victim unfortunate enough to be so injured is literally torn apart in a few minutes, with practically nothing but the skeleton remaining. Dermal barbels on the snout and lower jaws, especially of catfishes, function as sensory organs for the purpose of locating food.

One very dark night in Boro Passage, Bikini Atoll, a group anchored a small boat. Tuna fish were passed through a small sausage grinder and the chopped meat and blood were slowly cast into the channel waters flowing out to sea. Very quickly, dozens of gray sharks were chummed to the boat by the presence of blood and fish food in the water. Then chunks of tuna meat were placed on steel hooks and cast into the sea. Although it was dark the sharks struck the baited hooks furiously and within 5 hours 29 sharks, ranging in length from 3 to 7 feet, were landed. Apparently these sharks were able to detect the bait by senses other than sight.

Eyes

The eyes of fishes in most respects are very similar to those of the higher vertebrates. They have rods, cones, and other nerve structures to enable them to detect colors. The chief difference in fishes is the very globular lens and flattish cornea, which probably causes them to be nearsighted. This may not be a handicap because even in the clearest of waters it is difficult to see objects 100 feet away.

The eyes of most fishes are located on the side of the head, causing them to have monocular vision as contrasted with binocular vision, which gives man the ability to judge distances accurately and to see in clear perspective. The eye functions very much like a photographic camera. The lens focuses the image on the retina at the back of the eye, where nerve endings stimulated by the different intensities of light transmit the image to the optic lobes of the brain.

The space between the lens and retina is filled with the transparent liquid substance known as the vitreous humor. The outer surface of the eye is covered with the cornea; the space between the cornea and lens is filled with the aqueous humor. The iris of the eye, capable of dilation and contraction, controls the amount of light passing through the pupil.

Fishes do not possess eyelids or tear glands as found in the higher land vertebrates. Some sharks have a membranous lid, the nictitating membrane or third eyelid, which can be drawn over the cornea from the bottom upward. In bony fishes this membrane is absent. An eyelid is not necessary as the eye is constantly bathed in a watery medium, except for a very few fishes which have aerial vision, and these bathe their eyes by dipping them in water frequently.

The habits of fishes are closely correlated with the development or degeneration of the eyes. Fishes that live in caves may be blind and some that live in the depths of the ocean have such small eyes that they see poorly or not at all. Certain fishes which live in the dim light at moderate depths or which are nocturnal have extremely large eyes.

At the present time blind or nearly blind species of fishes have been reported in 16 families, exclusive of deep-sea fishes. Among these, 29 species do not have any external evidence of eyes in the adults.

To gather food, the loss of vision must be compensated for by some other organ that will acquaint the fish with the location of its prey. Barbels are long tactile dermal organs developed for this purpose. They are very sensitive to touch and possibly to chemical stimuli in certain fishes. The lateral line system receives low vibrations made by other animals in the water.

The olfactory organs detect odors in the water. By means of such stimuli fishes are able quickly to locate food-producing substances or odors. Luminous organs are used for the attraction of prey; in the deep-sea ceratid fishes light may also function to attract males to the females for reproduction.

Aerial vision occurs in at least two widely divergent kinds of fishes, one a blenny, *Dialommus fuscus*, living in the Galapagos Islands, and the other, the four-eyed fish, *Anableps*, one of the toothed carps or cyprinodonts of Central and South America.

The eye of *Dialommus* is divided by a vertical septum, evident as a dark line running across the cornea. This black line is a modification of the umbulacrum, or eyeshade, a little flap of the iris that partly covers the pupil in many kinds of fishes living in shallow sandy areas exposed to bright sunshine. Light passes through both openings in the iris, making this a "four-eyed fish." This blenny lives in potholes in the upper part of the reef, clinging to the rocks in a vertical position, apparently able to see above and below the water surface.

Anableps, the celebrated four-eyes, or cuatro-ojos, from southeastern Mexico to the Guianas in South America, has its eyes divided not vertically but horizontally by a black pigmented band. This adapts *Anableps* to swim horizontally, which it does almost constantly at the surface. The upper or aerial part of the eye focuses horizontally and obliquely upward, whereas the lower or aquatic part of the eye focuses obliquely downward below the water surface. The four-eyed fish is thus equipped to see enemies approaching in the water and in the air.

Without eyelids and tear glands to moisten the eyes as in higher land vertebrates, *Anableps* has solved the problem for its aerial eye by dipping it into the water every few moments.

Ears

The ears of fishes lie entirely within the skull. They are paired, and consist of a membranous sac or vestibule constricted to form two portions, the dorsal or utriculus and the ventral or sacculus. The utriculus has one, two, or three semicircular canals—one in hagfishes, two in lampreys, and three in sharks and bony fishes. These canals lie in all three dimensions of space, two vertically, one horizontally, except that the horizontal canal is lacking in lampreys (Petromyzonidae). The utriculus may be connected to the exterior by means of the endolymphatic duct, a small tube that remains open only in the sharks and the chimaeras. It may end just below the skin in a bulb, the endolymphatic sinus. It is closed in the bony fishes.

The sacculus contains the earstone, or otolith. This bony concretion is secreted by delicate glandular tissue which is deposited in proportion to the rate of growth of the fish. The crystalline structure of the otolith varies with different rates of growth, which makes it possible to distinguish the age of fishes living in temperate and arctic regions. The internal part of the ear is filled with a liquid, the endolymph, whereas the bony capsule surrounding the auditory organs contains perilymph.

Reproductive Systems and Methods of Reproduction

The reproductive system of fishes is closely connected with the excretory system. The gonads are the sexual glands. They consist of the female ovaries and the male testes. Each sex is normally found in separate individuals; thus fishes are dioecious, similar to other vertebrates.

The testis when partly matured is a triangular, flattened, elongated organ, usually whitish or creamy in coloration, considerably fissured. It is a paired organ and lies in the body cavity usually dorsolateral to the digestive tract. It is homogeneous, not granular, in texture. The germ cells, microscopic in size, occur in follicles of irregular shape. They are not spherical like the ova, which aids in the recognition of sex in microscopic examination. The sperm are retained in the seminal vesicles and sperm sac until they are discharged at spawning time.

The ovaries are usually paired organs that appear pinkish or amber in color at maturity. They have a granular texture, caused by the presence of spherical eggs. The ovaries are usually rounded and plump, lacking all fissures. The sex may be recognized by mounting the tissue on a glass slide with cover glass and examining it under a microscope with a magnification of 15 to 30 times. The eggs are visible as small globules, resembling many tiny droplets. Eggs are retained in the ovary until mature, at which time they lose their opaqueness and become almost transparent. They are either discharged into the body cavity and picked up by the funnel of the oviduct or discharged directly to the exterior.

In the female shark the ovaries are elongated soft lobulated bodies, lying a little to the right and left of the mid-line of the body cavity and suspended by folds of the peritoneum. On the surface are rounded elevations or follicles of various sizes, each containing a bright yellowish ovum. The two oviducts or Müllerian ducts are entirely unconnected with the ovaries. Each oviduct is an elongated tube that extends through the entire length of the body cavity of the shark. At the front the two unite just behind the pericardium to form a wide median funnel that opens into the body cavity. Just before the oviducts unite, they form a large swelling, the shell gland, posterior to which is the uterine chamber. The two uteri join to enter the cloaca as a single aperture, or, in some sharks, each uterus has its own opening. In bony fishes, the oviducts are continuous or almost continuous with the ovary, except in those forms that are viviparous.

The male shark has two elongated soft, lobulated testes, each attached to the wall of the abdominal cavity by a fold of the peritoneum. From each testis a small number of efferent ducts pass to the anterior end of the kidney;

they enter the vas deferens, which runs along the entire length of the non-renal part of the kidney. Posteriorly it dilates to form a thin-walled sac, the seminal vesicle, which connects with the urogenital sinus, from which the sperm sac arises. The urogenital sinus opens into the cloaca.

External Sexual Organs

There are several kinds of external genital organs in fishes. Best known among these are the claspers of sharks, rays, and skates. The claspers are paired appendages on the male of elasmobranchs, which arise at the inner base of the pelvic fins and form a part of them. Their distal tips are folded and cartilaginous. Each clasper has a channel through which the sperm flows during the act of copulation with the female.

The holocephalians or chimaeras also have pelvic claspers, or myxopterygia; in addition, the males have a cephalic or frontal clasper. This is a clublike appendage, armed with curved spines, which can be lowered into a depression in the skin of the head when not required. It is used as a clasping organ, probably holding onto the female chimaera at the base of the dorsal fin during copulation. The frontal clasper is also known as the nuptial horn.

Genital papillae occur in various groups of fishes. This organ is a fleshy projection from the genital aperture of the male. It is especially prominent during the breeding season of such fishes as lampreys (Petromyzonidae) and sculpins (Cottidae). In the egg-laying act of some sculpins, the genital papilla is probably inserted into the egg mass when laid by the female.

A modified anal fin of the male has been observed in such families of fishes as the viviparous perches (Embiotocidae) and the top minnows (Poeciliidae). Related to the silversides is the family Phallostethidae, known as the "viviparous silversides." The males of the latter possess a complicated fleshy appendage, the priapium, suspended from the head and shoulder girdle and supported by a complex skeleton. It has anal, urinary, and genital openings and bears certain long free, slender, curved bony structures, presumably used as claspers. One of these bony processes, the toxactinium, projects from the anterior part of the priapium, and one or two others, the ctenactinia, project from the posterior part.

The anal fin of the Poeciliidae is modified into the intromittent organ in the male. This structure serves the purpose of introducing the spermatozoa into the body of the female where internal fertilization of the eggs occurs. The third, fourth, and fifth anal rays are modified and elongated. They form a groove or tube into which the genital duct opens. The tips of these rays may be curved, and barbed or smooth, perhaps as an aid in keeping the intromittent organ in place during copulation.

Certain fishes have developed other means of ensuring the fertilization of the eggs and the incubation of their young. The European bitterling,

Rhodeus, and the carplike fish, *Acheilognathus* of Japan, both cyprinids, have developed in the female an ovipositor, a tubular elongation from the genital opening. This is inserted in the gill chambers of mussels for the purpose of depositing eggs in the porous gills of the host mussel. The larvae hatch there and remain in their protected environment for a time before escaping to the outside world.

The males of pipefishes and sea horses have a brood pouch on their ventral sides. This is one of the few cases in nature where the males are responsible for the incubation of the young. This external abdominal brood pouch receives the eggs from the female during the breeding act. The eggs become embedded in a sort of "placenta" which is highly vascular, thus furnishing the necessary oxygen for development. When the young pipefish are ready to swim, they escape from the pouch by swimming off in the same slow motion as their parents.

Eggs of Fishes

The eggs of fishes may be divided into three categories: (1) oviparous, (2) ovoviviparous, and (3) viviparous, according to their embryonic development and the method of reproduction.

The majority of fishes are oviparous, producing eggs that are fertilized externally and that develop outside the body. Such fishes may spawn in sand, gravel, or among weeds, depositing their eggs in nests or in open water.

The oviparous type of eggs may be divided into three subcategories, demersal, pelagic, and egg cases. Demersal eggs, which sink because they have a specific gravity a little greater than that of water, are of at least three kinds: (1) eggs with adhesive membranes, which when laid usually stick to sand, gravel, or to the sand in nests; (2) eggs with adhesive threads, which are chiefly adapted to cling to vegetation; and (3) nonadhesive eggs, which usually are cared for by the parents in some special method such as buccal incubation in the gaff-topsail catfish, *Felichthys felis,* and the cardinal fishes (Apogonidae).

Pelagic fish eggs have a specific gravity about the same as water. They are, therefore, suspended in it and float at various depths. This type of egg is commonly produced by marine fishes. Pelagic fish eggs may or may not have oil globules, the number and size of which aid in maintaining the proper specific gravity, causing the eggs to float at an optimum depth for each species.

Egg cases or egg baskets vary greatly in size and form. These horny cases are commonly deposited by sharks, skates, and chimaeras. They possess many tough filaments at each end, which cling to seaweeds or on the bottom of rocks when laid. Shark and skate egg cases measure from 2 inches up to several inches in length. They are of various shapes, boxlike and flattened, twisted into spirals, or long and narrow with long streamers at the corners. From one to several eggs may occupy a single egg case. Fertilization of eggs occurs internally in the female, after which these horny baskets are deposited. The young develop within the case. When all or most of the large yolk has been absorbed, the case ruptures and the fully developed young escape.

In the ovoviviparous type of reproduction, the eggs are fertilized internally in the female and develop in the ovary or uterus. This type of egg has sufficient yolk to meet the needs of the embryo without receiving additional nourishment from the mother.

In the viviparous type of reproduction, the eggs are fertilized internally in the female. The mother has a placentalike organ in the ovary-uterus which furnishes nourishment to the developing embryo, since this type of egg does not contain enough yolk to feed the embryo until it is born.

These two types of reproduction are not easily distinguished from each other in fishes. In many cases the young do receive nourishment and oxygen from the mother and as a result most fishes that give birth to their young are called viviparous, such as the poeciliids or top minnows, rockfishes in the genera *Sebastes* and *Sebastodes,* and the viviparous perches (Embiotocidae).

There is no evolutionary relationship among bony fishes in regard to the three types of reproduction, oviparous, ovoviviparous, and viviparous, since all three types occur in the class Osteichthyes.

The relationship between number of eggs produced and parental care is an indirect one. The more parental care given eggs and young, the fewer the eggs produced. For example, nest-building fishes such as the gouramis, paradisefishes, and the Siamese fighting fish produce a few thousand eggs, whereas pelagic fishes such as halibut and cod produce a few million eggs. The least number of eggs produced occur in viviparous fishes, or in fishes that have some special type of incubation such as mouthbreeders, pipefishes, and sea horses.

Excretory System

The excretory system of fishes is closely associated anatomically with the reproductive system. In the bony fishes the kidneys are two reddish-colored straplike organs, lying on the dorsal side of the coelomic or body cavity next to the body mass and covered by the peritoneum. The kidney of the adult fish is a massive gland of deep red color, made up of Malpighian bodies, urinary tubules, and a copious supply of blood vessels.

The kidney is a highly complex organ capable of sorting from each other chemical substances that occur in the blood, retaining those which are valuable to the body and must be saved, and removing those which are waste products and must be excreted.

The microscopic functional unit of the kidney in fishes, the Malpighian body, is similar to that of higher vertebrates. It is divisible into distinct parts. The tip is expanded to form Bowman's capsule, which contains the glomerulus. This is an elaborate tuft of capillaries whose walls are so thin that through them water and dissolved substances can be filtered from the blood very rapidly. Attached to the capsule is the uriniferous tubule, which is greatly convoluted. Cilia aid in the movement of liquids along these minute tubules, which connect to form larger ones, which in turn unite to form the ureter, the duct that carries waste products away from the kidney to the cloaca or to the outside.

Homer W. Smith states that there is good reason to believe that the first fishes were evolved in the fresh waters of the Cambrian or Silurian continents. The most primitive kidney consisted of a series of bilateral segmentally arranged tubules draining the primitive body cavity and opening into this cavity by nephrostomes. These renal tubules functioned by picking up substances from the blood and transporting them directly into their lumina, from which they drained to the exterior. No doubt the protovertebrates, with their blood rich in salts and bearing the impress of long residence in an aquatic environment, drew water into their bodies through osmotic pressure. This may have entered from the intestinal tract, respiratory membranes, and through the skin. The early fishes had to resist this constant influx of water by excreting it some place or they would swell up. This was accomplished by the heart pumping the blood past the tubules and the gradual formation of the numerous glomeruli.

With the formation of the glomeruli, there was a need for conservation of valuable substances that would be lost. This was accomplished by reabsorption, the usable material being withdrawn from the filtrate as it moved along the tubules on its way to the exterior. As long as the early vertebrate remained in fresh water, as do numerous fishes and many amphibians, this filtration-reabsorption process was efficient because the early fishes were osmotically superior to their aquatic medium and could absorb all the water needed.

When conditions became favorable for the early aquatic vertebrates to develop into land and sea forms, the kidney no longer could get all the water it needed. In the sea, in a salty environment, the fish found itself in a solution having a higher osmotic pressure than its blood, with a reversal in osmotic gradient. As a result it tended to lose water to its environment; thus the need arose for conserving every bit of water that it could get. In this marine environment the glomerular filter and tubules were too efficient.

Smith states that several modifications occurred in the kidneys of salt-water fishes to conserve water in the blood: (1) In the majority of marine fishes the glomeruli are reduced in size, poorly vascularized, and function under some undetermined physiological inhibition; (2) in specialized instances, the glomeruli have disappeared completely, as found for toadfishes, the sea horse, the pipefish, and certain deep-sea fishes; (3) the elasmo-branchs have overcome the osmotic pressure difficulty of living in salt water by a renal development which is simple and unique. They reabsorb from the glomerular filtrate the chief product of protein metabolism, urea, and return it to the blood. This conservation of urea raises the osmotic pressure of the blood to a level above that of their environment; thus elasmobranchs, like their Silurian ancestors, are at a constant advantage in respect to their marine habitat.

The presence of extra amounts of urea in the blood of sharks and rays makes it necessary to wash this substance out of the flesh when prepared for food; otherwise it may have a distinctive taste.

The Aquarium and Its Management

AN *aquarium* is the container in which live fishes are maintained. Aquaria vary in size, shape, and material from which they are constructed, according to the use they are to serve.

TYPES OF AQUARIA

Aquaria that hold up to 5 gallons of water may be all glass or may have a metal frame with glass sides and a glass or slate bottom. The advantages of the metal-framed aquarium are many: if a side glass should crack, it can usually be replaced easily; the plane sides make viewing easy as compared with the refraction of light caused by the variable thickness of glass in an all-glass aquarium. An all-glass aquarium is delicate and easily cracked, and therefore undesirable as a permanent home for tropical fishes.

The bottoms of aquaria are usually made of glass or slate. Several grades of slate are available, and the type selected is a major factor in the manufacturing cost. The poorer grades of slate, usually recognized by their rough and unpolished finish, may be porous and contain microscopic fissures which in time will begin to leak water.

Aquaria larger than 5 gallons create new problems. Water weighs about 8⅓ pounds per gallon, and simple multiplication can demonstrate the need of a strong frame for large tanks. Several types of materials are used for aquaria up to 50 gallons capacity: angle iron, galvanized iron, aluminum, stainless steel, brass, and copper. The more common materials, angle iron painted or galvanized, aluminum, and stainless steel, are preferred. Angle iron, though the least attractive, is the strongest of the materials; it is used almost exclusively for aquaria of over 50 gallons capacity. Every few years it is wise to repaint the angle-iron frame and to use a heavy wire brush to remove the rust, which begins to eat the metal away. It is wise to use a prime coat of red lead on all surfaces which are not to be in contact with water (or the condensation of water). Any metal paint will be suitable for a second coat. Metal should never be in contact with aquarium water.

Galvanized iron, painted, is usually the most inexpensive framing. When given proper treatment, it will last just as long as any other frame, but care should be exercised so that the finish is not scratched. Galvanized frames, too, after a few years, need refinishing if they are to be preserved.

This aluminum-framed aquarium measures over 6 feet long and 3 feet wide. It has a center section for small fish and delicate plants. This photograph was supplied by O. Tutwiler, Tampa, Florida, who had the tank made to order for his office.

A top view of an aluminum-framed aquarium of the type used by dealers, where a removable partition allows plants to be separated from fishes so that dealers can easily net the fish and handle the plants for sale. This type of aquarium can also be used for separation of species, isolation of sexes or sizes of fish, breeding purposes, and the propagation of delicate plants which must be maintained with destructive fishes.

A side view of the dealer's-type aquarium showing a school of *Puntius tetrazona* separated from some soft-leafed plants which they would tear apart were they able to reach them. This type of aquarium was invented by O. Tutwiler.

A decorative type of home aquarium with stainless steel frame. The elaborate wrought-iron stand lends beauty to the setup.

Only recently aluminum has become a popular framing material. It is strong, light, easily cut and riveted, and does not oxidize to any great extent. Most commercial hatcheries in Florida use aluminum-framed aquaria, which they have found very desirable.

Stainless steel for the frames of aquaria takes a high buffing, is rust-resistant and very strong. It requires little care and is used extensively by wholesalers, jobbers, breeders, and storekeepers. Its cost is higher than angle iron, aluminum, or galvanized iron. Brass and copper are rarely used, and the few dealers that stock them refer to these frames as "super-deluxe jobs." They are not very satisfactory.

Aquaria are made watertight by the use of special aquarium cement to form a bond between the metal frame and the glass. A good cement must hold metal and glass equally well, not dry out, be relatively pliable to allow for the difference in pressures as the aquarium is emptied or filled, and be easily applied. Commercial preparations are available from nearly any aquarium shop. Should an aquarium develop a leak, it may be possible to stop the flow of water. If the leak is not organic—that is, if the leak is not caused by a cracked glass or porous slate—then a first-aid treatment is to place the aquarium in a sink or bathtub and fill it with the hottest water available. This tends not only to soften the aquarium cement, but it expands the glass sufficiently to tighten the joints. This usually works, but should it fail try the following: Dry the aquarium out thoroughly. Allow at least 24 hours for all the moisture to be evaporated and then pour asphaltum varnish (usually called liquid cement) along all the joints on the inside of the aquarium. Allow this to dry for a day or two and gradually refill the aquarium. If the aquarium still leaks, it may be necessary to remove all the glass and the bottom and recement the entire tank. This is hardly to be recommended for smaller aquaria, as they are inexpensive and not worth the effort. Larger aquaria are easier to handle, as the glass is of a heavier gauge. If possible, send the aquarium back to the manufacturer or have an experienced operator make the repair for you.

For cracked glass, a piece of plastic waterproof adhesive tape on the outside over the crack, after the aquarium has been thoroughly dried, will help.

All operating aquaria should be fitted with covers. The cover may either be suspended inside the top with special handles or it may rest on top of the aquarium. A notch should be cut in a corner to accommodate heaters and thermostats and for feeding. Small pieces of rubber or plastic tubing fitted over the edges of the frame, under the glass, will lessen the rusting of the frame.

The glass for the aquarium should be special sun glass or any type of commercial clear glass that allows the desirable rays of the sun to pass through. Tinted glass should be avoided.

When a stand is required for an aquarium, the weight it is to support should be taken into consideration. Wooden stands may be used but warpage should be borne in mind. Commercial stands are available for every type of aquarium found in stock sizes. They are usually constructed of angle iron which has been painted. Some types have a lower shelf either for another aquarium or for storage purposes.

SIZE

The shape and size of the aquarium are very important. The objective in selecting an aquarium, whether it is for a laboratory, breeding, show, or storage, must be based upon a solid understanding of certain principles. There is a limit to the number of fishes a given aquarium can maintain and this limit varies not only with the size, species, and condition of the fishes that are to be kept in it, but with the temperature of the water and the aeration factor (artificial or natural) as well.

Mechanical water aerators do help in the overpopulation problem, but not in the manner in which one might think. It is a common error to believe that mechanical aerators give oxygen to the water. The actual purpose is twofold: First, they aid in the circulation of the water, thus reducing the possibility of stratification (warmer water on top, cooler below), and help

A laboratory-type aquarium with angle-iron frame. The advantage of this type of aquarium is the relative ease with which a broken glass may be replaced.

the water to rid itself of harmful gases and to pick up soluble atmospheric oxygen. Second, they actually remove gases which are in greater concentration in the water than in the atmosphere. This latter phenomenon is accomplished by the many bubbles which pick up gases in the water as they make their way to the surface. The reason for the emphasis on aeration is that the limiting factor in a crowded aquarium is not how much oxygen but how much carbon dioxide is dissolved in the water. The objective is to have as low a carbon dioxide content as possible.

Shallow aquaria offer the greatest surface area for a given volume of water; therefore, without artificial or mechanical aeration, shallow aquaria are to be desired. To attempt to offer a simple formula for the optimum ratio of surface area to volume of water would be perilous, for there would always be some fishes which would not do well in that size of aquarium. A sound general rule is to have the aquarium wider than it is deep. Then it is relatively easy to prescribe the formula for the number of fishes a given aquarium can maintain: Allow 1 inch (of body) of fish per gallon of water. With artificial aeration, this figure can be doubled for intermittent aeration and tripled for constant aeration. Some aquarists rely on the surface area formula: Allow 24 square inches of surface area for each fish (in an aquar-

An inside view of a Florida tropical-fish hatchery. Note that all the aquaria are fairly shallow in comparison with their length. Fry are raised from the egg in these aquaria and, after they are able to take dry foods, in order to hasten their growth they are placed in the huge concrete aquaria built into the floor.

ium without mechanical aeration). Certain air-breathing fishes like the Anabantidae can be more crowded than the formula will allow because they do not rely solely upon dissolved oxygen for respiration.

In the breeding aquarium, for egg-laying fishes, it is usually not the size of the breeders that must be considered but the size and number of the spawn. It should be remembered that unless the aquarium is large enough to support the newborn fish for the first 8 weeks of their lives, they will suffer greatly because they cannot be moved safely prior to that age. In the breeding of live-bearing species, the purpose of a larger aquarium is not to support a great many fry, but to enable the small fry to hide better from their cannibalistic parents.

LIGHT

Light is necessary for the successful maintenance of tropical fishes. Just how much light, the quality of the light, and the direction from which the light comes are matters for much speculation.

The amount of light necessary is a variable that is not always easily controlled. Direct sunlight for any extended period of time is not beneficial to fishes or to plants. A northern exposure is ideal for an aquarium that does not receive any artificial light, though artificial light will provide light just as well.

Fishes need light in order to see. Sight is an important factor in reproduction and in feeding. Plants need light for other reasons (see page 101). Studies have shown that the intensity, amount (in hours), and quality of light have important effects upon reproduction in certain fishes. It has been demonstrated that in the medaka, *Oryzias latipes,* light periodicity has a positive effect on ovulation. If kept under continuous light, guppies will have broods every 3 weeks instead of every month. Yet in the killifish, *Fundulus,* no positive effects from changes in light periodicity were found.

Light has a definite effect on the color of fishes. A simple example is to view fishes that have spent many generations in lightless caves. These fishes, such as the popular blind cave characins, are lacking entirely in pigment.

Ordinarily, fishes are diurnal and need about 12 hours of light per day. The intensity of light must vary with the size of the aquarium, and a few practical experiments will easily show just how much light is necessary. An allowance of about 2½ watts per gallon of water is ample for an aquarium hood light. In smaller aquaria the problem of overheating owing to the use of an electric light must be considered. Fishes maintained in the northern parts of the country definitely need artificial light during the winter months. During the summer when there are 15 hours of sunlight these fishes do not show any adverse effects.

If leafed plants grow well in an aquarium, then the aquarium is receiv-

In the commercial tropical-fish hatcheries in Florida, various methods are used to cut down on the light which open pools receive from the direct sunlight. Here is an outdoor concrete pool, common in the Miami area, which utilizes a fine screening to cut down the sunlight entering the water.

Sometimes large floating plants, or bushy plants, are used to keep the light down.

The large open pools dug into the ground, as in this Tampa-area hatchery, must have running water in order to keep the fishes cool. The water in Tampa runs from the ground at about 74°F, an ideal temperature for raising tropical fishes. Is it any wonder that 90 per cent of the world's supply of live-bearing fishes comes from this area?

ing enough light. Green water, water which is filled with green plankton, is usually caused by too much light. To rid the aquarium of this unpleasant condition it is necessary to remove the fishes and place dark paper all about the aquarium. Add some live *Daphnia* to the aquarium to eat the algae. The use of taller aquatic plants also aids in keeping water from becoming green.

TEMPERATURE

The optimum temperature for individual fresh-water aquarium fishes varies. Most aquarists would disagree on the limits of temperature tolerance since experiences vary as much as the conditions under which fishes are maintained. In the discussion of each species of fish the optimum temperature range has been noted. These ranges should be taken as a general guide, not as an absolute amount. Many factors must be considered when temperature variations are under investigation.

Certain facts are known, however, which have led to the suggestion of an optimum temperature for each individual species. The suitable temperature range most common to all tropical fishes lies between 74 and 78°F. With the higher temperatures it must be borne in mind that there is less dissolved oxygen in the water available for fishes, whose need for oxygen increases directly with the rise in temperature. Although no controlled experimentation has been reported on the subject, it is common knowledge

This is an indoor view of a Tampa-area hatchery. Even in this tropical climate the rare live bearers and egg layers are raised indoors with adequate heating facilities in case the air temperature takes a sudden drop. Note the gas heater, upper right.

that 100 small goldfish easily can be maintained in a 20-gallon aquarium (12 × 12 × 33 inches) if the temperature is 40°F. Should the temperature rise to 70°F then the tank would be seriously overcrowded.

In the large outdoor pools in Florida, where breeders raise huge quantities of platyfishes, it is a common sight to see the fishes congregating near the place where the spring water is being constantly added. The temperature in this area is usually near 72°F while in the farthermost distances from this spot, where the water temperature may be as high as 90°F, few, if any, fishes will be found.

Then, too, bacterial action and bacterial abundance are nearly directly proportional to a temperature rise from 70 to 85°F. The lower the water temperature, the lower the bacterial count.

Fishes raised in colder water (water at a temperature of 72°F as compared to 85°F) show some slight variations from those raised in warmer water. The colder water fishes may have higher ray, scale, and vertebrae counts, grow larger, live longer, and mature less rapidly. Aquarists claim that fishes raised in the colder water are healthier and are more resistant to the ordinary aquarium diseases.

All in all, we may conclude that other than for some slight variations, the temperature of the water in which tropical fishes are to be maintained should be in the range of from 72 to 80°F. Fluctuations in temperature are hazardous and will tend to lower resistance to disease. A sudden drop in temperature is not good for tropical fishes.

Aquarium heaters with built-in thermostats are available for suitable maintenance of the aquarium temperature. When purchasing heaters several mechanical factors should be considered: outside adjustment of the temperature control, mechanical guarantee, a sturdy device to fasten the heater to the side of the aquarium, easily replaceable parts, and correct wattage. To calculate the amount of wattage necessary, merely multiply the amount of water the aquarium contains by 5. Thus a 20-gallon tank requires a 100-watt heater.

Practice has shown that it is better to raise the temperature of aquarium water rapidly if for some reason it has dropped below 65°F, than to raise the temperature slowly to the proper reading. Thus, if a shipment of fishes arrives in very cold water, it is better for the fishes if they are immediately placed into water of the proper temperature than if they are allowed to experience the colder water for a longer period of time while the water is being heated slowly.

WATER

Water is composed of the two elements hydrogen and oxygen chemically bonded together. The hydrogen and oxygen are not readily freed, and fishes are unable to utilize the oxygen that is in the water molecules. Where then does the oxygen which fishes need for respiration come from?

Water, like most other liquids, is capable of having dissolved in it certain solids and gases. The amounts and kinds of these solids and gases depend upon two factors, temperature and pressure. The oxygen which the fishes are able to utilize is the oxygen which has been dissolved into the water from the atmosphere. Water without dissolved solids and gases is flat to the taste and is unsuitable for the maintenance of aquarium fishes. It is called distilled water.

Through their gills fishes are able to utilize dissolved oxygen and excrete their carbon dioxide waste. In this manner gills are comparable to lungs.

Conditioned Water

Water drawn directly from the tap, fetched straight from a brook or lake, or caught in a rain barrel, is not the best type of water to use in the home aquarium without further treating it, or "conditioning" it.

The process of conditioning water has several purposes: to aerate the water properly so that there will be a maximum amount of oxygen dissolved in it and a minimum amount of carbon dioxide and other harmful gases; to remove the extremely toxic chlorine gas which is nearly always present in water drawn freshly from the tap; to allow fine organic matter which is in suspension to settle out; to allow fish parasites to persist and die without finding a host; and to give the bacteria a chance to "balance" themselves out. Newly used water will always show an increased bacterial count for the first week or so; this is the cause of the "cloudy" water in newly set up aquaria.

Conditioning tap water is easily done by merely allowing the water to stand for a week or so in an open glass container, preferably in direct sunlight. Aeration by means of an air-stone (or other air release) and compressed air will hasten this conditioning process. Some aquarists claim that putting some plants in the water will also hasten conditioning. Although no positive proof can be offered on behalf of this theory, it certainly works out well in practice.

Water taken directly from a brook or lake should be used with great care. The chance of introducing parasites or other harmful organisms is so great that it is recommended that water taken from a lake be allowed to "age" for at least 2 weeks, in direct sunlight and under constant observation for parasites and other organisms. If possible never use untreated water.

Rain water or the water from melted snow may be used at once if 1 teaspoonful of Epsom salts is added to each gallon of water. Do not use chemically pure salts if possible. Also add 1 tablespoon of coarse table salt to every 5 gallons of water to add a further mineral content to this very soft water.

pH of Water

To understand the true meaning of "pH of water" would necessitate a thorough knowledge of basic chemistry. For the purpose at hand, let us define acidity and alkalinity in terms of the number of *ions* found in the water. By ion is meant a charged atom or group of atoms. If there is an excess of hydrogen ions H⁺ (that is, charged hydrogen atoms), then water is said to be acid. If on the other hand there is an excess of the negatively charged hydroxyl ion (OH⁻), then an alkaline condition is said to exist.

The pH scale, as used by its originator Sörensen, expresses the concentration of hydrogen ions as the "logarithm of the reciprocal of the normality of free hydrogen ions." Mathematically written this means:

$$\text{pH} = \frac{1}{\log_{10} \text{H-ion concentration in gram equivalents per liter}}$$

The scale is usually used on a range from pH 0.0 to 14.0 with three points of interest:

pH of 0.0, the lowest point on the scale, represents a solution normal in hydrogen ions, that is to say, the strongest acid.

pH of 7.0 is the middle or neutral point at which there is an equal number of hydroxyl and hydrogen ions.

pH of 14.0, the strongest alkaline solution, means the solution is normal in hydroxyl ions.

When pH is written as "pH 7.0," it is read as "The pH is 7.0." To say that the pH is getting higher means that the solution is becoming more alkaline; as the pH gets lower the solution becomes more acid.

The symbol pH itself has an interesting history. Sörensen, the first to use this symbol, proposed the use of the negative power of 10, or a power of 10^p where p stands for any negative number. The symbol was to refer to the "power of hydrogen" so the symbol H for hydrogen was added. Since all chemical symbols are capitalized in the first letter, the symbol became 10^{pH}. This was reduced to merely pH, though actually the H should be inferior to the p, as p_H. It is easiest to credit typographers with the more easily written pH. Thus typesetters may have made their mark in chemical science!

There are several methods of measuring the pH, or hydrogen-ion concentration of a solution. All methods are easily categorized into two broad groups: electrometric and colorimetric. Electrometric methods, by use of a "pH meter," merely measure the ability of a given liquid to conduct an electric current. These methods are extremely accurate. Colorimetric methods require the addition of a dye which varies in color with the pH, and comparison with a fixed standard, either electrically in a "colorimeter" or by the eye. Several inexpensive pH testing sets are available through aquarium shops.

To reduce the acidity in aquarium water sodium bicarbonate is usually added. If fishes are present in the water while the pH is being adjusted, it is wise to make the adjustment slowly over a period of a week or so. To adjust the pH to the acid side use sodium acid phosphate, tannic acid, or filter the water through peat moss. *All pH changes must be made gradually. Rapid changes of pH will affect the fishes.* Experience has shown that a pH of 6.8 seems to be the best average pH for an aquarium. A variation of 0.2 on either side of the optimum is a normal fluctuation.

Hardness of Water

As pH was the measure of the free ions in solution, so DH is the measure of the salts dissolved in the water. The effect of extremely hard aquarium water upon both fishes and plants is only lately coming into the spotlight. Experiments have shown that water which is too soft or too hard may be the cause for many aquarium troubles.

Measuring the hardness of aquarium water has been made easier with the advent of several new testing kits. Two types of kits have been devised; one, which operates like a colorimetric pH kit, necessitates the use of a dye and a color comparator chart. The other and more reliable is the standard soap solution method. As is commonly known, it is difficult to obtain a "sudsing" with hard water, and much soap is wasted when clothes are washed in hard water. A standard soap solution, technically known as "B and B Soap Testing Solution" (available from the Permutit Corporation of 330 West 42nd Street, New York) is added dropwise to a measured amount of aquarium water to be tested. Each time a drop is added the bottle is shaken to see if a permanent lather has been developed. Once the water has been softened sufficiently by the soap solution, soap bubbles will result from the shaking process. By counting the drops of soap necessary to make the water suds one can ascertain by a formula just how hard the water is in "ppm," parts per million, that is, how many water molecules there are per salt molecule. Once the water has been judged as too hard, chemicals such as Zeolite or Zeocarb can be added to the filter, which will tend to soften the water. Water should be softened gradually.

If a source of soft water is desirable, rain water, melted snow, or the melted ice that gathers about the coils of most refrigerators will usually serve the purpose. Mix this water with the hard water. Distilled water too may be added in small amounts (no more than 50 per cent) in order to soften the aquarium water.

Cloudy Water

There are several factors which cause aquarium water to become discolored and cloudy, all of which are easier to prevent than to cure.

Green water, the most common discoloration of aquarium water, is nearly always caused by the presence of an overabundance of microscopic green plant organisms, usually called *algae,* which are found in nearly all aquarium water. The factors which make them reproduce so vigorously and in numbers great enough actually to color the water green are excessive light and an environment rich in plant foods. To ensure against green water the aquarium must be sufficiently planted with rooted and floating plants, receive no more than 5 hours direct sunlight daily, and not be overrich in plant foods from overfeeding the aquarium inhabitants.

Once the water has become green nearly all remedies require the removal of the fishes from the aquarium. However, first aid for green water is to cover the aquarium so that it is unable to receive any light. This starves the algae as they need light to manufacture their food. Should the fishes be left in the aquarium at this time they will be endangered by the great amounts of carbon dioxide which the algae will give off in their darkened environment, so use artificial aeration if possible. Usually it helps if some *Daphnia* are added to the aquarium as these small animals are reputed to feed upon the algae.

An extremely dangerous method of ridding the aquarium of these plants is to add some copper sulfate to the water. This is best done without using the raw chemicals. Obtain an old copper screen and immerse it in the aquarium water. As soon as the plants start to die and the water begins to clear up, the screening should be removed. Once this has occurred it is wise to change as much of the water as possible.

The best method of getting rid of green water is to change the water in its entirety. Most aquarists agree that this is the easiest and safest way to be rid of the problem.

Green water is not to be considered as a valueless entity. Not only is it rich in food for newborn fishes but it is ideal for a breeding tank (provided the tank receives plenty of light) as the water is so cloudy that the mother fish will be unable to see her newborn fry and thus will be unable to eat them. Care should be exercised that if fishes are maintained in green water, the water is given plenty of light. *Daphnia* cultures are easily propagated in green water.

Gray water, a sign of overfeeding, is a great annoyance to many beginning aquarists. The abundance of uneaten fish food is utilized by bacteria and infusoria and their increased numbers will cause the clouding and fouling of the water. Steps should be taken to keep the floor of the aquarium siphoned free of all excess food. Fishes should be fed less frequently if this phenomenon occurs.

Clearing up gray water is usually accomplished merely by siphoning all uneaten food particles off the bottom of the aquarium and keeping the fishes unfed for a week or 10 days. Sometimes 50 mg of aureomycin per gallon of aquarium water helps to bring about a clearing up in shorter time. If the condition is not remedied within 10 days the water should be changed.

A freshly set up aquarium might become cloudy for a few days, even before any fishes have been added to it. Conditioning by allowing it to age will clear the water.

Dirty water, caused by a constant stirring up of the muck that has accumulated on the bottom of the aquarium, can only be alleviated by siphoning off the muck. The bottoms of aquaria should be siphoned clean at least once a month.

SAND

Sand is only necessary in aquaria which are to have rooted plants as part of their "aquascaping." An aquarium which is to be maintained for purposes other than decorative need not have a sandy bottom.

Commercial grade No. 2 or 3 gravel, in a light color, is best for aquarium use. If the gravel is of too small a caliber the plant roots will have a difficult time in poking their way through it. Gravel which is too coarse creates lodging places for uneaten food and thus is unsatisfactory for aquarium use.

The ideal planting medium is a combination of fine and coarse sand. If a larger grain gravel is placed under a thin coating of very fine sand then each type of gravel is being utilized to its full advantage. The disadvantage of this arrangement, however, is that when the plants are taken up or the sand is otherwise disturbed this arrangement is easily upset and the whole planting medium must be readjusted.

Rocks, shells, pieces of wood, and other ornamental pieces have no place in the aquarium, unless their surfaces are extremely smooth and they cannot provide lodging places for uneaten food particles.

When sand and gravel turn dark it is a sure indication that the fishes are being overfed. Blackened gravel or sand should be removed with a siphon,

This is the side view of an aquarium which is being prepared to accommodate tropical fishes. Note that the sand is level and about an inch above the metal frame base. This is *not* the correct way to place the sand in the aquarium.

This same side view shows the correct way to arrange the sand in the aquarium. Note that the front is bare of any sand. When the aquarium is filled, the ledge of the sand will fall, thus forming a natural slope on which all the dirt will accumulate and be readily available and compact to be siphoned off.

The sand should be thoroughly washed in running water to be sure that all the dust and dirt is removed. Placing the sand in a large, shallow pot and stirring it as the water from a tap runs into it does the job simply but efficiently.

When filling the aquarium with water after it has been filled with sand, be sure that the sand is first covered over with a clean piece of heavy paper. Then place a small saucer over the paper to hold the paper down and to prevent the sand from being stirred up.

This is what happens when the saucer and paper are not used.

Plants should not be introduced into the aquarium until it is nearly full of water. Do not fill the aquarium to the utmost until it is planted, for it will overflow when your arm displaces water during planting.

Initial planting should be done in this manner. Use your index finger to clear the way for the roots into the sand. Do not try to force the plants into the sand without this assistance, or the roots will be damaged and the stems will probably break.

Once the aquarium is set up and a plant becomes loose, it can easily be adjusted by means of some sort of planting stick or tong.

thoroughly washed, and replaced. Washing gravel is easily accomplished in a large container with plenty of hot running water. The sand should be thoroughly rinsed until the water that runs off it is perfectly clear regardless of the amount of agitation. Sand which has been taken from another aquarium should be thoroughly cleaned in boiling hot water to remove the spores of harmful organisms.

Earth, humus, or other fertilizing materials should never be added to the home aquarium.

FOODS AND FEEDING

The present aquarium market is all but flooded with different brands of tropical-fish foods. With few exceptions, they contain in varying amounts fish meal (usually menhaden, *Brevoortia tyrannus,* which is dried and ground for animal feeds and is readily available), crab or clam meal, beef meal, and possibly some wheat meal or other filler. Shrimp and vegetable matter, very nutritive in a fish food, are usually found only in the better brands.

Not only is the content of a fish food important, but the way the food is prepared is a factor of great significance. Foods should be sifted according to size, for particles which are too large will be uneaten until they have

Gordon's formula being prepared for the fishes at the New York Aquarium. Note the use of the blendor.

become soft, and particles which are too small can only benefit the plants and smaller organisms. A well-prepared food should be screened and sifted for particle size and cleaned of all dust. The most economical way to do this on a large scale is for the ingredients to be added in the form of a meal, mixed well, and then be prepared into a batter by adding water. This should then be baked, dehydrated (so it will float and not rot or get moldy), and then ground. An ordinary coffee grinder will serve the purpose. Each grind size should be sifted for smaller particles. Some organizations sell the fine dust that comes with every grinding procedure as a food for fry.

Fishes in captivity do suffer from dietary deficiency diseases. The number of tropical fishes dying from such disorders is probably slight, although a poorly balanced diet would certainly be responsible for a drop in the fishes' ability to fight off harmful organisms. The following suggestions outline in general the essential factors in fishes' diet. One caution cannot be overemphasized: the easiest way to aquarium mismanagement is through overfeeding. Adult fishes should be fed every other day; fry should be fed, in small amounts, as often as possible. *Never feed your fishes more food than they can eat in 15 or 20 minutes.*

Gordon's Formula for Wet Food*

"The liver-cereal food described below is designed for feeding as a thick wet mash. Under ordinary conditions, with adult fishes, feed each group of fishes early in the morning enough for them to work on for 15 minutes. It is wise to check the aquarium to be sure that the food has been taken. Uneaten food should be siphoned off the same day it was introduced, if possible, at any rate other food should not be offered until old food has been cleaned up. By feeding the fishes in the morning they have the advantage of all the daylight hours in which to finish their meal before the food has time to decompose.

Ingredients: 1 pound of fresh beef liver, 20 tablespoonfuls of Pablum or Cera-vim, 2 teaspoonfuls of salt. [The authors prefer to leave the salt out, though either formula is satisfactory.]

Apparatus: Waring Blendor, 2-ounce measuring cup, jars of 1- to 4-ounce size for storing formula.

1. Skin the liver of its connective-tissue covering; remove the larger blood vessels and other tough or fibrous tissues.
2. Cut the liver into ½-inch cubes.
3. Measure 2 ounces each of cubed liver and cold water. Place in blendor and liquidize. Pour liquidized liver through strainer into a 2-quart bowl. Repeat until all the liver is liquidized and strained. Add salt.

* Gordon, *The Care and Breeding of Laboratory Animals,* John Wiley & Sons, Inc., New York, 1950, p. 376.

4. Add Pablum, Ceravim, or any other similar dry, precooked cereal, stirring thoroughly all the time. Add as much cereal as the liquidized liver will take or until a thick peanut-butter-like consistency is attained.

5. Fill 1-, 2-, or 3-ounce glass containers, the size depending on the amount used for a single day's feeding of the liver paste.

6. Place the filled glass jars in water. Heat until water begins to boil, turn off heat and allow the jars to stand in hot water for about half an hour.

7. Cool and cover the glass containers and place in the coldest part of a refrigerator. Some may be frozen.

"Heating the liver mixture is necessary to coagulate the liquid elements of the gland. If the heat were not applied, the liver fluids would separate from the paste, and when placed into the aquarium water the fluids would foul the water just as quickly as ordinary liver particles do."

By using this basic formula, occasional feedings of live foods will supplement the diet, and the fishes will have a well-balanced fare. Gordon has observed that this food is excellent for very young live-bearing fishes.

It seems common knowledge that the best food for fishes is other fishes. This statement, long the password of fish nutritionists in both hobby and science, has recently been challenged. Warren H. Yudkin in 1949 wrote an article entitled "Thiaminase, the Chastek-paralysis Factor."[*] In this paper he warns that feeding raw fish is dangerous, especially the meat of cyprinids, since raw fish meat contains an enzyme, thiaminase, which destroys the vitamin thiamine. More work is needed in the field of fish nutrition before anyone can be certain of just what fishes should be fed and what they should not. It would be an easy matter, however, to name a score of fishes whose sole diet in nature is other fishes.

A suitable prepared diet is as follows: Measure out the following formula by weight:

	PER CENT
Liver or beef	13
Precooked cereal, wheat germ, or zwieback	40
Shredded shrimp, fish meal, or salmon-egg meal	17
Lettuce, spinach, or other greens	13

The meat should be placed in a pot with as little water as possible and boiled for 20 minutes. The meat should be removed and in the same sauce the remainder of the ingredients boiled. The meat is then ground or liquefied into smaller particles and added to the whole stew. After boiling for as long a time as it takes to evaporate most of the moisture from this mixture, pour the contents into a large flat pan for cooking and drying. If cooked, it should be in an oven not over 200°F. When the mixture has been thoroughly dried it should be ground in a coffee grinder or mill and sorted ac-

[*] *Physiol. Rev.*, vol. 28(4), pp. 389–402.

cording to particle size, using a wire-mesh screen. If all the moisture has been removed this dried food can be stored, preferably in glass containers.

Live Foods

Although it is entirely possible and feasible to raise many different species of fishes in outside pools without any intentional feedings of live foods, fishes raised indoors in small aquaria require regular and constant feedings of living organisms.

Live foods not only have a nutritional advantage over prepared diets but they add necessary bulk and natural laxative to the fishes' fare. Care should be taken when feeding live foods to ensure that harmful organisms are not being introduced. Crayfish, dragonfly larvae, water boatsman, and other aquatic larvae do feed upon small fishes and can do a great deal of harm if introduced into an established aquarium.

Daphnia

The most popular and desirable of live foods for aquarium fishes is *Daphnia*. This generic name includes several species, the most common of which are *D. pulex, D. longispina,* and *D. magna.* This listing is according to their size, an important factor when baby fishes must be fed. All species breed in the same manner and require the same general care. Gordon[*] reports that "when *Daphnia* are fed to the (live-bearing) fishes just after they are born, they subsequently grow better on other foods."

Raising *Daphnia* is a simple matter if their life cycle and requirements are completely understood. Sex in the *Daphnia* is rather easily ascertained as the female carries eggs in a brood sac. These eggs appear as tiny dark spots when the animal is held in a small glass container and light is allowed to pass through it. Initial cultures should have a dozen pairs as a starter, at least. Experience has shown that a culture will reach its peak of productivity about 3 weeks after the culture has been initiated.

The indoor culture requires at least a long 20-gallon aquarium. The water should preferably be that which has been siphoned from the bottom of an aged aquarium. Dirt and fecal matter are advantageous to the culture. Plenty of light is necessary, and a solid growth of algae or green water is ideal. A few yeast tablets, some bone or soybean meal, or even the brown leaves of decaying lettuce tend to produce the foods upon which the *Daphnia* will feed. Algal and bacterial foods are necessary for *Daphnia*. A few *Tubifex* worms can be introduced if there is to be sand on the bottom of the culture tank. Once the culture tank has become cloudy or green, then the time has arrived for the introduction of the *Daphnia*. Temperature fluctuation is only important as it affects the amount of oxygen dissolved in the water. Artificial aeration is desirable if it is available. Cultures should not be al-

[*] *Op. cit.,* p. 380.

lowed to grow too rich, as overpopulation will ruin them. If the culture shows signs of decreasing in productivity it probably means that certain unknown daphniacidal agents have developed and the entire culture should be started over again. Sometimes a partial change of water helps to get the culture running well again. Decaying aquatic plants have been used successfully as a fertilizer for *Daphnia* cultures, but direct sunlight is important in small cultures.

If possible cultures should contain several species of daphnioid organisms, as sometimes a given species will not take to a particular environment. Tropical fishes cannot be overfed with *Daphnia,* but too great a feeding might appreciably diminish the available dissolved oxygen supply and cause an overcrowded condition in the aquarium. *Daphnia* will usually live in the aquarium until they are eaten by the fishes, so regular small feedings of this organism have their advantages.

Outside cultivation of *Daphnia* is much easier. Pools should be fertilized with sheep, cow, or horse manure. A week or so later some *Daphnia* should be introduced. If the pool does not freeze, the culture should be available all year round. Frequent addition of lettuce leaves is helpful. Earth-bottom pools or all-concrete pools are used to equal advantage. The parasite problem is manifest in the outdoor situation.

White Worms

White worms, *Enchytraeus albidus,* are easily cultured in a loamy, loose soil. The humus which comes neatly packaged in 5-pound sacks at most floral shops makes an ideal culture medium.

The container in which these worms are to be raised should be wooden and have dimensions approximately the size of a cigar box. Successful cultures have been maintained in every type of container from a cigar box to a cheese box (about 5 inches square on the ends and 10 inches long), or a fruit box. The larger the box, the larger the culture.

Soil, to a depth of about 5 inches, is ideal. It must be kept moist and cool, but not wet and cold. A temperature of about 55 to 60°F seems to suit these worms well. If the container is large cultures should be introduced into all parts of the container by evenly spreading the worms over the surface of the earth and gently covering them with an inch of rich humus. Food for the worms should be very starchy; bread, oatmeal, cooked cereal, or any cereal mash seems to be favored. If the food is placed into several pockets and barely covered with humus, there will be less chance for the culture to become moldy. If mold does plague the culture, a bit of Moldex should be added to the cereal before it is cooked. Certain breads already contain Moldex. So that the culture may remain moist, it is advisable to fit a piece of glass over the top of the wooden container, resting right on top of the soil. If several cultures are established at the same time and put up in uniform containers, then stacking one container atop the other will help maintain an even moisture content. Wet cloth towels or even a thick blanket of wet newspaper will serve this purpose, but glass is by far the best.

In warm climates the cultures are best maintained in a refrigerator which has a high setting, say of 50°F if possible. Dehydration of the culture is of the greatest significance in a refrigerator.

Once the culture has been well seeded, usually 6 weeks after introduction of the worms it will be ready for harvesting. The food supply should be checked periodically, as well as the moisture content; food or water should be added as necessary. Constant stirring and mixing of the soil is not desirable until harvesting. After each harvest the soil should be completely loosened and refertilized.

Usually the worms can be removed in a semisolid ball, clinging to loose particles of earth about the food. Removing the worms from the earth is done with a separator which needs the following components: a screen with a mesh large enough for the worms to crawl through, under which there is cool water and over which a light bulb can be placed. The worms are placed on the screen and the light is put on top of them. The heat from the bulb will drive the worms away to the bottom of the screen and finally through the screen into the water, where they may easily be picked up with an eye dropper. It is possible to store the worms for a few days in wet moss or cotton in a refrigerator. They will not last long in water.

Since constant feedings of white worms result in a fatty degeneration of the reproductive organs, they should not be a steady diet for any kind of fish. They have value as a supplementary food, once or twice a week, when fed in conjunction with other foods.

Often when cultures are kept in damp, dark basements (which are usually ideal places for them), they become overrun with other organisms, usu-

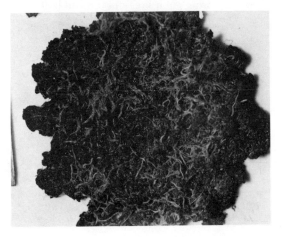

White worms, *Enchytraeus albidus,* as they appear in a bit of the humus in which they are propagated. A small matchstick lies alongside for comparison of size.

ally mites and the larvae of gnats. These organisms are not harmful either to the culture or to the fishes. Ants and small vertebrates (rats, mice, etc.), however, are harmful and destructive and they should be avoided if possible.

Tubifex Worms

The *Tubifex* worm represents, in the aquarium field, the greatest "overplayed" food for fishes. The worms are used by unknowing hobbyists as if they were entirely harmless organisms, and further, as if their fishes just could not live without them. Any number of aquarists will swear by these worms, but they never seem to have an answer when their fishes start perishing in large numbers.

This statement is not to imply that the worms have no value as a fish food. They do! But only after they have been treated and cleaned. Usually *Tubifex* worms can be purchased in aquarium shops where they have been stored in large shallow trays in which special water inlets and outlets enable them to be subjected to a steady flow of fresh, cold water. This flow of water serves three purposes: first and foremost, it keeps the worms cool, which enables the *Tubifex* to live on a minimum amount of oxygen as their metabolic processes are slowed down by the lower temperature; second, it assures the worms of a sufficient supply of well-aerated water; third, it constantly works to remove dead worms, excreted matter, and harmful bacteria. A ball of *Tubifex* the size of a baseball contains hundreds of thousands of worms and each worm needs its own supply of aerated water. This can only be accomplished in running water.

In small amounts the worms may be stored in shallow water in a cold refrigerator. The water must be changed at least twice a day and the dead worms washed free. This is easily done by pouring off the water from the massed worms, then breaking up the ball by a high-pressure stream of wa-

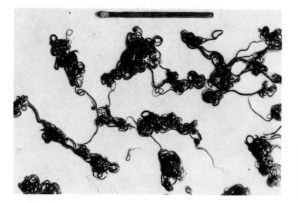

Tubifex worms, a fish food of great value, but one which must be used with caution.

ter. Allow the worms to settle and pour off the whitish debris which remains in suspension. This whitish matter is dead and decaying worms. Once the mass of worms starts to decay the whole ball will be endangered. Some persons keep the worms in a jar in their toilet storage tank, so that every time the toilet is used the worms get a change of water.

Keeping the worms in running water is important in washing the worms also. Not only are the worms covered with bacterial filth, but their entire digestive tract may be loaded with harmful organisms. Worms must be washed in fresh running water for at least 48 hours before they are fit for feeding to fishes.

Healthy worms manifest a blood-red color, form tight balls, and are not stringy. As the worms begin to die they get long, whitish, and stringy and impart an odor which, once experienced, is not easily forgotten.

Collecting your own worms is not a desirable side line. Techniques are difficult and the type of water in which the worms are found must, of necessity, be laden with raw sewage. In Japan, where the populace is not fortunate enough to have an underground sewage system, long drainage ditches pass through the cities for the deposition of waste materials. These ditches are laden every inch of the way with *Tubifex* worms. In their normal environment these worms perform the very important function of utilizing the organic wastes, thus providing food for larger organisms.

The worms should preferably be fed to fishes with a floating worm feeder. This can be a plastic floating dish with small holes perforated in the bottom, thus allowing only a few worms to escape at a time. The fishes soon learn to congregate about this worm feeder and few worms survive to burrow into the aquarium gravel.

In gravelless aquaria the worms can simply be thrown in without regard for their falling to the bottom uneaten. However, if large numbers of uneaten worms are allowed to remain in an aquarium for any length of time they will be sure to cloud the water in a way that defies clearing. It is a necessity that uneaten worms be siphoned within 8 hours from the bottom of aquaria into which they have been introduced.

Sometimes when a few worms escape into the sand of a very large aquarium they are able to survive and even to reproduce, but it is not too long before either they perish or the fishes in the aquarium eat them. The catfishes of the genus *Corydoras* show a special preference for these worms, and they are able to burrow down to the slate bottom after a single worm.

Brine Shrimp

Brine shrimp, *Artemia* species, have been used successfully for years as a food for aquarium fishes. The eggs of *Artemia* are noted for their viability, and they have been packaged and sold throughout the world, ready for hatching and feeding to small fishes of all species. Many claim that there is

Collecting brine shrimp in the salt ponds near Redwood City, California.

no better food for newborn fishes, and the authors are inclined to agree with this school of thought. The use of newly hatched brine shrimp as a first food for fishes has several advantages: first, they are easily hatched and available at the time they are needed; secondly, since they are a marine form they do not carry fresh-water parasites or other organisms which might be harmful to baby fishes; thirdly, they are so small that even if they are overfed to the baby fishes they will not use up much oxygen should they live in the fresh water, nor will they cloud the water if they should succumb.

Of late there has been made available to aquarists the frozen form of the adult *Artemia*. These are greedily taken by larger fishes but, like frozen *Daphnia*, they seem to lose much of their food value once they have been frozen. The organism does not remain intact when frozen, but bursts its ectoskeleton and

Male and female brine shrimp copulating.

there really is nothing left for the fishes to feed upon except empty shells.

The method of collecting the eggs is well known to anyone living near a brine pit. The brown eggs, are nearly as plentiful in some areas as pebbles on a beach, and all one needs to do is to scoop them up. This practice has resulted in some very disappointing experiences, for the eggs collected in this manner are only 10 to 30 per cent viable; the rest have no chance of hatching. The whole trick seems to lie in the manner in which the eggs are handled after they are collected. The San Francisco Aquarium Society, which has this process down to a science, remains one of the prime sources of fine brine shrimp eggs. A firm in Ogden, Utah, now supplies brine shrimp eggs from Great Salt Lake. The process of separating the good or heavy eggs from the lighter or bad ones is accomplished by blowing air through a thin stream of eggs in an air separator. Once the good eggs have been separated from the poor eggs, there should be an 80 per cent hatching. Eggs can last for at least 10 years if they are stored in a cool, dry place. Glass containers serve this purpose best.

Hatching the eggs is no problem at all. A solution of brine should be made up using 6 tablespoonfuls of coarse salt to a gallon of water. Enough eggs are then introduced into this water so that they barely cover the sur-

Robert P. Dempster (left) and Maurice Rakowicz collecting and examining brine shrimp eggs that have washed up on the beach at one of the salt ponds near Redwood City, California.

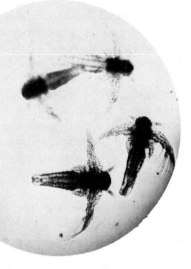

Brine shrimp nauplii a few hours after hatching. The large oarlike appendages are used as swimming organs.

face of the water. Artificial aeration helps in the hatching. When the newly hatched shrimps are to be collected the aeration must be taken off the hatching pan and a bright light placed in such a position that only one small corner of the aquarium is lighted. The light attracts the brine shrimps and they will congregate in a small area from which they can easily be siphoned off. The siphon should be run through a very fine net. If the shrimps are collected in an eye dropper their constant addition to a small aquarium will greatly increase the salinity of the water and gradually have an effect upon the fishes to whom they are being fed.

For all practical purposes it is impossible to raise brine shrimps to any size; they usually die after a few days. Sea water should be used if experiments are to be conducted which require the shrimps to be kept alive for longer periods.

Mature male brine shrimp showing the large claspers on the head region.

Freshly collected eggs showing the debris that usually accompanies them.

A satisfactory method of separating fertile and nonfertile *Artemia* eggs was published by Robert P. Dempster, Steinhart Aquarium, in *California Fish and Game,* 39(3):355–364, figs. 1–8, 1953.

With Robert Dempster's permission we quote his published account:

"Considerable thought was given to the problem of separating the heavy eggs from the light ones because of the desirability of having a pure culture of heavy eggs—and thereby establishing a quality standard for brine shrimp

Brine shrimp eggs magnified 50 times. Note that they are concave on one side. This is characteristic of all dry brine shrimp eggs. When they are submerged in salt water they become round.

eggs. It was hoped that, by taking advantage of a differential in weight, the light eggs could be separated from the heavy (or fertile) ones by the use of air currents.

"The equipment used is a vacuum sweeper (reversed to act as a blower) and three lengths of ordinary stovepipe with a few fittings. The lengths of pipe are sealed together, forming a tube 6 inches in diameter and 6 feet high. A plug, which serves as a base for the tube, is soldered to one end, and near this end in one side is inserted an elbow placed so as to point downward into the tube. The blower is connected to this elbow by a hose and a short piece of pipe. A valve is placed between the blower and the tube to control the volume of air directed on the eggs. Eggs that are about to be separated are poured into the top of the tube. After they have settled on the bottom, the blower is turned on and air which is forced into the bottom of the tube agitates the eggs quite vigorously and blows the light ones out of the open end. After a short period, the light eggs will have blown out and only the heavy eggs will remain. These in turn may be poured off into a suitable container

Brine shrimp egg separator in action. The eggshells are being blown out of the top of the tube. In the average collection of eggs, about 25 per cent is shells.

for storage. It takes about 20 minutes to separate a gallon of eggs by this method. Not more than one gallon should be separated at one time.

"Brine shrimp eggs cling together very tenaciously when they have become dry. Even though they are sifted through a moderately fine mesh screen (32 meshes to the inch) they come through in clusters which resemble miniature bunches of grapes. Since clusters consist of heavy eggs and light eggs in all proportions, adhering tightly together, an accurate separation cannot possibly be effected with the blower unless these clusters are broken up.

"After experimenting with several grades of wire screens, it was found that one with 60 meshes to the inch worked most satisfactorily. A screen of this grade allows only single eggs or, at most, clusters of two or three to go through. Eggs treated in this manner are readily separated with the blower. When a sample of the material that blows out of the separator is set up in a culture, no hatch results. This material, when observed under a microscope, is found to consist of infertile eggs and egg shells."

Microworms

Microworms, *Anguillula silusiae*, are threadlike organisms about ⅛ inch long. They make an excellent supplement to a brine shrimp diet for baby fishes but by no means are they a satisfactory substitute for the brine shrimps.

Cultures are best maintained in refrigerator jars of about 1-quart capacity. The culture medium is usually a mixture of 3 parts Pablum or Ceravim to 1 part of yeast, made into a paste with the addition of water. This food is poured to ½-inch depth in each refrigerator jar and a few worms inoculated into the medium. Since most of the microworms are females which reproduce, seemingly without the aid of a male, by giving off living young, it is not too long before the culture is ripe enough for harvesting. Usually when the culture is properly growing the excess worms will start to climb up the sides of the container and from this position they are easily scraped, either with a finger or a stick, and introduced to the small fishes. The worms will live for hours in aquarium water.

The refrigerator jars should be fitted with covers and the covers should be sealed to the containers with a plastic or cloth tape. This ensures that the medium will not dehydrate. Once the culture diminishes in productivity it is time to change the medium. One small culture may be used to inoculate hundreds of other cultures. It is wise to have several cultures running at the same time as accidents do happen and every so often a culture may turn sour. Never maintain a culture for more than 2 weeks.

Once fishes like guppies, white clouds, and neons have been introduced to the worms when they are hungry, they will usually eagerly await their introduction at later times. Under no conditions should these worms be offered as a sole diet, for they are lacking in many of the essential constituents of a balanced diet.

Mosquito "Larvae"

Mosquito pupae, or mosquito larvae as they are called by the aquarium trade, make fine foods for tropical fishes. They are usually found in the summer along with *Daphnia*. Being surface breathers, they do not offer the same problems as *Daphnia*, and they may be stored in small containers and kept alive a longer period of time than the daphnioids. Care should be exercised that the pupae are not kept long enough for them to hatch into mature mosquitos.

Earthworms, Bloodworms, and Sandworms

Earthworms, bloodworms, and sandworms make excellent fish food for animals which are large enough to ingest them. This feat is usually attributable only to the larger cichlids. To make the worms small enough for the normal run of aquarium fishes it is necessary to chop them into small pieces, wash them thoroughly in a fine net, and feed them in small amounts.

Drosophila

Fruit flies, *Drosophila*, are becoming quite popular as an aquarium fish food. They are easily cultured in small cream bottles with a piece of banana as a culture medium. The top of the bottle should be covered with a gauze to prevent the flies from escaping. A mutant variety with vestigial wings makes excellent fish food. Any high school or college which offers courses in biology will be able to supply the initial culture.

Infusoria

An ordinary drop of pond or aquarium water looks quite clear and lifeless to the naked eye, but actually the small drop of water may contain living organisms, both plant and animal. This group of organisms is loosely defined as infusorians. They are excellent food for baby fishes and are practically a necessity for every newborn tropical fish.

Most of the infusorian animals are classified in the phylum Protozoa (pro-toe-zoe'-a: meaning first animals). In this gigantic phylum are found species which live not only in fresh water but in salt water, species that live in dry desert sands, species that live inside the bodies of humans and animals as parasites, species that live in and on the soil, and species that live alone or in colonies. For the tropical-fish breeder all that really is necessary is to be able to recognize infusorians when present. The technique of pure cultures is too bothersome for the ordinary aquarist, and a mixed infusorian culture serves well to feed the fry in their various sizes.

An ordinary low-power microscope magnifies enough to enable one to

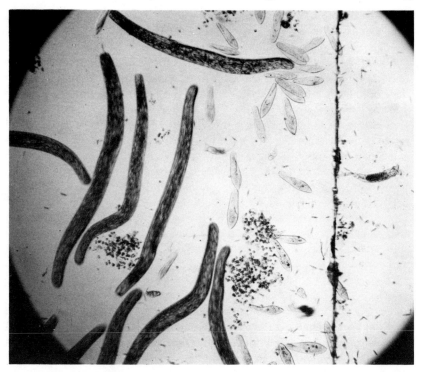

A microscopic view of infusoria.

distinguish when a culture is teeming with life or when there is barely an infusorian present. Sometimes larger protozoans can be observed with an ordinary hand lens when the culture is held up to a strong light.

More important for the hobbyist is how to obtain infusoria and how to culture them. The prime source of an infusorian culture is a pond; preferably a pond with green water. A cupful of this green water should contain millions of living organisms. Other sources are the bottom ooze of ponds, decaying aquatic plants, and ordinary air, for the spores and cysts of protozoans are found everywhere. They are only outnumbered by the bacteria, molds, and possibly the algae.

Once some living specimens have been found there will be no trouble, but in the wintertime when ponds are frozen over and when outdoor collection is difficult, there is still another method of starting an infusoria culture. On the market in most aquarium shops there is such a thing as "infusoria pills." When placed into conditioned aquarium water these pills issue forth a volume of infusoria. Then again, if these pills aren't available, try a few pieces of dried or decaying lettuce.

Place the lettuce, infusoria pills, or green water in quart jars or enamel pans or any other suitable *rustproof* container. If the material is dry add enough water to cover it. Maintain this container in a warm place, preferably not in direct sunlight. Within 48 hours the culture will progress and if they are properly fed will continue to multiply until after about 15 days they become overpopulated and start to die off. At this time the culture must be changed.

Feeding the infusoria is easy. Boil lettuce, grass, or leaves of some kind for 20 minutes in just enough water to cover. When cool add the vegetation and liquor remaining in small amounts to the culture. The culture need be fed only once, when it is first set up. Sometimes lima beans or rice can also be used without boiling. Set these grains in the culture dishes a few days before they are inoculated with the culture.

At times a culture will grow so rapidly that it will start to give off an odor; it should be changed at this time.

THE SALT-WATER AQUARIUM

The successful maintenance of a salt-water or marine aquarium depends almost entirely upon a thorough understanding of the differences between fresh and salt water and the effect of salt water upon the aquarium and its occupants. A marine aquarium is much more difficult to maintain than a fresh-water one. This statement might be sufficient to discourage the potential marine enthusiast. However, once he has had a successful experience with a marine aquarium, he will have the unsatiable desire to expand his salt-water collection, because marine coral fishes are undoubtedly the most colorful aggregate of fishes known to man.

Salt water holds much less oxygen than fresh water. According to Welch,[*] *oxygen is about one-fifth less soluble in sea water than in fresh water.* This means that the aeration factor is critical when dealing with the marine aquarium and aerating equipment is most necessary. Turbulence helps release the carbon dioxide from the water.

Salt water is more chemically active than fresh water. The aquarium should be inspected to be sure that no metal is in contact with the salt water. Condensation of water on the glass top of a marine aquarium will usually be fresh water, but the spray from an air release will be salt water, which must not be allowed to act upon the metal frame of the aquarium. Care should be exercised to see that all metal surfaces have been painted with a neutral asphaltum paint (like liquid aquarium cement), or a waterproof varnish that does not react with sea water. Metal air releasers or ornaments should be avoided.

[*] Paul S. Welch, *Limnology,* 2d ed., McGraw-Hill Book Company, Inc., New York, 1952, p. 98.

Fresh-water plants will never survive in the marine aquarium and will only foul the water if introduced. Decorations in the form of bleached coral pieces, shells of marine animals, sea fans, and sand are permissible if they have been thoroughly washed, cleaned, and perhaps boiled for a short time to remove soluble salts clinging to them. Fine white sand should be used so that uneaten particles of food may easily be seen and siphoned out of the tank. Then, too, the smaller particles of sand allow fewer pieces of uneaten food to fall into inaccessible places. It is safer for the beginning marine aquarist to do without sand or decorations in his aquarium until he is sure of his feeding techniques. Uneaten particles of food should be removed within 10 minutes of their introduction, since pollution of water is one of the chief problems in marine aquaculture.

Mrs. Helen Simkatris of Washington, D.C., has been very successful in maintaining a marine aquarium in direct sunlight and without any filtration or change of the water for about a year. Green algae have grown in her tank, along with other marine plants, on which her butterflyfish and French angelfish feed. The water is in part continually agitated by means of a circulating pump.

Feeding Marine Fishes

The needs of marine tropical fishes are the same as the familiar fresh-water tropicals. Feedings should be once a day, or once every other day for mature fishes, with only small amounts of food being offered at a time. When the fishes have consumed the small offering, more can be fed.

Tubifex worms, brine shrimps, *Daphnia*, bits of fish, clam, and meat are all accepted by marine fishes. Live *Daphnia* will not last long in the marine water but brine shrimp will endure until eaten; thus they are the most desirable food for salt-water fishes.

Temperature of Marine Aquaria

If tropical coral fishes are to be maintained in the marine aquarium then the water temperature is of vital concern. The ordinary thermostatically controlled aquarium heaters will be acceptable for use in the marine aquarium if they have no metal parts in contact with the water. *Chrome heaters are not to be used.*

Marine fishes cannot tolerate too high a temperature in the aquarium. Fishes normally living in water of 80°F cannot tolerate this same temperature when maintained in a small aquarium. This is partly due to the more limited amount of oxygen available. The temperature of the marine aquarium should never be allowed to go above 78°F nor below 65°F. Marine forms can tolerate the lower limit better than fresh-water forms.

During summer months when aquarium water temperatures are apt to rise above the 78°F mark, additional aquaria should be available to spread out the fishes. There is a drastic death rate when marine fishes are crowded at higher temperatures. Air conditioning is nearly a necessity in commercial marine houses handling wholesale lots of coral fishes and other marine forms, if the water temperature in the aquarium rises much above 80°F.

Filtration

Elaborate systems of filtration have been worked out in various public aquaria. Owing to the great care and difficulties inherent in showing marine fishes and the scarcity of suitable specimens, the New York Aquarium has not contained any marine forms for several years. Since it has an excellent filtration system and still finds the job a difficult one, the hobbyist should proceed fairly cautiously.

A filter system is a necessity for a successful marine aquarium. The principles and equipment are the same as for the fresh-water aquarium, but only plastic filters should be used. It is better to use a molded filter than one with cemented joints. If there must be a decision as to whether aeration *or* filtration should be used, aeration is the more important. Aeration *and* filtration, as a team, go far toward making the marine aquarium a success.

Water

Water for the marine aquarium may present a problem. The ideal water for use in the home aquarium would be filtered sea water. As the water evaporates it should be refilled with distilled water preferably. If distilled water is not available use tap water, but *never use sea water to replace evaporated water from the marine aquarium.* This would cause a more saturated solution of sea salts and gradually build up the specific gravity of the water to the point where it would kill the fishes. Using a small hydrometer to measure the specific gravity of the sea water will help maintain the proper amount of salts in the water. Full-strength sea water should have a specific gravity (sp gr) of between 1.020 and 1.025.

Artificial sea water may be made by the addition of commercial sea salt mixed with distilled water until the proper specific gravity has been reached. There is no really good substitute for natural sea water. Certain trace elements are needed by marine fishes and other sea life which are

	GRAMS PER KILOGRAM OF WATER
Sodium chloride, NaCl	23.476
Magnesium chloride, $MgCl_2$	4.981
Sodium sulfate, Na_2SO_4	3.917
Calcium chloride, $CaCl_2$	1.102
Sodium bicarbonate, $NaHCO_3$	0.192
Potassium bromide, KBr	0.096
Boric acid, H_3BO_3	0.026
Strontium chloride, $SrCl_2$	0.024
Sodium fluoride, NaF	0.003

never present in their proper proportions in artificial sea water. Several formulas have been developed for artificial sea water. The easiest to prepare, and one that is just as satisfactory as the others, is that of John Lyman and R. H. Fleming.* This formula is shown on page 96. Enough tap water then should be added to make a total of 1,000,000 cc.

Chemically pure compounds should be used, if possible. Since trace elements are not included, this formula should not be considered more than an emergency substitute for sea water.

The water in a marine aquarium should be changed in its entirety every 8 to 10 months and must be changed after 1 year.

The pH of good sea water is about 8.2. There is considerable doubt about the importance of the pH in marine work, but if trouble occurs the pH should be checked. Checking the pH of marine water requires special testing paper and chemicals. If possible use liquid chemical comparators rather than paper comparators.

Diseases

Diseases of marine fishes require the same treatments as fresh-water forms, except where an osmotic change is required for small parasites. Then, instead of treating the fish with a salt-water bath, a fresh-water bath is used. Very little has been published on the treatment of diseases of marine animals in captivity. Diseased fish should be isolated and treated in a separate aquarium.

Marine Forms Other than Fishes

There are many marine animals, other than true fishes, which make interesting additions to the home aquarium. Their care is the same as for higher marine forms with the exception of satisfying their feeding habits.

Sea anemones are members of the subclass Anthozoa of the class Coelenterata. Anthozoa, meaning "flower animals," are marine polyps related to the jellyfishes. The sea anemone has a large muscular trunk with a larger upper extremity forming a disk. The disk has a mouth surrounded by tentacles in several concentric circles. The tentacles, usually arranged in multiples of six, contain thread capsules for holding captured fishes. The main diet of the sea anemone is small fishes, but it will eagerly accept bits of fish or meat dropped into its mouth.

The basal end of the animal is a muscular basal disk that is used for locomotion and security. So tenaciously can the animal cling to rocks with this disk that unless a gentle continuous pressure is maintained when freeing the animal it will surely be pulled apart.

Anemones are capable of reproducing sexually or asexually. Asexual reproduction is vegetative, and the animal merely pulls itself apart into two

* *Jour. of Mar. Res.*, vol. 3, pp. 134–146, 1940.

nearly equal pieces. Some species are capable of regeneration when cut into several pieces, and bits of anemones are capable of growing into large, complete animals. In sexual reproduction sperm and egg cells are ejected from the mouth and each fertilized egg forms an anemone.

Anemones occur in many beautiful colors. Tropical and temperate species are found throughout the world. There are reports of their having bred in captivity.

Since their movements are so very slow, it might be difficult to realize that the animals are alive and can move. They require little oxygen and can easily be kept alone in small aquaria. Since their locomotion is based upon a firm attachment, they can hardly travel about over a sandy bottom.

When shipping these animals it is best to send them without water, wrapped in damp moss. They can, however, be sent along with fishes in regular shipping containers.

At times, especially when maintained in glass containers, they are practically impossible to dislodge. Take a knife blade and pass it between the animal and the glass very carefully, and gradually work the animal free. Do not use jerky pressure as it will tear the animal apart.

Crabs, clams, mussels, oysters, and snails add variety to the scene in a marine aquarium. They do not require special feeding but manage to get along on bits of food in the water and on the aquarium floor. If the bottom of the aquarium is covered with sand, the mollusks should be examined every day, for they are less easily observed when buried and should one die it will surely pollute the water. Crabs are by far the best of the group, and the smaller the better. Fiddler crabs, so named because the male has an overgrown left pincer which he continually moves in much the same manner as a fiddler would move his bow arm, make an interesting addition to the marine aquarium. They are scavengers and live in burrows along the sandy ocean beaches. Hermit crabs, which are not true crabs at all, live with their soft abdomens protected by the empty shell of some marine gastropod. They have a pair of hooked abdominal appendages which serve to anchor the body inside the shell. The cephalothorax can be extended and the crab can carry its shell when walking about, if it so desires. Should danger threaten the crab it will immediately retreat into the shell. These animals are acceptable for the marine aquarium and are easily obtained.

Plants in the Home Aquarium

THE importance of plants in the home aquarium has only recently been fully explained and documented. Charles M. Breder, Jr., James W. Atz, and other workers have been untiring in their efforts to put before the aquarium world the true value of plants in the aquarium.

According to Breder and Atz, plants are of limited value as "oxygenators." They do have several other important functions, however, as follows:

1. As a decoration for the aquarium. Most aquaria would look rather shabby and bare without the addition of aquarium plants, much like a picture without a frame.

2. As a conditioner and test of the water. If the water is so "raw" as to be unable to support plant life, then it is certainly unsuitable for fishes.

3. As an inhibitor of the growth of algae. Large-leafed plants seem to slow the growth of smaller plants and algae by shading, which helps starve them.

4. As a food for fishes, both directly and indirectly as food for the organisms upon which the fishes feed.

5. As a shelter and hiding place for the smaller fishes and less aggressive species.

6. As a spawning medium for many types of egg-laying fishes.

7. As a security factor. Plants make the aquarium more like "home" to the fishes.

Plants are not an absolute necessity for the well-being of fishes. Many commercial breeders maintain their fishes without plants; often the first time they come into contact with any plants at all is when they arrive in the home aquarium. The reason that plants are not used by commercial breeders is twofold: They get in the way when the fishes must be netted, and they hinder a close inspection for size and health. Small parasites are harder to see in a planted aquarium.

Plants and fishes do have something like a "symbiotic relationship." The fishes' wastes are excellent fertilizer for the aquatic plants, which utilize them as such. This helps rid the aquarium of an otherwise useless by-product from fishes. Although plants do give off oxygen during photosynthesis, their more important function lies in absorbing and utilizing dissolved carbon dioxide. Photosynthesis can only take place in the presence of light. It is nec-

For exhibition tanks it is often desirable to identify the fishes contained within the aquarium. Drawings or photographs are extremely helpful in this respect.

essary either to give the plants direct exposure to daylight or to substitute an equivalent amount of artificial light.

Aquatic plants in general are divided into three main groups: rooted plants, bunch plants, and floating plants. Rooted plants are those which require individual planting, have long roots, and are purchased in a rooted condition. Bunch plants are a type of rooted plant; however, they are purchased without roots, by the bunch, and are best planted by the bunch. They will usually develop roots as they grow. Floating plants are those which normally float upon the surface of the water and are not planted in sand.

Plants for the aquarium should be positioned according to their height. Note that the smaller plants are in the front, while tall plants are further rear. The use of bushy plants in the front or center of an aquarium merely distracts from the beauty of the fish and is annoying to observers.

In large aquaria with rockwork backgrounds, tall plants are situated on the sides of the aquarium, while the center is planted with very small foliage. This highlights the fish nicely as the top light shines right into the center section of the aquarium.

A new aquarium in England featured large aquaria with aquatic, semiaquatic, and terrestrial plants. Water filled about one-third of the aquarium, and fishes, lizards, and frogs were also on display.

The Amazon sword plant, formerly *Echinodorus intermedius*, is now identified as *E. brevipedicellatus*.

ROOTED PLANTS

Amazon Sword Plant

The Amazon sword plant, most popular in the group, is *Echinodorus brevipedicellatus* [eh'-kin-o-dor'-us brev'-i-ped'-i-sel-lay'-tus]. It may have from 30 to 40 leaves coming off the main stem, much like a stalk of celery. It is rather delicate and must not be subjected to plant-molesting cichlids or plant-eating snails. It reproduces by runners, which should be weighted into the sand at the various points at which baby plants begin to sprout. It does well in moderate to strong light or in 8 to 10 hours of electric light daily. As the leaves turn brown they should be removed. If other than outer leaves begin to discolor, the plant is not receiving enough light and should be exposed to either more or stronger light.

Fertilizers are not necessary to propagate this beauty, but it will do better in a large flowerpot half filled with very rich black soil, then filled with sand. Once the plant has been set it should not be removed unless absolutely necessary. When planting, make sure that the crown of the plant is above the sand level, though all the roots must be buried beneath the sand. If algae grow upon the leaves, the plant is receiving too much light. These algae may be removed by rubbing the leaves gently between the fingers.

A broad-leafed Amazon sword plant is also available.

(Above) The junior sword plant, *Echinodorus tenellus,* from Brazil.

(Left) The ruffled sword plant, *Echinodorus martii.*

Pygmy Chain Sword Plant

The pygmy chain sword plant, *E. intermedius* [in'-ter-me'-dee-us], is a miniature of the Amazon sword plant. Although it tends to reproduce faster than the larger plant, it makes an ideal centerpiece for the 1-, 2-, or 5-gallon aquarium because it rarely gets higher than 4 inches. Runners should be cut as soon as they start growing if the plant is used for a centerpiece. This will make the plant grow more bushy instead of being extended. In the larger aquarium, if left uncut, it will cover the whole bottom of the tank in a few months. This hardy plant does as well in relatively weak light as in strong light. It should be planted, like all rooted plants, with its crown above the sand level.

Echinodorus cordifolius

Another member of the large genus *Echinodorus* is the beautiful plant, *E. cordifolius* [cord'-i-fo-li'-us]. At one time the plant was mistakenly called

The pygmy variety of *Echinodorus tenellus* is from Florida.

The pygmy chain sword plant, formerly *Echinodorus tenellus,* is now identified as *E. intermedius.*

a *Sagittaria*. It is not recommended for the large aquarium because it tends to grow into lilylike plants with aerial and floating leaves, with nothing much except stems below the water level. If little light is given to the plant, thus retarding its growth, there is a fair chance that the plant will maintain its leaves below the water mark, but this is not easy to accomplish. Many aquarists grow the plant in a small aquarium; when it has many leaves they transfer it to the larger aquarium where the longer leaves are still submerged and the plant shows up very well. This plant flowers easily and the seeds are easily propagated. It requires little light.

Madagascar Sword Plant

The Madagascar or ruffled sword plant, *Aponogeton undulatus* [a-pon'-oh-gee'-ton un'-dew-lay'-tus], is only a recent import. Propagation is difficult; though the plant flowers easily few seeds develop. Most plants in home aquaria came to this country as small bulbs imported from the Far East. The bulbs are fairly large and may develop into as many as three separate plants. The plant does best in a well-lighted aquarium, which it soon fills with many leaves. Unfortunately, the leaves tend to float on the surface and the stems get longer and longer. By constantly transplanting, it may be kept in a semiconstant state of flowering.

Brown outer leaves should be removed as soon as possible. The plant should always be kept trimmed. It is fast-growing and does well without fertilizers. The plant grows to 30 inches in length in an 18-inch-high aquarium.

The "Madagascar sword plant" as a popular name is misleading, since it is not endemic in Madagascar.

The beautiful Madagascar lace plant, *Aponogeton fenestralis.*

Madagascar Lace Plant

This beautiful plant, *A. fenestralis* [fen-es-tray'-lis], is only now coming into the price range where it can be appreciated by all aquarists. No one seems to understand the handling of these plants as well as Hans Tusche of Germany. The following is an excerpt from an article which appeared in *Datz*, the German magazine for aquarists:

"In the Summer of 1952, the Swedish Aquarium Society, 'Stockholm Akvarievarening,' was able to import *Aponogeton fenestralis* directly from Madagascar. The bulbs were packed damp in tin boxes and air-mailed to Stockholm, and were then cultivated to healthy plants by . . . Paul Jacobson. These plants, with their tough, almost leathery, lush green leaves which have a unique, lattice-like structure have never failed to make the aquarist's heart beat faster. . . . Up to now, the popularity of this plant was hindered by two reasons: the enormous price, and the natural assumption that a plant which is so expensive must necessarily be extremely sensitive. . . . There is no other plant which compares with the Madagascar lace plant in toughness and adaptability. . . . When the first few lace plants were imported into Germany from Sweden after the war, they were delayed for 14 days and lay unplanted in the station in a water-basin. This, and further transportation, they withstood perfectly and one plant found its way to my community tank which was populated with small peaceful fishes. As a precaution, the plant was placed in a small flowerpot which was 3 inches high and about 2¼ inches in diameter. The bulb with its white roots was pressed into coarse gravel, which was mixed with powdery clay and fine bits of dried cow-

A close-up of the leaf of this plant. Leaves are very tough, but terribly brittle.

manure. Even while it was planted a weak spot was discovered. This was the leaf stems, which although they are thick and strong, are also quite brittle. One of the six leaves had to carry on. So, one must take great care when planting or removing, that these lovely leaves are not damaged. . . .

"The plant . . . was placed in my 15-gallon community tank and requires a space of 8 to 12 inches for its horizontally spreading leaves. It is obvious that this, like other species of *Aponogeton*, can not . . . be stuck into a bunch of *Cryptocoryne*. There the plant would surely waste away. No other plants should be placed at least within 6 to 8 inches. In this way only can the Madagascar lace plant spread out to its full beauty. Mine received only electric lighting of 50 watts for 10 hours daily. Because of this, the new leaves showed coloring. The plant started growing immediately, sending out snow-white rootlets into the bottom soil and also sending up a rhubarb-colored sprout, which soon opened up into a beautiful latticed leaf. Only after 14 days did the leaves gradually turn green. The *Aponogeton* sprouted a new leaf every month on an average; sometimes when fresh water was added one would appear every two weeks. As long as these leaves are not fully developed they turn toward the light and often are pointed steeply upwards after the dark of night. Once the leaves attain their length, which may vary according to light conditions, this length is held and cannot be changed. One can then rub off any settlings or light growths of algae between the thumb and index finger, without any fear of damaging the leaf. . . .

"If *Aponogeton fenestralis* is provided with fluorescent lighting [Sylvania soft white], or daylight is provided, then the new shoots are immediately a bright green in color. In the latter case, one must be very careful of a growth of algae.

"The next happy change in this one was noted when an offspring appeared. Unfortunately, the plant made no attempt at blooming, but at least made an effort to propagate. . . . It was not noticed that the lovely leaves of the lace plant were being slowly but surely covered with a strong growth of brown algae. A quick change was made into a smaller container which was totally free of algae. The plant began to grow again, but the leaves which were covered with the strongest growth decayed. Of the 16 leaves originally on the double plant, only 9 remained which could be cleaned. While in this condition, the plant was given a fresh supply of bottom soil of the same mixture originally used, and replaced in its old home, the community tank, where the place of honor was still waiting. There it made an entirely satisfactory comeback, and showed itself as having weathered the storm.

"Mother and daughter each put out a beautiful green leaf, both of which were larger than almost any before. It could also be noticed that the two plants had grown further apart, and that now a space of about an inch was measured between them. The time seemed ripe to separate the two bulbs. So the plant was carefully removed at the roots, so as not to break off the leaves again, and it was observed that the hitherto small bud had grown into a small bulb about ½ inch in diameter. The cutting away with a razor blade was easily accomplished without injuring the other buds, which according to A. Wendt could have had serious consequences. The cut places were rubbed with powdered charcoal to prevent decay. However, this dust came off when the plant was put back, but the bulbs healed well in the meantime and became fully hard. Naturally, the young bulb had already sprouted its own roots and was already producing—a grandchild! It was a small sprout, which had not yet put in an appearance above ground. . . . While the young plant flourished immediately in the fine, clayish sand, producing new shoots and leaves, the parent plant stopped growing and even lost the large leaves. However, even here, after a long rest, fresh growth began again, and a small, light brown swelling formed at the cut end began to produce new shoots. Although thus far we have recommended only coarse gravel, to which clay and cow-manure have been added, this is not to say that no other bottom is possible. For instance Mr. Pinter has kept his lace plants in clean sand only."

Water Orchid

A native southeastern American bog plant, *Spiranthes odorata* [spy-ran'-thees o'-dor-ay'-ta], has recently been adapted to the aquarium. Not really an aquatic plant, it grows on bogs and marshes, semisubmerged, fully submerged, or even wholly above water. Its well-being in the aquarium seems directly dependent upon the amount of light it receives. At least 8 hours of

The water orchid, *Spiranthes odorata.*

good strong light is required. The heavy, fleshy roots are necessary for the plant to live; do not buy this species unless it has a fully developed root system.

Undoubtedly the water orchid does best in a soil-sand medium, but a well-aged aquarium with plenty of fish waste on the bottom is a fair substitute. In this environment the plant will flower upon occasion.

Spatterdock or Cow Lily

The spatterdock or cow lily, *Nuphar advena* [new'-far ad-ven'-a], is one of the more popular of the indigenous plants. It has beautiful green, delicate leaves, not too dissimilar to the Amazon sword plant leaf. Propagation is

both vegetative and sexual. The root or rhizome (like a tuber) is usually purchased from the store and planted in the sand. Most of the time it grows beautifully into a grand, 8-inch-high plant; other times the root begins to rot and the plant is worthless. When purchasing these plants be sure that a luxurious growth of leaves has already been started. Squeeze the root to be sure that it is not soft and mushy. Smell the root; if it has a foul odor look for another. If possible dip the root into some plant hormones manufactured just for this purpose. This seems to stimulate growth and retard decay. The plant requires an acid condition, preferably a pH as low as 5.0.

Another spatterdock or cow lily is *Nuphar sagittifolia.*

Cryptocoryne

There are many species of *Cryptocoryne* [crip'-toe-core'-een] now available to the aquarist. Not too long ago these Far and Middle Eastern plants were a rarity, but now that local breeders have the knack of raising them they are in profusion. The plants do well in a slightly acid environment (pH 6.8 to 6.4). Propagation is usually by runners; a good plant will produce 20 plants a year if they are not overcrowded. The plant requires little light, but it must be from overhead. Side lighting does not seem to suit it. If only limited light is available, try one of this variety of plants.

It is not uncommon for a single plant to grow two different kinds of leaves. Several plants have been observed with a few mottled underside leaves, while other leaves are a bright, unmottled green.

If kept in the large aquarium some species will tend to grow large, while

Left to right, *Cryptocoryne cordata*, *C. beckettii*, and *C. willisii*.

Cryptocoryne ciliata.

Cryptocoryne griffithii, from Malaya.

Cryptocoryne hartelliana is the name given this plant by aquarists.

other species will always be small. The popular smaller species are *C. beckettii*, *C. willisii*, *C. cordata*, while *C. griffithii* and *C. ciliata* grow to 8 or 10 inches in length. New *Cryptocoryne* arrive every year, as the plant ships easily if kept in moist newspapers. Breeders use a soil-sand mixture in propagating the "cryps"; this is not necessary for the home aquarium.

Eel Grass

Vallisneria spiralis [val'-is-nair'-ee-a spy-ral'-is], is often called eel grass or Italian val. It is a straight grasslike plant which reproduces rapidly by runners in a well-lighted environment. It does well if planted densely. When in a well-lighted aquarium this plant covers the floor if conditions are favorable. Planting should be carried out with care, as the crowns of the plant must be above the soil level.

Several varieties of *Vallisneria* are available. The corkscrew variety is the same as the Italian except that the leaves curl around like a corkscrew. Giant val is a Florida variety which grows 2 feet long with a leaf over ½ inch wide. These plants are widely used by breeders in pools of live bearers. Both fishes and plants are harvested at the same time.

Sagittaria or Arrowheads

Another favorite grassy-type plant is *Sagittaria* [sag'-i-tare'-i-a], several species of which are cultivated for the home aquarium. They all have the same requirements and differ only in their size. All reproduce principally by runners and are fast-growing plants when in a suitable environment. Their

(Left) *Vallisneria spiralis,* corkscrew val, is probably only a form of the ordinary species.

(Below) Left to right, *Sagittaria subulata, S. natans,* and *S. subulata.*

needs are simple: clean, clear, aged water, plenty of light, and a tank well stocked with fish.

The giant sagittaria, S. *sagittifolia* [sa-git′-ti-fol′-i-a], a large variety, grows to 2 feet long and over ½ inch wide and is best suited for the larger aquarium, over 20 gallons. Its growth is less rapid than the smaller varieties and it is harder to maintain, probably because it is cultivated in the wild and not under aquarium conditions. S. *natans* [nay′-tans] is the familiar, popular "sag" which grows about 8 inches long and is easily cultivated. It has long been an aquarium favorite. S. *subulata* [sub-you-lay′-ta] is a species similar to S. *natans,* though its leaves are narrower and thicker. It takes on a much greener and more sturdy appearance than S. *natans.*

All sagittarias should be carefully planted so that the crowns of the plants are not buried beneath the sand. With proper lighting this genus makes a beautiful arrangement. Many aquarists set up an aquarium simply with varieties of this genus of plants. The tall grass should form the background, the shorter species the foreground.

Water Fern

Water fern, *Ceratopteris thalictroides* [ser′-a-top′-ter-us thal-ik-troy′-des], is one of the in-between plants which does equally well as a rooted or as a floating plant. When the leaves become longer and float to the surface baby plants appear on them; soon the top is covered with the floating water fern. Once this happens the bottom plant begins to die and must be replaced. The plant is fast-growing and is a favorite with many of the advanced hobbyists. Its general appearance reminds one of a carrot top.

Sagittaria sagittifolia, giant sag. This illustration is of a young plant.

Water fern, *Ceratopteris thalictroides.*

Hygrophila polysperma, often incorrectly spelled *Hydrophilia*.

Needle grass or spike rush, *Eleocharis acicularis*.

Hygrophila

This plant, *Hygrophila polysperma* [hi'-gro-fil'-a pol'-ly-sperm'-a], often wrongly spelled *Hydrophilia*, is only now becoming an aquarium favorite. It is a rooted plant which does well when planted in bunches. Small rootlets come out of every leaf-stem junction and the lower leaves begin to fall off when the plant is first introduced into a new environment. After a week or so of settling down the plant begins to come into its own and before long it shows magnificent growth. Interestingly enough, this plant, like other members of its genus, will grow as a terrestrial in wet places.

Cabomba caroliniana, two varieties. Left, the red form; right, the green form.

Spike Rush

Spike rush, *Eleocharis* [ell'-ee-oh'-kar-is], sometimes called needle grass, is something different for the aquarium. The plant looks much like ordinary grass except that the "blades" are cylindrical rather than flat. A good growth is almost entirely dependent upon sufficient light; unless light is available at least 8 hours a day there is little use in even attempting to grow this plant.

When purchased, plants are bunched and tied together with a lead strip or rubber band. The brown stems should be removed and the grass planted in clumps. It makes excellent spawning grass for both live bearers and egg layers.

A species often used comes from Georgia and Florida, growing on the banks of exposed ponds and streams. Most of the commercial grass available is from wild stock; therefore, examine it carefully for parasites and other harmful organisms.

BUNCH PLANTS

Fanwort

Fanwort, *Cabomba caroliniana* [ka-bom'-ba car'-oh-lin-ee-an'-a], is one of the oldest, most versatile friends of the aquarist. This fast-growing plant, needing 8 hours of strong light a day, may reach lengths of 2 or 3 feet.

Planting should be accomplished by cutting off the lower inch of the bunch as it comes from the dealer. Next strip off the leaves from the bottom inch of the plant and press it firmly into the gravel, in a bunch, fastened with a strip of lead or tied with a rubber band. In no time at all it will take hold and grow beautifully.

The plant is a popular spawning grass and is useful in breeding both egg-laying species and the live bearers. Inspection of the bunch prior to purchase should reveal crisp, green stems and leaves, without odor and not slimy to the touch. If the plant is turning brown it should not be bought.

Elodea

Elodea, *Anacharis canadensis* [el'-oh-dee'-a, an-ack'-ar-is can'-a-den'-sis], is in the same category as *Cabomba*. It comes in bunches and should be planted in bunches with the lower parts of the plant being treated as for *Cabomba*. It requires at least 8 hours of good light or it will grow into a stringy mess. If the leaves are turning brown when the plant is purchased it will soon perish and the leaves will foul the tank in short order. Only very crisp, dark green plants should be selected. If possible try to obtain tank-bred varieties, even if the price is a little higher.

When breeding live bearers some bunches of elodea may be planted while others should be allowed to float about on the surface of the water.

The giant anacharis, cultivated type, **Ana-*** *charis gigantea*, often called elodea.

Myriophyllum spicatum (or *M. pinna-* *tum*), often called foxtail by the trade.

Most fishes seem to enjoy picking at the leaves, but the plant is so fast-growing that there never seems to be any permanent damage.

Milfoil

The long, fine leaves of this plant, *Myriophyllum spicatum* [mir'-ee-oh-file'-um spy-cay'-tum], afford maximum efficiency in catching the ova of the egg-laying fishes. It needs plenty of strong light to maintain its closely knit leaves. When such light is available the plant will grow astoundingly fast, sometimes as much as 3 or 4 inches per week. Should growth be too rapid the plant may be trimmed and the lower part disposed of, using the upper part to replace it.

Myriophyllum should be planted the same way as *Cabomba;* many inexperienced aquarists might even mistake this plant for *Cabomba,* so closely do they resemble each other. However, the leaves of *Myriophyllum* are much finer and more closely knit than those of *Cabomba.*

Ludwigia

Though not a true water plant, *Ludwigia* [lud-wig'-i-a] has, nevertheless, found its way into those aquaria where light and richly fertilized sand are available. *Ludwigia*, like the other bunch plants, tends to become very stringy and die if sufficient light is not available. The beautiful red-under-leaf species, grown so successfully in greenhouses and ponds in Florida, rarely maintains itself in a home aquarium.

Needle-leaf ludwigia, *Ludwigia natans.*

Green ludwigia, *Ludwigia palustris.*

The fact that *Ludwigia* does best in a rich soil culture bears out the fact that it is primarily a bog plant. Reproduction can be accomplished vegetatively, that is, the parent plant can be divided into smaller plants by merely snipping off a piece and planting it in a suitable environment.

Water Hyssop or Bacopa

Bacopa, *Hydrotrida caroliniana* [hy′-dro-tri′-da car′-oh-lin-ee-an′-a], is much like *Ludwigia.* It requires more light than the latter and its leaves are slightly fragrant. The plant is not quite as popular as it has a right to be. It does well in aquaria with at least 6 hours of light per day. Its lack of popularity is possibly due to the Florida breeders, who do not favor the plant because it is a slow grower and does not fare well in the brightly lit pools in which they raise other plants.

Wide-leaf ludwigia,
Ludwigia palustris var. *americana.*

Hornwort

This submerged aquatic plant, *Ceratophyllum demersum* [ser-at'-oh-fill'-um dee-mer'-sum], is one of the best spawning grasses available to the aquarist. The plant itself has weak stems and grows to 8 feet in length in nature. There are never any roots. The plant does well in hard water with little light. It gives off an odor at times and for that reason is not too welcome in most aquaria, but its finely knit leaves and dense growth make it a superior plant for spawning fishes. If the bottom of the plant is weighted down or stuck into the gravel, it will grow beautifully up to the surface of the water in a magnificent spray. The hornwort has a world-wide range in temperate and tropical regions.

Fontinalis

For a breeding grass, easily found in the New York metropolitan area, there is none better than *Fontinalis gracilis* [fon'-tin-a'-lis gra-sill'-is], as it needs very little light and is ideal for breeding the "panchax" fishes.

The plant is commonly known as willow moss and is easily collected in the northeastern United States and adjacent areas. It attaches itself to any kind of base, an old water-soaked log, a bit of stone, or even a tin can, from which it is easily picked up by the handfuls. Wild plants should be thoroughly washed and sterilized.

FLOATING PLANTS

Water Hyacinth

One of the pest plants of the South is water hyacinth, *Eichhornia crassipes* [eye-kor'-nee-a krass'-i-pes]. So rapidly and densely does this plant propagate that it may make waterways impassable. As a plant in the outdoor pool it is ideal, both for the shading effect it has on other submerged plants and as a spawning medium. Its dense, fine roots suit the purpose of many fishes, especially the bubble-nest builders and goldfish. Although it is quite commonly sold in pet shops, it is impossible to maintain this plant in the home aquarium for any length of time, for it needs many hours of direct sunlight every day. When it blooms the flowers are beautiful and may grow to a foot in height. Flowers last only a day in the aquarium.

Spanish Moss

This aerial plant, *Tillandsia usneoides* [till-and'-si-a yous'-nee-oi'-des], is used in the aquarium only after it is dead and cured. The plant itself is several feet long and is found hanging in irregular profusion from all sorts of projections—tree limbs, telephone wires, or almost anything. The plant is common from Virginia south to Florida and west to Texas.

Ceratophyllum demersum.

Fontinalis gracilis.

The plants on the left are water hyacinths, *Eichhornia crassipes*. The plant on the right is water lettuce, *Pistia stratiotes*.

Spanish moss is commercially valuable to the furniture industry, where it is used as upholstery stuffing. Some packers even use it for insulation. Aquarists use it after the outer skin has been taken off and only the fine, dark inner strands are left. After the color has been boiled out of it the plant makes the best known breeding grass, for after each use it can be washed out and hung up to dry until it is needed again. Since the plant is dead when it is being used it requires no light and does not decay even after many years of use.

If used without a series of boilings, Spanish moss will discolor the water and tend to make the pH slightly lower, toward the acid side. This has certain value and American aquarists are finding it a suitable substitute for peat moss. Only recently has it been put up in special packages for aquarists. If unavailable at a pet shop it may easily be obtained from an upholsterer.

Nitella

Nitella gracilis [ni-tell'-a gra-sill'-is] is a form of stonewort, or Charales, family Characeae, an alga. It looks much like emaciated *Cabomba*. It has a fine, long main stem from which thin filaments protrude in all directions. It does not root and is excellent for use when spawning egg layers and live

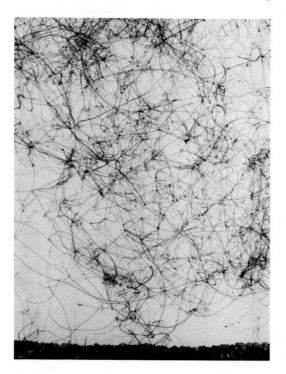

Nitella gracilis,
an excellent spawning grass.

bearers. Most fishes—*Scatophagus*, barbs, swordtails, and some cichlids particularly—enjoy eating the plant.

This is one of the best plants for aging and testing aquarium water. If a handful of crisp, green *Nitella*, placed in the newly set-up aquarium, flourishes for a few days, then the tank may be assumed to be safe for fishes. If, however, the *Nitella* starts to turn brown and decay, then another clump of *Nitella* must be introduced. It is certain that when the first clump was put in the water was unsafe for fishes, but that first clump might have treated the water sufficiently for it to be safe.

Nitella is a fast-growing plant and should be kept thinned out. It is just about impossible to keep any flourishing growth in a tankful of *Puntius nigrofasciatus*, for they eat the new shoots as fast as they sprout.

Crystalwort

Riccia [rik'-ki-a] is a floating plant with many and varied uses. It is ideal for the bubble-nest builders; it is soft enough for newborn live bearers to creep into for protection; it can be used as a food for the vegetarians among fishes; it can be used as a shading plant; and it can also be used in breeding certain egg-laying species if it is held down under the water in some manner.

Riccia needs plenty of light; unless it gets at least 6 hours of strong light a day it will stop growing and may decay. The form often used occurs in the eastern Atlantic states from Virginia south to Florida in nearly all the pools and lakes. Care should be taken when collecting the wild plants to ensure that no parasites are introduced with the plants.

Duckweed

Duckweed, *Lemna minor* [lem'-na my'-nor], appears as one or more egg-shaped, thin floating plants with only a single root. It is found in nature floating on the top of stagnant waters or washed on the shores of slow-moving bodies of fresh water, from Nova Scotia to Florida and westward to the Pacific, and in the Old World.

This flowering plant propagates vegetatively at terrific speeds and in a

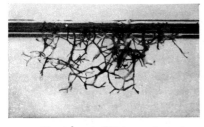

Crystalwort, *Riccia* species.

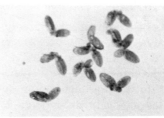

Duckweed, *Lemna minor.*

Dwarf Madagascar lily, *Nymphaea micrantha*. This photograph is of a young plant which might possibly be a hybrid between *N. micrantha* and *N. caerulea*.

sunny, humid environment it will cover the surface of the water. The plant serves as a food for ducks and pheasants in the wild; when introduced into a *Daphnia* pond it greatly increases the yield of "bugs" but makes them difficult to separate from the plants.

Dried duckweed when ground makes an excellent culture medium for infusoria. Merely add a few pinches to aged aquarium water and place it in the sun.

Salvinia

Salvinia [sal-vin'-i-a] is really a fern, but has a superficial resemblance to the widespread duckweed. Its leaves are a bit more circular, but it certainly is not to be considered better than our own American plant by any means. It requires the same care as duckweed and propagates in exactly the same manner.

Water Lettuce and Water Lilies

Water lettuce, like water lilies, has little value in the home aquarium. In nature these plants are considered as pests but for ponds they are attractive and controllable. Many hybrids of the water lily have been developed and some of the flowers are extremely beautiful.

In the breeding pool during the summer months these plants may be used for shade and hiding; otherwise they have little value for aquarists.

The water lettuce is in the genus *Pistia,* and the white water lily is *Nymphaea.*

Diseases of Fishes and Their Cure

BY C. VAN DUIJN, JR.

A.M.TECH.I.(GT. BRIT.), F.R.M.S., M.I.P.T.

ALL living beings can in certain circumstances become subject to disease and fishes are no exception. Generally fishes have a great resistance against disease so long as they are not weakened by bad treatment, such as unsuitable food, lack of oxygen, too high or too low temperature, or other weakening influences. Thus, to avoid diseases, the first essential is to keep your fishes in optimal condition so that they have good resistance if any infection should occur.

Most infections, however, can be avoided. If a new tank has been supplied with plants that have grown in absence of fish, and completely healthy fishes are put in this tank, any parasite which causes a disease later on must have been introduced from the outside, either with new plants or living food or a new fish.

DISEASES OF THE SKIN

The skin of a fish consists of two layers, namely, the *epidermis* (upper part) and the *cutis* (the underlayer). The epidermis consists of epithelial cells with slime cells in between. The slime cells excrete a slimy substance covering the whole surface of the skin with a thin protective film. Some fishes are more "slimy" than others; for example, tench and eels excrete much slime, while this is considerably less in dace. It seems likely that the slime on the skin protects the fish more or less against bacterial infections; consequently, fishes with a very slimy skin are apt to be more resistant to infection than others. The excretion of the slime cells becomes greater when they are irritated, for example, by certain parasites. Abnormal slime excretion is an important symptom to be considered in diagnosis.

The cutis consists of fibers of binding tissue and is rich in blood vessels. The upper part of the cutis contains the scales, which are mounted in small pockets. Both sides of this part of a scale are covered with binding tissue and the whole is covered once more by epithelial cells. If pathogenic bacteria penetrate into the scale pockets, an inflammation is caused and the scale pockets are filled with an exudate. Pressure of this exudate against the scales causes protrusion.

Beneath the cutis fat cells are situated, while between the cutis and the epidermis *chromatophora* (color cells) are present. The black ones, *melano-*

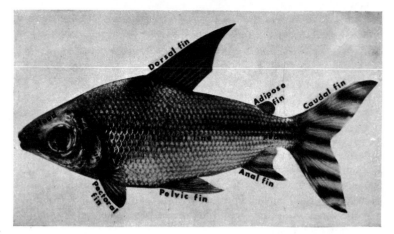

The fins of fishes.

phora, are generally called pigment cells. The colors of a fish may vary between some limits; a completely healthy fish will be normally colored. Fading of colors is often a sign of disease, but it may sometimes be due to shock; if fishes are frightened they often grow pale. The same phenomenon will occur when tropicals are kept at too low temperatures.

Fish Louse (*Argulus foliaceus and Related Species*)

The fish louse is about as large as a water flea and it belongs also to the Crustacea. It has eight legs that are used for swimming and a small fishlike tail that acts as a rudder while swimming. The tail contains the reproductive organs, namely, the testes in the male and the *receptaculae seminis* in the female (small sacs in which the semen is preserved after mating). Females may reach a length of 6 to 7 mm, males about 4 to 5 mm.

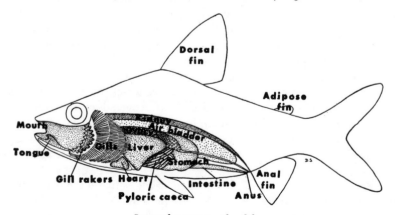

Internal anatomy of a fish.

The fish louse has two large suckers for attaching on the skin of its host. Above these two facet eyes are present. A hollow sting is inserted under a scale of the fish into the cutis and by means of this the parasite feeds on the blood of the host.

The chance of introducing fish lice is greatest during the hatching time of the eggs, which takes place from May to September. The eggs have a citron-yellow color and are deposited in long flat lines on stones. In an aquarium they are often deposited on the glasses. The females die after spawning and the eggs hatch about 1 month later. The number of eggs averages 185.

Bruno Hofer mentions that minnows, *Phoxinus laevis*, in an aquarium will eat fish lice, while other fishes try to escape from their neighborhood as soon as they see the parasites.

TREATMENT

Since the fish louse is a rather large creature, the parasites may be removed by a pair of forceps, while holding the fish in your left hand. If there are many of them, they can be removed by gently rubbing over the skin of the fish, always going from the head to the tail. Parasites that are sucking so fast that they are not removable in this way may be paralyzed by touching them with a small pencil or brush dipped into a strong solution of ordinary table salt. Then they may be rubbed off too.

In ponds it is impossible to remove all fish lice by individual treatment of the fishes. This would also be ineffective because the eggs and the hatching young parasites would not be removed so that new infections should occur very soon. In such cases, treatment with *potassium permanganate* may be tried (0.2 to 0.25 grains per gallon). Never on any account add crystals of permanganate directly to the water; the chemical must be dissolved first in a small amount of water and then the solution added to the pond or tank. Dosage of the chemical must be as accurate as possible, since too strong solutions may cause casualties among the fishes.

Anchor "Worm" (*Lernaea cyprinacea and Related Species*)

This is not a worm but also a crustacean related to *Cyclops*. It reaches a length of about 20 mm (¾ inch). By means of the anchorlike head appendages the parasite sticks to the fish; since the anchor penetrates deep under the skin into the muscles, the fish becomes badly injured. Only female anchor worms are parasites on fish; the males are parasites on the females.

TREATMENT

It is impossible to remove the parasites by forceps only; they must always be paralyzed and softened before removal. This is done by touching them with a small pencil or brush dipped into a 0.1 per cent solution of *potassium permanganate*. The parasites are killed by this treatment and softened so that they can then be removed by forceps. The sore spots are touched afterward with 1:10 diluted *mercurochrome* solution for disinfection.

If there is a possibility of new infections, as is the case when the parasites are in the breeding season (May) and are showing full egg sacs, it is advisable to place the fishes in another tank for some weeks. Then the young parasites, unable to find a host, will die. After a period of 3 to 4 weeks, depending on water temperature, the tank may be considered safe again. (At higher temperatures the parasites will die sooner.)

In ponds, *permanganate* treatment is the only possible cure (0.2 to 0.25 grains per gallon).

Leeches

Fishes that are attacked by leeches swim restlessly and try by all means to get rid of the torturers feeding on their blood. Usually they try in vain. Leeches are also dangerous as bearers of blood parasites (*Trypanoplasma* and *Trypanosoma* species) that cause a sleeping sickness in fish.

TREATMENT

Since the leeches are sucking very fast, they cannot be removed directly by forceps without causing serious damage to the fish. The best treatment is to place the fish in a *2.5 per cent salt solution for 15 minutes.* In this solution, the fish will at first become restless, but this will do no harm. The parasites are paralyzed and most of them will fall off. Specimens that are still adhering to the fish will be sufficiently affected to allow removal by forceps without injury to the fish skin. For ponds no special treatment is known at present.

Although the salt solution paralyzes the leeches, it does not *kill* them. Therefore, do not throw them into any water!

Flukes (Gyrodactylus and Dactylogyrus)

At first the colors fade and the fish grows very pale; then the fins are folded and gradually become torn, while the skin becomes more slimy than normal and shows some small blood spots. Small blood spots may also show at the base of the fins. Generally, breathing frequency is increased, even in cases where the gills are not affected. If all these symptoms are present, it is wise to treat the diseased fish as being infected with *Gyrodactylus,* even if there is no opportunity to confirm diagnosis by microscopic examination of the slime from the skin. The diseased fishes become dull and feeble; they rest very much, generally near the surface of the water, with every movement becoming more and more difficult until at last the animals die from complete exhaustion.

Dactylogyrus is a typical parasite of the gills and even more dangerous than *Gyrodactylus*. Fishes infected with *Dactylogyrus* gape for breath and their gill coverings are stretched open widely. The gills are expanded and very pale. Often parts of the gill sheets become protuberant and will show as a small fleece outside the covering.

The flukes belong to the flatworms, Platyhelminthes, of the class of the sucking worms, Trematoda. At the front end there are two conical projections which bear the openings of glands. These glands secrete a thick, sticky liquid, which enables them to cling to the skin or the gills of the fish. At the hind end a strong attachment organ is situated. This organ is disk-shaped and has two large hooks in the middle, surrounded by a ring of smaller hooks. The parasite first attaches itself by means of the small hooks and then drives the two larger hooks into the fish skin.

Gyrodactylus is a live-bearing parasite with a peculiar life history. In the body of the embryo, produced by a true sexual process, another embryo may be seen. Often this "grandchild" contains still a "great-grandchild" so that in one *Gyrodactylus* already four generations may be preformed. *Dactylogyrus* is an egg-laying organism. It has four eyes, while *Gyrodactylus* is blind.

TREATMENT

Treatment must be started as soon as possible. If the fishes have already been weakened too much they cannot be saved.

Methylene Blue (Medical Quality). Stock solution: 1 gram in 100 ml of water. For use: 0.8 to 1.6 ml per gallon. This may be increased to 3.25 ml per gallon if necessary. The higher concentrations will affect the plants.

Formalin. Stock solution: 10 ml formalin B.P.,* 990 ml water. For use: 6 to 7 ml per liter, 22 to 26 ml per gallon. Use only *fresh* formalin, not showing any white precipitate of paraformaldehyde, which is harmful to fishes. After 3 days a partial change of water is made and then a second addition equal to the first is made. *Use artificial aeration during treatment.* This valuable treatment, which has proved efficacious against both *Dactylogyrus* and *Gyrodactylus*, was suggested by Ian M. Rankin.

Black-spot Disease (*Diplostomiasis*)

In fishes with little pigment, the spots may be brownish instead of black. The spots contain a light-colored cyst of binding tissue in which a slowly moving worm lies rolled up. The cyst is surrounded by an accumulation of pigment cells, which causes the black spot to be seen from the outside.

The worm in the cyst is a larval stage of a sucking worm, known as *Neodiplostomum cuticola*. The adult parasite lives in the intestines of water birds. The eggs reach the water with the excreta of the bird, where they hatch. A further part of their life history takes place in aquatic snails. The

* British Standard of Purity, or chemically pure.

parasites then infect fish. If an infected fish is eaten by a water bird, the larvae penetrate into its intestine and the cycle may start anew.

As the life cycle of the parasite relies on the presence of aquatic snails, the absence of snails from tanks and ponds removes the possibility of black-spot disease occurring in the fishes. All species of *Limnaea* must be suspected in cases of infection. There is, of course, always the possibility of a fish being introduced to new quarters after it has been infected; in this instance the disease may manifest itself after a short time even though snails are absent.

TREATMENT

Picric Acid. Stock solution: 1 gram in 100 ml water. For use: 7 to 24 ml per gallon or 2 to 7 ml per liter. Fishes are bathed in this for about *one hour*, unless they show signs of distress, when they must be removed from the bath at once.

White Spot (*Ichthyophthiriasis*)

Ichthyophthirius multifiliis means "fish louse with many children"; it was so named because one parasite may produce as many as 600 to 1,200 youngsters.

The parasite penetrates the mucous coat and the upper layer of the epidermis. By its movements the epidermis is irritated and reacts by augmentation of the epithelial cells, resulting in a covering of the parasite by a layer

A scat infected with ich, or white-spot disease.

of the skin of the fish. Thus the swelling is a pathological production of the fish skin as a reaction to the activity of the parasite and not the parasite itself. The ich is always situated between the epidermis and the cutis, where it feeds on red blood corpuscles and disintegrated epithelial cells.

When after some days in the fish skin the parasites have matured, they bore through the epidermic "bladder" and leave the fish for reproduction. Then they will have a diameter of 0.2 to 0.5 mm. Sometimes even larger specimens, up to 1 mm, are found.

The mature parasite, having left its host, sinks to the bottom of the water, where it secretes a soft, jellylike cyst. Here a series of rapid divisions takes place. The speed of this process depends on the temperature of the water; it increases with higher temperature. At 64 to 68°F the division process takes about 12 to 18 hours. Approximately 36 hours after the mature parasite has left the fish, the youngsters will be swimming in a lively manner through the water in search of a host. Thus, in an aquarium the parasites leave the fishes periodically, but fishes are infected again and again by ever-increasing numbers of parasites.

Development of ich in the skin of the fish takes different times, depending on the temperature of the water. From 70 to 80°F the parasite will leave the fish 3 to 4 days after the white spot became visible to the naked eye. At 50°F this period will be 4 weeks or more! Thus, raising the temperature will decrease the time that the parasites remain in the fish skin, but it also shortens the time before reinfection occurs. Raising the temperature should therefore always be combined with some suitable treatment for killing the parasites. Heat alone will *not* kill them.

The young parasites cannot live long free in the water. If they cannot find a host, they die within a few days. According to Schäperclaus, at 68°F no free-swimming young parasite will survive longer than 55 hours. Thus, if all fishes are removed from an infected tank, after 3 days this tank will be safe again. Complete treatment of the diseased fish will take a longer period, so that after treatment in a separate tank the fishes may be put back in their original home directly.

Most cases of ich occur in autumn and winter. This may be due to a decreased resistibility against disease owing to lack of light (causing less oxygen production by the plants) and lack of suitable live foods. If a completely healthy fish is infected by one or two ich parasites it will not suffer much, and if the tank is not crowded the chances of reinfection are not too great. In such cases, infection may remain in a latent stage for a long period, since the parasites in the skin of the fish will grow very slowly and consequently no symptoms of disease will appear. However, if the resistance of the fish is weakened by unsuitable conditions the parasites will have a better chance and then an epidemic may occur. This explains why epidemics often appear when tropicals are kept at too low temperatures, while, on the contrary, in cold-water fishes epidemics may occur at too high temperatures.

Cysts of ich can often be found on water plants, which explains how these parasites can be smuggled into the aquarium by plants from an infected tank.

To make sure that newly obtained fish have no latent ich infection, a long quarantine period is required: 4 to 8 weeks for cold-water fish, 2 to 4 weeks for tropicals. It is also possible to give the fish a prophylactic treatment with *Methylene Blue*.

TREATMENT

No chemical available will kill the ich in the skin of the fish, without killing the fish too, because the parasite is protected by the layer of epidermis growing over it. Consequently one must wait for the moment when the ich leaves the fish for reproduction. The unprotected parasite, the cysts, and the youngsters in search of a host can be attacked successfully. Treatment must always be extended over a period sufficiently long to make sure that all parasites have left the fish.

Quinine Hydrochloride. Stock solution: 3 grams in 300 ml. The total amount is sufficient for treatment of 25 gallons of water. For smaller tanks use 12.5 ml per gallon. This amount is not added all at once but in three equal parts with an interval of about ½ day. The fishes must remain in this bath until every white spot has disappeared. Recommended temperature is 70 to 80°F for tropicals, 60 to 68°F for cold-water fish.

The shortest period after which the fishes may be replaced in the original tank is 1 week. However, it is advisable to extend treatment to 2 weeks. Changing of water after treatment is necessary because too long a contact with quinine salts has a bad effect on fish, especially on their fertility. Most plants will be affected, too. The quinine bath will kill ich parasites that have just left the fish, within 3 hours; the long period of treatment is necessary because not all parasites will leave the fish at the same time.

Methylene Blue (Medical Quality). For use add 0.8 to 1.0 ml of 1 per cent stock solution per gallon, repeat after 1 or 2 days. No coal filter is allowed since it would remove the dye from the water. Use artificial aeration only with coarse bubbles near the surface. Since a dirty bottom would inactivate the medicament by absorption, remove all dirt from the bottom before treatment.

Methylene Blue hinders reproduction of the parasite, forcing it to simple division; after a short period the ich dies. Methylene Blue is completely harmless even to young fishes. In the weaker concentration, it does not affect the plants.

Mepacrine Hydrochloride (Atabrine). 300 mg per 100 liters = 165 grains per gallon. This should be used for very stubborn cases of ich, which are resistant both to quinine hydrochloride and Methylene Blue. Use in the same manner as quinine; a water change after treatment is necessary. Like quinine, the cure may affect fertility.

Velvet or Rust Disease

The disease is also sometimes called "gold dust" disease. Symptoms may resemble white spot. Infected fish show a "dusty" appearance of the skin. The skin looks like a surface which has been dusted with powdered sulfur or with talcum powder of a dark shade. The dust is of a pale yellowish color and may move over the skin surface.

The causative organism is *Oodinium limneticum,* a dinoflagellate. It appears in a free-living, motile stage of about 13 microns length (1 micron equals 0.001 mm). When this stage contacts a fish, it adheres with its longer flagellum, but this is only a temporary stage. Several outgrowths (pseudopodia) are produced that grow into the skin and the gills of the fish. The flagella and the transverse groove disappear and the body shape changes into a pearlike form. Both the free-swimming and the parasitic form of the organism contain some chlorophyll, which enables it to obtain food by the process of photosynthesis.

Reproduction takes place inside a cyst. A series of divisions may give rise to more than 200 young parasites in the course of a few days. Unlike *Ichthyophthirius,* this parasite reproduces also while on the skin of the fish.

The infection is most dangerous for young fishes; adult specimens having a higher resistance may carry the parasites for long periods. Therefore, most casualties will occur in batches of young fish, unless the victims are treated as soon as signs of disease have become apparent.

TREATMENT

Methylene Blue (Medical Quality). Use in the same way as for white spot. It may be necessary to raise the concentration to 3.5 ml of 1 per cent stock solution per gallon. Treatment has to be prolonged for 2 or 3 days more than is required for cleaning the skin of the fishes from the yellowish dust. Generally 6 to 10 days will be sufficient. The temperature should be kept between 75 and 80°F.

Acriflavine Neutral (Trypaflavine). Stock solution: 1 tablet in 330 ml of hot water. For use: 8 ml of this stock solution per gallon is added to the water. For very obstinate cases the strength may be doubled. Temperature should be raised to 80°F and use of artificial aeration is strongly recommended.

Treatment is extended over a period of 3 days, then the water is changed, and at the sixth day this treatment is repeated for another 2 to 3 days. Repeated treatment is necessary to avoid reinfection, because the encysted forms are not killed by the chemical. *Too long a contact of fish with acriflavine must be avoided,* since it is not completely harmless. It has been observed by Earle E. Patterson that acriflavine produces a temporary sterility in both egg-laying and live-bearing fish. In egg layers, although spawning takes place normally, most of the eggs fail to hatch, while such fry as may still emerge from some eggs are weak and generally die within a week after attaining the free-swimming stage. Female live bearers after treatment with acriflavine produced only one to three youngsters at two subsequent deliveries and these lived only for a brief time. However, normal fertility is restored after a period of several months.

Darkness. Since the causative organism, *Oodinium limneticum,* is in reality an alga containing chlorophyll, it needs a certain amount of light in order to manufacture its food. Thus by treating the fishes in darkness with either of the two dyes mentioned above, or merely by keeping the fishes without light in an ordinary untreated environment, there is a chance that the parasites will starve before the fishes will.

Total darkness can best be obtained by completely covering the aquarium with a dark photographer's cloth or with carbon paper. Be sure that not the slightest ray of light is allowed to enter. Remove all plants, as they will give off carbon dioxide in the darkness and thus be detrimental to the fishes. Sterilize the plants in a *potassium permanganate solution* prior to introducing them into any other aquarium.

The fishes should not be fed while they are being kept in the darkness, as they will be unable to see the food and it will merely contaminate the water. If well fed prior to being kept in the darkness, fishes can easily stand a week or 10 days of complete dark isolation without food. If possible, maintain aeration during this isolation period.

Knot or Pimple Diseases (*Morbus Nodulosus*)

This is a collective name for several diseases caused by sporozoans. Symptoms are the formation of little "knots" in the skin, often closely resembling those caused by *Ichthyophthirius,* or larger pimples or bumps originating from a process in the muscles. If there are only small knots in the skin, as is usually the case in carps and related groups, it is difficult to distinguish between this disease and white spot. However, since the disease cannot be cured by either quinine or Methylene Blue, the difference will show on treatment.

Sporozoans are a group of the protozoans characterized by the production of spores. The normal form of the parasite is amoeboid and for reproduction it encysts and produces hundreds or even thousands of spores. All sporozoans are parasites. The life cycle of several of them is quite intricate, but to give further details would be beyond the scope of this work.

The spores have a size of 0.004 to 0.020 mm (4 to 20 microns). The germ (sporozoite) lies inside together with one or two polar cells with a spirally rolled nettle thread which can be pushed out. This thread generally has a length of 2, 5, or 25 times that of the diameter of the spore. Under favorable conditions the sporozoite leaves the spore and lives for a time in the amoeboid stage. After some time a new cyst is produced and the cycle starts anew.

Sporozoans may be found in all organs of fishes but in the skin they are relatively rare; they include *Myxobolus exiguus* (spores with two polar capsules) in carps; *M. dispar* in bleak, *Alburnus lucidus; M. oviformis* in dace, *Leuciscus rutilus; Glugea anomala* (oval-shaped spores with one polar capsule) in sticklebacks and other fishes; and *Henneguya* species (spores with two polar capsules).

TREATMENT

At present no methods are known of curing infected fishes. The main difficulty is that we cannot administer drugs in such concentration as would be required to kill the parasites in the body of the fish without killing the fish too. Fortunately these diseases do not appear often in aquaria.

Neon Tetra Disease

In neon tetras a disease sometimes occurs in which some blemish or spot is formed in the blue-green line, which will gradually extend over a larger

Neon tetras infected with the dreaded neon disease. This disease manifests itself first in the fading area below the lateral line and immediately above the anal fin. The two pale yellow dots on the caudal peduncle (here retouched for emphasis) indicate that this fish is also suffering from fish tuberculosis.

area and grow into a light-colored band, which shows generally perpendicular to the longitudinal axis of the body. The initial spot may appear anywhere in the course of the line.

Although the disease was first observed in neon tetras, *Hyphessobrycon innesi*, it is not confined to this species only. It has also been observed in glow-light tetras, *Hemigrammus gracilis*, and rosy tetras, *Hyphessobrycon rosaceus*.

Upon microscopic examination of thin sections from the region of the pathological band it may be observed that its cells are necrotic, that is, the tissues consist of dead and dying cells.

The disease seems to be due to an infection with sporozoans belonging to the genus *Plistophora*. These have also been found in swordtails.

TREATMENT

Methods for prevention and cure are still unknown. It has been claimed that a cure could be effected with a rather strong dosage of *Methylene Blue* (*medical quality*), namely, 1 gram in 100 liters or 5.7 grains per gallon. This is about five times the amount used for treatment of white spot, and the plants will not stand it. In experiments by other investigators Methylene Blue failed to cure the disease.

Sliminess of the Skin

Sometimes a disease occurs characterized by the formation of a slimy secretion on the skin of the fishes. The colors of the infected fish are pale, while the slime covers the whole skin surface like a thin gray fog. The fins are usually folded up. The symptoms may be observed most easily in dark-colored fishes; in others it does not show so clearly, since there is less contrast between the gray fog of slime and the parts of the body that have not yet been affected.

On inspection under the microscope, unicellular parasites may be found in the slime. The most common species found in aquaria is *Cyclochaeta domerguei*. It is a relative of the bell animalcules. It measures from 40 to 50 microns, but sometimes specimens as small as 9 microns have been found. Seen from above, the organism shows a ring of relatively large hooks, 20 to 32 in number. This ring of hooks is part of a kind of sucker. *Cyclochaeta* may be found on all kinds of fish, but it attacks goldfish and other members of the carp family most frequently. In tropical tanks, paradisefish, guppies, and brachydanios are the most common victims.

The same symptoms of disease may be caused by *Chilodon cyprini* or the closely related species *C. hexastichus*. The length of these parasites is approximately 50 to 70 microns. Although these parasites appear frequently, they do not often cause epidemics. In good conditions, an infection may remain latent for weeks or even months. If the fishes are weakened by unfavorable conditions, however, the parasites may multiply in a rapid tempo and if they affect the gills too, they can do considerable harm. In such cases, an epidemic may occur.

A third parasite causing sliminess of the skin is *Costia necatrix*. Although this is the smallest (15 to 20 microns), it is nevertheless the most dangerous of the three. Reproduction goes on very rapidly. The parasite can also form cysts of high resistibility. In small fishes, death may occur in a few days, while large ones can stand the infection for a longer period. Without cure, all infected fishes will die in the end.

TREATMENT

Salt. The affected fishes are bathed in a 1.5 to 2.5 per cent solution of salt for ¼ to ½ hour. Since it is possible that the parasite produces cysts with a higher resistance, treatment must be repeated after 2 days. In *Costia* infections three or four repetitions may be required for a complete cure.

Quinine Hydrochloride. This is used in the same way as against ich (1.3 to 2.6 grains per gallon). The fishes must be kept in the quinine solution until they have been cured. If the tank is fully planted, it is advisable to add another dosage of 0.85 grains of quinine per gallon after 3 days, but it is much better to separate the fish from the tank and to treat them in another tank without plants, since quinine generally has a bad effect on plant growth. Experiences with the use of quinine salts in *Costia* infections are not yet available, but it is very likely that quinine hydrochloride could be useful as a cure for them.

In Holland some other treatments for *Chilodon* infections have been suggested by a physician (Dr. Van Dommelen), namely, *tryparsamide* 1 gram per 100 liters and *stilbamidine* 150 mg per 100 liters. Since these chemicals have not yet been sufficiently tested, one has to be careful in using them; at first try them on a few fish only.

If these treatments should be ineffective for *Costia*, a *formalin* treatment can be applied. Use 2 to 3 ml of B.P. formalin in 10 liters of water (0.85 to 2.2 ml per gallon) for bathing the fishes during ¼ hour. Treatment must be repeated every 2 days until complete recovery.

It would be worth trying the formalin treatment after Rankin, which has proved to be so effective against *Gyrodactylus,* in combatting *Costia.* Stock solution: 10 ml formalin B.P. in 990 ml of water. For use: 6 to 7 ml of stock solution per liter, or 22 to 26 ml per gallon. Partially change the water after 3 days and then make a second addition.

Disinfection of tanks is not necessary, since the parasites will die within a period of ½ to 1 hour in the absence of fishes.

Fungus Diseases

Fungus is characterized by the growth of thin threads on the skin or the fins of the fish. If fungus growth is very abundant, it may resemble tufts of cotton wool. Fungus is due to a great many kinds of molds of the family Saprolegniaceae. The most common members of the family are the species of the genera *Saprolegnia* and *Achlya*. They can only attack fishes that have been wounded or whose resistance has been weakened by other parasites or certain unfavorable conditions, such as too low or too high a pH.

Molds consist of threads, called *hyphae*, which are often branched. The lower parts of the hyphae are thinner and grow into the skin or other parts of the fish, like roots. This part of the fungus is called the *mycelium*. For reproduction, *sporangia* are usually formed at the end of the hyphae and in these a large number of spores (up to 800) are produced. Each spore has two cilia (thin threadlike processes) with which it can move through the water like a little animal; therefore, this form of spore is called the *zoospore* (from the Greek word *zoon*, meaning animal). Each zoospore can produce a new mycelium, which forms new hyphae. A second form of reproduction consists in the formation of so-called *conidia*, which are club-shaped swellings at the end of the hyphae. These divide themselves into several parts, which may produce new fungus plants, just like the zoospores, if they reach a suitable substratum.

These reproduction processes are all asexual, but a true sexual process may take place, too. For this purpose, larger and immovable *oöspores*, from the Greek word *oön*, meaning ovum, are formed in *oögonia* (ova producers), which may or may not be fertilized by spermatozoids. The oöspores are the

Two tetras attacked by fungus where scales have been torn from their bodies. Generally, fungus infections on live fishes are restricted, initially, to the site of infection.

most resistant forms in the life cycle of a fungus. After a period of rest they may produce a new fungus thread directly or a large number of zoospores; which process will actually take place depends on conditions.

After infection of the fish's skin, at first a mycelium will be formed, growing between the cells of the epidermis and penetrating from there into the cutis and even to the underlying muscles. Meanwhile hyphae are formed which grow not only upon the skin but also through the skin and into the muscles too. By their action the cells of the skin and the muscles begin to degenerate and eventually die. In very bad cases, the fungus may even penetrate into the skeleton.

Fishes that are completely healthy and undamaged do not get fungus, even though the spores of these parasites are present in the water. Were this not so, probably no fishes would exist at all, since fungus spores are present in nearly all natural waters where fishes live. Fungus is not an obligatory parasite. It can live very well without the presence of fish, provided that sufficient organic matter is available, such as decaying plants or dead bodies.

Since fungus is not infectious to healthy and undamaged fish, it is not necessary to remove an infected fish from the community tank, although this might be advisable to give it a suitable treatment.

The condition of the water is also important. Very alkaline waters, such as often are found in ponds where the concrete has not been matured properly, have a bad effect on the mucous coat of fishes, thus increasing the susceptibility to fungus infections. Sudden changes of water may have a bad effect; fishes that have been living in slightly acid water must not be transferred suddenly to alkaline water. If the change is gradual, fishes will be able to adapt themselves and then no harm will be done.

For most fishes the best conditions are present if the pH of the water is in the range from pH 6.8 to 7.2; in sea water a suitable pH range is 7.6 to 8.0.

TREATMENT *

If only a small part of the skin is covered by fungus, take the fish in the hand and touch the moldy places with a solution of a good disinfectant, such as commercial *iodine solution*, diluted 1:10; commercial *mercurochrome* solution diluted 1:10, or *potassium dichromate*, 1 per cent.

Iodine and mercurochrome have the strongest activity, but for very delicate fishes it is advisable to use potassium dichromate. Use a small pen-

* The use of Malachite Green for control of *Saprolegnia* was first reported from Wisconsin by Foster and Woodbury (1936) and later by O'Donnel (1941), who successfully eliminated fungus from 18 species of fish by dipping them for 10 to 30 seconds in a 1:15,000 solution of the chemical. Leonard N. Allison of the Michigan Institute for Fisheries Research recently reported that a pond treatment with a 1:180,000 solution of Malachite Green successfully controlled *Saprolegnia* on trout.

cil or brush dipped into the disinfectant. Take care not to touch healthy parts of the skin of the fish, since this would have a bad effect.

After this treatment place the fish in a tank containing potassium dichromate in a strength of 1 gram in 7½ gallons of water. This treatment should continue for 7 to 10 days (not longer) unless complete recovery should occur before this time.

If necessary, the primary treatment of touching the fungus with the stronger chemicals may be repeated. The water must be well aerated, while for tropicals raising the temperature to 80 or 82°F is recommended.

Potassium dichromate may also be used in fully planted tanks; its activity will not suffer, while plants are not affected. After the period of treatment, the water must be changed. In ponds that cannot be streamed through with fresh water, potassium dichromate cannot be used. Therefore, it is advisable to catch infected fishes from the pond and treat them in an aquarium.

Rankin has obtained very good results in curing fungus by means of *phenoxyethanol* (phenoxethol). Stock solution: 1 ml in 99 ml of water. For use: 10 to 20 ml per liter or 37½ to 75 ml per gallon.

Further, there have been reports that fungus might be cured with *sulfanilamide, 10 to 25 grams per 100 liters* (5½ to 14 grains per gallon) and with *penicillin,* 100,000 international units or more per 100 liters (4,000 I.U. per gallon) for 5 to 7 days.

It has been stated that *Methylene Blue* is effective against fungus also but this has not been verified.

Eye Fungus

Eye fungus is a true fungus disease and a very dangerous one, since the fungus may easily penetrate the brain. It requires treatment different from other fungus diseases.

TREATMENT

The best method is to touch the infected eye with a pencil or brush dipped into a 1 per cent solution of *nitrous argentum (silver nitrate)* in distilled water. After this touch the eye with a tuft of cotton wool dipped into a 1 per cent solution of *potassium dichromate.* A red precipitate will form on the eye, which prevents the nitrous argentum from attacking the eye by restricting its activity to the fungus alone. It is also effective against the fungus.

To avoid new infections, the fish should be placed in a solution of potassium dichromate (1 gram per 7½ gallons) until complete recovery. It is advisable to repeat the touching with nitrous argentum at intervals in the meantime.

BACTERIAL INFECTIONS

Tail Rot and Fin Rot

These are not true fungus diseases but are due to bacterial infections. Symptoms are putrefaction of the tail or other fins, or both. In most cases, small red spots are showing as well. The tail becomes torn and is gradually eaten away by the activity of the bacteria. Frequently a secondary fungus infection occurs. Fishes that have much pigment are more susceptible to this pest than others. In black mollies this disease appears often.

Tail rot is a very serious complaint. If the infection penetrates into the body of the fish it will be too late to rescue it from death.

TREATMENT

In early stages, the victims may be treated by touching the sore spots with an *acriflavine solution* (1 tablet in 330 ml of water) and then placing the fish for three days in a container with 8 ml of this acriflavine stock solution per gallon. Then the water is changed, the diseased places are touched again, and the fish is placed in clean, fresh water for 1 day. Next day the fish is replaced in the acriflavine solution for a further 3- to 5-day treatment.

If after this period no complete recovery has been attained, surgical treatment should be applied. This consists in cutting the tail or infected fins with a pair of scissors. The cutting must be done through the healthy part of the tail or fin to ensure that all infected regions are eradicated. The wounds are touched with a small pencil or brush dipped into a 1 per cent *silver nitrate* (nitrous argentum) solution, followed by a touching with a 1 per cent *potassium dichromate* solution, as described for treatment of eye fungus. The fish should be placed in fresh water with 1 gram of potassium dichromate in 7½ gallons of water. In advanced cases of tail rot it is advisable to use surgical treatment at once and acriflavine during 3 to 5 days as an aftertreatment.

By far the safest and surest treatment of tail rot is with the new wonder drugs, *aureomycin, terramycin,* and *chloromycetin.* These antibiotics are practically specifics for the bacterial infections causing tail and fin rots.

A minimal treatment with 250 mg of aureomycin per 5 gallons of water will positively remove the symptoms of the bacterial infections, but there is serious question as to whether it will cure the fish infected. A heavier dosage and more frequent treatment is by far the sounder procedure and should be followed if the drug is available. Most wholesalers of tropical fish use 500 mg per 15 gallons of any of the three antibiotics mentioned in their treatment of the bacterial diseases. However, they are only interested in ridding the fishes of the symptoms of the disease while the fishes are on their premises. Fishes known to have been treated with an antibiotic should be purchased with the calculated risk that they might not have been thoroughly treated.

Dosage for *chloramphenicol* (*chloromycetin*) should be 25 to 40 mg per gallon. Treatment should not be continued for more than 48 hours.

Phenoxethol and derivatives do not affect fertility, which is a definite advantage over the acriflavine treatment. Phenoxethol has been used for preventing fungus from attacking eggs of angelfish, *Pterophyllum;* the fry hatched and became free-swimming in the normal manner.

Cottonmouth Disease ("Mouth Fungus")

This disease is characterized by a funguslike growth resembling white cotton at the cheeks and mouth of the fish. Its lips may become swollen and gradually take on an almost macerated appearance. Infected fishes lose their appetite and their movements become sluggish. If no adequate treatment is given, the whole frontal part of the head may be eaten away and finally the fish dies. The popular name "mouth fungus" is wrong and should be discarded, since this disease is caused by a slime bacterium, *Chondrococcus columnaris.* The disease is contagious.

TREATMENT

Both *terramycin* and *aureomycin* are effective. A dosage of 50 mg per gallon of water can be expected to be successful after 48 hours.

Swabbing the mouth of the victims with *Lilly's tincture of merthiolate* seems instantly to arrest the disease, according to Clarence H. Butler. Disinfection of the tank is accomplished by adding 1 ml of merthiolate to 3 to 5 gallons *with the fishes removed.* After disinfection of the tank, the water has to be changed completely.

Further, a treatment with *Brilliant Green* has been recommended, in which 4 grains of the dye are dissolved in just sufficient ethanol (ethyl alcohol) and added to 1 gallon of water. The diseased fish may be dipped into this solution for not more than *45 seconds;* however, it is preferable to apply the dye solution locally, swabbing the mouth of the fish with a small pencil, brush, or a tuft of cotton wool dipped into it, rather than dip the whole fish. It is claimed that one treatment will cure the most stubborn cases of the infection.

Dropsy

In recent years serious epidemics of dropsy have occurred in Poland and Germany, causing heavy losses. The epidemics have started in Poland and spread westward. They occur in spring or early summer, when the water is growing warm. Symptoms of the disease may vary somewhat. The Polish form is characterized by the occurrence of ulcers and lesions in the skin with slight production of exudate or even without exudate formation. If the fish are dissected, they have a disagreeable sweet smell. Apart from the inflammation of the intestines, discoloration of the liver can be observed, while several internal organs may grow together. Fish that have recovered may show deformities of the skeleton and the fins. If ulcers in the skin were present, they will leave scars.

In fishes diseased from dropsy, Schäperclaus discovered a bacterium that is a variety of an already well-known species, which can be found in water and milk. This bacterium is *Pseudomonas punctata,* a small rod-shaped microorganism with one flagellum at the end of its body. It is not affected by either terramycin or aureomycin, though Chas. Pfizer & Co., Inc., has announced plans to produce a compound of terramycin which will control this virulent organism.

Although *P. punctata* can be isolated from the liquid in the belly and from the organs of the diseased fish, later investigations have given rise to doubt whether this bacterium is the one and only cause of the disease. Russian and Yugoslavian scientists have gathered evidence in favor of the opinion that a virus is the primary cause of the disease, the bacteria coming into play as secondary invaders. This opinion has been confirmed by recent investigations with the electron microscope by the Germans Sophia Roegner-Aust and F. Schleich. They found virus globules, having a size up to 0.1 micron, in the liquid from the belly and also in the sap pressed from the internal organs of the diseased carp. These liquids were filtered through ultrafilters, retaining all ordinary cell constituents and bacteria as well. If the filtrate was injected into healthy carps, they developed the exudative form of dropsy.

The incubation time of the disease depends on the temperature of the water and on the age of the fish. At 68°F the course of the disease is rather rapid, the fish dying a few days after having been injected with the virus suspension. At 50 to 55°F infected fish may survive for months. Further, the course of the disease is more rapid in young fish than in adult ones. This is in agreement with observations made in other virus infections, namely, that viruses multiply most rapidly in tissues that are themselves still in full growth.

From these investigations it was concluded that dropsy is due to a primary virus infection, which is usually further complicated by a secondary infection with *Pseudomonas punctata.*

TREATMENT

Most treatments that have been suggested in the past are unreliable. Although sometimes it was possible to rescue one or two fish from death, generally the most to be hoped from treatment was some lengthening of the victim's lifetime. Recently, however, good results have been obtained by application of modern drugs.

Chloromycetin, in a dosage of 50 mg per gallon of water, may cure the infection in a period of 3 to 7 days. Chloromycetin is known to be effective against some virus infections as well as against bacteria.

Since the rate of multiplication of the virus is increased at higher temperatures of the water, it is advisable to keep cold-water fish at as low a temperature as possible. For tropicals, it will be difficult to make temperature adjustments. Certain species of fish that can stand relatively low temperatures, such as most live-bearing tooth carps, *Puntius conchonius,* and paradisefish, can be kept at 60°F until recovery. No food should be given.

In bad cases of dropsy, where already a great volume of exudate has accumulated in the belly, surgical treatment should be applied to remove the liquid before starting the chloromycetin cure, provided that the fish is large enough to allow manipulation of a hypodermic needle without damaging internal organs. A syringe with a very thin needle is used. The fish is taken in the left hand, and, with great care, the needle is pricked into the belly. Then the liquid is drawn away. The needle must be introduced a few millimeters before the anal opening and into the belly in the direction of the head.

Recently, Ian M. Rankin found *para-chlorophenoxethol* effective in treatment of dropsy; 50 cc of a 0.1 per cent stock solution per quart of aquarium water were added gradually in a period of 24 hours. Prior to putting the fish in this solution, the belly was punctured with a hypodermic needle and syringe to remove the accumulated liquid, as described above. Recovery of diseased fishes was obtained after 7 days of treatment. During 4 months after recovery no signs of recurrence of the disease were observable, which is a long enough period to make sure that a real cure had been obtained and not a mere temporary improvement.

Scale Protruding

In many cases all the scales of the body stick out, while in others only some of the scales are in this condition. Besides the protrusion of the scales, there are generally some red spots (*ecchymoses*) on different parts of the body or the fins. In some cases the fins are torn as well. The scales may be so loose that they fall off if the body of the diseased fish is rubbed. If the scales are pressed a little, a watery exudate appears, which has been formed in the pockets of the scales. The pressure of this liquid causes the scales to rise.

Scale protruding may occur as an accompanying symptom of another disease, generally dropsy, or it may appear as an independent complaint. The disease may be caused by *Vibrio piscium;* then it is highly contagious. Most cases occurring in aquaria, however, are due to *Bacterium lepidorthosae.*

Generally, the disease progresses very slowly. Sometimes it is 3 to 4 weeks before the scales protrude all over the body. At first the victims do not show much discomfort, but later their movements become slower, while the frequency of breathing increases. Next the tail becomes paralyzed and immovable. Hanging near the surface of the water, the animals die in a few days.

If a fish has been infected very badly, the characteristic symptom of scale protruding does not show at all, but the red patches on the skin of the belly and on the fins are obvious. Such badly infected fishes generally die in a few days after the outbreak of the disease. The disease is contagious but epidemics never occur. Infection takes place from the skin, but completely healthy and undamaged fishes cannot be infected. Most cases of scale protruding in aquaria occur in labyrinth fishes (especially bettas and paradise-fish) and in live-bearing tooth carps.

TREATMENT

A sure cure is not known at present. Experimenting with *chloromycetin* (250 mg per gallon of water) or with *sulfanilamide* (250 mg per quart) might be worthwhile.

For disinfection of a tank the following treatment may be used: Add 2 to 2½ grains of *potassium dichromate* and ¾ oz of *salt* per gallon, and another ¾ oz of salt the next day. After 1 week change half the water and 10 days after the first addition make a complete change of water. The chemicals must be dissolved before they are added to the water.

To prevent scale protruding it is important to keep the tank clean and avoid damaging the fishes by handling. Do not place stones with sharp edges in a tank. Do not keep fishes at too high a temperature. Avoid lack of oxygen.

Spottiness of the Skin in Labyrinth Fishes

In this infection the skin shows "corroded" spots, sometimes blood-colored, while red spots on fins and skin show clearly. Generally, these symptoms are accompanied by a secondary fungus infection.

The condition is caused by *Pseudomonas fluorescens*. This is a rod-shaped bacterium, 1.6 to 3 microns long and about 0.5 microns wide. The organism has 2 to 6 cilia situated at the ends, with which it moves through the water. The bacteria can be isolated only from the skin of infected fishes.

P. fluorescens is one of the commonest water bacteria. It is only faculta-tively parasitic and the nonparasitic strains are by far the commonest. It appears also that the organism can exist on the fish in a latent state. *P. fluorescens* has also been found in eels which had been injured and subsequently developed tumors and ulcers. In labyrinth fishes infected with these bacteria no ulcers or tumors were ever found.

TREATMENT

Cures for these infections are still lacking; the antibiotics are of no value in treating *Pseudomonas* infection.

Tuberculosis

In some cases of disease in fishes, bacteria have been found which are related to the tubercle bacterium (*Mycobacterium tuberculosis*) of warm-blooded animals. Aronson has given reports about two species of bacteria of this group which he found in fish, namely, *M. piscium* (pathogenic to fresh-water fish only) and *M. marinum* (pathogenic to marine fish only). The first-mentioned bacterium has been found in the intestines of golden carp (Hi-Goi), *Cyprinus carpio* var. *auratus;* pike perch, *Lucioperca sandra;* European catfish, *Siluris glanis;* and also axolotls, *Ambystoma mexicanus.* These bacteria are nonpathogenic to man and other warm-blooded animals.

It is possible that a number of instances of disease in fishes in which the symptoms are lack of appetite, progressive thinness, and sluggish movements may be caused by fish tuberculosis. Growing thin may be due to internal parasites such as worms, of course, but in many cases no internal parasite can be found. A certain diagnosis would only be possible after a specialized bacteriological investigation.

TREATMENT

As in human tuberculosis, streptomycin and PAS (para-aminosalicylic acid) could be expected to be effective, but these drugs are of prohibitive cost and further, they are not available for unqualified persons; cooperation of a physician or a veterinarian would be required. Dosage should probably be 1 to 2 grams of streptomycin or 2 grams of PAS per 100 liters of water (5.7 to 11.4 grains per gallon).

DISEASES OF THE EYES

Exophthalmus or Protruding Eye

Sometimes a disease occurs in fish in which the eye swells and, becoming too large for the orbit, protrudes.

An interesting case once occurred in a double-tail goldfish. This animal developed a gradually increasing exophthalmus of one of its eyes. At last the swelling became so great that the eye was pushed out of the orbit and was lost. The yawning wound healed without infection. After some time, the remaining eye also developed exophthalmus and was also pushed out of the orbit. This wound, too, healed without infection, which is very remarkable since no disinfectants were administered. The goldfish, now completely blind, nevertheless seemed to suffer very little from its defect and lived for several years, evidently being in good health.

Exophthalmus can be caused by bacteria, namely, some strains of *Pseudomonas punctata*, but in several cases no bacteria can be found and for these the real cause is not yet known. Hofer states that exophthalmus can be produced experimentally by blows or pushes on the head, but it is hardly believable that such injuries could be a natural cause of this disease.

TREATMENT

Cures are not known.

Worm Cataract

This is caused by the larvae of sucking worms, such as *Hemistomum spathaceum*. The adult parasite lives in water birds, where eggs are produced that are discharged into the water with the excrements of the bird. The eggs hatch in the water, producing larvae that are taken up by the fish. Infection from one fish to another is impossible. In an aquarium the disease can occur only if either eggs or larvae have been introduced with live foods or plants originating from natural waters.

TREATMENT

Sulfamerazine Sodium. 1 gram per liter of water for 2 to 3 weeks has been reported to be effective.

Fuadin (Stibophen). 5 ml of commercial solution per 100 liters of water.

Potassium Antimonyl Tartrate (Tartar Emetic). 150 mg per 100 liters of water. This chemical has to be used with caution.

Parachlorometaxylenol and *phenoxyethanol* seem promising. These chemicals have also been used successfully by Rankin in some cases of intestinal worms.

DISEASES OF THE INTERNAL ORGANS

Worms

Several species of tapeworms may be found in the belly of fishes, but they occur very seldom, if at all, in aquarium fish. Infections with intestinal worms always result from live food, since these parasites are living in some stage of their life cycle in different animals that are eaten by fish. Freshwater shrimp (*Gammarus pulex*), *Tubifex* worms, and red mosquito larvae can all act as carriers of worm parasites. *Cyclops* may carry *Cucullanus elegans*. Other worms often met with are *Paramermis crassa* and *Clinostomum complanatum*.

Clinostomum is introduced by snails. It forms cysts under the skin.

Cures have been effected by making a small incision in the cyst with a small lancet needle and removing the worms with a pair of fine-pointed tweezers. The incisions are then painted with *mercurochrome* and the fishes returned to the aquarium. This treatment has been reported by G. F. Hanson of Minneapolis.

Paramermis crassa lives in the internal organs but will cause a swelling, generally near the dorsal side of the body, when the time comes for it to leave the fish. Suggested treatment is *phenoxyethanol.* A 1 per cent stock solution in water is prepared. For use: 10 ml per liter, or 37½ ml per gallon. For adult fishes only, the strength may be increased to 30 ml per liter or 110 ml per gallon. Further, the infected fishes are fed with dried food that has been soaked in the 1 per cent stock solution. Treatment will only be effective if the internal organs are not yet damaged too severely by the parasite.

Ichthyophonus Disease

This parasite belongs to the Chytridiaceae, a group of organisms similar to both algae and fungi. In living fish diagnosis is difficult, since no very characteristic symptoms appear. Diseased fishes swim with sluggish movements as if they were benumbed. Then they lose their equilibrium and finally die, without showing other particular signs of disease. In cases where the parasites have penetrated into the brain, the victims make tumbling movements. Some cases have been reported where ulcerous growths, about the size of a pea, appeared in the skin. The ulcerous parts contained many cysts of *Ichthyophonus.* Generally, however, the parasites are found in the internal organs, in the heart, liver, kidneys, spleen, reproductive organs, stomach, intestines, and muscles. The cysts appear as whitish-gray or sometimes orange granules, lying between the tissues. They contain a mycelium that grows out periodically and penetrates through the entire organ.

If organs containing many cysts are taken with forceps, they feel hard like stone and sand.

The disease runs a long course. It may take months or even years before the victims die as a result of the gradual destruction of the infected organs. During this period they will slowly grow meager while they become dark-colored.

Infection may occur if a fish eats an infected fish that has died, or if it eats cysts that have been lost into the water from the skin or the gills of an infected fish. In the stomach the cysts open and produce a number of plasmodia having a size of 10 to 20 microns. These penetrate into the mucous coat of the stomach after a day, then into the blood; then they are transported by the blood stream to all internal organs. The cysts may reach a size of 150 microns or more.

The parasites reproduce in the organs of the host if the temperature is sufficiently high (thus in cold-water fishes during the summer months, in tropicals the whole year through). In some cases reproduction may be so fast that in a week or so an organ may be totally filled up with cysts. If the organ is indispensable for life, death may occur in a very short time. Sterility may result from the infection, even if cure is effected, owing to the damage which may have been done to the reproductive organs.

TREATMENT

Ichthyophonus infection is a very serious disease which until recently was incurable. If a cure is started before too much damage is done to the organs of the fish, it is possible to obtain recovery by a treatment with phenoxyethanol (phenoxethol) after Ian M. Rankin. The fishes are fed with dried food soaked in a 1 per cent solution. Further, 10 ml of this 1 per cent solution per liter of aquarium water is added. For *adult* fish this may be increased to 30 ml per liter.

Recently Rankin has found a related compound, namely, *para-chlorophenoxethol*, even more effective than phenoxethol itself. A stock solution is made by adding 1 ml to 1 liter of distilled water, thus making a 0.1 per cent solution. Of this stock solution, 50 ml per liter is added (190 ml per gallon) gradually over a period of 24 hours. *Ichthyophonus hoferi* cysts, spores, and plasmodia were found to be completely degenerate after 100 hours' exposure to this concentration. Para-chlorophenoxethol destroys *Ichthyophonus* more rapidly than does phenoxethol.

NONPARASITIC AFFLICTIONS OF THE INTERNAL ORGANS

Inflammation of the Stomach and Intestines

This is in most cases due to incorrect feeding. No fish can live on dried foods alone for a long period, and continuous feeding of only one kind of live food may also have bad results. Such diseases can consequently be completely avoided by giving fishes a suitable mixed diet.

Inflammation of the Intestines

Signs of an intestinal inflammation cannot be seen externally, although general symptoms such as lack of appetite, darkening of colors, etc., may give a warning that fishes are not healthy. From a section of a fish that has died from the disease, the condition may be easily recognized. Healthy intestines of most fishes have a whitish or pink color, whereas an inflamed intestine is red, due to a widening of the blood vessels. The exterior of the intestinal wall will swell so that the organs appear enlarged; they may be 1½ times their normal size. Inside the intestine a bloody, puslike liquid is usually present, which flows from the anal opening when light pressure is applied to the belly wall. Bloody or yellowish-colored excrements are therefore a certain sign of inflammation of the intestine.

TREATMENT

The remedy is simple. If bloody excrements have been found in a tank, feeding must cease immediately and the fishes be subjected to 4 or 5 days fast. After that, they must be fed with gradually increasing quantities of another kind of food than was given before the disease occurred. Complete recovery will be effected if these recommendations are observed. In severe cases the period of fast must be increased; this may even be extended to several weeks, if necessary. Feeding may be recommenced when no more bloody excrements are found.

Inflammation of the Stomach

This is generally due to excessive amounts of salt contained in the food; therefore, when live food is given, this disease will not often occur. All salted artificial foods should be soaked in water to remove the salt.

Smoked beef, which is sometimes used as a nourishing food rich in proteins, must be dried thoroughly; most of the salt will crystallize and form a white layer on the surface which can be removed easily. The beef should not be used as long as salt crystallizes; it may then be rasped and used for feeding, although it is not satisfactory to use it as the only food for a long period. A better policy is to mix the rasped beef with other kinds of food which contain fats and carbohydrates.

The chief symptom of inflammation of the stomach is a reddening of the mucous coat of this organ. Treatment is the same as that recommended for inflammation of the intestines.

Fatty Degeneration of Internal Organs

This is one of the commonest causes of death in aquarium fishes, as has been proved by examining sections from many fishes which have died without external signs of disease. This disease may also be caused by incorrect feeding. If too many foodstuffs containing excessive fats and carbohydrates in comparison to proteins are given (as would be the case when *Enchytrae* are fed continuously without varying the diet with other foods poor in fat content) fatty degeneration of several internal organs will take place.

The disease takes a very slow course and does not present many symptoms but it finally causes death of the fish.

Fatty degeneration of the liver can be recognized by the presence of white portions between the normal liver tissue, which is of a reddish-brown color. If the process develops to a great extent, dropsy may occur. (As has been set forth previously, dropsy may also be due to bacterial infection; see page 143.) In the spleen and the kidneys, fatty degeneration is recognizable by small yellow bodies lying in the tissue.

In fishes having a very compact liver, a lipoid degeneration of the liver may occur, in which case this organ becomes yellowish gray, yellowish, or spotted.

In fatty degeneration of the ovaries the ova become affected and are whitish gray in color; when normal they are translucent and pink or reddish. In further development of the disease the ovary may harden so that it is visible as a swelling from the outside, or at least may be felt when the fish is taken between the fingers. Fatty degeneration of this organ will cause infertility. A cure is impossible.

Since the causes of the disease are known, it is easy to avoid it by choosing a varied diet; it should be borne in mind, however, that not only may unsuitable foods cause distress but also overfeeding of fishes. Breeders of fish often subject their fishes to a few days' fast prior to mating, and this policy may prove beneficial.

Constipation

This is another complaint that may result from incorrect feeding. Some fishes are more susceptible to constipation than others; in aquaria it will be met mostly in angelfish and other varieties that possess a compressed body. Symptoms are lack of appetite and some swelling of the body.

Constipation particularly occurs after long periods in which only dried foods or *Enchytrae* have been fed. If sufficient *Daphnia*, mosquito larvae, and other natural foods are given in addition, fishes will not become affected.

TREATMENT

Constipation may be cured by giving the fish some dried food which has been soaked in *medicinal paraffin oil*. If it will not take this, some drops of paraffin oil may be applied directly into the mouth by means of a small syringe. In obstinate cases, the laxative can be applied into the anal opening, but this must only be done with large fishes and with great care to avoid perforation of the intestinal wall. The fish is held in the left hand, with its head to the left, so firmly that it cannot sprawl. Then the syringe is introduced into the anal opening, making an angle of about 45 degrees with the horizontal axis of the body. It should not be inserted more than a few millimeters. The amount of laxative to be injected must be chosen in relation to the size of the fish and may vary from 1 drop to 0.5 to 1 ml. Paraffin oil, glycerol, or castor oil may be used. The laxative activity increases from the first-mentioned to the last.

Catarrh of the Intestine

This may occur when fishes have eaten decaying food. Symptoms are lack of appetite and thinness, with thin, slimy excretions being produced. The disease occurs more often in young fish than in adults. Fishes showing such symptoms should be fasted for a few days and then fed with only dried food until the abnormal excretions have disappeared.

Ovarian Cysts

In this complaint the ovaries are swollen to a bladderlike extent and are filled with yellowish or reddish liquid. Histological examinations show a degeneration of the follicles of the ova. Generally, both ovaries have grown together and grown to the peritoneum too. The intestines are pressed together and the body swells, so that one must be careful not to confuse this disease with dropsy. With ovarian cysts, the swelling will be much nearer the hind part of the belly, which is generally not rounded, while in dropsy the greater swelling will be near the center of the belly, which will show a gradual rounding.

Under aquarium conditions the disease occurs chiefly in veiltails, which are always susceptible to diseases of the internal organs. The exact cause is not known, although it seems that not allowing the fish to spawn may be responsible to a greater or lesser extent.

Petrifaction of the Ovaries

In this disease the ovaries show degeneration with an extensive formation of binding tissue in which they become very hard. From the outside a swelling of the belly may be seen, resembling that described in ovarian cysts but not reaching such proportions. While the belly of a fish with ovarian cysts feels soft, in petrifaction of the ovaries the belly feels hard and the swelling cannot be pressed in. Sometimes parts of the ovary may be affected by petrifaction while in other parts ovarian cysts may be present.

In aquaria the disease occurs mainly in egg-laying tooth carps and members of the Characidae. It occurs generally when spawning has not been possible, but the way in which it is caused is not yet known. Diseased fishes may live for a long period but they are infertile. To avoid this disease, give the fishes an opportunity for spawning if they show ripeness, and do not overfeed.

Swim-bladder Disease

Tropical fishes are often kept at low temperatures in transit, and afterwards swim-bladder complaints sometimes occur. These are recognizable by the behavior of the fishes. Specimens thus afflicted have difficulty in maintaining their equilibrium and sometimes fall "head over heels," making tumbling movements. Finally they rest at the bottom or, in other cases, they float at the surface. In such cases the disease is obviously due to chilling, which may cause inflammation of the bladder wall.

Other causes of swim-bladder trouble are pressure from some internal organ, such as may result from constipation or other afflictions in which the volume of the internal organs increases. Alternatively, it may be due to a fatty degeneration of the tissues of the swim bladder itself. Swim-bladder disease is not fatal and under good conditions the fishes suffering from it may live for long periods.

Swim-bladder troubles are best prevented by giving fishes a varied diet with sufficient supplies of fresh foods. Sudden changes of temperature must be avoided, as should subjecting the fishes to too low temperatures for long periods.

Catalogue of Fishes

THE KINDS OF AQUARIUM FISHES

Arranged according to their classification, except that genera are in alphabetical order under each subfamily or family

Phylum Chordata
Subphylum Craniata
Superclass Gnathostomata
Class Osteichthyes (bony fishes)
Subclass Actinopterygii

COUNTS

Under each species a line is headed "Counts." These counts are needed in the identification of fishes and it is important for the hobbyist to know how to verify the counts.

Fin-ray Counts

The position, shape, and number of spines and rays in the various fins of fishes are important items of information. Fin-ray counts are usually slightly variable above and below an average for each species of fish. When variations are great and two modes occur in a series of counts, there may be two species or two subspecies involved.

The spines are bony rays, designated by Roman numerals. Even the smallest spine is counted. The soft rays are either unbranched or branched, and always show articulations when magnified. The soft-ray count is designated by Arabic numerals and in cases where there are both spines and rays on the same fin, as in the illustration of *Aequidens portalegrensis*, here used as an example, the Roman and Arabic numerals are separated by a comma. In cases where there are two or three separate dorsal fins, the counts are separated by a dash or long hyphen. There are never any spines in the adipose fins of characins or any other fish. In this book we have used lower-

Fin-ray and scale counts of *Aequidens portalegrensis*.

case Roman numerals to represent unbranched or simple soft rays, whereas the Arabic numerals refer to branched soft rays. See the Glossary under *fin-ray formula* for an example.

Scale Counts

One of the interesting facts about fishes is that, regardless of their age, the number of scales remains the same throughout the life of the individual fish. There are times when a fish might lose some scales through a mishap, but these missing scales regenerate rapidly.

Nearly every fish mentioned in this book has its scale count listed. Usually the scale count will read "scales 22 to 23," or some such number. This means that we have actually counted the scale rows on the body of the fish. This is easily done by counting the scales in a single line between the upper edge of the opercular opening and the base of the caudal fin rays, as illustrated by the white scales on the photograph of *Aequidens portalegrensis*. We count 24 rows of scales. There is usually a slight variation between different individuals of each species, but this variation seldom exceeds more than a few scales. Thus, if you read "scales 24 to 26" you will know that if you have a specimen of the fish described, it should have between 24 and 26 scale rows. See *scale formula* in the Glossary for an example.

FAMILY **POLYPTERIDAE**: Lobe-finned Fishes

[Po-lyp'-ter-i-dee]

GENUS *Polypterus* Lacepède

[Po-lyp'-ter-us: *poly* = many; *pterus* = fins]

Polypterus retropinnis Vaillant

[re'-tro-pin'-nis: *retro* = behind; *pinnis* = fins]

Polypterus retropinnis Vaillant, Bull. Mus. Paris, p. 219, 1899 (type locality, Alima River)

RANGE: Upper Congo, Africa.

SIZE: 8 inches.

TEMPERAMENT: This species is best kept by itself.

TEMPERATURE REQUIREMENTS: 60–75°F.

SEX DIFFERENCES: Not known.

COUNTS: Dorsal VI or VII separate spines; anal 12 to 15; scales 58 to 59.

This fish is currently known as *Polypterus palmas*.

[No-top'-ter-i-dee]

GENUS *Xenomystus* Günther

[Zen'-o-mys'-tus: *xeno* = strange; *mystus* = mystic]

AFRICAN KNIFEFISH / *Xenomystus nigri* (Günther)

[ni'-gri: named after the Niger River]

Notopterus nigri Günther, Catalogue of the Fishes in the British Museum, 7:481, 1868 (type locality, Niger River)

RANGE: Bahr-el-Jebel, Bahr-el-Ghazal, Chad Basin, Liberia, Niger, and Gabon, Africa.

SIZE: 8 inches.

TEMPERAMENT: This species is best kept by itself.

TEMPERATURE REQUIREMENTS: 65–80°F.

SEX DIFFERENCES: Not known.

COUNTS: Anal 108 to 130; scales 120 to 142.

The African knifefish is an interesting species which has been imported recently. Its nocturnal habits require feeding copious amounts of *Tubifex* worms at night or during darkness.

Half a coconut shell, overturned and with a small aperture for an entrance, makes the fish feel more at home.

[Os'-tee-o-gloss'-i-dee]

This family is found in South America, southeast Asia, Borneo, Australia, and Africa. In South America two species occur. The one illustrated and the giant pirarucu, *Arapaima gigas* (Cuvier), inhabit the coastal rivers from the Guianas to Baía, including the Amazon Basin.

The pirarucu has been measured at 8 feet in length and some reports place its maximum length at 15 feet.

The bony-tongued fishes are related to the early primitive fishes such as the clupeoids.

Genus *Osteoglossum* Vandelli, in Cuvier

[Os'-tee-o-gloss'-um: *osteo* = bone; *glossum* = tongue]

Bony-tongued Fish / *Osteoglossum bicirrhosum* Vandelli

[bi'-sear-ho'-sum: *bi* = two; *cirrhosum* = "filaments" or barbels]

Osteoglossum bicirrhosum Vandelli, in Spix and Agassiz, Selecta genera et species piscium . . . Brasiliam, p. 47, pl. 25, 1829 (type locality, Rio Amazon)

RANGE: Guianas to Brazil; Peru.

SIZE: 1½ feet; breeding not observed.

TEMPERAMENT: A species best kept by itself.

TEMPERATURE REQUIREMENTS: 65–80°F.

SEX DIFFERENCES: Not observed.

COUNTS: Dorsal 43 to 48; anal 53 to 57; scales 3 + 35 + 2 or 3.

Oral gestation or buccal incubation has been reported by Haseman, and it is known that other osteoglossids practice this method of parental care. The eggs and embryos are carried in the mouth of one of the parents in a pouchlike space between the bones of the lower jaw.

The pectoral fins are blackish in the young of this species. The two barbels shown in the illustration are attached to the tip of the lower jaw.

The family Pantodontidae [pan'-toe-don'-ti-dee] is represented by a single bizarre species usually known as the butterflyfish. It occurs in western Africa and is most closely related to the bony-tongued fishes (Osteoglossidae) with representatives in the fresh waters of South America, Africa, and Australia. Both families belong to the order of isospondylous fishes, which contains the herring and salmonid fishes.

The family is characterized by having 7 rays with free tips, forming the pelvic fins, a short dorsal fin placed far back, a large winglike pectoral fin with the lower ray adnate to a fleshy process, a large lizardlike mouth with small sharp teeth on jaws, tongue, vomer, palatines, and pterygoids.

Genus *Pantodon* Peters

[Pan'-toe-don: *pan* = all; *odon* = tooth; meaning teeth occur on all the tooth-bearing bones of the mouth]

Butterflyfish / *Pantodon buchholzi* Peters

[book'-holts-eye: named in honor of the naturalist R. W. Buchholz]

Pantodon buchholzi Peters, Mon. Berlin Acad., pp. 195–196, pl., figs. 1–4, 1876 (type locality, Victoria River, Cameroons, Africa)

RANGE: Western Africa, Nigeria to upper Zambezi.

SIZE: 5 inches; breeds at 3 inches.

TEMPERAMENT: This fish is inclined to nip the fins of other fishes, and it eats small fishes when available. Not a community tank fish. It needs at least a 15-gallon tank, not heavily planted.

TEMPERATURE REQUIREMENTS: 72–85°F.

SEX DIFFERENCES: Male is much slimmer than the female and his modified pectoral fins are seemingly larger than the "butterfly wings" of the female. When the female *Pantodon* is ripe with eggs there is little doubt about the sex, but all too often an empty female may be mistakenly selected as a male.

COUNTS: Dorsal i,5; anal ii,13; pectoral i,7; pelvic vi; caudal ii,9,ii; scales 4 + 25 to 29 + 3.

Breeding the butterflyfish is a difficult achievement. The single spawning that has been recorded merely states that the eggs are large and that they float. Eggs hatch after 7 days at 75°F. Parents should be removed after spawning. Young have been likened to tadpoles; they stay at the surface of the water at all times. Parents, too, are strictly surface feeders. Since this fish is reported to leap out of the water after winged insects, it should be maintained in a covered aquarium at all times. It is very tame once it has become acclimated to an aquarium and will eagerly grab pieces of meat, fish, worms of all sorts, and live fishes from the fingers.

The fry require an abundance of live food in the form of *Daphnia, Cyclops,* brine shrimp, or any live food that does not immediately drop to the bottom. It is advisable to lower the water level to a few inches in depth so that the fry may have a better chance of getting the live food. Small amounts of floating prepared food may be offered to the young as a variation in the diet.

[Mor-mir'-i-dee]

GENUS *Marcusenius* Gill

[Marc'-u-seen'-i-us: *marcusenius* = weak or feeble]

Marcusenius longianalis Boulenger

[lon'-gi-a-na'-lis: *longi* = long; *analis* = anal fin]

Marcusenius longianalis Boulenger, Proc. Zool. Soc. London, no. 1, p. 5, pl. 3, fig. 1, 1901 (type locality, Sapele, lower Niger River)

RANGE: Lower Niger Basin.

SIZE: 6 inches; breeding not observed.

TEMPERAMENT: Suitable in the community tank when small.

TEMPERATURE REQUIREMENTS: 65–85°F.

SEX DIFFERENCES: Not known.

COUNTS: Dorsal 14 to 16; anal 31 to 33; scales 60 to 66.

The "worm-jawed" mormyrid, *Gnathonemus petersi* (Günther), also known from western tropical Africa, makes an interesting aquarium oddity. It requires feedings of *Tubifex* worms.

The name of this species currently is *Brienomyrus longianalis*.

The family Characidae [kar-ace'-i-dee] belongs to the primary group of fresh-water fishes of the world; other related members are the carps and cat-fishes. The family is commonly called characins [kar-a'-sins], and the genera and species are very numerous in South America and in Africa. They are distributed throughout South America except the southern part, the arid Pacific slope of Chile, and northward to the Rio Grande of Texas. In continental Africa they are lacking only in the southern part and in the Sahara Desert. At the present time no one has made an accurate count of the number of kinds of characins in the world but the number of species in South America approaches 1,500, with an additional 100 or 200 more in Africa.

The members of this family have become modified to occupy nearly every kind of habitat available. In addition, their habits vary from delicate timid species to those which are voracious and pikelike, or bloodthirsty such as the piranha. Some are plant feeders, whereas others live wholly on a fish or protein diet. A few have learned to fly.

Characins differ from the carps and minnows in having an adipose fin and teeth in their jaws, whereas the carps (family Cyprinidae) lack the adipose fin and the jaw teeth but have toothed pharyngeal bones in their throats.

The numerous species of the family are oviparous and lay demersal eggs. In general, eggs are deposited on vegetation or other objects. The breeding habits of only a small percentage of characins are known.

Many characins are valuable aquarium fishes because of their bright colors and small size. They are peaceful in community tanks and will breed in captivity. The young are easily fed suitable live foods and grow rapidly. Adults thrive on a dried-food diet varied with live foods.

On the anal fin of the adult males of certain characins occur little retrorse hooklike processes which have been dubbed "the characin hooks." These little spines are well-developed on some of the Cheirodontinae, but they are so small that without magnification the hobbyist might not see them. In addition, on certain characins such as *Cheirodon*, the adult males may have numerous tiny spines projecting from the ventral edge of the caudal peduncle. These too are called "characin hooks," but not all characins develop these tiny spinules.

The family Characidae has been divided into the following subfamilies: Erythrininae, Anostominae, Characinae, Cheirodontinae, Serrasalminae, Glandulocaudinae, Crenuchinae, Hemiodontinae, and Citharininae. For the purposes of this book we are not arranging the species according to subfamily but are following our usual alphabetical arrangement.

GENUS *Abramites* Fowler

[A'-bray-my'-tease: *abramis* = mulletlike fish]

HEADSTANDER / *Abramites microcephalus* Norman

[mi'-crow-sef'-a-lus: *micro* = small; *cephalus* = head]

Abramites microcephalus Norman, Ann. Mag. Nat. Hist., (9)18:92, 1926 (type locality, near mouth of Amazon River)

RANGE: Lower Amazon.

SIZE: 5 inches; breeding size unknown.

TEMPERAMENT: A peaceful species desirable in the community aquarium.

TEMPERATURE REQUIREMENTS: 75–85°F.

SEX DIFFERENCES: Not known.

COUNTS: Dorsal ii,10; anal ii,11; pectoral i,13; pelvic i,8; scales 6½ + 36 + 6.

This fish has never been bred in the community aquarium. It is known for its ability to maintain itself at a characteristic 45-degree angle, thus earning the name headstander, which has also been given to several other fishes. Its color varies from a dull gray to a dark brown. Caudal, anal, and pectoral fins are light yellow; the pelvic fins are black. The adipose fin is yellow with a black edge. This fish is a powerful jumper.

This fish is currently known as *Abramites hypselenotus*.

FAMILY CHARACIDAE

GENUS *Alestes* Müller and Troschel

[A-les'-tease: *a* = (intensify meaning); *lestus* = a robber]

CHAPER'S CHARACIN / *Alestes chaperi* Sauvage

[chap'-er-eye: named in honor of the collector M. M. Chaper]

Alestes chaperi Sauvage, Bull. soc. zool. France, 7:320, pl. 5, fig. 2, 1882 (type locality, Cania River, Assini, Gold Coast)

RANGE: West Africa, Upper Guinea; Gold Coast to the Niger Basin.

SIZE: 4 inches; breeding not observed.

TEMPERAMENT: A peaceful species when kept with fishes of same size.

TEMPERATURE REQUIREMENTS: 70–85°F.

SEX DIFFERENCES: The male has a more pointed dorsal fin than the female.

COUNTS: Dorsal iii,8; anal iii,18 to 20; pelvic i,5 or 6; scales $5\frac{1}{2} + 25$ to $28 + 3\frac{1}{2}$.

This species is not sufficiently desirable to warrant an all-out attempt at propagation. It has not been available in the past few years. Its color is simple, much like an ordinary killifish with the dull guppy green broken up only around the belly region where a pale yellow covers the area. Fins in the male are colored with a faint yellowish edge, which is more obvious on smaller specimens than on mature fish.

The chief food is mosquito larvae. This fish requires a large aquarium; a 5-gallon tank will barely meet the minimum requirements of a large pair. Because it is a great jumper, the aquarium must be covered.

This fish is currently known as *Brycinus chaperi.*

GENUS *Anoptichthys* Hubbs and Innes

[Ann'-op-tick'-thees: *an* = without; *optic* = eye; *ichthys* = fish]

BLIND CAVE CHARACIN / *Anoptichthys jordani* Hubbs and Innes

[jor'-dan-eye: named in honor of the ichthyologist David Starr Jordan]

Anoptichthys jordani Hubbs and Innes, Occas. Pap. Mus. Zool. U. Michigan, no. 342, pp. 1–7, pl. 1, 1936 (type locality, San Luis Potosí, Rio Panuco system, Mexico)

RANGE: San Luis Potosí (La Cueva Chica), Panuco system.

SIZE: 3½ inches; breeding size 2½ inches.

TEMPERAMENT: The small specimens are "perfect gentlemen" but larger ones become aggressive and are satisfactory only for the larger community tanks.

TEMPERATURE REQUIREMENTS: They do well at temperatures from 68 to 90°F. Optimum breeding temperature 75°F.

SEX DIFFERENCES: Only the fullness of the ripe female is a guide to the sex.

COUNTS: Dorsal ii,8 or 9; anal iii,18 to 21; pectoral i,11 or 12; pelvic i,6 or 7; scales 7 + 35 + 6.

The spawning behavior is interesting. A pair of blind cave characins will circle each other for a few hours until finally the male will pull alongside the female and vibrate rapidly. The female expels eggs at this instant and the male fertilizes them. The male is the first to stop the process and withdraw, whereas the female may ignore his absence and continue expelling her ova. Immediately after spawning the blind characin will go after the eggs and eat them. Naturally, since the fish has no eyes, its hunt for the eggs is quite unusual but highly successful, as the fish is seemingly aided by some sort of extrasensory organ. The parents should be removed after spawning. The young fish are able to filter infusoria from the water, and plentiful supplies of these tiny animals should be offered. The constant hunt for food has induced aquarists to consider this fish as an excellent scavenger. Even though the fish cannot see, it moves away from light.

This fish is currently known as *Astyanax mexicanus*.

GENUS *Anostomus* Scopoli

[Ann'-os-toe'-mus: *ano* = upward or high; *stomus* = mouth]

STRIPED ANOSTOMUS / *Anostomus anostomus* (Linnaeus)

Salmo anostomus Linnaeus, Systema naturae, ed. 10, p. 312, 1758 (type locality, "Indüs")

RANGE: Guianas and Amazon Basin.

SIZE: 7 inches; breeding size not known.

TEMPERAMENT: A moderately peaceful species, which has been accused of nipping the fins of fishes. Sometimes they fight among themselves.

TEMPERATURE REQUIREMENTS: 72–85°F.

SEX DIFFERENCES: None apparent.

COUNTS: Dorsal ii,10; anal ii,8 or 9; pectoral i,13; pelvic i,8; scales 4 or 5 + 39 or 40 + 4.

This species has not been bred. However, recently when an exporter of fishes in Trinidad was able to obtain it, large numbers of specimens were shipped to the United States and the price dropped from $25 per pair to about $5 per pair. Many full-grown specimens were offered for sale, and before long someone may successfully spawn this species.

The brilliant coloration and odd shape of this fish make it very popular. Over 8,000 fish were sold in New York within a few weeks. The reddish golden-green color and the dark stripes add interest to a long pencil-shaped fish. The mouth opens at the top and the fish is quite comical when it must turn upside down in order to dig a worm out of the sand or pick up a bit of food from the bottom. For a while it is shy and hides among the plants. The diet should contain plenty of algae, *Nitella,* and bits of grass, spinach, or lettuce.

THREE-SPOT ANOSTOMUS / *Anostomus trimaculatus* (Kner)

[tri-mack'-you-lay'-tus: *tri* = three; *maculatus* = spotted]

Schizodon trimaculatus Kner, Sitzb. Akad. Wiss. Wien, 30:78, 1858; Denks. Akad. Wiss. Wien, 27:161, pl. 6, fig. 12, 1859 (type locality, Mato Grosso, Brazil)

RANGE: Guianas and Amazon Basin.

SIZE: 8 inches; breeding size not known.

TEMPERAMENT: A moderately peaceful species that makes a good member of a community tank.

TEMPERATURE REQUIREMENTS: 72–85°F.

SEX DIFFERENCES: No apparent sexual differences.

COUNTS: Dorsal ii,10; anal ii,8 or 9; pectoral i,13; pelvic i,8; scales 4 or 5 + 42 to 44 + 4½.

The large scales are marked with horizontal rows of black dots below the lateral line. The three spots are obvious: a large black spot on the gill cover, one on the middle of the side, and the third at the base of the caudal fin. The caudal fin shows a reddish tinge.

FAMILY **CHARACIDAE**

GENUS *Aphyocharax* Günther

[Ap'-hy-o-kar'-axe: *aphyo* = small; *charax* = a kind of fish]

BLOODFIN / *Aphyocharax rubropinnis* Pappenheim

[ru'-bro-pin'-nis: *rubro* = red; *pinnis* = fin]

Aphyocharax rubropinnis Pappenheim, Sitzb. Gesell. Nat. Freunde Berlin, p. 36, 1922 (type locality, Rosario, Argentina)

RANGE: Rosario, Argentina.

SIZE: 2 inches; breeds at 1½ inches.

TEMPERAMENT: A mild-mannered species highly desirable in a community aquarium.

TEMPERATURE REQUIREMENTS: 65–85°F.

SEX DIFFERENCES: Only the plumpness of the female and the slenderness of the male are signs of sex.

COUNTS: Dorsal ii,8; anal iii, 17 or 18; pectoral i,10; pelvic i,6; scales 32 or 33.

This species is no problem to breed if one has been able to breed the zebrafish, *Brachydanio rerio* (page 271). It lays nonadhesive eggs in a manner similar to that of the zebrafish. The breeding tank should be as long as possible, with clear, shallow water at a pH of 7.2 to 7.4 and temperature of 75°F. Care must be exercised in selecting only very plump females for breeding. Males are more slender and show slightly more color than the females. Some breeders use special tanks constructed with a false bottom of glass rods so spaced that the eggs can easily fall through between them, but the adult fish cannot pass. Since uneaten particles of food are also trapped from the adult fish, care in feeding must be exercised. *Tubifex* may be offered in special worm feeders, which are floating pieces of glass or plastic with holes on the bottom to allow the worms to escape a few at a time. *Daphnia* should be fed sparingly from an eye dropper with a wide mouth. The fish will usually spawn within 48 hours after introduction to the breeding tank if the males and females have been conditioned separately. Eggs hatch in 36 hours.

The name of this species currently is *Aphyocharax anisitsi*.

GENUS *Arnoldichthys* Myers

[Ar'-nold-ik'-thees: named in honor of Johann Paul Arnold, aquarist]

RED-EYED CHARACIN / *Arnoldichthys spilopterus* (Boulenger)

[spy-lop'-ter-us: *spilo* = spot; *pterus* = a fin]

Petersius spilopterus Boulenger, Catalogue of the Fresh-water Fishes of Africa, 1:239, fig. 182, 1909 (type locality, mouths of Niger River and Lagos coast).

RANGE: West Africa, vicinity of Niger River delta.

SIZE: 2½ inches; breeding not observed.

TEMPERAMENT: A peaceful species when among fishes of its own size.

TEMPERATURE REQUIREMENTS: 70–86°F.

SEX DIFFERENCES: The plumpness of the mature female indicates the sex.

COUNTS: Dorsal ii,10; anal iii,11; pectoral i,13 or 14; pelvic i,7; scales 4½ + 18 to 20 + 3½ above lateral line, 28 to 30 along lateral line.

This characin has not been bred but success in spawning this fine aquarium species would be worth all the trouble and time expended.

The male is the more colorful of the two sexes. The back is brownish, the sides dazzling blue, and the belly silvery. Two light stripes run horizontally above and below the dark lateral line from the eye to the caudal fin. The female shows little color in her fins and only on occasion is the eyespot visible. The rose-colored eye suggested the common name.

This fish feeds readily on all kinds of live food and dried preparations. It is timid and frightened when first introduced into the home aquarium but soon settles down to a quiet life.

FAMILY CHARACIDAE

GENUS *Asiphonichthys* Cope

[A-si'-fun-ik'-thees: *a* = without; *siphon* = tube; *ichthys* = fish]

Asiphonichthys stenopterus Cope

[sten-op'-ter-us: *steno* = narrow; *pterus* = fin]

Asiphonichthys stenopterus Cope, Amer. Nat., p. 67, January, 1894 (type locality, upper waters of Rio Jacuhy).

RANGE: British Guiana to Argentina.

SIZE: 3 inches; breeding size not observed.

TEMPERAMENT: This characin has habits similar to those of *Charax gibbosus* (page 185).

TEMPERATURE REQUIREMENTS: 70–85°F.

SEX DIFFERENCES: The swelling of the female indicates her sex.

COUNTS: Dorsal ii,9; anal iv,41 or 42; pectoral i,14; pelvic i,8; scales 43, transverse row 21 to 22.

This species has been confused with *Charax gibbosus* (page 185) by aquarists. Upon careful comparison it may be noted that *Charax* has a deeper body.

GENUS *Astyanax* Baird and Girard

[As-tie'-an-ax: named in honor of the son of Hector and Andromache of Greek mythology]

Astyanax bimaculatus (Linnaeus)

[bi'-mack-you-lay'-tus: *bi* = two; *maculatus* = spotted]

Salmo bimaculatus Linnaeus, Systema naturae, ed. 10, p. 311, 1758 (type locality, South America).

RANGE: Trinidad, eastern Venezuela, Guianas, Brazil to Argentina.

SIZE: 6 inches; breeding size 3 inches.

TEMPERAMENT: A rather peaceful species. It eats small fishes, hence is suitable only in a large community tank.

TEMPERATURE REQUIREMENTS: 70–85°F.

SEX DIFFERENCES: The swelling of the female indicates her sex.

COUNTS: Dorsal ii,9; anal iii,24 to 32; pectoral i,11 to 13; pelvic i,7; scales 7 to 9 + 36 to 42 + 6 or 7.

This species is much like *Astyanax mexicanus* (page 178) in habits and breeding.

Astyanax mexicanus (Filippi)

[mex'-a-can'-us: named after Mexico]

Tetragonopterus mexicanus Filippi, Guerin's Rev. Mag. Zool., p. 166, 1853 (type locality, Mexico).

RANGE: Mexico and the Rio Grande of southern United States.

SIZE: 3 inches; breeding size 2½ inches.

TEMPERAMENT: A fairly peaceful species but large-toothed, thus potentially dangerous to small fishes such as guppies even of considerable size. It may be kept only in a large community tank.

TEMPERATURE REQUIREMENTS: 68–85°F. Optimum breeding temperature 75°F.

SEX DIFFERENCES: Mature male is usually smaller than the mature female. The swollen female, bearing ripe eggs, is the most accurate indication of sex.

COUNTS: Dorsal ii,9; anal iii,19 or 20; pectoral ii,12 or 13; pelvic i,7; scales 8 + 36 or 37 + 6.

The fact that this fish, native to Mexico and the Rio Grande, is easily obtained has been responsible for the lack of interest by commercial breeders, but aquarists have bred it. It is not a popular fish because the color is drab. Spawning is much like that of other characins; adhesive eggs are laid in bunches on plants. It is an ardent egg eater unless a copious amount of live food is offered during the spawning period.

The young are fast-growing but need plenty of infusoria and finely powdered dry foods. They will eat brine shrimp as soon as they are large enough to take them. A 15-gallon tank should be supplied for their growth; otherwise, a great many of them will be lost because of overcrowding. This species reaches breeding size at about 9 months to 1 year of age, depending upon the size of the aquarium in which it is reared and the types of food fed. This is the only characin found in the United States.

Astyanax fasciatus (Cuvier) is a closely related species also used in the home aquarium.

Astyanax mutator Eigenmann

[mew-tay'-tor: *mutator* = changeable]

Astyanax *mutator* Eigenmann, Ann. Carnegie Mus., 6(1):18, 1909 (Savannah Landing, upper Potaro River)

RANGE: British Guiana.

SIZE: 6 inches; breeding size 3 inches.

TEMPERAMENT: A moderately peaceful species that eats small fishes; therefore, it is suitable only in a large community tank.

TEMPERATURE REQUIREMENTS: 65–90°F. Optimum breeding temperature 74°F.

SEX DIFFERENCES: Both sexes are similarly colored, so that the intensity of coloration is not a sexual distinction. The male is sometimes the proud possessor of a reddish glow to his anal and caudal fins. The male is slimmer and smaller than the plump female.

COUNTS: Dorsal ii,9; anal iii,20 or 21; pectoral ii,11 or 12; pelvic i,7 or 8; scales 6 or 7 + 34 or 35 + 4 or 5.

This characin is easy to breed. If a pair of well-conditioned fish, about 3 inches long, are placed in a thickly planted aquarium with a few water hyacinths, they may start spawning. Parent fish should be well-fed to prevent them from eating the spawn. All characins require the same treatment for prevention of infanticide.

The fry hatch in a few days at 74°F and the young are fairly large. Several broods have been successfully reared on powdered foods and infusoria, but the larger living foods are certainly necessary for robust growth and health. The fry are about 2 inches long when they are 6 months old. They will greedily take all kinds of dry and live foods. The many reports that young fishes have been raised on dry food only are probably not true. They are founded on the premise that dry foods are *purposely* supplied; however, live foods, in the form of weaker fish that die and are eaten by the larger fish, are always accidental supplements to the dry-food diet.

Genus *Carnegiella* Eigenmann

[Car-neg'-i-el'-la: named in honor of Margaret Carnegie]

The most striking feature of the hatchetfishes is their "hatchetlike" appearance, formed by a sort of keel along their lower thoracic edge.

Most hatchetfishes are able to leap and glide for fairly long distances and they hop about from aquarium to aquarium, or out of the aquarium onto the floor with perfect grace and ease. Their jumping ability is superior to that of many other fishes; thus the aquarium must be covered at all times.

The hatchetfishes are considered by many as delicate. They are! Not only are they susceptible to the ich, but they are likely to starve to death if not fed properly. The best food for hatchetfishes is *Daphnia. Tubifex* worms may be offered if placed in a floating worm feeder. It is almost impossible for a hatchetfish to feed on the bottom.

Once hatchetfishes are accustomed to their surroundings, if no other fishes are in the same aquarium, they may take dry, floating foods. The hatchetfishes are so meek that they can scarcely compete with other fishes when feeding.

The hatchetfishes have been divided into three genera: *Carnegiella, Gasteropelecus,* and *Thoracocharax,* all of which occur in South America. Although several species and subspecies have been described in these genera, we are illustrating only those that have been used in aquaria.

BLACK-WINGED HATCHETFISH / *Carnegiella marthae* Myers

[mar'-thi: named in honor of Martha Ruth Myers]

Carnegiella marthae Myers, Bull. Mus. Comp. Zool., 68(3):119, 1927 (type locality, vicinity of Caicara, Venezuela) RANGE: Orinoco and Amazon Basins. SIZE: 1½ inches; breeding size not known. TEMPERAMENT: A very peaceful and desirable species for the community tank. TEMPERATURE REQUIREMENT: 70–85°F. Optimum about 75°F. SEX DIFFERENCES: Unknown. COUNTS: Dorsal ii,8; anal total rays 22 to 24; pectoral i,9 or 10; pelvic v or vi; scales 26.

This species has not been bred in captivity. It is the most hardy of all the hatchetfishes but for some reason is not the most plentiful. This hatchetfish has been known to live for two years in a home aquarium before meeting an untimely end by a fast jump out of it. A storekeeper placed his hatchetfishes in a tank in the highest tier of three staggered rows of aquaria. A few days after putting fish into the top tank he found the majority had leaped out and were in aquaria as far as 16 feet from their original home. Whether or not the fish got from one tank to another in a single leap is not known.

MARBLED HATCHETFISH / *Carnegiella strigata* (Günther)

[stri-ga'-ta: *strigata* = streaked]

Gasteropelecus strigatus Günther, Cat. Fish. Brit. Mus., 5:343, 1864 (no locality given)

RANGE: Guianas and Amazon Basin to above Manaus.

SIZE: 2 inches; breeding size 1¾ inches.

TEMPERAMENT: A peaceful species but not a hardy one.

TEMPERATURE REQUIREMENTS: 75–90°F.

SEX DIFFERENCES: A ripe female may be recognized from a top view by her plumpness.

COUNTS: Dorsal ii,8; anal xxvii to xxxii; pectoral i,8; pelvic v or vi; scales 27 to 32.

Only one unconfirmed spawning has been reported for this species. The breeder, who reported that this fish spawned more than once for him, states that a temperature of about 85° is necessary. The male courted the female by a rapid circling and dashing about the prospective mate. Several attempts to leap were described. The pair finally aligned themselves in a parallel head-to-tail position and deposited small transparent eggs among floating plants. The eggs were not eaten.

Genus *Chalceus* Cuvier

[Kal′-ce-us: *chalceus* = a kind of fish]

PINK-TAILED CHALCEUS /
Chalceus macrolepidotus Cuvier and Valenciennes

[mack′-row-lep′-i-do′-tus: *macro* = large; *lepidotus* = scaled]

Chalceus macrolepidotus Cuvier, Mem. Mus. Hist. Nat., 4:454, 21, fig. 1, 1818 (type locality, Essequibo)

RANGE: Guianas; Amazon and Rio Negro Basins.

SIZE: 1 foot; breeding size not observed.

TEMPERAMENT: An active species, peaceful when 2 inches or shorter and suitable for a community tank; not suitable when larger.

TEMPERATURE REQUIREMENTS: 70–90°F.

SEX DIFFERENCES: See below. Male is more colorful.

COUNTS: Dorsal ii,10; anal iii,9; pectoral i,15; pelvic ii,8; scales 4 + 20 to 23 + 2.

This fish has not been bred, because it is fairly rare and not too desirable. The fish is sensitive and usually does not last very long in the home aquarium.

FAMILY **CHARACIDAE**

GENUS *Characidium* Reinhardt

[Kar'-a-sid'-i-um: *charac* = a kind of fish; *idium* = small]

DARTER CHARACIN / *Characidium fasciatum* Reinhardt

[fas'-ci-ay'-tum: *fasciatum* = banded]

Characidium fasciatum Reinhardt, Overs. Dansk. Vid. Selsk, Forh. Kjøbenhavn, p. 56, pl. 2, figs. 1, 2, 1866 (type locality, Lagoa Santa, Rio das Velhas)

RANGE: Orinoco to La Plata Basins.

SIZE: 3 inches; breeding size 2 inches.

TEMPERAMENT: A peaceful species desirable in the community aquarium.

TEMPERATURE REQUIREMENTS: 65–75°F.

SEX DIFFERENCES: The fullness of the female and the slimness of the male indicate sex.

COUNTS: Dorsal iii,9; anal iii,6; pectoral iii,7 to 9; pelvic i,8; scales 3½ to 4½ + 32 to 36 + 3 to 3½.

This characin is easy to spawn, easy to feed, hardy, peaceful, . . . yet unpopular! Well, it is not too hard to see why. This fish is just homely! Some fishes are so ugly that they are collected for their oddity, but this poor fellow is neither odd-shaped nor ugly enough to display. If a tankful were exhibited, it is doubtful that they would bring a remark from anyone, with the possible exception of "Where did you get those killies?"

Spawning *C. fasciatum* is only a matter of selecting a pair and placing them in a heavily planted aquarium. The spawning grasses most suited are *Nitella, Fontinalis,* or Spanish moss (artificial grass). The young hatch in 3 days at 70°. This species also does well at higher temperatures.

GENUS *Charax* Scopoli

[Kar'-ax: *charax* = a kind of fish]

HUMPBACKED HEADSTANDER / *Charax gibbosus* (Linnaeus)

[gib-bow'-sus: *gibbosus* = humpbacked]

Salmo gibbosus Linnaeus, Systema naturae, ed. 10, p. 311, 1758 (type locality, Surinam)

RANGE: Guianas and Amazon Basin.

SIZE: 4 inches.

TEMPERAMENT: A peaceful species that is desirable in a community tank and does well.

TEMPERATURE REQUIREMENTS: 74–85°F.

SEX DIFFERENCES: None apparent.

COUNTS: Dorsal ii,9; anal iii,46 to 54; pectoral i,14; pelvic i,7; scales 13 to 15 + 53 to 56 + 10 to 12.

This species has not been bred in captivity. It has a sluggish behavior and lacks luster. It has little appeal except for the odd angle at which the head is attached to the body. Normally the head of a headstander is in line with the lateral line, but in this species the head is oblique to that line. The humpback makes this fish appear monstrous.

It is a huge eater and is useful as a scavenger since it eats all kinds of fish foods.

FAMILY CHARACIDAE

GENUS *Chilodus* Müller and Troschel

[Ky-low'-dus: *chil* = edge; *odus* = teeth]

SPOTTED HEADSTANDER / *Chilodus punctatus* Müller and Troschel

[punk-tay'-tus: *punctatus* = spotted]

Chilodus punctatus Müller and Troschel, Horae ichthyologicae, pts. 1, 2, pp. 10, 26, pl. 4, fig. 2, 2*a*, 1845 (type locality, Lake Amacu, British Guiana)

RANGE: Guianas.

SIZE: 4 inches; breeding size unknown.

TEMPERAMENT: A moderately peaceful species, desirable in a community tank.

TEMPERATURE REQUIREMENTS: 75–85°F.

SEX DIFFERENCES: No external differences.

COUNTS: Dorsal ii,9 or 10; anal ii,10 or 11; pectoral i,13 to 15; pelvic i,8; scales 4½ + 25 or 26 + 3.

This species has not been spawned in captivity and it is difficult to keep alive. Many dealers are not too enthusiastic about handling this attractive fish owing to the losses they suffer and the high price tag which must be put on it. Hobbyists too agree that this fragility is a great hindrance to its popularity.

Some authors state that this fish must be fed small food particles, but this claim is obviously made by inexperienced aquarists. The spotted headstander is quite capable of ingesting coarse particles and should be encouraged to eat the larger pieces of food.

The angle at which the fish maintains itself is about 45 degrees. As yet there is no satisfactory explanation for this adaptation.

GENUS *Colossoma* Eigenmann and Kenedy

[Kol'-os-so'-ma: *coloss* = large; *soma* = body]

BLACK-FINNED COLOSSOMA / *Colossoma nigripinnis* (Cope)

[ni'-gri-pin'-nis: *nigri* = black; *pinnis* = fin]

Myletes nigripinnis Cope, Proc. Amer. Phil. Soc., 17:693, 1878 (type locality Peruvian Amazon)

RANGE: Peruvian Amazon.

SIZE: 8 inches; not yet bred in captivity.

TEMPERAMENT: A moderately dangerous fish.

TEMPERATURE REQUIREMENTS: 72–88°F.

SEX DIFFERENCES: The swollen abdomen indicates a mature female with eggs.

COUNTS: Dorsal iii or iv,13 to 14; anal iii,22 to 23; pectoral about i,16 to 17; pelvic i,7; scales 70 to 77; 8 or 9 from adipose fin to lateral line.

The younger fish have large brown spots on their sides and their fins are reddish in color. These spots almost disappear on the larger fish and the fins and head become darker, nearly blackish.

Live foods in the form of baby fishes, pieces of meat or fish, shrimp, and liver are necessary for its welfare. Dry food is not very readily taken and the fish may be near starvation before it shows any eagerness to eat prepared foods.

The name of this species currently is *Colossoma oculus*.

FAMILY **CHARACIDAE**

GENUS *Copeina* Fowler

[Kope-i′-na: named in honor of the naturalist Edward D. Cope]

The male *Copeina arnoldi*, showing the longer and more pointed dorsal fin, a sex difference shown to various degrees by many aquarium fishes.

SPRAYING CHARACIN / *Copeina arnoldi* Regan

[ar′-nold-eye: named in honor of Johann Paul Arnold]

Copeina arnoldi Regan, Ann. Mag. Nat. Hist., (8)10:393, 1912 (type locality, Amazon)

RANGE: Caripito, Venezuela to Brazilian Amazon.

SIZE: 3 inches; breeds at 2 inches.

TEMPERAMENT: A peaceful species desirable as a community tank fish.

TEMPERATURE REQUIREMENTS: 72–85°F.

SEX DIFFERENCES: Male is much larger than the female; female shows a red spot on the dorsal fin. Characteristic fullness of the ripe female indicates sex. The deep yellow ova of the female may be seen through her abdominal wall when a strong light is behind her.

A 10- to 15-gallon tank is required for breeding. Neutral (7.0) to acid (6.8) pH, water at 75°F is advised. The pair should be placed together in a tank with a few small bunches of floating plants. Seasoned water should fill only half the tank and a piece of slate should slant so that half of it sticks out of the water. The spawners should be fed heavily on live foods and scraps of raw beef and fish. The female should develop the characteristic fullness, at which time both fish should show signs of interest in each other, and the male will be seen to inspect the slate. As soon as he approves (he rarely disapproves) of the spawning site, he will drive the female to within an inch or so of it and suddenly they will leap out of the water, lock their fins in a manner which will facilitate fertilization of the extruded ova, and cling to the slate for a few seconds by fin suction, leaving a small, gelatinous mass of eggs at the spot where they have adhered. Usually the number of eggs so deposited is between 6 and 12. Repeated, this process may take as long as 90 minutes (the average is 45) during which nearly 125 eggs are deposited. Subsequent deposits are usually all in the same general area, non-overlapping, and before the spawning is complete the entire clump is joined together in a 2-inch diameter. Fertilization, seemingly haphazard, is well-coordinated and complete. The developing embryos are kept moist by the male. He makes a dash for the eggs every 15 minutes or so and splashes water onto them by a vigorous thrashing of his tail fin. The fry hatch after 3 days at 75°F and fall into the water; immediately they go to the bottom where they like to hide and hunt infusoria. After about a week they come out and congregate in schools looking for sifted *Daphnia*, brine shrimp, *Cyclops*, and dried foods. Parents should be removed after the young are hatched.

Copeina arnoldi: (*above*) male; (*below*) female.

BEAUTIFUL-SCALED CHARACIN / *Copeina callolepis* Regan

[kal'-o-lep'-is: *callo* = beautiful, *lepis* = scales]

Copeina callolepis Regan, Ann. Mag. Nat. Hist., (8)10:393, 1912 (type locality, Amazon)

RANGE: Amazon Basin.

SIZE: 2 inches; breeds at 2 inches.

TEMPERAMENT: A peaceful species, but it may jump out of the tank.

TEMPERATURE REQUIREMENTS: 72–85°F.

SEX DIFFERENCES: The dorsal fin of the male is more pointed than that of the female; the upper part of the tail on the male is longer than that of the female; the pelvic fins on the male are dark-tipped.

COUNTS: Dorsal ii,8; anal iii,8; pelvic i,7; scales 21.

Breeding this species is quite different from its close relative, *Copeina arnoldi*, since it spawns like ordinary characins.

Pairs should be conditioned on live food, preferably *Daphnia. Tubifex* is taken, as are dry foods. The eggs are deposited on submerged broad-leafed plants. Usually about 50 eggs are produced per spawning attempt. The eggs hatch in a day at 74°F but the young take about 2 days to absorb their yolk sac; then they are free-swimming and require copious amounts of rotifers or they will die within a week. This species is not in great demand and is seldom bred commercially. It is imported occasionally but is generally scarce.

The over-all color is light gray with a tannish shading. The sides show horizontal rows of dark red and black dots (due to this marking on each scale). The dorsal fin has a black ocellate spot at its base. The pelvic fins of the male have dark edges.

The name of this species currently is *Copella nattereri.*

RED-SPOTTED COPEINA / *Copeina guttata* (Steindachner)

[gut-tay'-ta: *guttata* = spotted]

Pyrrhulina guttata Steindachner, Sitzb. Akad. Wiss. Wien, 72:10, pl. 2, figs. 6, 6a, 1875 (type locality, Amazon and Rio Negro Rivers)

RANGE: Brazilian Amazon and Rio Negro Rivers.

SIZE: 4 inches; breeds at 3 inches.

TEMPERAMENT: A peaceful species that is recommended for the community aquarium.

TEMPERATURE REQUIREMENTS: A wide temperature range is enjoyed by this species since it does well at temperatures from 60 to 90°F, but it will show the best coloring only at temperatures of 75°F and up. It breeds at 75°F. If it is maintained at the higher temperatures it should be fed more heavily.

SEX DIFFERENCES: The male is more slender than the female and shows clear red spots during the breeding season. Female has few of these spots or dots and her colors are lighter than those of the male.

COUNTS: Dorsal ii,7 or 8; anal iii,8 or 9; pectoral 15; pelvic i,7; scales 23 or 24.

A pair of fish should be placed in a medium-sized (5 gallons and up) aquarium and then conditioned on live food in the form of chopped white worms, *Daphnia, Tubifex,* mosquito larvae, and pieces of beef or liver. When the parents start paying attention to each other, they will begin to dig a depression in the sand, where the eggs are deposited and fertilized. Unlike most other characins, the male will then drive the female away and, in cichlid fashion, will commence to fan the eggs with his pectoral fins. The female should be removed after spawning as the male may become upset by her presence in a small aquarium.

The eggs hatch in 48 hours and the male may be removed. The spawn are large and number about 250. Sometimes while the young are free-swimming the male may suddenly decide to make a meal out of them, but he usually ignores them. Youngsters need the usual diet of infusoria followed by freshly hatched brine shrimp, sifted *Daphnia,* and microworms.

Many times these fish will spawn in the community aquarium only to have some larger fish ignore the protests of the male parent fish and gobble up the spawn or youngsters.

The species is slow-moving and sluggish, though at the slightest provocation it may take a headlong dive out of the aquarium. It is not so timid as it looks and is highly recommended for the beginning aquarist if available.

FAMILY CHARACIDAE

GENUS *Corynopoma* Gill

[Cor'-i-no-po'-ma: *coryno* = club; *poma* = a cover]

Young swordtail characins, two males and two females. The fish to the left are males; the more rounded fish to the right are females. The extension of the caudal fins has not been fully developed.

SWORDTAIL CHARACIN / *Corynopoma riisei* Gill

[rice'-e-eye: named in honor of A. H. Riise, a Danish zoologist]

Corynopoma riisei Gill, Ann. Lyc. Nat. Hist., 6:66, 1858 (type locality, Trinidad)

RANGE: Trinidad and Venezuela.

SIZE: 3 inches; breeding size 2 inches.

TEMPERAMENT: A peaceful and desirable species for the community aquarium.

TEMPERATURE REQUIREMENTS: 68–88°F.

SEX DIFFERENCES: The male has a clublike extension on his gill plate.

counts: Dorsal ii or iii,8; anal iii,23 or 24; pelvic i,7 or 8; scales 6 or 7 + 38 to 44 + 6 or 7.

The swordtail characin is an extremely interesting characin to spawn. The parents seem to ignore both spawn and fry. Sex is easy to determine and the selection of breeders is merely a matter of recognizing when both sexes are sexually mature and in breeding condition. This fish is prolific, and successful spawnings have been recorded recurrently in the stock 20-gallon tank, 12 × 12 × 30 inches, which is large enough to raise 300 to 400 youngsters.

During the actual spawning, the male is very active, dancing around his female much like a guppy. After a short time his "corynopoma" (the clublike extension on his gill plate) will become distended and project out perpendicularly in contrast to its normal position close to the body.

Quite suddenly the male will curve his body in such a way as to direct a bundle of sperm at the vent of the female. No contact seems necessary for this fertilization, though it is possible that the corynopoma may be used to help direct the ball of sperm in some manner. The bundle of sperm, if immediately pipetted from the female's body, is closely packed and seems to be fused with some sort of glue or matrix. The female apparently contains the necessary solvent for this substance, for if the sperm packet is left inside her for any considerable period of time the sperm become dissociated and are free to complete their mission of fertilizing the eggs. This internal fertilization is in direct contrast to statements that the female carries the sperm in her mouth. Any spawning female can be hand-stripped of her eggs; they can be fertilized artificially by squeezing a matured male.

GENUS *Creagrutus* Günther

[Cree'-a-gru'-tus: *creagrutus* = to seize flesh]

GOLD-STRIPED CHARACIN / *Creagrutus beni* Eigenmann

[bey'-ne: named after the Rio Beni]

Creagrutus beni Eigenmann, Ann. Carnegie Mus., 8(1):172, pl. 6, fig. 2, 1911 (type locality, Villa Bella on Rio Beni)

RANGE: Venezuela, Colombia, and Amazon Basin.

SIZE: 3 inches; breeds at 2½ inches.

TEMPERAMENT: A mild-mannered species that does not attack small fishes in the community tank.

TEMPERATURE REQUIREMENTS: 74–85°F. Optimum breeding temperature 76°F.

SEX DIFFERENCES: Sex is difficult to distinguish except when the female is heavy with eggs. She is also the more brilliantly colored at that time.

COUNTS: Dorsal ii,8; anal iii,10 or 11; pectoral i,10 to 12; pelvic i,7 or 8; scales 5 + 35 to 38 + 3 or 4.

Although this fish has been bred several times, its actions are still a mystery. A pair will isolate itself from others present in the aquarium and swim about each other for hours at a time. This swimming behavior appears to be a sexually stimulated dance, during which the female will spawn her eggs on bushy plants. After spawning she should be removed, along with the male. The 3 or 4 dozen eggs will hatch in about 3 days at 75°F and the fry should be cared for with a diet of infusoria, followed by brine shrimp.

The species is hardy, though subject to attack by the parasite *Ichthyopthirius* if the water temperature is allowed to drop suddenly. The fish itself is colorful, with an olive-green back, silvery sides, and white belly. A black stripe traces the lower half of the lateral line and is margined on both edges with a fine gold stripe, from which the popular name is derived. The dorsal and anal fins are reddish but the other fins show little color. The female is more brilliantly colored during breeding time than the male.

Genus *Creatochanes* Günther

[Cree-a′-to-chan′-ees: *creato* = fleshy; *chanes* = wide gaping mouth]

ORANGE-FINNED CHARACIN / *Creatochanes affinis* (Günther)

[af-fi′-nis: *affinis* = neighboring]

Tetragonopterus affinis Günther, Catalogue of the Fishes in the British Museum, 5:327, 1864 (type locality, British Guiana)

RANGE: Guianas, Amazon, Rio São Francisco, Paraguay.

SIZE: 6 inches; breeding not observed.

TEMPERAMENT: A strongly predaceous fish not suitable for the community tank.

TEMPERATURE REQUIREMENTS: 70–86°F.

SEX DIFFERENCES: The male is more colorful than the female and possesses a longer dorsal fin.

COUNTS: Dorsal ii,9; anal iii,25 or 26; pectoral i,11 or 12; pelvic i,7; scales 7½ + 43 to 47 + 3 or 4.

The vicious temperament of this species makes it undesirable for any type of community aquarium. Individuals fight among themselves when there are no other kinds with which to fight. They are pretty, showing the characteristic guppy green on the back which becomes an elegant metallic blue on the sides, turning silvery yellow on the belly. A dark line more or less follows the lateral line from the gill cover to the tail fin. The dorsal fin is magnificent, in the males especially, having a brilliant red color with a darker crimson base. The tail fin shows many colors, mostly yellow on the lower part and a red- and yellow-dotted black upper lobe. The adipose fin is a brilliant orange, suggesting the popular name "orange-finned characin."

This characin is extremely hardy. Its diet must be carnivorous; it refuses prepared foods and only takes small fishes, worms, and the like.

The name of this species currently is ***Bryconops (Creatochanes) affinis.***

GENUS *Crenuchus* Günther

[Kren'-oō-kus: *cren* = a notch; *nuchus* = neck]

SAILFIN CHARACIN / *Crenuchus spilurus* Günther

[spy'-lure-us: *spil* = spot; *urus* = tail]

Crenuchus spilurus Günther, Ann. Mag. Nat. Hist., (3)12:442, 1863 (type locality, Essequibo)

RANGE: Amazon Basin and Guianas.

SIZE: 4 inches; breeding size 2½ inches.

TEMPERAMENT: Moderately peaceful with larger fishes, but nervous and shy. Does best by itself.

TEMPERATURE REQUIREMENTS: 72–85°F. Breeding temperature 74°F.

SEX DIFFERENCES: Mature male is very colorful; has much longer fins and is an inch longer than the female.

COUNTS: Dorsal iii to vi,15 or 16; anal ii,9; pectoral i,11 or 12; pelvic i,8; scales 28 to 32; transverse row 11 to 13.

Unless there is plenty of room for this fish, it does not pay to acquire a pair. The minimum need is a 10-gallon tank.

Males get much larger than females; after they mature, which takes a few years, the males become exceptionally colored. Their fins grow to an enormous size, becoming attractively mottled with blushing-red colors.

Breeding must take place in a large aquarium, and it is best to use the aquarium to which the pair has become accustomed. Separate the sexes with a glass partition and condition them on live foods for at least a week. When the males stay close to the glass partition they are ready to spawn. The females usually require a few more days before they show any sign of interest in the males. After the partition is removed both sexes will keep to themselves for a few hours, then quite suddenly a pair will dart off into some spawning grass and deposit adhesive pinkish eggs. They will not eat their own eggs, but will go after the fry. Parents should be removed after spawning.

Eggs hatch in 72 hours at 74°F. Fry are very tiny and require infusoria. Brine shrimp and sifted *Daphnia* should follow. The pair that spawned should be isolated for future matings.

GENUS *Ctenobrycon* Eigenmann

[Teen'-o-bry'-con: *cteno* = comb; *brycon* = tear in pieces]

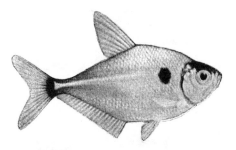

SILVER TETRA / *Ctenobrycon spilurus* (Cuvier and Valenciennes)

[spy'-lure-us: *spil* = spot; *urus* = tail]

Tetragonopterus spilurus Cuvier and Valenciennes, Histoire naturelle des poissons, 22:156, 1849 (type locality, Surinam)

RANGE: Venezuela to Guianas.

SIZE: 3½ inches; breeding size 2½ inches.

TEMPERAMENT: A peaceful species for its large size, which makes it popular.

TEMPERATURE REQUIREMENTS: These hardy fish do well at temperatures from 68 to 90°F. Optimum breeding temperature 75°F.

SEX DIFFERENCES: The female, besides being the larger and plumper of the two fish, also has a red cast to her anal fin. The male shows no color in this area.

COUNTS: Dorsal ii,8 or 9; anal iii,39 or 40; pectoral i,12 or 13; pelvic i,7; scales 12 or 13 + 46 to 49 + 10 or 11.

This fish is easily bred and is always in constant demand. Dealers do not call it a best seller, but it is one of the constant movers. Spawning occurs when two conditioned parents-to-be are placed in a large tank heavily stocked with plants of the bushy varieties. Spawning usually takes place as soon as the breeders have acclimated themselves to their new habitat. Spawning pairs should be kept together, as they show much affection for each other. A pair is ready to spawn when the two fish are observed doing a "loop-the-loop" together. A few days after this phenomenon the pair dashes among the plants, shedding hundreds of eggs. These hatch in a few days at 75°F, and very favorable results are obtained when green water is used to supplement the diet of infusoria for the young fry. Brine shrimp are eaten after a week of free swimming.

Conditioning the spawners is largely dependent on the food offered. A mash made of spinach, liver, and Pablum, boiled in a double boiler after being whipped in a blendor, is excellent food. The silver tetra needs plenty of plant material in its diet.

GENUS *Curimatopsis* Steindachner

[Cu′-ri-ma-top′-sis: meaning of name not known]

ROSE-COLORED CURIMATOPSIS / *Curimatopsis saladensis* Meinken

[sa′-la-den′-sis: named after the Rio Salada]

Curimatopsis saladensis Meinken, Blät. Aquar.-Terrak., 44:71, fig., 1933 (type locality, Rio Salada, tributary of Rio Parana, Argentina)

RANGE: Argentina.

SIZE: 3 inches; breeding at 2½ inches.

TEMPERAMENT: A peaceful species desirable for the community tank. They show up beautifully in schools.

TEMPERATURE REQUIREMENTS: 72–86°F. Optimum breeding temperature 76°F.

SEX DIFFERENCES: Female is broader and heavier and also shows a red margin on the front of the anal fin.

COUNTS: Dorsal ii,9; anal ii,7; pectoral iii,12 or 13; pelvic i,8; scales 30 to 32, transverse row 9 to anal origin.

This species has the general coloration of the rosy barb; the dark olive-brown dorsal fin is edged with a metallic shining aqua blue, and the sides at times are decorated with a rosy-red glow which extends along the belly and throat. The large, shining scales give a reticulated effect and a dark streak follows the lateral line. The tail is rosy red throughout, varying to a slightly darker color near its edges.

Breeding is comparatively easy. A pair should be placed in a clean aquarium in which there is no sand or plants other than some spawning grass on which the pair will deposit eggs. Parents are inclined to eat their eggs, so they should be removed as soon as possible after they have finished spawning.

This species has not been popular in the United States; however, now that German imports are coming in there is good reason to believe this beauty will soon grace many aquaria.

There is no feeding problem. Dry food and all types of live foods are eagerly taken.

Genus *Exodon* Müller and Troschel

[Ex'-o-don: *exo* = outside; *odon* = tooth]

Exodon paradoxus Müller and Troschel

[par'-a-dox'-us: *paradoxus* = strange]

Exodon paradoxus Müller and Troschel, Arch. Naturges. Wiegmann, 1:91, 1844 (type locality, Guiana)

RANGE: Amazon Basin to Guianas.

SIZE: 3 inches; breeding size about 2½ inches.

TEMPERAMENT: Moderately peaceful among large fishes, but they fight among themselves.

TEMPERATURE REQUIREMENTS: Very hardy. They can withstand temperatures of 68 to 90°F, but the optimum is probably about 75°F.

SEX DIFFERENCES: Male has slightly longer anal and dorsal fin rays than female. The fullness of the female indicates her sex.

COUNTS: Dorsal ii,9; anal ii or iii,17 to 21; pectoral i,14; pelvic i,7; scales 33 to 35; gill rakers 7 + 1 + 9.

The sparkling beauty of this species has led many experienced aquarists to try their hand at breeding this rarity. In the first printing of the *Handbook* we reported that no one, to date, had been successful. In 1955 Miss Martha Tutwiler, age 17, daughter of O. Tutwiler, owner of Tutwiler's Tropical Fish Hatchery in Florida, bred these fish for the first time. In order to verify this report we flew down to Tampa and saw a spawn of about 20 fry.

Tutwiler kindly gave us the pair of breeders, shown in the plate above.

Breeding is very difficult, for the pair are constantly moving. Their huge mouths match their enormous appetite, and in short order they eat half their weight in live foods. It is impossible to keep any other fishes in the same aquarium with *Exodon* because of their fin-nipping habits. In a matter of hours they can tear the fins of breeding-size angelfish to shreds.

Miss Tutwiler spawned the fish in a ten-gallon aquarium densely filled with artificial spawning grass (Spanish moss). There were only two inches of clear water above the plants, and the breeders raced back and forth spewing eggs every which way and eating their spawn nearly as quickly as they laid them. It is assumed that if a much larger aquarium were available, more eggs could have been saved, but such was not the case. The fry hatched from the eggs in "about 48 hours" at 74°F. Breeders must be removed after spawning.

In the male, the dorsal, anal, and pelvic fins are reddish, adipose yellow, caudal yellowish basally, lobes pink; back brownish, silvery ventrally, tinted yellowish. The female is generally yellowish. *Exodon* is in reference to external teeth on both jaws.

GENUS *Gasteropelecus* Scopoli

[Gas'-ter-o-pel'-e-kus: *gastero* = belly; *pelecus* = hatchet-shaped]

SILVER HATCHETFISH / *Gasteropelecus sternicla* (Linnaeus)

Clupea sternicla Linnaeus, Systema Naturae, ed. 10, p. 319, 1758 (type locality, Surinam)

RANGE: Amazon Basin.

SIZE: 2½ inches; breeding in captivity not known.

TEMPERAMENT: A peaceful species, desirable in the community tank.

TEMPERATURE REQUIREMENT: At least 75° and up to 90°F.

SEX DIFFERENCES: None apparent.

COUNTS: Dorsal ii,8 or 9; anal ii,28 to 30; pectoral i,9 or 10; pelvic i,5; scales 29 to 32.

This fish has not been bred in captivity. It is susceptible to the ich and dealers have lost entire tankfuls in a matter of days. It is a timid speices and will jump out of an uncovered tank. It seldom lives a year in the home aquarium. The main diet consists of *Daphnia* and fruit flies, *Drosophila*, which are easy to culture in a milk bottle. Drop the vestigial-winged *Drosophila* onto the surface of the water, and the eagerly waiting hatchetfish will swoop up and grab them.

Pterodiscus levis Eigenmann, Ann. Carnegie Mus., 6(1):12, 1909 (type locality, Pará) is a subspecies of G. sternicla.

Gasteropelecus maculatus Steindachner, Anz. Akad. Wiss. Wien, 16:151, 1879; Denks. Akad. Wiss. Wien, 41:168, pl. 1, fig. 4, 1879 (type locality, Mamoni River at Chepo) is another species.

GENUS *Gephyrocharax* Eigenmann

[Ge-fi'-ro-kar'-ax: *gephyro* = a bridge (connecting link); *charax* = a kind of fish]

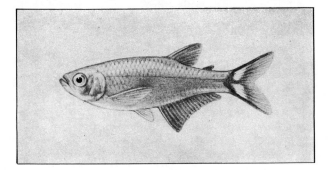

PLATINUM TETRA / *Gephyrocharax atracaudatus* (Meek and Hildebrand)

[at'-ra-cow-day'-tus: *atra* = black; *caudatus* = tailed]

Deuterodon atracaudata Meek and Hildebrand, Field Mus. Pub. Zool. Ser., 10(6):68, 1912 (type locality, Rio Frijoles, Canal Zone, Panama)

RANGE: Both slopes of Panama, except the Rio Chame.

SIZE: 3 inches; breeding size 2 inches.

TEMPERAMENT: An active but peaceful species suitable for a large community aquarium.

TEMPERATURE REQUIREMENTS: Does well at temperatures from 70 to 90°F.

SEX DIFFERENCES: Female is fuller and more rounded than the male. Both are colored alike.

COUNTS: Dorsal ii,7 or 8; anal iv or v,25 to 31; pectoral i,10; pelvic i,7 or 8; scales 9 or 10 + 36 or 37 + 7.

Success in breeding this fish has been attributed to the use of rain water, but any soft water will yield the same results. Soft water, at a pH of 6.8, with a temperature around 80°F, is all that is needed to breed it. For an unknown reason this fish is more prolific when about 2¼ inches than when larger. Unfortunately, one pair that spawned for us was broken up because of the untimely death of the male. He was able to jump through the small

hole in the cover of the aquarium where a heater would normally be fitted.

Pairs should be carefully conditioned on live foods, and none is better than *Daphnia*. When the pair is in good condition it should be placed in the breeding tank, containing the proper water, and the temperature should be slowly raised to 80°F. The bottom of the tank should be covered with marbles or stones, over which there should be a layer of Spanish moss or a fine-leafed plant. The eggs are not very sticky and seem to fall off the plants as the currents from the moving fish are brought to play against them. The crevices hide the eggs from the parents. This fish is very prolific; several hundred eggs are laid at each spawning. The water level should be low, no more than 3 inches above the pebbles.

The parents should be removed as soon after spawning as possible. The eggs hatch in about 4 days. They seem to be fairly impervious to fungus but they die if the water is hard, thus care should be exercised in choosing chemicals to adjust the pH. If the usual biphosphate and sodium bicarbonate are not effective, try acetic acid or sodium hydroxide.

FAMILY CHARACIDAE

GENUS *Glandulocauda* Eigenmann

[Glan'-dew-lo-cow'-da: *glandulo* = glandular; *cauda* = tail]

CROAKING TETRA / *Glandulocauda inequalis* Eigenmann

[in'-e-qual'-is: *inequalis* = unequal]

Glandulocauda inequalis Eigenmann, Ann. Carnegie Mus., 8(1):169, pl. 5, fig. 5, 1911 (type locality, Porto Alegre)

RANGE: Rio Grande do Sul Basin, southeastern Brazil.

SIZE: 2½ inches; breeding size 2 inches.

TEMPERAMENT: A peaceful species suitable for all sizes of community tanks.

TEMPERATURE REQUIREMENTS: 65–90°F, with an optimum breeding temperature of 75°F.

SEX DIFFERENCES: The plump body of a mature female indicates her sex.

COUNTS: Dorsal i,8; anal iv,25 to 27; pectoral i,9 or 10; pelvic i,7; scales 39 or 40, transverse row 14 or 15.

The breeding of *Glandulocauda inequalis* is something of a controversy at the present time. Some reports claim that internal fertilization takes place, and the lack of an intromittent organ is by no means sufficient to rule out this possibility. It is quite possible that when the male and female go through the spawning act, sperm are retained in her cloaca; she is capable of continuing the spawning by herself and deposits eggs on the underside of leaves. If both sexes are removed as soon as the eggs are discovered, the young may be raised in the conventional manner.

This fish makes an odd noise when it comes up for a gulp of air. The sound is loud enough to be heard when one is sitting anywhere in a quiet room. This noise is quite intriguing until one finds out the cause. In related families, many species which live in pools containing much decaying vegetation and having a high carbon dioxide content come to the surface to obtain oxygen from the surface film and to gulp air.

Genus *Gymnocorymbus* Eigenmann

[Jim'-no-cor-im'-bus: *gymno* = naked; *corymbus* = head]

Black Tetra; Blackamoor; Petticoatfish /
Gymnocorymbus ternetzi (Boulenger)

[ter'-nets-eye: named in honor of the collector Carl Ternetz]

Tetragonopterus ternetzi Boulenger, Proc. Zool. Soc. London, p. 528, 1895 (type locality, Mato Grosso)

RANGE: Paraguay and Guaporé Basins.

SIZE: 3 inches; breeding size 1½ inches.

TEMPERAMENT: An active and semi-aggressive species; not recommended for community tanks containing small fishes but satisfactory for the community tank containing large fishes.

TEMPERATURE REQUIREMENTS: This species is hardy at temperatures from 70 to 90°F but is apt to develop the ich or other diseases at lower temperatures.

SEX DIFFERENCES: Only the characteristic plumpness of the female indicates her sex.

COUNTS: Dorsal ii,9; anal iv, 35; pectoral i,12; pelvic i,6; scales 7 + 31 or 32 + 9.

Successful breeding of the black tetra is more a matter of successfully conditioning the pairs than a matter of technique. The heavy-bodied females should be separated from the males and placed for a week in an aquarium all to themselves. They should be allowed to gorge themselves on live foods. When freshly caught flies or other small insects (which should be killed first), are dropped onto the surface of the water, they make a quick strike at them. After a week of heavy feeding and conditioning, the females should be placed in a freshly set up aquarium, of at least the 10-gallon size (the larger the better). The entire tank should be heavily planted with dense bunch plants or artificial spawning grasses, of which Spanish moss is the best. One male should be placed with each female after the latter have been in the spawning tank for at least 24 hours. The tank should not contain any snails because they will eat the eggs. Spawning takes place as the male and female dash into the clumps of plants and deposit many eggs. If they do not eat the eggs as they lay them, they will surely devour the youngsters as soon as they hatch out. The eggs are semiadhesive and are rather easily seen under a good light.

All adult fish should be removed after spawning and the young raised in the spawning tank. Infusoria should be cultured as soon as the spawning is completed and chopped lettuce added to the culture. When the young hatch out they should be left in an aquarium which will receive plenty of light all day and artificial light all night. This constant light is necessary until they are large enough to take freshly hatched brine shrimp and sifted *Daphnia*. Most youngsters starve to death in the early stages of development.

GENUS *Hemibrycon* Günther

[Hem'-i-bry'-con: *hemi* = half; *brycon* = to tear in pieces]

GUPPY'S CHARACIN / *Hemibrycon guppyi* (Regan)

[gup'-py-eye: named in honor of Lechmere Guppy, Jr., the collector]

Tetragonopterus guppyi Regan, Proc. Zool. Soc. London, 1:384, pl. 21, fig. 1, 1906 (type locality, foot of northern range of hills, Trinidad)

RANGE: Trinidad.

SIZE: 5 inches; breeding not observed.

TEMPERAMENT: A fairly peaceful species when small.

TEMPERATURE REQUIREMENTS: 62–90°F.

SEX DIFFERENCES: None observed.

COUNTS: Dorsal ii,8; anal iii,26 to 29; pectoral i,10 to 13; pelvic i,6 to 8; scales 8½ + 38 to 40 + 7½ to 8½.

This fish has not been spawned in captivity. It is not a commercially valuable fish, although in large specimens the color is attractive and the fish is very hardy. The sides show in reflected light a metallic-blue sheen, changing to silver on the belly. The back is olive. An attractive gold stripe runs from behind the gill covers along the sides to the caudal peduncle and to the middle of the caudal fin, where it becomes blackish.

Feeding Guppy's characin is no problem as it eagerly takes all kinds of foods.

GENUS *Hemigrammus* Gill

[Hem′-i-gram′-mus: *hemi* = half; *grammus* = line]

GOLDEN TETRA / *Hemigrammus armstrongi* Schultz and Axelrod

[arm′-strong-eye; named in honor of Joseph Armstrong, who gave the specimens to the authors]

Hemigrammus armstrŏngi Schultz and Axelrod, Trop. Fish Hobbyist, 3(3): 72–75, fig., 1955 (type locality, near Georgetown, British Guiana)

RANGE: British Guiana, South America.

SIZE: 1½ inches, breeding size 1 inch.

TEMPERAMENT: A peaceful species that is desirable in the community tank.

TEMPERATURE REQUIREMENTS: 70–85°F.

SEX DIFFERENCES: None observed.

COUNTS: Dorsal ii,8 or 9; anal iv,19 to 21; pectoral i,9 to 11; pelvic i,7; pores in lateral line 6 to 10; scales 5 + 31 to 33 + 3.

Breeding is similar to that of other members of the genus. An intensely colored male with red caudal fin spots should be conditioned in a 5-gallon aquarium, one end of which is heavily planted with *Myriophyllum, Nitella,* or artificial spawning grass. Maintain the temperature at 74°F for two days, then introduce a heavy female. Usually the male will court the female almost at once, pursuing her about the tank. If the pair is slow to spawn in the plants, raise the temperature slowly to 80°F. The eggs hatch in about 36 hours at 78°F. The fry require infusoria for the first week.

Hemigrammus armstrongi is a **pathological variety of** *H. rodwayi.*

Hemigrammus caudovittatus Ahl

[cow'-do-vit-tay'-tus: *caudo* = tail; *vittatus* = striped]

Hemigrammus caudovittatus Ahl, Zool. Anz., 58(11,12):360, 1924 (type locality, Buenos Aires)

RANGE: Buenos Aires.

SIZE: 4 inches; breeding size 3 inches.

TEMPERAMENT: This species is somewhat vicious and is not suitable in a community tank since it attacks the smaller fishes. The female must be kept separated from the male or she may kill him.

TEMPERATURE REQUIREMENTS: Does well at temperatures from 65 to 90°F. Optimum breeding temperatures from 72 to 80°F.

SEX DIFFERENCES: The fullness of body of the female swollen with eggs is the best basis for recognition of sex.

COUNTS: Dorsal 11; anal 24 to 26; scales 32 or 33.

This interesting species is easy to breed. It presents much the same problem in breeding as does the Siamese fighting fish (page 532). The sexes must be kept separate until breeding time or the female (this is rather odd!) will tear the male apart. Not uncommonly the male is killed in this one-sided battle, as he never seems to fight back. The breeding fish have enormous appetites, which can only be satisfied with clumps of *Tubifex*, strips of beef, or fish.

A large breeding tank is necessary for successful spawning. A standard-size 15-gallon (12 x 12 x 24 inches) aquarium should be used, or a larger one. Plenty of vegetation should be afforded the pair, for protection not only of the eggs but also of the male fish.

Spawning is similar to other characins. When the male is ready to fertilize the eggs he gathers the courage to nudge the female a little bit. During the spawning act the eggs are sprayed out and fertilized. Since the eggs are sticky when first deposited, they are found clinging to all parts of the foliage. If left in the tank the parents will eat the eggs soon after they are laid, the female usually devouring the bulk of the spawn. Parents should be removed after spawning and the fry brought up on the standard diet of brine shrimp, *Daphnia*, and microworms.

GLOW-LIGHT TETRA / *Hemigrammus gracilis* (Reinhardt)

[gras'-i-lis: *gracilis* = slender]

Tetragonopterus gracilis Reinhardt, in Lutken, Overs. Dansk. Vid. Selsk. Forh. Kjøbenhavn, pp. 133, 141, 1874; Overs. Dansk. Vid. Selsk. Skrift. Kjøbenhavn, 12(2):217, pl. 5, fig. 16, 1875 (type locality, Lagoa Santa)

RANGE: Guianas to Rio das Velhas, Paraguay.

SIZE: 1¾ inches; breeds at 1½ inches.

TEMPERAMENT: A peaceful species that is desirable in the community aquarium.

TEMPERATURE REQUIREMENTS: 70–80°F. Optimum breeding temperature 75°F.

SEX DIFFERENCES: The female is more plump than the male, but the male is more brilliantly colored.

COUNTS: Dorsal ii,8; anal iii,16; pectoral ii,11; pelvic i,7; scales 5 + 29 + 4.

This tetra is becoming very popular. Undoubtedly this results from the new "tricks" being devised to spawn this beauty. Unlike most other characins, they do not like foliage too dense. The glow lights lock fins when spawning. They embrace or clasp in a rolling-over process which results in the extrusion of about a dozen eggs. This cavorting usually takes place among the plants; should the foliage be too dense and thick, it will push one of the fish out of position. A low rate of fertilization and consequently few young will result. An ideal spawning medium is *Nitella* or *Myriophyllum* in large, loosely woven clumps. The eggs are not very sticky and many will fall to the bottom where they will hatch if they do not fungus. It is a good idea to add 2 drops of a 5 per cent aqueous solution of Methylene Blue to each gallon of water in the propagating aquarium. It is possible to get as many as 200 fry at a time from these little fish. The free-swimming fry require infusoria, which should be cultured as soon as the parent fish have completed their spawning acts and been removed.

Lack of success in spawning these fishes is usually attributable to the inability to distinguish sex when selecting pairs. Keeping the eggs in the dark is helpful at times.

Fraser-Brunner (*The Aquarist*, p. 56, 1954) identifies the glow-light tetra as *Hemigrammus erythrozonus* (Durbin), but this species has about 2 more anal rays and 2 or 3 more scales than *H. gracilis*.

The name of this species currently is *Hemigrammus erythrozonus.*

SILVER-TIPPED TETRA / *Hemigrammus nanus* (Lutken)

[nan'-us: *nanus* = dwarf]

Tetragonopterus nanus Lutken, Overs. Dansk. Vid. Selsk. Forh. Kjøbenhavn, pp. 133, 141, 1874 (type locality, Lagoa Santa and vicinity); Overs. Dansk. Vid. Selsk. Skrift. Kjøbenhavn, 12(2):218, xiv, pl. 5, fig. 17, 1875 (Lagoa Santa)
RANGE: Southeastern Brazil in Rio das Velhas; São Francisco Basin.
SIZE: 1½ inches; breeding size 1¼ inches.
TEMPERAMENT: A peaceful and desirable species in a community tank.
TEMPERATURE REQUIREMENTS: 70–85°F. Optimum breeding temperature 75°F.
SEX DIFFERENCES: Only plumpness of the female indicates her sex. The male has more intense white tips on his fins than the female, but this feature is not easy to observe.
COUNTS: Dorsal ii,8 or 9; anal iii or iv,14 or 15; pelvic i,6; scales 4 + 30 to 32 + 4.

The silver-tipped tetra is produced in wholesale quantity by several breeders in the United States. It was once considered a difficult task to breed these fish in large numbers, but now it is a simple matter. *Soft water is required.* This water should half fill a 10-gallon breeding tank without sand but half full of bushy plants. Careful selection of two plump females and two colorful males will determine the success of the spawning attempt. A dealer or breeder has the advantage over the average hobbyist of having many more fish from which to select his breeding stock. The prime consideration in choosing the pairs is that they be of good color, in excellent health, and that the female be gravid with eggs.

They should be fed *Daphnia* continuously prior to placement in the breeding area and while in the breeding tank. Overfeeding of tropical fishes with these little water fleas is an impossibility. Pairs will spawn within 48 hours of introduction to the breeding tank.

Young fish should be fed copious amounts of infusoria, followed by brine shrimp and sifted *Daphnia*. Microworms are also very well taken by the younger fish.

The name of this species currently is *Hasemania nana*.

HEAD-AND-TAIL LIGHT / *Hemigrammus ocellifer* (Steindachner)

[os-el'-lif-er: *ocellifer* = bearing an eyelike spot]

Tetragonopterus ocellifer Steindachner, Denks. Akad. Wiss. Wien, 46:32, pl. 7, fig. 5, 1843 (type locality, Amazon River at Villa Bella and Cudajas)

RANGE: British Guiana and Amazon Basin.

SIZE: 2 inches; breeding size 1½ inches.

TEMPERAMENT: A peaceful and desirable species for the community aquarium.

TEMPERATURE REQUIREMENTS: 70–85°F. Optimum breeding temperature 75°F.

SEX DIFFERENCES: The plumpness of the female indicates her sex. The white spot in the middle of the anal fin of the male is characteristic for him, but it is not always obvious.

COUNTS: Dorsal ii,9; anal iii,20 or 21; pectoral i,11 or 12; pelvic i,7; scales 32 or 33; transverse row 9½ or 10.

This species is comparatively easy to breed. It deposits adhesive eggs in great numbers on bunches of plants or spawning grass. Most professional breeders use the new spawning grass called Spanish moss (new in the sense that now many are using it). Any type of fine-leafed plant, such as *Fontinalis, Cabomba, Myriophyllum,* and *Nitella,* is suitable for breeding purposes.

Select a very plump female and a male that has exceptionally bright color. Make sure that the male shows a tiny white dot in the middle of his anal fin prior to spawning. This "sex spot" seems to indicate the maturity and condition of the male fish.

The pair of fish should be placed in the spawning tank the evening prior to the day they are expected to spawn. Let them stay in the dark overnight, and they will usually spawn the following morning. The parents should be removed as soon after spawning as possible. Start an infusoria culture in the breeding tank and at the same time prepare a brine-shrimp hatching tray. The youngsters need brine shrimp a week after they are hatched out. It is possible to obtain 300 fry from a single spawning pair.

PRETTY TETRA / *Hemigrammus pulcher* Ladiges

[pul'-ker: *pulcher* = beautiful]

Hemigrammus pulcher Ladiges, Zool. Anz., 124:49, 1938 (type locality, Amazon between Tabatinga and Iquitos = Peruvian Amazon)

RANGE: Peruvian Amazon.

SIZE: 2 inches; breeding size 1½ inches.

TEMPERAMENT: A peaceful species that is desirable for the community tank.

TEMPERATURE REQUIREMENTS: 70–85°F.

SEX DIFFERENCES: A gravid female may be recognized by her rounded belly.

COUNTS: Dorsal ii,8 or 9; anal iii,20 or 21; pectoral i,11; pelvic i,7; scales 29 or 30; transverse row 10½.

This little beauty is becoming one of the aquarium favorites in the New York area and other localities. It does so well in the water of the New York area that serious attempts are being made to spawn it in commercial quantities, without suc-

cess as yet. The tank-raised fish of *Hemigrammus pulcher* are more intensely colored than the wild specimens, which may lose their color in captivity.

Breeding is accomplished in true characin manner; the breeding tank is heavily stocked with plants at one end, and the parents-to-be are placed in it at night. The breeding tank should be 5 gallons in size or larger and half filled with slightly hard water at a pH of 6.8. The entire success of the spawning is attributed to the selection of the female. She must be exceptionally plump and rounded or any attempt at spawning will be frustrating. The older the female the better. If a pair is put up to spawn and nothing happens within 72 hours (and the female is still as heavy as she was before), try another male.

Young fish need infusoria for 3 days after the free-swimming stage, then plenty of brine shrimp and sifted *Daphnia*.

RED- or RUMMY-NOSED CHARACIN / *Hemigrammus rhodostomus* Ahl

[ro-doss'-toe-mus: *rhod* = red; *ostomus* = mouth]

Hemigrammus rhodostomus Ahl, Wochschr. Aquar-Terrak., 21(18) no page, fig., 1924 (type locality, Pará)
RANGE: Pará, Brazil.

SIZE: 2 inches; breeding at 1½ inches.

TEMPERAMENT: A peaceful and desirable species in the community tank, but it does best alone in a well-planted aquarium.

TEMPERATURE REQUIREMENTS: 72–90°F. Optimum breeding temperature 74–80°F.

SEX DIFFERENCES: The fullness of the female indicates her sex. The female is about ½ inch longer than the male.

COUNTS: Dorsal ii,9; anal ii,13 or 14; pectoral i,12 or 13; pelvic i,7; scales 33 or 34; transverse row 9½.

Breeding the red- or rummy-nosed characin has been accomplished in a 10-gallon tank three-fourths filled with freshly conditioned tap water (pH 6.8, zero hardness) at 74°F. The entire bottom of the tank and half of the top were com-pletely stocked with *Nitella*, which grew luxuriantly.

Two males and three females were conditioned separately, each in a separate guppy tank; plenty of live *Daphnia* were available to them at all times. Late one evening they were placed in the breeding tank and were left there 24 hours. After small yellowish eggs were observed among the *Nitella*, the parents were removed. It was summer and the air temperature rose to over 90°F, causing the water to reach 79°F.

An infusoria culture was started. Since a few eggs fungused, the next eggs spawned were treated with 5 per cent Methylene Blue (2 drops per gallon). About 150 young hatched out; after 6 months only 47 fish were left. Subsequent spawnings produced a total of 490 fry, of which 187 were brought past the 6-month mark. It is significant that most of the losses were in the months of December and January when *Daphnia* were no longer available and *Tubifex* were fed to them instead.

FEATHER FIN / *Hemigrammus unilineatus* (Gill)

[u-ni-lin'-e-ay'-tus: *uni* = one; *lineatus* = lined]

Poecilurichthys unilineatus Gill, Ann. Lyc. Nat. Hist. New York, 6:60, 1858 (type locality, Trinidad)

RANGE: Trinidad, eastern Venezuela, Guianas, and Amazon Basin.

SIZE: 2 inches; breeding size 1½ inches.

TEMPERAMENT: A peaceful and desirable species in the community tank.

TEMPERATURE REQUIREMENTS: 65–90°F. Optimum breeding temperature 75°F.

SEX DIFFERENCES: The female is more plump and larger than the male.

COUNTS: Dorsal ii,8 or 9; anal iii or iv,26 to 28; pectoral i,11 or 12; pelvic i,7; scales 34; transverse row 12 or 13.

The feather fin is one of the easily spawned characins. A clean breeding tank, about the 10-gallon size, three-fourths filled with freshly conditioned water and densely stocked with fine-leafed plants or spawning grass (Spanish moss) at one end of the tank is all that is necessary. The layout of the breeding tank is simple; no sand is needed on the bottom, but the grass at one end should be in the shadows with a light over the other end.

Select the male fish for his slenderness, bright colors, and fast motion, the female for her plumpness and large size. Older females are more desirable than younger or smaller ones. The parents should be well-fed with *Daphnia*. Spawning should take place within 24 hours. The parents may devour their own eggs if there are not plenty of *Daphnia* available for the satisfaction of their appetites.

The young fry are rather fast-growing and need plenty of infusoria. If a few *Daphnia* remain after the parents have been removed, leave them in. The infusoria culture will aid the growth of *Daphnia* and the change-over from the infusoria diet to a sifted *Daphnia* diet will be more readily made by the fry; thus the faster-growing youngsters have the *Daphnia* to eat, while the smaller brothers and sisters have the infusoria upon which to feed. This double-culture method has long been used by successful European breeders.

FAMILY CHARACIDAE

GENUS *Hemiodus* Müller

[Hem'-i-oh'-dus: *hemi* = half; *odus* = tooth]

Hemiodus semitaeniatus Kner

[sem'-eye-tee'-nee-ay'-tus: *semi* = half; *taeniatus* = striped]

Hemiodus semitaeniatus Kner, Sitzb. Akad. Wiss. Wien, 30:77, 1858; Denks. Akad. Wiss. Wien, 7:154, pl. 4, fig. 7, 1859 (type locality, Rio Guaporé)

RANGE: Guianas and Amazon Basin.

SIZE: 5 inches; breeding size not known.

TEMPERAMENT: A moderately peaceful species that is desirable in the community tank.

TEMPERATURE REQUIREMENTS: 74–85°F.

SEX DIFFERENCES: No apparent differences.

COUNTS: Dorsal ii,9; anal iii,8 or 9; scales 7 + 44 or 45 + 4.

This colorful fish has not spawned in captivity. The black stripe contrasts sharply with the whitish background.

This fish is a fine jumper and must be handled with care; when netted it does not hesitate to leap out. Feeding it is no problem and it seems to adapt itself well to an aquarium environment. As it enjoys nibbling on plants in the aquarium, pieces of *Nitella* should be offered.

The name of this species currently is *Hemiodopsis semitaeniatus*.

GENUS *Hyphessobrycon* Eigenmann

[Hi'-fess-o-bry'-kon: *hyphesso* = small; *brycon* = to tear in pieces]

YELLOW TETRA / *Hyphessobrycon bifasciatus* Ellis

[bi-fas'-see-ay'-tus: *bi* = two; *fasciatus* = banded]

Hyphessobrycon bifasciatus Ellis, Ann. Carnegie Mus., 8(1):156, pl. 2, fig. 4, pl. 3, fig. 1, 1911 (type locality, southeastern Brazil)

RANGE: Southeastern Brazil.

SIZE: 2½ inches; breeding size 1½ inches.

TEMPERAMENT: A peaceful species, desirable in the community tank.

TEMPERATURE REQUIREMENTS: This species does well at a temperature from 65 to 85°F; optimum temperature 75°F.

SEX DIFFERENCES: The male is more deeply colored than the female with the two dark bands much more pronounced. The female is heavier when ripe with eggs. The male's fins are colored; the female has no color in her fins. The male has a convex anal fin, the female concave.

COUNTS: Dorsal ii,9; anal iii or iv,29 to 32; pectoral i,9 to 12; pelvic i,6; scales 34 to 36; transverse row 15.

The brass, gold, or bronze tetra is a color variety.

These characins are very easy to induce to spawn. Two pairs of fish should be conditioned, with males and females separated. The females should be introduced into a 10-gallon breeding tank which lacks gravel but which is densely stocked with bunch plants, fine-leafed plants, or the artificial spawning grasses. If the fish are properly conditioned and ripe females selected, spawning should take place within 24 hours after the introduction of the males. The temperature in the breeding tank should be raised to about 78°F after the males are introduced. A 50-watt heater will raise the temperature at the proper rate in a 10-gallon aquarium.

The youngsters and eggs should be protected from their parents, and for this reason the pairs should be removed after spawning. If the parents cannot be observed spawning, the plants should be checked for eggs periodically. If eggs are discovered they should be removed as they are found, or the parents should be taken out of the breeding tank. Infusoria should be cultured immediately after removing the parent fish. As soon as the youngsters are free-swimming they should be offered infusoria, freshly hatched brine shrimp, sifted *Daphnia*, microworms, and fine powdered dry foods, in that order.

JEWEL TETRA / *Hyphessobrycon callistus* (Boulenger)

[cal-lis'-tus: *callistus* = very beautiful]

Tetragonopterus callistus Boulenger, Boll. Mus. Zool. Anat. Comp. Univ. Torino, 15(370):2, 1900 (type locality, Río Paraguay, Mato Grosso)

RANGE: British Guiana, Brazil, to Río Paraguay.

SIZE: 1½ inches; breeding size, 1¼ inches.

TEMPERAMENT: A fairly peaceful community tank fish that may nip fins.

TEMPERATURE REQUIREMENTS: This species does well at temperatures from 70 to 85°F.

SEX DIFFERENCES: The fullness of the female indicates her sex. The male has brighter colors.

COUNTS: Dorsal ii,9; anal iii,25 to 26; pectoral i,10 or 11; pelvic i,6 or 7; scales 32 to 35; transverse row 12 or 13.

Females should be carefully selected, since some do not produce eggs every season. It has been observed that some females which spawned once never filled up with ova again. It may be that they spawn only a short period of time in their lives, quite possibly a single season. A breeding tank, 15-gallon size if possible, should be filled about 6 inches deep with freshly conditioned water. Optimum breeding temperature is 75°F; the pH should be as close to 7.0 as possible; a water hard-ness of zero is desirable. Half the tank should be stocked with spawning grass, *Myriophyllum*, *Fontinalis*, *Nitella*, or *Cabomba*. When a heavy female is found she should be placed in this tank and conditioned for a few days. Care should be exercised in selecting a male. The parents should be fed a substantial amount of *Daphnia* prior to the entrance of the male fish in the tank and *Daphnia* should be present during the spawning period. The pair will spawn by dashing into the thickets, lining up to each other, and then with a trembling motion expelling and fertilizing a dozen or so eggs.

After spawning the parent fish should be removed and the infusoria culture started. The few *Daphnia* left will propagate along with the youngsters and the newly hatched *Daphnia* will be greedily taken by the fry as they get large enough to ingest them. Since *Daphnia* eat infusoria also, lettuce or lima beans should be added to the tank for the propagation of the infusoria.

DAWN TETRA / *Hyphessobrycon eos* Durbin

[ee'-oss: *eos* = Greek goddess of dawn]

Hyphessobrycon eos Durbin, Ann. Carnegie Mus., 6:69, 1909 (type locality, between Potaro Landing and Kangaruma; Tukeit, British Guiana)

RANGE: British Guiana.

SIZE: 2 inches; breeding size $1\frac{1}{2}$ inches.

TEMPERAMENT: A moderately peaceful but active community tank fish which loses its bright coloration when frightened.

TEMPERATURE REQUIREMENTS: 70–85°F. Breeding temperature 75°F.

SEX DIFFERENCES: The female may be recognized by her plumpness, whereas the male is smaller and more brilliantly colored.

COUNTS: Dorsal ii,9; anal iii,17; pectoral i,11; pelvic i,7; scales 33; transverse row 11.

The female dawn tetra is strikingly more robust and plump than the male, and large females should be isolated and conditioned for reproduction by constant feedings of *Daphnia* and *Tubifex*. When they show signs of "bursting with eggs" they should be placed in the breeding tank which contains freshly seasoned water. One end of the breeding tank must be heavily stocked with fine-leafed bunch plants or artificial spawning grass. When males are introduced they should show immediate interest in the females. After 4 to 8 hours pairs will be seen cavorting among the thickets, during which eggs are extruded and fertilized. The parent fish eat their spawn, so they should be removed after spawning.

The young fry require plenty of infusoria, after which the standard diet of freshly hatched brine shrimp, sifted *Daphnia*, and microworms should be offered in great quantities. No snails should be present in the breeding tank, but after the young have hatched a few snails in the tank will do no harm.

This species shows magnificent breeding colors, which consist more or less of a blending of brassy colors in the fins with two extremes of yellow and red.

FIRE or FLAME TETRA; RED TETRA / *Hyphessobrycon flammeus* Myers

[flam'-me-us: *flammeus* = flame-colored]

Hyphessobrycon flammeus Myers, Fish Culturist, 4(3):330–331, 1924 (type locality, Rio de Janeiro, Brazil)

RANGE: Rio de Janeiro, Brazil.

SIZE: 2 inches; breeding size 1¼ inches.

TEMPERAMENT: A timid and peaceful species, whose coloration is pale unless placed in an aquarium free from disturbing influences. This species does not show up well in pet shops because of too many passers-by disturbing them.

TEMPERATURE REQUIREMENTS: 70–80°F.

SEX DIFFERENCES: A comparison of the anal fins of the two sexes will show that the female's is more concave than the male's, the male's having a straighter outline. A ripe female is always heavier and plumper than a male. Pelvic fins of the male are redder than the orange ones of the female.

COUNTS: Dorsal ii,9; anal iii,21 to 23; pectoral i,9; pelvic i,6; scales 34 or 35; transverse row 12 or 13.

Pairs of fish should be placed in a breeding tank abundantly stocked with fine-leafed plants or spawning grass. Conditioning of one sex may take place in the breeding tank by feeding plenty of *Daphnia* and keeping them constantly available during the actual attempts to induce the fish to spawn. The male drives the female into the dense plants, where she extrudes a few eggs which are fertilized just as the male gets alongside her. After the female extrudes each batch of eggs she dashes out of the thickets and has to be coaxed back in by the male. Usually a pair will make about 10 trips into their private nesting place. They seem to ignore the eggs until they are finished spawning, after which they will actually hunt and devour them unless there are plenty of *Daphnia* to satisfy their hunger.

The very small embryos hatch out in 72 hours at 75°F. They require copious amounts of infusoria and green water, if available. As they grow it is safe to assume that they are ready for the larger live foods in the form of freshly hatched brine shrimp, sifted *Daphnia,* and microworms. They mature in 9 months.

Hyphessobrycon heterorhabdus (Ulrey)

[het'-er-o-rab'-dus: *hetero* = different; *rhabdus* = streaked or striped]

Tetragonopterus heterorhabdus Ulrey, Ann. New York Acad. Sci., 8:286, 1895 (type locality, Pará, Brazil)

RANGE: Lower Amazon Basin of Brazil.

SIZE: 2 inches; breeding size 1½ inches.

TEMPERAMENT: A peaceful and desirable species for the community tank.

TEMPERATURE REQUIREMENTS: 70–85°F. Optimum breeding temperature 75°F.

SEX DIFFERENCES: The plumpness of the female, the curve in the anal fin of the female, and the brighter colors of the male indicate sex differentiation.

COUNTS: Dorsal ii,7 or 8; anal iii,20 or 21; pectoral i,9 to 11; pelvic i,7; scales 37; transverse row 10 or 11.

Well-distended females and colorful, active males should be placed in a tank of clear, freshly conditioned water with a pH 6.8 to 7.2 and zero hardness. Plants like *Myriophyllum, Nitella,* and artificial spawning grass should cover half the bottom of the aquarium. The tank should be so placed that the plants are in semidarkness at all times. The male chases the female into the thicket of plants where semiadhesive eggs are deposited on the leaves and stems. Immediately after they have spawned, the parents will ignore the eggs, but they will go after them as they prepare to spawn a fresh clutch. It is not known why the darkness at the bottom of the tank is beneficial, whether it makes the eggs harder to see or whether it gives the parent fish that little privacy they desire.

The parents should be removed after spawning. To ascertain whether the fish have spawned or not may necessitate lighting the bottom of the tank and looking for eggs. Methylene Blue, 2 drops of 5 per cent solution per gallon of water, should be added to the water in which the eggs are hatching. The fry need plenty of infusoria, then brine shrimp, sifted *Daphnia,* microworms, and dried foods. Snails should be added after the eggs have hatched.

Neon Tetra / *Hyphessobrycon innesi* Myers

[in'-nis-eye: named in honor of William T. Innes, bionomic ichthyologist]

Hyphessobrycon innesi Myers, Proc. Biol. Soc. Washington, 49:97, 1936 (type locality, Peruvian Amazon)

RANGE: Peruvian Amazon.

SIZE: 1½ inches; breeding size 1 inch.

TEMPERAMENT: The peaceful disposition of this species makes it one of the most desirable of community tank fishes.

TEMPERATURE REQUIREMENTS: 70–80°F.

SEX DIFFERENCES: The male is slimmer than the female. Only heavy, plump females should be selected for breeding.

COUNTS: Dorsal ii,9; anal iii,18 or 19; pelvic i,7; scales 32 to 35; transverse row 10 to 12.

The neon tetra is one of the most interesting fishes adorning the aquarium today. Its story should be of interest not only to the aquarist but to the financier also.

The story goes that the famous collector of fishes, Auguste Rabaut, sent a Frenchman, J. S. Neel, several specimens of a new and rare type of fish. Neel in turn wrote to Innes, a publisher of aquarium literature, telling him of this most beautiful fish. Innes accepted several specimens. A test run showed that there was a fantastic market for these fish. Therefore, Fred Cochu of Paramount Aquarium made arrangements with the Brazilian government for the sole rights for their importation (along with that of *Discus*). The American market was then controlled by Paramount Aquarium of New York City, and the European market by Aquarium Hamburg, of Hamburg, Germany. The price has been rather high, even in Brazil, since long treks are required to bring these fish to a place suitable for transportation to an airport. However, recently their transport has become less expensive and the savings have been passed on to the consumer. Only now are the neons becoming the medium-priced fish everyone has hoped they would be. Very few neons are tank-bred, but two successful methods of propagation have been developed, one of which is described below.

In May, 1952, G. Bartmann revealed

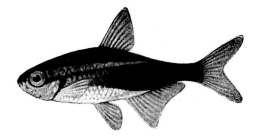

Neon tetra.

some of the secrets of the usually tight-lipped German aquarists. The Germans have been extremely successful in propagating the hard-to-breed species of fishes, but few of their techniques have been made known to the American aquarists. Bartmann's method is as follows:

An all-glass aquarium, about 12 x 10 x 10 inches, should be cleaned and sterilized. It should then be filled with 4½ inches of distilled water and be allowed to age for 2 weeks. A special solution in a glass jar should be prepared as follows: Pour some distilled water over dried oak or elm bark. Filter the solution through glass wool until it is as clear as possible. Add this solution to the aged water until a recording of 6.5 on the pH meter is reached. Sterilize a bunch of *Fontinalis* in a solution of 1 tablespoon of alum to 1.75 pints of distilled water for 5 minutes. Rinse the *Fontinalis* and place in the center of the breeding tank, leaving space for

the fish to swim freely. Maintain a temperature of 73.5 to 74.0°F. Choose a fine pair of neons, over 9 months old, transferring them in a dip tube. Keep the breeding tank in subdued light. Remove the parents after spawning. Cover the tank for 24 hours so that no light or other disturbance will enter. Prepare brine shrimp to feed the youngsters 3 days after hatching. If after 4 days the parent fish have not spawned, take them out and start all over again.

Sometimes these fish show two yellowish dots on the caudal peduncle. Nigrelli claims these are manifestations of tuberculosis. The whitish discoloration often seen in the brain area of the neon has been identified as a thick mass of sporozoan cysts; *Plistophora* is the guilty sporozoan. It causes tissue degeneration, for which there is no known treatment. Neon diseases are discussed on pages 135 and 136.

The name of this species currently is *Paracheirodon innesi*.

LEMON TETRA / *Hyphessobrycon pulchripinnis* Ahl

[pul′-kri-pin′-nis: *pulchri* = beautiful; *pinnis* = fin]

Hyphessobrycon pulchripinnis Ahl, Zool. Anz., 120:235–236, 1937 (type locality, Amazon Basin)

RANGE: Amazon Basin.

SIZE: 1¾ inches; breeding size 1½ inches.

TEMPERAMENT: A peaceful and mild species, thus a good community tank fish.

TEMPERATURE REQUIREMENTS: 70–85°F.

SEX DIFFERENCES: The female is fully distended when she is ripe, as contrasted to the slimmer male.

COUNTS: Dorsal ii,8; anal about ii,24 to 26; scales 32 or 33.

This characin is not as new as some authors supposed. Actually it is not as colorful as many of our more popular aquarium fishes, and, for economic reasons, it is not spawned, nor imported in any large quantities. Surprisingly enough it is easy to spawn.

Pairs look for thick clumps of vegetation in the form of artificial spawning grass, bunches of *Nitella, Fontinalis,* or *Myriophyllum.* The dense roots of water hyacinths are also a good spawning medium. Very small transparent eggs are shed as the pairs squeeze through the denser parts of the foliage and vegetation, and a few eggs are fertilized. The parents eat their eggs as they fall to the bottom unless one part of the bottom of the aquarium is thickly covered with grass. This area should be shaded and without direct light at all times. The lemon tetras are induced to spawn by raising the temperature from normal (72°F) to 80°F. The young require plenty of infusoria and brine shrimp.

ROSY-FINNED TETRA / *Hyphessobrycon rosaceus* Durbin

[ro-sa'-shus: *rosaceus* = rose-colored]

Hyphessobrycon rosaceus Durbin, Ann. Carnegie Mus., 6:67, 1909 (type locality, Gluck Island and Rockstone, British Guiana)

RANGE: Lower Amazon Basin and British Guiana.

SIZE: 1¾ inches; breeding at 1½ inches.

TEMPERAMENT: This peaceful species is desirable as a community tank fish.

TEMPERATURE REQUIREMENTS: 70–85°F.

SEX DIFFERENCES: The male has a longer dorsal fin than the female but lacks a red tip to his dorsal fin which the female possesses. The anal fin of the male is also a sure key to sex differentiation as it too is longer and more concave in shape than the female's.

COUNTS: Dorsal ii,9; anal ii,24 to 26; pectoral i,10; pelvic i,7; scales 33, transverse row 12.

It is not difficult to breed this species if one has patience. A 7- to 10-gallon or a larger tank should be half filled with clear, freshly conditioned water. The end of the tank toward the light should be without vegetation, whereas the other end should be thick with fine-leafed plants or artificial spawning grasses. A pair of carefully selected fish should be introduced into the breeding tank. The criteria for selection should be fullness and youth of the female, activity and color of the male. The temperature should be raised to 80°F in the breeding tank to induce spawning.

The fish usually spawn within 72 hours after they are introduced into the breeding tank. They should be removed after spawning, at which time an infusoria culture should be started in the breeding tank. The fry hatch in 72 hours at the higher temperature and require plenty of infusoria. Freshly hatched brine shrimp should be fed these youngsters after a week of free swimming. Maintain the temperature at 80° until they are able to take finely sifted *Daphnia*.

The name of this species currently is *Hyphessobrycon bentosi rosaceus*.

H. rosaceus Durbin. Male has longer dorsal fin.

Hyphessobrycon scholzei Ahl

[shoal'-zee-eye: named in honor of the aquarist P. N. Scholze]

Hyphessobrycon scholzei Ahl, Sitzb. Gesell. Nat. Freunde, p. 445, April, 1937 (type locality, Amazon Basin at Pará)

RANGE: Amazon Basin.

SIZE: 3 inches; breeding at 2 inches.

TEMPERAMENT: A moderately peaceful but actively swimming species which should be kept with faster-swimming fishes, because it has a tendency to nip the fins of less active fishes.

TEMPERATURE REQUIREMENTS: 65–90°F.

SEX DIFFERENCES: The female when ripe develops a dark area near her vent; otherwise, she may be distinguished by her fullness resulting from mature eggs.

COUNTS: Dorsal 11; anal 25 or 26; scales 32 or 33.

This easily bred characin deposits its eggs on fine-leafed plants whenever given the opportunity. It is a simple matter to select a good pair of fish, condition them for a few days, and place them in the spawning tank, one side of which should be heavily stocked with bunches of fine-leafed plants or artificial spawning grasses. The male may nip the female if she does not spawn. In this event they should be separated.

This species is now propagated in enormous quantities in pools all year round in the South, and during the summer months in the northern part of the country. Their prolificacy has made them reasonably inexpensive, and nearly every aquarist has had a pair at one time or another. They seem to be fashionable one year and unfashionable the next, probably because they are bred one year, then left alone the following because some dealers were unable to dispose of the previous year's spawn.

The fry need an abundance of infusoria for 3 or 4 days after hatching, then freshly hatched brine shrimp, microworms, or chopped sand worms.

Hyphessobrycon ulreyi (Boulenger)

[ul′-ray-eye: named in honor of the biologist Albert B. Ulrey]

Tetragonopterus ulreyi Boulenger, Proc. Zool. Soc. London, p. 529, 1895 (type locality, Descalvados, Mato Grosso)

RANGE: Paraguay Basin.

SIZE: 2 inches; breeding size, 1½ inches.

TEMPERAMENT: A peaceful and desirable species for the community aquarium.

TEMPERATURE REQUIREMENTS: Does well at temperatures from 70 to 85°F.

SEX DIFFERENCES: Plumpness of the female indicates her sex.

COUNTS: Dorsal ii,8; anal iii,20 to 22; scales 32 to 33; transverse row 10.

The breeding of this species has been somewhat of a problem, no doubt for two significant reasons. First, the identification of living specimens is practically impossible because they look so much like *Hyphessobrycon heterorhabdus* that any superficial identification is without value. Second, since even *H. heterorhabdus* is difficult to induce to spawn, no doubt mixing of species has occurred. Nevertheless, aquarists should continue trying to spawn these fishes and perhaps one day they will succeed. Then, in order properly to identify fishes after they have spawned, some should be preserved and sent to an expert taxonomic ichthyologist for positive identification. The help of aquarists is much needed here.

The name of this species currently is *Hemigrammus ulreyi*.

GENUS *Laemolyta* Cope

[Lee'-mo-ly'-ta: *laemo* = throat; *lyta* = little]

Laemolyta taeniatus (Kner)

[tee'-nee-ay'-tus: *taeniatus* = striped]

Schizodon taeniatus Kner, Denks. Akad. Wiss. Wien, 17:159, pl. 5, fig. 10, 1859 (type locality, Rio Guaporé; Barra do Rio Negro)

RANGE: Rio Negro and Amazon Basins, Brazil.

SIZE: 9 inches; breeding size unknown.

TEMPERAMENT: A peaceful, mild-mannered species suitable for the community aquarium.

TEMPERATURE REQUIREMENTS: 72–85°F.

SEX DIFFERENCES: Unknown.

COUNTS: Dorsal ii,10; anal ii,8; pectoral i,11 or 12; pelvic i,8 or 9; scales 5 or 5½ + 43 to 45 + 4 or 5.

This fish has not been spawned in captivity. The area above the lateral line is dark aquamarine, with the belly under the lateral line silvery green. The lateral line is accentuated with a broad black band that extends forward through the eye. The adipose fin is blackish, and the body may have dark cross bars.

GENUS *Lebiasina* Cuvier and Valenciennes

[Lee'-bi-a-sine'-a: *lebias* = a kind of fish suitable for cooking in a kettle; *ina* denotes likeness]

TWO-SPOTTED LEBIASINA / *Lebiasina bimaculata* Cuvier and Valenciennes

[by-mack'-you-lay'-ta: *bi* = two; *maculata* = spotted]

Lebiasina bimaculata Cuvier and Valenciennes, Histoire naturelle des poissons, 19:531, pl. 587, 1846 (type locality, Rio Rimac, near Lima, Peru)

RANGE: Western slopes of Peru and Ecuador.

SIZE: 5 inches; breeding size not observed.

TEMPERAMENT: A predaceous species not suitable for the community tank.

TEMPERATURE REQUIREMENTS: 72–85°F.

SEX DIFFERENCES: Not known.

COUNTS: Dorsal ii,8; anal iii,9; pectoral i,13; pelvic i,7; scales 30 or 31, transverse row 7.

This fish has not been bred in captivity. It is not common in aquaria in the United States and there is not much hope that it will ever become popular. The over-all body color is much like the golden tetra with the back olive and the sides golden or brassy. Each scale has a dark tip, giving the fish a reticulated appearance. There are two bold spots, purple-black in color, one located on the caudal peduncle, the other just above the pectoral-fin base. All fins are blushed with blue. All in all, this species is an attractive one but owing to its pugnacity, scarcity, and cost it is not widely distributed.

Genus *Leporinus* **Agassiz**

[Lep′-o-rin′-us: *lepor* = rabbit; *"rinus"* = snout]

Black-banded Leporinus / *Leporinus fasciatus* (Bloch)

[fas′-see-ay′-tus: *fasciatus* = banded]

Salmo fasciatus Bloch, Ichthyologie, histoire naturelle . . . poissons, 11:17, pl. 379, 1797 (type locality, Surinam)

RANGE: Amazon to the Apure Basin and the Guianas.

SIZE: 8 inches (larger in natural habitat); breeding size not known.

TEMPERAMENT: A peaceful species that makes a good community tank fish when only a few inches long.

TEMPERATURE REQUIREMENTS: 72–85°F.

SEX DIFFERENCES: None apparent.

COUNTS: Dorsal ii,10; anal ii or iii,8; pectoral i,15 or 16; pelvic i,9; scales 8 + 41 or 42 + 5.

Although this species has never been bred, it is popular whenever available. Not many are imported except when they are accidentally trapped with other species. It is hardy and ships well.

The main part of the diet is vegetable, since it requires algae or greens in the form of *Nitella*, duckweed, lettuce, or spinach. Commercial molly food is also good for this species.

It gives the impression of being a slow-moving species and maintaining a position much like that of the headstanders, but it is capable of jumping long distances and the aquarium should be covered at all times.

The young fish are yellowish-red, turning orange as they grow older. The baby fish manifest only 5 vertical bars but after about a year the first band splits in two; every half-year or so this happens again until the 5 bands become 10. The age of the specimen can usually be judged by the number of bands on its body. It takes about three years for a complete change to the adult color pattern.

Leporinus friderici (Bloch)

[frid'-er-i-see: named in honor of an unknown Mr. Frederic]

Salmo friderici Bloch, Ichthyologie, histoire naturelle . . . poissons, 11:75, pl. 378, 1797 (type locality, Surinam)

RANGE: Guianas; Apure, Orinoco, Amazon, and La Plata Rivers of South America.

SIZE: 12 inches; breeding size not known.

TEMPERAMENT: A peaceful and desirable community tank fish when only a few inches long.

TEMPERATURE REQUIREMENTS: 72–85°F.

SEX DIFFERENCES: None apparent.

COUNTS: Dorsal ii,10; anal ii,8 or 9; pectoral i,15 or 16; pelvic i,8; scales $5\frac{1}{2}$ + 36 to 39 + 4 or 5.

Since this fish has never been bred, it is worth the efforts of some ambitious aquarist to try to induce it to spawn.

BLACK-LINED LEPORINUS / *Leporinus melanopleura* Günther

[mel'-an-o-ploo'-rah: *melano* = black; *pleura* = side]

Leporinus melanopleura Günther, Catalogue of the Fishes in the British Museum, 5:310, 1864 (type locality, Baía; Cipo River, Brazil)

RANGE: Brazil.

SIZE: 10 inches; breeding size not known.

TEMPERAMENT: A peaceful and desirable species for the community aquarium.

TEMPERATURE REQUIREMENTS: 72–85°F.

SEX DIFFERENCES: None apparent.

COUNTS: Dorsal 12; anal 11; pelvic 10; scales 37.

This fish has never been bred. Its color is quite attractive. As would be surmised from the name, it is darker than other *Leporinus*. The darkest area is on the back while the color lightens as it reaches the silvery-gray belly. A dark band runs from the snout to the tail. The dark brown back has a reddish tinge; the upper sides are somewhat dark barred; periodically these colors become quite intense, usually in May or early June.

GENUS *Metynnis* Cope

[Me-tin'-iss: *met* = with; *hynnis* = plowshare]

SPOTTED METYNNIS / *Metynnis maculatus* (Kner)

[mack'-u-lay'-tus: *maculatus* = spotted]

Myletes maculatus Kner, Denks. Akad. Wiss. Wien, 18:26, pl. 2, fig. 5, 1860 (type locality, Rio Guaporé)

RANGE: Guianas; Amazon and Paraguay Basins.

SIZE: 8 inches; breeding size not known.

TEMPERAMENT: A moderately peaceful species for its size, which may be kept in a community tank but not with small fish.

TEMPERATURE REQUIREMENTS: 72–85°F.

SEX DIFFERENCES: None apparent.

COUNTS: Dorsal ii,15 or 16; anal iii,34 to 36; pectoral i,13; pelvic i,6; scales very fine; ventral serrae 24 to 26 + 7 to 11.

In full color its general shade would be a yellowish green. The back is darker than the rest of the body and the ventral side of the fish is silvery. The scales are extremely small for such a large fish.

If the spotted *Metynnis* is maintained in the community aquarium it should be offered plenty of live foods mixed with a vegetable diet.

Metynnis schreitmulleri Ahl (*Mitth. Zool. Mus. Berlin*, 11:19, 1923, type locality, Amazon) appears to be a synonym of this species. The identification of the numerous species of this genus is difficult and depends largely on obtaining extensive data as to the number of fin rays and scales. For interpretation of these counts, they must be arranged in statistical tables.

Metynnis roosevelti Eigenmann

[roos'-e-velt-eye: named in honor of Theodore Roosevelt]

Metynnis roosevelti Eigenmann, Ann. Carnegie Mus:, 9:268, pl. 55, 1915 (type locality, Santarém, Bastos, Manaus)

RANGE: Amazon Basin.

SIZE: 6 inches; breeding size not known.

TEMPERAMENT: A moderately peaceful species that may be kept with any fish over 2 inches long.

TEMPERATURE REQUIREMENTS: 72–85°F.

SEX DIFFERENCES: None apparent.

COUNTS: Dorsal ii,13 to 15; anal iv,34 to 39; pectoral i,14; pelvic i,5; scales, very fine; ventral serrae 22 or 23 + 9 or 10.

This fish has never been bred and not much is known about its habits. It is a fairly abundant and hardy species. It ships well. Some specimens have been known to live for seven or eight years.

From a casual look at its mouth, one would conclude that this fish is predominantly a carnivorous animal, living on the flesh of other animals. Such is not the case, however, as it requires an abundance of vegetation in its diet. *Vallisneria* and *Sagittaria* are its favorites; it is practically impossible to maintain both *Vallisneria* and *Metynnis* in the same aquarium. Spinach, lettuce, and duckweed make fairly good substitutes for its favorite plants.

The name of this species currently is *Metynnis lippincottianus*.

GENUS *Mimagoniates* Regan

[Mi'-ma-gon-ee-a'-tease: *mima* = mimic; *goniates* = angled]

BLUE TETRA / *Mimagoniates microlepis* (Steindachner)

[my'-crow-lep'-iss: *micro* = small; *lepis* = scales]

Paragoniates microlepis Steindachner, Sitzb. Akad. Wiss. Wien, 74:33, 1876 (type locality, Rio de Janeiro, Rio Macacos)

RANGE: Rio Macacos to Iporanga, southeastern Brazil and Paraguay.

SIZE: 2½ inches; breeds at 1½ inches.

TEMPERAMENT: A peaceful, delicate fish.

TEMPERATURE REQUIREMENTS: It requires temperatures of 72 to 79°F; optimum 76°F.

SEX DIFFERENCES: The fullness of the female and the pointed dorsal fin of the male are clues to sexual distinction. The dorsal fin of the female is rounded.

COUNTS: Dorsal ii,8; anal iii,28 to 30; pectoral i,10; pelvic i,6; scales 41 to 44; transverse row 13 or 14.

Several individuals of this species were placed in a 20-gallon aquarium which was in direct sunlight during the major part of the day. The entire bottom and sides of the aquarium were thick with algae and the water was so green that it was impossible to see through it. The main purpose of this aquarium was to supply green water for newborn fry. After several months it was noticed that many more fish were in the tank than the original two or three. Great care was exercised in removing the small fish and 38 blue tetras were taken out. At first glance they looked like the young of the pearl danio, *Brachydanio albolineatus* (page 269), but as soon as the adipose fin was spotted a great interest was taken in the young specimens and they were nurtured. They were placed in a different aquarium and soon all perished. The parent fish did very well in the environment just described and when they were removed and observed in the net, they had a brilliant bluish sheen like the pearl danio.

German writers claim that these fish spawn like *Astyanax* (Ahl and Arnold, *Fremdländische Susswasserfische*, p. 100, 1936). Hermann Meinken (*The Aquarist*, October, 1950) says that though *Mimagoniates* has reproductive mechanisms similar to *Corynopoma*, the female usually places eggs on plants before the male fertilizes them. He claims that when they breed this way few eggs hatch.

Mimagoniates barberi Regan (*Ann. Mag. Nat. Hist.*, (7)19:402, 1907, type locality, Estacion Caballero, Paraguay) is a synonym of this species.

The name of this species currently is *Coelurichthys microlepis*.

GENUS *Moenkhausia* Eigenmann

[Monk-house'-i-a: named in honor of the biologist William J. Moenkhaus]

GLASS TETRA / *Moenkhausia oligolepis* (Günther)

[ol'-ee-go-lep'is: *oligo* = few; *lepis* = scales]

Tetragonopterus oligolepis Günther, Catalogue of the Fishes in the British Museum, 5:327, 1864 (type locality, British Guiana)

RANGE: Brazilian Amazon north to the Guianas.

SIZE: 4 inches; breeds at 3 inches.

TEMPERAMENT: The smaller sizes are mild-mannered, but larger ones will eat small fishes. They are useful in the larger community tank.

TEMPERATURE REQUIREMENTS: 70–85°F.

SEX DIFFERENCES: Only the fullness of the female indicates her sex.

COUNTS: Dorsal ii,9; anal iii,23 or 24; pectoral i,13 or 14; pelvic i,6; scales 5 + 28 to 30 + 4 or 5.

The great size, the amount of food consumed, and the absence of intense colors probably account for the lack of enthusiasm shown for this species. During the past 10 years few *Moenkhausia oligolepis* have been seen in pet shops although this fish was at one time a big import from Europe.

Breeding is easy, in typical characin style. Successful conditioning consists of daily feedings of raw beef scraps, pieces of cooked chicken, raw or cooked fishes, shrimps that have been carefully cut into small pieces, *Tubifex*, and dry food. It is of the utmost importance that the conditioning be continued for at least 2 weeks; otherwise, the female will not develop ripened ova and the male will not be strong enough for successful spawning.

The male nudges the female into thick clumps of spawning grass, where they assume a side-by-side position. The male then begins rapid undulating motions, soon followed by the female. She extrudes a dozen or more eggs, which are fertilized by the male as they are expelled. After the spawning act she rapidly leaves the spawning site, with the male in pursuit. Parent fish should be removed after spawning and rested at least 60 days before they are bred again. The eggs, which may run in the hundreds, adhere to the plants and hatch in 72 hours at 75°F. The newly hatched fry require infusoria, brine shrimp, egg infusion, and microworms in copious amounts.

Moenkhausia pittieri Eigenmann

[pete'-tea-ay'-eye: named in honor of the naturalist Henri Pittier]

Moenkhausia pittieri Eigenmann, Indiana U. Stud., 7(44):10, pl. 3, 1920 (type locality, Concejo, Rio Tiquirito; Rio Bue, Maracay, Venezuela)

RANGE: Lake Valencia Basin, Venezuela.

SIZE: 2½ inches; breeds at 2 inches.

TEMPERAMENT: A moderately peaceful fish for a community tank.

TEMPERATURE REQUIREMENTS: 70–85°F.

SEX DIFFERENCES: The male has longer, more pointed and flowing dorsal and anal fins. The female, when ripe with eggs, is very swollen and heavy. The male maintains his slender appearance at all times.

COUNTS: Dorsal ii,9; anal iii,24 to 27; scales 7 + 35 + 6.

This species is closely related to *Moenkhausia oligolepis*, both in structure and in habits. Although not popular in the United States, owing to its lack of bright colors, it is a favorite of the Germans and Dutch, probably because it is fairly challenging to breed and is very graceful and hardy.

Breeding takes place in dense vegetation where the eggs are fertilized as they are extruded. Nearly 400 eggs are laid at a spawning. Given reasonable treatment, the great majority will hatch. Failure in spawning this fish results from mismatching of pairs. Fish of the same age and size should be selected. Conditioning should be prolonged and thorough, with sustained feedings of scraped beef, chicken, small fishes if possible, and *Tubifex*. Dried foods, though taken liberally, are not favorable for conditioning unless they are substantially supplemented with the live foods. The parents should be removed after spawning.

The fairly large eggs, easily visible with top light, hatch in a few days, depending upon the temperature. Sometimes they hatch a day earlier when the temperature is raised to 80°F from the optimum breeding temperature of 74°F. This shortened period of incubation results in fewer eggs being lost to active fungi and bacteria.

GENUS *Mylossoma* Eigenmann and Kennedy

[My′-los-so′-ma: *mylos* = millstone; *soma* = body]

GOLDEN MYLOSSOMA / *Mylossoma aureum* (Agassiz)

[our′-ee-um: *aureum* = golden]

Myletes aureus Agassiz, in Spix and Agassiz, Selecta genera et species piscium . . . Brasiliam, p. 74, *Tetragonopterus aureus* on pl. 31, 1829 (type locality, rivers of equatorial Brazil)

RANGE: Orinoco to La Plata Rivers.

SIZE: 4 inches; breeds at 3 inches, since mature females have been observed at that size.

TEMPERAMENT: A desirable species in a community tank containing large fishes.

TEMPERATURE REQUIREMENTS: This fish thrives at 74°F.

SEX DIFFERENCES: The mature female has a larger abdomen than the male.

COUNTS: Dorsal ii,14 to 16; anal iii or iv,28 to 34; pectoral i,16 to 18; pelvic i,6; scales very fine; ventral serrae 27 to 33 + 10 to 15.

This fish has not been bred and we have no record of successful spawning in an aquarium.

GENUS *Nannaethiops* Günther

[Nann-ee'-thee-ops: *nann* = dwarf; *aethi* = unusual; *ops* = appearance]

ONE-STRIPED AFRICAN CHARACIN / *Nannaethiops unitaeniatus* Günther

[you-ni-tea'-nee-ay'-tus: *uni* = one; *taeniatus* = striped]

Nannaethiops unitaeniatus Günther, Proc. Zool. Soc. London, p. 670, pl. 65, fig. C, 1871 (type locality, Gabon, Africa)

RANGE: Africa in Nile, Congo, and Niger Rivers.

SIZE: 3 inches; breeds at 2 inches.

TEMPERAMENT: An active but peaceful species, well suited for the community aquarium.

TEMPERATURE REQUIREMENTS: 75–85°F.

SEX DIFFERENCES: The female is much rounder than the male, while the male has the intense color. The lower half of the caudal fin becomes very bright on the male during breeding season.

COUNTS: Dorsal iii,10 to 12; anal iv,7; scales 5 + 35 + 7.

Not too many of the popular fishes come from Africa. This is partly due to the lack of sufficient desirable fish in any single location, coupled with the greater distance from the United States.

Since breeding this attractive fish is not too difficult, more advanced aquarists should be encouraged to spawn it. Breeding occurs in a large aquarium heavily stocked with spawning grass (*Nitella, Cabomba, Myriophyllum,* or Spanish moss). The female lays about 500 adhesive eggs which hatch about 48 hours later at 80°F. The parents should be removed.

This interesting African fish is exceptionally hardy and eats dry as well as live foods, both of which keep it active and healthy.

GENUS *Nannostomus* Günther

[Nan'-no-sto'-mus: *nann* = small; *stomus* = mouth]

GOLDEN PENCILFISH / *Nannostomus anomalus* Steindachner

[a-nom'-a-lus: *anomalus* = exceptional or irregular]

Nannostomus anomalus Steindachner, Sitzb. Akad. Wiss. Wien, 74:81, 1876 (type locality, mouth of Rio Negro; Amazon at Óbidos)

RANGE: Amazon and Rio Negro Basins.
SIZE: 2 inches; breeding size 1¼ inches.
TEMPERAMENT: A peaceful and shy species.
TEMPERATURE REQUIREMENTS: 75–85°F.
SEX DIFFERENCES: The male has white tips on his pelvic, anal, and caudal fins.
COUNTS: Dorsal ii,8; anal iii,8 or 9; pectoral i,10 or 11; pelvic i,7; scales 25; transverse row 7.

This species has been bred in quantity by aquarists. Systems of breeding cover many techniques, which indicates that it is easy to breed. The common technique is to select a choice pair and place it in a half-filled aquarium with freshly conditioned water at a pH of 6.8 to 7.2, using soft water if possible. Temperature should be near 78°F. Spanish moss and *Nitella* seem to be the best plants. The eggs are deposited on the plants, and after 48 hours of incubation the young hatch and soon may be seen clinging to all parts of the glass and whatever else may be in the tank (like heaters or thermometers). After a week the fry are free-swimming and should be offered quantities of infusoria, the culture of which should be started as soon as the eggs are laid. Remove the parents after spawning and thin out the young after 2 weeks.

In a community aquarium large fishes of other species will eat the food before this meek fish gets a chance at it.

The name of this species currently is *Nannostomus beckfordi.*

BROWN PENCILFISH / *Nannostomus aripirangensis* Meinken

[a′-ri-pir′-an-gen′-sis: named after an island in the lower Amazon]

Nannostomus aripirangensis Meinken, Wochschr. Aquar.-Terrak., p. 553, 1931 (type locality, Aripiranga Island, lower Amazon)

RANGE: Lower Amazon.

SIZE: 2 inches; breeds at 1¼ inches.

TEMPERAMENT: A peaceful species, suitable for the community tank.

TEMPERATURE REQUIREMENTS: 70–87°F.

SEX DIFFERENCES: The male has a slight blue tinge and red blush to his pelvic fins. The female's pelvic fins are clear.

COUNTS: Dorsal ii,9; anal iii,7 to 9; scales 23 or 24; transverse row 5 or 6.

This small species is attractive and much in demand when available. Viewing them from the top, in large tubs, one gets the impression that little chocolate-colored cigars are moving about. They are perfectly camouflaged among scattered twigs. The back is a chocolate brown and the underside silvery white. An attractive stripe runs from the snout, through the eye, thence along the lateral line, right through the tail fin. The upper margin of this stripe is beautifully traced with a fine golden line. The dorsal and caudal fins have brilliant red spots on them, and the anal fin is red with a dark margin.

In breeding the brown pencilfish, two males should be used for a single female. An aquarium of about 5-gallon capacity should be filled with old, slightly acid water. The females should be put into the breeding tank first, after having been thoroughly conditioned on newly hatched brine shrimp. The males may be introduced a few days later. Females will deposit one or two eggs at a time upon fine spawning grass, at which moment the males will fertilize them. It is best to remove the breeders after spawning has been completed. Seldom are more than 100 eggs produced from a community spawning.

The name of this species currently is *Nannostomus beckfordi*.

ONE-LINED PENCILFISH / *Nannostomus marginatus* Eigenmann

[mar'-gi-na'-tus: *margin* = border or edge; *atus* = suffix meaning provided with]

Nannostomus marginatus Eigenmann, Ann. Carnegie Mus., 6(1):41, 1909 (type locality, British Guiana)

RANGE: British Guiana.

SIZE: 1½ inches; breeds at 1¼ inches.

TEMPERAMENT: A peaceful species, desirable in the community aquarium.

TEMPERATURE REQUIREMENTS: 75–85°F.

SEX DIFFERENCES: The dark bands are more prominent on the male than on the female and the female is more robust.

COUNTS: Dorsal ii,8; anal iii,9; pectoral i,11; pelvic i,8; scales 20; transverse row 6½ or 7.

This species once was called simply the pencilfish. It is becoming more popular, probably because of successful spawning by professional breeders. Breeding will occur in a large aquarium (about 10 gallons) with freshly conditioned water. Plenty of *Nitella* or spawning grass should be used. Very colorful males and extraordinarily plump females should be selected for spawning. A pair will enter the thickets and deposit their eggs near the surface in the thicker parts of the plants. Some of the eggs float. The parents are not likely to eat the eggs. Hatching time is 72 hours at 78°F.

The young require the usual diet of infusoria and brine shrimp for a long time, as they are very small and their mouths will not open wide enough for any larger particles of food.

This fish lacks an adipose fin.

FAMILY CHARACIDAE

GENUS *Neolebias* Steindachner

[Nee'-o-leeb'-e-as: *neo* = new; *lebias* = a kind of fish]

Neolebias ansorgei Boulenger

[an-sorg'-ee-eye: named in honor of W. J. Ansorge, the collector]

Neolebias ansorgei Boulenger, Ann. Mus. Congo, Zool., 2(3):8, pl. 17, fig. 2, 1912 (type locality, marshes near Luculla River, Luali River, Chiloango, Africa)

RANGE: West Africa.

SIZE: 2 inches; breeds at 1½ inches.

TEMPERAMENT: A shy, peaceful species, requiring a densely planted aquarium.

TEMPERATURE REQUIREMENTS: 80–85°F.

SEX DIFFERENCES: The male is slightly more colorful than the female; the female's heaviness is also a clue to her sex.

COUNTS: Dorsal iii,8; anal iii,6; pectoral about i,12; pelvic about i,7; scales 29 to 32; transverse scales 9 or 10.

This species is so timid and easily frightened that it should be placed in a small aquarium as high above the floor of the fishhouse as possible, which gives it a higher water temperature and more pri-

vacy. The aquarium should be heavily stocked with *Nitella* and *Cabomba*.

An inquisitive friend happened to spy these little fish and thought that the author was hiding something. Looking in, he saw that the tank was loaded with youngsters. Nothing would convince this friend that the spawning was accidental. Later, in a controlled situation, pairs were observed going to a very heavily stocked corner of the aquarium and depositing eggs on the vegetation. The slightly hard water had a temperature of 82°F and a pH of 6.8. The fry hatched in 52 hours. The parents seemed to ignore the eggs and did not go after the young until they were free-swimming. Parents were conditioned on *Daphnia*, microworms, and *Tubifex*, in addition to their regular diet. The young were matured on infusoria, brine shrimp, and sifted *Daphnia*.

GENUS *Phago* Günther

[Fay'-go: *phago* = to eat]

PIKE CHARACIN / *Phago maculatus* Ahl

[mack'-u-lay'-tus: *maculatus* = spotted]

Phago maculatus Ahl, Blät. Aquar.-Terrak., p. 23, 1922 (type locality, Niger River)

RANGE: West Africa in Niger River.

SIZE: 8 inches; breeding not observed.

TEMPERAMENT: A predaceous species not suitable for the community tank.

TEMPERATURE REQUIREMENTS: 72–82°F.

SEX DIFFERENCES: None known.

COUNTS: Dorsal ii,9 to 11; anal iii,8 to 9; scales 1½ + 47 or 48 + 2½ or 3½.

There are few kinds of fishes as vicious as this one. The *Betta* is an angel by comparison. The well-developed jaws and teeth of this fish are there for a purpose. With this carnivorous "hardware" it refuses all types of dry foods but eagerly accepts fishes of all sizes, dead or alive, bits of meat, and even some clams now and then. Its growth is rapid and in direct proportion to the size of the aquarium in which it is maintained and the amounts of fresh live food available. The minimum requirement is a 6- to 7-gallon aquarium, kept covered.

The coloring of the fish is drab. The back is olive, becoming silvery on the lower sides and the belly. A series of irregularly shaped spots forms an attractive longitudinal stripe. The dorsal and caudal fins are striped, with other fins brownish.

GENUS *Phenacogrammus* Eigenmann

[Feen'-a-ko-gram'-us: *phenaco* = an impostor; *grammus* = line]

This genus is distinguished from *Micralestes* on the basis of an interrupted lateral line.

LUFUNDI (native name); CONGO TETRA or CHARACIN /
Phenacogrammus interruptus (Boulenger)

[in'-ter-rupp'-tus: *inter* = between; *ruptus* = a break]

Micralestes interruptus Boulenger, Ann. Mus. Congo, Zool., 1:88, pl. 36, fig. 6, 1899 (type locality, Stanley pool, upper Congo)

RANGE: Upper Congo Basin, Africa.

SIZE: 3 inches; breeding size not known.

TEMPERAMENT: A species sufficiently peaceful for the home aquarium, although it may bite small fishes.

TEMPERATURE REQUIREMENTS: 72–85°F.

SEX DIFFERENCES: The fullness of the mature female indicates her sex.

COUNTS: Dorsal ii,8; anal iv,17 or 18; scales 21 to 23.

The following account of the breeding of this species appeared in *Datz* by E. Meder as translated by William Vorderwinkler for *Tropical Fish Hobbyist,* 2(1):9–10, September–October, 1953.

"The congo tetra needs plenty of elbow-room. Only when they are provided with this do the males develop their full beauty. A top-lighted tank is preferable; in no case should the light be directed at the front or shining through the rear glass. The fish always finds itself comfortable in a subdued, indirect light. The composition of the water is also important. The fish retains its health only in a lightly amber-

Hemigrammopetersius caudalis, African tetra related to *Phenacogrammus interruptus.*

colored water which has been filtered through peat-moss; coconut shells also lend this amber coloring to the water, and also provide the fish with convenient hiding-places. In any other water, the fry are very sensitive to fungus infections. The native waters of this fish are soft, and one should not allow the hardness to go higher than 6 degrees. The best temperatures lie between 74 and 78 degrees F. Foods do not present a problem. They enjoy *Daphnia* but also take *Enchytrae* and *Tubifex.* The surface is watched constantly, and any floating insects, such as freshly shed mealworms or the larvae of **wax-moths,** are eagerly consumed. Dried foods may also be fed, as well as tiny bits of beef-heart.

"I have spawned *Micralestes* with an addition of tannic acid, ($\frac{1}{10}$ grains to 10 liters of water). The breeding pair should not be introduced into the tank until the second or third day after the addition of the tannic acid. If they are introduced immediately, they are in great danger of

suffocation by the action of the acid upon the gills. Tannic acid has been found to be preferable; at least the water is made practically free of all bacteria and infusoria for a time. I have already stated in previous articles that pH value has only an indirect importance. The specific effect of the tannic acid, not the concentration of hydrogen ions, is what makes the difference. It is therefore assumed that the discussions over pH values will slowly quiet down. The importance of organic acids, most of all tannic acid, is not only that there is a strong bactericidal action, but that there is also a formation of non-soluble calcium salts which have no further effect on the fish, eggs, sperm and later on, the fry. In this way, tannic acid is proving to be the key to success in the breeding of fishes which are sensitive to bacteria and infusoria. Our Dutch friends have been telling me this for a long time.

"A more popular method seems to be the use of water which has been filtered through peat-moss; here the effect is achieved with the extracted substances from peat-moss, rather than the addition of tannic acid. I have also spawned the *Micralestes* in this type of water with great success.

"It is becoming increasingly evident that the peat-moss filter has become a standby for the modern aquarist. It has become as important as the addition of salt (a heaping teaspoonful to 10 liters of water) in the care and breeding of *Aphyosemion, Cynolebias* and especially *Telmatherina*. These beautiful creatures kept dying in our tanks solely because, knowingly or unknowingly, the importance of an addition of salt was kept quiet. Although I was once opposed to adding salt

to aquarium water, experience has taught me differently. It was without doubt to the credit of Mr. Tushe that we old breeders were shown the wisdom of this practice. The action of salt seems to result in an increase of mucous secretion, thereby inhibiting bacterial action on the gills. As a result, 'Aphyosemion disease' has been eliminated, and *Saprolegnia* infections have also stopped.

"Although these findings have been known to some for a long time, they cannot be reiterated often enough.

"In closing, I hope that *Micralestes interruptus* has the same success which has been won by *Hyphessobrycon innesi.*"

Phenacogrammus interruptus.

GENUS *Phoxinopsis* Regan

[Fox'-i-nop'-sis: *phoxin* = an unknown kind of riverfish; *opsis* = appearance]

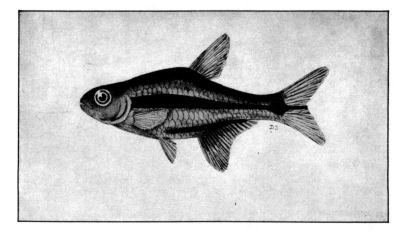

Phoxinopsis typicus Regan

[typ'-i-kus: *typicus* = typical]

Phoxinopsis typicus Regan, Ann. Mag. Nat. Hist., (7)19:262, 1907 (type locality, Argentina)

RANGE: Rio de Janeiro, Argentina.

SIZE: 1½ inches; breeds at 1 inch.

TEMPERAMENT: A mild-mannered species desirable in a community tank that does not contain large species.

TEMPERATURE REQUIREMENTS: 70–90°F.

SEX DIFFERENCES: The male has brighter colors than the female; she is plumper when mature.

COUNTS: Dorsal ii,8 or 9; anal iv,14 or 15; pectoral i,10; pelvic i,5; scales 32 to 34; transverse row 12.

The color of this fish is a brownish green with a dark horizontal lateral line which blends with the reddish tint to the fins. It loses most of its color when kept under unfavorable conditions. Its preference is a small well-planted aquarium with reflected light; it is not happy in strong overhead light and a bare tank.

The adults will feed on brine shrimp and microworms.

An exceptionally plump female, conditioned on *Daphnia* and brine shrimp, will deposit adhesive eggs on *Nitella* or Spanish moss from April to October. This fish does not seem to eat the young but will go after the eggs. Once a pair which apparently did not spawn was taken out of the spawning tank and conditioned. A week later the pair was reintroduced to the same aquarium. In a few hours many small fishes were seen. Obviously these must have resulted from the previous spawning, and the eggs had gone unnoticed. The fish were left in with the young for 3 or 4 days and did not eat the young. About 50 fry were raised to maturity. The main diet was brine shrimp and microworms, aided by the usual dry, finely powdered foods.

Spintherobolus broccae Myers (*Ann. Carnegie Mus.*, 16(1):143, pl. 10, 1925, type locality, Rio de Janeiro) is a valid genus and species according to Dr. Travassos.

Genus *Poecilobrycon* Eigenmann

[Pea'-sil-o-bry'-con: *poecilo* = many-colored; *brycon* = a kind of fish]

Three-striped Pencilfish / *Poecilobrycon trifasciatus* (Steindachner)

[tri-fas'-see-ay'-tus: *tri* = three; *fasciatus* = banded]

Nannostomus trifasciatus Steindachner, Sitzb. Akad. Wiss. Wien, 74:75, pl. 9, fig. 2, 1876 (type locality, Amazon River near mouth of Rio Negro and at Tabatinga)

RANGE: Guianas; Amazon Basin and lower Rio Negro.

SIZE: 2 inches; breeding at 1½ inches.

TEMPERAMENT: A peaceful species desirable in the community aquarium.

TEMPERATURE REQUIREMENTS: 72–88°F. Optimum 80°F.

SEX DIFFERENCES: Only the heaviness of the female and the slenderness of the male indicate sex at maturity.

COUNTS: Dorsal ii,8; anal ii,9; pectoral i,9; pelvic i,7; scales 1½ + 24 or 25 + 3.

Spawning this is difficult but many aquarists have accomplished it. An aquarium should contain well-conditioned water with a pH of 6.8, in which *Cryptocoryne* has taken root. The water should be soft (zero hardness) such as rain water. The female will deposit nearly 50 eggs on the underside of the *Cryptocorne* leaves. The male and female both stay in the area in which they spawned. The eggs hatch in 48 hours at a temperature of 82°F. The small fry need plenty of infusoria and grow rapidly. They reach spawning size in 8 months. A peculiarity of this fish is its poise at a 30-degree angle, head up.

Poecilobrycon auratus Eigenmann (*Ann. Carnegie Mus.*, 6(1):42, 1909) from British Guiana is a synonym of this species.

The name of this species currently is *Nannostomus trifasciatus*.

After Innes

ONE-LINED PENCILFISH / *Poecilobrycon unifasciatus* (Steindachner)

[u-nee-fas'-see-ay'-tus: *uni* = one; *fasciatus* = banded]

Nannostomus unifasciatus Steindachner, Sitzb. Akad. Wiss. Wien, 74:79, pl. 9, fig. 1, 1876 (type locality, mouth of Rio Negro, Amazon at Teffé)

RANGE: Guianas; Amazon and Rio Negro Basin.

SIZE: 2 inches; breeds at 1½ inches.

TEMPERAMENT: A peaceful and desirable species in the community aquarium.

TEMPERATURE REQUIREMENTS: 70–82°F.

SEX DIFFERENCES: None apparent.

COUNTS: Dorsal ii,9; anal iii,9; pectoral i,9 or 10; pelvic i,7; scales 25 to 28; transverse row 5½ or 6.

This species was classified as breeding at 1½ inches because several females at that length were observed to contain mature eggs. It has not been spawned in captivity although females appear to be ready for spawning.

The one-lined pencilfish is difficult to keep alive in captivity. It is best to maintain it alone in an aquarium where the competition for food is not keen, since it is slow in habit and the last to get the food. It maintains an inclined position at 45 degrees with the head up. It is an excellent scavenger in the aquarium and will go after food tidbits that have fallen to the bottom. It may be seen "digging in the sand" with its small pointed mouth.

The name of this species currently is *Nannostomus unifasciatus*.

A school of one-lined pencilfish make an attractive picture with their characteristic 45-degree-angle poise.

FAMILY **CHARACIDAE**

GENUS *Prionobrama* Fowler

[Pry'-o-no-bray'-ma: *priono* = a saw; *brama* = a bream, a kind of fish]

GLASS BLOODFISH / *Prionobrama filigerus* (Cope)

[fi-lig'-er-us: *fil* = a filament; *gerus* = suffix for bearing or carrying]

Aphyocharax filigerus Cope, Proc. Amer. Phil. Soc., p. 564, 1870 (type locality, Pebas)

RANGE: Amazon Basin from Pebas to Villa Bella; Madeira Basin.

SIZE: 2 inches; breeding at 1½ inches.

TEMPERAMENT: A peaceful species desirable in a community tank.

TEMPERATURE REQUIREMENTS: 68–85°F.

SEX DIFFERENCES: The first anal rays of mature males are elongate, with whitish outer edges.

COUNTS: Dorsal ii,8; anal iv,28 to 34; scales 26 to 30, transverse row 10.

We have no record of the successful spawning of this species. Most fishes which have never been recorded as spawned in the home aquarium are either lacking in economic or æsthetic value and thus not worth the effort, or they are spawned by persons who prefer to keep their breeding methods secret. The demand for this fish is limited since it looks, to the casual observer, like *Aphyocharax rubropinnis* in poor color. The size is about that of the bloodfin too, and since the bloodfin is so easy to raise and so very hardy and well-tempered, the demand for this weak relative is slight. Lately this fish is receiving more attention since some hobbyists are looking for the scarcer fishes, which are more challenging to spawn. This species can withstand temperature extremes very well.

The name of this species currently is *Prionobrama filigera.*

GENUS *Pristella* Eigenmann

[Pris-tell'-a: *prist* = saw; *ella* = little]

Pristella riddlei (Meek)

[ridd'-lee-eye: named in honor of the collector Oscar Riddle]

Holopristes riddlei Meek, in Eigenmann and Ogle, Proc. U.S. Nat. Mus., 33:11, 1907 (type locality, Los Castillas, Venezuela)

RANGE: Eastern Venezuela, Orinoco Basin, and Guianas.

SIZE: 2 inches; breeding at 1½ inches.

TEMPERAMENT: A peaceful species.

TEMPERATURE REQUIREMENTS: 70–90°F.

SEX DIFFERENCES: The female is much heavier and plumper than the male. If the fish are viewed with a strong back light, the air bladder of the male will be noted to be more pointed than that of the female.

COUNTS: Dorsal ii,9; anal ii,20 or 21; pectoral i,9 or 10; pelvic i,7; scales 30; transverse row 9.

This discussion applies to the albino variety as well as the normally colored *Pristella*. At this particular time the albino variety is in much greater demand and supply than the colored variety, possibly because it has been found easier to breed than the normal strain.

Breeding is accomplished in a 5-gallon tank three-fourths filled with clear, slightly hard water with a pH of 6.8 to 7.2. Optimum breeding temperature is about 76°F. Raising the temperature to 79 or 80°F may induce spawning if the fish will not spawn at the lower temperatures. Prepare the tank so that one entire end is well stocked with plants. A thin strip of glass separating the tank into two equal parts tends to keep the front of the tank free of vegetation. The pair will dash off into the vegetation, come up next to each other, and tremble for a few seconds, with 5 to 10 eggs being laid at that time. If the parents are well fed on *Daphnia* they usually ignore their own eggs. However, should they be left in the breeding tank for any length of time after they have spawned they will eat the eggs. Therefore, they should be removed as soon after spawning as possible.

The youngsters need infusoria in large amounts, followed by the standard brine shrimp, sifted *Daphnia*, and dried-food diet. The young grow faster if the temperature is maintained at 80°F.

The name of this species currently is *Pristella maxillaris*.

GENUS *Prochilodus* Agassiz

[Pro-kil′-o-duss: *pro* = in front of; *chil* = margin; *odus* = tooth]

Prochilodus insignis Schomburgh

[in-sig′-nis: *insignis* = well-marked]

Prochilodus insignis Schomburgh, in Cuvier and Valenciennes, Histoire naturelle des poissons, 22:88, 1849 (type locality, Rio Branco)

RANGE: Amazon and Rio Negro Basins; Guianas.

SIZE: 1 foot (larger in natural habitat); breeding size not known.

TEMPERAMENT: A peaceful species very desirable in the community aquarium.

TEMPERATURE REQUIREMENTS: 72–85°F.

SEX DIFFERENCES: None observed.

COUNTS: Dorsal ii,9; anal iii,8; pectoral i,14 or 15; pelvic i,8; scales 10 or 11+ 48 to 50 + 8.

Several individuals of this species were included in a shipment of *Crenuchus spilurus* from South America. At first difficulty in identifying these silvery fish was experienced. Fortunately (or unfortunately as case may be) one of them jumped out of the tank and flopped on the floor in an inaccessible corner where it died before it could be rescued. From this specimen identification was possible.

As a community fish it has few peers, provided the tank is large and well lighted. The fantastically large lips are well adapted to scrounging around for algae. Four of these beauties have been kept in a 50-gallon tank located in front of a window in the living room. Although the back of this tank was never shaded by a coat of paint and a light was left on nightly, these fish kept the green algae down to a minimum. Only the brown algae needed the steel-wool treatment every few months. In a smaller aquarium, this fish does not thrive well, but in a big tank it forms schools. It is a bottom feeder as well as a glass cleaner and eats meat, bits of fish, and other organic material. It is a good jumper and should be watched.

Prochilodus taeniurus (Valenciennes)

[tee'-ni-ur'-us: *taeni* = striped; *urus* = tail]

Curimatus taeniurus Valenciennes, in Humboldt, Recueil d'observations de zoologie . . . l'Océan Atlantique . . . 1799–1803, 2:166, 1811 (type locality, rivers of tropical America)

RANGE: Amazon Basin.

SIZE: 1 foot; breeding size not known.

TEMPERAMENT: A peaceful species desirable in the community tank.

TEMPERATURE REQUIREMENTS: 72–85°F.

SEX DIFFERENCES: Not apparent.

COUNTS: Dorsal ii,9; anal ii,8; pectoral i,15; pelvic i,8; scales 14 or 15 + 70 + 10.

This fish has not been spawned. It has the same general habits as *Prochilodus insignis*. The back is a dark aquamarine which tinges to silvery green as it approaches the lateral line.

The name of this species currently is *Semaprochilodus taeniurus*.

GENUS *Pseudocorynopoma* Perugia

[Sue'-dough-ko-rin'-o-po'-ma: *pseudo* = false; *coryno* = a club; *poma* = a cover]

DRAGON-FINNED CHARACIN / *Pseudocorynopoma doriae* Perugia

[dor'-y-ee: named in honor of the collector G. Doria]

Pseudocorynopoma doriae Perugia, Ann. Mus. Civ. Stor. Nat. Genova, ser. 2a, 10:646, fig., 1891 (type locality, Rio Jacuhy, Brazil)

RANGE: La Plata Basin to Rio Grande do Sul.

SIZE: 3½ inches; breeding size 2½ inches.

TEMPERAMENT: A peaceful species, desirable in the community aquarium, which should be covered to keep this fish from jumping out.

TEMPERATURE REQUIREMENTS: 70–85°F.

SEX DIFFERENCES: The female is indicated by her fullness and plumpness. The male's fins are much larger than those of the female.

COUNTS: Dorsal ii,9; anal iii,30 to 38; scales 7 + 41 to 43 + 6.

This fish can be easily spawned in groups. If an aquarium about 12 x 12 x 30 inches is available, set it up with large pebbles or marbles on the bottom in such a way that there are many holes and crevices into which the eggs may fall, thus protecting them from the parent fish. Conditioning is done by constant feedings of *Daphnia*, strips of beef, fish, liver, and shrimp. Naturally, these foods must be cut into bite-size pieces so they can be ingested whole before they settle to the bottom. The aquarium should be in a position where it will receive not direct sunlight but plenty of reflected light. The fish will more or less school together for a few days, then quite unexpectedly a pair will separate from the school and do a "frenzied dance about each other," which is part of the spawning act, also described for *Glandulocauda inequalis*. During this behavior the eggs are extruded and fertilized. They fall to the bottom where some adhere to the fine-leafed plants; those that do not adhere fall on the bottom of the aquarium and find protection among the pebbles or marbles.

Since the other fish will eat the eggs of the spawning fish if they have the opportunity, the water must be maintained at a low level so that the eggs may reach safety in as short a time as possible. The ova hatch in 48 hours at 75°F. The young are extremely tiny. The adult fish should be removed within 48 hours after the first pair have spawned.

Meinken reports that this fish spawns like *Mimagoniates*.

GENUS *Pyrrhulina* Cuvier and Valenciennes

[Pir'-hew-li'-na: *pyrrh* = flame-colored; *lina* = line]

HALF-BANDED PYRRHULINA / *Pyrrhulina laeta* (Cope)

[lee'-tus: *laetus* = pleasing]

Holotaxis laetus Cope, Proc. Acad. Nat. Sci. Philadelphia, p. 257, 1872 (type locality, Rio Ambyiacu)

RANGE: Guianas; Orinoco and Amazon Basins, Paraguay.

SIZE: 3 inches.

TEMPERAMENT: A peaceful species desirable in the community tank.

TEMPERATURE REQUIREMENTS: 72–85°F.

SEX DIFFERENCES: Mature male has a more elongate upper caudal fin lobe than the mature female.

COUNTS: Dorsal ii,8; anal iii,8; pectoral i,13 or 14; pelvic i,7; scales 23 or 24; transverse row 5½.

There is no record of breeding this species in captivity but the feat is believed possible. Few fish come up from South America at one time. When they do they are usually mixed in with other fishes and get lost in the shuffle. By the time the storekeeper receives a shipment from his supplier these fish are so widely distributed that it is nearly impossible to try to select pairs. The species is not attractive enough to warrant a thorough and intensive effort at breeding, yet with the great contrast of breeding habits in this family it might be interesting to try to induce them to spawn in captivity.

The ocellated dorsal fin is the most attractive attribute. The back is pale olive, becoming silvery toward the belly. A fine black line runs from the snout, through the eye to the end of the gill cover, then thickens to a wide band along the body, which suggests its common name, the *half-banded pyrrhulina*. Other fins show blushes of red.

Pyrrhulina semifasciata Steindachner (Sitzb. Akad. Wiss. Wien, 72:2, pl. 1, figs. 1, 1*a*, 2, 2*a*, 1875) is a synonym of this species.

FANNING CHARACIN; RACHOW'S PYRRHULINA /
Pyrrhulina rachoviana Myers

[rak-cho'-ve-ann'-a: named in honor of the German aquarist Arthur Rachow]

Pyrrhulina rachoviana Myers, Blät. Aquar. Terrak., no. 18, p. 441, 1926 (type locality, Rosario, Argentina)
RANGE: Rosario, Argentina.
SIZE: 2 inches; breeds at 1½ inches.
TEMPERAMENT: This peaceful species is so small that it should not be kept with larger aquarium fishes.
TEMPERATURE REQUIREMENTS: 70–90°F. Breeding at 75°F.
SEX DIFFERENCES: Male has a dark spot on the tip of the dorsal fin while the homologous spot on the female is more toward the center of the fin. The edges of the pelvic and anal fins are red in the male, while the female has only a very pale border on her fins (usually so pale that it cannot be seen). The male has the characteristic orange-red dots.
COUNTS: Dorsal i,9; anal ii,9; scales 21.

A pair should be placed in a small aquarium, heavily planted with broad-leafed plants such as the giant *Sagittaria*, Amazon sword plant, and *Cryptocoryne*. Conditioning should start immediately by feeding such live foods as brine shrimp, microworms, chopped white worms, earthworms or sandworms, and fine dried foods. When a female shows fullness, she should be selected along with a male that shows activity and bright colors.

The pair will select a leaf upon which she will deposit her spawn. The male will then take the spotlight, chase the female away, and start fanning the eggs, at which time the female should be removed. After 24 hours of constant fanning, at a temperature of 75°F, the young will hatch out and sink to the bottom where they will hide and hunt infusoria for 3 or 4 days. They should be fed sifted *Daphnia*, brine shrimp, and fine dried foods when they start to swim freely about the aquarium.

It is possible to detach the leaf upon which the pair has spawned and hatch the young in a separate container. This is done by adding 2 drops of 5 per cent Methylene Blue solution to each gallon of water in the hatching tray and by playing a stream of air bubbles against the eggs to imitate the fanning of the parent fish.

GENUS *Schizodon* Agassiz

[Shiz'-o-don: *schiza* = a cleft; *odon* = tooth]

BANDED ANOSTOMUS / *Schizodon fasciatum* Agassiz

[fas'-see-a'-tus: *fasciatus* = banded]

Schizodon fasciatus Agassiz, in Spix and Agassiz, Selecta genera et species piscium . . . Brasiliam, p. 66, pl. 36, 1829 (type locality, rivers of Brazil)

RANGE: Caracas, Venezuela, Orinoco Basin, Guianas, Amazon Basin to Rio Paraguay.

SIZE: 18 inches, but only about 5 inches in an aquarium; breeding size not known.

TEMPERAMENT: A peaceful species when small.

TEMPERATURE REQUIREMENTS: 72–85°F.

SEX DIFFERENCES: No apparent differences externally.

COUNTS: Dorsal ii,10; anal ii,8; pectoral i,15 to 16; pelvic i,8; scales 4½ + 41 or 42 + 4.

This fish has never been bred. The fact that it is kept in an aquarium probably accounts for its lack of growth to the maximum size of 18 inches. There are 5 dark blue spotlike bars on its sides. A black spot occurs on the caudal peduncle. The background color is greenish yellow, with a yellowish-white belly.

GENUS *Serrasalmus* Lacepède

[Ser'-ra-sal'-mus: *serra* = a saw; *salmus* = salmon, a kind of fish]

SPOTTED PIRANHA / *Serrasalmus rhombeus* (Linnaeus)

[rom'-bay-us: *rhombeus* = rhomboid in shape]

Salmo rhombeus Linnaeus, Systema naturae, ed. 12, p. 514, 1766 (type locality, Surinam)

RANGE: Guianas and Amazon Basin.

SIZE: 14 inches; not bred in captivity.

TEMPERAMENT: A ferocious species, very dangerous to have with other fishes.

TEMPERATURE REQUIREMENTS: 70–85°F.

SEX DIFFERENCES: Not known.

COUNTS: Dorsal ii,14 or 15; anal iii,30 or 31; pectoral i,14 or 15; pelvic i,6; ventral serrae 22 to 24 + 9 or 10.

This species, like all others of the genus *Serrasalmus*, has the same habits as the dark-banded piranha, although it grows to a larger size in the aquarium.

DARK-BANDED PIRANHA / *Serrasalmus spilopleura* Kner

[spy'-low-ploo'-rah: *spilo* = spots; *pleura* = the sides]

Serrasalmo spilopleura Kner, Denks. Akad. Wiss. Wien, 18:43, pl. 5, fig. 11, 1860 (type locality, Mato Grosso, Rio Guaporé, Bogotá)

RANGE: La Plata, Amazon, Orinoco, and Apure Basins.

SIZE: 9 inches; breeding size in captivity not known.

TEMPERAMENT: A vicious and dangerous species that should not be placed with other fishes. When handled in a net, care should be taken not to let it bite one's hands.

TEMPERATURE REQUIREMENTS: 72–85°F.

SEX DIFFERENCES: Not externally apparent.

COUNTS: Dorsal ii,14; anal iii,30 to 32; pectoral i,13 or 14; pelvic i,6; ventral serrae 22 or 23 + 9 or 10.

The vicious nature of this species is becoming legendary. There are numerous accounts of its savage attacks on animals, such as cattle being reduced to bones in a short time by a school of piranhas.

At the present time there are many piranhas in the United States. Most dealers believe that they are lacking something if they do not "keep one of the monsters." This has led to the import of many of these bloodthirsty fellows and much has been learned about handling them.

The razor-sharp teeth of the piranha are capable of destroying the best of the usual nets. A special net must be used, such as one made of plastic materials. These fish must be shipped separately and maintained apart from each other or they will surely tear each other apart. This is in direct contrast to their natural schooling habit.

Most dealers feed the piranha on their dead fishes. As they pull the dead fishes out of their tanks they merely throw them into the piranha's tank and in a short time they disappear. Some aquarists have put their hands into a piranha tank without any bad consequences, but this is not recommended.

Serrasalmus nattereri (Kner).

Another piranha that occurs from the Guianas to the La Plata system is a convex-headed species, *Serrasalmus nattereri* (Kner). It has the same bloodthirsty habits as other members of the genus.

GENUS *Thayeria* Eigenmann

[Thay-air′-i-a: named in honor of Nathaniel Thayer, sponsor of the Thayer expedition to the Amazon]

BLACKLINE / *Thayeria obliquus* Eigenmann

[ob-lik′-us: *obliquus* = slanting]

Thayeria obliquus Eigenmann, Bull. Mus. Comp. Zool., 52(6):94, 1908 (type locality, Óbidos)

RANGE: Amazon Basin.

SIZE: 3½ inches; breeding at 2½ inches.

TEMPERAMENT: A fairly peaceful fish. Such a large species, however, armed with sharp teeth, is a potential menace. It will swallow with a single gulp any fish small enough to catch.

TEMPERATURE REQUIREMENTS: 70–85°F. Optimum breeding temperature 75°F.

SEX DIFFERENCES: The plumpness of the female indicates her sex.

COUNTS: Dorsal ii,8 or 9; anal iii,13 or 14; pectoral i,11 or 12; pelvic i,7; scales 30 to 32; transverse row 9.

Selection of a plump female and a spirited male is almost insurance that this fish will spawn. The breeding tank should be as large as possible so that the prolific offspring will be able to grow properly. Usually when a school of fish is placed in a tank of its own a pair will separate from the rest and become rather secretive, like any two young lovers. They slowly circle about each other, keeping away from the other fish, until quite suddenly they will move rapidly, almost dashing, to a clump of plants where they rub against each other, nudging with their mouths. Spawning is accomplished by the trembling motion of the female, who sheds a dozen or so eggs which are fertilized by the male. After each spawning act they rush out of the foliage and then repeat the process.

The fry appear in 48 hours at 75°F. Parents should be removed after spawning, as they will surely make a meal out of the young if left with them.

It is surprising how small these fry are. They require an abundance of infusoria and brine shrimp. After 6 months they are nearly 2 inches long and will breed at 8 months of age, if given plenty of room and live food during their growth and maturity.

Thayeria sanctaemariae Ladiges is another popular species.

The name of this species currently is *Thayeria obliqua.*

Thayeria boehlkei.

FAMILY CHARACIDAE

GENUS *Thoracocharax* Fowler

[Tho'-ra-co-kar'-ax: *thoraco* = breast plate; *charax* = a kind of fish]

Gasteropelecus securis (Filippi)

RANGE: Amazon basin.

SIZE: 3 inches; breeding size not known.

TEMPERAMENT: A peaceful species but it may jump out of the tank unless covered.

TEMPERATURE REQUIREMENTS: 72–85°F.

SEX DIFFERENCES: Not observed.

COUNTS: Dorsal ii,10 to 15; anal iii,31 to 41; pectoral i,10 or 11; scales 19 to 22; pelvic i,5.

This fish has not been bred and is seldom seen in aquaria any more. It is delicate and difficult to keep alive when netted. It requires copious amounts of mos-quito larvae and other floating or surface foods. It is a jumper and must be kept in a covered aquarium.

Gasteropelecus securis Filippi, Guer. Rev. Mag. Zool. 5:165, 1853 (type locality, not known)

T. stellatus has a black spot at front base of dorsal fin and only 2 or 3 rows of scales over front of rays of anal fin base, whereas *T. securis* lacks the blackish spot at base of dorsal fin and has 5 or 6 rows of scales over base ray at front of the anal fin.

Thoracochorax and *Gasteropelecus* have an adipose fin, but the latter is lacking on *Carnegiella*.

The name of this species currently is *Thoracocharax securis*.

SILVER HATCHETFISH / *Thoracocharax stellatus* (Kner)

[stel-la′-tus: *stellatus* = with starlike spots]

Gasteropelecus stellatus Kner, Denks. Akad. Wiss. Wien, 18:17, pl. 1, fig. 2, 1859 (type locality, Rio Cuiabá)

RANGE: Amazon, Paraguay, Orinoco Basins to Rio Apure, Venezuela.

SIZE: 3 inches; breeding size not known.

TEMPERAMENT: A peaceful species, desirable for the community tank.

TEMPERATURE REQUIREMENTS: 74–85°F.

SEX DIFFERENCES: Unknown.

COUNTS: Dorsal ii or iii,11 or 12; anal ii or iii,37 to 40; pectoral i,10 or 11; pelvic i,5; scales 19 or 20.

This fish is often confused with *Gasteropelecus levis;* without a preserved specimen the two species are nearly impossible to distinguish. The silver hatchetfish has been seen to jump or fly for a distance of 2 yards.

Genus *Triportheus* Cope

[Try-por'-the-us: *tri* = three; *portheus* = to destroy]

Triportheus angulatus (Agassiz)

[ann'-gu-lay'-tus: *angulatus* = having corners]

Chalceus angulatus Agassiz, in Spix and Agassiz, Selecta genera et species piscium . . . Brasiliam, p. 67, 1829 (type locality, Brazil)

RANGE: Amazon, Orinoco Basins to the Paraguay.

SIZE: 10 inches; breeding not observed.

TEMPERAMENT: A peaceful species when small, and desirable in the community tank, which should be covered to keep this species from jumping out.

TEMPERATURE REQUIREMENTS: 74–85°F.

SEX DIFFERENCES: Not known.

COUNTS: Dorsal ii,9; anal iii,29; pectoral i,10; pelvic i,6; scales 31 to 33.

This fish has not been bred in captivity. The larger fish show a distinct preference for bits of meat, the larger *Daphnia,* and brine shrimp (adults). They are becoming quite popular lately because of the color that the imported specimens take on after they have become acclimated to their new surroundings. The dark sword-like extension of the caudal fin becomes trimmed with a rust red, with the dark bands and silver background as contrast. *Triportheus angulatus* is a shy, retiring fish until it has been in a large aquarium for a few weeks at least.

In most aquarium books on fishes this species has been misidentified as *T. elongatus* (Günther), which has 40 to 43 scales, the middle rays of the caudal fin not elongate and blackish, and the body much more slender than in *T. angulatus.*

[Jim-no'-ti-dee]

GENUS *Gymnotus* Linnaeus

[Jim-no'-tus: *gymno* = naked; *notus* = back]

BANDED KNIFEFISH / *Gymnotus carapo* Linnaeus

[ka-ra'-po: meaning not known]

Gymnotus carapo Linnaeus, Systema naturae, ed. 10, p. 246, 1758 (type locality, South America)

RANGE: Guianas, Trinidad, Amazon and Orinoco Basins south to the Rio de la Plata and Rio São Francisco; Guatemala and Panama.

SIZE: 1 foot; breeding size not known.

TEMPERAMENT: A carnivorous species that should be kept by itself in an aquarium.

TEMPERATURE REQUIREMENTS: 65–85°F.

SEX DIFFERENCES: No external sex differences observed.

COUNTS: Dorsal fin absent; anal 200 to 260; pectoral i,14 or 15; pelvic absent; scales very numerous.

Little is known about the breeding habits of this species. It has not been spawned in captivity and anyone attempting this feat would need plenty of guppies and other live fishes upon which to condition it.

During the daytime the banded knifefish is usually lying in hiding. Its habits are strictly nocturnal and food offered in the morning is usually ignored; sometime during the night it is gobbled up, as there are never any traces the following morning. Large pieces of meat, shrimp, and fish should be offered prior to leaving the fish in complete darkness so the food will not foul the water next day.

It has a unique ability to swim in reverse. Dorsal, pelvic, and caudal fins are missing, and the pectorals are small. The anal fin is, however, greatly developed and it may be seen to undulate even when the fish is not swimming forward or backward.

FAMILY **APTERONOTIDAE**

[Ap-ter'-o-no'-ti-dee]

GENUS *Hypopomus* Gill

[High'-po-po'-mus: *hypo* = below; *pomus* = cover]

SPECKLED or MOTTLED KNIFEFISH / *Hypopomus artedii* (Kaup)

[are'-te-de'-eye: named in honor of Peter Artedi, the father of ichthyology]

Rhamphichthys artedii Kaup, Catalogue of Apodal Fishes in the British Museum, p. 128, fig. 3, 1856 (type locality, Mona, French Guiana)

RANGE: Guianas.

SIZE: 7 inches; breeding size not known.

TEMPERAMENT: A carnivorous species that should be kept by itself.

TEMPERATURE REQUIREMENTS: 65–85°F.

SEX DIFFERENCES: None observed.

COUNTS: Dorsal fin lacking; anal rays 204 to 238.

The habits of this species are nearly the same as its close relative *Gymnotus carapo*.

[Si-prin'-i-dee]

GENUS *Brachydanio* Weber and de Beaufort

[Brak'-i-dan'-i-o: *brachy* = short; *danio* = probably a native name]

A recent analysis of the species referrable to the *Danio* group indicates that *Brachydanio* should have generic status.

PEARL DANIO / *Brachydanio albolineatus* (Blyth)

[al'-bow-lin'-e-a'-tus: *albo* = white; *lineatus* = streaked]

Nuria albolineata Blyth, Jour. Asiatic Soc. Bengal, 29:163, 1860 (type locality, Tenasserim)

RANGE: Sumatra, Burma, Siam.

SIZE: 2½ inches; breeds at 2 inches.

TEMPERAMENT: An active though peaceful species, desirable in the community tank.

TEMPERATURE REQUIREMENTS: 70–85°F.

SEX DIFFERENCES: Only the plumpness of the female indicates the sex.

COUNTS: Dorsal ii,7; anal iii,13; pectoral i,11; pelvic i,6; scales 31 to 33, transverse 8½.

There are two color varieties of this species. The pearl danios now available are nearly always a golden variation from tank-raised stock developed by selective breeding. This golden pearl danio is more attractive than the normal strain, although the blue coloring is much less intense.

Spawning is the same as for the zebrafish. The main problem with the production of the pearl danio is the selection of gravid females. The females get heavy quite suddenly and spawn immediately, before they can be picked out and controlled. Community spawning is practiced by most breeders in screened-bottom containers floating in large breeding troughs.

SPOTTED DANIO / *Brachydanio nigrofasciatus* (Day)

[ni'-gro-fas'-see-a'-tus: *nigro* = black; *fasciatus* = banded]

Barilius nigrofasciatus Day, Proc. Zool. Soc. London, p. 620, 1869 (type locality, Pegu and Moulmein)

RANGE: Burma.

SIZE: 1½ inches; breeds at 1¼ inches.

TEMPERAMENT: A peaceful species desirable in the community tank.

TEMPERATURE REQUIREMENTS: 70–85°F.

SEX DIFFERENCES: Only the fullness of the female indicates her sex.

COUNTS: Dorsal ii,7; anal ii,11; pectoral i,14; pelvic i,6; scales 30 to 32.

Breeding is very similar to the zebrafish, *Brachydanio rerio*. The females tend to become egg-bound, and this has offered the author opportunity to hand-strip a female of her eggs. If the female is picked up in a net her eggs may be gently massaged from her by a slight pressure on her abdomen, rubbing in the direction of the anus from the gills. Too much pressure is dangerous. The eggs should be collected in a small watch glass and as soon as they are expelled a male should be similarly treated for his sperm, then water added.

Ordinarily breeding should be encouraged in the same arrangement as for zebrafish. The actual breeding is a variation that has not been observed in other cyprinids. The male and female come to each other head on. They suddenly swoop up into a vertical position, embrace for a short time, and expel their eggs. Sometimes this embrace may be a mere bump or even a glancing blow. Artificial spawning, or hand-stripping, should only be practiced on very heavy females.

Eggs hatch in 24 hours at 78°F. The young are free-swimming about 2½ days after hatching.

ZEBRAFISH; ZEBRA DANIO; RERIO /
Brachydanio rerio (Hamilton = Buchanan)

[rare'-i-o: after a native name]

Cyprinus rerio Hamilton = Buchanan, Fishes of the River Ganges, pp. 323, 390, 1822 (type locality, Ganges River)

RANGE: Bengal to Coromandel Coast of India.

SIZE: 2 inches; breeds at 1½ inches.

TEMPERAMENT: A peaceful species, desirable in the community tank.

TEMPERATURE REQUIREMENTS: 70–90°F. Optimum temperature 75°F.

SEX DIFFERENCES: The plumpness of the female indicates her sex.

COUNTS: Dorsal ii,7; anal ii or iii,12 or 13; pectoral i,12; pelvic i,7; scales 26 to 28.

Next to the guppy, this species is the best seller in fish of this class. It is inexpensive, hardy, and easy to breed.

Breeding this fish is a simple matter. The method used by breeders during the summer is to place a dozen pair in a heavily planted pool that also contains green algae and is partially shaded. After 3 months there will be thousands of zebrafish. Feedings should be of dried foods and *Daphnia*, as there will be plenty of mosquito larvae. *Tubifex* are usually eagerly taken.

Tank breeding is accomplished by making a false bottom of screen or rods which is so designed as to allow the eggs to fall through to the bottom where the parents will not have a chance to get at them. It is best to use a glass-bottom aquarium without any sand so the eggs may easily be seen.

Professional breeders use long tanks, like the *Betta* tanks, which have 6 or 7 compartments. Since the parents like to eat their own eggs as they fall down through the water, it is wise to keep the water level as close to the screen or rodded bottom as possible and still leave enough water for the fish to swim. About 2 inches of water above the false bottom is the minimum.

After the spawners have done their job they should be removed and the eggs hatched in the same aquarium in which they were laid. Although these eggs are not too susceptible to fungus, they do better if treated with 2 drops of a 5 per cent water solution of Methylene Blue (Gentian Violet). Eggs hatch in 48 hours, and the young are free-swimming in another 2 days.

GENUS *Caecobarbus* Boulenger

[See'-co-bar'-bus: *caeco* = blind; *barbus* = a kind of fish]

BLIND BARB / *Caecobarbus geertsi* Boulenger

[geerts'-eye: named in honor of the discoverer, M. G. Geerts]

Caecobarbus geertsi Boulenger, Rev. Zool. Africa, 9:252–253, fig., 1921 (type locality, cave at Thysville, Lower Congo)

RANGE: Lower Congo.

SIZE: 3 inches; breeding not known.

TEMPERAMENT: A peaceful species suitable in the community tank.

TEMPERATURE REQUIREMENTS: 70–85°F.

SEX DIFFERENCES: Not known.

COUNTS: Dorsal iii,7 or 8; anal iii,5; scales 28 or 29.

This species has not been observed to spawn in captivity. It is able to move around the aquarium by means of its long tactile barbels which function as "feelers." It lives in caves in complete darkness, much like numerous other blind fishes.

GENUS *Carassius* Nilson

[Kar-a'-shus: probably derived from the name Karass of Gesner]

GOLDFISH / *Carassius auratus* (Linnaeus)

[au-ra'-tus: *auratus* = overlaid with gold]

Cyprinus auratus Linnaeus, Systema naturae, ed. 10, 1:322, 1758 (type locality, China)

RANGE: Temperate Asia; introduced into all temperate parts of the world.

SIZE: 12 inches; breeds at about 3 inches.

TEMPERAMENT: This species is suitable in the community tank.

TEMPERATURE REQUIREMENTS: 40–80°F. The fancier the fish, the higher the temperature requirements.

SEX DIFFERENCES: The fullness of a ripe female indicates her sex.

COUNTS: Dorsal iii,15 to 18; anal iii,5 or 6; scales 26 to 35.

There is no doubt that this species has more varieties than any other aquarium fish. The intense interest that the Chinese and Japanese have shown in domesticating the goldfish goes back possibly 1,350

(Left) Adult veiltail goldfish at 2 years of age. (Right) Lateral view of veiltail at 8 years of age. Note that the height of the dorsal fin *exceeds* the length of the body, as do the ventral and anal fins.

This unusual head-on view of a pearl-scaled fantail gold-fish is one of the best pictures of the famous British photographer of fishes, Laurence E. Perkins.

Male goldfish showing the nuptial tubercles on his gill cover. Only male goldfish show this sex characteristic, and it is the only sure indication of sex in goldfish.

years to the T'ang dynasty (618–907 A.D.) in China. Since then many new forms have been developed. Sometimes color varieties of goldfish are referred to as without scales. This is an erroneous reference, as all goldfish have scales. There may have been some confusion with the "mirror carp," which does lack some of its scales. The large scales on the goldfish may be pigmented or unpigmented; it is these unpigmented varieties which give the scaleless appearance. Aquarists have shifted from the term "scaleless" to "cal-

ico," to define those goldfish lacking black pigment in their scales. All the shubunkins are calico, while the moors are scaled. The other varieties appear as either calico or scaled. Color varieties of goldfish are caused by the varying amounts and arrangement of the pigment cells in the skin.

The breeding season for the goldfish is in the late spring and early summer. Usually it is over 3 inches long before the sex is recognizable and it will breed. Males may get "nuptial tubercles" on their head, body, and fins. These tubercles appear as

(Left) A pond in a small garden, having extended sides and shallow side basins for spawning. The depth at the middle is 4 feet 6 inches. (Right) An informal goldfish pool designed for limited spaces.

Short-tailed common shubunkin. This fish is so fine that it won first prize in an English goldfish show.

hard white pimples, about the size of a pinhead, and look much like the ich or other parasites. A fish bearing these tubercles is always a male. Females may be recognized by their abdomens swollen with mature eggs. For best results put 3 males with 2 females. Prepare an aquarium with fresh water at a temperature slightly higher than that to which the fish are accustomed. Thus if

pairs have been maintained in a tank or pool at 60°F, set them up to breed in a tank at 70°F. Never go above 80°F.

Since goldfish scatter sticky eggs haphazardly over the aquarium, it should be well stocked with aquarium plants. Try to arrange the aquarium with floating rooted plants like water hyacinth, bottom plants like Nitella, and artificial spawning grass. When the pair is ready to breed it will be

Chinese-bred telescope-eye veiltail goldfish.

Adult celestial goldfish.

noticed that the male will be staying quite close to the female and finally the two come together in a spawning act, at which moment the eggs are laid and the male fertilizes them. The eggs adhere to the first thing they touch as they settle. Infertile eggs are sticky too, but they turn white in a few hours and begin to decay. If possible remove all white eggs. The fertilized eggs are about $\frac{1}{16}$ inch in diameter and are amber-colored when first laid. Spawnings are usually large, from about 500 to 2,000 eggs, depending upon the size and condition of the female. The parents should be removed immediately after spawning, which usually lasts about 3 hours. Eggs should be incubated for 8 or 9 days at 65°F. Five drops of 2 per cent Methylene Blue should be added to each gallon of well-aerated aquarium water. Although the eggs will hatch after 5 days, the embryo needs 3 days or so to absorb all the yolk.

Once the fry have digested the yolk, they require copious amounts of infusoria. Keep them on an infusorian diet for at least a week and then offer them freshly hatched brine shrimp, sifted *Daphnia*, and finely powdered dry food.

GENUS *Chrosomus* Rafinesque

[Crow-so'-mus: *chro* = colored; *somus* = body]

RED-BELLIED DACE / *Chrosomus erythrogaster* Rafinesque

[ee-rith'-row-gas'-ter: *erythro* = red; *gaster* = belly]

Chrosomus erythrogaster Rafinesque, Ichthyologia Ohiensis, p. 47, 1820 (type locality, Ohio River)

RANGE: Eastern United States, west of the Alleghenies and in the Mississippi Basin.

SIZE: 3½ inches; breeds at 2½ inches.

TEMPERAMENT: A somewhat predaceous species not suitable in the community tank.

TEMPERATURE REQUIREMENTS: 60–70°F, no higher than 74°F.

SEX DIFFERENCES: Male has the brilliant red belly and nuptial tubercles.

COUNTS: Dorsal i,6; anal i,7; pectoral i,9; pelvic i,7; scales 77 to 91.

This species was very popular during the 1951–1952 season. The over-all impression of the brilliant red on the belly is that the fish has been injured and is bleeding. This color does not persist, unfortunately, after spawning time. The fish is too large to be successfully acclimated to a small aquarium and will soon die. A few specimens kept with goldfish, in an unheated, large aquarium, lasted much longer than those kept in a heated aquarium. The fish is not peaceful and it attacks other species of fish.

Schultz gives an account of their spawning in his book *The Ways of Fishes:* ". . . during mid-May to mid-June schools of red-bellied dace congregate in pools. Then several males pursuing one female, they swim up a riffle. As the foremost gain position alongside the female, their speed is almost lightning-like. Then a male presses against each side of a female; the positions are maintained both by the stones between which the fish squeeze and by the nuptial tubercles. The trio forces upstream and vibrates rapidly for an instant, during which the eggs are laid and fertilized. The males immediately relax their hold. The eggs adhere to bottom pebbles." The nuptial tubercles are white, wartlike excrescences. They are as large as a pinhead and are usually found on the head and head area of the males, though at times they are found also on their sides and back, or even on their pelvic fins. They disappear when spawning is over. Their function may be as weapons, or as tools in breeding or nest building.

To breed in captivity, this species needs a very elaborate setup, approximating conditions in a rapidly flowing stream with a gravelly bottom.

GENUS *Danio* Hamilton = Buchanan

[Dan'-i-o: probably a native name]

Danio devario (Hamilton = Buchanan)

[de-va'-ri-o: probably after a native name]

Cyprinus devario Hamilton = Buchanan, Fishes of the River Ganges, pp. 341, 393, pl. 6, fig. 94, 1822 (type locality, Ganges River)

RANGE: Northern India.

SIZE: 4 inches; breeds at 2½ inches.

TEMPERAMENT: A peaceful species desirable in the community tank.

TEMPERATURE REQUIREMENTS: 68–85°F. Temperature should be raised to 80°F to induce spawning.

SEX DIFFERENCES: Only the fullness of the female as contrasted to the slender male indicates sex.

COUNTS: Dorsal iii,15 or 16; anal iii,15 or 16; pectoral i,12; pelvic i,7; scales 41 to 48.

This danio has, for some reason, become quite uncommon of late. The fish itself is pretty, its color being aquamarine dorsally and silvery below. The upper part of the caudal peduncle is steel blue with some yellow markings. Three beautiful blue bands run from the middle of the body through the caudal peduncle, where they converge into a large blue stripe that runs into the dorsal lobe of the caudal fin. The dorsal fin has a white edge; the anal and pelvic fins are bluish.

Breeding this fish is very simple. A large aquarium, heavily stocked with plants at one end, furnishes a suitable place for the parents to dash into and expel their spawn. This fish breeds as does *Danio malabaricus*, except the eggs are not nearly so sticky, though they adhere to the plants. Spanish moss seems to be the best spawning medium. The parents should be removed after spawning. The young require infusoria and brine shrimp as soon as they are free-swimming.

GIANT DANIO / *Danio malabaricus* (Jerdon)

[mal'-a-bar'-i-cus: named after the type locality]

Perilampus malabaricus Jerdon, Madras Jour. Lit. Sci., 15:325, 1849 (type locality, Malabar)

RANGE: Western coast of India; Ceylon.

SIZE: 6 inches; breeds at 2 inches.

TEMPERAMENT: A desirable species for the community tank that does not contain fishes small enough for it to ingest whole.

TEMPERATURE REQUIREMENTS: 72–85°F. Optimum breeding temperature 80°F.

SEX DIFFERENCES: The male is smaller, much slimmer, and has more intense coloration.

COUNTS: Dorsal ii,10 to 13; anal iii,12 to 16; pectoral i,14; pelvic i,7; scales 35 to 37.

This gorgeously colored fish has been popular with aquarists for a long time. The breeding of the giant danio is no problem at all, as certain techniques have proved to be fairly successful for controlled spawning. A 20-gallon tank (12 × 12 × 30 inches) has been successful for spawning of this large prolific species. The aquarium must be heavily stocked with artificial spawning grass. Such plants as *Fontinalis, Cabomba, Myriophyllum,* and the like also make fine spawning media. The sticky eggs adhere to the plants.

Some breeders prefer to use more males than females, but a prolonged breeding table has shown that the use of a separate pair is most economical. They should be well conditioned on live foods and introduced into the breeding tank the evening prior to the day on which breeding is expected to take place. If the fish have been conditioned in separate aquaria they should spawn the following morning as soon as they have become acclimated to the light. It is of value to increase the temperature gradually from 74 to 80°F. Remove the parents after spawning, and feed the young quantities of infusoria in order to keep them going; then brine shrimp eggs after 10 days of growth will hasten the time when they are able to take *Daphnia.* The youngsters will need plenty of space in which to grow and may require thinning out at intervals.

GENUS *Esomus* Swainson

[Ee-so'-mus: *e* = out of, from; *somus* = body]

FLYING BARB / *Esomus danrica* (Hamilton = Buchanan)

[dan'-ri-ka: after a native name]

Cyprinus danrica Hamilton = Buchanan, Fishes of the River Ganges, pp. 325, 390, pl. 16, fig. 88, 1822 (type locality, Bengal)

RANGE: India, Ceylon.

SIZE: 5 inches; breeds at 4 inches.

TEMPERAMENT: A peaceful species, desirable in the community tank.

TEMPERATURE REQUIREMENTS: 72–90°F.

SEX DIFFERENCES: The male, when properly conditioned, shows more red in his lower half than the female. The female is fuller.

COUNT: Dorsal ii,6; anal iii,5; pectoral ii,13; pelvic i,8; scales 30 to 34.

In his great book, *The Fauna of British India* (vol. 1, p. 335, London, 1889), Francis Day records two instances where collectors discovered these fish in hot streams at temperatures of 112°F. Since one incident took place in Ceylon and one in India there seems to be some veracity to the report. The author raised the temperature of the water containing this species to that temperature, but they died at about 104°F. The collectors may have taken the temperature of the top layer of water without bothering to take it at the level where the fish were swimming. This fish is noted for its fast moving and jumping ability. Thus it is particularly suited to make a dash into the air, through the hottest layer of water, for a flying insect, then quickly return to the cooler water. Usually in such warm springs, the upper water is at a temperature 6 to 10 degrees higher than that on the bottom. It is best to keep the tank covered for these fish.

The flying barb is a prolific breeder. It lays semiadhesive eggs among the floating plants with the male and female nudging each other during the spawning and egg-laying acts. The eggs are not lighter than water, and unless they are firmly anchored to the plants they fall to the bottom. Since the parents make fast dips to eat the falling eggs, the same precaution must be taken as with the zebrafish, *Brachydanio rerio*—the water level should be as low as possible. The eggs hatch in 48 hours at 76°F and the fry must be fed rotifers as their first food.

MALAYAN FLYING BARB / *Esomus malayensis* (Mandee)

[may'-lay-en'-sis: named after the locality where it occurs]

Nuria danrica var. *malayensis* Mandee, Jahrb. Aquar.-Terrak., 5:11, 1909 (type locality, Malaya)

RANGE: Malay Peninsula.

SIZE: 4 inches; breeds at 3½ inches.

TEMPERAMENT: A peaceful species suitable for the community tank. Its habit of jumping requires a cover over the tank.

TEMPERATURE REQUIREMENTS: 74–90°F.

SEX DIFFERENCES: The female is fuller than the male and shows more intense red colors.

COUNTS: Dorsal ii,6; anal iii,5; scales 29 or 30.

Esomus danrica, the flying barb, breeds the same way and has the same temperament as this species. It is distinguished by its slightly smaller size and by the fact that its lateral stripe is much paler, whereas the spot on the caudal peduncle is a deeper red. A feature that distinguishes *E. malayensis* is the dark spot at the base of the anal fin, which may disappear when the fish is excited, nervous, or out of condition.

GENUS *Labeo* Cuvier

[Lay'-be-o: *labeo* = large lips]

RED-TAILED BLACK "SHARK" / *Labeo bicolor* Smith

[bi-co'-lor: *bi* = two; *color* = color]

Labeo bicolor Smith, Proc. U.S. Nat. Mus., 79(7):9, fig. 4, 1931 (type locality, Menam Chao Phraya, Siam)

RANGE: Siam.

SIZE: 5 inches; breeding at 3 inches.

TEMPERAMENT. A peaceful species, suitable in the community tank.

TEMPERATURE REQUIREMENTS: 72–85°F.

SEX DIFFERENCES: Only the heaviness of a female full of ripe eggs is an indication of her sex.

COUNTS: Dorsal ii,13; anal iii,5; scales 34.

This is a recent importation that has not been bred, but sexually ripe females (3 inches long) have been found. The fish has been described as abundant in central Siam, especially in the Menam Chao Phraya Basin. It is high-priced at this time, though it is not rare in the native habitat.

The coloration makes it a desirable species. Nearly the whole body except the caudal and pectoral fins is a deep rich velvety black, the tail and pectoral fins being a bright reddish-orange. These contrasting colors make the fish attractive to the people of Siam who call it *pla song kruang,* meaning "full-dress fish."

It is a bottom feeder, taking *Tubifex* worms and other organic foods.

Genus *Morulius* Hamilton = Buchanan

[Mo-ru'-li-us: *Morulius* = dark-colored]

Black "Shark" / *Morulius chrysophekadion* (Bleeker)

[cry'-so-feak'-a-de-on: *chryso* = golden; *phekadion* = lens-shaped spots]

Rohita chrysophekadion Bleeker, Bijdrage . . . Ichthyologische fauna van Middenen Oost-Java, Verh. Batavia Gen. 23:20, 1850 (type locality, Surabaya, Java)

RANGE: Java, Borneo, Sumatra, Siam.

SIZE: 14 inches; breeding not observed.

TEMPERAMENT: Not suitable for the community aquarium.

TEMPERATURE REQUIREMENTS: 72–85°F.

SEX DIFFERENCES: Not known.

COUNTS: Dorsal iii,15 to 18; anal iii,5; pectoral i,15 to 17; pelvic i,8; scales 8 + 41 to 43 + 8 or 9.

In the summer of 1952, Charles Horvath, one of the newer importers of fish in Brooklyn, New York, brought back a few dozen of these fish. The storekeeper who was able to buy the whole lot thought himself lucky and ran a large advertisement in the newspapers proclaiming that these $1,000 fish were for sale at a much lower figure. He had to sell them several times because they were so vicious that customers brought them back. This is in direct contrast to what most European writers say about this species; therefore, it is possible that his species was misidentified. Although this fish has never been spawned, it should be tried. The smaller specimens show that soft, velvety black which is so desirable in the molly. As they grow larger the caudal fin takes on a golden hue, which may indicate maturity.

The hardiness of this species is emphasized by Horvath, who collected them. He says when he got on the boat he saw the black sharks making life miserable for several other species of fishes in the same can; having no extra can he placed them in an old pail, without aeration, and they all survived the 2½-month trip from Singapore.

GENUS *Osteochilus* Günther

[Oss'-tee-o-kil'-us: *osteo* = bony; *chilus* = lip]

BONY-LIPPED BARB / *Osteochilus vittatus* (Cuvier and Valenciennes)

[vit-tay'-tus: *vittatus* = striped]

Rohita vittata Cuvier and Valenciennes, Histoire naturelle des poissons, 16:267, 1842 (type locality, Java)

RANGE: Java, Borneo, Sumatra, Malay States, Siam.

SIZE: 2½ inches; breeding not observed.

TEMPERAMENT: A somewhat aggressive species but suitable in the community tank with fishes of its own size.

TEMPERATURE REQUIREMENTS: 70–80°F.

SEX DIFFERENCES: Not observed.

COUNTS: Dorsal iii,10 to 13; anal iii,5; pectoral i,13 to 16; pelvic i,8; scales 5½ to 6 + 33 to 34 + 6½.

The back is olive, becoming bright silver below. A black stripe runs from the snout through the eye to the tips of the middle rays of the bifurcate caudal fin. The fins are translucent or clear. Barbels are small.

Genus *Puntius* Hamilton = Buchanan

[Pun'-chus: *puntius* = boat-shaped]

The classification of the Old World fishes usually assigned to the genus *Barbus* as proposed by Cuvier and Cloquet in 1816 has been highly unsatisfactory. Weber and de Beaufort, and also Hugh M. Smith, after splitting off several genera, have adopted the generic name *Puntius* for that group of barbs usually referred to as *Barbus* from the East Indian region. Their reasons seem more valid than any others presented, especially since the name *Barbus* was used for a bird by Cuvier in 1798, which antedates its use for a fish. Ornithologists seriously question the use of *Barbus* by Cuvier in 1798 in the generic sense. To further complicate this matter of nomenclature, this "catch-all" genus *Barbus* Cuvier and Cloquet 1816 was based on *Cyprinus barbus* Linnaeus also known as *Barbus vulgaris*, a cyprinid inhabiting northern and central Europe which on closer study does not appear to be in the same phyletic line as the tropical barbs.

Since these matters are far from being settled, it seems best to follow the lead of Weber, de Beaufort, and Smith and use the name *Puntius*.

SPOTTED BARB / *Puntius binotatus* (Cuvier and Valenciennes)

[bi′-no-tay′-tus: *bi* = two; *notatus* = marked or spotted]

Barbus binotatus Cuvier and Valenciennes, Histoire naturelle des poissons, 16:168, 1842 (type locality, Java)

RANGE: East Indies, Malaya, Siam.

SIZE: 7 inches; breeds at 4 inches.

TEMPERAMENT: This active species is recommended for a community tank containing only large fishes.

TEMPERATURE REQUIREMENTS: 70–85°F.

SEX DIFFERENCES: Only the heaviness of the female indicates her sex.

COUNTS: Dorsal iv,8; anal iii,5; pectoral i,15 to 17; pelvic i,8 or 9; scales 4½ or 5 + 23 to 27 + 4½.

This easy-to-breed species should be placed in an aquarium with freshly conditioned water, heavily stocked with spawning grass. Select a very colorful male and a heavy female and feed great portions of *Daphnia* and *Tubifex;* chopped earthworms are of some value too. When the pair is ready it will dash into the thickets and spawn. The adhesive eggs will cling to the plants. The parents will ignore the eggs for a short time, but they should be removed as soon after spawning as possible. The young need plenty of *Infusoria,* brine shrimp, and microworms. Green water is very helpful for all fry of the barbs.

The over-all color of the fish is silver with a bluish tinge. There are black spots on the base of the dorsal, caudal, and anal fins. The younger fish show various markings which disappear as they get older. The size and intensity of the spots are variable.

The name of this species currently is *Barbodes binotatus.*

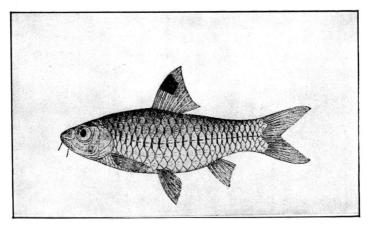

Puntius callipterus (Boulenger)

[kal-ip'-ter-us: *calli* = beautiful; *pterus* = a fin]

Barbus callipterus Boulenger, Ann. Mag. Nat. Hist., (7)20:486, 1907 (type locality, Kribi River, at Akok, South Cameroon)

RANGE: Cameroon and Niger River, West Africa.

SIZE: 3 inches; breeds at 2½ inches.

TEMPERAMENT: An active species, but suitable in the community tank.

TEMPERATURE REQUIREMENTS: 72–85°F.

SEX DIFFERENCES: Male is slimmer than the female, and with more colorful fins.

COUNTS: Dorsal iii,8; anal iii,5; scales 3½ + 23 to 26 + 2½.

This species breeds like other barbs but they are difficult to induce to spawn. Success on one occasion is not tantamount to subsequent successes. The selection of pairs is very important. The aquarium should be well stocked with artificial spawning grass or *Nitella*. Parent fish should be well fed on live foods, *Tubifex* and *Daphnia* being preferred.

The background color is yellowish brown, with the large scales darker brown at the base. The basal half of the caudal and dorsal fins is a shade of red which fluctuates to orange at times. The dorsal fin has a black spot that varies in size.

The name of this species currently is *Barbodes callipterus*.

SWAMP BARB / *Puntius chola* (Hamilton = Buchanan)

[cho'-la: a native Indian name]

Cyprinus chola Hamilton = Buchanan, Fishes of the River Ganges, pp. 312, 389, 1822 (type locality, Ganges River)
RANGE: India and Burma.
SIZE: 4½ inches; breeds at 3 inches.
TEMPERAMENT: An active species, suitable for the community aquarium.
TEMPERATURE REQUIREMENTS: 72–85°F.
SEX DIFFERENCES: The male has color in his anal and pelvic fins, whereas these fins are clear in the female.
COUNTS: Dorsal iii,8; anal ii,5; pectoral ii,13; pelvic i,8; scales 26 to 28.

This species has been confused with *Puntius conchonius* and has the same shape and color; therefore it is a very attractive fish. *P. conchonius* is more slender and lacks barbels. The gill covers of the swamp barb have a beautiful purplish-golden spot and there is a dark mark at the base of the dorsal fin.

This fish is more difficult to breed than the rosy barb, *P. conchonius*, but it follows the same general barb pattern. It requires large pieces of live food in the form of earthworms, sandworms, *Tubifex*, and the like. It takes *Daphnia* and dried food as well. Breeding is nearly always accomplished in ponds or large pools.

The name of this species currently is *Capoeta chola*.

ROSY BARB; RED BARB / *Puntius conchonius* (Hamilton = Buchanan)

[kon-chon'-i-us: probably a native name]

Cyprinus conchonius Hamilton = Buchanan, Fishes of the River Ganges, pp. 317, 389, 1822 (type locality, Ganges River)

RANGE: Assam, Bengal, Orissa, Bihar, Punjab, Deccan, all India.

SIZE: 5 inches; breeds at 2½ inches.

TEMPERAMENT: A peaceful but active species, suitable for the home aquarium.

TEMPERATURE REQUIREMENTS: 72–85°F.

SEX DIFFERENCES: The male is more colorful, the female having no color in her fins.

COUNTS: Dorsal iii,8; anal ii,5; pectoral ii,9; pelvic i,8; scales 24 to 26.

The rosy color is so distinct and beautiful that during this season storekeepers sell them by the scores. They are very hardy and easy to breed according to the standard methods for breeding barbs. Sexes should be separated at all times except when spawning. This keeps the fish in good color longer and also aids in selecting properly conditioned spawners. The rosy barb is prolific and should be spawned in a large tank, as many hundreds of fry will need a large amount of room. It may be spawned with ease in outdoor pools.

Cuming's Barb / *Puntius cumingi* (Günther)

[kum'-ing-eye: named in honor of an unknown Mr. Cuming]

Barbus cumingii Günther, Catalogue of the Fishes in the British Museum, 7:155, 1868 (type locality, Ceylon)

RANGE: Ceylon.

SIZE: 2 inches; breeds at 1¼ inches.

TEMPERAMENT: A peaceful species suitable for the community tank.

TEMPERATURE REQUIREMENTS: 72–85°F.

SEX DIFFERENCES: Male is more colorful than the female.

COUNTS: Dorsal ii,8; anal iii,5; pectoral i,11; pelvic i,7 or 8; scales 19 to 21.

Imported specimens are much larger than those tank-bred. Males in Ceylon reach a full 2 inches in length, but tank-raised fish rarely grow beyond the 1½-inch mark. This does not in any way affect their brilliant coloration or spawning, as the 1¼-inch fish are as active and colorful as the larger specimens. Though not a scavenger, this fish likes to feed off the bottom. Live food will keep the male in color nearly all year. This species breeds like all the barbs.

P. E. P. Deraniyagala, director of the National Museum of Ceylon, has recently illustrated this species. The two black bars cover 3 vertical rows of scales, the one behind the head reaching from 3 rows above the lateral line to opposite the pelvic base. The specimens illustrated may be a variety or a variation of the normal color pattern.

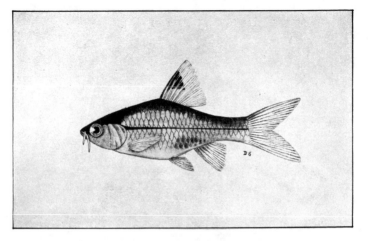

Puntius dorsimaculatus (Ahl)

[dor'-see-mack'-you-lay'-tus: *dorsi* = back; *maculatus* = spotted]

Barbus dorsimaculatus Ahl, Zool. Anz., 56(7,8):183, 1923 (type locality, Sumatra)

RANGE: Sumatra.

SIZE: 1½ inches; breeding not observed.

TEMPERAMENT: A peaceful species, excellent for the community tank.

TEMPERATURE REQUIREMENTS: 72–85°F.

SEX DIFFERENCES: Unknown.

COUNTS: Dorsal iii,8; anal iii,5; pelvic i,7; scales 24 to 26.

German literature states that this small species "probably spawns like other barbs." We are unable to verify this.

This barb has a brownish back, turning silvery on the lower sides and on the belly. A narrow black line follows the lateral line from the gill cover to the caudal peduncle. The dorsal fin has an obvious black spot. The fish is reputed to eat well on all sorts of foods, both live and prepared.

The name of this species currently is *Barbodes dorsimaculatus*.

Duncker's Barb / *Puntius dunckeri* (Ahl)

[dunk'-er-eye: named in honor of George Duncker, a German ichthyologist]

Barbus dunckeri Ahl, Das Aquarium, p. 165, fig., 1929 (type locality, Singapore)

RANGE: Malay.

SIZE: 5 inches; breeds at 3 inches.

TEMPERAMENT: A peaceful species when small, but adults should not be kept with other species.

TEMPERATURE REQUIREMENTS: 72–85°F.

SEX DIFFERENCES: Only the fullness of a ripe female indicates her sex.

COUNTS: Dorsal iii,8; anal iii,5; pelvic i,8; scales 23 or 24.

This species is easily bred but there is not much demand for it; therefore, commercial breeders do not pay much attention to it. The conditioning of the pairs is of the utmost importance. If one of the two sexes is ready to breed before the other it may become impatient and drive the other fish too hard.

There is a large blotch on the rosy-tinted back which looks like the shadow of the dorsal fin on the body. There are two pair of barbels, the maxillary (upper) pair being shorter than the posterior pair. The fins are yellowish, with the anal fin showing some red at the tip.

The name of this species currently is *Barbodes everetti.*

After Innes

CLOWN BARB / *Puntius everetti* (Boulenger)

[ev'-er-ett'-eye: named in honor of the collector, an unknown Mr. Everett]

Barbus everetti Boulenger, Ann. Mag. Nat. Hist., (6)13:248, 1844 (type locality Poeah, Sarawak, Borneo)

RANGE: Singapore, Borneo, Bunguran Island.

SIZE: 5 inches; breeds at 4 inches.

TEMPERAMENT: A peaceful species when small, but it should not be kept in the community aquarium except with fish its own size.

TEMPERATURE REQUIREMENTS: 72–85°F.

SEX DIFFERENCES: Only the fullness of the female indicates her sex.

COUNTS: Dorsal iv,8; anal iii,5; pectoral i,13; pelvic i,7; scales 3½ + 22 to 25 + 4½.

The difficulty in breeding this beauty lies in the incorrect method of conditioning. The most satisfactory method includes complete isolation of the males while offering both sexes enormous quantities of live foods and green plants. Chopped earthworms, sandworms, bloodworms, *Tubifex*, and fairy shrimp are well taken by the large fish. The breeding tank should be one of the long 20-gallon types (12 × 12 × 30 inches), heavily stocked with breeding grasses. Green water is best for the young, and if it is possible to allow one part of the tank to get direct sunlight this should be done.

Quite a mix-up has been caused by the improper identification of this species. It was incorrectly called *Barbus lateristriga*.

The name of this species currently is *Barbodes everetti*.

STRIPED BARB; ZEBRA BARB / *Puntius fasciatus* (Bleeker)

[fas'-see-a'-tus: *fasciatus* = banded or striped]

Barbus fasciatus Bleeker, Nat. Tijdschr. Ned. Indie, 5:190, 1853 (type locality, Bangka)

RANGE: Sumatra, Bangka, Borneo.

SIZE: 5 inches; breeding not observed.

TEMPERAMENT: A hardy, peaceful species suitable for the community tank.

TEMPERATURE REQUIREMENTS: 72–85°F.

SEX DIFFERENCES: Female shows less intense coloration than the male and is fuller.

COUNTS: Dorsal iv,8; anal iii,5; pectoral i,14 to 16; pelvic ii,8; scales 27.

This fish has not been bred, but not because aquarists have not tried. There are so many variables when trying to induce a fish to spawn that all tricks have a fair chance. The standard method of breeding barbs does not seem to work. When a pair is together the female and male simply ignore each other.

The sides of this fish are adorned with 6 stripes, which run nearly parallel from the head to tail. The female's stripes are not so clear as the male's. The fins are an attractive reddish to yellowish color. Two pair of barbels are obvious.

The name of this species currently is *Puntius lineatus*.

AFRICAN BANDED BARB / *Puntius fasciolatus* (Günther)

[fass'-see-o-lay'-tus: *fasciolatus* = a band]

Barbus fasciolatus Günther, Catalogue of the Fishes in the British Museum, 7:108, 1868 (type locality, Fluilla, Angola)

RANGE: Angola, West Africa.

SIZE: 2½ inches; breeding not observed.

TEMPERAMENT: An active species, suitable in the community tank.

TEMPERATURE REQUIREMENTS: 72–85°F.

SEX DIFFERENCES: Not apparent.

COUNTS: Dorsal iii,8; anal iii,5; scales 3½ + 25 + 2½.

Like many other African species, this one is not plentiful, because it occurs in a region that is not readily accessible to collectors of aquarium fishes and it is very difficult to induce to spawn. (No record exists of its having been spawned.) The color of the fish is attractive. A bluish sheen covers the entire body; the back is darker and the belly silvery. The side has 12 or 13 vertical bars.

The name of this species currently is *Barbodes fasciolatus*.

Black-spot Barb / *Puntius filamentosus* (Cuvier and Valenciennes)

[fil'-a-men-to'-sus: *fila* = a thread; *mentosus* = the chin]

Leuciscus filamentosus Cuvier and Valenciennes, Histoire naturelle des poissons, 17:96, pl. 492, 1844 (type locality, "Alypey")

RANGE: Ceylon, India, and Burma.

SIZE: 7 inches, breeding at 5 inches.

TEMPERAMENT: Not to be trusted with fishes small enough to be eaten whole.

TEMPERATURE REQUIREMENTS: 70–86°F.

SEX DIFFERENCES: Male is smaller than the female and shows the nuptial tubercles on his face when ready to spawn.

COUNTS: Dorsal iv,8; anal iii,5; pectoral i,15; pelvic i,8; scales 22 or 23.

This barb breeds in ponds like its close relative, the goldfish; however, a very large aquarium, heavily laden with plants, will serve the same purpose. The aquarium should be set up with half of one end filled with plants. Condition the parents on earthworms, *Tubifex* worms, and other meaty live foods. Dry foods are taken also. The female should be distended with eggs and the male should have the characteristic sexual tubercles (pimples) on his face. The female will deposit her eggs on the plants. Spawns are usually large, sometimes running into thousands of eggs. When spawning is completed the parents must be removed.

The fry require infusoria for a few days, then brine shrimp and *Daphnia*. The fry and young pass through a series of color changes scarcely resembling their parents. This has led to their confusion with *Puntius mahecola*.

GOLDEN DWARF BARB / *Puntius gelius* (Hamilton = Buchanan)

[gell'-i-us: probably a native name]

Cyprinus gelius Hamilton = Buchanan, Fishes of the River Ganges, pp. 320, 390, 1822 (type locality, Ganges River)

RANGE: Ganjam, Orissa, Bengal, Assam.

SIZE: 2 inches; breeds at 1½ inches.

TEMPERAMENT: A peaceful and shy species suitable for the community tank.

TEMPERATURE REQUIREMENTS: 65–85°F. Optimum at 70°F.

SEX DIFFERENCES: Male is ½ inch smaller than the female. The color is deeper in the male; the female is fuller.

COUNTS: Dorsal ii or iii,8; anal iii,5; pectoral ii,13; pelvic i,8; scales 23 or 24.

This species, though named over 100 years ago, is not well known to many hobbyists. The dwarf barb lives in one of those out-of-the-way places which makes importation impractical. Although it is fairly easy to induce these fish to spawn, they eat their eggs just as soon as they drop them. A special technique must be developed whereby adhesive eggs of this type may be protected from the eager parents. The Germans use a wire screen with holes just large enough to keep out the adult fish. This wire is suspended high enough above the floor of the breeding tank to allow the eggs to fall through without the parents having too great an opportunity to gobble up their own spawn.

The color of this fish is not outstanding. The back is olive green, becoming silvery as it approaches the belly. The sides have a golden tint.

Tiger Barb / *Puntius hexazona* (Weber and de Beaufort)

[hex'-a-zone'-a: *hex* = six; *zona* = bands]

Barbus (*Barbodes*) *hexazona* Weber and de Beaufort, Alfr. Maass: Dur. Zentral-Sumatra, 2:527, 1912 (type locality, Sumatra)

RANGE: Sumatra, Malay Peninsula.

SIZE: 2½ inches; breeds at 2 inches.

TEMPERAMENT: A peaceful but active species suitable for the community tank.

TEMPERATURE REQUIREMENTS: 70–85°F.

SEX DIFFERENCES: More intense color occurs in the male, especially in the fins.

COUNTS: Dorsal iv,8; anal iii,5; pectoral i,14; pelvic i,8; scales 5½ + 23 to 25 + 4½.

This species breeds in the same manner as other barbs. It is difficult to induce to spawn so all tricks must be tried: raise the temperature, feed ample supplies of *Daphnia,* and separate with a glass partition. When it does spawn it is prolific, producing nearly 300 eggs, which hatch in 56 hours at 80°F. The fry require copious amounts of infusoria, followed by the usual brine shrimp.

Puntius hexazona lacks color until it is of breeding size, but once it has attained sexual maturity it shows colors much like *P. tetrazona,* though with less gold. The males show a beautiful red around their fins, which they keep for the greater part of the year. The meaning of the name *hexazona* is easily verified by counting the stripes: one at the base of the tail and one through the eye mark the first and the sixth of the stripes which divide the body into six zones.

P. hexazona may be the same species as *P. pentazona.* About the only difference noted is that *pentazona* lacks the black bar through the eye.

The name of this species currently is *Barbodes pentazona hexazona.*

SPANNER BARB / *Puntius lateristriga* (Cuvier and Valenciennes)

[lat′-er-i-stri′-ga: *lateris* = side; *striga* = a streak]

Barbus lateristriga Cuvier and Valenciennes, Histoire naturelle des poissons, 16:161, 1842 (type locality, Java)

RANGE: Java, Borneo, Sumatra, Malay Peninsula, and Siam.

SIZE: 8 inches in native habitat but only 5 inches in captivity; breeds at 3 inches.

TEMPERAMENT: A peaceful species, desirable in the community tank.

TEMPERATURE REQUIREMENTS: 70–85°F.

SEX DIFFERENCES: The fullness of the female and the intense color of the male indicate sex.

COUNTS: Dorsal iv,8; anal iii,5; pectoral i,14 or 15; pelvic i,8; scales $4\frac{1}{2} + 23 + 3\frac{1}{2}$.

The Englishman who gave this fish its popular name "spanner barb" did so after noticing the dark horizontal stripe and two short vertical bars which form what the English call an "adjustable spanner." The American equivalent would be "monkey-wrench barb."

The general color is an olive gold—more gold than olive. The fins have a rosy tint.

Breeding is a rare occurrence, with the pairs dashing into thickets and expelling several hundred eggs. The young are very large at hatching and a week afterward are free-swimming and can take brine shrimp, microworms, and sifted *Daphnia*. They grow very rapidly on this diet.

The name of this species currently is *Barbodes lateristriga*.

Black Ruby or **Purple-headed Barb** / *Puntius nigrofasciatus* (Günther)

[ni'-grow-fas'-see-a'-tus: *nigro* = black; *fasciatus* = banded]

Barbus nigrofasciatus Günther, Catalogue of the Fishes in the British Museum, 7:155, 1868 (type locality, Ceylon)

RANGE: Ceylon.

SIZE: 2½ inches; breeds at 2 inches.

TEMPERAMENT: An active species, yet desirable in the community tank.

TEMPERATURE REQUIREMENTS: 72–82°F.

SEX DIFFERENCES: Male is much redder than the female.

COUNTS: Dorsal iii,8; anal iii,5; pectoral i,12; pelvic i,6; scales 20 to 22.

This species breeds in the typical barb style. The temperature for spawning should be slightly higher (about 80°) than for the majority of other barbs. The eggs hatch in 2½ days at this temperature and the young grow faster than those of other barbs.

CHECKERED BARB; IRIDESCENT BARB / *Puntius oligolepis* (Bleeker)

[ahl'-i-go-lep'-is: *oligo* = few; *lepis* = scales]

Capoeta oligolepis Bleeker, Nat. Tijd-schr. Ned. Indie, 4:296, 1853 (type local-ity, Sumatra)

RANGE: Sumatra.

SIZE: 2 inches; breeds at 2 inches.

TEMPERAMENT: A peaceful species, highly desirable for the community tank.

TEMPERATURE REQUIREMENTS: 72–85°F.

SEX DIFFERENCES: See below.

COUNTS: Dorsal iv,8; anal iii,5; pectoral i,12; pelvic i,7 or 8; scales $3\frac{1}{2}$ + 17 + $3\frac{1}{2}$.

This barb breeds like other barbs. No trick is needed; none is advised. The parent fish are very prolific and lay several hundred eggs among fine-leafed plants. The young hatch out in $2\frac{1}{2}$ days at 80°F. Green water and rotifers are a necessity for the growth of the newly hatched fry and the entire success of the spawning is dependent on the first week. Sometimes community spawning is practiced in hatcheries. The sexes should be in the ratio of three males to two females. As males become ready to breed they get much darker, while the females get very heavy and their checkerlike spots become more vivid.

The name of this species currently is *Capoeta oligolepis*.

BANDED BARB; TIGER BARB / *Puntius partipentazona* (Fowler)

[par'-ti-pen'-ta-zone'-a: *parti* = divided; *penta* = five; *zona* = bands]

Barbus partipentazona Fowler, Proc. Acad. Nat. Sci. Philadelphia, 86:344, fig. 8, 1934 (type locality, Krat River, Siam) RANGE: Siam, Malay States.

SIZE: 2 inches; breeds at 1½ inches.

TEMPERAMENT: A peaceful species desirable in the community aquarium.

TEMPERATURE REQUIREMENTS: 72–86°F.

SEX DIFFERENCES: The bright red in the dorsal fin is much brighter in the male than in the heavier female.

COUNTS: Dorsal iv,8; anal iii,5; pectoral i,13 or 14; pelvic i,8; scales 5½ + 20 to 22 + 5½.

This species breeds like other barbs but is not nearly so prolific as its cousins. Since many eggs are prone to fungus, the Methylene Blue treatment may be of value. This species has been confused with *Puntius tetrazona* and with *P. hexazona*. It became a famous aquarium fish under the name *Barbus tetrazonus*, but its nomenclature has been corrected by Weber and De Beaufort and especially Hugh M. Smith. *P. partipentazona* is a pleasing fish which is colored much like *P. tetrazona* (see color plate) except that the black dorsal fin bar does not extend on the body. The name refers to the 5 blackish bars seen in the illustration, counting the half band in the dorsal fin as the reason for its being called *partipentazona*.

The name of this species currently is *Capoeta tetrazona partipentazona*.

FIVE-BANDED BARB; BELTED BARB / *Puntius pentazona* (Boulenger)

[pen'-ta-zone'-a: *penta* = five; *zona* = bands]

Barbus pentazona Boulenger, Ann. Mag. Nat. Hist., (6)13:248, 1894 (type locality, Baram River, Sarawak, Borneo)

RANGE: Singapore, Borneo, Malay Peninsula.

SIZE: 2 inches; breeds at 1½ inches.

TEMPERAMENT: A peaceful species highly desirable in the community aquarium.

TEMPERATURE REQUIREMENTS: 74–85°F.

SEX DIFFERENCES: The male is more intensely colored than the female, who has no color in her pectoral fins.

COUNTS: Dorsal iii,8; anal iii,5; pelvic i,8; scales 5½ or 6 + 22 to 25 + 4½.

Easily bred, this fish does not have the place in the American aquarists' heart that it should. This is probably caused by lack of quantity. Few fishes are currently imported from Borneo and the Malay Peninsula. True barb-style breeding is manifest in the spawning of this species. The young are fast-growing and require brine shrimp after 10 days of the free-swimming infusoria stage.

The background color is copper-red on the back and red on the sides, with the belly a golden yellow. There are 5 bluish-black bars running around the body. The fins are all blood red at the base, losing their brilliance toward the edge, which is pinkish. The pectoral fins are very light pink.

The name of this species currently is *Barbodes pentazona*.

DWARF BARB; PYGMY BARB / *Puntius phutunio* (Hamilton = Buchanan)

[fu-tun'-i-o: probably a native name]

Cyprinus phutunio Hamilton = Buchanan, Fishes of the River Ganges, pp. 319, 390, 1822 (type locality, Ganges River)

RANGE: Ganjam, Orissa, Bengal, Burma.

SIZE: 2 inches; breeds at 1¼ inches.

TEMPERAMENT: A peaceful and desirable species for the community tank.

TEMPERATURE REQUIREMENTS: 72–85°F.

SEX DIFFERENCES: See below.

COUNTS: Dorsal ii or iii,8; anal iii,5; pectoral ii,13; pelvic i,8; scales 20 to 23.

These barbs are fairly easy to induce to spawn if maintained in an aquarium of about 5 gallons. Select a heavy female and a slim, active, colorful male. These are the only secondary sex characteristics. The aquarium should contain plenty of spawning grass so that the parents will not devour the eggs as soon as deposited. The percentage of fertilization is high. The dwarf barb readily takes all kinds of food, whether it is too large to ingest or not. Avoid large-particled foods.

The eggs hatch in 48 hours at 75° and the young are free-swimming within 72 hours after hatching. Rotifers are a preferred diet, after which brine shrimp and microworms should be offered.

HALF-STRIPED or GREEN BARB / *Puntius semifasciolatus* (Günther)

[sem'-i-fas'-see-o-lay'-tus: *semi* = half; *fasciolatus* = banded]

Barbus semifasciolatus Günther, Catalogue of the Fishes in the British Museum, 7:140, 484, 1868 (type locality, China)

RANGE: Southern China.

SIZE: 2½ inches; breeds at 2 inches.

TEMPERAMENT: A peaceful species suitable for the community tank.

TEMPERATURE REQUIREMENTS: 72–85°F.

SEX DIFFERENCES: The male becomes very red during breeding time. At this same time several ripe females will be noted to be heavier than males.

COUNTS: Dorsal iii,8; anal ii,5 or 6; pelvic i,7; scales 22 to 24.

The over-all color of this fish is light coppery brown with an olive-green shade. The fins have a yellowish-red tinge to them. There are 5 black vertical bars on the upper half of the body. A golden color variety has appeared which (according to Frederick Stoye in The Golden Variety of *Barbus semifasciolatus, The Aquarium*

Journal, June, 1950) has been credited to a golden sport raised by Thomas Schubert of Camden, New Jersey, a professional breeder. It seems that some of these sports were inbred and found to breed true, thus producing many thousands of the "new" fish. W. Ladiges, one of Germany's best aquarium writers and ichthyologists, was able to obtain a few of these sports. His report (*Wochenschrift für Aquarien und Terrarienkunde,* October, 1949) states that the new fish the Germans have been calling the brocaded barb is *Barbus schuberti.* He also states that this fish appeared in the United States after the war as *Puntius schuberti.* He credited Schubert with being the first "one to market the fish." Ladiges lists some important physical differences between *B. schuberti* and *B. semifasciolatus.* He states further that it is not a hybrid and it is not identical with *B. semifasciolatus* but seems to be closer to *B. sachsi.*

This is the fish which is called, unofficially, *Barbus schuberti*, after Tom Schubert of Camden, N.J. According to Ladiges, there are important physical differences between this fish and the fish from which it supposedly arose as a sport. Accordingly Dr. Ladiges has named the fish *Puntius sachsi*, although he has been unable to fix the type locality.

STOLICZKA'S BARB / *Puntius stoliczkai* (Day)

[sto-licks'-key-i: named in honor of the collector Stoliczka]

Danio stoliczkae Day, Proc. Zool. Soc. London, p. 621, 1869 (type locality, Burma)

RANGE: Burma, Siam.

SIZE: 2 inches; breeds at 1½ inches.

TEMPERAMENT: A peaceful species, desirable in the community tank.

TEMPERATURE REQUIREMENTS: 72–85°F.

SEX DIFFERENCES: The dorsal fin of the male is always reddish.

COUNTS: Dorsal iii,8; anal iii,5; pelvic i,8; scales 4½ or 5 + 22 to 25 + 3 to 3½.

This species is nearly identical with *Puntius ticto* in color pattern; however, a careful examination of the lateral lines will give a clue to the difference between them. The lateral line in *P. ticto* is incomplete, while in this barb it is complete. Hora states that the predorsal scales of *P. stoliczkai* number 8 or 9 whereas its closest relative *P. ticto* has 11 predorsal scales. This species lacks the usual barbels on the maxillary.

In current aquarium books the species name is misspelled *stoliczkanus*.

The name of this species currently is *Puntius ticto*.

ONE-SPOT BARB / *Puntius terio* (Hamilton = Buchanan)

[tare'-i-o: after a native name]

Cyprinus terio Hamilton = Buchanan, Fishes of the River Ganges, pp. 313, 389, 1822 (type locality, Ganges River)

RANGE: Orissa, Bengal to Punjab.

SIZE: 4 inches; breeds at 2 inches.

TEMPERAMENT: A peaceful species suitable for the community tank.

TEMPERATURE REQUIREMENTS: 72–85°F.

SEX DIFFERENCES: The deep orange color of the male at breeding time and the fullness of the female indicate sex.

COUNTS: Dorsal iii,8; anal ii,5; pectoral 1,14; pelvic i,8; scales 22 or 23.

Although this barb spawns readily in the aquarium, it is slightly more difficult to induce to spawn than the rosy barb. An attempt should be made to cross various species of barbs to see what kind of hybrids might be produced. Not much work has been done with crossing the egg layers.

The reddish spot on the gill cover, the punctated lateral line running from the dark ocellus lying over the last rays of the anal fin, and sometimes a dark streak in the dorsal fin are sufficient to characterize this species for aquarists. The color of the breeding male is a brilliant orange.

SUMATRAN or TIGER BARB / *Puntius tetrazona* (Bleeker)

[tet′-ra-zone′-a: *tetra* = four; *zona* = bands]

Capoeta tetrazona Bleeker, Nat. Tijdschr. Ned. Indie, 9:262, 1855 (type locality, Palembang)

RANGE: Sumatra, Borneo (not in Siam).

SIZE: 3 inches; breeds at 2 inches.

TEMPERAMENT: A peaceful species suitable for the community tank when small, but the adults may nip fins of small fishes.

TEMPERATURE REQUIREMENTS: 70–90°F.

SEX DIFFERENCES: The male has a typical "cherry nose." The female is less brilliantly colored and is heavier.

COUNTS: Dorsal iv,8; anal iv,5; pectoral i,13 or 14; pelvic i,8; scales 23.

This barb without doubt is one of the most beautiful of the group. The contrasting colors stay with it more or less throughout the year, depending on the amount of algae available to it to eat. True enough, live food will also color this fish, but a school of these barbs was left at the laboratory when one of the authors left on a Far Eastern trip. For 17 months these fish received nothing but the prepared food they had been getting intermittently when their keeper was there. Upon his return to the laboratory he noted that a thick blanket of algae had grown all along the bottom of the tanks and every male Sumatran barb was in full color! This was exceptional as it was out of their season. A closer observation verified the fact that these barbs made a steady meal of the algae, while the algae kept the aquarium immaculately clean of the fish's droppings, utilizing the rich store of nitrogen and other compounds in the fecal matter. The barbs maintained their brilliant colors, the males their cherry-colored noses throughout the year without any extra live foods. Repeated spawnings took place in this community tank. When pairs were taken out and conditioned further on live food for controlled spawning, they did so readily. They prefer some direct sunlight in part of their aquarium and like the stringy type of algae which is promoted by direct sunlight.

This species is represented in Siam by *Puntius partipentazona*. This species is

also known as *Barbus sumatranus* on the basis of Bleeker's redescription (*Systomus Capöeta sumatranus, Ichthy. Arch. Ind. Prod.*, 2:354, 1860) from Sumatra, but this name is a synonym of *P. tetrazona*.

The name of this species currently is *Capoeta tetrazona*.

Two-spot Barb or Tic-tac-toe Barb /
Puntius ticto (Hamilton = Buchanan)

[tick'-toe: after a native name]

Cyprinus ticto Hamilton = Buchanan, Fishes of the River Ganges, pp. 314, 389, pl. 8, fig. 87, 1822 (type locality, Ganges River)

RANGE: Southern India and Ceylon.

SIZE: 4 inches; breeds at 2 inches.

TEMPERAMENT: A peaceful species when small and suitable for the community tank, but when of full adult size it may attack smaller fishes.

TEMPERATURE REQUIREMENTS: 72–85°F.

SEX DIFFERENCES: Male has more brilliant color.

COUNTS: Dorsal iii,8; anal ii,5; pectoral i,14; pelvic i,8; scales 23 to 26.

This is one of the barbs without barbels. Closely compared with *Puntius stoliczkai*, it will be noted that the only external difference is the incomplete lateral line of this fish. The male is the handsome member of the family, with a beautiful dorsal fin.

Breeding is comparatively easy and is in typical barb style.

CHERRY BARB / *Puntius titteya* Deraniyagala

[tit-tay´-a: after a Ceylonese name]

Puntius titteya Deraniyagala, Spolia Zeylanica, 15:73, 1929 (type locality, Ceylon)

RANGE: Ceylon.

SIZE: 2 inches; breeds at 1½ inches.

TEMPERAMENT: A peaceful species suitable in the community tank.

TEMPERATURE REQUIREMENTS: 75–90°F. Optimum breeding temperature 80°F.

SEX DIFFERENCES: The mature female may be recognized by her distended body; the male has brighter colors.

COUNTS: Dorsal iii,7; anal iii,5; pectoral i,10; pelvic i,8; scales 19 or 20.

This fish is easy to spawn but the young are hard to raise. Most losses occur in the first week of life when there are insufficient small infusoria for them to eat. A pure culture of rotifers is practically a necessity for any success at all.

Parent fish are so active during spawning that they are continually splashing around, often jumping clear out of the water and onto the floor. Covers must be provided for all tanks containing these barbs.

The name of this species currently is *Capoeta titteya.*

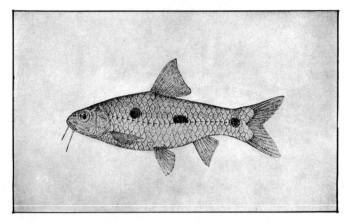

AFRICAN THREE-SPOT BARB / *Puntius trispilos* Bleeker

[try-spy'-lus: *tri* = three; *spilos* = spots]

Puntius (*Barbodes*) *trispilos* Bleeker, Nat. Verh. Vet. Haarlem, 18(2):113, pl. 23, fig. 3, 1863 (type locality, Dabo-Crom, Guinea)

RANGE: Guinea, Gold Coast, Liberia, West Africa.

SIZE: 2½ inches; breeding not observed.

TEMPERAMENT: A peaceful species suitable for the community tank.

TEMPERATURE REQUIREMENTS: 75–90°F. Optimum breeding temperature 80°F.

SEX DIFFERENCES: Male is slimmer and more colorful.

COUNTS: Dorsal iii,8 or 9; anal iii,5 or 6; pectoral i,14; pelvic i,8; scales 4½ + 25 to 28 + 3½.

The only report of the spawning of this species is not very complete. It is said to spawn like other barbs. Because this African barb has been scarce in home aquaria, not much has been written about it.

The back is light brown; the rest of the body is silvery. There are three dark oval spots on the side.

The name of this species currently is *Barbodes trispilos.*

RED-FINNED BARB / *Puntius unitaeniatus* (Günther)

[you-ni-tee'-ni-a'-tus: *uni* = one; *taeniatus* = striped]

Barbus unitaeniatus Günther, Zool. Rec., p. 151, 1866; Catalogue of the Fishes in the British Museum, 4:103, 1868 (type locality, Angola)
RANGE: Angola, Transvaal, Zululand, Natal.
SIZE: 3 inches; breeds at 2 inches.
TEMPERAMENT: A peaceful species, suitable in the community tank when small, but it nips fins when of adult size.
TEMPERATURE REQUIREMENTS: 75–88°F.
SEX DIFFERENCES: Male is slimmer and more colorful than the female.

COUNTS: Dorsal ii,8; anal ii,5; scales $4\frac{1}{2}$ to $5\frac{1}{2}$ + 30 to 33 + $4\frac{1}{2}$.

Breeding is reported to be the same as for other species of the genus *Puntius*. The over-all color is brownish yellow, with the back brownish, becoming yellow on the belly. A dark stripe runs along the side which may end in a round blackish spot on the caudal peduncle. Sometimes there are rows of dots on the sides. The fins have a reddish tinge.

The name of this species currently is *Barbodes unitaeniatus*.

Puntius vittatus (Day)

[vit-tay'-tus: vittatus = striped]

Barbus vittatus Day, Proc. Zool. Soc. London, p. 303, 1865 (type locality, Malabar)

RANGE: Indian Peninsula, Ceylon.

SIZE: 2 inches; breeds at 2 inches.

TEMPERAMENT: A peaceful species, rather active but suitable in the community tank.

TEMPERATURE REQUIREMENTS: 68–88°F.

SEX DIFFERENCES: The fullness of the mature female indicates her sex. There is more color in the male.

COUNTS: Dorsal ii,8; anal ii,5; pectoral i,11; pelvic i,8; scales 20 to 22.

This species is easy to breed and does so in typical barb manner. The body is a shiny yellowish green. The side is peppered with tiny dark dots. There is a dark oval spot in a yellow background on the caudal peduncle. The fins are quite clear except for the dorsal, which has a stripe through it and an orange edge. The young are streaked.

WERNER'S BARB / *Puntius werneri* (Boulenger)

[wer'-ner-eye: named in honor of F. Werner]

Barbus werneri Boulenger, Proc. Zool. Soc. London, no. 1, p. 63, 1905 (type locality, Lower Nile River)

RANGE: Nile River of Egypt, Sudan, and East Africa.

SIZE: 2 inches; breeds at 1½ inches, although it has not been bred in captivity.

TEMPERAMENT: A peaceful species suitable in the community tank.

TEMPERATURE REQUIREMENTS: 72–85°F.

SEX DIFFERENCES: The female is more robust than the male when she is mature and with eggs.

COUNTS: Dorsal iii,8; anal iii,5; pelvic i,5; scales 24 to 26.

Although this barb has never been bred, there is a preserved specimen of a ripe female which attained a length of only 1½ inches.

The color is olive green or yellowish on the back, with silvery sides. The fins have a bluish cast to them at times. The middle of the side has from 3 to 8 small round black spots along a narrow dark streak.

The name of this species currently is *Barbodes werneri*.

318   Family CYPRINIDAE

Genus *Rasbora* Bleeker

[Ras-bor'-a: a native fish name]

Silver Rasbora / *Rasbora argyrotaenia* (Bleeker)

[arr'-gy-row-tee'-ni-a: *argyro* = silvery; *taenia* = band or stripe]

Leuciscus argyrotaenia Bleeker, Verh. Batavia. Gen., 23:21, 1850 (type locality, Java)

RANGE: East Indies, Malaya, Annam, Siam.

SIZE: 7 inches; breeding not observed.

TEMPERAMENT: A peaceful species when small but not desirable in the community aquarium when adult.

TEMPERATURE REQUIREMENTS: 72–85°F.

SEX DIFFERENCES: Mature female is more robust than the male.

COUNTS: Dorsal ii,7; anal iii,5; pectoral i,12 or 13; pelvic i,7 or 8; scales 29 or 30.

This species was successfully maintained by Herbert Axelrod while in Japan and in Siam. It is seldom offered for sale in any quantity in the United States, probably because it is so hard to breed. It certainly is a colorful and pleasing fish for the aquarium. Hardiness and ease of feeding make it remarkably desirable. Specimens do not grow larger than 4 inches when maintained in the home aquarium.

The coloration is interesting: the area around the dorsal fin is brownish yellow, becoming orange laterally. A brilliant brownish-red stripe runs from its snout to the caudal peduncle.

Slender Rasbora / *Rasbora daniconia* (Hamilton = Buchanan)

[dan'-i-co'-ni-a: probably after a native name]

Cyprinus daniconius Hamilton = Buchanan, Fishes of the River Ganges, pp. 327, 391, pl. 15, fig. 89, 1822 (type locality, Ganges River)

RANGE: India, Ceylon, Burma, Andaman Islands.

SIZE: 7 inches; breeds at 3 inches in the aquarium.

TEMPERAMENT: A peaceful species, suitable in the community aquarium.

TEMPERATURE REQUIREMENTS: 70–85°F.

SEX DIFFERENCES: Only the roundness of the female is a clue to any sexual difference, and this is rather hard to discern.

COUNTS: Dorsal ii,6 or 7; anal ii,5; pectoral i,13 or 14; pelvic i,7 or 8; scales 30 to 34.

This is one of the easier species of *Rasbora* to breed. It spawns much like the barbs, laying eggs on fine-leafed plants or on the popular artificial spawning grass, Spanish moss. If difficulty is encountered in inducing the fish to spawn, it may be attributed to such factors as: (1) the fish are both of the same sex; (2) the pH is too high; or (3) the water is too hard. This species is difficult to sex and only a careful study of the roundness of the female will offer any clue. Heavy females should be immediately isolated. A pH as low as 5.6 is necessary for spawning this *Rasbora*. A temperature of about 79 to 82°F should be maintained. Soft water or water of zero hardness is necessary. Zeolite softeners should be added to the filtering unit if the water is too hard.

The young vary in size and should be sorted as they grow to prevent cannibalism. Infusoria should be offered as soon as the young are free-swimming (about 3 days after the eggs hatch). Rotifers are best for the first few days.

This species has been confused with *Rasbora einthoveni* (Bleeker) (page 321) but differs in having 9 instead of 7 rows of scales between the lateral lines counted over the dorsal part of the caudal peduncle; 14 or 15 scales between the head and the origin of the dorsal fins instead of 12 or 13.

Eyespot Rasbora / *Rasbora dorsiocellata* Duncker

[dor'-see-os'-sel-lay'-ta: *dorsi* = back; *ocellata* = eyelike spot]

Rasbora dorsiocellata Duncker, Mitth. Naturh. Mus. Hamburg, 21:182, pl. 1, fig. 2, 1904 (type locality, Malay Peninsula)

RANGE: Sumatra, Malay Peninsula.

SIZE: 2 inches; breeding not observed.

TEMPERAMENT: A peaceful species suitable in the community tank.

TEMPERATURE REQUIREMENTS: 70–85°F.

SEX DIFFERENCES: The mature female is larger than the male and much fuller.

COUNTS: Dorsal ii,7; anal iii,5; pectoral i,15; pelvic i,7; scales 28 to 30.

This fish has not been bred in captivity although it undoubtedly breeds the same way as other *Rasbora*. The habitat of this species is in the smaller streams and ponds in the Malay country, where large schools of eyespots are to be found. This great prolificacy may be due to the pH of the native waters (which is 5.6), the temperature of 76°F, the softness of the water (zero hardness), or the fact that in the three areas which have been investigated there were very thick growths of *Cryptocoryne*, in which millions of fry could be seen hovering for protection.

The natural food of the parents is mosquito and other insect larvae. The area thick with *Cryptocoryne* was dense with fine infusoria and rotifers. It has often been stated in the German literature that rotifers are the best foods to offer young fishes.

Natives do not collect these fish for any reason except to use as fertilizer.

In the aquarium this fish is very hardy and, with the exception of the eyespot in the dorsal (which so reminds one of a strain of guppy that has appeared with an ocellated dorsal), the fish is just plain silvery.

Rasbora dusonensis (Bleeker)

THE BRILLIANT RASBORA / *Rasbora einthoveni* (Bleeker)

[ine-tho'-ven-eye: named in honor of I. Einthoven, the collector]

Leuciscus einthovenii Bleeker, Nat. Tijdschr. Ned. Indie, 2:434, 1851 (type locality, Sambas, Borneo)

RANGE: Dutch East Indies, Singapore, Malaya, Siam.

SIZE: 4 inches; breeds at 3 inches.

TEMPERAMENT: A peaceful species desirable in the community tank.

TEMPERATURE REQUIREMENTS: 72–85°F.

SEX DIFFERENCES: The male has a broader stripe and a purplish cast to the body. The female is best described as being greenish. All the female's fins are clear, except the caudal which is yellowish. The male has a soft red in the dorsal fin (which darkens with conditioning) and has a sort of "wagtail," substituting red for the familiar black. The female has a hyaline caudal fin.

COUNTS: Dorsal ii,7; anal iii,5 or 6; pectoral, i,12; pelvic i,8; scales 29 to 32.

How this fish was ever given the name "brilliant rasbora" is somewhat of a mystery, as the fish is anything but brilliant. The colors are "striking," but that is as enthusiastic as one can get. The fish is dark gray on the back, getting lighter below the lateral line. The scales are edged with black. A striking black stripe runs from the lower jaw through the eye to the fork of the caudal fin. The eye is red.

Spawning is rather easily accomplished. The water should be soft and somewhat acid (pH 6.4) and a temperature of 76° should be maintained in the heavily planted aquarium. Fine-leafed plants (for example, *Myriophyllum, Nitella, Cabomba,* and artificial spawning grass) should be packed into an area at one end of the aquarium. The eggs are reported to fungus rather easily. When 2 drops of a 5 per cent aqueous solution of Methylene Blue is added to each gallon of water few eggs are lost.

YELLOW RASBORA; ELEGANT RASBORA / *Rasbora elegans* Volz

[el′-e-gans: *elegans* = fine, beautiful]

Rasbora elegans Volz, Zool. Anz., 26:558, 1903 (type locality, Palembang, Sumatra)

RANGE: Sumatra, Borneo, Singapore, Malaya.

SIZE: 5 inches; breeds at 3 inches.

TEMPERAMENT: A peaceful species, desirable in the community tank when small; when of adult size it will attack small fishes.

TEMPERATURE REQUIREMENTS: 70–85°F. Optimum breeding temperature 76°F.

SEX DIFFERENCES: The anal fin of the male is yellow but that of the female is hyaline.

COUNTS: Dorsal ii,7; anal iii,5; pectoral i,14; pelvic i,6; scales 24 to 29.

This species is becoming more popular in the smaller sizes. Early imports were either 4 inches long or they easily grew that large in a few months of good care.

As the fish was tank-bred, time after time, it kept maturing at smaller sizes until now mature and fully grown specimens rarely become longer than 3 inches. With this decrease in size has come an increase in popularity; owing to increased demands native stocks are being imported again, a situation that may upset the size of the domesticated stocks.

The back is an olive brown which gradually changes to lighter shades as it approaches the belly. There is a fine bluish line connecting the two spots, clearly seen in the illustration. Some of the fins show tinges of color.

Breeding is in true barb style with the depositing of eggs in thick bunches of plants, a characteristic method of propagation. The young hatch in 3 days and grow rapidly. Some larger fry are able to make a meal out of their smaller brothers and sisters.

HARLEQUIN FISH; THE RASBORA / *Rasbora heteromorpha* Duncker

[het'-air-o-mor'-fa: *hetero* = different; *morpha* = form or shape]

Rasbora heteromorpha Duncker, Mitth. Naturh. Mus. Hamburg, 21:182, pl. 1, fig. 5, 1904 (type locality, Singapore; Malaya)

RANGE: Eastern Sumatra, Malaya, Siam.

SIZE: 2 inches; breeds at 1½ inches.

TEMPERAMENT: A peaceful species and one of the most desirable in the community tank.

TEMPERATURE REQUIREMENTS: 70–85°F. Temperature changes must be very gradual as these fish get the ich very easily.

SEX DIFFERENCES: The male shows more gold all over than the female. This is especially true of the dorsal base and the top part of the triangular black marking so characteristic of this species.

COUNTS: Dorsal ii,7; anal iii,5; pectoral i,12; pelvic i,7; scales 26 or 27.

In Singapore this species was the least expensive of those for sale. The current price of this most desirable fish was less than 3 cents each. They are so plentiful and available that they are caught by thousands and made into a pancake-like delicacy. They are also used for fertilizer. In America, however, they command a high price and are easily sold. The fact that they must travel 2½ months by boat from Singapore is probably responsible for this great increase in price. There is a maxim in the fish-importing business that "the rasbora (meaning *R. heteromorpha*) pays for the trip." This is meant to imply that enough rasboras are brought back to enable the importer to pay all his expenses incurred in the trip. The rest of the fishes brought in are his profit. Anywhere up to about 70,000 rasboras are brought in four times a year. If a larger shipment arrived there would not be sufficient space for them and prices would come down.

Breeding the rasbora is not a simple matter since only a few experienced breeders have been able to perform the feat repeatedly. The selection of a pair, well-conditioned on white worms, *Tubifex*, and *Daphnia*, is a necessity to successful spawning. A pair should be placed in a tank of freshly conditioned soft water with a pH of 6.4 and a temperature of 76°F. The male will swim around the female and soon they will start to hunt for a broad leaf upon which to attach their eggs. The female will finally locate a site and rub her belly against the underside of the leaf, at which moment the male will embrace her and they will deposit their spawn on the site selected. They have prolific spawns of up to 300 at a time. Parents should be removed after spawning. The eggs are very clear for the first few hours, then they cloud. The young hatch in 24 hours. The young, once they hatch, are very hardy and need rotifers and other pond infusoria, followed by brine shrimp.

Rasbora espei.

Rasbora species

Spotted or Pygmy Rasbora / *Rasbora maculata* Duncker

[mack'-you-lay'-ta: *maculata* = spotted]

Rasbora maculata Duncker, Mitth. Naturh. Mus. Hamburg, 21:182, pl. 1, fig. 6, 1904 (type locality, Bandar Maharani, Malay Peninsula)

RANGE: Malay Peninsula.

SIZE: 1 inch; breeds at 1 inch.

TEMPERAMENT: A peaceful species, most desirable for the community tank.

TEMPERATURE REQUIREMENTS: 72–85°F.

SEX DIFFERENCES: The female has two spots above the anal fin while the male has only one.

COUNTS: Dorsal ii,6; anal iii,5; pectoral i,13; pelvic i,7; scales 31.

This species is one of the favorites. It has an enchanting beauty when about 100 spotted rasbora are kept alone in a 20-gallon aquarium.

Breeding is no feat at all. The selection of a full female and an active male ensures spawning. Sexes should be maintained in separate aquaria for the seasoning process. An aquarium should be arranged with a profuse growth of *Cryptocoryne* and *Sagittaria*. The water should be half changed with soft water and adjusted to a pH of 6.4. The females should be placed in the aquarium the evening before the males are introduced. Brine shrimp and sifted *Daphnia* should be offered at this time. The next morning the males should be introduced. Spawning should take place within 48 hours with the male driving the female to a clean leaf and constantly dancing about her. The female will select a spot to lay her adhesive eggs, usually the underside of a *Cryptocoryne* leaf. When the female assumes her position the male will immediately nudge her; he fertilizes the egg cluster as laid. Depositing of eggs goes on for many hours; as many as 200 eggs have been counted. The aquarium should be given the Methylene Blue treatment after spawning, and the parents should be removed. The eggs hatch in 24 hours at 78°F. It is absolutely essential that rotifers be offered the young, as the larger infusoria choke the fry. Sometimes it is of value to raise the temperature if the pairs are reluctant to spawn.

Although Weber and de Beaufort place this species as a synonym of *Rasbora kalochroma* (Bleeker), it is a valid species with one less anal ray and a different color pattern.

MEINKEN'S RASBORA / *Rasbora meinkeni* de Beaufort

[mine'-ken-eye: named in honor of the aquarist Hermann Meinken]

Rasbora meinkeni de Beaufort, Das Aquarium, p. 8, June, 1931 (type locality, Sumatra)

RANGE: Sumatra.

SIZE: 3 inches; breeds at 2½ inches.

TEMPERAMENT: A peaceful species, desirable in the community tank.

TEMPERATURE REQUIREMENTS: 75–90°F.

SEX DIFFERENCES: The great fullness of the female indicates her sex.

COUNTS: Dorsal ii,7; anal iii,5; pectoral i,12; pelvic i,6; scales 25.

This species is rather rare at the present time in aquaria, although previously it was very common in the market.

There are claims that this species is easy to breed, but they must come from people who have not seen the fish. Many top aquarists in England, France, Germany, and Holland have tried to breed it, without consistent success. Most breeding records are incomplete and inaccurate, but evidence indicates it spawns like other *Rasbora*. The eggs are deposited on the leaves of plants.

The back is olive green, becoming yellowish ventrally. A black band runs from the gill cover to the fork of the caudal fin; a second band is along the middorsal line of the back; a third short band is on the base of the anal fin. The anal fin is yellowish; the dorsal and caudal fins have a rusty tinge.

High temperatures are enjoyed by this fish, a good temperature for it being 80°F.

Dr. Martin R. Brittan thinks *R. trifasciatus* Popta may be the same species as *R. meinkeni*.

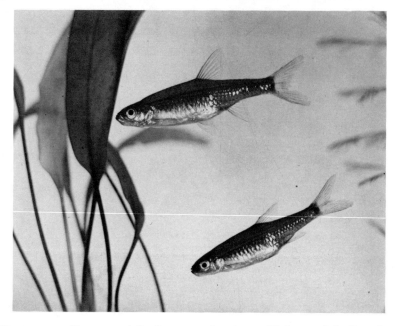

RED-STRIPED RASBORA / *Rasbora pauciperforata* Weber and de Beaufort

[pau'-see-purr'-for-a'-ta: *pauci* = few; *perforata* = perforated]

Rasbora pauciperforata Weber and de Beaufort, Fishes of the Indo-Australian Archipelago, 3:78, fig. 28, 1916 (type locality, Sumatra)

RANGE: Sumatra.

SIZE: 3 inches; breeding not observed.

TEMPERAMENT: A peaceful species, desirable in the community tank.

TEMPERATURE REQUIREMENTS: 72–85°F.

SEX DIFFERENCES: Unknown.

COUNTS: Dorsal ii,7; anal iii,5; pectoral i,11 or 12; pelvic i,8; scales 32 or 33.

The breeding of this fish is still a mystery. Very few specimens have been reported and few have reached America. Several breeders in Europe have a few specimens. The authors have seen only one pair of these fish (living).

The background color of this fish is aquamarine. A thin golden stripe which turns reddish at times runs from the head to the base of the caudal fin. It is edged by a fine black line.

Rasbora steineri Nichols and Pope

[sti'-ner-eye; named in honor of J. F. Steiner]

Rasbora cephalotaenia steineri Nichols and Pope, Bull. Amer. Mus. Nat. Hist., 54:364, fig. 30, 1927 (type locality, Hainan)
RANGE: Hainan, China.
SIZE: 3 inches.
TEMPERAMENT: Peaceful.

TEMPERATURE REQUIREMENTS: 72–85°F.
SEX DIFFERENCES: Not observed.
COUNTS: Dorsal 9; anal 7, scales 27 to 29.

This species has never been bred. It should receive standard Rasbora care.

BLACK-STRIPED RASBORA / *Rasbora taeniata* Ahl

[tee'-ni-a'-ta: *taeniata* = striped]

Rasbora taeniata Ahl, Blät. Aquar.-Terrak., p. 295, 1922; Zool. Anz., 46:181, 1923 (type locality, Sumatra)

RANGE: Sumatra.

SIZE: 3 inches; breeds at 2 inches.

TEMPERAMENT: A peaceful species desirable in the community tank.

TEMPERATURE REQUIREMENTS: 74–88°F.

SEX DIFFERENCES: The base of the caudal fin of the male is orange; sometimes an especially colorful female will show this orange, but never is it as deep as the male's.

COUNTS: Dorsal ii,7; anal iii,5; scales 31.

This is one of the easiest of the species of *Rasbora* to spawn. The eggs are large and hardy and the young do well on infusoria. Although this fish spawns like some barbs, the aquarium should be no smaller than a 10-gallon size and as long and flat as possible. The entire back half and one full end of the aquarium should be thickly stocked with spawning grass, the finer the better. This aquarium should have a pH of 6.6 and zero hardness of water. The temperature should be raised to 80°F from the minimum of 74° at which the fish do well. Community spawning of these fish is worth trying. Conditioning should take place with the females in the breeding tank and the males separated. Twice as many males should be placed in with the females, when they are showing fine color and when the females are full. They spawn in pairs, with the adhesive eggs sticking to the plants.

Rasbora vaterifloris.

Rasbora sumatrana.

THREE-LINED or SCISSOR-TAILED RASBORA / *Rasbora trilineata* Steindachner

[try-lin'-e-a'-ta: *tri* = three; *lineata* = streaked]

Rasbora trilineata Steindachner, Sitzb. Akad. Wiss. Wien, 61(1):637, 1870 (type locality, Johore; Pengulon Patie)

RANGE: Borneo, Sumatra, Siam.

SIZE: 8 inches; breeds at 3 inches.

TEMPERAMENT: A peaceful species, desirable in the community tank when small.

TEMPERATURE REQUIREMENTS: 74–88°F.

SEX DIFFERENCES: Only the fullness of the female indicates the sex.

COUNTS: Dorsal ii,7; anal iii,5; pectoral i,15; pelvic i,7; scales 29 to 33.

This species breeds in the same manner as the White Cloud Mountainfish, *Tanichthys albonubes* (page 334). A well planted aquarium should be supplied with fresh water. After a few days the pairs should be put in and kept well fed. Since spawning occurs at night or in the dark, keep the tank covered except when feeding. Do not change the environment from

darkness to light very rapidly (that is, do not turn on a light when the fish has acclimated itself to absolute darkness). The breeders will not eat too many fry or eggs if they are well fed on *Daphnia* and *Tubifex* and some dry foods. The youngsters require infusoria as soon as they are free-swimming.

The body is nearly translucent and silvery with a brownish cast. The back is darker, as a protective coloration. A dark brown stripe runs along the lateral line until it meets a spot on the caudal peduncle. Another darker line runs along the bottom of the fish from the anal fin to the base of the caudal fin. Each lobe of the caudal fin is distinctly marked, with hyaline tips, a black triangular spot in the center, and an orange base. The caudal fin is compressed after each stroke in swimming and this action is compared to a scissorlike motion, thus the popular name "scissortail."

GENUS *Rhodeus* Agassiz

[Roe'-dee-us: *rhodeus* = pertaining to a rose]

BITTERLING / *Rhodeus sericeus* (Pallas)

[se-ri'-shus: *sericeus* = silky sheen]

Cyprinus sericeus Pallas, Reise durch verschiedene Provinzen des russischen Reiches, 3:208, 704, 1776; Zoographia Rosso-Asiatica, 3:320, 1811 (type locality, southern Europe)

RANGE: Central and southern Europe.

SIZE: 3 inches.

TEMPERAMENT: A peaceful species, but not entirely suitable in the community tank.

TEMPERATURE REQUIREMENTS: 40–75°F.

SEX DIFFERENCES: Male is beautifully colored in spring and early summer.

COUNTS: Dorsal ii,9 to 11; anal iii,8 to 10; pectoral i,11 or 12; pelvic i,7; scales 34 to 40.

The bitterling is one of the smaller European fresh-water fishes. Its breeding habits are remarkable: The female injects her eggs into the inhalant siphon of a fresh-water mussel. This feat is accomplished by means of a 2- or 3-inch-long ovipositor (egg depositor). The eggs are then washed into the gill chamber of the host. There is doubt that this relation can be called parasitic or symbiotic, for the eggs are merely protected from the outside world by the shell of the mussel; they take nothing from the mussel and the latter receives nothing from the developing fry. The young have large yolk sacs from which they derive their food. A male will carefully investigate many mussels before he selects a fine specimen and drives the female to it. He will not select a dead mussel even if there are no live ones in the aquarium. The female swoops down rapidly on the mussel, with her ovipositor immediately coming to position. She invariably is able to locate the right spot to insert her ovipositor. The male releases his sperm over the inhalant siphon and the milt is carried down to fertilize the eggs inside the mussel. Eggs are laid singly or a few at a time. Numerous mussels may be used by the same female and spawning may cover several days.

After spawning the parent fish should be removed. The fry will appear in 35 days at 70°F.

The parents like plenty of live food; sandworms, bloodworms, and earthworms are their favorites. The fish should be fed twice a week.

FAMILY CYPRINIDAE

GENUS *Tanichthys* Lin

[Tan'-ik-thees: named in honor of a Chinese boy named Tan, who brought the fish to the attention of Lin]

WHITE CLOUD MOUNTAINFISH / *Tanichthys albonubes* Lin

[al'-bow-new'-bees: *albo* = white; *nubes* = clouds]

Tanichthys albonubes Lin, Shu-yen, Lingnan Sci. Jour. 11(2):379, 1932 (type locality, White Cloud Mountain, Canton, China)

RANGE: White Cloud Mountain, Canton, China.

SIZE: 1½ inches; breeds at 1 inch.

TEMPERAMENT: A peaceful species desirable for the community tank.

TEMPERATURE REQUIREMENTS: 40–85°F. Best breeding temperature 70°F.

SEX DIFFERENCES: Female is much heavier and less brilliant than the male.

COUNTS: Dorsal ii,7; anal iii,8; scales 30.

This species is not truly tropical, but it is so beautiful and easy to breed that it has won a place in every home aquarium. Breeding is so simple that it may be called the easiest egg layer to spawn. A pair may be placed in anything from a milk bottle to a lake and spawn will be noticed. The best way to spawn the pair is to feed it heavily with brine shrimp, *Daphnia, Tubifex,* microworms, or white worms and place the pair in a heavily planted aquarium with little light and no snails. The female will deposit adhesive eggs in all directions and will not bother eggs or young if kept well-fed.

The young are easily mistaken for neons and are very hardy.

[Co-bit′-i-dee]

GENUS *Acanthophthalmus* Van Hasselt

[A-can′-thof-thal′-mus: *acanth* = thorn or spine; *ophthalmus* = eye]

COOLIE LOACH; LEOPARD "EEL"; STRIPED LOACH; PRICKLY EYE /
Acanthophthalmus kuhli (Cuvier and Valenciennes)

[ku′-lye: named in honor of Heinrich Kuhl]

Cobitis kuhlii Cuvier and Valenciennes, Histoire naturelle des poissons, 18:77, 1846 (type locality, Batavia)

RANGE: Java, Borneo, Sumatra, Singapore, Malaya, Siam.

SIZE: 3½ inches; breeds at about 3 inches.

TEMPERAMENT: A peaceful and useful scavenger in the community aquarium.

TEMPERATURE REQUIREMENTS: 72–80°F.

SEX DIFFERENCES: The female is more robust than the male.

COUNTS: Dorsal ii,7 or 8; anal ii,6 or 7; pectoral i,8; pelvic i,5.

This species has been reported to spawn during a nuptial embrace, but details are lacking. It is sensitive to light, but not so much so as *Acanthophthalmus semicinctus*. It is wise to offer this loach a coconut shell similar to that for the half-banded loach.

This loach swims with an eel-like motion. It has 6 obvious barbels which look like whiskers. A short spine in front of each eye accounts for the name *Acanthophthalmus*, meaning with a spine near the eye. The dorsal and the pelvic fins are set well back. The anal fin is located behind the end of the base of the dorsal fin. The background color is pinkish yellow, crossed by several vertical dark brown bars extending to the belly. The number of these bars varies from 12 to 17 on the body and 3 on the head.

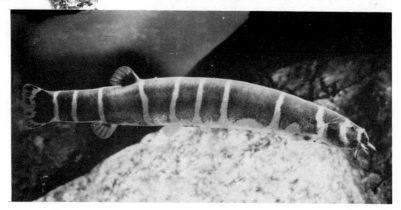

Acanthophthalmus myersi Harry

[my'-ers-eye: named in honor of G. S. Myers]

Acanthophthalmus myersi Harry, Proc. Biol. Soc. Washington, 62:69, 1949 (type locality, southeast Siam)

RANGE: Siam.

SIZE: 2½ inches; breeding not observed.

TEMPERAMENT: A peaceful species suitable for the community tank.

TEMPERATURE REQUIREMENTS: 70–76°F.

SEX DIFFERENCES: Robustness of a mature female indicates sex.

COUNTS: Dorsal ii,8; anal ii,6 or 7; pectoral i,9; pelvic i,5.

This species has been confused with *Acanthophthalmus kuhli* and *A. sumatranus,* so that methods of spawning may actually apply to this species as well as to the other loaches.

HALF-BANDED LOACH or COOLIE /
Acanthophthalmus semicinctus Fraser-Brunner

[sem'-eye-sink'-tus: *semi* = half; *cinctus* = encircled]

Acanthophthalmus semicinctus Fraser-Brunner, Ann. Mag. Nat. Hist. (11) 6:172, fig. 3, 1940 (type locality, Malacca, Johore, Malay Peninsula)

RANGE: Malay Peninsula.

SIZE: 3 inches; breeding not observed.

TEMPERAMENT: A peaceful species and a good scavenger for the community aquarium.

TEMPERATURE REQUIREMENTS: 70–76°F.

SEX DIFFERENCES: Male has rose-colored belly when sexually stimulated.

COUNTS: Dorsal ii,6; anal ii,6; pectoral i,10; pelvic i,5.

This species has just been bred. The background color is pink. The upper part of the body is marked with a variable number of blotches which may or may not have consistent intensity of coloration. This loach is uncomfortable during the daylight hours, and it is most unkind to place it in an aquarium where hiding places from the light are lacking. In native haunts it burrows into the mud during the day; in order to trap it a native walks through the mud or drags a rake through to stir it out. Many kind dealers and hobbyists have taken to placing half a coconut shell with a few holes in it on the bottom of the aquarium. This gives the loach a place to hide from the light.

This fairly hardy species should not be kept at a temperature over 80°F; at 95°F they die.

Herbert Axelrod (*Tropical Fish Hobbyist*, 3(2): 17–20, 1954) reports that the parents make a bubble nest. Each egg is enclosed in a single large bubble.

SHELFORD'S PRICKLY EYE / *Acanthophthalmus shelfordi* Popta

[shell'-ford-eye: named in honor of R. W. C. Shelford, director of the Sarawak Museum]

Acanthophthalmus shelfordii Popta, Notes Leyden Mus., 23:231, 1901–1903 (type locality, Sarawak River near Kuching, Borneo)

RANGE: Borneo.

SIZE: 3 inches; breeding not observed.

TEMPERAMENT: A peaceful species and a good scavenger for the community aquarium.

TEMPERATURE REQUIREMENTS: 72–80°F.

SEX DIFFERENCES: Unknown.

COUNTS: Dorsal 6; anal 5; pectoral i,8; pelvic 6; scales 220.

This yellow loach is decorated with the familiar black blotches.

Genus *Botia* Gray

[Boat'-i-a: meaning not known]

Botia hymenophysa (Bleeker)

[hi'-men-o-fy'-sa: *hymeno* = a membrane; *physa* = a bladder]

Cobitis hymenophysa Bleeker, Nat. Tijdschr. Ned. Indie, 3:602, 1852 (type locality, Palembang, Sumatra)

RANGE: Sumatra, Siam, Malay Peninsula, Java.

SIZE: 1 foot; breeding not observed.

TEMPERAMENT: A peaceful species, rather shy, preferring dim light.

TEMPERATURE REQUIREMENTS: 72–85°F.

SEX DIFFERENCES: None apparent.

COUNTS: Dorsal i,12 to 14; anal ii,6; pectoral i,11 to 14; pelvic i,7.

This species along with other *Botia* is called a loach, but the body is much deeper and more laterally compressed (more narrow than high) than most other loaches. The tail is forked, unlike other loaches whose tails are rounded. It usually stops growing as soon as placed in the aquarium. All attempts at breeding have been futile.

At the present time this fish is very expensive, costing nearly 50 times the price of the rasbora in Singapore and about 10 times the price of the rasbora in New York.

The over-all color of this particular species is pearly gray with a striped side. These irregular stripes are dark grayish brown with a black border. The stripes on the head are nearly horizontal; as they progress backward they get more oblique until finally at the caudal peduncle they are vertical.

CLOWN LOACH; TIGER BOTIA / *Botia macracanthus* (Bleeker)

[mack'-rah-can'-thus: *macr* = large; *acanthus* = spine]

Cobitis macracanthus Bleeker, Nat. Tijdschr. Ned. Indie, 3:603, 1852 (type locality, Sumatra)

RANGE: Sumatra, Borneo.

SIZE: 1 foot; breeding not observed.

TEMPERAMENT: A peaceful species when small, but not suitable in the community aquarium when large.

TEMPERATURE REQUIREMENTS: 72–85°F.

SEX DIFFERENCES: Not known.

COUNTS: Dorsal i,10; anal ii,6; pectoral i,13 to 15; pelvic i,8.

This species is imported at a size of about 1½ inches since that size ships best.

A movable spine lies in a groove under the eye; this is believed to protect the eye when the fish burrows into the mud, which it does so frequently in nature.

Since this species dislikes light also, it is advisable to place a piece of coconut shell in the aquarium so it can go inside where it is dark. This fish is nocturnal; feed it in the evening before turning out the lights.

GENUS *Cobitis* Linnaeus

[Co-bi'-tis: a kind of loach]

SPOTTED WEATHERFISH; SPINED LOACH / *Cobitis taenia* Linnaeus

[tee'-ni-a: *taenia* = band]

Cobitis taenia Linnaeus, Systema naturae, ed. 10, 1:303, 1758 (type locality, Europe)

RANGE: Great Britain, Europe; central Asia, Japan to Siam.

SIZE: 4 inches; breeds at 3 inches.

TEMPERAMENT: A peaceful species suitable for the community tank.

TEMPERATURE REQUIREMENTS: 40–80°F.

SEX DIFFERENCES: Female is fuller than the male and has a paler color.

COUNTS: Dorsal ii,7 to 11; anal ii,5 to 7; pectoral i,9; pelvic i,6.

This genus has the movable hinged and forked spine under the eye and 3 pairs of barbels, the pair on chin lacking. The general color is buff, with regular rows of dark blotches on the side and another quite similar row on the back. The underside is white and has no markings.

Breeding the weatherfish is difficult, as there seem to be many more males than females (out of 87 fish, 4 were females). Spawning takes place over a muddy bottom and the parent fish wriggle about each other as hundreds of eggs are deposited. The small eggs, which look like midget salmon eggs, are heavy and fall to the bottom. The parents continually swim around them until they are all covered with mud. Eggs hatch in a few weeks, depending upon the temperature. Specimens rarely last more than a year or two at the most.

This widely ranging species has been broken into several subspecies, some of which are *Cobitis taenia taenia* Linnaeus, from Europe; *C. t. meridionalis* Karamen, from Macedonia; *C. t. dalmatina* Karamen, from southern Europe; *C. t. paludica* de Buen, from Spain; *C. t. maroccana* Pellegrin, from Marokko; *C. t. sinensis* Sauvage and D. de Thiersant, from China; *C. t. gracilentus* (Smith), from Siam.

FAMILY COBITIDAE

GENUS *Lepidocephalus* Bleeker

[Lep'-i-do-cef'-a-lus: *lepido* = scales; *cephalus* = head]

LOACH / *Lepidocephalus thermalis* (Cuvier and Valenciennes)

[ther'-mal-is: *thermalis* = pertaining to heat]

Cobitis thermalis Cuvier and Valenciennes, Histoire naturelle des poissons, 18:78, 1846 (type locality, Ceylon)

RANGE: Southern India, Malabar coast, Ceylon.

SIZE: 3 inches; breeding not observed.

TEMPERAMENT: A peaceful species that is shy and does not do well in the light.

TEMPERATURE REQUIREMENTS: 72–85°F.

SEX DIFFERENCES: Unknown.

COUNTS: Dorsal ii,6; anal ii,5; pectoral i,6; pelvic i,6.

This species resembles *Cobitis taenia* but it has 4 pairs of barbels instead of 3. It also has small spots on the side and bears a distinctive ocellus (eyespot) on the caudal peduncle.

This species likes to burrow into the sand or mud and stay that way until dark, with only its little snout exposed. Another usual pose is a walking position, standing on its pectoral fins with its head high like a watchdog sniffing the air.

GENUS *Misgurnus* Lacepède

[Mis-gurn'-us: a French native name for this loach]

JAPANESE WEATHERFISH or WEATHER LOACH /
Misgurnus anguillicaudatus (Cantor)

[ann-gwil'-li-cow-da'-tus: *anguilla* = an eel; *caudatus* = tailed]

Cobitis anguillicaudata Cantor, Ann. Mag. Nat. Hist., 9:485, 1842 (type locality, Chashan)

RANGE: North China, Japan.

SIZE: 8 inches; breeds at 5 inches.

TEMPERAMENT: This species is a little too large for the community tank.

TEMPERATURE REQUIREMENTS: 35–75°F.

SEX DIFFERENCES: Female is more rotund and paler than the male.

COUNTS: Dorsal ii to iv,5 to 7; anal ii to v,5 or 6.

This eel-colored fish swims in an eel-like manner. The general color is olive gray with slightly darker blotches on the sides. It is a good scavenger but is so large and unpredictable in its actions that it is useless for the home aquarium. The name "weatherfish" stems from its sensitivity to barometric changes. When the barometer drops you can expect this fish to be swimming about wildly trying to get out of the water. The now rare *Misgurnus fossilis* (Linnaeus), a European weatherfish, was so sensitive to barometric changes that it was kept throughout Europe as a living barometer. Some writers claim this fish is capable of giving 24-hour notice of a storm.

This fish spawns in exactly the same way as *Cobitis taenia*.

FAMILY **COBITIDAE**

GENUS *Noemacheilus* Van Hasselt

[Ne'-ma-ky'-lus: *noema* = a thread; *cheilus* = edge or lip]

Noemacheilus fasciatus (Cuvier and Valenciennes)

[fas'-see-a'-tus: *fasciatus* = banded]

Cobitis fasciatus Cuvier and Valenciennes, Histoire naturelle des poissons, 18:25, 1846 (type locality, Java)

RANGE: Sumatra, Batoe Islands, Java, Borneo.

SIZE: 4 inches; breeding not observed.

TEMPERAMENT: A peaceful species suitable for the community tank.

TEMPERATURE REQUIREMENTS: 72–85°F.

SEX DIFFERENCES: Unknown.

COUNTS: Dorsal iii,9; anal iii,5; pectoral ii,9; pelvic i,7.

This odd species has a greenish-olive color on its back, becoming yellowish on the side and pink ventrally. There are from 10 to 20 tapering coppery bars extending from the back to the lateral line. The side has a fine stripe running along the lateral line. The yellow fins are attractive, especially the tail and dorsal fins, which are punctuated with coppery dots.

[Doe-rad′-i-dee]

Genus *Acanthodoras* Bleeker

[A-kan′-tho-dore′-as: *acantho* = spine; *doras* = a leathery skin]

Talking Catfish /
Acanthodoras spinosissimus (Eigenmann and Eigenmann)

[spi′-no-sis′-i-mus *spinos* = spiny; *issimus* = the most]

Doras spinosissimus Eigenmann and Eigenmann, Proc. California Acad. Sci., 1:161, 1888 (type locality, Rio Coary)

RANGE: Amazon and Guaporé Basins.

SIZE: 8 inches; breeding at 6 inches.

TEMPERAMENT: Not suitable for the community tank because of its predaceous habits, although larger fishes are safe.

TEMPERATURE REQUIREMENTS: 70–85°F.

SEX DIFFERENCES: Not observed.

COUNTS: Dorsal I,5; anal ii,9; pectoral I,5; pelvic i,6; plates 21 to 23.

This species is a member of the family Doradidae, along with *Astrodoras asterifrons* (Heckel). Both are heavy-bodied catfishes. The body, covered with bony plates, is an example of natural protection. Each plate has a stiff spine capable of piercing the hand. The pectoral fin has a strong first spine armed with a set of pointed spines on the inner margin so that it may be used as a defensive weapon. There is an adipose fin, which is spineless, unlike close relatives in the family Loricariidae.

This fish is capable of emitting a sound both in and out of the water. The sound, a low grunt, is produced by means of special adaptations of the air bladder, perhaps aided by the movements of the pectoral spine.

GENUS *Astrodoras* Bleeker

[As'-tro-dore'-as: *astro* = a star; *doras* = skin]

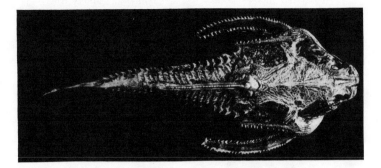

Astrodoras asterifrons (Heckel)

[as-ter'-a-frons: *aster* = a star; *frons* = forehead]

Doras asterifrons Heckel, in Kner, Sitzb. Akad. Wiss. Wien, 27:123, pl. 2, fig. 2, 1855 (type locality, Barra do Rio Negro and Rio Guaporé)

RANGE: Amazon Basin.

SIZE: 8 inches; breeding size not known.

TEMPERAMENT: The predaceous habits of this species exclude it as a community tank fish.

TEMPERATURE REQUIREMENTS: 72–85°F.

SEX DIFFERENCES: Not observed.

COUNTS: Dorsal I,6; anal ii,10; pectoral I,5; pelvic i,6; scales 24 to 26.

This dark gray fish has a white belly. The side and fins are marked with a series of irregular blotches and bars. The fins are tan. The barbels are barred.

Its habits are similar to those of *Acanthodoras spinosissimus*.

[Pim'-ee-lod'-i-dee]

GENUS *Microglanis* Eigenmann

[Mi'-crow-glan'-is: *micro* = small; *glanis* = a kind of fish]

HARLEQUIN or MANY-COLORED CATFISH / *Microglanis poecilus* Eigenmann

[pea-sil'-us: *poecilus* = variegated or many-colored]

Microglanis poecilus Eigenmann, Fishes of British Guiana, p. 155, 1912 (type locality, below Packeoo Falls)

RANGE: British Guiana; Rio Apure and Rio Orinoco, and Amazon Basin.

SIZE: 3 inches; breeding size not observed.

TEMPERAMENT: A peaceful species and a good scavenger in the community tank.

TEMPERATURE REQUIREMENTS: 72–80°F.

SEX DIFFERENCES: Not observed.

COUNTS: Dorsal I,6; anal iv or v,6 to 8; pectoral i,6 or 7; pelvic i,5.

This many-colored catfish has nocturnal habits. It does most of its scrounging around after dark, and during the day it is quiet. The coloring is interesting and attractive. It has the color scheme of the bumblebeefish, *Brachygobius xanthozonus* (page 672), but is nearly twice the size of that goby. The body is a light yellowish brown when placed on a light-colored sand. There are 3 pairs of barbels.

Microglanis parahybae Steindachner, also known as *M. cottoides* (Boulenger), is another species close to *M. poecilus* in habits and coloration. The figure was compared with types of *M. poecilus* and was found to be identical with that species.

348 FAMILY **PIMELODIDAE**

GENUS *Pimelodella* Eigenmann and Eigenmann

[Pim'-ee-low-del'-la: *pimel* = fat; *odella* = a little tooth]

STINGING CATFISH; GRACEFUL CATFISH /
Pimelodella gracilis (Cuvier and Valenciennes)

[gras'-il-is: *gracilis* = slender]

Pimelodus gracilis Cuvier and Valenciennes, Histoire naturelle des poissons, 15:181, 1840 (type locality, Buenos Aires)

RANGE: Venezuela; Amazon, Uruguay, and La Plata Basins.

SIZE: 5 inches; breeding not observed.

TEMPERAMENT: This species is predaceous and thus not suitable for the community tank.

TEMPERATURE REQUIREMENTS: 74–80°F.

SEX DIFFERENCES: Not observed.

COUNTS: Dorsal I,6; anal v,7 or 8; pectoral I,8 or 9; pelvic i,5; caudal branched rays 15.

This species, like its close relative *Pimelodella chagresi*, occurs from Venezuela to Panama. It has a dark streak along the middle of the side, contrasting sharply with the silvery or whitish background; the dorsal rays are blackish in a translucent fin. The pectoral spines are venomous, causing severe pain in one's fingers if pierced by them, thus the name "stinging catfish." Individuals have been seen to bite at active fishes, such as the paradisefish.

This species is sensitive to salt water. One specimen with the ich was placed in the usual salt-water bath and died very quickly.

Pimelodella chagresi.

Genus *Pimelodus* Lacepède

[Pi-mel'-o-dus: *pimel* = fat; *odus* = tooth]

Polka-dot Catfish / *Pimelodus clarias* (Bloch)

[klar'-i-as: *clarias* = clear]

Silurus clarias Bloch, Naturgeschichte der Ausländischen Fische, pl. 35, figs. 1, 2, 1785 (type locality, restricted to Magdalena River)

RANGE: Panama to the La Plata system.

SIZE: 1 foot; breeding not observed.

TEMPERAMENT: Because of its predaceous habits not suitable in the community tank.

TEMPERATURE REQUIREMENTS: 72–85°F.

SEX DIFFERENCES: Unknown.

COUNTS: Dorsal I,6; anal v,8 or 9; pectoral I,8 to 10; pelvic i,5; branched caudal rays 15.

The smaller individuals of this species, 3 inches long, are more distinctly colored than the adults. The popular name was derived from the numerous dark brown polka dots which cover the body and contrast sharply with the light golden skin. Specimens kept in the home aquarium for 3 or 4 months start to lose these dots, since they fade away unless dark pebbles are placed on the bottom. Six barbels are obvious and the adipose fin is large.

This species is greedy and will eat almost anything available. Schultz in 1944 stated that in Lake Maracaibo, Venezuela, it abounds around the docks in the oil fields and along the waterfront. It is a scavenger, eating any refuse it can get. Often it sweeps its long blackish maxillary barbels forward and backward under the film of oil in search of food. It feeds both at night and in the daytime.

GENUS *Sorubim* Agassiz

[So-ru'-bim: *sorus* = mound or head; probably meaning two humps]

SHOVEL-NOSED CATFISH / *Sorubim lima* (Bloch and Schneider)

[li'-ma: *lima* = a file]

Silurus lima Bloch and Schneider, Systema ichthyologiae, p. 384, 1801 (type locality, Maranhão, Brazil)

RANGE: Magdalena to the La Plata systems.

SIZE: 1½ feet; breeding not observed.

TEMPERAMENT: A peaceful species but capable of eating small fishes.

TEMPERATURE REQUIREMENTS: 72–85°F.

SEX DIFFERENCES: Not observed.

COUNTS: Dorsal I,6; anal v,14; pectoral I,8; pelvic i,5; caudal 20 to 23 branched rays.

This species may be recognized by the greatly depressed head and almost paperthin snout, with the eye lateral in position. The color is olivaceous, with two dark stripes, the one on the side being the most distinct.

Feeding is no problem since it eats almost anything but prefers live worms and bits of meat; it is a scavenger. It is not an active eater or swimmer during the daylight but is more so at night. It should have plants among which to hide during the day.

[Bew'-no-sef-al'-i-dee]

GENUS *Bunocephalus* Kner

[Bew'-no-sef'-a-lus: *buno* = mound; *cephalus* = head]

TWO-COLORED BANJO CATFISH / *Bunocephalus coracoideus* (Cope)

[core'-a-coi'-dee-us: *coracoideus* = like a raven]

Dysichthys coracoideus Cope, Proc. Acad. Nat. Sci. Philadelphia, p. 133, 1874 (type locality, Nauta, upper Amazon)

RANGE: Amazon Basin to Nauta, Ecuador and Rio Negro; Uruguay.

SIZE: 6 inches; breeds at 4 or 5 inches.

TEMPERAMENT: A species desirable in the community tank.

TEMPERATURE REQUIREMENTS: 72–85°F.

SEX DIFFERENCES: A mature female may be recognized by her fuller and rounder belly.

COUNTS: Dorsal i,4 or 5; anal ii,5; pectoral i,5; caudal i,4,4,i.

When this species reaches the 5-inch size it should be well fed on an abundance of live foods (*Tubifex* and earthworms seem to be favorites). Place the heavily planted breeding tank in a corner that will not receive much direct light. Clean sand should be 3 inches deep, without debris. The water should have a pH of 7.6 and a temperature of 75°F. Select a plump female and a slim, active male. Heavy feedings should be continued through the fall months as this fish seems inclined to breed in early spring and requires several months of conditioning. The parent fish may scoop out a small depression under a rock or plants in subdued light. Natural small rock caves make good breeding sites. If these sites are not provided, the spawning fish will tear up the vegetation in order to drop leaves under which they may spawn. The parents should be removed after spawning, although they do not eat their own young. The fry require rotifers, microworms, white worms, and small *Tubifex*. This diet will bring them up to maturity.

Bunocephalus bicolor Steindachner (*Denks. Akad. Wiss. Wien,* 46:8, pl. 2, figs. 1, 1b, 1883, Huallaga) is the same as this species. Another species that has been kept in aquaria is *B. kneri* Steindachner.

FAMILY CALLICHTHYIDAE

[Kal'-ik-thy'-i-dee]

GENUS *Callichthys* Agassiz

[Kal-ik'-thees: *call* = beautiful; *ichthys* = fish]

ARMORED CATFISH; HASSAR / *Callichthys callichthys* (Linnaeus)

Silurus callichthys Linnaeus, Systema naturae, ed. 10, p. 307, 1758 (type locality, "American rivers")

RANGE: Eastern Venezuela, Trinidad to Buenos Aires.

SIZE: 5 inches; breeds at 4 inches.

TEMPERAMENT: A peaceful species, incapable of harming any fish except tiny ones, thus desirable in the community tank.

TEMPERATURE REQUIREMENTS: 72–85°F.

SEX DIFFERENCES: Mature females are plumper than the males.

COUNTS: Dorsal i,6; anal i,5; pectoral i,7; pelvic i,5; plates 26 to 29.

This species in the catfish genus *Callichthys* has its robust body armored with overlapping bony plates. There is a stiff spine in the dorsal and adipose fins. The mouth is small with fine teeth. The lips are not modified to allow the fish to attach itself to rock surfaces. Two pairs of barbels are present; the upper pair of barbels points downward, while the lower pair points upward (as upper teeth point downward, and lower teeth upward).

This fish is a good scavenger, but as it may eat small fishes, it should be kept out of tanks containing baby fishes.

There is a record of a Russian named Scheljuzhke, who in 1910 spawned a pair and raised the fry. The spawning took place in a tank 6 feet long, 3 feet wide, with 10 inches of water. The male built a bubble nest and protected the eggs. A German aquarist 24 years later reported a similar action, though the parents ate the eggs. American aquarists have since spawned this species. Bubble nests are reported to be built under the leaf of a floating plant, like water lettuce.

J. J. Hoedeman, Zoological Museum, Amsterdam, says, "It has been proved that even in large tanks with plenty of water, and a good supply of oxygen, a sudden shower is the only way of inducing these fishes to reproduce, to start building their nests. Only water introduced from above like a shower in nature, seems to be the sign that the coast is clear for offspring. It need not even be fresh water or rain water, for water taken from the tank and brought back by means of a watering can works quite the same."

GENUS *Corydoras* Lacepède

[Kor'-y-dore'-as: *cory* = a kind of fish; *doras* = a leathery skin]

This genus of armored catfishes has numerous species, many of which are difficult to identify because they are so similar to others. *C. punctatus* (Bloch) is not sufficiently well described to be identifiable, according to Gosline. Thus it is omitted in this book.

These bottom-dwelling catfishes are droll creatures, feeding on live worms and prepared foods. Some species are scavengers, but they should be fed regularly to keep them healthy.

BRONZE CORYDORAS / *Corydoras aeneus* (Gill)

[ee-nee'-us: *aeneus* = bronze or copper-colored]

Hoplosoma aeneus Gill, Ann. Lyc. Nat. Hist. New York, 6:403, 1858 (type locality, Trinidad)

RANGE: Eastern Venezuela and Trinidad to São Paulo, westward to Bolivia.

SIZE: 3 inches; breeds at 2 inches.

TEMPERAMENT: A peaceful species, popular in the community tank.

TEMPERATURE REQUIREMENTS: 70–90°F.

SEX DIFFERENCES: Mature female is much plumper than the male.

COUNTS: Dorsal I,7; anal i,6; pectoral i,8; pelvic i,5; branched caudal rays 12; plates 22.

This hardy catfish has been bred more frequently than any other *Corydoras*. There are reports of spawning but it is not raised commercially, and it is too cheap to be imported.

Young healthy pairs should be obtained and fed plenty of *Tubifex* and *Daphnia*. This fish must not be considered a scavenger but must be fed a normal, substantial diet. Keep each fish separated if possible. It does not need much space and a gallon jar is sufficient for any single catfish. Females have been known to lay eggs without males so fish of the same sex should be separated. Arrange the largest tank available for the breeding event. An aquarium smaller than 15 gallons will not support the entire brood. Clean sand should be placed in a clean aquarium with fresh water and allowed to age for a day or so. *Do not put any salt into the water;* pH is of no consequence. In the tank place three males and one plump female. Fish should spawn within the next 2 weeks. They usually spend a week looking around for a clean spot upon which to place their spawn. Males congregate away from the female and wait for her to join them when she is ready to spawn. As soon as she joins them they swim all about her, seeming to pay particular attention to the back of her head. The males will then clean a small spot on the glass or on the leaf of a plant with the mouth. The female is accompanied to the cleaned spot and soon deposits her eggs there. Parents should be removed after spawning. Eggs hatch in 72 hours at 80°F. The fifth day after spawning the young should be fed a mash which will fall to the bottom of the tank, where they pick it up. They should also receive microworms and brine shrimp until they are able to take regular foods.

Agassiz's Corydoras or Catfish / *Corydoras agassizi* Steindachner

[ag'-a-siz-eye: named in honor of Louis Agassiz]

Corydoras agassizi Steindachner, Sitzb. Akad. Wiss. Wien, 74:90, pl. 12, figs. 2, 2*a*, 1876 (type locality, Amazon River at Tabatinga)

RANGE: Amazon Basin.

SIZE: 4 inches; breeding not observed.

TEMPERAMENT: A peaceful species, suitable in the community tank.

TEMPERATURE REQUIREMENTS: 70–90°F.

SEX DIFFERENCES: Not known.

COUNTS: Dorsal i,7; anal i,6 or 7; pectoral i,9; pelvic i,5; plates 21 to 23.

This good-looking *Corydoras* has not been spawned, but the fact that it was named after Agassiz should make it an attractive fish, for Louis Agassiz was one of the greatest natural history teachers ever to come to the shores of the United States. Agassiz was famous for his teaching methods, especially his rigid discipline. He did much work on fishes but also was versed in ornithology (birds), geology, herpetology (snakes, lizards), botany (plants), and many other phases of nature.

The two pairs of barbels and the leopardlike color might lead to a mistaken identity. This *Corydoras* is not in supply, but an occasional one is caught and shipped with *C. aeneus* or *C. paleatus*. It makes a good scavenger but requires an occasional feeding of *Tubifex* worms.

ARCHED CORYDORAS / *Corydoras arcuatus* Elwin

[ar'-ku-a'-tus: *arcuatus* = arched]

Corydoras arcuatus Elwin, Ann. Mag. Nat. Hist., (11)3:126, pl. 3, 1939 (type locality, Teffé, Amazon)

RANGE: Amazon Basin.

SIZE: 2½ inches; breeding not observed.

TEMPERAMENT: A peaceful species suitable in the community tank.

TEMPERATURE REQUIREMENTS: 70–85°F.

SEX DIFFERENCES: Not known.

COUNTS: Dorsal i,7; anal i,6; pectoral i,8 or 9; pelvic i,5; plates 22 to 24.

The color contrasts sharply with other members of the same genus. The black arching streak looks much like an archer's bow, thus the name *arcuatus*. The gill plates are decorated with two bright golden spots. It is a good scavenger.

Corydoras pygmaeus.

BANDED CORYDORAS / *Corydoras barbatus* (Quoy and Gaimard)

[bar-bay'-tus: *barbatus* = bearded]

Callichthys barbatus Quoy and Gaimard, Voyage autour du monde . . . *Uranie* et la *Physicienne*, . . . 1817–1820, Zoologie, p. 234, 1824 (type locality, Rio de Janeiro)

RANGE: Southeastern Brazil.

SIZE: 5 inches; breeding not observed.

TEMPERAMENT: A peaceful species suitable for the community tank.

TEMPERATURE REQUIREMENTS: 72–85°F.

SEX DIFFERENCES: Unknown.

COUNTS: Dorsal i,7; anal ii,6; pectoral i,9; pelvic i,5; caudal 12; plates 23 or 24.

This attractive species is light brown with a pinkish belly. The head has a distinctly golden tinge with numerous irregular blotches of black which extend to the sides. The pelvic fins are dark brown while the other fins are clear with dark curving bands, from which the fish gets its popular name. It is a good scavenger and should be treated like other *Corydoras*.

C. kronei M. Ribeiro (*A. Lavoura*, 11(5):189, 1907, southeastern Brazil) is a synonym of this species.

Corydoras elegans Steindachner

[el′-e-gans: *elegans* = choice, fine]

Corydoras elegans Steindachner, Sitzb. Akad. Wiss. Wien, 74:93, 1876 (type locality, Cudajas, Teffé, Peru)

RANGE: Upper Amazon Basin at Cudajas, and Teffé, Peru.

SIZE: 2 inches; breeding not observed.

TEMPERAMENT: Suitable in the community tank.

TEMPERATURE REQUIREMENTS: 72–85°F.

SEX DIFFERENCES: Unknown.

COUNTS: Dorsal I,7; anal i,6; caudal 12; pectoral I,7; pelvic i,5; plates 22.

This species has habits and water and temperature requirements similar to other species of *Corydoras*.

The figure was accurately drawn from the types in the United States National Museum.

Corydoras hastatus is by far the most simple member of this very popular genus of aquarium catfishes. This variety, bred from selected stock, is rapidly becoming so popular that it has already overshadowed all other *Corydoras* in sales in Europe. There is more color in this species than the native variety.

Dwarf or Pygmy Corydoras /
Corydoras hastatus Eigenmann and Eigenmann

[hass-tay'-tus: *hastatus* = spear-shaped]

Corydoras hastatus Eigenmann and Eigenmann, Proc. California Acad. Sci., 1:66, 1888 (type locality, Villa Bella)

RANGE: Amazon Basin, Mato Grosso, Paraguay.

SIZE: 1½ inches; breeds at 1¼ inches.

TEMPERAMENT: A peaceful species, suitable in the community tank.

TEMPERATURE REQUIREMENTS: 70–85°F.

SEX DIFFERENCES: The mature female is plumper than the male.

COUNTS: Dorsal i,7; anal ii,5; pectoral i,8; pelvic i,5; plates 21 or 22.

The over-all color is a light brown. There is a dark black band running along the lateral line from the pectoral fin to the base of the caudal fin. The caudal peduncle is decorated with an arrowhead or spearhead pattern, thus the name *hastatus*. The body is covered with fine black dots.

It has spawned unobserved in an aquarium. Plenty of live foods are required in the form of white worms, or *Tubifex*. Several stones in a pile make a suitable spawning site. Large eggs, about a dozen or so, are placed singly on the glass, on stones, or on plants. Parents do not eat the eggs if they are well-fed. Young are the size of newborn guppies when they hatch; they go after dwarf white worms, microworms, brine shrimp, and newly hatched *Daphnia*.

LEOPARD CORYDORAS / *Corydoras julii* Steindachner

[ju'-li-eye: named in honor of a now unknown Julius]

Corydoras julii Steindachner, Anz. Akad. Wiss. Wien, 43:480, 1906 (type locality, Parahim River, Paranaguá, and at Vitória)

RANGE: Piauí and Maranhão, Brazil; upper basin of Amazon.

SIZE: 3 inches; breeding not observed.

TEMPERAMENT: A peaceful species suitable for the community tank.

TEMPERATURE REQUIREMENTS: 72–85°F.

SEX DIFFERENCES: Unknown.

COUNTS: Dorsal i,7; anal ii,5; pectoral i,7 or 8; pelvic i,5; plates 22 or 23.

The over-all color is gray with olive stripes. The dark spot on the dorsal fin is black. Running through the center of the body are 3 distinct dotted or solid lines. The adipose and anal fins are dotted. The tail has 6 regular dotted bands and is normally bifurcated.

This is one of the best aquarium species of *Corydoras*. It is active, very pretty, and does not grow very large. It is a good scavenger.

An examination of the holotype and paratype of *Corydoras leopardus* Myers (*Aquarium,* 2(8):188, fig., 1933; *Proc. Biol. Soc. Washington,* 48:10, 1935, type locality, coastal rivers south of the Amazon) by both Gosline and Schultz shows it to be a synonym of this species.

BLACK-SPOTTED CORYDORAS / *Corydoras melanistius* Regan
[mel'-a-nis'-ti-us: *melanistius* = black]

Corydoras melanistius Regan, Ann. Mag. Nat. Hist., (8)10:216, 1912 (type locality, Essequibo, British Guiana)

RANGE: Eastern Venezuela to British Guiana.

SIZE: 2½ inches; breeding not observed.

TEMPERAMENT: A peaceful species suitable for the community tank.

TEMPERATURE REQUIREMENTS: 72–85°F.

SEX DIFFERENCES: Not known.

COUNTS: Dorsal i,7; anal iii,5; pectoral i,8; pelvic i,5; plates 21 or 22.

This catfish is coming into the United States in quantity now that it has been found in large numbers in Venezuela.

Many people like it because it is more colorful than other available species of *Corydoras*. Its body is pinkish and covered with many small black spots. There are two large blotches, one running around the eye and another at the base of and extending slightly into the dorsal fin. If this fish is well fed and cared for it is known to develop golden areas in beautiful contrast to the pink.

A variant of this species was named as a subspecies, *Corydoras melanistius brevirostris*, by Fraser-Brunner (*Proc. Zool. Soc. London*, 117(1):244, 1947, from the Orinoco River). It differs in having a shorter snout and larger and fewer spots than *C. m. melanistius* Regan.

MYERS' CORYDORAS / *Corydoras myersi* M. Ribeiro

[my′-ers-eye: named in honor of George S. Myers]

Corydoras myersi M. Ribeiro, Rev. Bras. Biol., 2(4):427, fig. 1, 1942 (type locality, Rio Javarí, Amazon)

RANGE: Rio Javarí, Amazon Basin.

SIZE: 3 inches; breeding not observed.

TEMPERAMENT: A peaceful species suitable for the community tank.

TEMPERATURE REQUIREMENTS: 72–85°F.

SEX DIFFERENCES: Not known.

COUNTS: Dorsal i,7; anal i,6; pectoral i,7; pelvic i,5; plates 20 or 21.

Though never bred, this colorful fish has generally been confused with *Corydoras rabauti*. It is about as colorful a catfish as *C. melanistius*.

The name of this species currently is *Corydoras rabauti*.

BLUE CORYDORAS / *Corydoras nattereri* Steindachner

[nat'-er-er-eye; named in honor of Johann Natterer, its collector]

Corydoras nattereri Steindachner, Sitzb. Akad. Wiss. Wien, 74:95, p. 11, figs. 1, 1*a*, 1*b*, 1876 (type locality, near Rio de Janeiro, Rio Paraíba, and Rio Jequitinhonha)

RANGE: Rio de Janeiro to São Paulo.

SIZE: 3 inches; breeds at 2¼ inches.

TEMPERAMENT: A peaceful species suitable in the community tank.

TEMPERATURE REQUIREMENTS: 72–85°F.

SEX DIFFERENCES: See below.

COUNTS: Dorsal i,7; anal i,6; pectoral i,8; pelvic i,5; plates 20 or 21.

This species has been reported to breed in the same manner as its close cousin *Corydoras aeneus.*

The general color is light olive-brown with a silver-blue tinge when the light strikes it just right. The sides are decorated with a dark stripe which extends from the gill cover to the base of the caudal fin. There is a dark spot at the base of the caudal fin, on the caudal peduncle. Fins are clear except at breeding time when the male's dorsal fin gets a black edge.

Peppered Corydoras / *Corydoras paleatus* (Jenyns)

[pay'-lee-a'-tus: *paleatus* = probably light-colored]

Callichthys paleatus Jenyns, Zoology of the Voyage of H.M.S. *Beagle*, 1832–1836, pt. 4, Fish, p. 113, 1842 (type locality, South America)

RANGE: Southern Brazil and northern Argentina.

SIZE: 3 inches; breeds at 2¼ inches.

TEMPERAMENT: A peaceful species suitable for the community tank.

TEMPERATURE REQUIREMENTS: 72–85°F. Optimum breeding temperature 75°F.

SEX DIFFERENCES: The female's belly takes on a pink hue when she is ready for breeding.

COUNTS: Dorsal i,7; anal i,5; pectoral i,7; pelvic i,5; plates 22 or 23.

This is a popular species which is in fair demand and constant supply. It breeds freely. During the few days before

spawning, courtship by the male consists of particular attention to the back of the head of the selected female. Finally the male rolls over on his back while the female lies across him, breast to breast. Her barbels are in contact with his pectoral fins and they stay in this position for nearly a minute. Quite suddenly the female will wiggle off and swim away carrying some eggs in her pelvic fins. She then looks for a clean leaf to place her eggs against. Prior to actually fastening the eggs against the spot she gives it a thorough going over with her mouth. She then assumes an upside-down position and clasps the leaf between her pelvic fins, fastening the sticky eggs there a few at a time until nearly 100 eggs have been deposited. Spawning may go on all morning.

Remove the parents and feed the young as for *Corydoras aeneus*.

DWARF or RABAUT'S CORYDORAS / *Corydoras rabauti* La Monte

[ra-bow'-eye: named in honor of the American collector Auguste Rabaut]

Corydoras rabauti La Monte, Zoologica, 26(1):5, 1941 (type locality Amazon River)

RANGE: Amazon near Manaus.

SIZE: 1 inch; breeds at 1 inch.

TEMPERAMENT: A peaceful species suitable in the community tank.

TEMPERATURE REQUIREMENTS: 72–85°F.

SEX DIFFERENCES: Not known.

COUNTS: Dorsal i,7; anal i,5 or 6; pectoral i,9; pelvic i,5; caudal i,12,i.

This droll species was bred in the New York Aquarium and has been confused with *Corydoras myersi* Ribeiro. Schultz has examined the holotype of *C. rabauti* La Monte, through Miss La Monte's kindness, and has compared this with specimens of *C. aeneus* Gill and with the detailed drawing of the type of *C. eques* Steindachner.

Contrary to the statements in various aquarium books and in aquarium magazines, all three species appear to be distinct and can be recognized by their basic color pattern of blackish or brownish shading. *C. eques* has a wedge-shaped dark bar through the eye; then beginning

in front of the dorsal fin is a blackish bar that joins with the blackish sides; the back is paler, and the belly very pale. *C. aeneus* Gill from Trinidad, Venezuela, and Brazil lacks the dark bar through the eye; the dark side is confined to a large oblong area mostly below the dorsal fin; the belly is whitish or pale. *C. rabauti* also lacks the dark bar through the eye but the dark sides occupy the entire area behind the head to the rear of the dorsal fin and completely encircle the body between the base of the pelvic and origin of the anal fin. *C. myersi* Ribeiro, illustrated on page 257 of Innes' *Exotic Aquarium Fishes*, 1950 and earlier editions, has been confused with both *rabauti* and *eques* in the text. It is our opinion that all four species mentioned above are distinct and valid.

Further information on the distinctness of *C. rabauti* from *C. myersi* is given in two letters dated January 26 and April 30, 1953, from Francesca La Monte, American Museum of Natural History, New York City:

"I am sending you [L. P. Schultz] tomorrow the type and two other specimens of *Corydoras rabauti*. . . . To the best of my knowledge no one else has seen this (type) specimen and I had three generations of tank-bred fishes from the New York Aquarium."

"I did not 'raise' any of the *C. rabauti*. I had them living in a tank here but the lots were raised in the New York Aquarium where they had an original lot and a second and third generation. I also had 7 preserved specimens in addition to the 3 living. Between the ones I had and the ones they had up there, I examined the parent fish and their young. The ones I had were adults. The ones I sent you were the same lot as the type—same generation and could have been called paratypes. They were not descendants of the type lot. They were the type lot! There was no change in color pattern with age. The largest we had were 19 mm. The largest living one was 18 mm. As Christopher Coates told you, Rabaut has not been able to go back to the locality. No more have been collected and the New York Aquarium lot has died out."

We conclude that *C. rabauti* is a dwarf species.

The drawing shown was made from the holotype and is an accurate representation.

RETICULATED CORYDORAS / *Corydoras reticulatus* Fraser-Brunner

[re-tick'-you-lay'-tus: *reticulatus* = colored like a net]

Corydoras reticulatus Fraser-Brunner, Proc. Zool. Soc. London, 117(1):245, figs. 4, 5, 1947 (type locality, Monte Alegre, River Amazon)

RANGE: Amazon Basin.

SIZE: 2 inches; breeding not observed.

TEMPERAMENT: A peaceful species suitable for the community tank.

TEMPERATURE REQUIREMENTS: 72–85°F.

SEX DIFFERENCES: Not known.

COUNTS: Dorsal i,7; anal i,6; pectoral i,10; pelvic i,6; plates 21 to 23.

This fish has an olive back with beautiful glistening metallic reflections from top lighting. The sides are light gray with a distinct netlike (reticulated) black pattern. The dorsal fin has a large black spot edged with white. Other fins are very clear. This species is rare and a search of the literature indicates it is a small *Corydoras*.

[Si-lur'-i-dee]

Genus *Kryptopterus* Bleeker

[Krip-top'-ter-us: *krypto* = hidden; *pterus* = fin]

Ghost or Glass Catfish /
Kryptopterus bicirrhis (Cuvier and Valenciennes)

[bi-sear'-is: *bi* = two; *cirrhis* = filament]

Silurus bicirrhis Cuvier and Valenciennes, Histoire naturelle des poissons, 14:367, 1839 (type locality, Java)

RANGE: Java, Sumatra, Borneo, southern Siam.

SIZE: 6 inches; breeding not observed.

TEMPERAMENT: A peaceful and shy species that is suitable in the community tank.

TEMPERATURE REQUIREMENTS: 72–82°F.

SEX DIFFERENCES: Unknown.

COUNTS: Dorsal i; anal ii,52 to 68; pectoral i,11 or 12; pelvic i,5 or 6.

This fish has not been bred in captivity. Even though all the anatomical structures can be seen right through the fish, one is unable to distinguish sexes.

When first introduced into a new aquarium it is shy and will head for the thickets and stay there for a few days until it is familiar with the surroundings. It has a peculiar ability to remain in one place and undulate only its large anal fin. The body is transparent, thus the name "glassfish." Every part of its skeletal system, viscera, brain, and air bladder is visible.

The glass catfish is quite hardy, and once acclimated it is a fair eater. The favorite foods are *Tubifex* and *Daphnia*. It rarely feeds from the bottom or the top; it stays in the middle stratum of the aquarium.

The genus *Kryptopterus* has about a dozen or so members ranging mostly in Java, Borneo, Sumatra, Siam, and Malaya. This is the only species so far imported. This fish has but a single pair of barbels, a rudimentary dorsal and a large anal fin, which nearly reaches to the caudal fin. The caudal fin is bifurcated.

GENUS *Ompok* Lacepède

[Om'-pok: meaning not known]

GLASS CATFISH / *Ompok bimaculatus* (Bloch)

[by-mack'-u-lay'-tus: *bi* = two; *maculatus* = spotted]

Silurus bimaculatus Bloch, Ichthyologie histoire naturelle . . . poissons, 11:17, pl. 304, 1797 (type locality, Malabar)

RANGE: Java, Borneo, Sumatra to Malaya, Siam, Indochina, Burma, India, and Ceylon.

SIZE: 18 inches; breeding not observed.

TEMPERAMENT: When over 4 inches long this species is not a safe member of the community aquarium.

TEMPERATURE REQUIREMENTS: 72–80°F.

SEX DIFFERENCES: Unknown.

COUNTS: Dorsal i,3; anal ii,56 to 58; pectoral 12; pelvic i,5.

Though never bred, this glass catfish is maintained as an oddity. This fish looks so much like *Kryptopterus bicirrhis* that only a close examination will show the differences. One apparent difference, however, is the distinct triangular dorsal fin in *Ompok*, whereas in *K. bicirrhis* we find a rudimentary one that looks more like a small spine than a fin. Two pairs of barbels are present. Those on the upper jaw are large; the pair on the mandible or just below the lower jaw are short.

It likes large pieces of meat, earthworms, and sandworms but does not care too much for dried foods. It will take them when not offered meat or live food.

This species is incorrectly known under the name *Callichrous bimaculatus*.

Family MYSTIDAE

[Mist'-i-dee]

Genus *Mystus* Scopoli

[miss'-tus: *mystus* = mystic]

Striped Catfish / *Mystus vittatus* (Bloch)

[vit-tay'-tus: *vittatus* = striped]

Silurus vittatus Bloch, Ichthyologie histoire naturelle . . . poissons, 11:40, pl. 371, fig. 2, 1797 (type locality, Tranquebar)

RANGE: India, Burma, and Ceylon.

SIZE: 8 inches; breeding not observed.

TEMPERAMENT: Up to 3 inches, this catfish is a safe member in the community tank but larger sizes will feed on smaller fishes.

TEMPERATURE REQUIREMENTS: 72–85°F.

SEX DIFFERENCES: Unknown.

COUNTS: Dorsal i,7; anal iv,9; pectoral i,8 or 9; pelvic i,5; caudal 14.

This interesting catfish is the only representative illustrated for the family Mystidae. Significant characteristics of this family (also known as Bagridae) are nonarmored body, normal dorsal, anal, pelvic, and pectoral fins, long adipose fin, and 4 pairs of barbels, the maxillary pair of which is very long.

This fish is extremely sensitive to salt and should not be placed in an aquarium with any salt in it. It prefers live worms to any other food. Many dealers sell different fishes under this name. Especially confused with this species is *Mystus tengara* (Hamilton).

[Lor'-i-ka-ri'-i-dee]

GENUS *Farlowella* Eigenmann and Eigenmann

[Far'-low-el'-la: named in honor of W. G. Farlow of Harvard University]

TWIG CATFISH / *Farlowella acus* (Kner)

[a'-kuss: *acus* = pointed, a needle]

Acestra acus Kner, Denks. Akad. Wiss. Wien, 6:93, pl. 8, fig. 1, 1853 (type locality, Caracas, Venezuela)

RANGE: Venezuela and Rio Meta of Colombia.

SIZE: 6 inches; breeding not observed.

TEMPERAMENT: A shy and peaceful species, suitable for the community tank.

TEMPERATURE REQUIREMENTS: 72–85°F.

SEX DIFFERENCES: None observed.

COUNTS: Dorsal i,6; anal i,5; pectoral i,6; pelvic i,5; caudal i,11,i.

This species has not spawned in captivity. It is quite a job to keep individuals alive since it feeds mostly on algae. A fair though unsubstantial substitute is lettuce and spinach, chopped into fine bits. The mouth is modified into a sucking device which enables the fish to cling to rocks in fast-moving streams and at the same time with its specially constructed teeth rasp off the algae. The shape and dark brown color of the twiglike fish camouflages it for a life among rocks, twigs, and green and brown algae. This species is an excellent example of protective adaptation for a specialized habitat.

Genus *Hypostomus* Lacepède

[High'-po-stom'-us: *hypo* = underneath; *stomus* = mouth]

CASCUDO; PANAQUE; ARMADILLO DE RIO /
Hypostomus plecostomus (Linnaeus)

[ple-cos'-to-mus: *pleco* = plaited; *stomus* = mouth]

Acipenser plecostomus Linnaeus, Systema naturae, ed. 10, p. 238, 1758 (type locality, Surinam) (= *Loricaria plecostomus* Linnaeus, Systema naturae, ed. 12, 1:508, 1766)

RANGE: Rio La Plata northward to eastern Venezuela and Trinidad.

SIZE: 2 feet.

TEMPERAMENT: A peaceful species suitable for the community tank.

TEMPERATURE REQUIREMENTS: 70–85°F.

SEX DIFFERENCES: Not known.

COUNTS: Dorsal i,7; anal i,4; pectoral i,6; pelvic i,5; caudal i,14,i; plates 25 or 26.

This fish has not been bred in the aquarium. It is easily the most popular species of the family Loricariidae.

Netting this fish from a planted aquarium is quite difficult. Though it looks like a slow-moving species this is only a hoax;

it moves very rapidly when touched by a net. During the day it hides as much as possible and if there is debris on the aquarium floor it will lie completely covered in that. It may be lifted out of the net by carefully getting a secure grip on the hard head. There are many small spines sticking out of the armored body so that the net is easily torn by carelessly dropping the fish into another aquarium. Frequently it makes croaking noises when lifted from the water. These vibrations, if not easily heard, are easily felt by the fingers when grasping the fish.

The large sucking disks or lips are peculiarly adapted for tenaciously clinging to rocks. This fish is mostly nocturnal; its actions are vigorous. It is almost entirely dependent upon algae for food, but wet prepared foods are also eaten at night.

This species has been incorrectly passing under the name of *Plecostomus plecostomus*.

SPOTTED ARMORED CATFISH / *Hypostomus rachovi* (Regan)

[ra-cove'-eye: named in honor of Arthur Rachow]

Plecostomus rachovii Regan, Ann. Mag. Nat. Hist., (8)12:555, 1913 (type locality, Rio de Janeiro)

RANGE: Rio de Janeiro.

SIZE: 8 inches; breeding not observed.

TEMPERAMENT: A peaceful species suitable in the community tank.

TEMPERATURE REQUIREMENTS: 65–90°F. Optimum 75°F.

SEX DIFFERENCES: Not known.

COUNTS: Dorsal i,7; anal i,4; pectoral i,6; pelvic i,5; plates 32.

This is not a popular catfish because few specimens are available. It is long-lived and a few remain healthy for several years.

This species is very sensitive to salt and it will die with as little as ¼ teaspoon per gallon dissolved in water. Otherwise it is hardy, standing extremes of temperatures for short periods of time. It feeds on algae.

Its over-all color is a dark gray. The body and fins are covered with small golden spots, but those on the body are smaller.

FAMILY LORICARIIDAE

GENUS *Loricaria* Linnaeus

[Lor'-i-ka'-ri-a: *loricaria* = coat of mail, a corselet]

WHIP-TAILED LORICARIA / *Loricaria parva* Boulenger

[par'-va: *parva* = small]

Loricaria parva Boulenger, Proc. Zool. Soc. London, p. 527, 1895 (type locality, Descalvados, Mato Grosso)

RANGE: Paraguay and southern Brazil.

SIZE: 5 inches; breeds at 3 inches.

TEMPERAMENT: A peaceful species suitable for the community tank.

TEMPERATURE REQUIREMENTS: 72–80°F.

SEX DIFFERENCES: Male has a broader head.

COUNTS: Dorsal i,7 or i,8; anal i,5; pectoral i,6; pelvic i,5; caudal i,10,i.

Carroll Friswold, Altadena, California, published in the February, 1937, issue of *The Aquarium* a description of the spawning and hatching of this species.

Conditioning of breeders was done with only dry foods. The temperature varied from 73 to 78°F, and aeration was supplied. The water was about 13 inches deep. A piece of petrified wood was used as the spawning site about 8 inches below the surface.

According to Friswold, about 72 hours of courtship occurred before spawning. Later, the female laid about 40 large amber-colored eggs, adhesive enough to stick to the rock upon which they were laid. The male incubated them, fanning and cleaning the eggs with his mouth. During the incubation of the eggs the male was noted to leave them but once, and then only for 5 minutes. Fungused eggs were eaten by the male.

Eggs hatched in 8 days at 78°F. The parents did not bother the fry. The hatched fry were 3/8 inch long. They grew rapidly on a diet of rotifers, mashed *Enchytrae,* and fine dried foods.

GENUS *Otocinclus* Cope

[Oh'-to-sink'-lus: *oto* = ear; *cinclus* = a latticework]

DWARF OTOCINCLUS / *Otocinclus affinis* Steindachner

[af-fi'-nis: *affinis* = related]

Otocinclus affinis Steindachner, Sitzb. Akad. Wiss. Wien, 76:5, pl. 1, figs. 1, 1*a*, 1*b*, 1877 (type locality, near Rio de Janeiro)

RANGE: Southeastern Brazil at Santa Cruz.

SIZE: 2 inches; breeds at 1½ inches.

TEMPERAMENT: A peaceful species suitable in the community tank.

TEMPERATURE REQUIREMENTS: 70–85°F.

SEX DIFFERENCES: Unknown.

COUNTS: Dorsal i,7; anal i,5; pectoral i,6; pelvic i,5; plates 23 to 24.

If the hobbyist has trouble with algae on plants, especially on Amazon sword then this is the algae-eating fish to use. Of special interest is its small size, which means it can fit itself easily on most leaves without the leaf drooping under its weight. A great deal of its time is spent in a restful position on the tops of leaves relieving them of their undesirable algae.

O. Beldt, a very capable breeder, has reported the successful spawning of this fish. He claims that it places its eggs against the glass of the aquarium, like *Corydoras aeneus,* except that single eggs are laid at a time. Eggs are the size of a small pinhead, hatching in 48 hours. The transparent young may be seen clinging to the sides of the glass for 2 days before they venture to the bottom looking for food.

There was a time when these fish were in great supply, but dealers, especially the larger ones, had terrific losses with them because they were treated like other catfishes and overcrowded and underfed.

ARNOLD'S SUCKER CATFISH / *Otocinclus arnoldi* Regan

[ar'-nold-eye: named in honor of Johann Paul Arnold]

Otocinclus arnoldi Regan, Ann. Mag. Nat. Hist., (8)3:234, 1909 (type locality, Rio La Plata)

RANGE: Rio La Plata Basin.

SIZE: 2½ inches; breeding not observed.

TEMPERAMENT: A peaceful species suitable for the community tank.

TEMPERATURE REQUIREMENTS: 72–85°F.

SEX DIFFERENCES: Unknown.

COUNTS: Dorsal i,7; anal i,5; pectoral i,6; pelvic i,5; plates 25.

This species has not been bred, but from all indications it should be treated exactly as its close cousin *Otocinclus affinis*.

The over-all color of this species is olive-brown with a broad longitudinal dark band along the middle of the side. The belly is gray, with darker gray blotches. The dorsal, anal, and caudal fins are adorned with 3 to 5 series of dark spots, while the other fins are the same color as the body. In *O. affinis* the vertical fins are unspotted.

Otocinclus vittatus Regan

[vit-ta'-tus: *vittatus* = striped]

Otocinclus vittatus Regan, Trans. Zool. Soc. London, 17(3):267, pl. 15, fig. 3, 1904 (type locality, Descalvados, Mato Grosso, Paraguay system)

RANGE: Rio Paraguay system.

SIZE: 2 inches; breeding not observed.

TEMPERAMENT: A peaceful species suitable for the community tank.

TEMPERATURE REQUIREMENTS: 72–85°F.

SEX DIFFERENCES: Not known.

COUNTS: Dorsal i,7; anal i,5; pectoral i,6; pelvic i,5; plates 21 to 23.

This catfish may be recognized by the dark streak on its side. It is an excellent scavenger as far as vegetable matter is concerned, with habits about the same as *Otocinclus affinis*.

Family LORICARIIDAE

Genus *Xenocara* Regan

[Zen'-o-car'-a: *xeno* = strange; *cara* = head]

Blue-chin Xenocara / *Xenocara dolichoptera* (Kner)

[doe'-lee-kop'-ter-a: *dolicho* = long or lengthy; *ptera* = wing or fin]

Ancistrus dolichopterus Kner, Denks. Akad. Wiss. Wien, 7:274, pl. 3, fig. 1, 1854 (type locality, Barra do Rio Negro)

RANGE: Guianas, Amazon Basin, and Rio Negro.

SIZE: 5 inches; breeding not observed.

TEMPERAMENT: A peaceful species suitable for the community tank.

TEMPERATURE REQUIREMENTS: 72–85°F.

SEX DIFFERENCES: Not known.

COUNTS: Dorsal i,8 or 9; anal i,4; pectoral i,5; pelvic i,4; caudal i,14,i; plates 24.

This dark-colored catfish, with a bluish tinge, is attractively decorated with small white spots. The belly is white with the same blue cast and light spots.

Not much is known about this species except that it is a good algae eater, possibly subsisting on mashes of fish and meat. Spinach should be offered in these mashes.

[Mo-coke'-i-dee]

GENUS *Synodontis* Cuvier

[Syn'-o-don'-tis: *syn* = together; *odontis* = teeth]

UPSIDE-DOWN CATFISH / *Synodontis nigriventris* David

[ni'-gri-ven'-tris: *nigri* = black; *ventris* = the belly]

Synodontis nigriventris David, Rev. Zool. Bot. Africaines, 28:3, 1936 (type locality, Congo Basin)

RANGE: Congo Basin.

SIZE: 4 inches; breeding not observed.

TEMPERAMENT: A peaceful species suitable for the community tank.

TEMPERATURE REQUIREMENTS: 72–80°F.

SEX DIFFERENCES: Unknown.

COUNTS: Dorsal about I,7; anal about III or IV,8.

This fish has not been bred, but its behavior of occasionally swimming upside down makes it an interesting aquarium inhabitant. In that manner it resembles the plecostomus which spends much of its time in an upside-down position, clinging to the underside of rocks and filters.

Fraser-Brunner suggests that the upside-down habit may have resulted from some change in the balancing organ of the ear which, through years of use, has become reversed and genetically fixed. As specimens grow older and their air bladders become larger, they spend more and more time in the inverted position. In its upside-down position this species is able to eat food from the surface of the water as its mouth is under its head. It prefers bottom feedings of *Tubifex*, though the main diet is algae.

This fish has a heavy-boned head and three pairs of barbels, two pairs of which are branched. The spine at the front of each pectoral fin and the one on the dorsal fin fit into special sockets that lock into position. This discourages any larger fish from ingesting it. The croaking noise this cat is capable of making has been attributed to the friction of these spines in their sockets, but it may be caused by air moving past thin partitions of the air bladder.

[Mal-ap'-ter-u'-ri-dee]

GENUS *Malapterurus* Lacepède

[Mal-ap'-ter-ur'-us: *mala* = soft; *pter* = fin; *urus* = tail]

ELECTRIC CATFISH / *Malapterurus electricus* (Gmelin)

[ee-lec'-tri-kus: *electricus* = electrical]

Silurus electricus Gmelin, Systema naturae, ed. 13, 1:1351, 1789 (type locality, tropical Africa)

RANGE: Tropical Africa, except Lake Victoria and the rivers of east Africa north of the Zambezi River.

SIZE: 2½ feet in native habitat; breeding at 1 foot.

TEMPERAMENT: A vicious species dangerous to all fishes, especially at night.

TEMPERATURE REQUIREMENTS: 72–80°F.

SEX DIFFERENCES: According to Rachow, the male's fins are elongated and pointed, those of the female rounded.

COUNTS: Dorsal fin not rayed; anal iii,6 to 10; pectoral i,8; pelvic i,5; caudal 8 + 7.

Small specimens are easily recognized by their characteristic colors consisting of a light ring around the caudal peduncle, a black bar at the base of the caudal fin, and a crescent-shaped black ring cutting the caudal fin in half. The electric discharge is capable of killing small fishes and stunning larger fishes and can make a man jump back with surprise. Thus it is sometimes called the "stunning fish."

A Chinese student of Egyptology once stated that the electric catfish was taken into captivity during the height of the old Egyptian culture. The fish reproduced in captivity and a supply of all sizes was available. It was used in a ritual performed when a dignitary passed on to the next world.

The great German aquarist Rachow states that this species is not difficult to spawn. It was reported in *The Aquarium* for November, 1934, that the parent fish shelter the fry in their mouths, but no further confirmation of this is available.

[Hem′-i-ram′-fi-dee]

GENUS *Dermogenys* Van Hasselt

[Der′-mo-gen′-ees: *dermo* = skin or membrane; *genys* = lower jaw]

One of Gene Wolfsheimer's most famous photographs, this fascinating illustration of a baby halfbeak being born head first.

WRESTLING HALFBEAK / *Dermogenys pusillus* Van Hasselt

[pu-sil′-lus: *pusillus* = very small]

Dermogenys pusillus Van Hasselt, Alg. Konst. Letterbode, 2:131, 1823 (type locality, Java)

RANGE: Java, Borneo, Sumatra, Malay Peninsula, and Siam.

SIZE: 3 inches; breeds at 2 inches.

TEMPERAMENT: This "fighting fish" may be kept in the community aquarium, since it only wrestles its own kind. It prefers quiet waters.

TEMPERATURE REQUIREMENTS: 72–85°F.

SEX DIFFERENCES: Male has a gonopodium.

COUNTS: Dorsal III,7 to 9; anal I,12 to 15; pectoral i,9 to 11; pelvic 6; scales 45 to 50.

The following account was taken from Bull. 188, United States National Museum, pp. 434–436, 1945, by H. M. Smith: "The pugnacious disposition of the little halfbeak *Dermogenys pusillus* is manifested in an entirely different manner from that of the *Betta*. The exhibition of strength and endurance, on which the encounters are decided, can best be described as wrestling; and as the fish had no distinctive English name Dr. H. M. Smith ventured in 1923 to suggest that it be called *wrestling fish*, a designation that has since been generally used.

"The chief interest in the fish arises from its viviparity (bearing living young) and from the extraordinary combativeness of the males. The fish has a more prominent place in Thailand than in any other country to which it is native, because it is there employed in contests of endurance and strength, and because it is cultivated in order to increase its pugnacious qualities.

"From early times the Thai people have had, as a national trait, the strongly developed desire to match various kinds of small animals in contests of strength and skill. Most noteworthy of these animals is the celebrated fighting fish (*Betta*). Next in importance is *Dermogenys*.

"The effects of cultivation and selective breeding have been manifested in a slight increase in the average size of the fish and in a very marked increase in the wrestling or fighting ability.

"Cultivated fish have a keener inclination to attack and exhibit a technique decidedly superior to that of wild fish, but the most striking result of cultivation is the improvement in the stamina and endurance. Fish collected in open waters and kept in suitable vessels for a few days will, when brought together, struggle actively for supremacy, but their ardor is of short duration; one or both of the contestants will soon tire or lose interest, and a combat lasting more than 15 or 20 minutes would be unusual. On the other hand, cultivated fish may fight on hour after hour, and the contest is decided only when complete exhaustion overcomes one or both of them.

"While the use of *Dermogenys* in matched contests began in a rather remote past, the cultivation of the fish was instituted about 1863 or 1864 and is now completely depended on for supplying candidates for pugilistic encounters.

"Cultivation as now conducted for this fish in Thailand consists in the retention for breeding purposes of fish of proved stamina, the holding of them in pure water in spacious vessels, and the administration of appropriate food in sufficient quantity.

"Only vessels of earthenware or other opaque material may be used for retaining the fish. Owing to inability to adapt themselves to the transparency, they break the lower jaw or otherwise injure themselves against the sides of glass vessels. Favorite receptacles are the large, wide-topped glazed or unglazed terra cotta water jars such as are to be found in every Thai household.

"A wrestling match is arranged by providing a large earthenware basin three-quarters filled with clear water and introducing therein two male fish that have been kept in separate vessels. Instantly, and with great rapidity, the fish dart at each other, maybe from opposite sides of the wide basin, and grasp each other by their jaws. The usual hold is an interlocking of jaws at their base, with the long axis of the bodies at right angles, but there is considerable variety in the holds, and the outcome of a contest may be determined by the particular hold that one fish obtains at the start or seeks to reobtain after each break. Effective and disabling holds, which some individuals are observed to strive for regularly, and which place their adversaries at a decided disadvantage, come from the exercise of a peculiar knack that may result from generations of selective breeding. No holds are barred by the rules under which wrestling-fish contests are held. One fish may grasp the other across the base of the jaws without interlocking, across the tip of the lower jaw, obliquely across the base of the lower jaw so that the adversary is kept on his side or back, across the eyes, across the gill covers, and from either above or below across the gill openings, so that respiration may be impaired and exhaustion be rapidly induced. Other holds that may be observed in the course of a series of contests are head on, with the lower jaw of one fish in the mouth of the other; the grasping by one fish of the pectoral or caudal fin of the other, and the closing of the jaws either straight or obliquely across the body.

"Only rarely is any injury done to either combatant. The lower jaw, perhaps inadvertently used for stabbing, may occasionally draw blood from the gills. The tip of the lower jaw may very exceptionally be broken. Very rarely one or both fishes, without having sustained any apparent injury, may die after being separated. The contest, in the great majority of cases, is ultimately decided by the ability of one fish to maintain, and, after a breakaway, to regain an advantageous hold that will cause exhaustion or affect the stamina. With evenly matched fish in a long-drawn-out struggle, determination of the victor may have to be based on points rather than on a single decisive act. Ordinarily the climax is reached when one fish shows unwillingness or inability to lock jaws with the other."

[Si-prin'-o-don'-ti-dee]

The killifishes or top minnows are small oviparous fishes that lay eggs which develop externally. No species gives birth to the young as in the Poeciliidae, which are viviparous.

The members of this family are distributed in the tropical zones and warm areas of the temperate ones in the old and new world, mostly in fresh and brackish waters, although some species are caught in the sea near shore. The genera and species are very numerous and in some groups it is most difficult to recognize the different kinds.

In general, killifishes are inclined to be aggressive, nipping fins, and most species should not be kept in a community tank; they are best by themselves or with fishes of the same size or larger. Their beautiful coloration, however, makes the top minnows valuable aquarium fishes, in spite of their undesirable aquarium habits.

Genus *Aphanius* Nardo

[A-fan'-i-us: *aphanius* = darkness; obscurity]

Aphanius dispar (Rüppell)

[dis'-par: *dispar* = unequal; dissimilar]

Lebias dispar Rüppell, Atlas zu der Reise im nördlichen Afrika, Fische, p. 66, pl. 18, figs. 1, 2, 1828 (type locality, Tor)

RANGE: Fresh and brackish waters of regions adjoining the Red Sea, Persian Gulf, and northwestern India.

SIZE: 3 inches; breeding at 2½ inches.

TEMPERAMENT: An active species not recommended for the community aquarium.

TEMPERATURE REQUIREMENTS: 70–80°F. Breeding range 75–80°F.

sex differences: The male is a gray color with a multitude of silvery-blue spots. Dorsal and anal fins are marbled. The tail is marked with a few crescent-shaped blue bars. The pectoral and pelvic fins are yellow. The female is plain with as many as 22 vertical bars on her side. Her fins are clear.

counts: Dorsal 8 or 9; anal 9 or 10; pectoral 16; pelvic 7; scales 25 or 26.

The various species of the genus *Aphanius* all breed in the same way. *A. dispar* thus serves to illustrate the typical breeding habits of this group.

Water requirements of *A. dispar* are somewhat rigid. It must be maintained in 20 per cent sea water. A suitable substitute may be made by the addition of 1 teaspoon of sea salt (or noniodized salt) to each gallon of aquarium water. Never replace evaporated water with sea water but use tap water.

Females and males should be conditioned in separate containers prior to breeding. The males are ardent suitors and the aquarium should be so planted as to provide plenty of cover and concealment for the female. The favorite spawning mediums are the roots of a water hyacinth or other floating plant. A fair substitute would be Spanish moss (artificial spawning grass) piled high enough to reach the surface of the water. Feed plenty of live food to the breeding pairs. Temperature should be about 75°F but may be raised to 80°F to induce spawning. Fry will hatch in 10 days at the higher temperature. The breeders should be removed after spawning and the young reared in a large aquarium. Fry are able to take sifted *Daphnia*, brine shrimp, and microworms at hatching.

Aphanius fasciatus (Valenciennes)

[fas'-see-a'-tus: *fasciatus* = banded]

Lebias fasciatus Valenciennes, in Humboldt and Bonpland, Recueil l'observations de zoologie . . . , 1799–1803, 2:160, pl. 51, fig. 4, 1811 (type locality, Cape Cagliari)

RANGE: Fresh and brackish waters of Italy, North Africa, Sardinia, Cyprus, and Asia Minor.

SIZE: 2½ inches; breeding at 2½ inches.

TEMPERAMENT: A species not suitable in the community aquarium.

TEMPERATURE REQUIREMENTS: 70–80°F.

SEX DIFFERENCES: The female has clear fins as contrasted with the more ornate fins of the male.

COUNTS: Dorsal 10 to 13; anal 9 to 13; pectoral 14 or 15; pelvic 6 or 7; scales 25 to 29.

This species breeds in the same manner as *Aphanius dispar*.

The over-all color of the male is aquamarine, darker on the back and lighter on the belly. The side is adorned with 10 to 15 dark vertical bars. The dorsal fin has a dark edge and the tail fin is banded. Other fins are yellowish. The female shows lighter colors than the male and the bars on her body are much narrower than those of the male; also, her fins are clear.

Aphanius iberus (Cuvier and Valenciennes)

[eye-bear'-us: *iberus* = Iberian region of Spain]

Cyprinodon iberus Cuvier and Valenciennes, Histoire naturelle des poissons, 18:160, pl. 528, 1846 (type locality, Spain)

RANGE: Spain and high plateau of Algeria.

SIZE: 2 inches; breeding at same size.

TEMPERAMENT: This species is not suitable in the community tank.

TEMPERATURE REQUIREMENTS: 70–80°F.

SEX DIFFERENCES: The female and male differ as noted below.

COUNTS: Dorsal 9 or 10; anal 9 or 10; pelvic 6; scales 26.

This species breeds in the same manner as *Aphanius dispar*.

The male is aquamarine, darker on the back and becoming yellowish on the belly. The sides have 16 to 24 vertical bars. The fins are yellowish. The dorsal fin has a beautiful bluish edge and a darker base. The tail fin is banded with from 3 to 6 bars. The female is light olive, glistening with red but sprinkled with brown. Her fins are clear.

Aphanius sophiae (Heckel)

[sof′-i-ee: probably named after Lady Sophia]

Lebias sophiae Heckel, in Russegger, Reisen in Europa . . . , 2(3):267, pl. 22, fig. 2, 1846 (type locality, Persepolis)

RANGE: Persia, Syria, and Asia Minor.

SIZE: 2 inches; breeding at same size.

TEMPERAMENT: This species is not suitable in the community aquarium.

TEMPERATURE REQUIREMENTS: 70–80°F.

SEX DIFFERENCES: See below.

COUNTS: Dorsal 11; anal 10; pectoral 13 to 15; pelvic 5 or 6; scales 27 to 30.

This species breeds in the same manner as *Aphanius dispar*.

The males are dark gray, speckled irregularly with silvery-blue shiny dots. These dots are present in the unpaired fins. The female is olive, though varying toward gray brown at times. Her belly is yellowish brown. The side markings of the male are not distinct on the female.

The name of this species currently is *Aphanius mento*.

GENUS *Aphyosemion* Myers

[Ap'-hy-o-se'-mi-on: *aphyo* = small fry; *semion* = mark]

ARNOLD'S LYRETAIL / *Aphyosemion arnoldi* (Boulenger)

[are'-nold-eye: named in honor of Johann Paul Arnold]

Fundulus arnoldi Boulenger, Ann. Mag. Nat. Hist., (8)2:29, 1908 (type locality, Warri, Niger Delta)

RANGE: Niger River Delta.

SIZE: 2 inches; breeds at 2 inches.

TEMPERAMENT: A species best kept by itself.

TEMPERATURE REQUIREMENTS: 72–80°F.

SEX DIFFERENCES: Male is reddish-brown, with a darker back and lighter belly. The body and head are irregularly marked with crimson lines and spots. Scales reflect the light beautifully. The tail fin of the male is yellowish-green spotted with crimson and has a brownish-red edge; it is very distinctive when compared to the female. The female is slightly smaller and not so colorful as the male.

COUNTS: Dorsal 15 or 16; anal 15 to 17; scales 25 to 27.

The breeding of this species of lyretail is not difficult, but it is a job for the advanced hobbyist. The majority of *Aphyosemion* come from Germany where "kitchen" breeders specialize on the varieties of this group.

The following is an account of the breeding habits of this species, as related by Hans Tusche, translated from the February, 1953, *Datz* by William Vorderwinkler:

"Lyretails should be spawned in pairs. . . . This bottom-spawning species is considerably more greedy than the more slender and harmless species such as A. *australe, bivittatum, singa* and *cognatum*, and they might be described as being in the middle position between this group and the real roughnecks, A. *coeruleum* and *sjoestedti*. Of course, they may be kept in community tanks in company with other fishes, even delicate ones, as long as they are not members of this genus. They will not harm them, and will not even pay any attention to them. However, as soon as they find a male of their own kind, there is an immediate end to all peace and quiet, . . . and the weaker one is driven away. However, if two males of the same size meet, the *arnoldi* spread their fins until they seem ready to rip, and fan at each other, bending the hind part of the body sideways. The first thing which usually happens is the loss of the long, drawn-out golden filaments of the dorsal and tail fins, which are sometimes forked. This loss of the fish's main attractions may be avoided by keeping mature males by themselves. . . .

"There were two distinct color forms brought back from the last expedition from Nigeria, . . . known as the "yellows" and "reds," and reference here is made only to the fins. The body color is almost always blue with reddish dots. These dots form an indefinable pattern which varies. . . . The "yellow" form has a delicately olive-green dorsal fin with carmine dots, as well as predominantly yellow to orange anal and caudal fins. Sometimes there is an area of yellow or even dark orange on the top and base of the dorsal fin. The others have these fins in blue, but here we also meet with pretty variations of color, for instance dorsal fins with violet to indigo dots on a yellow background. Besides, the "blue" variety has an anal fin which carries a stripe through the middle, of the same color as the dots in the dorsal. Furthermore, the anal and caudal fins are edged with bright yellow. Mother Nature dipped generously into her paint-pot in providing this fish with colors. . . .

"Whoever wishes to meet with success in spawning this fish must provide himself with several pairs or with extra females. . . . If no eggs are laid after 14 days, another female must be substituted. . . .

"The small containers often referred to as 'refrigerator dishes' are much too small

for this fish; *A. arnoldi* are much too shy and excitable for these. The long, shallow tanks which have been recommended for *A. australe*, *A. bivittatum*, *A. singa* and *A. cognatum* would be preferable, but not for extended periods of time. However, 6 to 10 gallon tanks are very well adapted for this. As these fish require heavy planting, a heavy bottom sediment and a dim lighting, this should be provided for the breeding period, which may extend over several weeks. Naturally, when more than one pair are available, they should be replaced from week to week, allowing the ones removed to rest in separate tanks. Dr. Meder has had good results using charcoal of 3 to 4 mm sizes in place of a sediment bottom of a breeding tank for bottom-spawning *Aphyosemion* species. This is better adapted for a short period of time, because the fish must be removed when they begin searching for eggs. For a longer set-up, the best results have been gotten with *Fontinalis*, spread out to form a heavy layer on the bottom of the tank. Even if this plant does not float, it should be anchored down with a few glass rods. Some floating plants should also be provided, in order to cut down the incoming light. As with all other *Aphyosemion* species, only soft, aged water should be used. Temperature should range between 72 and 76 degrees Fahrenheit. Salt should be added, a heaping teaspoonful for every 3 gallons. . . . Water depth is sufficient at 4 to 5 inches. Because the eggs of bottom-spawning species are exceptionally sensitive to light, and the densest layer of *Fontinalis* is not enough to cut out all light, a sheet of green or black paper should be fastened to within an inch of the water surface on three sides, leaving the front glass open. It will now be noticed that there are light as well as dark portions of the tank, and the observer will soon see that his *A. arnoldi* will stay in the darker sections, and prefer to lay their eggs there. They willingly accept the plants on the bottom as a substitute for a sedimentary bottom. One should not substitute a pillow of algae for the *Fontinalis*, as it would be quite a tedious job searching for eggs.

"Soon after being introduced, the fish begin their first spawning, which may take upwards of an hour. In this time, depending upon age and size of the breeders, 10 to 30 eggs have been laid in the plants on the bottom. In the evening, the eggs may be easily removed. This is how it is done: first, the top plants are lifted out; then the glass rods which hold down the *Fontinalis*. Then the *Fontinalis* is shaken, in order that any eggs in it may fall to the bottom; they do so readily, because they are non-adhesive. Most of the eggs may already be observed on the bottom, having been shaken through by the hard driving of the male. This is more likely to happen because only a few sites are chosen for spawning, and the fish keep returning to them. Now it will be found that there is some difficulty in seeing the eggs on the bottom, the tank having been shaded with dark paper. If the paper is fastened with cellulose tape, it can be easily removed for the egg-removing operation.

"When the plants have been shaken out and removed, they had best be placed where they will not drip on the rug and incur the wrath of the lady of the house. Then the paper which has been removed may be placed under the bottom, and the eggs may be seen with a light shining through. And what are our *Aphyosemions* doing all this time? Nothing, if all is done without too much disturbance. They wait shyly in a corner, paying little attention to the removal of their eggs, which may be performed with the aid of a thin glass tube. Of course, the jars which will hold the eggs have been prepared previously. They have been filled to a depth of ½ to 1 inch with aged, clean rain-water, which has been made acid with peat moss, (pH 6). If one is fortunate enough to locate some spring water of acid value, so much the better. Why? The eggs of Arnold's Lyretail take 5 to 6 weeks to hatch in the summer months, and in the winter may take as long as 2½ to 3 months. This is a long period of time, during which the eggs are open to attack by bacteria or infusoria. It has been found, however, that acid water minimizes, perhaps even eliminates this danger. For instance, 70 eggs kept in spring water of 1-degree hardness and a pH of 5.8, as is found in the Helmstedt region on the border, resulted in only a few fungused eggs, which were probably sterile to begin with. However, eggs placed in neutral rain-water resulted in hatchings of only 30% to 50%. Of course, the addition of chemicals such as Cilex, Trypoflavin or IM66 also suggest themselves as a possibility, as has been mentioned in previous articles. Well, back to the removal of the eggs: the eggs are picked up with a glass tube, using it like a dip-tube. When one or more eggs are picked up in this manner, they are held in this tube above the incubating jar and allowed to sink to the bottom of the tube, while the water is kept in by keeping the upper end closed. Then the tube is inserted into the water of the incubating jar and the eggs drop out by their own weight.

"The water in the tube is then returned to the breeding tank. In this way it is possible to avoid to a great extent the contamination of the water in the jars. *A. arnoldi* are astonishingly productive. One can figure on a daily average of 15 to 25 eggs. In one case there were 38 in one day, and about 400 in one month, all from one female. Of course, the breeders must be fed during these long breeding periods. Besides large *Daphnia*, which should be constantly in the breeding tank, white worms, tubifex and mosquito larvae may be offered. This food must first be carefully rinsed. Besides, only as much should be fed as the fish can dispose of. This applies especially to white worms and tubifex, which only too often get into the bottom plants if fed too freely. Uneaten worms should be removed with tweezers.

"Back again to the incubating jars: even if the spoiled eggs are removed daily, the amount added daily brings the total constantly higher. After about 4 weeks there are hundreds of eggs, all of different ages. This makes no difference here, because *A. arnoldi* hardly ever have the power to burst their shells after the incubation period is over. It can be assumed that in their natural state, after the end of the dry season, during which the eggs lie in the swampy mud of the ponds and brooks, the enormous rainfalls supply the eggs not only with water, but also with microorganisms which assist the completely developed fry out of their shells. The reason is that bacteria cause the outer shells to dissolve. This process must be brought about in the incubating jars by artificial means. This was already accomplished before the war by scattering artificial dried food over the surface of the water. We have been especially successful after the war with Wedo or Wawil. This is how it is done: for this purpose an additional container is put into use as a 'hatching dish,' and is filled with equal parts of aged and fresh rain-water. In this are placed the over-ripe eggs. These may be distinguished by a light golden glitter of the eyes through the shell. Then the surface is strewn with dried food, which sinks slowly to the bottom and clouds the water in a half-hour. A pinch of food is sufficient. Then at least 80% emerge, to be picked up carefully with the glass tube and placed into a rearing tank, (preferably all-glass, without bottom gravel). Again we should avoid introducing water, as we did with the eggs. This is quite simple. The tube is again held upright in the clean water of the rearing tank, and the youngsters soon wriggle out. Care must be taken not to leave the unhatched eggs, as well as the fry in the cloudy water for any longer than 3 hours or they will surely suffocate, the fry in the eggs as well as the hatched fry. The unhatched eggs are placed in clear water and should be 'treated' again on the next day or the day after. A more radical treatment would be to stir the eggs in the 'hatching dish' occasionally with a glass rod. This will usually help in stubborn cases. The fry, as well as the eggs, are quite distinguishable in size. The 'yellow' variety produces an egg which is only about half the size of *Aphyosemion bivittatum*, while the 'blue' variety fry and eggs are considerably larger. Feeding is begun immediately in the rearing tanks; (you will soon require a number of them). At first, only small infusoria may be used; (banana-peel cultures, etc.). The fry grow enormously during the first week, after which they may be fed the *nauplii* of Crustacea, (newly hatched brine shrimp, or sifted cyclops), for which they make regular dashes. By no means is it advisable to raise other fishes, even those of the same genus such as *A. bivittatum* or *A. australe* with them; they would soon disappear. When they are only ½ cm in length, the young *arnoldi* already have heavy bellies if fed well daily, and show a delicate violet tint. If 3 rearing tanks are provided, two of them about 12 inches in length, and the other about 20 inches in length, and the fry divided among them according to size, the fry will be well accommodated.

"Sorting the fry is especially important, otherwise the larger ones will keep their smaller brethren away from their fair share of the food, and if the disparity in sizes is too great, are even likely to disregard brotherly love altogether and make a meal of the smaller ones. Further raising instructions are the same as for other members of this family; chopped tubifex worms and white worms should be fed frequently as soon as they are large enough to take them.

"Translator's note: Two substitutes for *Fontinalis* which are more easily available come to mind: Spanish moss and nylon yarn. The artificial dried foods mentioned are German products, in which the main ingredient is powdered milk. Any grocer will sell you powdered milk, and it will do just as good a job. Two drops of Methylene Blue, 5% solution, in the incubating jars, will give you ample protection and is otherwise quite harmless."

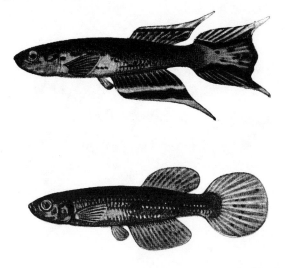

After Innes

CAPE LOPEZ LYRETAIL / *Aphyosemion australe* (Rachow)

[aus-tra'-le: *australe* = southern]

Haplochilus calliurus australe Rachow, Blät. Aquar.-Terrak. pp. 129, 275, 1920; Hauptkat. Verein. Zierfischzucht. Rahnsd. Mühle, 1922–1923, 2:428, 1923; Handb. Zierfischk., Stuttgart, p. 63, 1928; p. 82, 1928 (type locality, Ogooué Delta, Cape Lopez; references not checked)

RANGE: Gabon, Africa.

SIZE: 2 inches; breeding at 2 inches.

TEMPERAMENT: A species best kept by itself.

TEMPERATURE REQUIREMENTS: 70–80°F.

SEX DIFFERENCES: Male is more colorful than the female.

COUNTS: Dorsal 10 to 12; anal 15 to 18; scales 31 to 33.

Breeding is same manner as for *Aphyosemion arnoldi*. Fred Corwin, a successful breeder of this fish, uses small refrigerator jars with *Fontinalis*. Every day he checks the grass for eggs and removes the eggs to another container. A basement is suggested for their domicile as it gets just the amount of light needed. Eggs take about 2 weeks to hatch and are protected from fungus by the addition of 2 drops of 5 per cent Methylene Blue per gallon of water. By the time the eggs hatch out the dye has lost its color and they are easily seen. These fish are not bottom breeders like *A. arnoldi*.

A few pieces of rock salt should be added to the breeding aquarium. German breeders advise about 5 per cent sea water for this species.

RED APHYOSEMION / *Aphyosemion bivittatum bivittatum* (Lönnberg)

[bi'-vit-tay'-tum: *bi* = two; *vittatum* = banded]

Fundulus bivittatus Lönnberg, Öfv. Akad. Forh. Stockholm, p. 190, 1895 (type locality, Ndian River, Cameroon)
RANGE: Lower Niger; Cameroons, West Africa.
SIZE: 2½ inches; breeds at 2 inches.
TEMPERAMENT: A species best kept in an aquarium by itself.
TEMPERATURE REQUIREMENTS: 70–80°F.
SEX DIFFERENCES: The female does not show as much color as the male.
COUNTS: Dorsal 11 to 13; anal 13 or 14; scales 26 to 29.

As with *Aphyosemion australe*, they should be bred in pairs only.

The male is brownish-red, with the lower half of the body darker olive tinged with greenish brown. The body is sprinkled with crimson dots. Two dark stripes occur: one from the snout to the base of the caudal fin, another from the mouth to the base of the caudal fin. The dorsal, anal, and tail fins, spotted with red dots, are long and pointed in comparison to those of the female. The anal and tail fins have a purple-red border.

Two color varieties of *Aphyosemion bivattatum*, with *A. b. hollyi* (male), left; *A. b. bivattatum* (male), center; and *A. b. hollyi* (female), right.

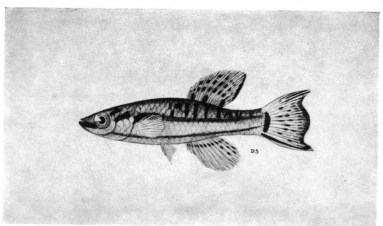

BLUE APHYOSEMION / *Aphyosemion bivittatum hollyi* Myers

[hol'-ly-eye: named in honor of Maximilian Holly]

Aphyosemion bivittatum hollyi Myers, Copeia, no. 4, p. 184, 1933 (new name to replace *Fundulopanchax bivittatus* var. *coerulea* Meinken 1930; preoccupied) (type locality, Equatorial West Africa)

RANGE: Equatorial West Africa.

SIZE: 2½ inches; breeding at same size.

TEMPERAMENT: Best kept with other *Aphyosemion.*

TEMPERATURE REQUIREMENTS: 70–80°F.

SEX DIFFERENCES: See below.

COUNTS: Dorsal 12; anal 14; scales 28 or 29.

This species breeds the same as *Aphyosemion bivittatum bivittatum.*

This is a blue color variety. The front half is predominantly blue, the rear half yellowish green. The gill covers and adjacent areas are blue with violet-tinted markings. The lower jaw is red. The side has a horizontal stripe with irregular bars decorating the body above this stripe. The dorsal fin is dark brown with violet dots at its base, and yellow and black in layers above the base. The anal fin is light blue basally, becoming greener distally. The tail fin is a beautiful shade of sky blue with violet dots, the lower edge showing a red stripe. The female is light brown with two stripes running along her sides. Her tail fin is edged in brown. She is slightly smaller than the male and is not brilliantly colored.

Blue Calliurum / *Aphyosemion calliurum ahli* Myers

[ahl'-eye: named in honor of Ernst Ahl]

Aphyosemion calliurum ahli Myers, Copeia, no. 4, p. 183, 1933, new name to replace *Panchax calliurus* var. *caeruleus* Meinken 1932; preoccupied (type locality not given)

RANGE: Probably Liberia to Luanda, Africa.

SIZE: 2 inches; breeds at 2 inches.

TEMPERAMENT: Same as *Aphyosemion calliurum calliurum* (page 397).

TEMPERATURE REQUIREMENTS: 70–80°F.

SEX DIFFERENCES: The coloration of the female is much less variable than that of the male.

COUNTS: Same as *A. c. calliurum.*

This fish is a subspecies of *A. c. calliurum* and has the same body shape, breeding habits, range, and size.

The male is a deep blue; the back is dark olive with a greenish reflected light. The head and body are decorated with blood-red bands, bars, and dots. The dorsal fin is a purplish blue with darker dots and edged with yellow. The anal fin is blue with darker dots and a purple edge. The caudal fin is blue with red dots, red bands, and yellow edges. The female is light purple; the markings on her body are much less intense than those of the male. Her unpaired fins are aquamarine with red dots.

The name of this species currently is *Aphyosemion ahli.*

RED-CHINNED PANCHAX / *Aphyosemion calliurum calliurum* (Boulenger)

[kal'-li-ur'-um: *calli* = beautiful; from *ura* = tail]

Haplochilus calliurus Boulenger, Ann. Mag. Nat. Hist., no. 8, p. 265, 1911 (type locality, Liberia)

RANGE: Liberia to Luanda, Africa.

SIZE: 2 inches; breeds at 2 inches.

TEMPERAMENT: This species is best kept by itself; males kept together may nip each other's fins.

TEMPERATURE REQUIREMENTS: 70–80°F.

SEX DIFFERENCES: The female is not so brilliantly colored as the male.

COUNTS: Dorsal 10 to 12; anal 12 to 14; pectoral 17; pelvic 6; scales 29 to 30.

This fish and its subspecies *Aphyosemion calliurum ahli* are bred in the same way as *A. australe*. A color description is necessary to distinguish this fish from its subspecies, both of which have the same breeding habits, size, habitat and shape.

The male shows mostly bluish green in the front part of the body, with the rearmost portions being reddish brown. The underside of the lower jaw is best described as a reddish brown. Gill covers are aquamarine. Sides show crimson dots arranged in irregular longitudinal lines that run from the snout to the caudal peduncle. The dorsal and anal fins are straw-colored with some red dots. The anal fin is decorated with a red and yellow edge. The aquamarine tail has a dark red border and is marked with red spots in its middle portion. The upper edge of the caudal fin is whitish and the lower edge is orange; pectorals are light blue edged with white; pelvics are yellowish brown with a dark red border. The female is tan-colored with red spots; her fins are greenish with some spots.

The name of this species currently is *Aphyosemion calliurum*.

Aphyosemion cameronensis (Boulenger)

[cam'-er-on-en'-sis: named after the locality where collected]

Haplochilus cameronensis Boulenger, Ann. Mag. Nat. Hist., (7)12:440, 1903 (type locality, Kribi River, southern Cameroon)

RANGE: Southern Cameroon, Gabon, lower Congo River, Africa.

SIZE: 2 inches.

TEMPERAMENT: A species best kept by itself.

TEMPERATURE REQUIREMENTS: 70–80°F.

SEX DIFFERENCES: See below.

COUNTS: Dorsal 11 or 12; anal 14 or 15; pectoral 17; pelvic 6; scales 30 to 34.

The color is yellowish to olive brown with carmine spots forming two lengthwise bands on the sides. These spots are more numerous in the male. This fish breeds in the same manner as *Aphyosemion australe*.

Amphyosemion cognatum.

Aphyosemion filamentosum (Meinken)

[fil'-a-men-to'-sum: *fila* = a thread; *mentosum* = the chin]

Fundulopanchax filamentosus Meinken, Blät. Aquar.-Terrak. 44:249, fig., 1933 (type locality, Tropical West Africa)

RANGE: Tropical West Africa, Lagos to Cameroons.

SIZE: 2 inches; breeds at 1¾ inches.

TEMPERAMENT: A species best kept by itself.

TEMPERATURE REQUIREMENTS: 70–80°F.

SEX DIFFERENCES: The female is much less intensely colored than the male.

COUNTS: Dorsal 13; anal 14; scales 28.

This species is often confused with *Aphyosemion gardneri*, but it is at least ½ inch smaller than that species. It is bred the same as *A. arnoldi*.

The coloration of the male is dark greenish yellow on the back, aquamarine on the head, and a beautiful blue on the belly. The head and body have numerous red dots. The dorsal fin is blue green with red markings; the fringed anal fin is sky blue in color with maroon spots. The tail fin is light blue with maroon-colored dots and a maroon band in the lower part.

STEEL-BLUE APHYOSEMION / *Aphyosemion gardneri* (Boulenger)

[gard'-ner-eye: named in honor of R. D. Gardner]

Fundulus gardneri Boulenger, Ann. Mag. Nat. Hist., (8)8:261, 1911 (type locality, headwaters Cross River, Calabar)

RANGE: West Africa, Lagos to Cameroons.

SIZE: 2½ inches; breeds at 2 inches.

TEMPERAMENT: A species best kept by itself.

TEMPERATURE REQUIREMENTS: 70–80°F.

SEX DIFFERENCES: See *Aphyosemion filamentosum* (page 399).

COUNTS: Dorsal 12 or 13; anal 14 to 16; pectoral about 15; pelvic 6; scales 28 to 32.

This fish is colored almost identically with *A. filamentosum.* The only apparent differences are its size and fin-ray count. It is bred the same way as *A. arnoldi.*

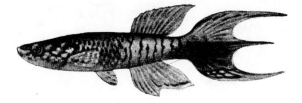

After Innes

BLUE GULARIS / *Aphyosemion gulare caeruleum* (Boulenger)

[see-rue'-lee-um: *caeruleum* = dark or sky blue]

Fundulus gularis var. *caerulea* Boulenger, Catalogue of the Fresh-water Fishes of Africa, 3:30, 1915 (on Arnold 1908)

RANGE: Niger Delta to Cameroon, Africa.

SIZE: 5½ inches; breeding at 4 inches.

TEMPERAMENT: A species best kept by itself. This species is a good jumper.

TEMPERATURE REQUIREMENTS: 70–80°F.

SEX DIFFERENCES: The female is a mud color, not nearly so colorful as the male and much smaller.

COUNTS: Same as for *Aphyosemion gulare gulare* (page 402).

This is one of the most beautiful of aquarium fishes. Unfortunately, American aquarists do not see many individuals, as they are more frequently found in Germany where they are bred in large numbers by the "kitchen" breeders. It breeds in the same manner as *A. arnoldi* except that a larger tank is used. Eggs require 2 to 3 months to hatch.

A single color pattern does not exist for this fish. There are several color varieties, although we know of only the one species described. Very few specimens now come from nature; most come from Germany where several color varieties occur. The color differences within the species are as variable as those of the male guppy.

The male shows a dark red back which shades to a straw brown on the sides. The jaws are dark blue; the gill covers are a light blue with red stripes which become dots farther along the body. The side, besides having these dots, has some vertical red bars. The dorsal fin is bluish green with a reddish base and has some spots of red in its main section. The anal fin is straw-colored. The tail fin shows three pointed lobes, each a different color. The upper lobe is usually 'blue with irregular red markings, the middle lobe yellow and red, and the lower lobe aquamarine and purple. Pelvic and pectoral fins are yellowish red.

The name of this species currently is *Aphyosemion sjoestedti*.

YELLOW GULARIS / *Aphyosemion gulare gulare* (Boulenger)

[gue-lar'-ee: *gulare* = pertaining to the throat]

Fundulus gularis Boulenger, Proc. Zool. Soc. London, no. 2, p. 623, pl. 37, figs. 2, 3, 1901 (type locality, Agberi, Cameroons)

RANGE: West Africa, Lower Niger to Cameroons.

SIZE: 2½ inches; breeds at 2 inches.

TEMPERAMENT: A species best kept by itself.

TEMPERATURE REQUIREMENTS: 70–80°F.

SEX DIFFERENCES: The female is of much less intense coloration and is slightly smaller.

COUNTS: Dorsal 15 or 16; anal 16 to 18; pelvic 6; scales 30 to 34.

The breeding habits of this species are the same as those of *Aphyosemion gulare caeruleum*.

The color of the male is a yellowish green peppered with purple marks on the gill cover and on the body. The belly is a straw color or whitish. The dorsal fin is pinkish with some red dots. The anal fin is a reddish yellow with darker dots. The tail fin is red with darker dots above the center line and yellowish beneath it.

LÖNNBERG'S APHYOSEMION / *Aphyosemion loennbergi* Boulenger

[loenn'-berg-eye: named in honor of A. J. E. Lönnberg]

Aphyosemion loennbergii Boulenger, Ann. Mag. Nat. Hist., (7) 12:440, 1903 (type locality, Kribi River, Cameroons)

RANGE: Niger to Cameroons, West Africa.

SIZE: 2 inches; breeds at 2 inches.

TEMPERAMENT: A species best kept by itself.

TEMPERATURE REQUIREMENTS: 70–80°F.

SEX DIFFERENCES: The male and female may be recognized by the different coloration described below.

COUNTS: Dorsal 11 or 12; anal 12 or 13; pectoral 15; pelvic 6; scales 26 to 28.

The breeding habits of this species are the same as *Aphyosemion australe*.

The male is dark brownish green on the front half of the upper sides and back. The edge of the back is a shiny gold, the sides reflect a bronze and green, and the belly is yellowish. The lower jaw is black or purple. The gill plate has irregular red lines decorating it. All the fins are yellowish green; the dorsal and anal fins are "oversized" with dark margins and yellow tips. The tail fin has a red middle portion and a blue upper part that is peppered with red dots; the tips of the rays are yellowish.

The female has the same over-all color, but her sides show two long stripes; the upper stripe runs from the snout through the eye to the base of the tail fin, the lower from the base of the pectoral to the lower base of the tail fin.

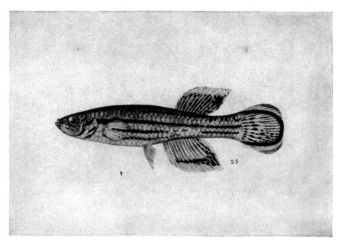

MEINKEN'S APHYOSEMION / *Aphyosemion meinkeni* Myers

[mine'-ken-eye: named in honor of Hermann Meinken]

Aphyosemion meinkeni Myers, Copeia, no. 4, p. 184, 1933, new name to replace *Panchax pictus* Meinken 1932 preoccupied (type locality, tropical West Africa)

RANGE: Tropical West Africa.

SIZE: 2 inches; breeds at 2 inches.

TEMPERAMENT: A species best kept by itself.

TEMPERATURE REQUIREMENTS: 70–80°F.

SEX DIFFERENCES: The female is not so intensely colored as the male.

COUNTS: Dorsal 12; anal 14; scales 29 or 30.

The breeding of this species is the same as for *Aphyosemion australe*.

The male is aquamarine in color. The gill covers are decorated with irregular red lines and dots that extend on the body as four horizontal dotted lines. These lines run to the tail fin. The dorsal fin is aquamarine with a yellowish cast, with a few red dots and a yellow margin. The anal fin is a yellowish green with a few red dots in the form of a triangle and a yellowish margin. The tail fin is aquamarine with a purple peppering throughout. The pectoral and pelvic fins are yellow of varying intensity.

The female is light brown and shows some red on her gill plates.

Many-colored Aphyosemion / *Aphyosemion multicolor* (Meinken)

[mul'-ti-col'-or: *multi* = many; *color* = color]

Fundulopanchax multicolor Meinken, Wochschr. Aquar.-Terrak., p. 18, 1930 (type locality, Cameroon)

RANGE: Lagos; Nigeria; Cameroons, West Africa.

SIZE: 2½ inches; breeding at same size.

TEMPERAMENT: This species should be kept by itself.

TEMPERATURE REQUIREMENTS: 70–80°F.

SEX DIFFERENCES: The female is plainer in color than the male and is smaller.

COUNTS: Dorsal 10; anal 13; scales 26.

This species breeds in the same way as *Aphyosemion australe.*

The male fish, the larger and more colorful of the two, has an olive-colored back, the sides are aquamarine, and the lower jaw shows a reddish cast when the fish is in good condition. The belly is a straw color. There are two horizontal stripes running along the side; the upper stripe runs through the eye to the lower base of the caudal fin, the lower one from below the eye to the lower base of the caudal fin. The median fins are somewhat enlarged. The dorsal fin is deep brown with red markings. The anal fin has a yellowish base, which becomes light yellow in the middle part and ends with a brilliant purple margin. The center of the tail is yellowish green with beautiful red dots and is bounded by light brown bands; its dorsal margin is yellow, green, and blue; the lower margin is lighter green with a deep vermilion border.

RED APHYOSEMION; GOLDEN PHEASANT /
Aphyosemion sjoestedti (Lönnberg)

[s-joe'-stedt-eye: named in honor of Y. Sjoestedt, the collector]

Fundulus sjoestedti Lönnberg, Öfv. Akad. Forh. Stockholm, p. 191, 1895 (type locality, Bonge and Ndian River, Cameroons)

RANGE: Sierra Leone to Cameroons in coastal region, West Africa.

SIZE: 3 inches; breeds at 2½ inches.

TEMPERAMENT: A species best kept by itself.

TEMPERATURE REQUIREMENTS: 68–80°F.

SEX DIFFERENCES: The male is intensely and beautifully colored. The female is a uniform color and not so intensely pigmented as the male.

COUNTS: Dorsal 17 to 19; anal 17 to 19; pectoral 16 or 17; pelvic 6; scales 33 to 36.

The name of this species currently is *Aphyosemion occidentalis*.

Breeding is much like *A. arnoldi*. One of the most successful of German breeders has indicated to the authors that the breeding of this species depends on the use of soft or rain water, or the water from ice which accumulates in a refrigerator. The breeding pairs are selected for their size and brilliant coloration. They should be placed in a small 2-gallon aquarium with *Fontinalis* or artificial spawning grass. The plants are removed every day to a large, shallow hatching tray with a white bottom so that the fry are more visible. Fresh plants should replace removed ones. The eggs are said to take up to 6 months to hatch and should never be allowed to develop in daylight. The eggs should be kept at 70°F. Some Methylene Blue should be added to the water (2 drops of 5 per cent solution per gallon) to protect them against fungus. Fry are large enough at birth to accept freshly hatched brine shrimp. Youngsters must be segregated according to their size.

Aphyosemion splendopleuris (Meinken)

[splen'-do-pleur'-is: *splendo* = luster or sheen; *pleuris* = sides]

Fundulopanchax splendopleuris Meinken, Wochschr. Aquar.-Terrak., p. 17, 1930 (type locality, Cameroon)

RANGE: Cameroons, West Africa.

SIZE: 2 inches; breeding at 2 inches.

TEMPERAMENT: A species best kept by itself.

TEMPERATURE REQUIREMENTS: 70–80°F.

SEX DIFFERENCES: See below.

COUNTS: Dorsal 11; anal 13; scales 26 to 27.

Breeding is the same as for *Aphyosemion australe*. Breeders about 8 months old seem to be the most successful and are least inclined to devour the spawn. This is one of the rarer members of the genus *Aphyosemion* and pairs are hard to find. They seldom live longer than a year in the aquarium, which leads one to suspect that this is an annual fish, but the beautiful colors shown by adult specimens are more than reward for their short lives.

The male shows a deep golden brown hue which becomes an aquamarine tinge on the posterior half of the body. Two horizontal lines run the length of the sides; the upper stripe is an olive to black color and runs from the snout through the eye to the caudal fin. The lower stripe is a green, iridescent line which runs from the gill cover back to the caudal fin. There are sprinkles of red in both these stripes and the red shows up well in the dorsal fin. The large anal fin is colorful with a blue color at its base, a golden center, and a dark green edge. The same gold and blue are mixed in the tail fin, the lower edge being a brilliant red.

The female is brownish green. There are a few red spots similar to the male's coloration on the sides of the female, but they are few in number and not too distinct. The fins have a translucent yellowish hue with several darker spots in them. These dark dots are not of a definite pattern, as some females have them in certain areas while others do not show them at all.

Aphyosemion vexillifer (Meinken)

[vex-il'-li-fer: *vexilli* = a flag; *fer* = carrying]

Panchax vexillifer Meinken, Blät. Aquar.-Terrak., p. 255, 1929 (type locality, tropical West Africa)

RANGE: Tropical West Africa.

SIZE: 2½ inches; breeds at 2 inches.

TEMPERAMENT: This species is best kept by itself.

TEMPERATURE REQUIREMENTS: 68–80°F.

SEX DIFFERENCES: See below.

COUNTS: Dorsal 9; anal 14; scales 32.

This fish comes from small intermittent pools in Africa. Its chief diet is probably mosquito larvae and small insects. It shows best color when in dirty, muddy water and is known to be an excellent jumper, so the aquarium must be kept covered.

Breeding this species is the same as for *Aphyosemion australe*. Pairs may be selected after 6 months of age, though optimum breeding age is probably about 8 months. Breeding should be done in very small aquaria containing old, green water. A single pair in a 1-gallon aquarium is ideal. Pairs put up for breeding should be well-conditioned and in good color. Females should be round and heavy. Since they do not breed in strong light, keep them in shaded areas.

The male is a beautiful blue, although there are forward areas which are nearly black. The gill plates are colorful and have a striped mosaic design. The sides are striped in this same nondescript pattern. The anal fin is a mustard color, deeper green in the center portion and with a brilliant red and white border. The dorsal fin is green with red spots, much like *Aphyosemion splendopleuris*. The tail fin is body color in the mid-region, with red spots as in the dorsal fin. The rear edge is dark, and the top and lower margins are colored like the outer edge of the anal fin.

GENUS *Aplocheilichthys* Bleeker

[Ap'-low-kile-ick'-thees: *aplo* = single or simple; *cheil* = margin or edge;
ichthys = fish]

YELLOW-FINNED PANCHAX / *Aplocheilichthys flavipinnis* Meinken

[flav'-i-pinn'-is: *flavi* = golden yellow; *pinnis* = fins]

Aplocheilichthys flavipinnis Meinken, Blät. Aquar.-Terrak., p. 54, 1932 (type locality, Lagos)

RANGE: Nigeria.

SIZE: 1½ inches; breeding at same size.

TEMPERAMENT: This species may be kept with fishes of its own size and larger, but it annoys smaller fishes.

TEMPERATURE REQUIREMENTS: 60–90°F. Optimum breeding temperature 72°F.

SEX DIFFERENCES: The female and male differ as noted below.

COUNTS: Dorsal 6 or 7; anal 13 or 14; scales 30 or 31.

Community breeding may be practiced with this species. The female extrudes a cluster of eggs, much like the medaka (page 444). As the male passes the cluster he releases a cloud of sperm. The sperm have been observed under a microscope to live for at least 15 minutes in water after discharge. Breeding is best accom-plished with about three pairs in a 5-gallon aquarium. The vegetation should be dense. Spanish moss (artificial spawning grass) serves this purpose very well. It is of value to have an excess of females since the males are capable of spawning with more than one female. The water should be of pH 6.8 at a temperature of 68 to 78°F. It is likely that this fish is an an-nual. The young mature rapidly, growing to full size in 3 to 4 months. They require copious amounts of live foods and bits of meat and fish. Dry food should be offered sparingly. They do best in a dark location and in shallow water. Because they are good jumpers, the aquarium should be covered.

The general coloration is greenish, the belly much lighter than the back. The dorsal and anal fins of the male have a beautiful blue trim. The pelvic fins of the male are reddish; those of the female are uncolored.

The name of this species currently is *Foerschichthys flavipinnis*.

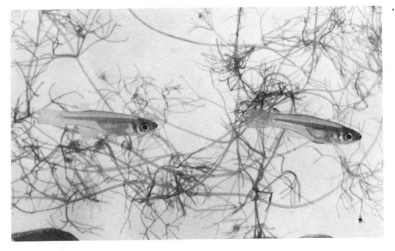

LAMP-EYED PANCHAX / *Aplocheilichthys macrophthalmus* Meinken

[mack'-roff-thal'-mus: *macro* = large; *ophthalmus* = eye]

Aplocheilichthys macrophthalmus Meinken, Blät. Aquar.-Terrak., p. 53, 1932 (type locality, Lagos)

RANGE: Nigeria.

SIZE: 1½ inches; breeds at 1½ inches.

TEMPERAMENT: This species may be kept with fishes larger than itself.

TEMPERATURE REQUIREMENTS: 65–90°F. Optimum breeding temperature 72°F.

SEX DIFFERENCES: Besides the differences in color noted below, the dorsal and anal fins of the male are pointed, while those of the female are rounded.

COUNTS: Dorsal 7; anal 11; scales 26.

The breeding habits of the lamp-eyed panchax are similar to those of *Aplocheilichthys flavipinnis*. The eggs, in clusters of about 10 to 15, hang from the vent of the female for a moment or so while the male fertilizes them, after which the female brushes them off onto some bushy plants. The best type of spawning grass is Spanish moss. Parents do well in a darkened corner where they receive little light. Shallow water is preferred with a pH of 6.8, and moderate hardness is desirable.

Breeders should be seasoned on worms (both *Tubifex* and white), *Daphnia*, bits of meat and fish, and fed sparingly on dried foods. After spawning parents should be removed and the eggs hatched in the dark. The water in which the eggs are hatched should be from the spawning tank, with 2 drops of 5 per cent Methylene Blue per gallon added. Eggs take about 2 weeks to hatch at 72°F.

The general color is light green, lighter on the belly. The back is marked with a dark band, the sides with two brilliant aquamarine bands. The upper stripe runs from the base of the pectorals to the base of the caudal fin, and the lower along the ventral edge from the gill cover to the tail fin. The tail fin of the male is light green adorned with red dots and an electric blue edging. The female lacks these dots. All the other fins in both sexes are clear. The popular name applied to this fish gives some idea of the way the giant eyes impress people. The eyes are large compared with the body size and they reflect a beautiful gold and green light. The eyes are not luminous (that is, they do not *give off* light; they just reflect it).

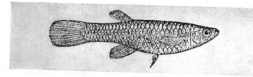

Aplocheilichthys schoelleri (Boulenger)

[shoell′-er-eye: named in honor of C. H. Schoeller]

Haplochilus schoelleri Boulenger, Ann. Mag. Nat. Hist., (7)14:136, 1904 (type locality, near Lake Marcotis, Egypt)

RANGE: Egypt.

SIZE: 1½ inches; breeding at 1½ inches.

TEMPERAMENT: A species not to be kept with fishes smaller than itself.

TEMPERATURE REQUIREMENTS: 60–90°F. Optimum breeding temperature 72°F.

SEX DIFFERENCES: The difference between male and female is noted below.

COUNTS: Dorsal 7 or 8; anal 12 or 13; pectoral 11; pelvic 6; scales 25 to 28.

As in *Aplocheilichthys flavipinnis,* the eggs hang from the female in clusters, where they are fertilized by the male. Breeding techniques are the same as with the other two species of this genus. The early maturity of this and the other two members of *Aplocheilichthys* indicates that they might be annual fishes. It is the exception rather than the rule for pairs to live more than 6 months. When specimens are about a year old they start to become emaciated and sick. To the authors' knowledge, no specimen of this genus has been kept alive more than 14 months. The eggs are large, tough, and extremely viable under adverse conditions. Normal hatching time is about 16 days at 72°F.

This species is aquamarine in coloration with a reticulated pattern formed by the delicately black-edged scales. The dorsal fin is light blue in both sexes. The tail fin of the female is light blue; that of the male is edged with red. The anal and pelvic fins are yellow in the male, light blue in the female. Females, as in guppies, are sometimes larger than males.

FAMILY CYPRINODONTIDAE; TOP MINNOWS

GENUS *Aplocheilus* McClelland

[Ap'-low-kile'-us; *aplo* = simple; *cheilus* = lip]

Hugh M. Smith has shown that the genus *Panchax* is a synonym of *Aplocheilus*. Further he has demonstrated that *Aplocheilus*, with a protractile upper jaw, forms a genus distinct from *Oryzias*, which does not have a protractile upper jaw.

DWARF or GREEN PANCHAX / *Aplocheilus blocki* (Arnold)

[block'-eye: named in honor of a Captain Block]

Haplochilus panchax var. *blockii* J. P. Arnold, Woch. Jahrb., 8:672, 1911 (type locality, Madras, India)

RANGE: Peninsular India and Ceylon.

SIZE: 2 inches; breeding at 1¾ inches.

TEMPERAMENT: This species should be kept only with fishes of its own size.

TEMPERATURE REQUIREMENTS: 68–88°F. Optimum spawning temperature 72°F. These fish may be kept in unheated indoor aquaria the year round. Temperatures as low as 50° are tolerated for a short time.

SEX DIFFERENCES: The coloration of the dorsal and anal fins as described below indicates the sex. The fins of the male are more pointed than those of the female.

COUNTS: Dorsal 7 or 8; anal 15 to 19; pectoral 12; pelvic 6; scales 26 to 30.

Breeding of this species is best accomplished in a small tank. Pairs may be put in anything from a quart jar up to a 2½-gallon tank. Success in breeding this fish in quantity has occurred by placing pairs in refrigerator jars (1-quart capacity) with a bit of Spanish moss. The jars were stacked about 5 high in a rather dark corner. Every day the jars were taken down and the grass with eggs attached was replaced with new spawning grass. The old grass containing the eggs was then placed in another quart container with a label telling the date. As soon as the first batch hatched it was easy to know, day by day, which jar would need attention the next day. The young are very small and require infusoria. Finely powdered food and egg infusion are also necessary for the first 2 weeks. As soon as brine shrimp can be taken growth will be rapid.

This species is nicely colored with a shiny dark green cast. The belly is greenish purple. The gill cover is decorated with a brilliant green spot which catches the light in a twinkling effect. The side is splendid with alternating rows of green and smaller red dots. These magnificent dots occur in the dorsal, caudal, and anal fins of the male. These fins in both sexes are orange-colored, but the female lacks the dots. The anal fin in the male is bordered with flaming red.

Aplocheilus parvus Sundara Raj has been referred to this species as a synonym by Arthur Rachow.

CEYLON KILLIFISH / *Aplocheilus dayi* (Steindachner)

[day'-eye; named in honor of Frances Day]

Haplochilus (*Panchax*) *dayi* Steindachner, Denkschr. Akad. Wiss. Wien, 59:376, pl. 1, fig. 2, 2a, 1892 (type locality, Ceylon)

RANGE: Ceylon.

SIZE: 3½ inches.

TEMPERAMENT: A species best kept by itself.

TEMPERATURE REQUIREMENTS: 68–88°F.

SEX DIFFERENCES: Males have larger and more expanded fins.

COUNTS: Dorsal 6 or 7; anal 15; scales 29 or 30.

This species is related to *Aplocheilus lineatus* and has similar breeding habits. Its eggs are about 2 mm in diameter and easily seen. Hatching occurs in 12 days at 75°F. The young are able to eat freshly hatched brine shrimp, sifted *Daphnia,* and rotifers.

Aplocheilus lineatus (Cuvier & Valenciennes)

PANCHAX LINEATUS / *Aplocheilus lineatus* (Cuvier and Valenciennes)

[lin'-ee-a'-tus: *lineatus* = to make straight or perpendicular]

Panchax lineatum Cuvier and Valenciennes, Histoire naturelle des poissons, 18:381, 1846 (type locality, Bombay)

RANGE: India and Ceylon.

SIZE: 3½ inches; breeding at 3 inches.

TEMPERAMENT: A species best kept by itself.

TEMPERATURE REQUIREMENTS: 68–88°F.

SEX DIFFERENCES: The female is usually darker than the male and has more numerous vertical bars on her body. Dorsal and anal fins of the male are more pointed than in the female. The female has a spot on the base of her dorsal fin.

COUNTS: Dorsal 7 or 8; anal 17; pectoral 14 or 15; pelvic 5; scales 32 or 33.

This fish is bred by the thousands in Germany and shipped to America, where specimens are easily found in most pet shops.

Breeding the *"Panchax lineatus"* requires the same technique as for other *Aplocheilus* and *Aplocheilichthys*. It breeds readily in gallon jars. *Keep this fish in subdued light. No more than 3 hours of light is needed.*

BLUE PANCHAX / *Aplocheilus panchax* (Hamilton = Buchanan)

[pan'-chax: *panchax* = a kind of fish]

Esox panchax Hamilton = Buchanan, Fishes of the River Ganges, pp. 211, 230, pl. 3, fig. 69, 1822 (type locality, Bengal)
RANGE: India, Burma, Malay Peninsula, Siam, Indo-Australian Archipelago.
SIZE: 3 inches; breeds at 3 inches.
TEMPERAMENT: This species is best kept by itself.
TEMPERATURE REQUIREMENTS: 70–85°F.
SEX DIFFERENCES: The female has more rounded dorsal and anal fins than the male. His are more brightly colored.
COUNTS: Dorsal 8; anal 16 or 17; pectoral 14 or 15; pelvic 6; scales 29 to 31.

This is another *Panchax* which is abundant in pet shops because it is colorful and easy to breed. Breeding occurs as in related species.

Great care should be exercised to maintain this and the related species of the genus in soft water of zero hardness.

The general coloration is a dark green. The scales are marked with aquamarine dots; the dorsal, anal, and caudal fins are orange colored with lighter borders, but vary in color and intensity. There is a large dark spot at the base of the dorsal fin.

GENUS *Chriopeops* Fowler

[Cry'-o-pe'-ops: *chriope* = an old common name; *ops* = appearance]

BLUE-FIN TOP MINNOW / *Chriopeops goodei* (Jordan)

[good'-eye: named in honor of George Browne Goode]

Lucania goodei Jordan, Proc. U.S. Nat. Mus., 2:240, 1879 (type locality, Arlington River, tributary of St. Johns River, Florida)

RANGE: Florida.

SIZE: 2 inches; breeds at 2 inches.

TEMPERAMENT: A moderately peaceful species that requires much tank space.

TEMPERATURE REQUIREMENTS: 55–75°F.

SEX DIFFERENCES: All the fins of the female are clear; those of the male are brilliantly colored.

COUNTS: Dorsal 11 or 12; anal 10 or 11; pectoral 10; pelvic 6; scales 27.

Selected pairs should be placed in a heavily planted 10-gallon aquarium, with slightly hard aged water at a temperature no higher than 72°F with a pH of 7.2, to which should be added 1 teaspoon of coarse salt. Parent fish eat all kinds of dried and prepared foods, but they should be conditioned only on live foods for a week prior to mating. Live foods should be offered all during the spawning time. Every day a few eggs will be expelled in the vegetation, and spawning may go on for a month or more.

Plants should be removed from the aquarium every day and carefully inspected for eggs. Spanish moss, the artificial spawning medium, is the best for this purpose. Eggs may be removed and placed in a small vessel containing only water of the original breeding tank. Two drops of 5 per cent Methylene Blue per gallon of water should be added to this vessel. Eggs hatch in 7 days at 72°F, but they are not harmed by lower temperatures and may be kept at any temperature above 55°F. Eggs are best kept in the dark until they hatch.

The name of this species currently is *Lucania goodei*.

Genus *Cubanichthys* Hubbs

[Cue'-ban-ick'-thees: *cuban* = after the island of Cuba; *ichthys* = fish]

Cuban Killie / *Cubanichthys cubensis* (Eigenmann)

[cue-ben'-sis: named after the island of Cuba]

Fundulus cubensis Eigenmann, Bull. U.S. Fish. Comm. 1902, 22:222, 1903 (type locality, Pinar del Rio, Cuba)

RANGE: Cuba.

SIZE: 2 inches; breeds at 1½ inches.

TEMPERAMENT: A moderately peaceful species.

TEMPERATURE REQUIREMENTS: 70–80°F.

SEX DIFFERENCES: The dorsal and anal fins of the male are edged with blue.

COUNTS: Dorsal 10 or 11; anal 10; pectoral 15; pelvic 6; scales 22 or 23.

The breeding habits of this species are practically the same as for the various members of the genus *Aplocheilichthys*. When spawning with the male, the female expels a few eggs which hang, grapelike, from her vent on a thin thread. These are brushed off, either accidentally or by design, against bunch plants or other suitable materials. Parents may or may not eat the eggs, depending upon their state of appetite. Hatching in water at 75° may take about 10 days. Spawning may last for weeks, with a few eggs being laid every day.

Fry are free-swimming and large enough upon hatching to take freshly hatched brine shrimp and fine sifted *Daphnia*. No infusoria are necessary.

GENUS *Cynolebias* Steindachner

[si′-no-leeb′-i-as: *cyno* = a dog; *lebias* = a kind of fish]

The genus *Cynolebias* has been divided into three subgenera: *Cynolebias* Steindachner 1876 is the typical subgenus; *Cynopoecilus* Regan 1912 contains only *C. melanotaenia; Leptolebias* Myers 1952 was established for the dwarf species of this group.

Cynolebias adloffi Ahl

[ad-loff′-eye: named in honor of an unknown Mr. Adloff]

Cynolebias adloffi Ahl, Blät. Aquar.-Terrak. no. 14, pp. 1–5, 1922 (type locality, Porto Alegre, Rio de Janeiro)

RANGE: Santa Catarina, Brazil.

SIZE: 2 inches; breeds at 2 inches.

TEMPERAMENT: This species should not be kept with fishes smaller than itself.

TEMPERATURE REQUIREMENTS: 65–90°F.

SEX DIFFERENCES: The sexes are distinguished as indicated below.

COUNTS: Dorsal: females 19, males 22 or 23; anal 26 or 27; pectoral 12 or 13; pelvic 5; scales 28 or 29.

These fish are annuals, like *Rachovia brevis* (page 447). Therefore, we might expect them to breed in the same manner as *R. brevis*. The male is known to dig holes in the mud and entice the female to expel eggs in each hole as the male shimmies next to her for a few seconds. Breeding may take place during the weeks that the water is evaporating. The parent fish are big eaters and require quantities of live foods. They are partial to mosquito larvae.

The color of the male is a beautiful electric blue with a dark stripe through the eye. The sides show between 9 and 12 vertical bars. The fins are deep blue; the dorsal and anal fins have a dark margin with lighter spots at the base. The female is light brown but the bars on her side are very indistinct. There are two black spots on the caudal peduncle and brown spots on the unpaired fins. The male and female look like two different species; they even have a different dorsal fin-ray count.

ARGENTINE PEARLFISH / *Cynolebias bellottii* Steindachner

[bel-lot'-tee-eye; named in honor of C. Bellotti]

Cynolebias bellottii Steindachner, Anz. Akad. Wiss. Wien, 18:98, 1881 (type locality, La Plata)

RANGE: Province of Buenos Aires, Argentina.

SIZE: 3 inches; breeds at slightly less than 3 inches.

TEMPERAMENT: This species is best kept by itself.

TEMPERATURE REQUIREMENTS: 65–90°F.

SEX DIFFERENCES: The male has the color. The male has fewer rays in the dorsal fin.

COUNTS: Dorsal: 17 on males, 23 on females; anal 28 to 30; pectoral 13; pelvic 5; scales 29 or 30.

The first importation of this very attractive fish into Germany was in 1906 but it arrived much later in America, exact date unknown.

So different are the two sexes that Steindachner incorrectly classified the female as a distinct species, *Cynolebias maculatus*. This difference was not merely in coloration, but in the entire genus the males have fewer rays in their dorsal fins than the females. This is quite an oddity and rarely occurs among fishes. Therefore, the great ichthyologist Steindachner should be forgiven for his mistake.

Breeding this fish is exactly the same as for *Rachovia brevis* (page 447), which also is an annual. The eggs require anywhere from 2 to 10 weeks to hatch, varying with the temperature—the warmer it is the sooner they hatch.

GENUS *Cynopoecilus* Regan

[Si'-no-pea-sil'-us: *cyno* = a dog; *poecilus* = variegated or spotted]

Cynopoecilus melanotaenia (Regan)

[mel'-an-o-teen'-i-a: *melano* = black; *taenia* = a band]

Cynolebias melanotaenia Regan, Ann. Mag. Nat. Hist., (8)10:506, 1912 (type locality, Paranagua)

RANGE: Southeastern Brazil.

SIZE: 2 inches; breeds at 2 inches.

TEMPERAMENT: A species best kept by itself, even though it is fairly peaceful.

TEMPERATURE REQUIREMENTS: 70–90°F.

SEX DIFFERENCES: The male's fins seem pointed when compared with the rounded ones of the female.

COUNTS: Dorsal 16 to 18; anal 17 to 20; pectoral 12 or 13; pelvic 6; scales 28.

This fish is an annual and may be expected to breed the same as *Rachovia brevis*.

The general color is dark maroon; the belly is yellowish, and a red band runs through the eye and lower jaw to the base of the caudal fin. A similar band runs from the base of the pectoral fin to the rear base of the anal fin. The gill cover is decorated with greenish-gold spangles and the body with three median series of scales which manifest the same color. Fins are spotted with red, especially the dorsal, anal, and caudal. The female is less intensely colored; her rounded dorsal and anal fins are in contrast to the male's pointed fins.

The name of this species currently is *Cynolebias melanotaenia*.

Genus *Cyprinodon* Lacepède

[Si-prin'-o-don: *cyprin* = a kind of carp; *odon* = tooth]

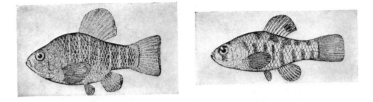

Sheepshead Minnow / *Cyprinodon variegatus* Lacepède

[va'-ri-e-gay'-tus: *variegatus* = variable]

Cyprinodon variegatus Lacepède, Histoire naturelle des poissons, 5:486, 1803 (type locality, South Carolina)

RANGE: Maine to Florida and west to Texas, in fresh water, but mostly in brackish and sea water.

SIZE: 3 inches; breeds at 2 inches.

TEMPERAMENT: This species is suitable in the community aquarium.

TEMPERATURE REQUIREMENTS: See text.

SEX DIFFERENCES: See text.

COUNTS: Dorsal 11; anal 11; pectoral 15; pelvic 7; scales 25 to 27.

Breeding occurs in slightly brackish water. A mixture of 20 per cent sea water and fresh water is well suited to this fish. A carefully selected pair will spawn readily in a large aquarium (about 15 gallons). Eggs are semiadhesive and are laid on sand, plants, glass, slate, or the sides of the aquarium. Hatching time varies greatly with the temperature, from 12 days at 55°F to 6 days at 75°F. The fish are uncomfortable at higher temperatures. Parents should be removed after spawning and the pair should be kept together for further spawnings. Immediately after hatching and absorption of the yolk sac, the fry are large and can take *Daphnia* and brine shrimp.

Cyprinodon nevadensis Eigenmann and Eigenmann.

GENUS *Epiplatys* Gill

[Ep′-e-play′-tees: *epiplatys* = broad at the top]

FIRE-MOUTH PANCHAX / *Epiplatys chaperi* (Sauvage)

[chap′-er-eye: named in honor of M. Chaper]

Haplochilus chaperi Sauvage, Bull. soc. zool. France, p. 323, pl. 5, fig. 5, 1882 (type locality, Gold Coast)

RANGE: Sierra Leone to Gold Coast, Africa.

SIZE: 2½ inches; breeding at 2½ inches.

TEMPERAMENT: A peaceful species when kept with fishes of its own size.

TEMPERATURE REQUIREMENTS: 65–90°F.

SEX DIFFERENCES: Male is the more colorful.

COUNTS: Dorsal 9 or 10; anal 14 to 16; pectoral 15 or 16; pelvic 5; scales 25 to 27.

This pikelike fish looks mean and vicious, but fortunately it does not attack other fishes unless they are small enough to be ingested whole.

Breeding is fairly easy. Place three females with a single male in a small 2½- to 5-gallon aquarium half filled with extremely old water and containing floating plants (bunches preferably) or some Spanish moss. The male will drive a female into the plants where she will expel a single sticky egg. He will fertilize it and quickly leave the spawning site looking for another female. This may continue all day until there are about 2 dozen eggs for each female present. It seems that once one female spawns the others follow suit rather easily. Breeding time is in the late fall and early winter.

The best technique for saving the spawn is to remove the plants from the aquarium every day and replace them with fresh plants. The egg-laden plants should be placed in a separate aquarium to hatch. Spawning may be kept up for a week or 10 days. It is best to hatch each day's spawning separately, as the young fish will eat their smaller brothers and sisters in the normal course of a meal. The fry are ready for newly hatched brine shrimp immediately after hatching, which is usually 2 weeks after having been spawned.

Females are ready for spawning again after a week's rest. Males seem always ready to spawn. Keep the sexes separate when not spawning.

The name of this species currently is *Epiplatys dageti.*

BANDED PANCHAX / *Epiplatys fasciolatus* (Günther)

[fas'-see-o-lay'-tus: *fascio* = bands; *latus* = to bear]

Haplochilus fasciolatus Günther, Catalogue of the Fishes in the British Museum, 6:358, 1868 (type locality, Sierra Leone)

RANGE: Sierra Leone, Liberia to Nigeria.

SIZE: 3½ inches, breeds at 2½ inches.

TEMPERAMENT: Suitable in the community tank with fishes of its own size.

TEMPERATURE REQUIREMENTS: 65–85°F.

SEX DIFFERENCES: See below for color differences.

COUNTS: Dorsal 11 or 12; anal 16 to 18; pectoral 16 or 17; pelvic 5; scales 27 to 29.

This species is bred the same way as *Epiplatys chaperi,* but it is best to place the fish in a 5-gallon aquarium. It is suggested that a little salt be added to the water containing this fish (about 1 teaspoonful per gallon).

The male shows a tannish maroon on the back; each scale seems to have a small red dot in it with a bit of shiny silver below the dot. The sides have a series of 10 dark vertical stripes or bands which run the entire length of the body from the area just back of the eye to the base of the caudal fin. The fins are aquamarine while the dorsal and caudal (and at times the pelvics) show a brilliant red peppering. The red border on the caudal and pelvics adds further brilliant color to the male.

The female is an olive brown with few variations in coloring. She shows no design in her fins.

Epiplatys longiventralis (Boulenger)

[lon'-gi-ven-tray'-lis: *longi* = long; *ventralis* = ventral or pelvic fins]

Haplochilus longiventralis Boulenger, Ann. Mag. Nat. Hist., (8)8:266, 1911 (type locality, Old Calabar)

RANGE: Southern Nigeria to Cameroons.

SIZE: 2½ inches; breeds at 2 inches.

TEMPERAMENT: Suitable in the community tank with fishes of its own size.

TEMPERATURE REQUIREMENTS: 65–90°F.

SEX DIFFERENCES: See differences below.

COUNTS: Dorsal 8 or 9; anal 15 or 16; scales 25 to 27.

This species breeds in the same manner as *Epiplatys chaperi*.

The male is a chocolate brown on the back blending with green on the sides. The belly is yellowish. The body and unpaired fins show an irregular pattern of red dots that disappear during periods of sexual inactivity. Accompanying these dots are irregular bands that run in all directions and at all angles to the median line, though nearly always below the lateral line. These bands vary from a maroon to a chocolate color. The fins are bluish yellow. The male has long, pointed pelvic fins; his pointed dorsal and anal fins are obvious when compared to the female.

The upper left is female of *Epiplatys dageti* Poll. Lower right, female of *E. macrostigma* (Boulenger).

SPOTTED EPIPLATYS or PANCHAX / *Epiplatys macrostigma* (Boulenger)

[mack′-row-stig′-ma: *macro* = large; *stigma* = spots]

Haplochilus macrostigma Boulenger, Ann. Mag. Nat. Hist., (8)8:268, 1911 (type locality, Lucola River near Cabinda)

RANGE: West Africa, southern Nigeria to Angola.

SIZE: 2½ inches; breeds at 2 inches.

TEMPERAMENT: Suitable in a community tank with fishes of its own size.

TEMPERATURE REQUIREMENTS: 70–85°F.

SEX DIFFERENCES: Though both male and female possess the red spots, they are more distinct and larger in the male. The male has longer and more pointed dorsal and anal fins. The female has a fuller body during breeding time than the male.

COUNTS: Dorsal 8 or 9; anal 16 to 18; pectoral about 16; pelvic 5; scales 27 to 30.

This species breeds the same way as *Epiplatys chaperi*, but it is not so easy to induce to spawn. A seasoning process may be necessary. The male and female should be separated by a glass partition while being fed quantities of live foods in the form of white worms, *Tubifex,* and the like. *Daphnia* seem to be particularly relished.

The richly colored red spots from which this fish derived the name *macrostigma* make it easily identifiable for hobbyists; however, *E. sheljuzhkoi* may be confused with *E. grahami* (Boulenger). The only way to distinguish between them is to count the dorsal rays. *E. sheljuzhkoi* has 8 or 9 rays, whereas *E. grahami* has 7 or 8, with 5 to 7 blackish bars on the body.

This fish is an excellent jumper and must be kept in a covered aquarium.

The upper fish is a female. The lower two fishes are males.

SPOTTED EPIPLATYS / *Epiplatys sheljuzhkoi* (Boulenger)

[shell-juz-ko-eye: named in honor of Leo Sheljuzhko]

Epiplatys sheljuzhkoi Poll, Rev. Zool. Bot. Africa, Vol. 48 Nos. 3, 4, p. 262, fig. 1, 1953 (type locality, Abidjan, Ivory Coast)

RANGE: Liberia to Congo, west Africa.

SIZE: 4 inches; breeding at 3½ inches.

TEMPERAMENT: This species should be kept with fishes of its own size; since it jumps, the aqarium must be covered.

TEMPERATURE REQUIREMENTS: 70–80°F.

SEX DIFFERENCES: See below.

COUNTS: Dorsal 10 to 12; anal 15 to 17; pectoral 16; pelvic 5; scales 28 to 32.

This species breeds the same way as *Epiplatys chaperi*.

The male, as usual, is the more colorful of the pair, with an olive-green back that becomes yellow as it approaches the belly. There are from 5 to 7 bars on the sides, but usually only 6 in mature adult specimens. These bars are only found beneath and slightly oblique to the lateral line. The fins of the male fish are a light yellow with a dark margin. The pelvics are long and pointed, much like *E. longiventralis*. The pectoral fins show a dark margin at all times but are lacking in color except at breeding time, when they are suffused with a pink glow.

Females are their usual drab selves with clear fins and fairly indistinct bands.

The name of this species currently is *Epiplatys chaperi sheljuzhkoi*.

GENUS *Fundulus* Lacepède

[fun'-du-lus: *fundulus* = the bottom]

GOLDEN EAR / *Fundulus chrysotus* Holbrook

[cry-so'-tus: *chrysotus* = golden ear]

Fundulus chrysotus Holbrook, in Günther, Catalogue of the Fishes in the British Museum, 6:317, 1866 (type locality, Charleston, South Carolina)

RANGE: South Carolina to Florida in fresh and brackish water.

SIZE: 3 inches; breeds at 2 inches.

TEMPERAMENT: A predaceous species not suitable in the community aquarium.

TEMPERATURE REQUIREMENTS: 60–90°F. Optimum about 72°F.

SEX DIFFERENCES: Female seldom has any red coloration.

COUNTS: Dorsal 8 or 9; anal 10 or 11; pectoral 13; pelvic 6; scales 32 to 34.

The over-all color is olive, which is made iridescent by the bluish-gold scales and red-gold dots, especially on the male. The eye is golden. Some specimens taken from the warmer waters of southern Florida show an extreme of these reddish gold dots and their fins are vermilion. The beautiful shiny gold spot on the gill cover gives the name "golden ear." Unfortunately, this beautiful fellow is vicious, a definite snail killer.

Breeding is comparatively easy. Parents should be conditioned on plenty of worms, baby fishes, and pieces of meat and beef. Plenty of fine plants should be available for the breeders, not only for the eggs, but for the female if she is slightly hesitant about spawning. Parents should be removed after spawning. Eggs are usually large and clear, hatching in about 2 weeks at 72°F. The fry are large enough when free-swimming to take freshly hatched brine shrimp, microworms, and sifted *Daphnia*.

This species may be acclimated to the marine brackish-water aquarium.

STAR-HEAD TOP MINNOW / *Fundulus dispar*   (Agassiz)

[dis'-par: *dispar* = unlike; dissimilar]

Zygonoectes dispar Agassiz, Amer. Jour. Sci. Arts, 17:353, 1854 (type locality, creeks opposite St. Louis, Beardstown, Illinois)

RANGE: Northern Ohio and Illinois south to Mississippi and Louisiana.

SIZE: 2½ inches; breeds at 2 inches.

TEMPERAMENT: This species is predaceous and should be kept by itself.

TEMPERATURE REQUIREMENTS: 65–85°F. Lower temperatures are tolerated but not advised.

SEX DIFFERENCES: See below.

COUNTS: Dorsal 7 to 10; anal 9 to 12; pectoral 13; pelvic 6; scales 33 to 36.

This species has the same breeding habits as *Fundulus chrysotus*, although the eggs hatch in a slightly shorter time, about 12 days at 72°F.

The male is dark aquamarine on the back and yellow green on the belly. The sides are adorned with horizontal rows of dark brown dots. A dark stripe crosses the eye. The fins are a mixture of yellow and aquamarine colors. The female is dull brown and lacks the 10 distinct bars running vertically on the sides of the male. Instead, she has about 9 lengthwise dark streaks on the sides.

This vicious fish should not be kept with other fishes, regardless of size. It is an excellent mosquito-larvae destroyer.

STAR-HEAD TOP MINNOW / *Fundulus dispar notti* (Agassiz)

[nott'-eye: named in honor of an unknown Mr. Nott]

Zygonectes notti Agassiz, Amer. Jour. Sci. Arts, 17:353, 1854 (type locality, Mobile, Alabama)

RANGE: Lowland streams of southeastern United States.

SIZE: 4 inches; breeding size 2½ inches.

TEMPERAMENT: A suitable species for the community tank.

TEMPERATURE REQUIREMENTS: 55–85°F.

SEX DIFFERENCES: The over-all color of the male is grayish-olive to brown. The belly is silvery; the sides have 6 horizontal dotted stripes and several short dark vertical bars. A wide dark band runs through the eye. The dorsal, anal, and caudal fins are maroon with dark dots. The female is drab and less intensely colored than her mate.

COUNTS: Dorsal 7 or 8; anal 9 or 10; pectoral 13; pelvic 6; scales 35 or 36.

Place a well-conditioned trio (two females, one male) in a well-planted aquarium. The male will drive a female into heavy vegetation, where she will deposit her eggs among the fine-leafed plants. Hatching takes place in 12 days at 73°F, which is a good breeding temperature. Usually a male will mate with one female, but as many as three females may be placed in the breeding tank since the male may drive a stubborn female rather strenuously and may injure her in his haste.

Remove the parents after spawning and prepare brine-shrimp cultures as soon as the eggs hatch. Free-swimming fry are able to take these tiny crustaceans as soon as they can maneuver for themselves.

The name of this species currently is *Fundulus notti.*

TEXAS KILLIE / *Fundulus grandis* Baird and Girard

[gran'-dis: *grandis* = grown large]

Fundulus grandis Baird and Girard, Proc. Acad. Nat. Sci. Philadelphia, 6:389, 1853 (type locality, Indianola, Texas)

RANGE: Texas.

SIZE: 6 inches; breeds at 4 inches.

TEMPERAMENT: Peaceful enough to be in the community tank with fishes of its own size.

TEMPERATURE REQUIREMENTS: 55–75°F. Breeds at 73°F.

SEX DIFFERENCES: Female is a straight olive brown. Her bars are wider and less distinct than the male. All her fins are colorless.

COUNTS: Dorsal 12; anal 10 or 11; pectoral 18; pelvic 6; scales 31.

The female is less intensely colored and sometimes is so drab that smaller specimens are easily mistaken for other species of the genus. Her background color, viewed from reflected light, is a sparkling olive green on the back which turns silvery on the belly. There is a beautiful troutlike yellow with silver-blue coloring on the sides. The males show a reddish tinge on their belly which contrasts nicely with the silver. There are 13 dark, narrow vertical bars on the sides. Fins are highly colored, with shiny green dots in all the unpaired fins and the pelvics; other fins have yellow margins.

This is a brackish-water fish which does better at cooler temperatures. The water should be 20 per cent sea water.

Robert R. Miller informs us that *Fundulus pallidus* Evermann is a synonym of this species.

ZEBRA or COMMON KILLIE / *Fundulus heteroclitus* (Linnaeus)

[het'-er-o-clit'-us: *hetero* = different; *clitus* = famous]

Cobitus heteroclitus Linnaeus, Systema naturae, ed. 12, p. 500, 1766 (type locality, Charleston, South Carolina)

RANGE: Maine to Rio Grande.

SIZE: 6 inches; breeds at 4 inches.

TEMPERAMENT: An active, somewhat predaceous species not suitable in the community tank.

TEMPERATURE REQUIREMENTS: 40–90°F. Optimum temperature 72°F.

SEX DIFFERENCES: See below.

COUNTS: Dorsal 11 to 13; anal 10 to 12; pectoral 18 or 19; pelvic 6; scales 33 to 38.

This species, common on the eastern coast, is stocked from time to time as something new by many dealers. The males show an olive-brown background coloration and a yellow-red belly. The sides are decorated with about 13 vertical steel-blue bars. The unpaired fins are dusky brown with numerous spots of the same color as the vertical bars on the sides. The dorsal fin is edged with dark vermilion; the anal fin is yellow. The tail is black. All the fins on the female are a pale yellow. The female may lack the vertical bars.

This fish breeds like *Fundulus chrysotus*. It is also a brackish-water fish which should have at least 1 teaspoon of coarse salt per gallon of aquarium water.

PLAINS TOP MINNOW / *Fundulus sciadicus* Cope

[si-ad'-i-cus: *sciadicus* = pertaining to a shadow]

Fundulus sciadicus Cope, Proc. Acad. Nat. Sci. Philadelphia, 17:78, 1865 (type locality, Platte River, Nebraska)

RANGE: South Dakota to Arkansas.

SIZE: 2½ inches; breeds at 2 inches.

TEMPERAMENT: Suitable in the community tank with fishes of its own size.

TEMPERATURE REQUIREMENTS: 55–75°F.

SEX DIFFERENCES: Female may be smaller than the male and her fins are not edged in maroon.

COUNTS: Dorsal 7 to 10; anal 10 to 12; pectoral 13 or 14; pelvic 6; scales 33 to 38.

This species breeds the same as *Fundulus dispar notti.*

The over-all color of the male is bright aquamarine. The belly is silvery white and the gill covers are silvery. The side has a dark spot above the pectoral fin, and a light blue streak runs from this spot to the end of the caudal peduncle. The fins are a contrasting maroon.

GENUS *Jordanella* Goode and Bean

[Jor'-dan-el'-la: named in honor of David Starr Jordan]

AMERICAN FLAGFISH / *Jordanella floridae* Goode and Bean

[flor'-i-dae: named after the state of Florida]

Jordanella floridae Goode and Bean, Proc. U.S. Nat. Mus., 2:117, 1879 (type locality, Lake Monroe, Florida)

RANGE: Florida.

SIZE: 2½ inches; breeds at 2 inches.

TEMPERAMENT: This species does best in a heavily planted aquarium of over 50 gallons capacity.

TEMPERATURE REQUIREMENTS: 68–80°F.

SEX DIFFERENCES: The male is the more colorful of the pair, showing brilliant red spots on his body and fins, which the female lacks.

COUNTS: Dorsal i,15 or 16; anal 12 or 13; pectoral 13 to 15; pelvic 6; scales 25 or 26.

This is a domestic fish that has become popular in the American market because it is good-looking and hardy. It is found in the native waters around the southern parts of Florida, where many commercial breeders have hatcheries. They often seine waters hoping to find different fishes which might have a commercial value to hobbyists. Few breeders actually breed them under controlled conditions, but they do collect them carefully from areas rich in this fish so that they never "bleed" an area and lose their breeding stock. This American flagfish has a long intestine, which is evidence that it is an algae eater. It must be supplied with "greens" in the form of *Nitella* or some other soft green plant. It does exceedingly well in green water with copious growths of algae on the glass and rocks.

The pair will dig a small depression in the sand and finally spawn therein. The male will give the eggs cichlid-like care, fanning and guarding them for about a week until they hatch. The female should be removed after spawning, although in the larger aquarium she may not eat her spawn. It is rare that the male will eat the spawn while he is guarding it.

GENUS *Leptolucania* Myers

[Lep'-to-lew-can'-i-a: *lepto* = delicate; *luc* = light; *ania* = distress]

SWAMP KILLIE / *Leptolucania ommata* (Jordan)

[om-may'-ta: *omma* = an eye; *ata* = provided with]

Heterandria ommata Jordan, Proc. U.S. Nat. Mus., 7:323, 1884 (type locality, Indian River, Florida)

RANGE: Georgia and Florida, in swamps.

SIZE: 1½ inches; breeds at 1¼ inches.

TEMPERAMENT: A peaceful species suitable in the community tank.

TEMPERATURE REQUIREMENTS: 55–85°F.

SEX DIFFERENCES: See below.

COUNTS: Dorsal 7; anal 11; pectoral 12 or 13; pelvic 5; scales 30.

This swamp fish is found in mudholes in swamps of southern Georgia (Okefenokee) and neighboring areas. It seldom lives longer than a year in captivity. Favorite foods are *Daphnia* and mosquito larvae. During spawning the eggs are deposited on plants or twigs, or if neither is present, on the muddy bottom. Normal hatching occurs in 12 days at 72°F. Spawning may go on continually all year around, although it is much heavier in the summer months, especially August.

The male is brownish yellow, having the sides decorated with a dark stripe which runs from the snout, through the eye, to the ocellus on the caudal peduncle. There are from 4 to 8 dark vertical bands on the lower half of the sides; the dorsal fin is tipped with blue, while basally the color is orange. The anal fin is yellow with a black edge. The female is less colorful and lacks the vertical bars except on rare occasions.

GENUS *Nothobranchius* Peters

[Noth'-o-brank'-ki-us: *notho* = spurious; *branchius* = fins or gills]

This genus is native to equatorial east Africa ranging from Somaliland and Mozambique to the central northern lakes and northern Nigeria. They are annual fishes which spawn much like their relatives in the genera *Aphyosemion* and *Aplocheilichthys*.

Though undoubtedly a fresh-water fish, they seem to fare better in an aquarium containing very old water which is 10 per cent sea water. They require plenty of live foods, semidarkness, plenty of hiding places, a muddy bottom, higher temperatures (say about 78 to 80°F), and privacy. These fishes are shy and are best observed from a distance.

Breeding is a complex procedure: Place a pair in a small aquarium with soft mud on the bottom and half full of water. A thermostatically controlled heater, set for 80°F, should be placed in the water. The objective is to have the water evaporate out of the aquarium slowly. As the water level gets lower there will be a sharp increase in the activity of the fish until the pair will start to dig a small depression in the soft mud on the bottom. When the hole is about ½ inch deep the pair will lie side to side, with their ventral surfaces in contact, and spawn. The eggs, which are not adhesive, will number about 2 dozen. After spawning the adults cover over the eggs with mud. Breeders die about 2 weeks after spawning.

The eggs hatch only after 45 to 75 days in damp warm mud. After the eggs have been laid, the water should be allowed to evaporate completely from the aquarium. After 2 months or so, fresh rain water should be added to the aquarium, about 1 inch per day. After the aquarium is half filled the temperature should be raised to 80°F again and the fry should appear in a few weeks. Fry mature rapidly, in about 3 months, and require infusoria, brine shrimp, and sifted *Daphnia* from the start.

Günther's Nothobranch / *Nothobranchius guentheri* (Pfeffer)

[gun'-ther-eye: named in honor of G. A. Günther]

Fundulus guentheri Pfeffer, Jahrb. Wiss. Anst. Hamburg, 10(2):39, 1893 (type locality, Zanzibar)

RANGE: Zanzibar; and African east coast from Mombasa to Pangani River.

SIZE: 3 inches; breeding at 2½ inches.

TEMPERAMENT: A species best kept by itself.

TEMPERATURE REQUIREMENTS: 74–84°F.

SEX DIFFERENCES: See below.

COUNTS: Dorsal 17 or 18; anal 18 or 19; scales 27 to 30.

This species is brilliantly colored. As with most annual fishes, this color is maintained throughout the short life span.

The male is the more colorful of the pair. He is a beautiful blue with a dark back and a golden anal-fin edge. Each scale when viewed microscopically will show a small red edge which macroscopically forms bars in the lower half of the body. The gill cover is beautiful with similar, though larger, bright red markings. The unpaired fins are a golden olive with dark red spots. The tail fin is the most beautiful part of the whole fish, with a crimson hue and chocolate edge. The paired fins are sky blue trimmed with white. Females are plain green and have no color in their fins.

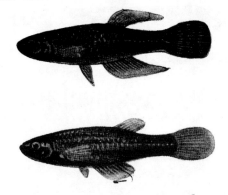

GORGEOUS FUNDULUS / *Nothobranchius orthonotus* (Peters)

[orth'-o-no'-tus: *ortho* = straight; *notus* = probably the back]

Cyprinodon orthonotus Peters, Mon. Berlin Acad., p. 35, 1844 (type locality, Mozambique)

RANGE: Eastern coast of equatorial Africa.

SIZE: 3 inches; breeds at 2½ inches.

TEMPERAMENT: A species best kept by itself.

TEMPERATURE REQUIREMENTS: 72–80°F.

SEX DIFFERENCES: See below.

COUNTS: Dorsal 15 or 16; anal 14 to 16; pectoral 12 or 13; pelvic 6; scales 28 to 30.

The male is the more colorful member of the pair. Some reports claim that the color varies, but the color is constant if the diet is adequate. Live foods in the form of *Tubifex*, white worms, *Daphnia*, and chopped earthworms are ideal. This fish should be fed daily. The male has varying shades of green and blue throughout the body, with crimson spots showing up irregularly. The fins are red, becoming darker toward their margin. The tail and anal fins show much darker margins, especially as the fish gets ready to spawn. The female is plain and shows color similar to the Japanese medaka (page 444).

This species breeds like other members of the genus. The eggs are variable in size and hatch after 4 weeks, first in mud, then covered with 4 inches of water. The eggs hatch out in lower temperatures, about 72°, but as soon as the fry appear they should be slowly acclimated to higher temperatures.

RACHOW'S NOTHOBRANCHIUS / *Nothobranchius rachovi* Ahl

[ra-cove'-eye: named in honor of Arthur Rachow of the Berlin Museum]

Nothobranchius rachovii Ahl, Blät. Aquar.-Terrak., 37(14):1, 1926 (type locality, Beira, Portuguese East Africa)

RANGE: Portuguese East Africa.

SIZE: 2 inches; breeds at 1½ inches.

TEMPERAMENT: This species should be kept by itself.

TEMPERATURE REQUIREMENTS: 72–80°F.

SEX DIFFERENCES: See below.

COUNTS: Dorsal 15 or 16; anal 15; scales 25 or 26.

This species breeds like other members of the genus.

The male is brilliant orange red with about 12 crimson-red vertical stripes running from back of the gill plates through the caudal fin. These stripes are not in strong contrast to the orange body color, but when they reach the sky-blue caudal fin they are extremely beautiful. The unpaired fins are sky blue with crimson and darker red bars irregularly patterning the fins. The caudal fin has a dark brown margin on the posterior edge. The female is yellowish orange.

Nothobranchius taeniopygus Hilgandorf (*Sitzb. Ges. Nat. Freunde Berlin*, p. 20, 1891, Lakes Tschaia and Victoria) may be the same species; at least it is very similar to *N. rachovi*. No one has made a close study of the relationships of these fishes.

GENUS *Oryzias* Jordan and Snyder

[O-ri'-zi-as: *oryzias* = rice]

Oryzias celebensis (Weber)

[sell'-ee-ben-sis: named after the locality where collected]

Haplochilus celebensis Weber, Zool. Ergebn. Reise niederl. Ost-Indien, 3:426, 1894 (type locality, Celebes Island)

RANGE: Fresh waters of Celebes.

SIZE: 2 inches; breeds at 2 inches.

TEMPERAMENT: This species should not be kept with fishes smaller than itself.

TEMPERATURE REQUIREMENTS: 68–88°F. Optimum breeding temperature 75°F.

SEX DIFFERENCES: The fins of the male show more color than those of the female. The dorsal and anal fins of the male are pointed in comparison to those of the female. The female is larger and more plump than the male.

COUNTS: Dorsal 7 to 10; anal 17 to 23; pectoral 13 or 14; pelvic 6; scales 30 to 36.

The breeding of this species is of the same pattern as that of the various species of *Aplocheilus* and *Aplocheilichthys*. Suggestions about a particular method of spawning merely point out one that has been satisfactory; they do not intimate that other methods are of no value. Sometimes one method succeeds where another fails.

This species is bred in small containers. A pair may be placed into a 1-gallon aquarium where it will deposit several eggs a day for weeks at a time. The spawning grass should be taken out every day, carefully patted dry, and scanned for eggs. Eggs should be hatched in a separate container for they require about 2 weeks to hatch. Fry are quite small and need the finest of foods.

The general coloration is aquamarine, with the underside silvery. A narrow dark line runs from above the pectoral fin to the base of the tail fin where it divides, one branch passing into each lobe of the caudal fin. Fins are light tannish yellow.

This fish may well be an annual fish.

JAVA MEDAKA / *Oryzias javanicus* (Bleeker)

[ja-van'-i-cus: named after the locality where collected]

Aplocheilus javanicus Bleeker, Nat. Tijdschr. Ned. Indie, 7:323, 1854 (type locality, Java)

RANGE: Singapore, Java, Malaya.

SIZE: 1½ inches; breeding at 1½ inches.

TEMPERAMENT: A peaceful species suitable in the community aquarium.

TEMPERATURE REQUIREMENTS: 65–90°F.

SEX DIFFERENCES: The male has longer dorsal and anal fins than the female. The plumpness of the female indicates her sex.

COUNTS: Dorsal 7; anal 21 to 23; pectoral 11 or 12; pelvic 6; scales 29 or 30.

This species is so closely related to *Oryzias latipes* that many aquarists do not know them apart. The lack of color has resulted in increasing unpopularity. This fish is somewhat smaller than *O. latipes*. It is best to keep the aquarium fully covered, since it does occasionally jump out.

When this fish is viewed in sunlight the scales are mirrorlike, showing dazzling reflections. It varies between golden and silvery pink. Every now and then a black sport appears, which might be inbred to produce a new strain.

Oryzias melastigma (McClelland)

[mel'-a-stig'-ma: *mela* = black; *stigma* = spot]

GEISHA-GIRL MEDAKA; RICEFISH /
Oryzias latipes (Temminck and Schlegel)

[la'-ti-peas: *lati* = broad; *pes* = a foot (fin)]

Poecilia latipes Temminck and Schlegel, *Fauna Japonica*, p. 224, pl. 102, fig. 5, 1846 (type locality, Japan)

RANGE: Japan, Korea, and adjacent coast of China.

SIZE: 2 inches; breeds at 1½ inches.

TEMPERAMENT: A peaceful species desirable in the community aquarium.

TEMPERATURE REQUIREMENTS: Above freezing to 90°F.

SEX DIFFERENCES: The male has a longer dorsal fin than the female and his anal fin is broader. The female is fuller, especially in the spring.

COUNTS: Dorsal 6; anal 19; pectoral 11; pelvic 6; scales 29.

This species is one of the easiest of the egg layers to spawn. It is hardy, inexpensive, takes all kinds of fish foods, and can get along without a thermostatically controlled heater in the aquarium.

The female, during the spring months, will be noted to have a bunch of eggs hanging from her vent, much like *Aplocheilichthys*. The male will dart against her, squirting his milt on the eggs and thus fertilizing them. After fertilization, there seems to be a sort of decay in the hairlike projections of the eggs, which are easily brushed off as the female darts among the plants. Even in a bare tank, once the eggs have been fertilized, they will drop off the female. Usually the parents ignore the eggs and young, but occasionally they will eat the fry.

In Japan this fish is used almost exclusively over other live fishes as a laboratory animal. It likes plenty of sunshine, and if a bit of *Nitella* is placed in the tank it does well.

There is no great color in this fish, though a melanistic strain has been developed in Japan and a mottled strain was produced when the black fish were crossed with the wild strain. It is usually billed as a "mosquito eater" in the rice paddies of the Far East.

Though *O. latipes* is almost immune to the ich infection, it does occasionally become stricken with the disease.

Genus *Pachypanchax* Myers

[Pak'-ee-pan'-chax: *pachy* = large or stout; *panchax* = a kind of fish]

Playfair's Panchax / *Pachypanchax playfairi* (Günther)

[play'-fair-eye: named in honor of R. L. Playfair]

Haplochilus playfairii Günther, Catalogue of the Fishes in the British Museum, 6:314, 1866 (type locality, Seychelles)

RANGE: Seychelles and Zanzibar.

SIZE: 4 inches; breeds at 3 inches.

TEMPERAMENT: A predaceous species best kept away from other fishes. The males should be isolated like male *Bettas*.

TEMPERATURE REQUIREMENTS: 75–85°F. Breeding temperature about 80°F.

SEX DIFFERENCES: Male is more colorful and has obliquely projecting scales.

COUNTS: Dorsal 11 or 12; anal 17 or 18; pectoral 18 or 19; pelvic 6; scales 29 or 30.

This species is found in fresh and brackish waters. If breeding is attempted, it is best to keep at least 2 tablespoons of sea salt in the breeding aquarium, which should be a minimum of 10 gallons. The male is vicious and will make fast work of both the female and the spawn unless there is ample room for all of them to keep their distance. It is essential that the pairs be removed as soon after spawning as possible. This means that the pairs should be checked every few hours for those unmistakable hints that breeding is going on. This is usually evidenced by intense coloration in both fish and an unusually attentive male. The breeding aquarium should be heavily stocked with hiding grass, of which Spanish moss has no equal. *Nitella, Myriophyllum,* and *Fontinalis* may also be used with good results.

The male shows much orange during breeding but his normal color is more olive. His sides are adorned with 5 attractive rows of red dots. The female is olive brown with a hint of yellow. She has irregular sprinklings of red dots. The male is easily recognizable, as his scales stand out obliquely from his body. Many hobbyists claim that this is an illness, but such is not the case.

GENUS *Pterolebias* Garman

[tear'-o-le'-bi-as: *ptero* = a wing or fin; *lebias* = a kind of fish]

PERUVIAN LONGFIN / *Pterolebias peruensis* Myers

[Pe-ru'-en-sis; named after Peru]

Pterolebias peruensis Myers, Aquar. Jour., 25(8): 175–177, fig., August, 1954. (Type locality, Peruvian Amazon).

RANGE: Peruvian Amazon, South America.

SIZE: 3 inches; breeding not observed.

TEMPERAMENT: Best kept by itself.

TEMPERATURE REQUIREMENTS: 68–88°F.

SEX DIFFERENCES: Males are larger and have greatly expanded and colorful fins.

COUNTS: Dorsal 8 or 9; anal 14 or 15; scales 33 or 34.

This is a newly introduced fish. It feeds on dry, prepared food, and on frozen or live brine shrimp. It does best in slightly acid water, with some boiled "Georgia peat" on the bottom.

Genus *Rachovia* Myers

[Ra-cove'-i-a: named in honor of Arthur Rachow]

Rachovia brevis (Regan)

[bre'-vis: *brevis* = short]

Rivulus brevis Regan, Ann. Mag. Nat. Hist., (8)10:496, 1912 (type locality, Colombia)

RANGE: Colombia.

SIZE: 2 inches; breeds at 2 inches.

TEMPERAMENT: This peaceful species does best in its own aquarium.

TEMPERATURE REQUIREMENTS: 72–90°F. Optimum breeding temperature 80°F.

SEX DIFFERENCES: The male is olive brown on the back, greenish blue on the sides, and yellowish on the belly. The scales are tipped with blue. Dorsal and anal fins are aquamarine and spotted, the tail is grayish with green dots, and the elongated rays are pink. The female is very drab and has no distinct marking.

COUNTS: Dorsal 8 or 9; anal 12 to 14; pelvic 6; scales 29 or 30.

It is quite a feat to keep this fish going for more than a year.

Breeding is accomplished only in very shallow water. It is best done when a tank is left partially exposed to the sun, with a bottom of soft sand, and the tank half filled with water which should be left to evaporate. By placing an electric fan over the tank to hasten evaporation, the spawning process will be speeded up a bit. A male and female should be used, though community spawnings might work. The pair will not be observed to spawn, but as the water gets lower and lower they will bury themselves partially in the sand. If the parents are removed after this spawning they will not live more than a few weeks. Allow the water to evaporate completely. Be sure that the sand is moist and allow the eggs to age for at least 2 weeks. Then fill the tank up again very slowly, at the rate of about ½ gallon per day. If possible let rain water be the first water used to refill the tank. The young are fairly large when they become free-swimming and will take brine shrimp and microworms. The adult fish like mosquito larvae, which is probably their natural food.

GENUS *Rivulus* Poey

[Riv'-you-lus: *rivulus* = a small stream]

GREEN or BROWN RIVULUS / *Rivulus cylindraceus* Poey

[cyl'-in-dra'-see-us: *cylindraceus* = cylindrical in shape]

Rivulus cylindraceus Poey, Memorias sobre la historia natural de la isla de Cuba, 2:308, 1861 (type locality, near Havana, Cuba)

RANGE: Cuba.

SIZE: 2 inches; breeds at 2 inches.

TEMPERAMENT: A peaceful species, slow-moving but fast-jumping, suitable in the community tank.

TEMPERATURE REQUIREMENTS: 65–85°F.

SEX DIFFERENCES: See below.

COUNTS: Dorsal 9; anal 12; pectoral 13; pelvic 6; scales 36.

The general color may be described as olive green or brownish. The back is chocolate brown and the body has green (olive) spots which change to red toward the caudal area. A maroon line runs from the snout to the base of the tail fin. A shiny blue spot adorns the area behind the gill cover. The forward chest area is reddish, shading to orange as it colors the belly region. Dorsal and caudal fins are bright green, with a beautiful blue and white margin. The anal fin is a lighter green, spotted with red dots at the base and with a maroon margin. This is a description of the male in breeding color. The female has typical drabness when compared with the male. Her fins are yellow and devoid of any markings. The typical "rivulus spot" of black on a white background is located on the upper edge of the caudal peduncle. This spot is sex-linked to the female.

This species breeds the same as *Rivulus urophthalmus* and is an easy fish to induce to spawn. Prior to spawning the female will exhibit her short ovipositor, as in many cichlids. Raise the temperature to about 80°F to induce spawning, but keep it low (70°) at other times.

Dorn's Rivulus / *Rivulus dorni* Myers

[dorn'-eye: named in honor of Richard Dorn]

Rivulus dorni Myers, Ann. Mag. Nat. Hist., (9)8:588, 1924 (type locality, Rio de Janeiro)

RANGE: Rio de Janeiro.

SIZE: 2½ inches; breeding at 2 inches.

TEMPERAMENT: A peaceful species but a good jumper. It may be kept in the community tank.

TEMPERATURE REQUIREMENTS: 68–85°F.

SEX DIFFERENCES: See below.

COUNTS: Dorsal 7 or 8; anal 11 to 13; pectoral 13 or 14; pelvic 7; scales 30 or 31.

This fish is not too popular, though it has appeared from time to time when it happens to be plentiful in Rio de Janeiro.

The female lacks the typical rivulus spot and is much paler than the colorful male, whose color is chocolate brown on the back, fading to light brown as it reaches the lateral line. The belly region is a grayish white. Each scale has a small aquamarine spot on it. There are two bright spots, similar to the smaller spots, at the base of the caudal fin. The lower part of the body is striped with 6 or 7 vertical bars. Fins are aquamarine, with the dorsal and anal fins showing dark brown bands and edges.

Breeding is rather difficult for a *Rivulus* and much live food is necessary for a long conditioning period. This fish breeds the same as *R. urophthalmus*.

HART'S RIVULUS / *Rivulus harti* (Boulenger)

[hart′-eye: named in honor of the collector P. N. Hart]

Haplochilus harti Boulenger, Proc. Zool. Soc. London, no. 1, p. 389, pl. 21, fig. 2, 1906 (type locality, Trinidad)

RANGE: Trinidad and Venezuela.

SIZE: 4 inches; breeds at 3 inches.

TEMPERAMENT: Eats fish small enough to ingest whole but gets along well with larger fish.

TEMPERATURE   REQUIREMENTS: 68–85°F.

SEX DIFFERENCES: See below.

COUNTS: Dorsal 8; anal 11 to 14; pectoral 13 to 15; pelvic 6 or 7; scales 35 to 38.

This fish is popular as food with some of the people of Trinidad; it is prepared in a local oil and is quite tasty. The meat is sweet but bony. Individuals are easily caught in large numbers when desired. It is capable of jumping a good 12 inches in any direction and can easily flip through cracks as large as itself. Care should be exercised in handling it. This is true of the entire genus *Rivulus*.

The male is brown on the back as a protective coloration when viewed from above against a muddy background. The belly is a grass green, the sides brownish green. There are rows of beautiful bright red dots running horizontally. The fins are light green with red dots and red bars. The female is much paler and her red dots are not nearly so bright as the male's. Her fins are colorless. The rivulus spot is present but indistinct, especially when live foods are not available.

OCELLATED RIVULUS / *Rivulus ocellatus* Hensel

[os'-ell-lay'-tus: *ocellatus* = provided with an eyelike spot]

Rivulus ocellatus Hensel, Arch. Naturges. 34:365, 1869 (type locality, Rio de Janeiro)

RANGE: Southeastern Brazil in coastal zone.

SIZE: 2½ inches; breeds at 2 inches.

TEMPERAMENT: A peaceful species suitable in the community tank.

TEMPERATURE REQUIREMENTS: 70–85°F.

SEX DIFFERENCES: See below.

COUNTS: Dorsal 8 or 9; anal 11 or 12; pectoral 13; pelvic 6.

This is a fine little fish, lacking only in color. It is a well-poised individual that maintains a characteristic position in the upper layers of the water, preferably among floating plants. Its aquarium must be carefully covered at all times. One was observed to dash against a top cover to catch a piece of dirt that rolled along the top of the glass like an insect.

The name *ocellatus* is apparently given for the rivulus spot, which is probably as distinct in this species as in any other in the genus. The male is olive-colored, varying in intensity over the body from the back to the lighter belly. The sides have an irregular pattern of blotches which give a mottled or marbled effect; the fins are yellowish to green. The dorsal and anal fins show a black outer edge lined with yellow. The female is brown, with lighter body markings than the male. The rivulus spot is distinct on the female.

Spawning is typical, as for **R.** *urophthalmus.*

Rivulus santensis Köhler

[san-ten'-sis: named after the locality where collected]

Rivulus elegans var. *santensis* Köhler, Blät., Aquar.-Terrak. pp. 407–408, 1906 (type locality, Santos, Rio de Janeiro)

RANGE: Santos, Rio de Janeiro.

SIZE: 2½ inches; breeds at 2 inches.

TEMPERAMENT: A peaceful species suitable for the community aquarium.

TEMPERATURE REQUIREMENTS: 68–85°F.

SEX DIFFERENCES: See below.

COUNTS: Dorsal 7 or 8; anal 12 or 13; pectoral 13; pelvic 6; scales 36.

Breeding is the same as *Rivulus urophthalmus*. This fish may be a little easier to breed than most of the other *Rivulus*, probably because there are so many tank-raised specimens available. German aquarists do well with this fish and produce great quantities.

The over-all color is an olive green, with a blackish back and a lemon-colored belly. Rows of red dots run horizontally along the sides. The dorsal and caudal fins are tinged and edged with white; the anal fin has a black edging. The female is less intensely colored than the male, but her fins show indistinct dots. Her rivulus spot usually is not too obvious.

HERRINGBONE RIVULUS / *Rivulus strigatus* Regan

[stri-gay'-tus: *strigatus* = streaked]

Rivulus strigatus Regan, Ann. Mag. Nat. Hist., (8)10:502, 1912 (type locality, Amazon)

RANGE: Middle Amazon Basin.

SIZE: 2 inches; breeds at 1½ inches.

TEMPERAMENT: A peaceful species, but best kept in its own tank.

TEMPERATURE REQUIREMENTS: 76–90°F.

SEX DIFFERENCES: See below.

COUNTS: Dorsal 8; anal 12; pectoral 13; pelvic 6; scales 33.

Breeding is almost the same as for *Rivulus urophthalmus* except that conditioning must take a little longer and the female must be carefully selected. The female should be chosen for her good vigor, size, and color. She will become swollen with eggs after a male has been placed with her after the conditioning process. The herringbone *Rivulus* is usually sold in trios (two males, one female) because females are scarce. Usually about 80 per cent of a hatching are males. Conditioning should be at 80°F and breeding at 85°F. It may take weeks to induce this fish to spawn, but it is well worth the effort.

The coloration of this species is unique in its genus. The back of the male is olive with brown blotches irregularly placed. The sides are beautifully colored with some V-shaped lines of brilliant red, in the "herringbone" pattern. Also there are some horizontal red lines. The throat is a contrasting orange or light red that diffuses to a yellow red on the belly. The yellow dorsal fin has red dots while the anal and pelvic fins are light orange with a red edge. Pectorals are yellow with the first few rays showing red. The tail fin shows the V-shaped red markings, plus the colors of yellow in top half and orange in the bottom. The caudal fin has a red margin.

The female has a dull rusty color with very little hint of the male's beautiful color pattern. It takes a lot of imagination to see the rivulus spot on some specimens.

SLENDER RIVULUS / *Rivulus tenuis* (Meek)

[ten'-you-is: *tenuis* = slender]

Cynodontichthys tenuis Meek, Field Columbian Mus. Zool., 5:101, 1904 (type locality, El Hule, Oaxaca, Mexico)

RANGE: Central Mexico to Costa Rica.

SIZE: 3 inches; breeding at 2½ inches.

TEMPERAMENT: A fairly peaceful species, but it will eat small guppies.

TEMPERATURE REQUIREMENTS: 72–85°F.

SEX DIFFERENCES: See below.

COUNTS: Dorsal 8; anal 11; pectoral 13; pelvic 6; scales 38.

This fish breeds the same as *Rivulus urophthalmus*.

The background color of the male is olive brown on the back, aquamarine on the sides, with a yellowish belly. The throat is carmine. The gill covers reflect an iridescent bluish green and the sides show irregular rows of red dots. The dorsal fin is yellowish with a brown edge. The green anal fin is edged with red. The tail fin is carmine, edged with a black band through it, except that the upper part is yellow green and the lower is orange, much like the color of the herringbone *Rivulus*. The pectoral and pelvic fins are yellow green.

The female is tan with irregular rows of darker dots, but there is no flaming beauty as manifested by the males.

Golden or Green Rivulus / *Rivulus urophthalmus* Günther

[your'-off-thal'-mus: *uro* = tail; *ophthalmus* = eyespot]

Rivulus urophthalmus Günther, Catalogue of the Fishes in the British Museum, 6:327, 1866 (type locality, Pará, Brazil)

RANGE: Guianas to Rio São Francisco, Brazil.

SIZE: 2½ inches; breeds at 2 inches.

TEMPERAMENT: A peaceful species desirable in the community aquarium.

TEMPÉRATURE REQUIREMENTS: 68–85°F.

SEX DIFFERENCES: See below.

COUNTS: Dorsal 6 or 7; anal 11 to 13; pectoral 13; pelvic 6; scales 37 to 42.

This interesting species shows what can be done to some of the less colorful egg layers to brighten them up. There exist two distinct color varieties. One should be called the golden *Rivulus* and the other the green *Rivulus*.

The golden *Rivulus* is lemon yellow with regular rows of bright red dots running horizontally along the sides from behind the gill cover to the caudal fin base. The female has fewer red spots and a more grayish chest. The dorsal and anal fins of the male are peppered with red dots while those fins are clear in the female. The female lacks the rivulus spot.

The green *Rivulus* is a brownish green with numerous rows of red dots running longitudinally along the sides. The unpaired fins are greenish with red dots. The dorsal fin has a dark margin and the tail fin has a cream brown upper edge and a dark brown lower edge. The female is brown and marbled. She possesses a clear eyespot, or rivulus spot, from which this species gets its name.

Breeding is best accomplished with two

males per female, in seasoned water at a temperature of 76°F, pH of 6.8 to 7.2, and zero hardness. The female should be conditioned in the breeding tank and only the males should be moved. A 15-gallon aquarium half-filled with water should be abundantly stocked with spawning grass, Spanish moss, and some floating plants like *Riccia*. If there is a natural sediment on the bottom some pairs will spawn in this material; other pairs select the plants. The female is driven into the plants by an active male. They assume a side-by-side position and shimmy next to each other for a few seconds. A single egg expelled by the female is fertilized by the male. This occurs every day for a few weeks. Eggs are large and easily seen. They should be picked off the plants and placed in a small jar floating in the same aquarium with the parents. A drop of five per cent Methylene Blue should be added to each quart of water. Eggs hatch in 2 weeks. Parents will eat the young but leave the eggs alone if they are well-fed. Young require infusoria and brine shrimp, followed by microworms and sifted *Daphnia*. Growth is rapid.

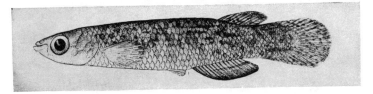

AUTUMN-LEAF RIVULUS / *Rivulus volcanus* Hildebrand

[vol-can'-us: named after an extinct volcanic lake where collected]

Rivulus volcanus Hildebrand, Field Mus. Nat. Hist. Zool., 22:317, fig. 8, 1938 (type locality, Laguna Grande, Chiriquí, Panama)

RANGE: Panama.

SIZE: 2 inches; breeding not observed.

TEMPERAMENT: Not known.

TEMPERATURE REQUIREMENTS: 68–85°F.

SEX DIFFERENCES: See below.

COUNTS: Dorsal 8 or 9; anal 13 to 15; pectoral 15; pelvic 6 or 7; scales 42 to 45.

About 30 specimens of this species were collected in Panama in February. The largest was about 2 inches long; among the several females none was with ripe eggs. Possibly this was due to the time of year. Some of the fish were sent to New York by air but after a rough ride only 3 specimens were alive on arrival. A careless assistant had placed them in an uncovered aquarium, and the next morning they were found at the end of the room. They had traveled about 30 feet from their aquarium and were practically dried stiff. Usually if they are able to keep moist they will survive many hours out of the water.

The male is colored like an autumn leaf with the beautiful colors of yellow, red, and brown tinging the whole body. The sides have red spots. The mouth and throat are carmine. The dark-tipped pointed dorsal fin has dark dots basally. The caudal and anal fins are reddish brown with a black edge. The female is similarly colored but is without the red spots. Her caudal and anal fins are light brown with black spots; her dorsal fin is rounded. The rivulus spot is distinct.

The name of this species currently is *Rivulus hildebrandi*.

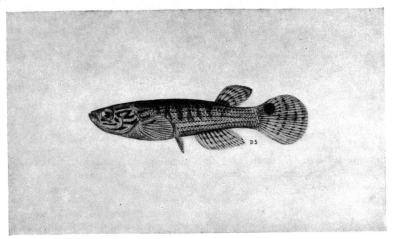

Yellowback Rivulus / *Rivulus xanthonotus* Ahl

[zan'-tho-no'-tus: *xantho* = yellow; *notus* = back]

Rivulus xanthonotus Ahl, Blät. Aquar.-Terrak., p. 315, 1926 (type locality, Amazon River)

RANGE: Amazon Basin.

SIZE: 3 inches; breeds at 2½ inches.

TEMPERAMENT: A peaceful species when kept with fish of its own size or larger.

TEMPERATURE REQUIREMENTS: 68–88°F.

SEX DIFFERENCES: See below.

COUNTS: Dorsal 6; anal 11 or 12; pectoral 13; pelvic 6 or 7; scales 40.

This species breeds the same as *Rivulus urophthalmus*.

The male is a golden yellow on the back but paler on the sides, becoming gray on the belly. The head is an olive brown and the sides have the red dots which are so common in this genus. Red dots also adorn the unpaired fins. Fins are yellowish green, the dorsal and anal fins being edged in black. The female has a distinct rivulus spot but the red dots are fairly indistinct.

Genus *Valencia*

[Va-len'-see-a: named after a locality in Spain]

Spanish Tooth Carp / *Valencia hispanica* (Cuvier and Valenciennes)

[his-pan'-i-ca: named after Spain]

Hydragyra hispanica Cuvier and Valenciennes, Histoire naturelle des poissons, 18:214, pl. 531, fig. 1, 1846 (type locality, Catalonia)

RANGE: Southeastern Spain.

SIZE: Female 3¼ inches, male 2¼ inches: female breeds at 3 inches, male at 2 inches.

TEMPERAMENT: This species nips fins and is not suitable in the community tank.

TEMPERATURE REQUIREMENTS: 70–90°F.

SEX DIFFERENCES: The male is grayish brown on the back, with a greenish-blue side. The belly is yellow. A large spot, darker than the surrounding area, is located above the base of the pectoral fin. About a dozen vertical bars run from the gill plate into the caudal fin. The dorsal, anal, and caudal fins are yellow with a red tinge; they have dark markings and a maroon edge. The female is less colorful; she lacks the shoulder spot and vertical bars. All her fins are clear. The female grows an inch larger than the male.

COUNTS: Dorsal 10 or 11; anal 12 to 14; pectoral 14; pelvic 6; scales 29 to 32.

Eggs are deposited one at a time among floating plants, or upon leaves or twigs which are close to the surface. They hatch in about 13 days at 75°F and should be removed as soon as the parents have completed spawning. Parent fish should be well-conditioned on live foods and their breeding tanks should be in a sunny location at a temperature between 75 and 80°F. Parents eat eggs and young. The free-swimming fry need infusoria as their first food.

[Good'-i-dee]

This small family of live bearers is found in the waters of central Mexico. They are small fishes, with the males having slightly modified anal fins. They are most closely related to the Cyprinodontidae and Poeciliidae. The familiar gonopodium of poeciliid fishes is not present in the Goodeidae; instead, the first few rays of the anal fin of the male are distinct from the other rays and are used as a copulatory organ.

Studies have shown that the mother is not capable of superfetation, that is to say, for each brood she must have a separate fertilization. A careful study of her anatomy indicates that she has a structure resembling a uterus, which does not occur in the poeciliids. This gives her the power to nourish the developing embryos, a trait of a true viviparous fish; most other live-bearing fishes are more correctly classified as "ovoviviparous."

Aquarists have raised two members of this family: *Girardinichthys innominatus* Bleeker and *Neotoca bilineata* (Bean), but the first member of this family is so rare and undesirable that few if any hobbyists are interested in it; therefore, it is omitted from this book.

The family Goodeidae was revised by Hubbs and Turner in 1939. They recognized the following subfamilies: Ataeniobiinae, Goodeinae, Characodontinae, and Girardinichthyinae.

GENUS *Neotoca* Hubbs and Turner

[Ne′-o-tok′-a: *neo* = new; *toca* = offspring]

TWO-LINED NEOTOCA / *Neotoca bilineata* (Bean)

[bi-lin′-ee-a′-ta: *bi* = two; *lineata* = with lines]

Characodon bilineatus Bean, Proc. U.S. Nat. Mus., 10:371, 1887 (type locality, Guanajuato, Rio Lerma, Mexico)

RANGE: Central Mexico.

SIZE: 2 inches; breeds at 2 inches.

TEMPERAMENT: A peaceful species with fishes of its own size.

TEMPERATURE REQUIREMENTS: 70–85°F.

SEX DIFFERENCES: The male has a modified anal fin.

COUNTS: Dorsal 13 to 15; anal 23 or 24; pectoral 15 or 16; pelvic 6; scales 29 to 33.

Since this is a live-bearing fish it is best that a pair be kept together. The male is more colorful than the female and is easily identified because the first rays of the anal fin are separated from the membranous part of this fin. The male is smaller than the female, in about the same proportion as male to female guppies.

The male is colored with the usual killie-like green. He has a dark bar running across the caudal peduncle. This bar is crossed irregularly with dark bands which originate in back of the gill cover and run the entire body length. The fins are colored like the body, but at certain periods they do show darker hues. The female is slightly more colorful, with an iridescent green band running along the side to the anal fin.

Although this fish is not an avid eater of its fry, it is not to be trusted. A well-planted aquarium kept in strong sunlight is advised. It is fond of an aquarium in which *Nitella* has been growing for some time; it is bred commercially in small tanks with so much *Nitella* that the fish has little room to swim but lies about near the surface resting on the plants.

The fry are very small when born and need infusoria; green water is best suited for their needs. With brine shrimp available they fare well and in a large aquarium they will mature and reproduce in 3 months.

The name of this species currently is *Skiffia bilineata*.

[Pea'-ci-li'-i-dee]

This family of live-bearing fishes is characterized by the males having the anal fin placed forward and modified into an intromittent organ known as the gonopodium. It is strictly an American fish family, found only on the North and South American continents. The genera of this family are recognized according to the development of their teeth and the structure of the male gonopodium.

These fishes are ovoviviparous—the developing young do not obtain any nourishment from the parents. They are capable of superfetation in that a single fertilization will be sufficient to enable the female to deliver several successive broods. The exact number of broods may vary from species to species but may number as high as eight in a single year.

Walter H. Chute, of the Shedd Aquarium, Chicago, reported that *Limia vittata* delivered 242 fry, of which only 4 were dead. That is a record. The average brood will vary with the size of the fish involved. It will even vary from one female to another of the same species. An average brood of 75 is expected for *Xiphophorus,* about 90 for the mollies, about 50 for the guppies, and only one or two for *Heterandria* each day. Hobbyists have passed the word along that the second brood of a female is her largest; this usually is not true, since the larger the female the larger the brood that may be expected.

Breeding live bearers is no great feat, but the successful rearing of the entire brood is not easy. The aquarist must devise means of keeping the parents from eating the fry and of having the proper foods, in the correct amounts, available for the young. Breeders must be carefully selected, for color variations in this family are greater than in any other family, with the possible exception of goldfishes and species of *Betta.*

As a family these fishes are easy to keep and generally peaceful, with a few noted exceptions. They are omnivorous, preferring bits of vegetable material with their meat. They are, without doubt, the most popular family to aquarists.

The family Poeciliidae has been divided into the following subfamilies: Gambusiinae, Poeciliinae, Xenodexiinae, Poeciliopsinae, Alfarinae, Tomeurinae, and the peculiar Jenynsiinae. For the purposes of this book we are not arranging the species according to subfamily but are following our usual alphabetical arrangement.

Genus *Alfaro* Meek

[Al-far'-o: named in honor of A. Alfaro]

This genus is distinguished by the scaly knifelike keel along the ventral edge of the body.

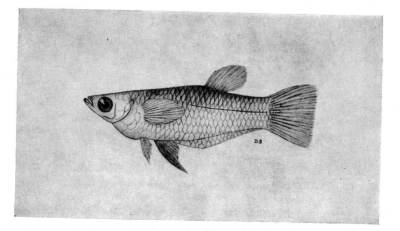

Knife Live Bearer / *Alfaro cultratus* (Regan)

[cul-tray'-tus: *cultratus* = knife-shaped]

Petalosoma cultratum Regan, Ann. Mag. Nat. Hist., (8)2:458, 1908 (type locality, Costa Rica)

RANGE: Costa Rica, Nicaragua, and Atlantic slope of Panama.

SIZE: 2½ inches, with female largest; breeds at 1½ inches.

TEMPERAMENT: This predaceous species is best kept in a tank by itself.

TEMPERATURE REQUIREMENTS: 60–80°F.

SEX DIFFERENCES: Male has a gonopodium.

COUNTS: Dorsal 8; anal 8 to 10; pectoral 12; pelvic 6; scales 34 or 35.

The color is light olive brown dorsally, becoming silvery white on the belly. There is a narrow dark line along the middle of the side. The fins are clear or light yellow.

Alfaro amazonum (Regan) is considered to be a synonym of this species by Rivero and Hubbs, who placed this species in a separate subfamily, Alfarinae.

GENUS *Belonesox* Kner

[Bee-lon'-ee-sox: *belone* = a needle; *esox* = a pikelike fish]

PIKE TOP MINNOW / *Belonesox belizanus* Kner

[bay-lee-zann'-us: named after Belize, British Honduras]

Belonesox belizanus Kner, Sitzb. Akad. Wiss. Wien, 40:419, fig., 1860 (type locality, Belize)

RANGE: Southern Mexico, Honduras to Costa Rica, Nicaragua, and Guatemala.

SIZE: At least 8 inches, the largest poeciliid fish; female breeds at 4 inches; male half the size of the female.

TEMPERAMENT: An active predaceous species with a vicious disposition.

TEMPERATURE REQUIREMENTS: 70–85°F.

SEX DIFFERENCES: Male has the gonopodium.

COUNTS: Dorsal 8 to 10; anal 10; pectoral 14 to 16; pelvic 6; scales about 52.

This live bearer presents certain difficulties because the vicious look and sharp teeth truly indicate its mean disposition. An 8-inch specimen will tear apart a fully matured platy or molly and will swallow smaller fishes in one gulp. It will attack its own kind occasionally. This fish is strictly carnivorous and will refuse dried foods to the point of starvation. Its ideal diet would be small fishes, but one may substitute flies, small worms, tadpoles, bits of raw meat and fish, or whatever else it becomes accustomed to while young. The newborn fry are nearly 1 inch in total length and quickly take worms, *Daphnia*, and baby fishes.

Pairs must be conditioned on live foods for at least 2 weeks prior to spawning. The female will deliver dead babies if she has not had the proper diet in profusion. The normal diet for a mature female is a molly a day, and a big one at that. The fry are eaten as soon as they are dropped unless precautions are taken against this. It is best to have them in large pools where they have lots of room. The water should be somewhat salty, about 1 tablespoon of salt per gallon of water.

GENUS *Brachyrhaphis* Regan

[Brack'-i-ray'-fiss: *brachy* = short; *rhaphis* = a needle]

THE BISHOP / *Brachyrhaphis episcopi* (Steindachner)

[e-pi'-scope'-eye: *episcopi* = an overseer]

Gambusia episcopi Steindachner, Sitzb. Akad. Wiss. Wien, 78:9, pl. 2, figs. 3, 4, 1878 (type locality, Obispo)

RANGE: Both slopes of Panama.

SIZE: Female 2 inches; breeds at 1 inch. Male is half the size of the female.

TEMPERAMENT: Not desirable in the community aquarium.

TEMPERATURE REQUIREMENTS: 70–85°F.

SEX DIFFERENCES: Male has gonopodium.

COUNTS: Dorsal 8 or 9; anal 10; pectoral 12; pelvic 6; scales 28.

This live bearer presents a challenge to the breeder. Though it is easily induced to breed in captivity, it needs lots of room in a long, low aquarium. It requires brackish water, 1 tablespoon of salt per gallon of water. It has an attractive maroon color.

Gambusia latipunctata Meek and Hildebrand, otherwise known as *Mollienesia latipunctata* from Panama, is a synonym of this species.

R. R. Miller warns that *Poecilia latipunctata* Meek, 1904, should not be confused with this genus and species since it is a valid species in another genus, *Mollienesia*.

GENUS *Cnesterodon* Garman

[Ness'-tear-o'-don: *cnester* = a knife; *odon* = teeth]

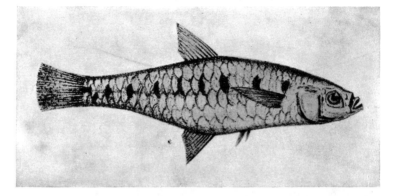

TEN-SPOTTED LIVE BEARER / *Cnesterodon decemmaculatus* (Jenyns)

[de'-sem-mack'-you-lay'-tus: *decem* = ten; *maculatus* = spotted]

Poecilia decemmaculata Jenyns, Zoology of the Voyage of *H.M.S. Beagle*, Pt. 4, Fish, p. 115, pl. 22, figs. 1, 1a, 1842 (type locality, Maldonado)

RANGE: Rio de la Plata system; Uruguay, Paraguay, and southern Brazil.

SIZE: 1½ inches; breeds at 1 inch. Male is smaller than the female.

TEMPERAMENT: This species is suitable in the community aquarium.

TEMPERATURE REQUIREMENTS: 70–84°F.

SEX DIFFERENCES: Male has gonopodium. The fins of the male have some pigmentation, lacking in the female.

COUNTS: Dorsal 8; anal 10; pectoral 9; pelvic 6; scales 24 or 25.

This live bearer produces small broods of young at regular intervals throughout the year. Many of the young are born crippled, as the parent fishes are easily frightened and the female may possibly injure her unborn fry. The crippled fish are, nevertheless, perfectly good spawners and seem to be less inclined to eat the young. The fry must be protected from their parents by a dense growth of vegetation or ample artificial spawning grass.

The coloration is dull green above, golden on the sides, and yellowish silver on the belly. From 5 to 12 small dark vertical bands run from the gill plate to the tail in regular patterns along the sides.

Genus *Gambusia* Poey

[Gam-bus'-i-a: *gambusia* = nothing or frustration; when fishermen came back empty-handed, the Cubans would say "he went fishing for Gambusinos."]

Spotted Gambusia; Mosquitofish / *Gambusia affinis affinis* (Baird and Girard)

[af-fi'-nis: *affinis* = neighboring or related]

Heterandria affinis Baird and Girard, Proc. Acad. Nat. Sci. Philadelphia, 6:390, 1854 (type locality, Medina and Salado Rivers, Texas)

RANGE: Gulf drainage, from Texas to Alabama.

SIZE: 2½ inches; breeds at 2 inches.

TEMPERAMENT: This species is predaceous and active for its size and will reduce the fins of other fishes to shreds.

TEMPERATURE REQUIREMENTS: Above freezing to 90°F.

SEX DIFFERENCES: Male has the gonopodium.

COUNTS: Dorsal 7 to 9; anal 9; pectoral 13 or 14; pelvic 6; scales 30 to 32.

A live bearer which has a great appetite for its own young. It can stand all types of foul water conditions, poor food, and overcrowding. It is pretty and has an interesting history. This is a mosquitofish that does wonders on mosquito larvae, eating its own weight of them per day. This fish has been sent to many parts of the tropical world for use in mosquito extermination.

There occur in nature several black sports of this species. The male looks like a small mottled (marbled) molly. He is black dotted. This is not a different species but is classified as a melanistic variety. Inbreeding has produced females with these same spots, which are considered by hobbyists more desirable than normal ones. There are, in nature, extremely rare cases of black females. In breeding *Gambusia* there has been produced a black sport illustrated here.

The habits and care are the same as for *Gambusia affinis holbrooki*.

Gambusia patruelis (Baird and Girard) was described as *Heterandria patruelis* (*Proc. Acad. Nat. Sci. Philadelphia*, 6:390, 1854) from the Rio Sabinal, Rio Nueces, and Elm Creek, all of Texas. It ranges from southern Indiana and Illinois southward to the Gulf Coast from eastern Texas to Tampa, Florida.

There occur in nature several black sports of *Gambusia affinis*. This drawing shows a pair of "marbled gambusia" which were developed from these sports by selective breeding.

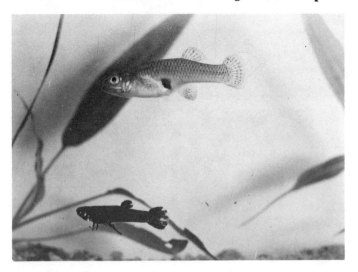

MOSQUITOFISH; GAMBUSIA / *Gambusia affinis holbrooki* (Girard)

[hol-brook'-eye: named in honor of the naturalist J. E. Holbrook]

Gambusia holbrookii Girard, Proc. Acad. Nat. Sci. Philadelphia, 9:61, 1859 (type locality, Charleston, South Carolina)

RANGE: New Jersey to Florida.

SIZE: 2 inches; breeds at 1½ inches.

TEMPERAMENT: This species is best kept in an aquarium by itself because it will shred the fins of other fishes.

TEMPERATURE REQUIREMENTS: Above freezing to 88°F.

SEX DIFFERENCES: The male has the gonopodium.

COUNTS: Dorsal 6 to 8; anal 9 or 10; pectoral 13 or 14; scales 30 to 32.

The adult male is much smaller than the female and has a long gonopodium, nearly as long as its head. Females normally give birth only during the months of May to October, but in some tank-bred strains the cycle extends the year round. Fry are about ⅓ inch long when born and can live fairly well with fine dried foods, newly hatched brine shrimp, and other fine-grained foods like powdered eggs and microworms. The females are easily mistaken for other species of fishes, especially *Fundulus* females. For a small female the normal brood is small, about 8, seldom including more than 2 males. For a large female 30 to 60 is an average brood. In nature the ratio of 6 females to 1 male is usual. Maturity is reached in about 4 months, depending on water temperatures and food supply.

Gambusia has been introduced into California, Burma, Siam, India, Hawaii, Tahiti, Formosa, the Philippines, and Japan as a most useful devourer of mosquito larvae. One individual fish has been credited by S. F. Hildebrand as having eaten 165 larvae in 12 hours.

It is extremely hardy and can live all winter under a thin sheet of ice. In winter it hibernates in mud, but even in the home aquarium when temperatures fall below 68°F it may be seen to gather on or near the bottom.

MOSQUITOFISH; GAMBUSIA / *Gambusia nicaraguensis* Günther

[nick′-a-ra-guen′-sis: named after Lake Nicaragua]

Gambusia nicaraguensis Günther, Catalogue of the Fishes in the British Museum, 6:336, 1866 (type locality, Lake Nicaragua)

RANGE: Atlantic drainage from southern Mexico to Panama.

SIZE: 2½ inches; female breeds at 2 inches, male at 1 inch.

TEMPERAMENT: Like other species of *Gambusia*, this one should be kept by itself.

TEMPERATURE REQUIREMENTS: 50–90°F.

SEX DIFFERENCES: Male has gonopodium.

COUNTS: Dorsal 7; anal 9 or 10; pectoral 13; scales 29.

This live bearer has a great fondness for eating its own young, or anything else which is small enough to be ingested whole. It is a successful mosquitofish because it can eat many larvae without showing the slightest discomfort.

The color is grayish olive with a metallic blue sheen on the sides. It is marked with scattered brown spots on all unpaired fins and the body.

Breeding is best done in a heavily vegetated aquarium, or out of doors during the summer season. In Central American countries these fish are kept in small stagnant pools, water barrels, marshes, and whatever other intermittent bodies of water might be breeding places for the aquatic larvae of the mosquito.

It is not a popular live bearer. At times it is brought in by an aquarist-tourist who thinks he has found a new live bearer.

Blue Gambusia; Spotted Gambusia / *Gambusia punctata* Poey

[punk-tay'-ta: *punctata* = spotted]

Gambusia punctata Poey, Memorias sobre la historia natural de la isla de Cuba, 1:384, 390, pl. 32, figs. 5–9, 1854 (type locality, Cuba)

RANGE: Streams of Cuba.

SIZE: 3 inches; female breeds at 2 inches; male is much smaller.

TEMPERAMENT: This species is best kept in a tank by itself as it will shred the fins of other fishes.

TEMPERATURE REQUIREMENTS: 65–90°F.

SEX DIFFERENCES: Male has gonopodium.

COUNTS: Dorsal 8 to 10; anal 11; pectoral 15; pelvic 6; scales 35.

This live bearer eats its own young and must be bred in a heavily planted aquarium where the youngsters have a chance to get away from the ever-hungry parents.

The popular name "blue gambusia" probably refers to the blue eyes, which are more or less unique in fishes. No doubt it should be dubbed the blue-eyed *Gambusia*. The body is a light metallic blue. The male has about 4 rows of dots running parallel to the lateral line.

FAMILY POECILIIDAE: Live-bearing Toothed Carps

GENUS *Girardinus* Poey

[Gi'-rar-din'-us: named in honor of Charles Girard, Smithsonian Institution naturalist]

THE GIRARDINUS / *Girardinus metallicus* Poey

[meh-tal'-li-cus: *metallicus* = metal-like]

Girardinus metallicus Poey, Memorias sobre la historia natural de la isla de Cuba, 1:387, pl. 31, figs. 8–11, 1854 (type locality, Cuba)

RANGE: Cuba.

SIZE: Female 3 inches, male 2 inches; female breeds at 2 inches, male at 1¼ inches.

TEMPERAMENT: Suitable in the community tank.

TEMPERATURE REQUIREMENTS: 72–85°F.

SEX DIFFERENCES: Male has long gonopodium.

COUNTS: Dorsal 9; anal 10 or 11; pectoral 10; pelvic 6; scales 29 or 30.

This live bearer needs little prompting to reproduce. The male has a characteristic double-pointed gonopodium like the *Glaridichthys*, whereas the female has a normal anal fin. The sides of this plain olive-sheened fish are marked with a dark horizontal stripe running along the lateral line. This stripe is regularly interrupted with a silvery bar from just behind the head to the end of the caudal peduncle. The dorsal fins have a small black basal spot. The name *metallicus* is derived from an observation of the fish in reflected light. There is a decided silvery gleam when viewed in this manner.

The fry should be removed from the parents and fed small-particled foods.

GENUS *Glaridichthys* Garman

[Glar'-id-ick'-thys: *glarid* = a chisel; *ichthys* = a fish]

YELLOW BELLY / *Glaridichthys falcatus* Eigenmann

[fal-kay'-tus: *falcatus* = scythe-shaped]

Glaridichthys falcatus Eigenmann, Bull. U.S. Fish. Comm. 1902, 22:224, figs. 2, 3, 1903 (type locality, San Cristobal, Cuba)

RANGE: Cuba.

SIZE: Female 3 inches; female breeds at 2 inches, male at 1½ inches.

TEMPERAMENT: Suitable for the community aquarium.

TEMPERATURE REQUIREMENTS: 68–80°F.

SEX DIFFERENCES: Male has extremely long gonopodium.

COUNTS: Dorsal 7 to 9; anal 10; pectoral 11; pelvic 6; scales 29 or 30.

This female live bearer looks like the common female guppy, except it has a slightly golden hue with a decidedly golden underside, hence the name "yellow belly." The male is small with a long double-pointed gonopodium. Actually the longer part of the gonopodium is a hooked hood, which may have some important part in the reproductive processes of this fish.

Parents go after their own fry; therefore, a heavily planted aquarium is a must if they are to be saved. About 25 fry per spawning is usual. They take about 120 days to mature if fed the proper foods. They are capable of eating enormous quantities of newly hatched brine shrimp.

FAMILY POECILIIDAE: Live-bearing Toothed Carps

GENUS *Heterandria* Agassiz

[Het'-er-an'-dree-a: *heter* = different; *andria* = male]

DWARF TOP MINNOW; MOSQUITOFISH / *Heterandria formosa* Agassiz

[for-mo'-sa: *formosa* = beautiful or finely formed]

Heterandria formosa Agassiz, in Girard, Proc. Acad. Nat. Sci. Philadelphia, 9:63, 1859 (type locality, Charleston, South Carolina; Palatka, Florida)

RANGE: North Carolina to Florida.

SIZE: Female 1 inch, male ¼ inch; breed at same size.

TEMPERAMENT: Suitable for a small tank with guppies, otherwise best kept by itself because of small size.

TEMPERATURE REQUIREMENTS: 50–90°F.

SEX DIFFERENCES: Male has gonopodium.

COUNTS: Dorsal 7 or 8; anal 10 or 11; pectoral 12; pelvic 6; scales 27 to 31.

This live bearer is easily bred. The parents when well-fed do not pay much attention to their fry. It is difficult to imagine this species as a mosquitofish since it is hardly larger than some mosquito larvae. However, the term mosquitofish may refer to its size rather than its diet. It has an enormous capacity for *Daphnia*, and if supplied with these little animals it will surely reproduce in great numbers. During breeding season females will drop two or three fry a day for about 10 days or so. They will stop for 4 weeks and then start dropping again. The fry are easily raised.

Although not very attractively colored, this fish is inexpensive and is stocked by dealers for that reason. The dark line along the lateral line is punctuated at regular intervals with a bar which runs one-quarter of the body depth above and below this line.

GENUS *Jenynsia* Günther

[Jen-in'-si-a: named in honor of the naturalist Leonard Jenyns]

This is the only genus in the subfamily Jenynsiinae. It is characterized by the gonopodium of the male being capable of movement to one side only on each male, either right or left.

ONE-SIDED LIVE BEARER / *Jenynsia lineata* (Jenyns)

[lin'-e-a'-ta: *lineata* = streaked]

Lebias lineata Jenyns, Zoology of the Voyage of *H.M.S. Beagle*, Pt. 4, Fish, p. 116, pl. 22, fig. 2, 1842 (type locality, Maldonado)

RANGE: Rio Grande do Sul and Rio de la Plata systems in southern Brazil and Argentina.

SIZE: Female 5 inches, male 1½ inches; female breeds at 2 inches, male at 1 inch.

TEMPERAMENT: Not suitable in the community aquarium.

TEMPERATURE REQUIREMENTS: 68–80°F.

SEX DIFFERENCES: Male has long, tubular gonopodium; female is about four times as large as the male.

COUNTS: Dorsal 9; anal 9; pectoral 13; pelvic 6; scales 25.

This is an odd species; with the other members of the same genus it has as its most distinctive characteristic the peculiar fact that the gonopodium is definitely limited to movement in one direction, either to the right or to the left. No single male can move his gonopodium in both directions. This means only right-

"handed" and left-"handed" males occur. Oddly enough, there is a similar anomaly in the female: her genital pore is blocked by a single large scale which hinges in either a right or a left direction, thus blocking advances from any but a complementary male. A right-handed male can only fertilize a left-handed female.

The fact that the males are so small in comparison with the females is the reason why the females are listed as the vicious members of the family. They show every desire to gobble up all the fry in their brood; the poor males are barely larger than 4-week-old female fry. Breeding should be accomplished in an extremely large and heavily planted aquarium. This gives the fry a fair chance to escape their vicious mother.

Feeding is no problem as the young and parents take all kinds of foods. They seem to be especially fond of *Daphnia*.

The over-all color is olive green with a bluish sheen to the sides. Several dark horizontal stripes adorn the sides as do some irregular spots. Fins show a dusky color when in good condition.

GENUS *Lebistes* Filippi

[Leb-is'-tees: *lebistes* = a kind of fish]

GUPPY / *Lebistes reticulatus* (Peters)

[re-tik'-you-lay'-tus: *reticulatus* = netlike]

Poecilia reticulata Peters, Monatsb. Akad. Wiss. Berlin, 1859:412, 1860 (type locality, Caracas in Rio Guaire)

RANGE: Venezuela, Trinidad, and Barbados. Introduced into many localities of the world as a mosquito-control fish.

SIZE: Female 2½ inches, male 1½ inches; female breeds at 1 inch, male at ¾ inch.

TEMPERAMENT: A peaceful species well suited for the community aquarium.

TEMPERATURE REQUIREMENTS: 58–90°F. Optimum 72°F.

SEX DIFFERENCES: Male is colorful, female dull. Male also possesses a modified anal fin or gonopodium.

COUNTS: Dorsal 7 or 8; anal 8 or 9; pectoral 13 or 14; pelvic 5; scales 26 to 28.

The males of this beautiful species have every conceivable color and color combination known, although it is difficult to fix a strain in which all males have the same color. Contrary to most authors (who say that "no two males look exactly alike") there are a few strains, notably the golden lacetail, in which all males and females look exactly alike. The wild-type female has a dull olive-green body, with a grayish appearance. She lacks color in all her fins.

The name of this species currently is *Poecilia reticulata*.

The guppy has broods every 4 weeks or so, with the brood size averaging about 45, although there may be variations of this number up to 187 youngsters. Guppies usually eat a few of their offspring. Each female spawner should be placed if possible in a separate container.

Males grow larger and faster if separated from females. Early sexing of guppies is easy if the anal fin is judged in comparison to its distance from the pelvics.

A female guppy, well rounded and about to give birth.

It should be noted that the anal fin of the female is far back of the pelvics while that of the male continually moves forward until at maturity it lies practically between the pelvic fins.

Eugenie Clark and Lester R. Aronson of the Animal Behavior Department, American Museum of Natural History, reported on Sexual Behavior in the Guppy (*Zoologica*, vol. 36, pt. 1, April 20, 1951) in a masterpiece of investigation. They stated that the most striking features of sexual behavior in this species are the manner in which the males persistently pursue the females, and the great frequency with which the males jab at the genital region of the female with a momentary thrust of the highly modified anal fin or gonopodium.

"By taking smears of females immediately after observations it was learned that actual inseminations are relatively infrequent. Inseminations occur during definite and recognizable types of contacts (copulations) between the male and female when the latter specifically halts in her swimming. Inseminations were not effected during the commonly observed non-contact and momentary contact thrusts.

"The action and function of the gonopodium were analyzed. During the swinging, thrusting and copulation the gonopodium is brought forward and to one side, together with a forward movement of one of the pelvic fins. The gonopodial hood is necessary for insemination. The presence of large numbers of nerve fibers and the extensive plexus at the tip of the

Junior takes a peek at the outside world through the diaphanous sides of the pregnant female.

A newborn fry giving the last wriggle to get free.

gonopodial hood suggest that it serves primarily in a sensory capacity. The absence of the distal segments of rays 3, 4 and 5 hinders and may completely prevent sperm-transfer to the female.

"It can be seen from this study that the male guppy inseminates the female only during the copulatory act which involves a definite contact between the tip of the male gonopodium and the female genital region. During these copulations the female remains stationary while the male pushes against her with his gonopodium. The contact may be very brief, or may last several seconds. The male's numerous non-contact jabs and contact jabs at a fleeting female, so commonly observed in aquaria of mixed sexes of guppies, are not acts of insemination as reported by many authors."

Further studies by other researchers have shown that there are many other misconceptions about this very popular fish. The question of superfetation is always of interest to the beginning aquarist. It is seemingly impossible that a female can drop several successive broods without the assistance of a male each time. However, there are several folds in the female genital organs in which sperm may be stored; thus after one brood has been born, another can immediately start developing. This is a phenomenon in which the sperm are actually used as needed.

Enlargement of anal fin of a male guppy.

Many different strains of guppies are now on the market. So many dealers and breeders claim to have their own strain that we would need a special volume to record the types to which a claim of "pure strain" has been made. The following color varieties are the most popular ones:

Golden guppy: bright yellow; both male and female show a uniform butter-yellow color.

Golden lacetail: a popular pure strain in which the female is colored plain yellow but the male has a beautiful lacelike pattern in his tail.

Blue guppy: a strain in which most of the colors in the male are blue. The tail is a dark blue and usually 75 to 80 per cent of the young are blue guppies. The female has a greenish cast to her tail.

Red guppy: a strain similar to the blue guppy except that red is the dominant color.

The shape of the tail and that of the dorsal fin are other variations that are in-bred in the guppy. Several different types of tail shapes are reported. All color varieties have specimens with these various fin shapes as follows:

Roundtail guppy: a strain in which the caudal fin is rounded. The dorsal fin may either be short or long.

Swordtail guppy: not a cross with *Xiphophorus,* but merely a variation in which the male guppy has a longer upper or lower lobe to his caudal fin. The guppy with both upper and lower lobes longer is usually referred to as a *lyretail guppy.* Most swordtails and lyretails have long, pointed dorsal fins.

Pintail guppy: a strain in which the males have longer middle rays on their caudal fins. The dorsal fin may or may not be long and pointed. The *speartail guppy* is a pintail which has not quite fully developed.

A mother guppy eating her own baby.

Lacetail gold guppies.

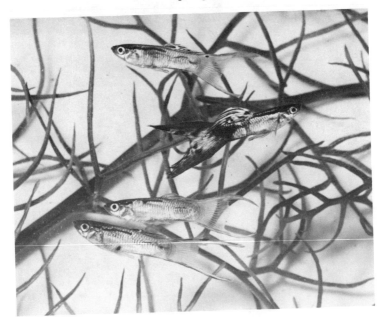

Sternke's lyretail or swordtail guppies.

Hahnel's magnificent veiltail guppies.

Sternke's lyretail guppies.

GENUS *Limia* Poey

[Lye-mi′-a: *limia* = mud]

This genus inhabits the West Indies, living in fresh water. Locally the species are abundant.

DWARF LIMIA / *Limia heterandria* Regan

[het′-er-an′-dri-a: *heter* = different; *andria* = male]

Limia heterandria Regan, Proc. Zool. Soc. London, p. 1017, pl. 101, figs. 3, 4, 1913 (type locality, La Guaira, Venezuela)

RANGE: La Guaira, Venezuela.

SIZE: Female 2 inches, male 1 inch; female breeds at 1½ inches, male at 1 inch.

TEMPERAMENT: A peaceful species suitable in the community aquarium.

TEMPERATURE REQUIREMENTS: 68–84°F.

SEX DIFFERENCES: Male has gonopodium.

COUNTS: Dorsal 8; anal 9; pectoral 13; pelvic 6; scales 26.

A live-bearing fish which is fairly prolific when kept under the best of conditions. It does eat its own fry as fast as it can catch them, so a heavily planted aquarium is necessary.

The wild strains of this fish seem to be a mud color, which is indicative of its habits of poking into the mud after food. The back is nearly a chocolate color and the belly shades from white to sky blue. A very fine stripe runs along the side. There are a few vertical bars on the male just above the caudal peduncle which run perpendicular to this stripe. The female does not show these bars clearly. The male's dorsal fin is flushed with orange. The female has a black ocellus with an orange ring near her vent.

This is about the smallest fish in the genus. There has been some confusion about where this species was first taken. Myers says it came from Santo Domingo but later study by Hubbs indicates that it actually came from La Guaira.

BLACK-BELLIED LIMIA; BLUE LIMIA / *Limia melanogaster* (Günther)

[mel'-an-o-gas'-ter: *melano* = black; *gaster* = belly]

Poecilia melanogaster Günther, Catalogue of the Fishes in the British Museum, 6:345, 1866 (type locality, probably Jamaica)

RANGE: Jamaica.

SIZE: Female 3 inches, male 2 inches; female breeds at 2 inches, male at 1 inch.

TEMPERAMENT: Except for nipping fins, this species is peaceful.

TEMPERATURE REQUIREMENTS: 70–85°F.

SEX DIFFERENCES: Male has gonopodium and orange color in dorsal and caudal fins. Female lacks much color in any fins.

COUNTS: Dorsal 8 to 10; anal 10; pectoral 13; pelvic 6; scales 26.

A live bearer which is capable of eating its own spawn. Several reports caution that such carnivorous habits are to be guarded against, but every fish has some tendency to eat its own spawn or young. It is wise to keep this fish in a heavily planted aquarium where there will not be too much tendency for the fish to swim rapidly all over the aquarium. The heavily planted aquarium seems to suit its personality too; in a bare aquarium the fish is nervous, jumps, and is in poor color, whereas in a planted aquarium the fish is colorful, active, and seems to breed more prolifically.

Colorwise the fish is attractive. The scales are tipped in metallic blue which glimmer in the light. The male shows a bit of orange in the dorsal fin with a small spot at its base. His caudal fin is similarly colored. The eyes of both sexes are golden.

Limia tricolor Stoye is a synonym of this species. *L. caudofasciata* Regan (*Proc. Zool. Soc. London*, p. 1017, pl. 101, fig. 6, 1913, type locality, Jamaica) probably also is a synonym of this species. About the only difference between the two species is the large black abdominal spot on the gravid female of *L. melanogaster*.

The name of this species currently is *Poecilia melanogaster*.

BLACK-BARRED LIMIA / *Limia nigrofasciata* Regan

[ni'-gro-fass'-see-a'-ta: *nigro* = black; *fasciata* = banded or barred]

Limia nigrofasciata Regan, Proc. Zool. Soc. London, p. 1015, pl. 101, figs. 1, 2, 1913 (type locality, Miragoâne, Haiti)

RANGE: Haiti.

SIZE: 2½ inches; breeds at 2 inches.

TEMPERAMENT: A peaceful species suitable in the community aquarium.

TEMPERATURE REQUIREMENTS: 70–85°F.

SEX DIFFERENCES: Male has color and gonopodium.

COUNTS: Dorsal 10; anal 9; pectoral 13; pelvic 6; scales 27 or 28.

This hardy species is a live bearer which eats its own fry. Pairs are best kept in heavily planted aquaria and fed well during that period when the female looks exceptionally heavy.

Colorwise the fish is attractive. The body is barred with about a dozen dark vertical bands on the sides, which extend on the male almost around the body. The bluish hue to the scales is fairly attractive when the species is in good health.

The male develops a hump on his back as he gets older. This hump is characteristic of many species of fishes as they approach their twilight age, but coupled with this humpback is a startling change in the dorsal fin. When the hump is finally fully developed the dorsal fin will have enlarged to nearly three times its original size and will be beautifully colored with a jet black outer margin and a brassy colored base. The female's dorsal fin is colorless.

The name of this species currently is *Poecilia nigrofasciata*.

Ornate Lima / *Limia ornata* Regan

[orr-nay'-ta: *ornata* = decorated]

Limia ornata Regan, Proc. Zool. Soc. London, p. 1016, pl. 101, fig. 7, 1913 (type locality, Haiti)

RANGE: Haiti.

SIZE: Female 2½ inches, male 1½ inches; female breeds at 2 inches, male at 1 inch.

TEMPERAMENT: A species suitable for the community aquarium.

TEMPERATURE REQUIREMENTS: 70–85°F.

SEX DIFFERENCES: Male has a gonopodium.

COUNTS: Dorsal 8 or 9; anal 10; scales 28.

This hardy species is a live bearer. It is not a colorful fish. The male is more colorful than the female, but they are so small that their color cannot be seen at any distance. The body is reminiscent of the marble molly, as this fish shows many irregular dark blotches all over its body and unpaired fins. The sides show some faint dark vertical bands and the lateral line is accentuated with a dim black line running for a short distance along its length. The male shows a beautiful dorsal fin, brilliant with orange or purple.

The name of this species currently is *Poecilia ornata*.

Limia vittata (Guichenot)

[vit-tay'-ta: *vittata* = striped]

Poecilia vittata Guichenot, in Ramon de la Sagra, Historia físcia política y natural de la isla de Cuba, pt. 4, Peces, p. 146, pl. 5, fig. 1, 1853 (type locality, Cuba)

RANGE: Cuba.

SIZE: Female 4 inches, male 2½ inches; female breeds at 2 inches, male at 1½ inches.

TEMPERAMENT: A peaceful species, though large enough to eat small guppies.

TEMPERATURE REQUIREMENTS: 74–85°F.

SEX DIFFERENCES: Male has gonopodium and larger dorsal fin.

COUNTS: Dorsal 9 to 11; anal 10; pectoral 13 or 14; pelvic 6; scales 26 to 28.

This live bearer is capable of eating its spawn. The Shedd Aquarium in Chicago has recorded the greatest number of living young ever delivered by a popular live-bearing fish, 242 youngsters. As large a brood as this may seem, the pair can completely ingest the whole mob in a matter of hours, and they seem to take great pains to get every last one. A very heavily planted aquarium is necessary for their successful breeding, in order to give the young a chance to survive. *Do not attempt to use any kind of breeding tank unless it is over 5 gallons in capacity.*

Though not a colorful species, the large size makes it interesting and a fairly good seller. It is hardy enough when kept at the proper temperature of 74°F. Fins of both sexes show a few splashes of black, and the male may have a few darker bars on his caudal peduncle, but all in all, the fish lacks luster. The dorsal fin of the male is larger than that of the female.

The name of this species currently is *Poecilia vittata.*

Genus *Micropoecilia* Hubbs

[Mi'-krow-pea-sil'-i-a: *micro* = small; *poecilia* = variegated]

Branner's Live Bearer / *Micropoecilia branneri* (Eigenmann)

[bran'-er-eye: named in honor of J. C. Branner]

Poecilia branneri Eigenmann, Ann. New York Acad. Sci., 7:629, 1894 (type locality, Santarém; Pará)

RANGE: Amazon Basin, Santarém, and Pará, Brazil.

SIZE: Female breeds at 1½ inches, male at 1 inch.

TEMPERAMENT: Best kept in an aquarium by itself as it is not too peaceful.

TEMPERATURE REQUIREMENTS: 68–80°F.

SEX DIFFERENCES: Male has gonopodium.

COUNTS: Dorsal 6 or 7; anal 8; pectoral 13; pelvic 6; scales 27 or 28.

This little live bearer may be found very often with a group of other live bearers. It is carnivorous and eats its own young as quickly as it drops them. It is not brightly colored but it does possess interesting color patterns: The dark olive back changes to silver on the sides, then lighter on the belly. There is a series of 7 to 9 dark vertical bars on the sides, less distinct on the female than on the male. There is an ocellus (eyespot) on the caudal peduncle of both sexes; the female shows a beautiful iridescence to her spot, while that of the male is decorated in a maze of concentric colored rings. This observation is only made under the best of lighting conditions. The male also shows a larger dorsal fin than the female.

TWO-SPOT LIVE BEARER / *Micropoecilia parae* (Eigenmann)

[par'-ee: named after the locality where collected]

Poecilia vivipara parae Eigenmann, Ann. New York Acad. Sci., 7:628, 1894 (type locality, "Rua das Mongubas of Pará")

RANGE: Amazon Basin and Guianas.

SIZE: Female 1½ inches, male 1 inch; breeds at slightly smaller sizes.

TEMPERAMENT: A species best kept in an aquarium by itself.

TEMPERATURE REQUIREMENTS: 58–85°F.

SEX DIFFERENCES: Male has color and gonopodium.

COUNTS: Dorsal 6; anal 8 or 9; pectoral 13; pelvic 6; scales 28.

This live bearer is best kept in slightly brackish water (1 teaspoonful of salt to every gallon of water).

The back is olive, becoming lighter on the sides and silvery white on the belly. A bluish sheen is. observed on the male when viewed from reflected light. Two spots are obvious on the male, one on the shoulder and another above the vent. The female lacks the vent spot. When the male is in good color the spot on the caudal peduncle is obvious and pretty. The dorsal fin of the male is colorful, showing red, black and tan markings with intermediate colors. The tail has a mustard color, greener at the base with a darker distal margin.

These fish, if bred, must be kept in heavily planted aquaria and fed on brine shrimp, *Daphnia*, and small worms.

GENUS *Mollienesia* Le Sueur

[Mol'-ly-en-ez'-i-a: named in honor of Mollien]

The familiar contraction of the generic name *Mollienesia* to molly is evidence of the popularity of the species in this genus. Most dealers claim that they sell more mollies than fishes of any other genus.

The reasons for the popularity of mollies are several: They are inexpensive, colorful, active, extremely peaceful, hardy, and do well in unheated aquaria. Although they are easy to induce to spawn, their youngsters are difficult to raise indoors. They make a fine addition to the community aquarium.

Nearly all the species of this genus have color varieties involving albinism and melanism. There are two groups of mollies, the common and the sail-fin. The large dorsal fin of the males indicates that the species falls into the "sail-fin molly" group, either *M. velifera* or *M. latipinna*. It may be necessary actually to count the rays on the dorsal fins to differentiate these species; if the count is near 18 rays it is *M. velifera*, but if it is closer to 14 it is *M. latipinna*. Only the males have the larger dorsal fin. All females may look alike, but interestingly enough, even though the males have huge dorsals in comparison to the females, both sexes have the same number of rays in the dorsal fin. If females have to be sorted, check the position of the dorsal fin. In *M. velifera* and *M. latipinna* the dorsal fin starts in front of the beginning of the anal fin, whereas in the common mollies, *M. sphenops* and *M. latipunctata*, it starts behind the anal fin. Other than this, ray counts must be taken.

Feeding the molly is important. While most fishes are carnivorous, the molly is mainly herbivorous. That is, in everyday language, the molly is mainly a vegetarian. True enough, mollies will greedily take worms, *Daphnia*, and other animal matter, but they will not last long when kept on this type of diet. Farms in Florida, where mollies are raised by the millions every year, feed their fishes strictly on a mash made up of Pablum and spinach, boiled together and blended in a Waring blendor. They do best when kept on this diet. A special molly food is on the market which contains these ingredients in a dry form.

The molly is found in nature all along the coastal waters of eastern America from South Carolina to Venezuela. It has been found far out in the ocean and inland in brackish and fresh water.

Mollies must be kept in a salt-water environment. If a teaspoon of Epsom salts per gallon of water, plus a drop of 5 per cent solution of Methylene Blue, is added to each gallon of aquarium water, the fishes will fare much better. They seem to prefer the lower 70's as far as temperature is concerned.

These fishes are prone to catch the ich, fungus, and shimmies. A very strong salt bath is recommended for their treatment. As much as 8 teaspoonfuls of salt per gallon of water, with heavy aeration and a slight rise in temperature, will be very helpful in treating them for specific diseases. Aureomycin seems to be helpful also. Two 250-mg tablets per 15 gallons of water seems to rid them of the symptoms of slime bacterial infection, which looks like a body fungus.

A salt-water environment will, without doubt, prevent most of these illnesses. For this reason it is advised that mollies be kept only with live-bearing fishes, as most of them can take the high salinity required to keep the mollies in the best of health.

SOUTH AMERICAN MOLLY / *Mollienesia caucana* (Steindachner)

[cow-can'-a: named after the Rio Cauca]

Girardinus caucanus Steindachner, Denks. Akad. Wiss. Wien, 42:87, pl. 6, figs. 4, 5, 1880 (type locality, Rio Cauca)

RANGE: Rio Cauca, lower Magdalena, of Colombia and Maracaibo Basin of Venezuela.

SIZE: Female 1½ inch, male 1 inch; breeds at slightly smaller sizes.

TEMPERAMENT: A species suitable in the community tank with fishes of the same small size.

TEMPERATURE REQUIREMENTS: 70–82°F.

SEX DIFFERENCES: Male is smaller and has a gonopodium.

COUNTS: Dorsal 8; anal 9; pectoral 12; pelvic 6; scales 26 or 27.

This live bearer is capable of eating its own fry. Owing to its very small size it is best to place it in a small aquarium, pre-ferably without other fishes. A tankful of these small fellows mounted in or on a wall with top lighting and a magnifying glass in front makes a beautiful display.

The coloration is reddish purple with brilliant blue gill covers. The dorsal and caudal fins are reddish brown edged with black; other fins are nearly translucent. Although the color pattern is attractive, the species is not commonly seen in home aquaria. It is abundant in its native habitat.

The name of this species currently is *Poecilia caucana*.

SAIL-FIN MOLLY / *Mollienesia latipinna* Le Sueur

[lat'-i-pinn'-a: *lati* = broad; *pinna* = fin]

Mollienesia latipinna Le Sueur, Jour. Acad. Nat. Sci. Philadelphia, 2:3, 1821 (type locality, New Orleans)

RANGE: South Carolina to Mexico in lowland streams.

SIZE: 4 inches; breeds at 2 inches.

TEMPERAMENT: A peaceful species suitable in the community aquarium.

TEMPERATURE REQUIREMENTS: 50–85°F. Optimum about 70°F.

SEX DIFFERENCES: Male has gonopodium and larger dorsal fin.

COUNTS: Dorsal 13 or 14; anal 9 or 10; pectoral 13; pelvic 6; scales 26 to 28.

This live bearer is familiar to every hobbyist, from beginner to advanced; however, many persons find this popular fish difficult to maintain. This species along with other mollies requires plenty of room, plenty of greens in its diet, and some salt added to the water. About a teaspoonful of Epsom salts and 2 teaspoonfuls of table salt per gallon of water seem to suit it perfectly. A few drops of

Methylene Blue, just enough to tint the water faintly, is advised also.

Mollienesia latipinna is the green sail-fin molly. The back is olive colored and the silvery sides are adorned with from 6 to 8 rows of black dots. The belly is whitish. The male has an extremely large dorsal fin, which may run the entire body length and up to 1½ inches in height. The female has a smaller dorsal, which has the same number of rays. In length the female may be somewhat larger than the male;

The name of this species currently is *Poecilia latipinna*.

Some black varieties have been found in nature. One of the successful aquarists, G. Schaumburg of Louisiana, has been able to inbreed the melanistic specimens into a pure black variety and finally into what we now know as the black sail-fin molly. This molly, further decorated with a beautiful orange edge to the dorsal fin, is also known as the orange dorsal sail-fin molly. Requirements for breeding this variety are the same as for the green sail-fin: lots of room, salt, greens, and some Methylene Blue.

Carl L. Hubbs, ichthyologist, has observed that the form often called *M. formosa* does not represent a distinct species but instead represents intergrades between *M. latipinna* and *M. sphenops*. Hybrid females that mate with males of either of the two parent species produce their own images. Thus is born a race of females, males of which are unable to exist.

This is a cross between the green sail-fin and the black sail-fin. The light areas on the dorsal and caudal fins of the male sometimes are bright orange, while at other times they are clear. These fish are sometimes called marble or sail-fin marble mollies.

This is a picture of the same fish as the sail-fin, but these specimens are tank raised.

THE MOLLY / *Mollienesia sphenops* (Cuvier and Valenciennes)

[svee'-nops: *sphen* = wedge; *ops* = appearance]

Poecilia sphenops Cuvier and Valenciennes, Histoire naturelle des poissons, 18:98, 525, 1836 (type locality, Vera Cruz, Mexico)

RANGE: Mexico and Central America and northern South America.

SIZE: 4 inches; breeds at 1½ inches.

TEMPERAMENT: A peaceful species suitable in the community aquarium.

TEMPERATURE REQUIREMENTS: 50–80°F.

SEX DIFFERENCES: Male has gonopodium and a larger dorsal fin.

COUNTS: Dorsal 8 to 11; anal 8 to 10; pectoral 14; pelvic 6; scales 25 to 30.

This species is found in salt, brackish, and fresh water. No significant difference other than size appears in specimens taken from any of the environments. It seems that the more salty the water, the larger it will grow. All kinds of color variations are found in this fish. The "wild" variety is a light gray green with a bluish cast. Small dark spots are unevenly spread all over the sides, and the belly may run from a gray white to a silver blue. Males show a faint series of vertical bars on their sides,

and extremes of colors in their caudal fins. Females are more uniformly colored and are usually plain; they get to be an inch longer than the males. Black varieties are not uncommon, and the short-dorsaled mollies commonly sold as inexpensive black mollies are usually this species. The popular liberty molly, once an aquarium favorite, is no longer being produced in great numbers. It is recognized by the brilliant reddish coloring in the dorsal and tail fins of the male, and the red blush of color in the corresponding fins of the female. Otherwise the fish is plain silvery blue.

The orange-tail molly, more commonly called *sphenops*, is another color variety of this species. It is recognized by the orange band in the caudal fin of the male. Body color has nothing to do with tail color and we find that either the plain silver-blue body or the mottled black and white body may be decorated with the beautiful orange tail. These are common, inexpensive mollies.

All varieties freely interbreed, but they are difficult to rear in small aquaria.

The name of this species currently is *Poecilia sphenops*.

SAIL-FIN MOLLY / *Mollienesia velifera* Regan

[ve-lif'-er-a: *velifera* = sail-bearing]

Mollienesia velifera Regan, Ann. Mag. Nat. Hist., (8)13:338, 1914 (type locality, Progreso, Yucatan)

RANGE: Yucatan.

SIZE: 5 inches; breeds at 2½ inches.

TEMPERAMENT: A peaceful species suitable in the community aquarium.

TEMPERATURE REQUIREMENTS: 50–80°F. Best kept at 70°F.

SEX DIFFERENCES: Male has gonopodium and larger dorsal fin; female may be black spotted.

COUNTS: Dorsal 18; anal 9; pectoral 14; pelvic 6; scales 26 to 28.

This is one of the rarer mollies, the reason being that there is little difference between this fish and *Mollienesia latipinna*. Since this species is from Yucatan and *M. latipinna* is from Florida, we usually obtain only the latter species.

The only easily apparent difference is that *M. velifera* has about 18 rays in the dorsal fin while *M. latipinna* has only 13 or 14.

All that has been said about the other mollies is applicable to this species. Broods of *velifera* run as high as 116 sometimes, though little luck is experienced with tank-raised broods. It seems that cramping these large fish into a small aquarium (and a dozen fish in a long 20-gallon aquarium is considered as cramping) causes them to lose their great size. The largest that we have been able to raise are a mere 3 inches, without the proud sailfins of their imported parents.

This molly has a great ability to jump and must be kept in a covered aquarium.

A cross between the black variety of *M. velifera* and the black variety of *M. latipinna* results in what the trade calls the "perma-black molly."

The name of this species currently is *Poecilia velifera*.

Genus *Phallichthys* Hubbs

[Fall-ick'-thees: *phalli* = penis; *ichthys* = fish]

Merry Widow / *Phallichthys amates* (Miller)

[a-ma'-tease: named after the locality where collected]

Poecilia amates Miller, Bull. Amer. Mus. Nat. Hist., 23:108, fig. 1, 1907 (type locality, Los Amates and affluent of the Motagua River, Guatemala)

RANGE: Motagua Basin, Atlantic drainage, Guatemala.

SIZE: Female 2 inches, male 1 inch; female breeds at 1½ inches.

TEMPERAMENT: A peaceful species suitable in the community aquarium.

TEMPERATURE REQUIREMENTS: 70–86°F.

SEX DIFFERENCES: Male has gonopodium.

COUNTS: Dorsal 13; anal 9 or 10; pectoral 13; pelvic 6; scales 26 to 28.

This live bearer is inclined to eat its own young. Breeding is best accomplished in large aquaria which are very heavily planted. It is necessary for the aquarium to be stocked rather heavily with artificial spawning grass.

This little fish is attractive, with its small crescent-shaped mark running vertically through the eye. Males have about a dozen or so vertical bars running down the sides. The gill cover and adjacent head areas show a brilliant blue green which is so characteristic of many cichlids. The name "merry widow" was given by Stoye, who noticed the dark margin on the dorsal fin. This looked much like a sign of mourning, quite in contrast to the activity of the fish.

Feeding is no problem as this fish eats almost anything offered.

ORANGE-DORSAL LIVE BEARERS / *Phallichthys pittieri* (Meek)

[pete'-tea-er'-eye: named in honor of P. N. Pittier]

Poecilia pittieri Meek, Pub. Field Mus. Zool. Ser., 10:71, 1912 (type locality, La Junta, Costa Rica)

RANGE: Costa Rica to Panama.

SIZE: Female 2½ inches, male 1½ inches; female breeds at 2 inches, male at 1 inch.

TEMPERAMENT: A peaceful species, suitable in the community tank.

TEMPERATURE REQUIREMENTS: 70–84°F.

SEX DIFFERENCES: Male has gonopodium.

COUNTS: Dorsal 9 or 10; anal 10; pectoral 11; pelvic 6; scales 26 to 28.

This is another fertile, easy-to-breed live bearer, ideal for the community aquarium. The fish is attractive but has not become popular, possibly because there has been so much demand for other live bearers that commercial breeders have not started breeding this species.

A crescent-shaped dark mark runs through the eye. The body glistens in all colors of the rainbow when light is reflected at a proper angle. The dorsal fin, slightly larger in the male than in the female, shows an orange margin, emphasized further by a black line underlying the orange margin. The gonopodium is extremely long, running about one-third the entire body length.

Feeding is simple as it eats almost anything. It has a better color when fed live foods intermittently, although it requires some green vegetation in the diet.

Phallichthys isthmensis (Regan), otherwise known as *Poeciliopsis isthmensis* Regan, is a synonym of this species.

GENUS *Phalloceros* Eigenmann

[Fal'-lo-ser'-os: *phallo* = penis; *ceros* = horned]

Phalloceros caudomaculatus reticulatus.

THE CAUDO / *Phalloceros caudomaculatus* (Hensel)

[cow'-do-mack'-you-lay'-tus: *caudo* = tail; *maculatus* = spotted]

Girardinus caudomaculatus Hensel, Arch. Naturges., 34:362, 1868; 35:89, 1869 (type locality, Costa da Serra, southern Brazil)

RANGE: Southeastern Brazil to Paraguay.

SIZE: Female 2¼ inches, male 1¼ inches; female breeds at 2 inches, male at 1 inch.

TEMPERAMENT: A peaceful species suitable in the community aquarium.

TEMPERATURE REQUIREMENTS: 65–80°F.

SEX DIFFERENCES: Male shows typical gonopodium.

COUNTS: Dorsal 7 or 8; anal 9 or 10; pectoral 10; pelvic 5; scales 28 to 30.

The spawns of this live bearer are fairly large for so small a fish and may run as high as 50 fry. The over-all color is a light olive green with a silvery belly. At the beginning of the caudal peduncle is a large black spot, which at times is ringed in gold. During breeding time when the males are in tiptop condition they may even show some dark bars after this spot, on the caudal peduncle. These bars are never very obvious.

A popular variety, shown above and described as *Girardinus januarius reticulatus* Köhler in 1906, has taken the limelight from its plainer sister fish. This variety looks much like a spotted molly. There are irregular black blotches strewn all over the body and fins in both sexes. The Germans produce them in large quantities. A golden variety, known as golden leopardfish, has also been reported, but this variation has become scarce.

GENUS *Phalloptychus* Eigenmann

[Fal-lop'-tie-chus: *phallo* = penis; *ptychus* = with folds]

BARRED MILLIONSFISH / *Phalloptychus januarius* (Hensel)

[jan'-you-a'-ri-us: named after the river in which collected]

Girardinus januarius Hensel, Arch. Naturges., 34:360, 1868 (type locality, southeast Brazil, Rio de Janeiro)

RANGE: Southeast Brazil; La Plata.

SIZE: Female 2 inches, male 1¼ inches; female breeds at 1½ inches, male at 1 inch.

TEMPERAMENT: A peaceful species suitable in the community tank.

TEMPERATURE REQUIREMENTS: 72–80°F.

SEX DIFFERENCES: The male has a very large gonopodium.

COUNTS: Dorsal 9; anal 9; pectoral 10 or 11; pelvic 5; scales 28.

This live bearer is rather rare. Although easy to induce to spawn, the young are very small and are nearly impossible to keep alive. Spawns are delivered for weeks at a time, with a few youngsters being spawned every day. Parents are inclined to eat their fry.

This fish has the typical killifish coloring of an olive green on the back. The silvery sides are decorated with about a dozen vertical bars that run the full height of the body. The fins are nearly colorless.

[Pea-cil'-i-a: *poecilia* = many-colored, variegated]

ONE-SPOT LIVE BEARER / *Poecilia vivipara* Bloch and Schneider

[vi-vip'-a-ra: *vivipara* = giving birth to living young]

Poecilia vivipara Bloch and Schneider, Systema ichthyologiae, p. 452, pl. 86, fig. 2, 1801 (type locality, Surinam)

RANGE: Venezuela to the La Plata system; Leeward Islands, Puerto Rico.

SIZE: Female 3 inches, male 1½ inches; female breeds at 2 inches, male at 1 inch.

TEMPERAMENT: A peaceful species suitable in the community aquarium.

TEMPERATURE REQUIREMENTS: 68–82°F.

SEX DIFFERENCES: Male has the gonopodium.

COUNTS: Dorsal 8 to 10; anal 7 to 9; pectoral 13 or 14; pelvic 6; scales 25 to 27.

This female live bearer may drop large broods of about 100 to 150 young at a time, but the usual number is closer to 75.

The fry are small and require infusoria a few hours after birth. They get along well on brine shrimp and microworms for the next few days; after 10 days they will eagerly accept the standard diet for small fishes.

The silver belly stands out in contrast to the olive-gray sides and deeper olive back. The dorsal fin is beautifully shaded in orange with a dark band near its base. Tank-raised specimens, selectively bred, have deeper orange coloring in their dorsal fins and the males show a beautiful flush of gold about the head and chest. Females usually have clear fins. There is a prominent dark spot high on the side. Local varieties show different color variations, but no work has been done on breaking these down into distinct varieties.

FAMILY POECILIIDAE: Live-bearing Toothed Carps

GENUS *Poecilistes* Hubbs

[Pea-cil-is'-tees: *Poecilistes* = a modification of the name *Poecilia*]

PORTHOLEFISH / *Poecilistes pleurospilus* (Günther)

[plur'-o-spy'-lus: *pleuro* = side; *spilus* = spots]

Girardinus pleurospilus Günther, Catalogue of the fishes in the British Museum, 6:353, 1866 (type locality, Lake Dueñas, Guatemala)

RANGE: Guatemala and southeastern Mexico.

SIZE: Female 2½ inches, male 1½ inches; female breeds at 2 inches, male at 1 inch.

TEMPERAMENT: A peaceful species suitable in the community tank.

TEMPERATURE REQUIREMENTS: 72–85°F.

SEX DIFFERENCES: Male has gonopodium.

COUNTS: Dorsal 8; anal 10; pectoral 12 to 14; pelvic 6; scales 28.

This live bearer is easily bred and raised. The parents might, if hungry, go after some of the fry but this is not an ordinary occurrence.

The adult fish is attractive with a trim appearance. The sides are neatly punctuated with evenly spaced dots, about 8 in all, along the lateral line. The chest of both sexes is a glistening silver. The male, much smaller than the female, does not have as distinct coloring.

Feeding is no problem, as the portholefish will take any type of food which is easily swallowed.

The name of this species currently is *Poeciliopsis gracilis*.

GENUS *Pseudoxiphophorus* Bleeker

[Sue'-doe-ziff'-o-for'-us: *pseudo* = false; *xiphophorus* = bearing a sword]

Pseudoxiphophorus bimaculatus (Heckel)

[bi-mack'-you-lay'-tus: *bi* = two; *maculatus* = spotted]

Xiphophorus bimaculatus Heckel, Sitzb. Akad. Wiss. Wien, 1(3):169, pl. 6, figs. 1, 2, 1848 (type locality, Mexico)

RANGE: Mexico, Guatemala, Honduras.

SIZE: Female 4 inches, male 1½ inches; female breeds at 3 inches, male at 1 inch.

TEMPERAMENT: An actively predaceous species not suitable for the community tank with small fishes.

TEMPERATURE REQUIREMENTS: 70–87°F.

SEX DIFFERENCES: Male has gonopodium.

COUNTS: Dorsal 13 to 17; anal 9 to 11; pectoral 15; pelvic 6; scales 30 to 32.

This species has been used extensively to illustrate to students and beginning aquarists how to differentiate between live bearers and egg layers, and to illustrate the structure of the gonopodium. The name *Pseudoxiphophorus* refers to the false swordlike gonopodium of the male.

It is not unusual for a female to repel the ever-amorous advances of the male by killing him with a vicious lunge. She seems perpetually to go after the male and to scorn his small size. The male is, however, quite nasty himself outside the family, and he is not to be trusted with fishes of any size. This fish is vicious and requires live food. It takes only small bits of dried foods, preferring live foods almost to the point of semistarvation. Smaller fishes are very suitable for them, but worms, *Daphnia*, and water bugs are greedily taken.

The fry are in constant danger from their parents and a breeding trap of sorts must be devised for successful culture.

This is a colorful fish with reticulated body scales and two large spots, one on the caudal peduncle and the other in back of the gill cover.

The name of this species currently is *Heterandria bimaculata*.

GENUS *Quintana* Hubbs

[Kwin-tan'-a: *quintana* = pertaining to the fifth anal ray]

BLACK-BARRED LIVE BEARER / *Quintana atrizona* Hubbs

[at'-ri-zone'-a: *atri* = black; *zona* = a band or belt]

Quintana atrizona Hubbs. Occas. Pap. Mus. Zool. U. Michigan, no. 301, p. 34, pl. 1, 1934 (type locality, Baracoa, near Havana, Cuba)

RANGE: Cuba and Isle of Pines.

SIZE: Female 2 inches, male 1 inch; breed at slightly smaller sizes.

TEMPERAMENT: A peaceful species suitable in the community aquarium.

TEMPERATURE REQUIREMENTS: 65–85°F. Optimum 74°F.

SEX DIFFERENCES: Male possesses long gonopodium.

COUNTS: Dorsal 8 or 9; anal 10; pectoral 8 or 9; pelvic 7; scales 27 to 29.

This live bearer may eat its spawn unless it has been heavily fed. The usual number of fry is about 15, which are delivered about every 2 months. The newborn are fairly large-sized and immediately look for bits of food on the bottom of the aquarium. Feeding is no problem as long as the foods are small enough to be ingested whole. Live as well as dried foods are welcome.

The body of this fish is translucent, and with a good back light they are extremely attractive. In reflected light they are silvery with a dark back. A variable number of bars divides the body into "zones" (thus the name *atrizona*) and the fins show slight bluish hues. The eye is pretty, having a black pupil trimmed with gold. The males are only half the size of females. The males are also fewer in number per brood but there is every reason to believe that the smaller fry are males and thus are easier prey for the parents.

Claims have been made that this species has successfully been crossed with the platy, *Xiphophorus maculatus* (page 510). An English author, Jack Hems, crossed this fish with the red platy and got a beautiful strain, which was lost during World War II. The young were fertile and he was able to breed the hybrids.

GENUS *Xiphophorus* Heckel

[Ziff'-o-for'-us: *xiphophorus* = bearing a sword, but refers to the gonopodium and not the caudal fin]

The genus *Platypoecilus* has been referred to the genus *Xiphophorus* as a synonym according to Myron Gordon and Donn Eric Rosen.

This popular genus contains the platies and swordtails. It is the most familiar group of fishes known to aquarists, and xiphophorine fishes occur endemically from Mexico through Guatemala.

Myron Gordon has specialized in this group in connection with cancer studies and has been able through specialized knowledge of genetics to breed several new varieties of platies. No doubt others will appear as more selection and breeding occur.

As a genus, all *Xiphophorus* have the same breeding habits. It is believed that actual contact is necessary for the male to effect a sperm transfer with the female. Internal fertilization results in superfetation, the phenomenon whereby a single contact with a male fish enables the female fish to deliver several broods of young. All members of the genus are live bearers and are easily propagated. Most platies drop their fry early in the morning. It is easy to remove the parents from the breeding tank at the proper time by watching them in the early daylight hours.

Contrary to popular belief, these fishes do not need a high temperature; a mean temperature of 74°F is enough. All the species of the genus *Xiphophorus* are capable of interbreeding.

SWORDTAIL / *Xiphophorus helleri* Heckel

[hell'-er-eye: named in honor of Carl Heller]

Xiphophorus helleri Heckel, Sitzb. Akad. Wiss. Wien, 1(3): 163, pl. 5, 1848 (type locality, Rio Chixoy, Guatemala)

RANGE: Atlantic slope of southern Mexico to Guatemala.

SIZE: 5 inches; breed at 2 inches.

TEMPERAMENT: A peaceful species desirable in the community aquarium.

TEMPERATURE REQUIREMENTS: 68–80°F.

SEX DIFFERENCES: Male has gonopodium and swordlike extension of caudal fin.

COUNTS: Dorsal 11 to 14; anal 8 to 10; pectoral 12 or 13; pelvic 6; scales 26 to 30.

This live bearer has received much recognition as one of the most popular swordtails. Wild specimens are large but the tank- and pool-bred specimens are smaller. The male has the characteristic tail spike which makes it easily recognizable as the swordtail. Interestingly enough, the fish was not named for its tail fin but for the swordlike appearance of the anal fin, which on the male is modified into a gonopodium. Parents are best removed from their offspring as soon after birth as possible.

There are several color variations of this fish, as follows:

Green swordtail: a green variety with a flash of red and yellow on the sides along the lateral line. The male has a swordlike extension on his caudal fin which may or may not be colored red and may or may not have black margins. The male also shows some color in his dorsal and caudal fins. The female lacks the caudal extension and color in the fins.

Green wagtail swordtail: a cross of the green swordtail with the wagtail platy. There is also a *green tuxedo wagtail swordtail,* which is a cross between the wagtail tuxedo platy and the green swordtail.

Red swordtail: a cross between the green swordtail and the red platy. There are, as in the platy, different shades of red. The trade calls the varieties bloodred, brick-red, and velvet-red. There are also varieties known as *red wagtail swordtails* and *red tuxedo wagtail swordtails.*

Variegated swordtail: a mixed swordtail with all types of color combinations and no fixed pattern of color.

Most of these crosses are between *Xiphophorus maculatus* and *X. helleri.*

A pair of green swordtails.

A pair of albino swordtails.

The green wagtail swordtail, a cross between the swordtail and the platy. Usually the growth of the "swordtail" on the male is stunted, and sometimes the caudal of the male is without the extended ray.

The red swordtail. (*After Innes*)

Red tuxedo swordtail.

Red wagtail swordtail.

Hybrid swordtail (swordtail × platy). No two fish are alike, but they are spattered with black, red, yellow, and green blotches. They are sometimes called "salt-and-pepper" platies if they don't have swordtails; if they have swords, they are called "hybrid swordtails." See salt-and-pepper platy.

Red moon platy, female above.

PLATY / *Xiphophorus maculatus* (Günther)

[mack′-you-lay′-tus: *maculatus* = spotted]

Platypoecilus maculatus Günther, Catalogue of the fishes in the British Museum, 6:350, 1866 (type locality, Mexico)

RANGE: Mexico to Guatemala.

SIZE: Female 3 inches, male 1½ inches; female breeds at 1½ inches, male at 1 inch.

TEMPERAMENT: An extremely desirable and peaceful community fish.

TEMPERATURE REQUIREMENTS: 70–80°F.

SEX DIFFERENCES: Male has gonopodium.

COUNTS: Dorsal 10; anal 8 or 9; pectoral 10 or 11; pelvic 6; scales 25 to 27.

This live bearer eats its own young unless heavily fed and kept in a large aquarium. The diet should contain some vegetation, chopped spinach, lettuce, or *Nitella*. It takes other foods too.

All platies do better with a bit of salt added to their water. About 1 teaspoonful per 2 gallons of water is sufficient. Since they have a high tolerance of salt, there is slight danger of harming them with a little too much salt.

Numerous color variations have been developed from the original stock of the wild fish. They are:

Red platy.

Red tuxedo platy.

Red platy: two subvarieties of the red are common. A deep, scarlet blood red, which is probably sex-linked as the males are the more usual possessors of this desirable color. A brick red is the common variety and is not nearly so scarlet as the blood-red platy. The *red moon* is a red platy with the characteristic "moon" of black on the caudal peduncle.

Red wagtail platy: a red platy (of either color red) with the caudal and dorsal fins delicately colored black. This is an extremely popular color variation.

Black platy: a name applied to several varieties. There is a green-colored platy with a black tuxedo, that is, the sides, from below the lateral line and from gill cover to tail, are black. This is called a black platy or *black* or *green tuxedo platy.* There is also a black platy which is plain black except the head.

Black wagtail platy: a black platy with a black wagtail.

Golden platy: a gold-colored platy without any pigmentation other than the bright yellow color. The *gold crescent* or *gold moon* is the gold platy with the familiar crescent of black on the caudal peduncle.

Golden wagtail platy: the gold platy crossed with the wagtail.

Blue platy or *blue moon:* a light-colored blue platy, closely associated with the green platy; either may be sold as the other.

Salt-and-pepper platy: a mixed-color platy with a little bit of every other kind of platy in it. Once they are mixed they seem to keep breeding true.

Mixed platy: a platy with no color that fits into any particular pattern. It is usually a throwback.

Mixed wagtail platy: merely a mixed platy crossed with a wagtail.

Red wagtail platies.

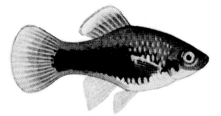

Green tuxedo platy. (*After Innes*)

Black wagtail platy, female.

Golden platy. (*After Innes*)

Gold wagtail platies.

A school of gold wagtail platies.

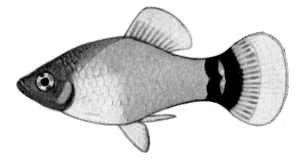

A blue moon or platy.

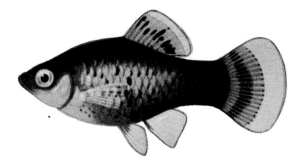

Salt-and-pepper platy.

MONTEZUMA SWORDTAIL / *Xiphophorus montezumae* Jordan and Snyder

[mon'-ta-zu'-mee: named in honor of an Aztec emperor of Mexico, Montezuma]

Xiphophorus montezumae Jordan and Snyder, Bull. U.S. Fish. Comm. 1899, 19:131, fig. 11, 1900 (type locality, Rio Panuco, Mexico)

RANGE: Rio Panuco, Mexico.

SIZE: Female 2½ inches, male 2 inches; breeds at 1½ inches.

TEMPERAMENT: A peaceful species suitable in the community tank.

TEMPERATURE REQUIREMENTS: 70–82°F.

SEX DIFFERENCES: Male has gonopodium.

COUNTS: Dorsal 11 to 13; anal 6 to 8; pectoral 12; pelvic 6; scales 27 to 29.

This drab little creature is a close relative of the very colorful swordtails herein described. Some hybridization between this species and *Xiphophorus variatus* has produced interesting strains that are colorful and fascinating.

Not many *X. montezumae* are seen now because it is a drab, olive-green color with dark reticulated scales; there is a series of dots and dashes on the otherwise clear dorsal fin. Other fins are clear and without markings. The male has the swordlike extension on his caudal fin, but this is much shorter than on other familiar swordtails.

Feeding this fish is quite easy, although it is shy in small aquaria.

VARIEGATED PLATY / *Xiphophorus variatus* (Meek)

[va′-re-a′-tus: *variatus* = variegated]

Platypoecilus variatus Meek, Field Columbian Mus. Zool., 5:146, pl. 10, 1904 (type locality, San Luis Potosí, Mexico)

RANGE: Rio Panuco to Rio Cazones, Mexico.

SIZE: 3 inches; breeds at 1½ inches.

TEMPERAMENT: A species suitable for the community aquarium.

TEMPERATURE REQUIREMENTS: 68–80°F.

SEX DIFFERENCES: Male has more color and a gonopodium.

COUNTS: Dorsal 10 to 11; anal 8 or 9; pectoral 12; pelvic 6; scales 25.

This live bearer is easy to propagate. It is one of the most colorful of live-bearing fishes. Several color varieties have been developed, which are:

Redtail variatus: a typical *variatus* except that the tail of the male fish is mostly red. The female lacks bright colors.

Yellowtail variatus: more easily bred than the redtail; a color variation with a yellow caudal fin in the male. The female is plain in color and it is impossible to distinguish her from the females of any other *variatus.*

Sunset variatus: merely a colorful variation in which the tail of the male has more than a single color, with yellow predominant. The female is plain in color.

Rainbow variatus: a strain in which there is no predominant color in the tail of the male fish but a variable mixture of different colors. This is more nearly like the wild *variatus.*

Feeding the *variatus* is no problem as it eats everything. It does better with a little salt in the water.

[Gas'-tare-o-ste'-i-dee]

GENUS *Apeltes* De Kay

[A-pel'-tes: *a* = without; *peltes* = a small shield]

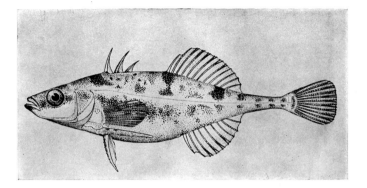

FOUR-SPINED STICKLEBACK / *Apeltes quadracus* (Mitchill)

[quad'-ray-cus: *quadra* = four; *acus* = spined]

Gasterosteus quadracus Mitchill, Trans. Lit. Phil. Soc., 1:430, 1815 (type locality, New York)

RANGE: Labrador to Virginia in brackish or salt water.

SIZE: 2 inches; breeds at 2 inches.

TEMPERAMENT: A predaceous species best kept in a tank by itself.

TEMPERATURE REQUIREMENTS: 50–70°F.

SEX DIFFERENCES: The male shows red pelvic fins during the spring breeding time.

COUNTS: Dorsal III-I,11 or 12; anal I,8 or 9; pectoral 10 or 11; pelvics I,1.

This is a fairly common species around the New York area where it is frequently seen in the spring when the males are in full color. It is a brackish-water fish that goes into the ocean when the brackish environment freezes up. It spawns in brackish water.

The male builds the nest, using bits of plant matter that are available. He secretes a waterproof glue to fasten his "vegetable bricks" together. There is a tunnel through the nest. After the female has laid her eggs within the nest, the male may be seen fanning and blowing water through the tunnel to circulate water about the eggs. It is not infrequent that a male will mate with several females in the same nest. He is to be trusted with the fry until they are free-swimming, but the female should be removed to save her from attack by the male after spawning.

This fish requires live foods, as does its close relatives. Brine shrimp seems to be the preference but it eats *Daphnia* whenever offered.

GENUS *Eucalia* Jordan

[You-kay'-li-a: *eu* = good; *calia* = nest]

BROOK STICKLEBACK / *Eucalia inconstans* (Kirtland)

[in-con'-stans: *inconstans* = variable]

Gasterosteus inconstans Kirtland, Boston Jour. Nat. Hist., 3:273, 1841 (type locality, brooks of Trumbull County, Ohio)

RANGE: Great Lakes region from New York to Kansas, central Ohio, Indiana, and Illinois; northward to the Saskatchewan Basin.

SIZE: 2½ inches; breeds at 2 inches.

TEMPERAMENT: A predaceous species best kept in a tank by itself.

TEMPERATURE REQUIREMENTS: 60–70°F.

SEX DIFFERENCES: The male has red pelvic fins during the spring breeding season.

COUNTS: Dorsal IV-I,9 or 10; anal I,10; pectoral 9 or 10; pelvic I,1.

The contrasting blackish and red pelvic fins make this a beautiful species, and a high-priced fish in some areas. Females are olivaceous, mottled and dotted. This fish prefers small streams and brooks. It likes bottoms with plenty of sticks and vegetation and requires the same care and feeding as *Apeltes*. The nest is similar to those of other sticklebacks, and the male guards the nest with eggs or young.

The name of this species currently is *Culaea inconstans*.

Genus *Gasterosteus* Linnaeus

[Gas'-tare-os'-tee-us: *gaster* = belly; *osteus* = bony]

Three-spined Stickleback / *Gasterosteus aculeatus* Linnaeus

[a-que'-lee-a'-tus: *aculeatus* = sharp-pointed]

Gasterosteus aculeatus Linnaeus, Systema naturae, ed. 10, p. 489, 1758 (type locality, Europe)

RANGE: Temperate Zone of Northern Hemisphere along coastal areas in fresh, brackish, and salt waters.

SIZE: 4 inches; breeds at 2 inches.

TEMPERAMENT: This predaceous little species should be kept in a tank by itself.

TEMPERATURE REQUIREMENTS: This is not a tropical fish; do not use a heater in the aquarium. 45–70°; optimum 60°F.

SEX DIFFERENCES: Male is brightly colored during breeding time.

COUNTS: Dorsal III-I,10 to 12; anal I,8 or 9; pectoral 10; pelvic I,1 or 2.

This species is an extremely beautiful one during the breeding season. Every ichthyologist living around coastal areas is familiar with it, for it can be found in many of the brackish-water regions and in tiny ponds and creeks.

Breeding habits are interesting as this is one of the few fishes that actually constructs a birdlike nest. The male will dig out a slight depression in the sand. Once the hole is of the proper size he will begin to fill it with bits of vegetation and bury or partly bury them in the sand so that they do not float to the surface. Then as the complex nest takes shape he will make a burrow or tunnel through the entire structure, which by now may be 2 inches around. While this is happening the female just looks on. By and by when the house is finished the male seeks the female and courts her, finally driving her into his tunnel. She deposits her eggs and he fertilizes them. He may drive her into the nest several times before the house is filled with eggs. When she has laid all her eggs the female moves away from the nest and then the male takes a position near the opening of the tunnel and carefully blows and fans water through it, thus keeping the eggs supplied with oxygen and fresh water.

Unless the tank is very large the female should be removed, because if she is in sight of the male he may attack and kill her. The male will remain on guard and tend eggs and fry until the baby fish are free-swimming. He may be left with them for some time, except that he will eat most of the freshly hatched brine shrimp which are needed to rear the fry.

A tablespoon of salt is needed for each gallon of water for this species.

FAMILY GASTEROSTEIDAE: Sticklebacks

GENUS *Pungitius* Costa

[Pun-gee'-ti-us: *pungitius* = sharp-pointed]

NINE-SPINED STICKLEBACK / *Pungitius pungitius* (Linnaeus)

Gasterosteus pungitius Linnaeus, Systema naturae, ed. 10, p. 296, 1758 (type locality, Europe)

RANGE: Northern Europe, northern United States, and southern Canada.

SIZE: 2½ inches; breeds at 2 inches.

TEMPERAMENT: This predaceous species is best kept in a tank by itself.

TEMPERATURE REQUIREMENTS: 50–70°F.

SEX DIFFERENCES: Male shows bright red on pelvic areas during breeding time.

COUNTS: Dorsal VIII or IX-I, 9 to 11; anal I,8 or 9; pectoral 10; pelvic I,1.

This stickleback breeds similarly to the three-spined stickleback, *Gasterosteus aculeatus*. It is included here because it is sometimes confused with other sticklebacks by persons who do not take the time to count the spines.

[Syng-nath'-i-dee]

GENUS *Hippocampus* Rafinesque

[Hip'-o-cam'-pus: *hippocampus* = a sea horse]

SEA HORSE / *Hippocampus hudsonius* De Kay

[hud-soan'-i-us: named after the Hudson River]

Hippocampus hudsonius De Kay, New York Fauna: Fishes, p. 322, pl. 53, fig. 171, 1842 (type locality, Hudson River, New York)

RANGE: Nova Scotia to Florida, Cuba, Gulf of Mexico.

SIZE: 6 inches; breeds at 3 inches.

TEMPERAMENT: This marine sea horse is suitable in the marine community tank.

TEMPERATURE REQUIREMENTS: 50–75°F.

SEX DIFFERENCES: Male has a brood pouch on underside of abdomen.

COUNTS: Dorsal 18 to 20; pectoral 15 to 19; plates 11 + 35 to 38.

This marine fish with a prehensile tail swims by movements of the dorsal-fin rays. It is one of the few fishes that depends on the dorsal fin for locomotion. Its tail is used as a holdfast around seaweed.

Sea horses mate in the spring and summer, at which time the female produces about 200 eggs. During a period of a day or two she places these eggs in the male's pouch, where they remain for a rather long incubation period, about 6 weeks.

When newly hatched, the fry swim about in a horizontal position. After about 90 days of free swimming, they develop sexual differences and then swim in a vertical position. They take a year to reach the stage of being able to reproduce.

Fry must be fed freshly hatched brine shrimp, which will live easily in the same marine water that is necessary for the developing sea horses. Adults require baby guppies, *Daphnia*, or adult brine shrimp.

The name of this species currently is *Hippocampus erectus*.

FAMILY ATHERINIDAE: Silversides

[Ath′-e-rin′-i-dee]

GENUS *Alepidomus* Hubbs

[A′-lep-i-doe′-mus: *alepid* = without scales; *omus* = shoulder]

CUBAN GLASSFISH / *Alepidomus evermanni* (Eigenmann)

[ev′-er-mann-eye: named in honor of B. W. Evermann]

Atherina evermanni Eigenmann, Bull. U.S. Fish. Comm., 22:228, fig. 9, 1902 (type locality, San Cristóbal, Cuba)

RANGE: Cuba and Isle of Pines.

SIZE: 2 inches.

TEMPERAMENT: A peaceful species suitable in the community tank.

TEMPERATURE REQUIREMENTS: 72–90°F.

SEX DIFFERENCES: None observed.

· COUNTS: Dorsal V-I,9 to 11; anal I,12 to 15; pelvic I,5; scales 32.

This attractive glassfish was introduced to aquarists by Albert Greenberg, Everglades Aquatic Nurseries, who supplied the photograph.

The Cuban glassfish has a light greenish tint. It should be fed live foods mostly, with some dry foods occasionally.

Genus *Melanotaenia* Gill

[Mel'-an-o-taen'-i-a: *melano* = black; *taenia* = a band]

Black-lined Rainbowfish / *Melanotaenia maccullochi* Ogilby

[mak-cull'-ok-eye: named in honor of Allen Riverston McCulloch]

Melanotaenia maccullochi Ogilby, Mem. Queensland Mus. 3:118, pl. 29, fig. 1, 1915 (type locality, Barron River, North Queensland)

RANGE: Northern Australia.

SIZE: 2¾ inches; breeds at 2 inches.

TEMPERAMENT: A peaceful species suitable in the community tank.

TEMPERATURE REQUIREMENTS: 70 to 88°F.

SEX DIFFERENCES: Male is more colorful than female.

COUNTS: Dorsal IV to VII-I,8 to 10; anal I,14 or 15; pectoral i,11 or 12; pelvic I,5; scales 33 or 34.

Breeding is easy. Place a group of them in a large aquarium (an old refrigerator lining does very well). Feed the fish tremendous quantities of *Daphnia* and *Tubifex* every morning. Leave them alone with as much *Nitella* or foxtail (*Myriophyllum*) as you can possibly put into the tank. After 8 weeks merely take out the half-grown fry. They must be bred out of doors where there is plenty of heat (78°F) and plenty of light (10 hours a day). Indoor breeding is not nearly so successful, although this fish may be seen spawning in the community aquarium. A pair will line up next to each other and tremble, at which moment a few eggs are laid, which the fish will eat immediately unless they are fully fed and heavy vegetation is present.

The dorsal and anal fins are pinkish distally whereas the entire caudal fin is pinkish.

AUSTRALIAN RED-TAILED RAINBOWFISH / *Melanotaenia nigrans*
(Richardson)

[ni'-grans: *nigrans* = black]

Atherina nigrans Richardson, Ann. Mag. Nat. Hist., 11:180, 1843 (type locality, Kings River, Victoria, near Port Essington)

RANGE: Australia.

SIZE: 3 inches; breeds at 2 inches.

TEMPERAMENT: A peaceful species suitable in the community tank.

TEMPERATURE REQUIREMENTS: 70–88°F.

SEX DIFFERENCES: Male is more highly colored than female.

COUNTS: Dorsal IV to VII-I,10 to 12; anal I,17 to 21; pectoral i,13 to 15; pelvic I,5; scales 34 or 35.

This attractive Australian species is not commonly seen because, though peaceful, hardy, and easy to breed, it does not attain bright colors until breeding and then only for a short period. It is a very delicate species; should it jump out on the floor it dies quickly.

The dorsal and anal fins are yellowish with red dots and the tips of the fin rays are blackish; the caudal fin lobes are red-tipped.

GENUS *Telmatherina* Boulenger

[Tell-math'-er-eye'-na: *telma* = a pond or swamp; *atherina* = a kind of fish]

CELEBES RAINBOWFISH / *Telmatherina ladigesi* Ahl

[la'-di-gees'-eye: named in honor of the famous German aquarist W. Ladiges]

Telmatherina ladigesi Ahl, Zool. Anz., 114:175, 1936 (type locality, Celebes, near Makassar)

RANGE: Celebes.

SIZE: 3½ inches.

TEMPERAMENT: A peaceful species suitable for the community tank.

TEMPERATURE REQUIREMENTS: 72–86°F.

SEX DIFFERENCES: Male has extended rays on the anal and second dorsal fins.

COUNTS: Dorsal V-I,7 to 8; anal I,11 or 12; pectoral i,11; pelvic I,5; scales 28 or 29; predorsal scales 9.

This fish, though seldom seen in home aquaria, is easy to breed, peaceful, hardy, and attractive. The sides are a yellowish blue, with a fine red line approximating the lateral line. The body is translucent enough so that the air bladder is plainly visible. There are two dorsal fins, the second being the larger. In the male, the first few rays on the second dorsal are elongated and are easily identified by their intense black coloring.

A pair should be well-seasoned on live foods, prepared foods, and plenty of green-plant foods. Should the aquarium be free of algae such as *Nitella*, the fish should be offered bits of spinach, lettuce, or celery tops. Some plant material seems to be a prerequisite to breeding.

Once the pair has been properly conditioned, allow it a large, well-planted aquarium. It spawns by depositing eggs in dense vegetation. The eggs are large and have a yellow color. They are not eaten by the parents if there is plenty of *Daphnia* around.

Water for these fish should have a pH of 7.6, zero hardness (or as close as possible), and a temperature of at least 78 to 80°F.

[An-a-ban'-ti-dee]

Genus *Anabas* Cuvier and Cloquet

[An'-a-bas: *anabas* = to go up]

Anabas; Walking Fish or Climbing Perch / *Anabas testudineus* (Bloch)

[tes'-tu-din'-e-us: *testudineus* = resembling a tortoise shell]

Anthias testudineus Bloch, Naturgeschichte der Ausländischen Fische, 6:121, 1792 (type locality, Japan)

RANGE: China, southeast Asia, India, Ceylon, Philippine Islands, and Indo-Australian Archipelago.

SIZE: 10 inches; breeds at 4 inches.

TEMPERAMENT: A predaceous species that should be kept only with individuals of its own species of about the same size in a covered tank.

TEMPERATURE REQUIREMENTS: 60–90°F.

SEX DIFFERENCES: Male has longer and more pointed dorsal fins.

COUNTS: Dorsal XVII,10; anal X,10; pectoral 15; pelvic I,5; scales 29.

The following account is quoted from H. M. Smith (*U.S. Nat. Mus. Bull.* 188, pp. 447–450, 1945).

"The fish lives in all kinds of fresh water, including large streams, but flourishes most in canals, ditches, lakes, ponds, and swamps. By means of its supplementary breathing apparatus, it can thrive in water deficient in oxygen, and has, in fact, ceased to depend entirely on its gills for its respiratory requirements. Associated with the air-breathing function is the habit of deliberately leaving the water and going considerable distances on dry land. Progress is jerky and ungraceful and is accomplished by lateral movements of the tail while the fish maintains an upright position supported by the spread paired fins.

"The fish is very hardy and able to live out of water for protracted periods, depending on the moisture of the air-breathing parts. In Thailand, where *Anabas* is an important and staple food fish over the whole country, it is the custom to take it to market in wicker baskets or in tubs with little or no water and to expose it for sale out of water on wooden or stone slabs, and the only attention during a long day in the market may be infrequent sprinkling with water.

"In 1791 a Dane named Daldorff, while in Tranquebar, at that time a Danish possession in India, came upon a fish which, during a heavy rainfall, was climbing a Palmyra palm and had reached a point 5 feet above the ground. There it was apparently enjoying itself in a little stream running in a fissure in the palm's trunk from a broad frond, which collected the rain water as in a funnel. Nearby was a swamp from which the fish had probably come.

"The name 'climbing perch' by which the fish has generally come to be known among English-speaking people and in English works of reference is somewhat inappropriate. The fish is not a perch and is not even remotely related to the true perches, common fresh-water fishes of America, Europe, and northern Asia.

"Other common names by which this fish has been called are 'climbing fish' and 'walking fish,' but these are borne also by several gobies, catfishes, serpentheadfishes and others. On the whole, it may be best to adopt the perfectly distinctive generic name as the common designation of the fish in European languages and call it *Anabas.*

"There are gills such as ordinary fishes possess, but the gills in the long process of evolution have become less important and now seem quite inadequate to sustain life. This is easily shown by putting a fish in an aquarium with a wire-mesh screen just below the surface. With inability to take in atmospheric air, the fish begins to suffer and will soon die. The reduced gills represent only a small proportion of the total respiratory surface, and the major part of respiration is carried on by means of a special structure occupying a cavity over the gills and consisting of a series of thin, concentrically arranged bony plates

covered by a vascular mucous membrane, which enables the fish to absorb atmospheric oxygen. Some writers have apparently failed to appreciate the exact role of the accessory branchial organ in *Anabas.* Thus, Dr. Francis Day, who spent many years in India and Burma and published a monumental work on the fishes of those countries, stated that the 'hollow superbranchial organ . . . enables the climbing perch to retain water for a considerable time, so that it can moisten its gills and live whilst out of its native element.' This enables the fish to breathe atmospheric air when the gills cannot be used. The gills function only when the fish is submerged; the superbranchial organ functions only when the fish is out of the water.

"The climbing powers of *Anabas* are exercised chiefly in leaving its home in a pond, swamp, or canal and seeking other waters that may afford better living conditions. In making this change of quarters the fish may have to travel on dry land, and it is this habit that is characteristic and well known to oriental people. In Siam, I not infrequently came upon an *Anabas,* usually at night, crossing a dusty road or traversing a dry lawn or field. It was easy to discover the water that a fish was leaving but it was not always possible to determine the particular water to which it was heading. In some cases the body of water to which the fish was obviously bound did not seem to the human observer to be more attractive than the water that had been left. The banks of drying canals and ponds, up which the fish has to climb, may be high and steep, and skill and patience may be required to negotiate them; but on arriving at a new body of water the fish may exercise much less care in descending, and I occasionally saw one, apparently deliberately, roll or fall down a steep bank and go into the water with a splash.

"As would be expected in a fish that regularly leaves the water and travels overland, *Anabas* displays no conspicuous color that might attract attention. The adult fish is of a uniform dark brown while the young is light brown, with a few blackish transverse stripes.

"The walking powers of *Anabas* seem to be exercised only when it is in quest of a new aquatic environment, and there appear to be no observations indicating that the fish feeds regularly when out of the water, although it may conceivably seize insects or worms that happen to be in its terrestrial path.

"The walking movements lack the grace and ease of those of a lizard and some of the gobies, such as the mudskipper (*Periophthalmus*). The gait is jerky but comparatively fast, and the efforts are usually persistent, so that a fish may travel a considerable distance in a short time. I have a note on the actually observed out-of-water movements of an *Anabas* in Peninsular Siam. This fish had been living in a small pool in a detached circular garden thickly planted with flowers and shrubs, but was removed when the pool was to be cleaned. It was taken by a servant for release in a stream on the edge of the compound. The servant, however, was called away and he put down the basket containing the fish just before reaching the stream. The fish immediately climbed out and, instead of entering the nearby stream, headed back in the direction of the pool. Its subsequent movements were partly conjectured but were under observation during the latter half of the journey. The fish first passed through grass and then over a metaled driveway between houses; and on arriving at the garden it continued on the driveway to the far side and then made a short turn, plunged through the flower beds, and re-entered the pool. The distance traveled was about 300 feet and the time occupied was about 30 minutes. This particular fish, in addition to progressing readily on dry land and breathing atmospheric air, had well-developed aerial vision (which is rare in fishes) and seemed to exhibit a homing instinct."

GENUS *Belontia* Myers

[Bee-lon'-ti-a: *belontia* = one of the native names for the species in Palembang]

COMB-TAIL PARADISEFISH / *Belontia signata* (Günther)

[sig-na'-ta: *signata* = marked]

Polyacanthus signatus Günther, Catalogue of the Fishes in the British Museum, 3:379, 1861 (type locality, Ceylon)

RANGE: Ceylon.

SIZE: 5 inches; breeds at 3 inches.

TEMPERAMENT: A predaceous species that should be kept with fishes at least of its own size.

TEMPERATURE REQUIREMENTS: 60–90°F. Optimum breeding temperature 75°F.

SEX DIFFERENCES: Male has longer rays projecting from caudal and dorsal fins.

COUNTS: Dorsal XVI to XVIII,8 to 10; anal XV to XVI,10 to 12; pectoral 10 to 12; scales 29 or 30.

The average loss on a shipment of fishes from Singapore by boat may run as high as 40 per cent. Once the fishes are taken from the boat, relocated in their own aquaria, and finally sold by a wholesaler, some 10 weeks after they left the Far East, more than 60 per cent may have perished, yet 99 per cent of this species survives even when imported under the worst conditions.

Once a tankful of this fish was kept in a large wholesale establishment. It so happened that a 4-inch *Astronotus ocellatus* jumped from its own tank into this tank full of comb-tails. No sooner had the fish hit the water than a couple of the ungracious hosts had torn it apart and were devouring it.

When frightened, this fish loses its attractive red color and shows a mosaic pattern. Basically the color is the same deep red as that of the paradisefish, *Macropodus opercularis*.

Large floating eggs are expelled into a flimsy bubble nest, which merely serves to hold the mass of floating eggs together. Spawns are usually large and are taken care of by both parents.

FAMILY ANABANTIDAE

GENUS *Betta* Bleeker

[Bet′-tah: named after a local native name]

Betta bellica Sauvage

[bell′-i-ca: *bellica* = beautiful]

Betta bellica Sauvage, Bull. soc. zool. France, 9:217, fig., 1884 (type locality, Kinta River, Malay Peninsula)

RANGE: Malay Peninsula.

SIZE: 4 inches; breeds at 3 inches.

TEMPERAMENT: This species is not suitable as a community fish.

TEMPERATURE REQUIREMENTS: 70–90°F. Optimum breeding temperature 76°F.

SEX DIFFERENCES: Male has longer fins.

COUNTS: Dorsal I,10; anal II,30 to 32; pectoral 12; pelvic I,5; scales 35.

This *Betta* breeds the same as *Betta splendens*. It is larger than the popular species, however, and does not have as much color as the domesticated varieties; however, in nature *B. bellica* is more colorful than *B. splendens*, for the tannish *B. bellica* has beautifully barred sides and each scale is beautifully marked with a metallic sheen that reflects an emerald green. The dorsal fin is a contrasting reddish brown with a greenish margin; the anal and ventral parts of the tail are a brilliant red.

MOUTHBREEDING BETTA / *Betta brederi* Myers

[bre'-der-eye: named in honor of Charles M. Breder, Jr., ichthyologist, American Museum of Natural History]

Betta brederi Myers, Proc. Biol. Soc. Washington, 48:25, 1935 (type locality, small stream in Johore)

RANGE: Johore, India.

SIZE: 3½ inches; breeds at 2½ inches.

TEMPERAMENT: This species is suitable in the community tank.

TEMPERATURE REQUIREMENTS: 70–90°F. Optimum breeding temperature 76°F.

SEX DIFFERENCES: Male has longer fins.

COUNTS: Dorsal II,8 or 9; anal II,23 or 24; pectoral 12; scales 29.

This is a surprising fish, for many persons, when they hear the name "betta" and are told that this fish is closely related to the famed Siamese fighting fish, expect to find a bubble-nest builder. However, this fish is a mouthbreeder.

The male actually embraces the female exactly as his cousin *Betta splendens* but, instead of taking the eggs in his mouth, he catches them in a nook he has prepared with his anal fin. The female then takes the few eggs in her mouth and blows them at the male. The male catches them all and stores them in his buccal cavity until they hatch and are able to swim freely, usually about 5 days. The male never attacks the female and conversely the female never attacks the male, but for the sake of the fry it is wise to remove the female as soon as she is finished spawning. Fry can take freshly hatched brine shrimp as soon as they are released by the male.

SIAMESE FIGHTING FISH / *Betta splendens* Regan

[splen'-dens: *splendens* = bright, glittering]

Betta splendens Regan, Proc. Zool. Soc. London, p. 782, 1909 (type locality, Siam)

RANGE: Siam.

SIZE: 2½ inches; breeds at 2 inches.

TEMPERAMENT: The females may be kept together; a single male may be kept in the community aquarium but no females; males, if kept together, will fight until one gives up.

TEMPERATURE REQUIREMENTS: 70–90°F. Breeds best at 80°F.

SEX DIFFERENCES: Male is more colorful and has longer finnage.

COUNTS: Dorsal IV,6; anal V,25; pectoral 12; pelvics I,5; scales 30.

The following account is quoted in part from H. M. Smith (*U.S. Nat. Mus. Bull.* 188, pp. 456–461, 1945)

"This, the celebrated fighting fish of Thailand, has a wide natural distribution in ponds, ditches, drains, and sluggish waters generally throughout the country. It does not appear to have been indigenous to any other country, but it is now to be found around the world because of its attractiveness, hardiness, and adaptability to small aquaria.

"The maximum length of wild fish is about 5 cm. for males, females being somewhat smaller. A length of 6 to 6.5 cm. is attained by male fish bred in captivity.

"Earlier references to this species were usually under the name of *Betta pugnax* (Cantor). It remained for Regan in 1910 to point out that *B. pugnax* is native to the island of Pinang and that the Thailand form is distinct.

The female *Betta* is less colorful and has shorter fins than the male.

"For several hundred years the fish has been used locally for sporting purposes, and for more than 100 years it has been domesticated and cultivated. Cultivation has increased the size, improved the colors, and enhanced the fighting qualities.

"In a wild state the fighting fish is an inconspicuous, retiring little creature, seeking protection from the glare of the sun's rays and from fish-eating birds like egrets, herons, and kingfishers by hiding beneath and among water plants.

"The general coloration of a quiescent fish is dull grayish brown or green with or without obscure dark lateral bands, and conveys no suggestion of the wonderfully brilliant hues assumed by the male under proper stimulation. Under the stress of excitement the male fish exhibits a remarkable change. All the fins are widely spread, the gill membranes are expanded and project like a frill or ruff suggestive of the raised hackles of fighting cocks, and the entire body and fins become intensely suffused with a lustrous blue or red color, which makes the fighting fish one of the most beautiful of all fresh-water fishes. The normal incitement to the display of latent colors is the approach of another male, but the same effect is produced when a fish sees his reflection in a mirror.

"Observations on fishes kept under the most favorable conditions in aquaria indicate that this species is normally short-lived. Possibly as a result of its strenuous activity and rapid metabolism, possibly because its span of life is predetermined by some immutable hereditary requirement, the fish in Siam appears to reach its age limit in 2 years, but under domestication in colder climates a somewhat greater age may be attained.

"Just how early in Siamese history the fighting fish acquired its reputation is not known, but for several hundred years its pugnacious qualities have been recognized and utilized in popular contests.

"Up to the year 1850 or thereabouts, the use of the fighting fish in sportive contests in Siam was confined to fishes obtained in open waters; but, in order to insure a regular supply for fighting and betting purposes, domestication and cultivation were then instituted and have since been conducted on an increasingly large scale.

"The fighting instinct is peculiar to the males and is so strong that a normal fish exhibits it under every condition and at every opportunity. One might reasonably infer that the fighting instinct would develop at the approach of maturity. As a matter of fact, the pugnacious tendency shows itself at an early age; and in captivity fish only 2 months old and less than half-grown should be separated to prevent continual scrapping.

"Because of their ever-present eager-

The only known color picture of an albino Siamese fighting fish, taken when still very young.

ness to fight, adult male fish must not only be kept in separate aquaria but the view of rivals in nearby vessels should be cut off by pieces of cardboard; otherwise their vitality and fighting ability will become impaired by incessant futile effort.

"The fighting fish has responded well to efforts to produce changes to meet the popular demand. Even in the hands of persons ignorant of the laws of heredity, noteworthy improvements in form, size, coloration, and fighting ability have been brought about; and there is reason to believe that still further improvements may be made.

"A person seeing for the first time a wild fighting fish would never suspect the wonderful possibilities in coloration that have been realized under cultivation. The most noteworthy of the color phases that have been established, in addition to intensified reds and blues, are lavenders,

iridescent greens, cornflower blue, blue and white, and yellowish and reddish creams with bright red fins. The latter, first produced about 1900, are known to the Siamese as *pla kat khmer* (Cambodian biting fish), probably from having originated among fanciers in French Indo-China.

"Along with the development of intensified and new colors, there has come about an increase in the size of the vertical fins, culminating in graceful crapelike effects, which vie with those in the veiltailed and other highly cultivated Japanese goldfish, so that there are now fighting fish whose caudal fins are about as long as the head and body combined.

"Fishes caught in open waters and taken indoors will after a few days readily respond to an opportunity to fight. The fighting stamina of the wild fishes, however, is not sufficiently developed for present-day requirements in Thailand.

"On the other hand, in fishes reared under careful domestication and intelligent selection of parents, the inherent desire and ability to fight are markedly strengthened. Well-matched fishes may continue their attacks hour after hour without intermission, with only brief excursions to the surface for air. There is a partial respite from active effort while the fishes are in a sparring position, but even then the fins are kept extended, the gill membranes remain expanded, the body muscles are taut, and an alert attitude is constantly maintained. Some of my own fishes have remained pugnacious after 6 hours of uninterrupted combat, but fights do not ordinarily last more than 3 hours. From reputable Siamese informants has come the information that fish have been known to struggle for a whole day and night.

"In Siam, as in the various countries into which the fish has been introduced, the usual procedure in arranging a fight is to select two males of approximately the same size, and bring them together in separate jars. If they spread their fins, show their colors, and make head-on efforts to reach each other, they are placed together in the same vessel. An ordinary porcelain or tin washbasin makes a good arena, but a rectangular glass receptacle, such as a battery jar, affords a better view. The fish immediately approach each other and indulge in a preliminary display of spread fins, expanding gill membranes, and color waves. A common sparring position finds the fishes side by side with the heads pointing in the same direction and with one fish slightly behind the other. This position may be held for a period varying from a few seconds to several minutes. Then, in quick succession, the fishes attack, their movements being so swift that the human eye can hardly follow the actual impact of the teeth, and the assaults are repeated with short intermissions, during which the same sparring attitude is taken.

"The most common points of attack are the anal, caudal, and dorsal fins. The ventral and pectoral fins may be practically untouched at the end of a protracted encounter, but may receive early attention from one or both contestants. The vertical fins, however, are always involved.

A male *Betta* will spread his fins in front of a female.

This is "Betta Row" in Tutwiler's Tropical Fish
Hatchery, Tampa, Florida.

The first evidence of a spirited encounter is likely to be torn or split fins. As the contest proceeds, there may be extensive loss of fin substance, and with well-matched fishes the vertical fins may ultimately be reduced to mere stubs.

"The loss or extensive damage of the fins impairs the swimming, steering, and balancing powers and hence places a fish at a disadvantage, but in evenly matched fishes this is not likely to be a final factor in deciding the issue.

"Another point of attack is the side of the body. Single scales or clumps of scales may be loosened or detached by a quick nipping act, but in many contests this kind of injury may not occur. Exceptionally

the gill covers may be bitten and slight injury may be done to the gills.

"An interesting variation in fighting tactics ensues when the fishes come together in a head-on assault and lock jaws. With their jaws firmly locked and their bodies extended, the fishes struggle while partly or completely rotating on their long axis. In my observations, the locked-jaw attack was always comparatively brief and was invariably terminated by the fishes settling to the bottom and remaining perfectly still for, say, 10 to 20 seconds. The hold was then broken and the fishes rapidly sought the surface for air, and then resumed their ordinary tactics. The lock-jaw position interferes with respiration and

Two male bettas in the characteristic fighting pose.

lasts only as long as the fishes can resist the call for extra oxygen.

"During the short interludes in fighting when the demand for oxygen forces the fishes to go to the surface for gulps of air, attacks are always suspended. I have never known one fish to assail another at such a time. It is literally a breathing spell provided for in the fighting fish's code of ethics.

"Fighting contests are decided by the general exhaustion and the failure of stamina in the combatants rather than by a definite injury or a knock-out assault. Sooner or later one fish shows a lack of ability or desire to continue the fight and swims away—literally turns tail when his rival assumes a position for attack. The engagement is then over, the fishes separated, the wagers, if any, are paid, and the owners put their charges into jars and go their respective ways.

"At the end of a protracted contest both fishes may present a most unattractive appearance because of their mutilated fins, but they seem to experience no discomfort and, if permitted, would fight again the next day. The fins regenerate rapidly and completely, and at the end of a few weeks may show no signs of injury. Loss of scales may be more serious, inducing the development of fungus.

The Tutwiler butterfly *Betta*.

"My experience, which extended over 12 years and covered many hundreds of exhibitions, coincides with that of most observers in finding nothing brutal, cruel, or repulsive in fighting-fish contests. The participants seem to get so much satisfaction from their encounters, their physical discomfort is apparently so negligible, and their recovery is so complete that there is little occasion to expend sympathy over them, while their graceful movements, muscular agility, acumen, tenacity, and wonderful color displays cannot fail to arouse enthusiasm even in the most sensitive spectators.

"Wholly erroneous impressions on this subject have been conveyed in some published articles. In an account that has often been quoted, one of the unfortunate combatants always terminates his fighting career and his very existence by literally bursting because of his futile efforts to reach his adversary kept in a separate jar.

Another description of the fish and their fights concludes with a statement which, if true, would enlist our sympathy:

" 'The two (fishes) are brought together in the same bowl and they forthwith begin to tear at each other with their mouths and sharp spines, until the one is overpowered. The victor seldom lives to enjoy his triumph.'

"As has been pointed out, fighting is done wholly with the teeth, and one fish is not overpowered. I never knew the victor, or even the vanquished, to succumb to a fight or to undergo serious injury.

"An outstanding peculiarity of the fish is its dependence on atmospheric air. In an open water course, just as in a well-aerated aquarium, the fish cannot obtain through its gills dissolved oxygen in amount sufficient for its needs, and hence it has to make frequent excursions to the surface to take in mouthfuls of air which it utilizes by its accessory respiratory ap-

The male embraces the female and squeezes the ova from her body. Fertilization takes place at the same time.

The female remains still for a few seconds after the embrace. This gives the male a chance to catch the slowly falling eggs and to blow them into his bubble nest.

paratus. The fish does not loiter at the surface where, in a wild state, it is exposed to attack by birds and other fish-eating animals. It projects its mouth for only an instant, expelling a bubble of vitiated air and taking in a new supply, and then rapidly retreats toward the bottom.

"The air-breathing apparatus is of simpler construction than in some related species, the 'climbing perch' for example, which can and do spend considerable time out of water. Above the gills there is in each side of the head a cavity lined with vascular epithelium, the absorptive surface being increased by several projecting laminae.

"The bubble-blowing habit is strongly developed in the male fish. At the time the bubbles are made there is a viscid mucous secretion of the mouth or pharynx, which strengthens and makes more last-

ing the walls of the bubbles and tends to keep the bubbles in a compact mass.

"The purpose of the bubbles—to serve as a nest for the eggs and a hover for the newly hatched young—is admirably achieved. As the bubbles gradually lose their stickiness and become scattered or ruptured, one may observe the male constantly engaged in renewing the supply.

"If one day a mature female fish is introduced into a vessel with a male fish that has been blowing bubbles, the probability is that next morning the bubble mass will be found to contain several hundred minute transparent eggs not easily distinguished from bubbles without a magnifying glass.

"At egg-laying time the fishes consort near the surface, and at short intervals the eggs are extruded in small batches. As the eggs slowly sink toward the bottom, both

Here the male guards his nest, now full of eggs.

the male and the female fishes go after them, gently take them in their mouths, and returning quickly to the surface blow the eggs into the bubble nest, repeating the performance as often as may be necessary to gather up all the eggs. This continues for several hours until all the ripe eggs have been voided.

"The role of the mother fish is almost entirely restricted to the production of eggs. After the eggs are once placed in the nest, her family duties cease, and all subsequent care of eggs and young devolves wholly on the male.

"The fish is rather prolific. At one spawning period from 200 to 700 eggs may be expelled, the average number for a fully developed normal fish being 400 to 500. A month after one batch of eggs has been produced, a given female may be ready to yield another lot, so that in the course of a year one fish may be responsible for 2,500 to 5,000 or more eggs.

"Aided partly by capillary attraction,

partly by the viscidity of the bubbles, the eggs are held in the nest until hatching ensues. The incubation period is remarkably short, covering only 30 to 40 hours in water at 80° to 85°F. Should any of the eggs drop from the nest and fall to the bottom, the male recovers them and blows them back.

"The newly hatched fishes find shelter under the bubble nest, and remain there while their yolk sacs are being absorbed and their fins are developing. If they stray from their proper place before they are old enough, the male carries them back to the nest and gently ejects them; and during the entire period of infantile helplessness the male repeatedly takes the young in his mouth and blows them out with new bubbles, thus insuring proper oxygenation.

"Throughout the nesting period the male fish is extremely busy and his vigilance never relaxes. In addition to making and maintaining the bubble nest, replacing eggs that may drop from the nest, rounding up the straggling young, and mouthing the young at intervals, he is constantly on the alert to protect the eggs and young from intruders that may devour them. The chief offender is the mother fish. In a wild state, she can be forcefully driven off and kept at a distance, but in the restricted quarters of an aquarium she must be removed as soon as egg-laying is completed.

"The presence of the male seems to be essential in the development and hatching of the eggs. If the male is removed from the aquarium, the eggs, or most of them, will fail to hatch. Those that fall to the bottom will suffocate; while the vitality of those that remain in the nest may be impaired by the lack of the aeration that comes from mouthing and bubble blowing.

"It is of interest to note that the for-bearance of the male from eating the eggs and young is not due to any temporary impediment to his digestive powers, such as a physiological closure of the esophagus. He can and does eat mosquito larvae throughout his period of guard duty.

"With all the solicitude shown by a male for his progeny, it may be noted that he cannot distinguish his own young from those of another parent introduced into his aquarium. Foster offspring receive the same care as his own.

"Another aspect of the interesting behavior of *Betta* is shown when a male parent is taken away from his nest and returned after a few days; he promptly devours his young. The fighting fish is a confirmed carnivore. This would be indicated by its dental equipment and short intestine even if not shown by direct observation on wild and domesticated fish."

GENUS *Colisa* Cuvier and Valenciennes

[Co-li'-sa: a native name]

GIANT GOURAMI / *Colisa fasciata* (Bloch and Schneider)

[fas'-see-a'-ta: *fasciata* = banded]

Trichogaster fasciatus Bloch and Schneider, Systema ichthyologiae, p. 164, pl. 36, 1801 (type locality, India)

RANGE: India.

SIZE: 5 inches; breeds at 3 inches.

TEMPERAMENT: A species suitable for the community tank.

TEMPERATURE REQUIREMENTS: 70–86°F. Optimum breeding temperature 80°F.

SEX DIFFERENCES: Male not only has longer dorsal fins but also more red color than the female.

COUNTS: Dorsal XV to XVII,9 to 14; anal XV to XVIII,14 to 19; pectoral 9 or 10; pelvic I,5; scales 31.

At one time this species was a popular gourami. It had "pet" names such as striped gourami and banded gourami. Many tales are told about the strange mating behavior as it does not seem to be obligated to spawn the same way twice. The male's bubble nests are poorly constructed and may be a mere mouthful of bubbles scattered at random over the surface of the water. Since the eggs are lighter than water this does not matter very much. Even after the fry have become free-swimming, now and then the male persists in letting loose a stream of bubbles. When the young have hatched out, or just prior to their hatching, he may be seen to take a few mouthfuls of sand and blow it among the eggs at the surface of the water. Eggs hatch in about 2 days at 80°F and the fry are free-swimming in another 3 days. Remove the female right after she has finished spawning and remove the male as soon as the young are free-swimming.

Thick-lipped Gourami / *Colisa labiosa* (Day)

[lay'-bi-o'-sa: *labiosa* = large-lipped]

Trichogaster labiosus Day, Fishes of India, 2:374, pl. 79, fig. 4, 1878 (type locality, Irrawaddy, Rangoon, Burma)

RANGE: Burma.

SIZE: 3 inches; breeds at 2½ inches.

TEMPERAMENT: This species is suitable for the community aquarium.

TEMPERATURE REQUIREMENTS: 70–86°F. Breeds best at 80°F.

SEX DIFFERENCES: Male has color and a longer, more pointed dorsal fin.

COUNTS: Dorsal XV to XVIII, 8 to 10; anal XVI to XVIII,17 to 20; pectoral 9 or 10; pelvic I,5; scales 29 to 31.

This bubble-nest builder is no longer popular. Only the male is colorful and this feature is only maintained while breeding. This species is peaceful, however, and aquarists claim that it can become very tame and can be taught to take food from between its keeper's fingers.

Herbert Axelrod has observed that this fish is shy.

The male has the sole responsibility for the construction of the bubble nest; the female does not aid in any way. Once the nest is built the male entices the female under the nest and fertilizes the clear eggs that flow from her vent. The eggs float to the surface and the male stands guard over them.

The female should be removed after spawning and the male as soon as the fry are free-swimming.

The male begins a bubble nest under floating plants.

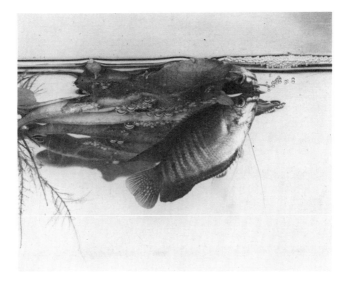

At first only large bubbles are blown.

Then smaller bubbles.

Now to get the wife to inspect the work.

She thinks it's swell! Just what the doctor ordered.

The female nudges the male.

He obliges by forming the C curve of the embrace.

As the eggs are expelled, they are fertilized and then float right up into the nest.

As the eggs hatch, the nest breaks up.

Young about four weeks old.

DWARF GOURAMI / *Colisa lalia* (Hamilton = Buchanan)

[lah'-li-a: a native name]

Trichopodus lalius Hamilton = Buchanan, Fishes of the River Ganges, pp. 120, 372, 1822 (type locality, River Ganges)

RANGE: India.

SIZE: 2½ inches; breeds at 1½ inch.

TEMPERAMENT: A species suitable in the community tank.

TEMPERATURE REQUIREMENTS: 70–86°F.

SEX DIFFERENCES: Male is more colorful and has longer dorsal fins.

COUNTS: Dorsal XVI,11; anal XV,18; pectoral 10; pelvic 1; scales 30.

The fact that *Colisa lalia* is the smallest of the gouramis, never longer than 2½ inches, explains the popular name "dwarf gourami." Its great popularity and abundance attest to its desirability as an aquarium pet. It is a very colorful fish, especially the male with his intense red stripes.

Most dwarf gouramis are rather shy and timid and will need coaxing to bring them into the open. It is usually advisable to withhold their food for the first few days in the new tank until hunger overcomes their shyness and they will appear for food.

Like *Betta splendens*, the dwarf gourami builds a bubble nest, but it goes one step farther than the *Betta* by weaving in bits of plants as a sort of superstructure. Owing to the added complexity of the nest it is common for the female to help the male in nest construction. The male is rather a vigorous lover and ardently courts any female prior to the actual spawning. He seems particular about the female with whom he will mate and it is not easy to discern the proper time to remove the female should you consider the match a poor one. Once the nest is being constructed by both fish, it is quite certain that they have propagation in mind. This fish is prolific. The ungrateful male will usually destroy the female after spawning unless she is removed or the tank is of a capacity over 25 gallons and is densely planted. The young, hatching out in a few days, need infusoria and brine shrimp. The adults are easy to feed and will take all kinds of food.

FAMILY ANABANTIDAE

GENUS *Helostoma* Kuhl and Van Hasselt

[He′-lo-sto′-ma: *helo* = a nail; *stoma* = mouth]

KISSING GOURAMI / *Helostoma temmincki* Cuvier and Valenciennes

[tem-mink′-eye: named in honor of the ichthyologist C. Temminck]

Helostoma temminckii Cuvier and Va- lenciennes, Histoire naturelle des poissons, 7:342, 1831 (type locality, Java)

RANGE: Java, Borneo, Sumatra, Malay Peninsula, and Siam.

SIZE: 12 inches; breeds at 5 inches.

TEMPERAMENT: This species should not be in a tank with fishes smaller than itself.

TEMPERATURE REQUIREMENTS: 68– 86°F. Breeding at 76°F.

SEX DIFFERENCES: Pairs over 5 inches are differentiated by observing them from above and noting the obvious swelling of the abdomen of the female.

COUNTS: Dorsal XIV to XVI,15 to 18; anal XIV or XV,17 or 18; pectoral 11 or 12; pelvic I,5; scales 38 or 39.

This species breeds similarly to *Betta splendens* except that no bubble nest is built. The pair will embrace, expel thou- sands of small lighter-than-water eggs, and then either eat or ignore them. It does not bother the fry, unless it must compete with them for food.

There are two varieties of this fish. The one known as *Helostoma temmincki* is de- scribed by Hugh M. Smith in his *Fresh- water Fishes of Siam* as follows: "While found in sluggish streams, it is essentially a fish of swamps, ponds, and lakes, and in Thailand (Siam) it is known particularly from the Tale Noi, near the Tale Sap, and other sluggish waters in the peninsula, and from Bung Borapet in Central Thai- land.

"A length of 30 cm (about 12 inches) is reached. The largest actually measured in Thailand was 25.5 cm (10 inches) over all. Several specimens, 21 cm long, obtained at Nakon Sritamarat Oct. 19th, 1923, were ripe males.

"Fish as long as 10 to 12 cm (4 to 5 inches) from Bung Borapet proved very attractive in small balanced aquaria in Bangkok. The general bright silvery skin is relieved by vertical black bars on the head, black longitudinal stripes on the body following rows of scales, a black vertical band at the base of the caudal fin, and black spinous dorsal and anal fins. They were very hardy and quickly adapted themselves to aquarium life, feeding on small bits of raw fish, insects, and shrimp."

The other variety, best known to aquarists as the golden variety, would appear to be an albino if it were not for the black eye. Other than the eye, the body seems entirely devoid of pigmentation. The golden variety has been named *Helostoma rudolfi* Machan (*Anz. Akad. Wiss. Wien,* 68:221, 1931) and came from Java.

Feeding this fish is a definite problem; unless it is fed regularly twice or three times a day there is little hope of survival. The preferred diet is salmon eggs and dried shrimp, but it eagerly takes worms and *Daphnia.*

FAMILY ANABANTIDAE

GENUS *Macropodus* Lacepède

[Mack'-row-po'-dus: *macro* = large; *podus* = foot]

ROUND-TAILED PARADISEFISH / *Macropodus chinensis* (Bloch)

[chin-en'-sis: named after China]

Chaetodon chinensis Bloch, Naturge-schichte der ausländischen Fische, 4:5, pl. 218, fig. 1, 1790 (type locality, China)

RANGE: Eastern China, Formosa, Korea.

SIZE: 2½ inches; breeds at 2 inches.

TEMPERAMENT: This species is not a suitable community fish.

TEMPERATURE REQUIREMENTS: 70–90°F. Optimum breeding temperature 76°F.

SEX DIFFERENCES: Male has longer dorsal fins.

COUNTS: Dorsal XVII,7; anal XIX or XX,9; pectoral 11 or 12; pelvic I,5; scales 28 or 29.

This species breeds like the paradise-fish, *Macropodus opercularis*. It has the same bad habits, unfortunately, and is not as colorful as its cousin. It is therefore in limited demand and may cease to be an aquarium fish.

Its general colors are more reddish than brown. It lacks the greens and blacks of *M. opercularis*.

SPIKE-TAILED PARADISEFISH / *Macropodus cupanus*
(Cuvier and Valenciennes)

[que-pan'-us: named after the "Coupang" River]

Polyacanthus cupanus Cuvier and Valenciennes, Histoire naturelle des poissons, 7:357, 1831 (type locality, Pondichéry)

RANGE: India along Malabar and Coromandel Coasts.

SIZE: 3 inches; breeds at 2 inches.

TEMPERAMENT: This species is suitable in the community aquarium.

TEMPERATURE REQUIREMENTS: 68–85°F. Optimum breeding temperature 76°F.

SEX DIFFERENCES: The male, more colorful and slender than the female, has longer and more pointed dorsal fins.

COUNTS: Dorsal XIV to XVII,5 to 7; anal XVI to XIX,9 to 11; pectoral 10; pelvic I,5; scales 29 to 32.

This species is a bubble-nest builder, breeding like *Betta splendens*. Though not considered to be a pretty fish, it has certain traits that make it desirable.

The over-all body shape, especially its pintail, gives it the general appearance of the dwarf cichlid, *Apistogramma agassizi* (page 606). Its general color is various shades of cinnamon brown. The head, gill covers, and adjacent areas show considerable amounts of a metallic green sheen usually associated with cichlids. There is a large black spot on the caudal peduncle. The dorsal and anal fins are aquamarine; when in breeding color they are sprinkled with tiny red dots. The pelvic fins, by far the most outstanding color manifestation on the fish, are bright red.

BROWN SPIKE-TAILED PARADISEFISH / *Macropodus dayi* (W. Köhler)

[day'-eye: named in honor of Francis Day, British ichthyologist]

Polyacanthus cupanus dayi W. Köhler, Blät. Aquar.-Terrak. 20:331, 1909 (type locality, not known)

RANGE: Ceylon, Sumatra, Malaya.

SIZE: 3 inches; breeds at 2 inches.

TEMPERAMENT: Suitable in the community aquarium but not with baby fishes.

TEMPERATURE REQUIREMENTS: 68–90°F. Optimum breeding temperature 78°F.

SEX DIFFERENCES: Male is more colorful and more slender. He also has a longer and more pointed dorsal fin.

COUNTS: Dorsal XIII to XVII,5 to 7; anal XVI to XIX,10 to 12; pectoral 10; pelvic I,5; scales 28 or 29.

This species differs in size and coloration from *Macropodus cupanus*, although its breeding habits and temperament are the same. It has two rather broad dark stripes running horizontally from the eye to the base of the caudal fin. Its color is brighter than that of *M. cupanus*, but it is still not a colorful fish.

PARADISEFISH / *Macropodus opercularis* (Linnaeus)

[op-per'-que-lar'-is: *opercularis* = a lid or cover]

Labrus opercularis Linnaeus, Systema naturae, ed. 10, p. 283, 1758 (type locality, China)

RANGE: Southeast China, Formosa, Ryukyu Islands, Korea.

SIZE: 3 inches; breeds at 2½ inches.

TEMPERAMENT: Not suitable as a community fish except when kept with fast-swimming species of same size.

TEMPERATURE REQUIREMENTS: 50–90°F. Optimum breeding temperature 74°F.

SEX DIFFERENCES: Male has more color and longer dorsal, anal, and caudal fins.

COUNTS: Dorsal XIII to XVII,6 to 8; anal XVII to XX,11 to 15; pectoral 11; pelvic I,5; scales 28 to 31.

The paradisefish, next to the famous Siamese fighting fish, is one of the most popular of the anabantids. Its native habitat is usually a stagnant stream or rice paddy.

Breeding the paradise is simple. A 4- or 5-gallon aquarium is set up without sand, the tank being divided into two equal parts by a glass partition. A male and female paradisefish are introduced into separate compartments, with a bunch of weighted bushy plants in each compartment as a hiding place. Once the actual courtship is allowed to progress, the fish should be conditioned for a few days on live foods, preferably *Daphnia* and white worms. When the male has constructed his bubble nest and the female shows signs of attention to the male through the glass partition, the glass should be carefully removed (so as not to destroy the bubble nest). Mating takes place by the male enticing the female under his nest of bubbles and wrapping his body about hers to squeeze out the eggs. The eggs are then captured in the mouth of the male and are blown into the prepared nest. The female should be removed after she seems to shy away from the male by hiding behind the foliage. The male may be left with the young until they are free-swimming. It is sometimes desirable to have a few floating plants in the aquarium to add something solid for the bubble nest. Many of the labyrinthfish seem to like a floating leaf or stick to center their nest about.

The young need small-particled food, like infusoria or newly hatched brine shrimp, as soon as they are free-swimming. If the yolk of a hard-boiled egg is strained through a piece of cloth and this finely divided yolk fed 4 or 5 times daily to the fry, in addition to the live food, the young develop much faster.

The albino paradise, a pink-eyed, pinkish-red-bodied variety of *Macropodus opercularis,* is quite popular now. The albino seems to be more peaceful than the wild colored fish.

The male may be distinguished from the female by a careful comparison of the fins. The male's are more flowing and more pointed than the female's. In full color, during the mating period, the male is more colorful.

Food for the paradise is no problem as it will take all types of dried foods and most live foods. It is fond of *Tubifex* but these red worms should be fed sparingly.

GENUS *Osphronemus* Lacepède

[Os'-fro-ne'-mus: *osphronemus* = to track by smell]

THE GOURAMI / *Osphronemus goramy* Lacepède

[gour-am'-i: a Javanese name]

Osphroneme goramy Lacepède, Histoire naturelle des poissons, 3:116, 117, 1802 (type locality, East Indies)

RANGE: East Indies; introduced into Siam, India, and China.

SIZE: 2 feet; breeds at less than 1 foot.

TEMPERAMENT: This predaceous fish is not suitable in the community aquarium.

TEMPERATURE REQUIREMENTS: 70–88°F.

SEX DIFFERENCES: Male has longer dorsal fin when mature than the females.

COUNTS: Dorsal XI or XII, 12 or 13; anal X,20; pectoral 12 or 13; pelvic I,5; scales 31 to 34.

This interesting fish is the only species with the name "gourami," which is a native name; thus it really is the only legitimate gourami. Also it is a "monster" for an aquarium fish and rapidly grows to a large size. It has been bred in the aquarium when only 10 inches long and that is much less than half-grown.

The over-all color is maroon, with a darker cast to the throat which gets bluish at times. The belly is whiter than any other part of the body.

Spawns are huge, running in the thousands, and success can only be had if the fry are raised in large pools. They should be given the standard fry fare of small-particled foods for the first month or so.

FAMILY ANABANTIDAE

GENUS *Sphaerichthys* Canestrini

[Sfere-ik'-thees: *sphaer* = a ball; *ichthys* = a fish]

CHOCOLATE GOURAMI / *Sphaerichthys osphromenoides* Canestrini

[os-from'-e-noi'-des: *osphromenoides* = to track by smelling]

Sphaerichthys osphromenoides Canestrini, Verh. Zool. Bot. Gesell. Wien, 10:707, 1860 (type locality, Indies)

RANGE: Sumatra, Malay Peninsula.

SIZE: 2½ inches; breeds at 1½ inches.

TEMPERAMENT: This peaceful species is suitable in the community aquarium.

TEMPERATURE REQUIREMENTS: 76–82°F.

SEX DIFFERENCES: Male has a patch of yellow in front of the dorsal fin.

COUNTS: Dorsal VIII to XII,7 to 10; anal VIII to X,18 to 22; pectoral 8 to 10; pelvic I,5; scales 26 to 29.

The chocolate gourami is a mouth-breeder; one parent carries the young in its mouth during some stages of development. Several aquarists say that it is a bubble-nest builder; but the Malayan people will tell you it carries its young. Much is still to be learned about this species.

Caring for the chocolate gourami is a problem. It is expensive to begin with, and sensitive to water changes. Water must be of pH 7.6 or 7.8. Food is no problem as it takes both dried foods and live foods. Once in a favorable environment it does well and is attractive with its chocolate-brown color.

GENUS *Trichogaster* Bloch

[Trik′-o-gas′-ter: *tricho* = a hair; *gaster* = belly]

PEARL GOURAMI / *Trichogaster leeri* (Bleeker)

[leer′-eye: named in honor of Leer]

Trichopus leerii Bleeker, Nat. Tijdschr. Ned. Indie, 3:577, 1852 (type locality, Palembang, Sumatra)

RANGE: Sumatra, Borneo, Malaya to Siam.

SIZE: 5 inches.

TEMPERAMENT: This peaceful species is suitable in the community tank.

TEMPERATURE REQUIREMENTS: 70–88°F.

SEX DIFFERENCES: Male has longer dorsal fin and red breast.

COUNTS: Dorsal V to VII,8 to 10; anal XII to XIV,25 to 30; pectoral 9; pelvic I,3 or 4; scales 30 to 37.

The parents are kind to their family, as they do not eat their eggs or their fry. Though they will usually build a sizable bubble nest, it is unnecessary as the ova of the pearl gourami are lighter than water and will float.

The fry are very small at birth and require plenty of room. Their first foods are most important. They require infusoria or brine shrimp from the first day they are free-swimming. This should be supplemented with the yolk of a hard-boiled egg squeezed through a porous cloth. The water level should not be higher than 5 inches until the fry are seen to be coming to the surface for air (about 6 weeks of age).

SNAKE-SKINNED GOURAMI / *Trichogaster pectoralis* (Regan)

[pek'-tor-al'-is: *pectoralis* = pertaining to the breast]

Trichopodus pectoralis Regan, Proc. Zool. Soc. London, p. 784, pl. 79, fig. 1, 1910 (type locality, Siam)

RANGE: Indochina and Siam.

SIZE: 10 inches; breeds at 5 inches.

TEMPERAMENT: This species is suitable in the community tank.

TEMPERATURE REQUIREMENTS: 70–88°F.

SEX DIFFERENCES: Male has longer dorsal fin than the female.

COUNTS: Dorsal VII,9; anal X,34; pectoral 11; pelvic I,2; scales 53 to 55.

Though not an attractive fish, this interesting bubble-nest builder is supposed to be the most peaceful member of the family. He does not eat the fry nor "beat" his wife, and all can live harmoniously in the same aquarium.

Spawns are unusually large; if the fry are to be brought up in a healthy condition they should be given ample room and plenty of the right kind of food, such as newly hatched brine shrimp and egg infusion.

The scales of this fish are so shaped that they give the impression that one is looking at the skin of a snake, hence the name "snake-skinned gourami."

Three-spot or Blue Gourami / *Trichogaster trichopterus* (Pallas)

[tri-kop'-ter-us: *tricho* = hair; *pterus* = fin]

Labrus trichopterus Pallas, Spicilegia Zoologica, no. 8, p. 45, 1770 (no locality given)

RANGE: Tropical Far East.

SIZE: 6 inches; breeds at 3 inches.

TEMPERAMENT: This species may be kept with fishes of its own size.

TEMPERATURE REQUIREMENTS: 70–88°F.

SEX DIFFERENCES: Male has longer and more pointed dorsal fin.

COUNTS: Dorsal VI or VII,7 to 9; anal IX to XII,32 to 38; pectoral 9 or 10; pelvic I,3 or 4; scales 40 to 52.

The three-spot gourami, *Trichogaster trichopterus,* is a popularly misnamed species, since it has only two spots on its body. The third spot is generally considered to be the eye. It builds a bubble nest and the eggs are lighter than water, floating to the surface. The young, too, when they hatch are lighter than water and float at the surface. A variety of this fish from Sumatra is covered with a hazy coat of whitish blue, which has caused it to be nicknamed "blue gourami." Scientifically it is designated as *T. trichopterus sumatranus* Ladiges. The fins of the male are longer and more flowing than those of the female.

Noted for its appetite for *Hydra,* the dreaded fry killers, this species is usually kept in the community tank for that purpose.

Breeding the blue gourami and the three-spot is a simple matter. A large tank is necessary, preferably the long type of 20-gallon capacity. Sand may or may not be used. There should be some vegetation for aid in the propagation of infusoria and also as a place of protection for the female. The male seldom is vicious but he does like to be left alone, and the female may annoy him at times and get nipped for her attentions.

The species is prolific, several hundred young being produced with little trouble. Fry should be fed infusoria, microworms, brine shrimp, and egg-yolk infusion.

GENUS *Trichopsis* Kner

[tri-kop'-sis: *trichopsis* = hairlike]

TALKING or **CROAKING** GOURAMI / *Trichopsis vittatus*
(Cuvier and Valenciennes)

[vit-tay'-tus: *vittatus* = striped]

Osphromenus vittatus Cuvier and Valenciennes, Histoire naturelle des poissons, 7:387, 1831 (type locality, Java)

RANGE: Java, Borneo, Sumatra, Malaya, Indochina, and Siam.

SIZE: 2½ inches; breeds at 2 inches.

TEMPERAMENT: This gourami is suitable in the community aquarium.

TEMPERATURE REQUIREMENTS: 74–88°F.

SEX DIFFERENCES: Male has a reddish color to the tip of his dorsal fin and a bit of the same on his tail. Breeding male has the large dark shoulder spot which is absent on the female.

COUNTS: Dorsal II to IV,6 to 8; anal VI or VII,25 to 28; pectoral 11; pelvic I,5; scales 28.

This bubble-nest builder breeds much like *Betta splendens,* with certain noteworthy exceptions. The nests are loosely constructed and quite a bit of effort is necessary to keep the heavy eggs in the nest. The female helps the male in caring for the eggs and also in placing the eggs in the bubble nest. Males do not molest the females too much and they are safe together. It is even safe to leave the parents in with the babies if the tank is large enough to ensure that the parents will not inadvertently hurt the fry while they swim about. Very small fry hatch in 2 days at 78°F and require the smallest of infusoria in great amounts, for the spawns of this fish are usually large.

The reason for the popular name "croaking gourami" is obvious if one has had a pair in his home aquarium, for during the night when the male comes up to the surface for air he makes a strange sound, like a frog. Females seem capable of this feat but they are rarely heard.

The Channidae are a small family, with most of its members noted for their good-tasting flesh. They have well-developed teeth, which they use on frogs, snakes, fishes, and just about any other live food they can swallow. Their extreme hardiness is attributed to the possession of a suprabranchial cavity which gives them the ability to live in the air, or buried in mud, provided they are able merely to stay damp.

Genus *Channa*

[Chan′-na: *channa* = a kind of wide-mouthed fish]

Snakeheadfish / *Channa asiatica* (Linnaeus)

[a′-shi-at′-i-ka: named after Asia]

Gymnotus asiaticus Linnaeus, Systema naturae, ed. 10, p. 246, 1758 (type locality, China)

RANGE: Southeastern Asia.

SIZE: Over 1 foot; breeds at 6 inches.

TEMPERAMENT: A predaceous species best kept with individuals of the same species and of the same size.

TEMPERATURE REQUIREMENTS: 50–90°F. Breeds readily at 70°F.

SEX DIFFERENCES: Not observed.

COUNTS: Dorsal 43 to 46; anal 28 to 30; pectoral 16 or 17; scales 52 to 55.

This species is dark brownish to olive green, with lighter green on the belly. The silvery spots on the side form a diamond-like pattern.

Large eggs are laid without the aid of a bubble nest since the eggs are lighter than water and float well. Eggs hatch within 72 hours at 80°F and larvae are quite large when hatched. In 4 days, once the yolk sac has been absorbed, they will double in size. For about a week or 10 days the fry must exert considerable effort to keep from floating up to the surface of the water, for they still seem to be much lighter than water. Most of the time they rest upside down in the water with their sac at the surface. It takes about a week for them to be able to right themselves.

[Per′-ci-dee]

Genus *Boleosoma* De Kay

[Bowl′-e-o-so′-ma: *boleo* = to dart; *soma* = body]

Boleosoma nigrum (Rafinesque)

[nye′-grum: *nigrum* = black]

Etheostoma nigra Rafinesque, Ichthyologia Ohiensis, p. 37, 1820 (type locality, Green River, Kentucky)

RANGE: Eastern United States west to Colorado and north to Manitoba.

SIZE: 2½ inches; breeds at 2 inches.

TEMPERAMENT: This active bottom-dwelling species is suitable in the community tank but may not live without good circulation of water.

TEMPERATURE REQUIREMENTS: A cold-water fish; the water temperature should not exceed 75°F.

SEX DIFFERENCES: The male is generally much darker in color than the female during the spring breeding season.

COUNTS: Dorsal VII to XI-10 to 14; anal I,6 to 9; pectoral 10 to 14; pelvic I,5; scales 38 to 52.

This American darter is not often found in the home aquarium. To induce it to spawn requires an elaborate setup involving flowing water. It is mentioned here because it has been sold, along with other American darters, by unscrupulous or ignorant dealers as some new, rare fish.

The name of this species currently is *Etheostoma nigrum*.

[Sen-trark'-i-dee]

This family contains about 40 species of fishes, all of which live in North America. Most of them are carnivorous and take the hook readily; thus they are considered game and food fishes. In general the sunfishes are more brilliantly colored than the basses, are of smaller size, and make more desirable aquarium pets. Both build nests on the bottom, usually on gravelly, sandy, or weedy bottoms.

After the nest is constructed by clearing a slight depression on the bottom in quiet water, the male in its most beautiful color will display his dazzling bright fins in attracting the female toward the nest. After a courtship the female lays her eggs in the nest and at that instant the male fertilizes them.

The eggs hatch in a few days. The newly hatched fry will take freshly hatched brine shrimp immediately. They grow rapidly and are ready to spawn at 1 or 2 years of age.

GENUS *Elassoma* Jordan

[El'-as-so'-ma: *elas* = little; *soma* = body]

DWARF or PYGMY SUNFISH / *Elassoma evergladei* Jordan

[ev'-er-glade'-eye: named after the Everglades of Florida]

Elassoma evergladei Jordan, Proc. U.S. Nat. Mus., 7:323, 1884 (type locality, St. Johns and Suwannee Rivers, Florida)

RANGE: North Carolina to Florida.

SIZE: 1⅓ inches; breeds at 1 inch.

TEMPERAMENT: A predaceous species suitable with fishes of its own size but best kept in a tank by itself.

TEMPERATURE REQUIREMENTS: 50–70°F.

SEX DIFFERENCES: Male has slightly larger dorsal fin. During breeding time he also has much more color than female.

COUNTS: Dorsal III or IV,8 or 9; anal III,5 to 7; pectoral 13; scales 27 to 30.

This species breeds freely in the same manner as other members of the family. It has been a fairly popular species although not so colorful as others of the family. Florida fish farmers have collected it and sent individuals along with other fishes, whether ordered or not, making it possible to sell it at a low price.

The general color is dark brown, with darker spots and a few vertical bands, which vary in intensity from specimen to specimen.

BANDED PYGMY or DWARF SUNFISH / *Elassoma zonatum* Jordan

[zo-nat'-um: *zonatum* = banded]

Elassoma zonatum Jordan, Bull. U.S. Nat. Mus., 10:50, 1877 (type locality, Little Red River, White County, Arkansas)

RANGE: Southern Illinois to Alabama, west to Texas.

SIZE: 1½ inches; breeds at 1 inch.

TEMPERAMENT: A predaceous species best kept in a tank by itself.

TEMPERATURE REQUIREMENTS: 50–75°F.

SEX DIFFERENCES: Male is more colorful during breeding time and has a slightly higher dorsal fin.

COUNTS: Dorsal IV or V,9 or 10; anal III,5; pectoral 16; scales 38 to 45.

This species has a general color of olive green. It is finely speckled; the sides have 11 dark bars, and a round black spot occurs on the side right behind the shoulder. Its fins are spotted and there is a bar at the base of the caudal fin. The eyes are large and the mouth is very small.

GENUS *Enneacanthus* Gill

[Een'-ne-a-can'-thus: *ennea* = nine; *canthus* = spined]

BLUE-SPOTTED SUNFISH / *Enneacanthus gloriosus* (Holbrook)

[glow'-ri-o'-sus: *gloriosus* = bright or handsome]

Bryttus gloriosus Holbrook, Jour. Acad. Nat. Sci. Philadelphia, 3:52, pl. 5, fig. 4, 1855 (type locality, Cooper River, South Carolina)

RANGE: New York to Florida in lowland areas.

SIZE: 3½ inches; breeds at 2 inches.

TEMPERAMENT: This predaceous species is best kept in its own aquarium.

TEMPERATURE REQUIREMENTS: 40–70°F. A cold-water fish.

SEX DIFFERENCES: See below for color differences.

COUNTS: Dorsal IX,10 or 11; anal III,9 to 11; pectoral 11; scales 30 to 32.

This very beautiful species breeds like other members of the family. Its over-all color is dark olive and its sides are strongly barred. There is a dark bar below the eye. The male has his head, body, and vertical fins covered with round sky-blue spots. The female is duller in color, shows little of the magnificent coloring of the male, and has larger though much fainter spots. The cross bars on the female are narrower and less distinct. The lateral line in this species is nearly always complete.

Enneacanthus obesus (Girard), the banded sunfish, is another beautiful species living in lowland areas from Massachusetts to Florida.

[Lee-po'-mis: *lep* = scale; *pomis* = a cover, the operculum]

RED-BELLIED SUNFISH / *Lepomis auritus* (Linnaeus)

[au-ri'-tus: *auritus* = eared]

Labrus auritus Linnaeus, Systema naturae, ed. 10, p. 283, 1758 (type locality, Philadelphia)

RANGE: Maine to Virginia, east of the mountains.

SIZE: 8 inches; breeds at 4 inches.

TEMPERAMENT: A predaceous species best kept in a tank by itself.

TEMPERATURE REQUIREMENTS: 40–70°F—*no higher than* 74°F.

SEX DIFFERENCES: The male is more colorful than the female.

COUNTS: Dorsal X,11 or 12; anal III,8 to 10; pectoral 13 or 14; scales 43 to 48.

This species breeds like the other members of the family. During the breeding season the red-bellied sunfish is most appropriately named because its belly and lower fins are deep red; scales on the sides have bluish spots, and there are bluish stripes on the head, especially before the eye.

The long bright-edged opercular flap is called the "ear" on sunfishes.

PUMPKINSEED SUNFISH / *Lepomis gibbosus* (Linnaeus)

[gib-bow'-sus: *gibbosus* = hunched or humped]

Perca gibbosa Linnaeus, Systema naturae, ed. 10, p. 293, 1758 (type locality, Carolinas)

RANGE: Great Lakes region to Maine, thence south to Florida; introduced into western United States and elsewhere.

SIZE: 8 inches; breeds at 3 inches.

TEMPERAMENT: A predaceous species best kept with fish of its own size.

TEMPERATURE REQUIREMENTS: 40–70°F—*no higher than* 74°F.

SEX DIFFERENCES: The male is brightly colored but the female has little coloring in her fins.

COUNTS: Dorsal X,10 to 12; anal III,10 to 11; pectoral 13; scales 40 to 47.

This species spawns in a nest, as mentioned for the family. It will defend its nest like a cichlid. It is best fed on *Tubifex* and smaller fishes; it will eagerly take bits of fish and meat but not dry food.

The back is greenish olive, the sides bluish, the belly and lower fins orange; the sides are profusely mottled with reddish orange. The dorsal fin is bluish with orange spots. Cheeks are orange with blue wavy streaks. The "ear" or opercular flap is blackish, broadly edged with red. This fish is a familiar inhabitant of clear brooks. Thoreau once said of this fish: "A very beautiful compact fish, perfect in all its parts, looking like a brilliant coin fresh from the mint."

LONG-EARED SUNFISH / *Lepomis megalotis* (Rafinesque)

[meg'-a-low'-tis: *megal* = great or long; *otis* = ear]

Ichthelis megalotis Rafinesque, Ichthyologia Ohiensis, p. 29, 1820 (type locality, Kentucky, Licking, and Sandy Rivers, Kentucky)

RANGE: Southern Michigan to Minnesota, southward to South Carolina and Texas.

SIZE: 6 inches; breeds at 4 inches.

TEMPERAMENT: A predaceous species best kept in a tank by itself.

TEMPERATURE REQUIREMENTS: 50–70°F.

SEX DIFFERENCES: The male is more brilliantly colored than the female.

COUNTS: Dorsal X,10 to 12; anal III,8 to 10; pectoral 12; scales 36 to 45.

This species breeds like other members of the family.

The over-all color is brilliant blue and orange. The lower parts are predominantly blue, with the orange occurring in spots. The blue, in wavy streaks, is exceedingly attractive. Fins have membranes of orange and the rays are blue. The pelvics are dusky-colored. This is a truly beautiful fish.

Several subspecies have been named in various parts of its range. This species is otherwise known as *Xenotis megalotis* and *Lepomis pallidus.*

GENUS *Mesogonistius* Gill

[Mes'-o-go-nis'-ti-us: *meso* = middle or half; *gonistius* = most-angled, referring to dorsal fin]

BLACK-BANDED SUNFISH / *Mesogonistius chaetodon* (Baird)

[key'-to-don: *chaet* = long bristle; *odon* = teeth]

Pomotis chaetodon Baird, Ninth Smithsonian Rep., p. 324, 1855 (type locality, Cedar Swamp Creek, New Jersey)

RANGE: New Jersey to northern Florida.

SIZE: 3 inches; breeds at 2½ inches.

TEMPERAMENT: A predaceous species best kept in its own aquarium.

TEMPERATURE REQUIREMENTS: 50–70°F.

SEX DIFFERENCES: The female is more lightly colored during breeding time and much heavier with eggs.

COUNTS: Dorsal IX to XI,10 to 13; anal III,12 or 13; pectoral i,10 to 12; scales 28 to 30.

This fish is without doubt the most beautiful of the sunfishes. The body is suborbicular, the mouth small, the fins high, and the scales large. Its body is straw color with from 6 to 8 very sharply defined, though irregular, black vertical bars crossing the body and fins; the first bar runs through the eye, the last through the tail.

Its breeding habits are truly cichlid-like and the male shows extreme devotion to his young. The female, though not very attentive, is said to drive the male back to the nesting area if he tries to leave.

The name of this species currently is *Enneacanthus chaetodon*.

[Sen'tro-pom'-i-dee; Am-bas'-i-dee]

The family of glassfishes known to aquarists as the *Ambassidae* is known to ichthyologists as the *Centropomidae*. This prolific group of fishes occurs in nearly every part of the tropical world from the eastern coastal waters of Africa to Australia and in most large volcanic islands in the Indo-West-Pacific.

GENUS *Chanda* Hamilton = Buchanan

[Chan'-da: *chanda* = a kind of wide-mouthed fish]

This genus was formerly known as *Ambassis,* but since this is not a valid name under the rules of zoological nomenclature it has been replaced with the older name *Chanda.*

The genus *Chanda* contains other species that might make nice aquarium fishes but they are more delicate than the now popular species. The species of *Chanda* need somewhat salty water (1 tablespoon of sea salt per gallon of water), shallow depths (not deeper than 12 inches), plenty of direct sunshine, copious amounts of live food (brine shrimp and *Daphnia* preferably), and a well-planted, crystal-clear aquarium. Under ideal conditions the genus is long-lived, peaceful, and extremely colorful.

All have two dorsal fins, the first a spiny one, the second soft-rayed and connected at the base. There are many kinds of glassfishes, but only three species have appeared for sale in any quantity.

EAST INDIAN GLASSFISH / *Chanda buruensis* (Bleeker)

[bu'-ru-en'-sis: named after Buru Island where first collected]

Ambassis buruensis Bleeker, Nat. Tijdschr. Ned. Indie, 11:396, 1856 (type locality, Buru Island)

RANGE: Siam, Malaya, Philippine Islands, Sumatra, Celebes, and Indo-Australian Archipelago.

SIZE: 2½ inches; breeds at 2 inches.

TEMPERAMENT: A peaceful species suitable for the community tank.

TEMPERATURE REQUIREMENTS: Best kept at 75°F at all times. Breeding is hastened at 85°F.

SEX DIFFERENCES: Female, especially during breeding time, has an enlarged belly.

COUNTS: Dorsal VII,I,8 or 9; anal III,8 to 10; pectoral ii,12; pelvic I,5; scales 27 to 29.

The original brackish-water habitat of this fish gives us an immediate hint that some salt (1 tablespoon to each gallon of water) is necessary to make this beautiful little creature feel at home. It has been imported by the hundreds, and finally in 1948 it was bred. Now that we know its breeding habits it is less expensive to breed than to import.

A well-planted aquarium, about the size of a long 20-gallon tank (12 × 12 × 30 inches) should be heavily stocked with any type of very dense spawning grass. The top of the aquarium should also contain a heavy growth of *Riccia* or other floating grass. A trio, two females to one male, should be selected, separated from the other fish and from each other, then heavily fed on *Daphnia*, brine shrimp, or *Tubifex*. The breeding tank should be half filled with water and placed in a very sunny position. After a week of conditioning, the trio should be placed in the aquarium soon after darkness in the evening and the temperature slowly raised to 85°F. The fish should spawn within 48 hours. Spawning is a pretty sight with the male courting the female by turning over in front of her. These antics continue until soon the female will sidle up to the male and do a somersault with him. When they are on their backs she will release some eggs which are fertilized immediately by the male. The discharge of eggs is usually made directly into the plants on the surface though some will fall down into the plants below. If the parents are well fed they will not eat eggs or spawn. Eggs hatch in 12 hours.

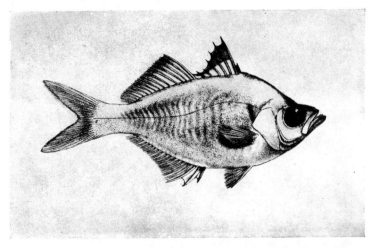

ELONGATED GLASSFISH / *Chanda nama* Hamilton = Buchanan

[na′-ma: *nama* = a flowing stream]

Chanda nama Hamilton = Buchanan, Fishes of the River Ganges, pp. 109, 371, pl. 39, fig. 37, 1822 (type locality, River Ganges)

RANGE: India and Burma.

SIZE: 4 inches; breeding not observed.

TEMPERAMENT: A species suitable in the community tank with fishes of its own size.

TEMPERATURE REQUIREMENTS: 75°F seems to be its most comfortable temperature.

SEX DIFFERENCES: Male has color in his fins.

COUNTS: Dorsal VII,I,16 or 17; anal III,16 or 17; pectoral i,10; pelvic I,5.

Not much is known about the breeding habits of this species. It is seldom imported even though it is hardy and ships very well.

There is a fine line of gold margining on the soft-rayed part of the dorsal fin, whereas the spinous dorsal has a black margin. Fins take on color in slightly salty water until they may be called flame-colored at the height of the breeding season, about Christmas.

GLASSFISH / *Chanda ranga* Hamilton = Buchanan

[ran'-ga: meaning of name not known]

Chanda ranga Hamilton = Buchanan, Fishes of the River Ganges, pp. 113, 371, pl. 16, fig. 38, 1822 (type locality, River Ganges)

RANGE: India and Burma.

SIZE: 2 inches.

TEMPERAMENT: A peaceful species suitable for the community tank.

TEMPERATURE REQUIREMENTS: 68–90°F. Best breeding temperature 85°F.

SEX DIFFERENCES: Male has color on his dorsal- and anal-fin margins.

COUNTS: Dorsal VII,I,12 to 15; anal III,13 to 15; pectoral i,9 or 10; pelvic I,5; scales 60 to 70.

This species is bred the same way as *Chanda buruensis* except that it might spawn in the community aquarium on thickets of plants near the bottom of the aquarium. Breeding seems to be at its best in a 50 per cent mixture of sea and fresh water. Since this species is now freely bred in Florida, few imported specimens are available.

The glassfish is more beautiful than *C. buruensis* because the males have more color edging the outer margin of their dorsal and anal fins, especially when kept in brackish or salt water (ocean water). This fish looks different in each environment in regard to coloration.

The large, silvery sac visible through the "glass" sides of this fish is the swim bladder. Nearly every fish has one, though its location and shape vary considerably from one species to another.

This fish requires small feedings of live foods at least three times a week. *Daphnia* and brine shrimp are the best.

C. lala Hamilton = Buchanan (*Fishes of the River Ganges*, pp. 164, 371, pl. 21, fig. 39, 1822) is a synonym of *C. ranga.*

[Ther'-a-pon'-i-dee]

Genus *Therapon* Cuvier

[Ther'-a-pon: *therapon* = a servant or shield-bearer]

Salt-water Zebrafish / *Therapon jarbua* (Forskål)

[jar-bu'-a: a native name]

Sciaena jarbua Forskål, Descriptiones animalium, pp. 12, 50, 1775 (type locality, probably Red Sea)

RANGE: Tropical Indo-Pacific in the sea, brackish water, and rivers.

SIZE: About 1 foot; breeding not known.

TEMPERAMENT: This species should not be kept with fishes smaller than itself.

TEMPERATURE REQUIREMENTS: 72–80°F.

SEX DIFFERENCES: Not known.

COUNTS: Dorsal XI or XII,10; anal III,8 or 9; pectoral 13; pelvic I,5; scales 80 to 90.

Not much is known about the breeding of this species since mature specimens are rarely imported. Although fairly attractive when small, it soon looses its distinctiveness and becomes bothersome with its big appetite and predaceous habits.

This fish is hardy and readily adapts itself to all salinities of water, from pure sea water to fresh water. It eats just about anything, though it prefers live foods, with clams undoubtedly its favorite.

Colorwise it is a shiny silvery fish with dark gray and black markings. It is not gaudily colored.

[Nan'-di-dee]

This family is interesting not only to aquarists but to ichthyologists and zoogeographers, as members of the family are found on three continents. One species, *Polycentropsis abbreviata,* occurs in western Africa; two species, *Polycentrus schomburgki* and *Monocirrhus polyacanthus,* are found in South America; and several species in southeastern Asia belong to the genera *Nandus, Badis,* and *Pristolepis.* These percomorph fishes probably represent a group of ancient fishes once more generally distributed, but now only relics of the past have survived in distant continents.

As a group of aquarium fishes, they are not very desirable. They possess large mouths, lack color (except *Badis*), and are slow-moving, preferring to hide among the vegetation. They are extremely vicious, especially at night when they will eat fishes at least three-fourths their own size. Even their smaller brothers are usually eaten *in toto* by the larger members present. They have been imported by the thousands and are usually in good supply.

Their habitat is an extremely slow-moving stream, pond, or ditch in which there are many pieces of dead twigs and leaves. The nandids blend perfectly with this background and thus some of them have been dubbed leaffishes.

Genus *Badis* Bleeker

[Bay'-dis: *badis* = probably a native name]

The Badis / *Badis badis* (Hamilton = Buchanan)

Labrus badis Hamilton = Buchanan, Fishes of the River Ganges, pp. 70, 368, pl. 25, fig. 23, 1822 (type locality, Ganges River)

RANGE: India and Burma.

SIZE: 3½ inches; breeds at 2 inches.

TEMPERAMENT: This species is the least vicious of the family and can be kept in the community aquarium with fishes of its own size.

TEMPERATURE REQUIREMENTS: 70–85°F.

SEX DIFFERENCES: Not known, except that the characteristic heavy body of the female indicates her sex.

COUNTS: Dorsal XVI or XVII,9; anal III,7; pectoral 13; pelvic I,5; scales 28 to 30.

This species has been bred repeatedly in this country. Inbreeding has, to some extent, fixed some wonderful color variations, but the color of this fish is as change-able as its temperament and we find that it is never the same color any two minutes.

This fish does not agree in color, disposition, mouth size, or breeding habits with any of the other nandids. It breeds much like some of the dwarf cichlids, though it definitely is not a cichlid. An inverted flowerpot or half a coconut shell seems to suit its purposes best of all. It likes to spawn on the undersurface of such an article and it has been known to spawn on the underside of a piece of slate left tilted on its side. When only two of this species are kept together they are never at peace, but when they are placed in a larger aquarium with other fishes, they get along rather well.

Lately the *Badis* has been in demand. This has resulted mainly from the publication of some excellent though exaggerated color photographs.

It requires live foods almost daily.

GENUS *Monocirrhus* Heckel

[Mon'-o-seer'-us: *mono* = single; *cirrus* = a curl]

SOUTH AMERICAN LEAFFISH / *Monocirrhus polyacanthus* Heckel

[pol'-y-a-can'-thus: *poly* = many; *acanthus* = spines]

Monocirrhus polyacanthus Heckel, Ann. Wien. Mus. Naturges., 2:439, 1840 (type locality, Rio Negro; Marabitanos)

RANGE: Amazon and Rio Negro Basins; British Guiana.

SIZE: 3 inches; breeds at 2 inches.

TEMPERAMENT: A predaceous species that will eat anything that it can get into its deceptively large mouth.

TEMPERATURE REQUIREMENTS: 73–90°F.

SEX DIFFERENCES: Male seems to have slightly larger fins.

COUNTS: Dorsal XVI or XVII,11 to 13; anal XII or XIII,11 to 14; pectoral 18 to 20; pelvic I,5; scales 34 to 38.

Any fish that eats its own weight in other fishes daily is obviously not a very desirable member of the home aquarium. It is necessary to feed this "monster" at least three grown guppies a day or it will soon starve to death. Nevertheless, as undesirable as this sounds, the leaffish is popular. Many people are fascinated by its ability to camouflage itself against the leaves of many aquatic plants. Even its movements are plantlike. It moves slowly and easily just as though a leaf were being carried by the water.

Spawning the leaffish is more a matter of luck than of design. When a pair is ready to spawn it will look for a leaf of a broad-leafed plant such as giant *Sagittaria*. The parents clean off the leaf and spawn thereon. The young hatch out under the watchful eyes of the parent fish.

After a few weeks, the variance in the sizes of the youngsters makes separation a must, otherwise they will gobble up each other. They are transparent when young. For a few months they are covered with whitish dots which lead one to believe they have the ich! However, these spots soon disappear. The youngsters need plenty of live food in the form of *Daphnia*, mosquito larvae, and, if available, baby fishes.

The barbel at the tip of the chin should be noted since the artist left it off the figure.

GENUS *Nandus* Cuvier and Valenciennes

[Nan'-dus: meaning of name not known]

THE NANDUS / *Nandus nandus* (Hamilton = Buchanan)

Coius nandus Buchanan = Hamilton, Fishes of the River Ganges, p. 96, pl. 30, fig. 32, 1822 (type locality, Gangetic provinces)

RANGE: India, Burma, and Siam.

SIZE: 8 inches; breeding not observed.

TEMPERAMENT: This predaceous species may be kept with active fishes larger than itself.

TEMPERATURE REQUIREMENTS: 70–85°F.

SEX DIFFERENCES: Female is slightly lighter in color than the male and her fins are somewhat smaller.

COUNTS: Dorsal XII to XIV,11 to 13; anal III,7 to 9; pectoral 15; pelvic I,5; scales 46 to 57.

This species has not been bred but it probably breeds the same as *Polycentrus*.

The over-all color is a dull brown, slightly punctuated with darker and lighter bands. The tail appears to lack pigment and from a distance the fish looks tailless. Upon closer examination, however, it will be seen that it keeps its tail widespread and the faint pigment is not easily seen. Other fins are more colorful.

It grows rather large but is usually imported at about 2 inches in length. It is extremely hardy and will live in brackish water very well. It does require copious amounts of live foods, although it will eat dead fish and bits of meat. In India it is considered a food fish.

THE CLOUDED NANDUS / *Nandus nebulosus* (Gray)

[neb'-you-low'-sus: *nebulosus* = clouded]

Bedula nebulosus Gray, Illustration of Indian Zoology . . . from the collection of General Hardwicke, pl. 88, fig. 2, 1830–1834 (type locality, India)

RANGE: Siam, Malaya, Sumatra, Borneo, and other East Indian islands.

SIZE: 4 inches; breeding not observed.

TEMPERAMENT: This predaceous species may be kept with active fishes larger than itself.

TEMPERATURE REQUIREMENTS: 68–85°F.

SEX DIFFERENCES: Not known.

COUNTS: Dorsal XIV or XV,11 or **12**; anal III,5 or 6; pectoral 16; pelvic I,5; scales 34 or 35.

This species has been confused with *N. nandus* but may be recognized by its larger scales and more distinct vertical "clouded" bars on the sides.

It has the same food and temperature requirements as *N. nandus*.

GENUS *Polycentropsis* Boulenger

[Pol'-y-cen-trop'-sis: *poly* = many; *centr* = spine; *opsis* = appearance]

AFRICAN LEAFFISH / *Polycentropsis abbreviata* Boulenger

[a-bree'-vee-ay'-ta: *abbreviata* = shortened]

Polycentropsis abbreviata Boulenger, Proc. Zool. Soc. London, no. 1, p. 8, 1901 (type locality, Ethiope River, Niger Delta)

RANGE: Lagos, Niger, and Ogooué, Africa.

SIZE: 4 inches; breeds at 2½ inches.

TEMPERAMENT: A predaceous species· that will eat fish of its own size, or any that it can get into its deceptively large mouth.

TEMPERATURE REQUIREMENTS: 70–85°F.

SEX DIFFERENCES: The female is heavier than the male during spawning time.

COUNTS: Dorsal XV to XVII,9 to 11; anal IX to XII,8 or 9; pectoral 18 or 19; pelvic I,5; scales 31 to 35.

This species has been bred and is in great supply, but it is not very popular. It has bad tricks. Its mouth opens wide very suddenly and it makes a fast lunge at anything swimming near it, usually downing the innocent passer-by with one gulp. It does not chase after its game but awaits its chance to catch the prey off-guard. Feeding this fish may at times be a problem as it requires live food. It can be fed crippled or dying fishes.

Breeding is interesting. The male will select the underside of a leaf, under which there is plenty of dense, dark vegetation. He will then begin to blow hundreds of sticky bubbles, much like a betta. Then the female will come by and place her eggs about the bubbles, attached to the leaf. After spawning, the male seems to turn on her; it is best to remove her from the breeding tank as quickly as possible. The male may be left with the fry as long as he does not start to eat them. To be safe, remove him after the fry are free-swimming.

FAMILY NANDIDAE

GENUS *Polycentrus* Müller and Troschel

[Pol'-y-cen'-trus: *poly* = many; *centrus* = spines]

SCHOMBURGK'S LEAFFISH / *Polycentrus schomburgki* Müller and Troschel

[skom'-burg-eye: named in honor of Richard Schomburgk]

Polycentrus schomburgki Müller and Troschel, Horae ichthyologicae, no. 3, p. 25, pl. 5, fig. 2, 1849 (type locality, Guianas)

RANGE: Guianas and Trinidad.

SIZE: 4 inches; breeds at 2 inches.

TEMPERAMENT: Not a community-tank species. Its deceptively large mouth enables it to ingest fishes its own length.

TEMPERATURE REQUIREMENTS: 68–90°F.

SEX DIFFERENCES: Male is darker than the female.

COUNTS: Dorsal XVI to XVIII,8 or 9; anal XIII,6 to 8; pectoral 15; pelvic I,5; scales 25 to 27.

This species breeds much like *Badis badis*. It requires a large flowerpot or coconut shell placed in the darkest corner of the aquarium, preferably hidden among dense vegetation. It has a feeling of insecurity when maintained in an unplanted aquarium and will not be happy without plants.

Imported specimens are not colorful; they have a typical dirty-brown color, but a few lighter and darker dots do make them more interesting than *Polycentropsis*. As they grow they pass through several color variations and soon are hardly recognizable as the faded, poorly colored fish they once were.

This species is slow-moving in the aquarium or remains motionless, waiting for unsuspecting prey. When hungry, it will dart sharply after worms but its favorite food is small fishes. Large specimens will eat smaller ones without chasing after them.

In the native habitat it is plentiful and extremely hardy. It ships well too.

The fry require plenty of infusoria and brine shrimp during their first few weeks. They also seem too lazy to chase after their food but prefer to catch it as it goes by.

[Tox-ot'-i-dee]

GENUS *Toxotes* Cuvier and Cloquet

[Tox'-o-tes: *toxotes* = a bowman or archer]

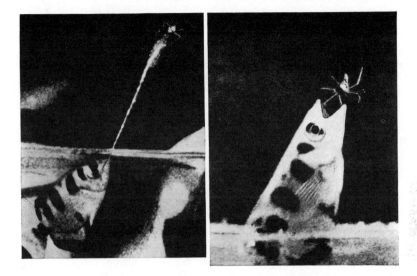

ARCHERFISH / *Toxotes jaculator* (Pallas)

[jack'-you-lay'-tor: *jaculator* = one that throws]

Sciaena jaculatrix Pallas, Phil. Trans. Roy. Soc. London, 56:187, 1766 (type locality, Batavia, Java)

RANGE: India, Burma, Malaya, East Indies, Philippines, Indochina, and Siam.

SIZE: 9 inches; breeding not observed.

TEMPERAMENT: A peaceful species suitable in the community tank if not too large.

TEMPERATURE REQUIREMENTS: 75–85°F.

SEX DIFFERENCES: Not observed.

COUNTS: Dorsal IV,11 or 12; anal III,15 or 16; pectoral 12 or 13; pelvic I,5; scales 28 to 30.

The archerfish, though rare in home aquaria because of difficulty in keeping it alive during long shipment, is one of the most remarkable fish species in the world.

Hugh M. Smith (*Bull. U.S. Nat. Mus.*, 188:490–497, 1945) gives the following information:

"The doubt shown by zoologists of the last century in regard to the reputed shooting powers of the fish was partly due to their failure to detect in the fish's mouth any special mechanism by which drops of water could be formed and expelled. It is, of course, obvious that there must be some peculiar adaptation or apparatus in *Toxotes* to account for its extraordinary accomplishment. By carefully watching the fish at close range on many occasions in Thailand, the writer formed an opinion of the probable propelling mechanism, and subsequently verified that opinion by holding the fish in a basin or bucket of water in the position regularly assumed when shooting and making them perform almost at will. This he accomplished by the quick, forceful compression of the gill covers with his fingers, and by so doing he was able to cause a fairly satisfactory imitation of the normal shooting act, and had no difficulty in propelling drops of water for distances up to 3 feet.

"This compression of the gill covers would in itself not account for the escape from the mouth of water in the form of individual drops of uniform size, and it is to the peculiar shape and structure of the mouth parts that we must look for the additional factors necessary for the complete and perfect performance.

"The mouth cavity of *Toxotes* is long but its diameter is much restricted by the projecting sides of the roof and by the large tongue, which when raised may completely close the passage to the pharynx. The anterior part of the tongue is free from the floor of the mouth, and its rounded tip is of paperlike thinness and fits snugly against the palate; posteriorly the tongue is thick, bears minute teeth, and has a conspicuous fleshy prominence. Extending along the median line of the roof of the mouth, from a point just behind the band of vomerine teeth to the pharynx, is a deep groove which, when the tongue is applied to the roof of the mouth, becomes converted into a tube. This groove-tube, which in a fish 7 inches long is less than a sixteenth of an inch in diameter, not previously described or referred to in ichthyological writings, may readily be seen when the tongue is depressed. That it should have been so long overlooked is something of a mystery when one recalls the vain efforts made by Oriental ichthyologists to discover any special adaptation for drop shooting.

"It is not difficult to discern the manner in which the shooting fish operates. With its tongue closely pressed against the palate, the sudden compression of the gill covers will force water from the pharynx into the palatine canal, and with the tip of the tongue acting as a valve, the flow of water under pressure from the anterior end of the tube is regulated. With the jaws partly separated and the mouth reaching or projecting slightly above the surface, the water is ejected with a force and for a distance that depends on the pressure. It is easy to understand how, with the pharyngeal cavity serving both as a reservoir for water ammunition and a compression chamber, it is possible for the fish to shoot drops of water in quick succession, to propel the water in the form of a jet when the valve is kept open longer.

"The drop-propelling function would be useless if *Toxotes* did not possess, in addition, the ability to use its eyes in the air and to gauge accurately the distance, size, and suitability for food of small creatures flying or resting near the water's edge. It is an outstanding point that, for a fish, the aerial vision of *Toxotes* is very keen, and it was always a surprise to the present author to note the readiness with which insects and spiders were sighted as the fish explored the vegetation on the bank of a pond or stream.

"The archerfish, with shapely, compressed body propelled by its broad caudal fin, is a graceful swimmer, moving quickly without apparent effort. It regularly swims at or just below the surface, and may go a long distance in a perfectly straight line, making a wake with the tip of its jaws. This wake is characteristic and enables an observer to detect the presence of a fish before he has actually seen it. The habit of swimming at the surface is ascribable to two circumstances: The food on which the fish chiefly subsists is obtainable there, and the eyes, on which the fish largely depends, could not otherwise function properly, for during most of the year the waters in which *Toxotes* lives are very muddy or turbid and aquatic vision is much restricted.

"One day in April, after a heavy rain, large winged termites appeared in great numbers in the yard of the author's residence in Bangkok and many flew low over a pond into which *Toxotes* had been introduced. The fishes were observed to follow the termites with great eagerness and often bring them down with a single shot or a series of shots. Marksmanship at moving insects was not nearly so accurate as when exercised against insects at rest on overhanging vegetation. On this occasion, when termites flew within a foot of the surface of the pond, the fishes sometimes jumped entirely out of the water, and caught them on the wing.

"The range, accuracy, and force of the shooting powers of *Toxotes* always cause surprise and admiration. In the author's experience in Thailand the distance within which the fish could always be depended on to score a direct hit was 3½ to 4 feet. A much longer effective range has been recorded. Two fishes in the New York Aquarium could without difficulty hit a small cockroach at a measured height of 5 feet above the water.

"Failure to hit a resting insect within proper range may be due to movements of the vegetation or, in the case of a spider dangling on a thread, to swaying caused by wind. When the first shot misses a mark, other shots usually follow in quick succession.

"The force with which the watery pellets may strike an object is sometimes most astonishing to a human observer. An insect may be knocked high in the air or may fall on the bank beyond a fish's reach. At short range the drops may strike a person's face with a distinctly stinging sensation. On many occasions, during exhibitions in Thailand, a spider at the end of a thread hanging from the end of a pole was knocked far up on the thread or even over the pole.

"The shooting habit begins to develop early and may be observed in fishes only an inch long. It is most amusing to see the inexperienced youngsters emulating the actions of their parents and sending out tiny drops that may go only 2 or 3 inches. In half grown fish the habit is well developed, but the highest expression of the shooting powers as regards accuracy, force, and range is to be seen only in the fully matured fish."

Toxotes jaculator

FAMILY **MONODACTYLIDAE**

[Mon'-oh-dak-tyl'-i-dee]

GENUS *Monodactylus* Lacepède

[Mon'-oh-dak'-ty-lus: *mono* = one; *dactylus* = a finger]

FINGERFISH / *Monodactylus argenteus* (Linnaeus)

[are'-gen-tee'-us: *argenteus* = covered with silver]

Chaetodon argenteus Linnaeus, Systema naturae, ed. 10, p. 272, 1758 (type locality, Indies)

RANGE: Tropical Indo-Pacific oceans from Polynesia westward to Africa, living in salt and fresh waters.

SIZE: 9 inches; breeding not known.

TEMPERAMENT: A peaceful species.

TEMPERATURE REQUIREMENTS: 72–85°F.

SEX DIFFERENCES: Not known.

COUNTS: Dorsal VII or VIII,28 to 30; anal III,27 to 32; pectoral ii,15; pelvic I,5; scales 50 to 60.

This fish has not been bred. Several reliable reports claim that it breeds in fresh water, though it is always trapped from salt or brackish water. It does have the ability to survive in the fresh-water aquarium, but it fares better when about 1 gallon of sea water is added to every 5 gallons of fresh water. Since it must come from open water, many individuals perish in the transition to smaller quarters. Keep this in mind when assigning it tank space. Each single fish needs at least 5 gallons of water, regardless of its size. The more room the better for the fish. Never subject it to unseasoned fresh water. It requires water which preferably has had fishes living in it for a few weeks, months, or years before it is introduced. This is true for a great many brackish-water fishes, especially the clown loaches and the monodactylids.

For a diet offer bits of meat, crabmeat, fish, worms of all kinds, and adult brine shrimp.

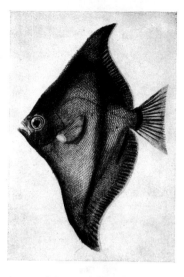

STRIPED FINGERFISH or MONODACTYLID / *Monodactylus sebae*
(Cuvier and Valenciennes)

[see'-bee: named in honor of the naturalist A. Seba]

Psettus sebae Cuvier and Valenciennes, Histoire naturelle des poissons, 7:241, pl. 189, 1831 (type locality, Senegal)

RANGE: West Africa from the Senegal to the Congo in salt and fresh waters.

SIZE: 8 inches; breeding not known.

TEMPERAMENT: A peaceful species.

TEMPERATURE REQUIREMENTS: 72–85°F.

SEX DIFFERENCES: Not known.

COUNTS: Dorsal VIII,32 to 36; anal III,37; pectoral ii,15; pelvic I,5; scales 50.

This fish has never been bred. Its care and habits are the same as for *Monodactylus argenteus*. It differs in having a dark black band that runs through the middle of its side. This fish has a greater depth for its length than any other fish kept in the aquarium, even deeper than *M. argenteus*.

Family SCATOPHAGIDAE

[Scat'-o-fay'-gi-dee]

Genus *Scatophagus* Cuvier and Valenciennes

[Scat'-o-fay'-gus: *scat* = combining form of dung; *phagus* = to eat]

THE SCAT / *Scatophagus argus* (Linnaeus)

[ar'-gus: *argus* = shining or glistening]

Chaetodon argus Linnaeus, Systema naturae, ed. 12, p. 464, 1766 (type locality, India)

RANGE: Tropical Indo-Pacific in salt and brackish waters.

SIZE: 10 inches; breeding not known.

TEMPERAMENT: A peaceful species.

TEMPERATURE REQUIREMENTS: 74–85°F.

SEX DIFFERENCES: Not known.

COUNTS: Dorsal XI,14 or 15; anal IV,14; pectoral ii,15; pelvic I,5; scales very fine.

This fish has never been bred, but its attractive coloration and interesting habits make it a desirable aquarium addition.

There is quite a bit of whispering in the trade about the name "Scatophagus," for the Greek word *scat* means dung. A search of the literature reveals that Francis Day, in *The Fishes of India* (vol. 1, footnote p. 115, London, 1878), remarks: "I have opened many specimens of *Scatophagus*, and those taken from near inhabited localities had, as a rule, their stomachs full of ordure." Thus we get the name for the fish as dung eater or garbage eater. This point is brought into prominence when the fish is kept in the aquarium, for there the fish will eat anything and everything. There seems to be a definite need, though, for vegetable matter of some sort; in the absence of *Riccia* and *Nitella*, lettuce should be offered. Otherwise *Tubifex* worms and some dried foods will eagerly be accepted.

The fish becomes fairly well acclimated to the aquarium after a few months of good food and it is inclined to be a good pet, showing remarkable powers of recognition for the person that feeds it.

The fish requires brackish water made either by the addition of 20 per cent sea water or about 2 teaspoonfuls of salt for every gallon of water. If kept in fresh water the pH must not get lower than 7.4. Use 250 mg of terramycin per 5 gallons of water if the fish gets body fungus and change to more brackish water.

AFRICAN SCAT / *Scatophagus tetracanthus* (Lacepède)

[tet′-ra-can′-thus: *tetra* = four; *acanthus* = spines]

Chaetodon tetracanthus Lacepède, Histoire naturelle des poissons, 4:726–727, 1802 (no locality)

RANGE: East African coastal area in salt and brackish waters.

SIZE: 10 inches; breeding not known.

TEMPERAMENT: A peaceful species.

TEMPERATURE REQUIREMENTS: 72–85°F.

SEX DIFFERENCES: Not known.

COUNTS: Dorsal XI,15 to 18; anal IV,14 or 15; pectoral ii,15; pelvic I,5; scales very fine.

This species is rarely seen in the United States, but it does from time to time appear in Germany and England. With air transportation it should not be long before the African scat is popular in America.

The general color of this species is a lemon shade, lightly sprinkled with spangles of pearly iridescence. There are 5 or 6 broad dark bars which distinguish this species from the spotted *Scatophagus argus*. The first of the bands passes through the eye, the next four lie between it and the sixth, which is the entire pigmented section of the caudal peduncle. The tail is lemon-colored and the first few spines of the dorsal fin are scarlet red.

This species, like the other scats, needs 20 per cent sea water.

Family SCATOPHAGIDAE

Genus *Selenotoca* Myers

[Sel'-e-not'-o-ca: *selen* = the moon; *otoca* = the ear]

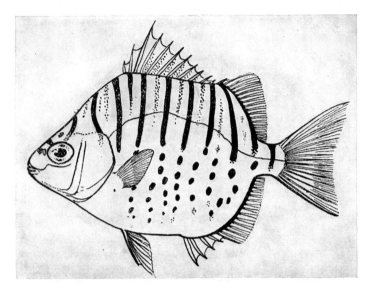

Many-banded Scat / *Selenotoca multifasciata* (Richardson)

[mul'-ti-fas'-see-a'-ta: *multi* = many; *fasciata* = banded]

Scatophagus multifasciatus Richardson, Zoology of the Voyage of the *Erebus* and *Terror*, Fish, p. 57, pl. 35, figs. 4–6 ,1844–1846 (type locality, King George's Sound, West Australia)

RANGE: East, north, and western coasts of Australia.

SIZE: 4 inches; breeding not known.

TEMPERAMENT: A peaceful species.

TEMPERATURE REQUIREMENTS: 72–85°F.

SEX DIFFERENCES: Not known.

COUNTS: Dorsal XII,16; anal IV,16; pectoral 16; pelvic I,5.

This fish closely resembles *Selenotoca papuensis* except for the fact that it has more bands, which break up into a continuous series of blotches on the lower sides. There are from 10 to 12 bands, depending upon the age of the individual.

It requires the same treatment as other members of the family Scatophagidae.

HALF-BANDED SCAT / *Selenotoca papuensis* Fraser-Brunner

[pap'-u-en'-sis: named in honor of the locality where collected]

Selenotoca papuensis Fraser-Brunner, Aquarist, 8(3):75, fig. 3, 1935; Ann. Mag. Nat. Hist., (11)2:78, figs. 1, 2, 1938 (type locality, New Guinea, Celebes)

RANGE: New Guinea and Celebes.

SIZE: 4 inches; breeding unknown.

TEMPERAMENT: A peaceful species.

TEMPERATURE REQUIREMENTS: 72–85°F.

SEX DIFFERENCES: Not known.

COUNTS: Dorsal XII,16; anal IV,16; pectoral 16; pelvic I,5.

Here again we have a silvery fish, typically scatlike in appearance, differing from its closest relative *Selenotoca multifasciata* only by having fewer but wider black bands.

The care of this species is the same as for the other scats. It does best in 25 per cent sea water which has been thoroughly filtered first.

[Po'-ma-sen'-tri-dee]

Genus *Amphiprion* Bloch and Schneider

[Am'-fie-pry'-on: *amphi* = on both sides; *prion* = a saw; referring to the two
serrated edges of the gill cover]

Clownfish / *Amphiprion percula* (Lacepède)

[per-que'-la: *percula* = a little perch]

Lutjanus percula Lacepède, Histoire
naturelle des poissons, 4:194, 239, 240,
1802 (type locality, New Britain)

RANGE: Coral reefs of tropical Indo-
Pacific oceans.

SIZE: 2½ inches; breeds at 2 inches.

TEMPERAMENT: A peaceful species.

TEMPERATURE REQUIREMENTS: 72–
80°F.

SEX DIFFERENCES: Not observed.

COUNTS: Dorsal X,15 or 16; anal II,12
or 13; pectoral 16; pelvic I,5.

This marine fish is brightly colored in
its native habitat on the coral reefs. The
background color is a vivid orange with
three broad blue bands encircling the
body. Sometimes in captivity the bright
colors fade into light tan or even become
whitish.

The clownfish lives in a symbiotic as-
sociation with the large sea anemone. It
swims about the stinging tentacles of
Discosoma without danger to itself. It is
said that the sting is fatal to *Amphiprion*,
but for some unknown reason it is not
stung. This relationship is profitable for
both. The clownfish attracts other fishes
to the anemone, which promptly paralyzes them by its stinging cells. Both then
share the food.

Recently it was determined that
although *Amphiprion percula* is indeed a
valid species, the fish often referred to by
that name within the aquarium trade is actually *Amphiprion ocellaris*, which is the
fish pictured here.

GENUS *Dascyllus* Cuvier

[Das-cyl'-lus: *dascyllus* = a kind of fish]

BLACK-AND-WHITE DAMSELFISH / *Dascyllus aruanus* (Linnaeus)

[are'-you-an'-us: named after the Aru Islands, East Indies]

Chaetodon aruanus Linnaeus, Systema naturae, ed. 10, p. 275, 1758 (type locality, Indies)

RANGE: Coral reefs of tropical Indo-Pacific oceans.

SIZE: 2 inches; breeding not observed.

TEMPERAMENT: Several individuals should be kept together in at least a 50-gallon tank. Two fish alone will fight each other.

TEMPERATURE REQUIREMENTS: 72–80°F.

SEX DIFFERENCES: Not observed.

COUNTS: Dorsal XII,14 to 16; anal II,13 or 14; pectoral ii,18 or 19; pelvic I,5; scales 27 or 28.

Remarks under *Dascyllus trimaculatus* hold true for this species also.

This coral fish is attractive with its bright white body banded by three wide black stripes. The stripes go through the fins (except the tail) and make an exceedingly interesting display.

Keep in mind that this species is strictly marine, and the more sea water available for it the better.

WHITE-SPOTTED DAMSELFISH / *Dascyllus trimaculatus* (Rüppell)

[tri-mack'-you-lay'-tus: *tri* = three; *maculatus* = spotted]

Pomacentrus trimaculatus Rüppell, Atlas Zu der Reise in Nördlichen Afrika, Fische, p. 39, pl. 8, fig. 3, 1828 (type locality, Massaua, Red Sea)

RANGE: Coral reefs of the tropical Indo-Pacific oceans.

SIZE: 3 inches; breeding not observed.

TEMPERAMENT: Several individuals should be kept together in at least a 50-gallon tank. Two fish alone will constantly fight each other.

TEMPERATURE REQUIREMENTS: 72–80°F.

SEX DIFFERENCES: Not observed.

COUNTS: Dorsal XII,15; anal II,14; pectoral ii,18 or 19; pelvic I,5; scales 27 or 28.

This species is strictly marine and has not been bred in the home aquarium. It must have full-strength sea water.

Feeding is no problem. It eats just about anything, such as bits of clam, shrimp, lobster, and crab. It should be fed regularly but sparingly every 2 days. Be careful not to overfeed it.

The body and fins are blackish and there are three brilliantly contrasting white spots (thus the name *trimaculatus*) one on each side of the body and one on the mid-line of the forehead. A black spot is located at the dorsal base of the pectoral fin.

GENUS *Pomacentrus* Lacepède

[Po'-ma-sen'-trus: *poma* = a cover; *centrus* = a point or spine]

BLUE DEVIL / *Pomacentrus fuscus* Cuvier and Valenciennes

[fus'-cus: *fuscus* = dark or dusky]

Pomacentrus fuscus Cuvier and Valenciennes, Histoire naturelle des poissons, 5:432, 1830 (type locality, Brazil)

RANGE: Key West, Florida, through West Indies to Brazil in marine waters.

SIZE: 5 inches; breeds at 3 inches.

TEMPERAMENT: This species should be kept by itself, with each individual in its own aquarium.

TEMPERATURE REQUIREMENTS: 72–80°F. Breed at 76°F.

SEX DIFFERENCES: Male shows a more deeply purplish sheen and has a more spangled effect.

COUNTS: Dorsal XII,15; anal II,13; pectoral ii,17; pelvic I,5; scales 28.

This is one of the few marine fishes that has been successfully spawned in the home aquarium. Its spawning habits are similar to those of the dwarf cichlids. It lays eggs inside a flowerpot. The fry hatch in a few days but usually die as soon as they become free-swimming, probably because of an insufficient supply of plankton for them to eat.

The body color is a beautiful royal blue with several rows of scales having a spangled effect. The intensity of this coloring varies with the condition of the fish but it is always very attractive.

Feeding is no problem if small baby guppies and bits of clam, shrimp, lobster, and crabmeat are made available to this fish.

Family CICHLIDAE

[Sick'-li-dee]

The great abundance of these fishes, coupled with their intense coloration and interesting breeding habits, has made the cichlid family popular among aquarists. Their chief faults are predaceousness and viciousness, but their hardiness and ease of propagation have made them a commercially valuable species.

Geographically this large family of fishes is found in Africa, South America, Central America, and the southwestern part of the United States, with one genus, *Etroplus*, found in Asia. They are extremely hardy and readily acclimate themselves to water conditions ranging from brackish to fresh. Several species (like *Tilapia macrocephala*) freely migrate from ocean water to fresh water. They are spiny-rayed fishes, with a single nostril on each side of the head; they have an elaborate mating pattern (bordering on monogamy). Much research has been done lately (mainly by animal behaviorists) on the "why" of their breeding habits.

In general the numerous species prefer live foods, but they willingly accept all sorts of substitutes. It is possible to raise them commercially without ever giving them any live foods other than the incidental infusoria and occasional cannibalism. They are fast-growing and give extreme care to their eggs and young.

Usually sexing the fishes is easy: males nearly always are more colorful than females and have more pointed anal and dorsal fins.

GENUS *Aequidens* Eigenmann and Bray

[Ee-qui'-dens: *aequi* = equal; *dens* = teeth]

FLAG CICHLID / *Aequidens curviceps* (Ahl)

[cur'-vi-ceps: *curvi* = curved; *ceps* = head]

Acara curviceps Ahl, Mitth. Zool. Mus. Berlin, 11(1):44, fig., 1924 (type locality, Amazon River)

RANGE: Amazon River.

SIZE: 3 inches; breeds at 2½ inches.

TEMPERAMENT: Suitable in the community tank when small, but it will eat fishes smaller than itself when adult.

TEMPERATURE REQUIREMENTS: 72–85°F. Optimum breeding temperature 76°F.

SEX DIFFERENCES: Male has longer and more pointed anal and dorsal fins.

COUNTS: Dorsal XV,7; anal III,7; pectoral ii,13; scales 2½ to 3 + 23 or 24 + 8 or 9.

This species spawns in typical cichlid fashion. Parents should be conditioned on *Tubifex* worms or other similar live food prior to their spawning. A pair will select a spawning site and then begin their housecleaning job. Once the site has been thoroughly scrubbed the breeding tubes (ovipositors) will appear at the anal pore and within a few hours the pair will spawn. Since this fish is shy, it should be provided with a heavily planted aquarium. It does not uproot plants as is the habit of many cichlids.

If disturbed, the parents may eat their eggs. If they repeatedly devour their spawn, it will be wise to remove them soon after they have completed spawning. The fry hatch in about 3 days at 76°F and are free-swimming in another 3 days. They require freshly hatched brine shrimp, microworms, sifted *Daphnia*, and Gordon's formula in fairly substantial amounts. Their growth the first three or four weeks is amazing if fed well; the fish are ½ inch long in less than a month.

KEYHOLE CICHLID / *Aequidens maroni* (Steindachner)

[ma-ron'-i: named after the river where first collected]

Acara maronii Steindachner, Denks. Akad. Wiss. Wien, 43:141, pl. 2, fig. 4, 1882 (type locality, Maroni River, French Guiana)

RANGE: Guianas.

SIZE: 3½ inches; breeds at 2½ inches.

TEMPERAMENT: Peaceful for a cichlid and suitable in the community tank.

TEMPERATURE REQUIREMENTS: 72–85°F. Optimum breeding temperature 80°F.

SEX DIFFERENCES: Male has longer and more pointed anal and dorsal fins.

COUNTS: Dorsal XV,10; anal III,9 to 11; pectoral ii,13; scales 22 to 24.

This is one of the more difficult cichlid species to spawn. It is timid and does well only in a heavily planted aquarium. One breeder produces this species in bare tanks but since there is little disturbance in his hatchery the fish do not seem to mind it. Spawns are not large. They may run to 300 at times, but the average is about 150.

Owing to its peaceful nature and serene beauty, this fish has come into great demand. Since it is hard to breed and scarce, it is high-priced. Colorwise it may be described as being brown, with various shades from mustard to dark brown. At about 2 years of age, spawners in good condition seem to develop a white border about their tail and dorsal fin, but this characteristic, like the keyhole spot, is variable and may scarcely be recognized.

THE PORT or BLACK ACARA / *Aequidens portalegrensis* (Hensel)

[por'-ta-lay-gren'-sis: named after the locality where first collected]

Acara portalagrensis Hensel, Arch. Naturges. Berlin, 36 yr. vol. 1, p. 52, 1870 (type locality, Porto Alegre)

RANGE: Porto Alegre, Rio Grande do Sul, Paraguay.

SIZE: 5 inches; breeds at 3 inches.

TEMPERAMENT: Moderately peaceful; may be kept in the community tank with fish of its own size.

TEMPERATURE REQUIREMENTS: 72–85°F. It will spawn at any temperature within this range.

SEX DIFFERENCES: Male is slightly more colorful, having longer and more pointed anal and dorsal fins than the female. The only really sure way of sexing specimens is to observe them from above and note the bulging sides of the female.

COUNTS: Dorsal XV,10; anal III,9; pectoral ii,12 or 13; scales 24 to 26.

This species is, without doubt, one of the easiest cichlids to induce to spawn. All that seems necessary is to have a male and female. They are not only very gentle with each other, but they show a gratifying affection for their spawn; seldom has a pair been reported to have eaten its eggs or young. So peaceful are they that most breeders keep the parents in with the fry until they are large enough to be sold. Many cases have been reported where the parents have spawned again while their previous spawn was still in the aquarium with them.

Because of the ease with which the port is bred, the market price is low. This has compelled many breeders to stop producing it. Only recently has it begun to be scarce, but it would only take a single pair to produce all the baby fish that are wanted in a very short time.

Blue acaras spawning.

BLUE ACARA / *Aequidens pulcher* (Gill)

[pul'-cher: *pulcher* = beautiful]

Cychlasoma pulchrum Gill, Ann. Lyc. Nat. Hist. New York, 6:382, 1858 (type locality, Trinidad)

RANGE: Panama, Colombia, Venezuela, and Trinidad.

SIZE: 6 inches; breeds at 4 inches.

TEMPERAMENT: Not suitable in the community tank except when kept with fishes of same size.

TEMPERATURE REQUIREMENTS: 72–85°F. Breeding best maintained at 78°F.

SEX DIFFERENCES: Male has more pointed anal and dorsal fins.

COUNTS: Dorsal XIV,9 or 10; anal III,7 rarely III,8; pectoral ii,12 or 13; scales 23 or 24.

Typically cichlid-like in its breeding habits, this species is an old-time favorite. It is easily spawned and takes good care of its fry. It competes with the port for popularity on this score, although this fish is certainly more attractive than the plain port.

Blue acaras "kissing."

Why this fish is called the blue acara is no mystery; its color is a steel-blue gray, which is typically cichlid. Many cichlids show this coloration around the gill cover but only this one and several species of *Apistogramma* show so much of this attractive pattern.

Pairs should be supplied with a large aquarium, the long type of 20-gallon capacity if possible. The bottom may be sanded or clear; this does not matter for the pair will dig into the sand until it reaches the bottom anyway. If conditions are right it will breed every 2 weeks like clockwork. Parents may be left with the fry, but this seems to keep them from breeding regularly.

Aequidens latifrons is a synonym of this species. It was originally published as *Acara coeruleopunctata latifrons* Steindachner (*Denks. Akad. Wiss. Wien*, 39:27, 1878, type locality, mouth of Rio Magdalena).

SADDLE CICHLID / *Aequidens tetramerus* (Heckel)

[tet'-ra-mer'-us: *tetra* = four; *merus* = pure or unmixed]

Acara tetramerus Heckel, Ann. Wien. Mus. Naturges., 2:341, 1840 (type locality, Rio Branco)

RANGE: Caripito, Venezuela, south to Paraguay and west to Bolivia and Peru.

SIZE: 8 inches; breeds at 5 inches.

TEMPERAMENT: Not suitable in the community tank except with fishes as large as itself.

TEMPERATURE REQUIREMENTS: 72–85°F.

SEX DIFFERENCES: Male has longer and more pointed anal and dorsal fins. Female is a bit plumper when filled with mature eggs.

COUNTS: Dorsal XV or XVI,10; anal III,8 to 10; pectoral ii,13; scales 26 or 27.

This species is not common because no one has taken the trouble to breed it. Small specimens lack attractive colors and for this reason it does not seem to be very desirable. If it were nicely colored when young, then it would be kept and bred regardless of what it looks like when older.

The older specimens are more beautifully colored. The dark spot on the back, when viewed from the proper angle, reminds one of a saddle, thus the popular name "saddle cichlid." This spot is common among the various kinds of *Aequidens; A. maroni* has a similar though larger spot. There seems to be a ring about the saddle mark at times, which may have a golden hue. Otherwise, the fish is colored like other *Aequidens* with browns and grays. The eye is large; compared to the bright red eye of the port, the eye is more golden brown.

The spawns are large and the breeders must be removed. Since they will tear up plants, they must be kept in unplanted aquaria.

The parents are so large that they take all kinds of food. A pleasant surprise is that they eagerly eat most dog and cat foods that have a base of meat and fish.

Acara diadema Heckel (*Ann. Wien Mus. Naturges.*, 2:344, 1840) from Rio Negro in Venezuela is a synonym of this species.

Genus *Apistogramma* Regan

[A'-pis-to-gram'-ma: *apisto* = false; *gramma* = lines]

The genus *Apistogramma* is a group of small cichlids, rarely longer than 3 inches, referred to as "dwarf cichlids" and native to South America. They are endeared to hobbyists because they manifest the extreme of parental care attributed to the larger cichlids. Their coloration is beautiful.

All species breed in much the same manner. A pair will look for a private site upon which to spawn. Many breeders prefer an overturned flowerpot, but coconut shells with two large holes in them are highly successful. Sometimes they may be inclined to spawn on a leaf if there is a stiff-leafed plant available and plenty of privacy. Once the female has spawned and the male has fertilized the eggs, it is wise to remove the male. The females seem to prefer their motherly tasks without the hindrance of the male.

Spawns are usually small and the fry require infusoria and freshly hatched brine shrimp as soon as they are free-swimming. They grow slowly, requiring constant feedings of live foods. They do better in large shallow aquaria.

AGASSIZ DWARF CICHLID / *Apistogramma agassizi* (Steindachner)

[ag'-as-siz-eye: named in honor of Louis Agassiz]

Geophagus (*Mesops*) *agassizii* Steindachner, Sitzb. Akad. Wiss. Wien, 71:111, pl. 8, figs. 2, 2a, 2b, 1875 (type locality, Curupirá; Cudajas; Rio Puty; Lago Maximo; Lago Manacápuru)

RANGE: Amazon Basin.

SIZE: 3 inches; breeds at 2 inches.

TEMPERAMENT: Fairly peaceful and suitable in the community aquarium.

TEMPERATURE REQUIREMENTS: 72–85°F.

SEX DIFFERENCES: Male is larger and has longer, more pointed anal, caudal, and dorsal fins.

COUNTS: Dorsal XV,7; anal III,6; pectoral 14; scales 23.

This species breeds the same as other members of the genus.

The over-all color of this species is a yellow brown. The back is a dark purple, with a brilliant sheen. There is a dark-brown line that runs from the eye along the sides to the end of the tail. This line continues forward of the eye to the snout but does not pass through the eye. The underside of the fish is flushed with red, but this varies in intensity as the fish approaches spawning time. There is a typical metallic sheen to some of the scales which adds to its attractiveness. The dorsal fin is beautifully colored with a slight edging in orange, with membranes colored in light purple. The tail is also edged in orange and has bluish membranes.

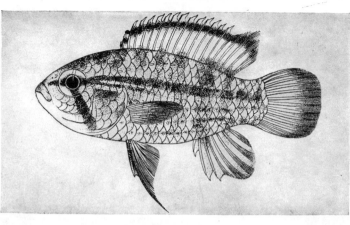

CORUMBA DWARF CICHLID /
Apistogramma corumbae (Eigenmann and Ward)

[cor-um'-bee: named after the locality where collected]

Heterogramma corumbae Eigenmann and Ward, in Eigenmann, McAttee, and Ward, Ann. Carnegie Mus., 4(2):146, pl. 45, fig. 3, 1907 (type locality, Corumba, Rio Paraguay)

RANGE: Brazil and Paraguay.

SIZE: 2½ inches; breeds at 2 inches.

TEMPERAMENT: A peaceful species suitable for the community aquarium.

TEMPERATURE REQUIREMENTS: 70--85°F.

SEX DIFFERENCES: Male has longer and more pointed fins. Female is a little smaller than the male.

COUNTS: Dorsal XVI,6; anal III,6 or 7; pectoral 11; scales 22.

This species breeds the same way as other members of this genus.

The coloration of this fish varies with its environment, but it may generally be considered to be a yellowish brown. The sides show a series of large dark dots and bars with a series of dark bands on the tail. This fish appears rounder than the other members of the genus and has the body contours of *Aequidens portalegrensis* (page 601). A curved dark bar runs through the eye from top to bottom. The fins show a reddish tinge, but this is variable. The rear parts of the dorsal and anal fins are speckled with small black dots.

ORTMAN'S DWARF CICHLID / *Apistogramma ortmanni* (Eigenmann)

[ort′-mann-eye: named in honor of the naturalist A. E. Ortman]

Heterogramma ortmanni Eigenmann, Mem. Carnegie Mus., 5:506, pl. 68, fig. 1, 1912 (type locality, British Guiana)

RANGE: Guianas.

SIZE: 3 inches; breeds at 2 inches.

TEMPERAMENT: Peaceful and suitable in the community aquarium.

TEMPERATURE REQUIREMENTS: 72–85°F.

SEX DIFFERENCES: Male has longer, more pointed dorsal and anal fins.

COUNTS: Dorsal XV,7; anal III,6 or 7; pectoral 12; scales 22 to 24.

This dwarf cichlid breeds like other members of the genus.

It has the same body form as *Apistogramma corumbae* and is easily mistaken for it. The over-all color is a brownish red with a tendency to yellowish brown on the underside. A black stripe runs from the snout, not through the eye but up each edge of it, and then continues to the tip of the caudal peduncle. About 6 dark vertical bars run over the back of the fish just past the lateral line. The scales are reticulated. The tail and the soft-rayed sections of the anal and dorsal fins are flecked with irregular dots, which again is similar to *A. corumbae*.

YELLOW DWARF CICHLID / *Apistogramma pertense* (Haseman)

[per-ten′-se: *per* = throughout; *tense* = slender]

Heterogramma taeniatum pertense Haseman, Ann. Carnegie Mus., 7(3,4): 359, pl. 66, 1911 (type locality, Manaus; Santarém, Rio Tapajos)

RANGE: Amazon Basin.

SIZE: 2 inches; breeds at 2 inches.

TEMPERAMENT: Peaceful and suitable in the community aquarium.

TEMPERATURE REQUIREMENTS: 70–85°F.

SEX DIFFERENCES: Male has much more color than the female. He also has longer, more pointed fins, especially the anal, dorsal, and caudal fins.

COUNTS: Dorsal XVI,6; anal III,6; pectoral 12 or 13; scales 23.

This species breeds in the manner described for other members of the genus.

The color of this cichlid is variable and a tankful of them emphasizes that point. The sides are more or less high-lighted by a single stripe that runs from the snout, through the eye, through a large dark spot in the center of the body, and ends at the dark spot on the caudal peduncle. A crescent-shaped dark mark runs above and below the eye but does not go through it. The individual scales are reticulated, giving the fish an over-all spotted appearance. This "checkerboard" effect is especially noticeable on the female because she lacks the other colorings on her sides. The tail fin of the male has a mosaiclike pattern which is more typical of certain anabantids (though several cichlids show this same type of marking).

Apistogramma pleurotaenia (Regan)

[pleur'-ow-teen'-i-a: *pleuro* = the side; *taenia* = striped]

Heterogramma pleurotaenia Regan, Ann. Mag. Nat. Hist., (8)3:270, 1909 (type locality, Rio de La Plata)

RANGE: Rio de La Plata.

SIZE: 3 inches; breeds at 2 inches.

TEMPERAMENT: A peaceful species suitable in the community aquarium.

TEMPERATURE REQUIREMENTS: 72–85°F.

SEX DIFFERENCES: Male is a little larger than the female and shows more pointed fins.

COUNTS: Dorsal XVI,6; anal IV,5; scales 23.

This species breeds the same as other members of the genus.

The general coloration is bluish. There is a dark stripe running from the snout, through the eye, to the spot on the caudal peduncle. Owing to reticulated edging on the scales, this stripe is not too obvious when the fish are in breeding color, but when they are kept with a light background, without any plants, the stripe is obvious. The crescent-shaped mark that runs above and below the eye seems to be much broader in this species than in the other members of this genus.

RAMIREZ'S DWARF CICHLID / *Apistogramma ramirezi* Myers and Harry

[ram'-i-rez'-eye: named in honor of the collector Manuel Vincente Ramirez]

Apistogramma ramirezi Myers and Harry, Aquarium, 17(4):77, frontispiece, pl, April, 1948; Proc. California Zool. Club, 1(1):1, 1948 (type locality, probably Rio Meta or Rio Apure or tributary in Venezuela)

RANGE: Venezuela in Rio Orinoco Basin.

SIZE: 3 inches; breeds at 2 inches.

TEMPERAMENT: A peaceful species suitable in the community aquarium.

TEMPERATURE REQUIREMENTS: 72–85°F. Optimum breeding temperature 78°F.

SEX DIFFERENCES: Male shows longer rays on the first part of his dorsal fin.

COUNTS: Dorsal XIV or XV,9; anal III,8; pectoral 11 or 12; scales 26 to 29.

More is known about the breeding habits of this dwarf cichlid than those of other members of the genus. Many commercial breeders prefer to remove the eggs from the breeders, much as with the angelfish, but it is safer for the eggs if the parents care for them until they hatch. Some parents are capable of taking care of their spawn but others continually devour them.

The adult fish is extremely fond of *Tubifex* worms, but it will also take small bits of meat, *Daphnia*, and other more common tidbits. It will not feed at the surface unless it is near starvation.

The beautiful coloration of this small fish has resulted in its increasing popularity and it may be dubbed the most popular of this genus.

The name of this species currently is *Microgeophagus ramirezi*.

YELLOW DWARF CICHLID / *Apistogramma reitzigi* Ahl

[rite-zig'-eye: named in honor of Herr Reitzig of Berlin]

Apistogramma reitzigi Ahl, Das Aquarium, p. 180, 1938; Zool. Anz., 127:81, 1939 (type locality, Amazon Basin in Brazil)

RANGE: Amazon Basin.

SIZE: 2½ inches; breeds at 2 inches.

TEMPERAMENT: A peaceful species suitable in the community aquarium.

TEMPERATURE REQUIREMENTS: 70–85°F. Optimum breeding temperature 80°F.

SEX DIFFERENCES: Male has extremely long fins. The female is a little smaller than the male.

COUNTS: Dorsal XVI,5; anal III,5; scales 21.

This fish spawns and breeds much the same as other members of the genus.

The fish is extremely beautiful. It has the body shape of *Apistogramma ramirezi* with a giant sail fin for a dorsal fin and a very sweeping anal fin (on the male fish only). The over-all color is greenish gray, with some copper and yellow on its underside, especially when it is in breeding color. The body is reticulated in effect. There are hints of the beautiful metallic blue all about the head and there are gleams of this same shade about the body.

GENUS *Astronotus* Swainson

[As'-tro-no'-tus: *astro* = a star; *notus* = the back]

OSCAR'S or VELVET CICHLID / *Astronotus ocellatus* (Cuvier)

[os'-sel-lay'-tus: *ocellatus* = spotted as with little eyes]

Lobotes ocellatus Cuvier, in Spix and Agassiz, Selecta genera et species Piscium . . . Brasilium, p. 129, pl. 68, pl. F, 1831 (type locality, "at ocean off Brazil")

RANGE: Eastern Venezuela, Guianas, Amazon Basin, to Paraguay.

SIZE: 1 foot; breeds at 7 inches.

TEMPERAMENT: A predaceous species that will eat fishes smaller than itself. Not suitable in the community tank.

TEMPERATURE REQUIREMENTS: 72–85°F. Optimum breeding temperature 78°F.

SEX DIFFERENCES: Male has more red color than the female.

COUNTS: Dorsal XII,19 to 21; anal III,15 to 17; scales 36 to 38.

The popularity of this fish has grown so much in the past few years that it might now be called one of the most popular cichlids. Youngsters are so stunning and attractive with their variable and beautiful shading that they have become best sellers. Many people have taken quite a liking to the larger individuals too, for they possess an intelligence rarely manifested by other fishes. They recognize their mas-

ter by rushing to meet him when he approaches their aquarium and spurn anyone else who comes near. They are playful for their master, and they have been known to rub themselves affectionately like a pussycat against the arm of their master when he put it into their aquarium.

Some of them make extraordinarily fine parents and produce spawn after spawn without bothering a single fry. Others do just the opposite and must be separated from their spawn. Their feeding habits too, are variable. One pair would only eat large goldfish or other live fishes and refused to eat dead fish or prepared foods. Another pair refused to eat live fishes and would only take crawfish. Other pairs refused anything but pieces of beef. Therefore, it is hard to generalize. All in all, a pair requires abundant food, ample room, and plenty of time (2 years) to grow up to breeding size. It is best to buy about six of them when they are quite small, raise them to sexual maturity, and then hope they will pair off. Males may treat females a bit roughly at times.

GENUS *Cichlasoma* Swainson

[Sick'-la-so'-ma: *cichla* = a kind of fish; *soma* = the body]

GOLDEN CICHLID / *Cichlasoma aureum* (Günther)

[au'-re-um: *aureum* = color of gold]

Heros aureus Günther, Catalogue of the Fishes in the British Museum, 4:292, 1862 (type locality, Guatemala; Mexico)

RANGE: Southern Mexico to Guatemala.

SIZE: 6 inches; breeds at 4 inches.

TEMPERAMENT: Not suitable in a community aquarium with fishes smaller than itself.

TEMPERATURE REQUIREMENTS: 68–85°F. Optimum temperature 74°F.

SEX DIFFERENCES: Male possesses more intense coloring and has longer and more pointed dorsal and anal fins than the female.

COUNTS: Dorsal XVI,9; anal VII,7 or 8; pectoral 13; scales 30 or 31.

This species breeds like other cichlids, laying its eggs either on a piece of flat rock or on the slate bottom of an aquarium. The care of the eggs seems to be shared by both parents, though often the male keeps away from the spawn and allows the female to assume full command.

Some breeders prefer to remove the parents from the eggs as soon as they have finished spawning, but it is probably best not to do so, as there is usually a tendency then for the eggs to be attacked by bacteria and fungus. Methylene Blue and some aureomycin (2 drops of 5 per cent Methylene Blue and 30 mg of aureomycin per gallon of water) are usually effective in combating these two invaders.

This cichlid is a rich golden brown (thus the name "golden cichlid") which under the proper lighting conditions looks more golden. There are about 6 darker vertical bars decorating the sides. A large ocellus occurs at the center of the side and a smaller one at the posterior end of the caudal peduncle. The unpaired fins are mustard colored with a slight hint of red and some blue dots.

TWO-SPOTTED CICHLID / *Cichlasoma bimaculatum* (Linnaeus)

[bi-mack'-u-lay'-tum: *bi* = two; *maculatum* = spots]

Labrus bimaculatus Linnaeus, Systema naturae, ed. 10, p. 285, 1758 (type locality, incorrectly given as Mediterranean)

RANGE: Trinidad, Venezuela, Guianas, and Brazil.

SIZE: 8 inches; breeds at 5 inches.

TEMPERAMENT: A vicious species not suitable in the community tank with fishes smaller than itself.

TEMPERATURE REQUIREMENTS: 68–85°F. Optimum breeding temperature 74°F.

SEX DIFFERENCES: Male has longer, more pointed dorsal and anal fins.

COUNTS: Dorsal XV,9 to 11; anal IV,8 or 9; pectoral 13 or 14; scales 26 to 27.

This vicious and active species breeds like other cichlids but is inclined to devour its own spawn. Aquarists have been known to return it to the dealer after purchasing it, as it will tear up the vegetation in an aquarium in a few hours after introduction into new surroundings. For this reason it is not a popular aquarium fish.

It has an over-all color of brownish olive and shows the typical metallic silvery-blue sheen. There are about 8 very dark vertical bars on the sides, with a stripe running from the operculum to the tail manifesting the same coloring. This stripe is punctuated with two large, obvious dark spots, one in the center of the body and the other on the caudal peduncle, thus the name *bimaculatus*. The fins are nicely tinted light blue and may show some spots.

The fry hatch in about 3 days at 74°F and require freshly hatched brine shrimp and infusoria.

JACK DEMPSEY / *Cichlasoma biocellatum* Regan

[bi-os'-sel-la'-tum: *bi* = two; *ocellatum* = eyespots]

Cichlasoma biocellatum Regan, Ann. Mag. Nat. Hist., (8)3:234, 1909 (type locality, Manaus, Rio Negro)

RANGE: Rio Negro and Amazon Basins.

SIZE: 8 inches; breeds at 5 inches.

TEMPERAMENT: A predaceous species not suitable in the community aquarium.

TEMPERATURE REQUIREMENTS: 68–85°F. Optimum breeding temperature 78°F.

SEX DIFFERENCES: Male shows more color and has longer anal and dorsal fins.

COUNTS: Dorsal XIX,9; anal VIII,8; pectoral 13; scales 31.

This species breeds like other cichlids and is probably one of the easiest cichlids to induce to spawn. As a parent this fish is extremely desirable. It takes excellent parental care of the eggs and seldom bothers the fry. Most breeders place the pair in an aquarium large enough for the entire family to be raised. Pool breeding of this cichlid is efficient. Once a pair of fish has been successful in mating it should be kept together for future spawnings. Males may get a bit rough at times, especially when a new female is introduced into the aquarium. Large groups of them are easier to keep in the same aquarium than a single pair.

The name "Jack Dempsey" may come either from its pugnacious habits or its puglike face.

Bits of meat, fish, and Gordon's formula should make up the bulk of this cichlid's diet, though it will greedily eat just about anything. It is destructive to plants and does better in an unplanted aquarium.

The name of this species currently is *Cichlasoma octofasciatum*.

Chocolate Cichlid / *Cichlasoma coryphaenoides* (Heckel)

[cor'-y-phe-noi'-des: *coryphaenoides* = a dolphinlike fish]

Heros coryphaenoides Heckel, Ann. Wien. Mus. Naturges., 2:373, 1840 (type locality, Rio Negro)

RANGE: Amazon and Rio Negro Basins of Brazil.

SIZE: 8 inches; breeds at 6 inches.

TEMPERAMENT: A vicious species when kept with its own kind, but otherwise fairly peaceful in the community aquarium.

TEMPERATURE REQUIREMENTS: 70–80°F.

SEX DIFFERENCES: Male has more intense red coloring and possesses longer dorsal and anal fins.

COUNTS: Dorsal XVI,12 to 14; anal VI or VII,9 to 11; pectoral 15; scales 33.

This cichlid was placed in a 50-gallon aquarium with a few *Astronotus ocellatus* the same size (about 1 inch long) and some angelfish. The entire group was allowed to grow up together and soon they were all about 4 inches long. The angelfish spawned in this community tank and the eggs were left in the tank. The eggs were not molested, the fry hatched out and swam about freely. About 20 grew to a fair size; the others mysteriously disappeared. This process was repeated a few more times but the parents started to eat the eggs so the eggs were removed. This new group continued to be kept together until the single chocolate cichlid was nearly 6 inches long.

He grew into a very handsome male with brilliant reddish-brown coloring, with dark stripes on his side and three black blotches spread out over his body irregularly. A female was found and he was moved to her tank to spawn. In less than 3 hours she was killed. After four other females met the same fate the male was again placed in his old aquarium. Upon his return the *Astronotus* showed signs of pairing and they were removed. Immediately after this the chocolate cichlid became very sedate, lost his color, and for the next 3 months only came out of his corner for food. A few weeks later another *Astronotus* was put into this aquarium, he then perked up a bit, started chasing the larger *Astronotus,* and killed it. When the original *Astronotus* were replaced he again became his normal self.

CUTTER'S CICHLID / *Cichlasoma cutteri* Fowler

[cut'-ter-eye: named in honor of Victor M. Cutter of United Fruit Company]

Cichlasoma cutteri Fowler, Proc. Acad. Nat. Sci. Philadelphia, 84:380, fig., 1932 (type locality, Lancetilla, Honduras)

RANGE: Honduras.

SIZE: 5 inches; breeds at 3 inches.

TEMPERAMENT: A fairly peaceful species if kept in a community aquarium with fishes no smaller than itself.

TEMPERATURE REQUIREMENTS: 68–85°F.

SEX DIFFERENCES: Male tends to lose intense barred pattern as he gets older while the female becomes more noticeably barred. Male has slightly longer and more pointed dorsal and anal fins.

COUNTS: Dorsal XVII to XIX,10 or 11; anal IX,8; pectoral 15; scales 30.

This peaceful cichlid is fully capable of rearing its young without harming either the eggs or the fry. Mama fish in this species seems to run the show as far as tending the young is concerned, but papa will usually be on guard against any possible invaders of his spawning site. Only during breeding time is there any inkling of temper. Males seem to tear up the vegetation during their preparation for spawning; this may be a protective response or merely an act incidental to the fish's quest for a suitable spawning site.

Colorwise the fish is not too beautiful, nor is it to be considered common. The barred sides makes it easily mistakable for the more common *Cichlasoma nigrofasciatum,* but a quick look at the eye will show it to be an attractive shiny blue color. *C. nigrofasciatum* has a brown eye.

Fry hatch in 4 days or less at 76°F, the optimum breeding temperature. They require newly hatched brine shrimp, sifted *Daphnia,* and microworms immediately upon becoming free-swimming. They also eat protozoans if they are large enough.

The name of this species currently is *Cichlasoma spilurum*.

Chanchito or Chameleon Cichlid / *Cichlasoma facetum* (Jenyns)

[fa-see'-tum: *facetum* = elegant]

Chromis facetus Jenyns, Zoology of the Voyage of *H.M.S. Beagle,* . . . 1832–1836, Pt. 4, Fish, p. 104, 1842 (type locality, Maldonado, Rio de La Plata)

RANGE: Brazil, Uruguay, Argentina.

SIZE: 10 inches; breeds at 6 inches.

TEMPERAMENT: A predaceous species that will ingest any fish small enough to swallow whole.

TEMPERATURE REQUIREMENTS: 65–85°F.

SEX DIFFERENCES: Male has more pointed anal and dorsal fins.

COUNTS: Dorsal XVI,9; anal VI,8; pectoral 13 or 14; scales 27.

This is an interesting fish. Colorwise it is so changeable that some people call it the "chameleon cichlid." The norm. il oli /e-green background has about a hal'-dozen darker blue-black vertical bars. With changing diets, moods, and backg.ounds this fish will change its colors often, i anifesting such intensely attractive shad s as blood red, purple, violet, gold, and green. There seems to be no sexual connection to this color change; however, the color is most intense during breeding time.

This fish is a good parent and may be left to care for its own young. The fry hatch in 4 days or so at 80°F and grow rapidly. Pool culture of these fish is extremely successful, and many breeders prefer to raise them in small outdoor pools during the warmer weather.

THE FESTIVUM / *Cichlasoma festivum* (Heckel)

[fes-tiv'-um: *festivum* = variegated with bright colors]

Heros festivus Heckel, Ann. Wien. Mus. Naturges., 2:376, 1840 (type locality, Rio Guapore)

RANGE: Amazon and Rio Negro Basins.

SIZE: 6 inches; breeds at 5 inches.

TEMPERAMENT: Peaceful for a cichlid; with its small mouth it does not bother other fishes very much.

TEMPERATURE REQUIREMENTS: 68–85°F. Optimum breeding temperature 80°F.

SEX DIFFERENCES: Male has longer, more pointed dorsal fin.

COUNTS: Dorsal XV,11 or 12; anal VIII,11; pectoral 11 or 12; scales 27.

This species is common in British Guiana and has become inexpensive since frequent airplane service to Georgetown, British Guiana, has made importation no problem at all. Although some writers claim this fish to be active, it is the authors' experience that the fish is timid. It likes to hide among the vegetation or in dark corners of unplanted aquaria. It does much better in a large community aquarium where other fishes tend to give it a sense of security.

It is difficult to induce to spawn, though once a pair has spawned it will continue to do so for a long time. This species is fairly long-lived and breeds prolifically if it is going to breed at all. Breeding can only be accomplished in a large, heavily planted aquarium. It likes plenty of direct sunlight but a part of the aquarium must be kept in subdued light. It requires the extreme of privacy if it is to spawn. It is the usual practice to paint all sides of the aquarium so that passing shadows will not disturb it. It likes pool life and this might be a good way to propagate it.

The fry are small at birth and require copious amounts of infusoria and freshly hatched brine shrimp. They are slow-growing unless fed continously on live foods.

Spotted Cichlid / *Cichlasoma maculicauda* Regan

[mack'-you-li-cow'-da: *maculi* = spotted; *cauda* = tail]

Cichlasoma maculicauda Regan, Ann. Mag. Nat. Hist., (7)16:227, 1905 (type locality, Rio Motagua, Lake Izabal, Guatemala, and Rio Chagres, Panama)

RANGE: Central America.

SIZE: 1 foot; breeds at 8 inches.

TEMPERAMENT: A predaceous species that will ingest fishes smaller than itself.

TEMPERATURE REQUIREMENTS: 68–85°F

SEX DIFFERENCES: Male has longer, more pointed dorsal fin.

COUNTS: Dorsal XVII,11 to 13; anal VII,8; pectoral 16 or 17; scales 30.

Not too much is known about the breeding of this cichlid. It may have been spawned but no breeding details are available.

The fish is attractive. Its over-all color is brownish with a mixture of blue green on the underside. There are numerous dark vertical bars on the sides, and there always seem to be a few forked bars. It is thought that as the fish becomes older and longer the bars split and double in number. The dorsal fin shows an attractive copper brown on the anterior section, and it may even turn to a mustard yellow at times. The anterior portion of the anal fin is a mustard yellow. A large dark spot decorates the caudal peduncle.

FIRE-MOUTH CICHLASOMA / *Cichlasoma meeki* (Brind)

[meek'-eye: named in honor of Seth Eugene Meek]

Thorichthys helleri meeki Brind, Aquatic Life, 3:119, 1918 (type locality, Progreso, Yucatan)

RANGE: Yucatan.

SIZE: 5 inches; breeds at 4 inches.

TEMPERAMENT: A predaceous species that is not suitable in a community tank with small fishes.

TEMPERATURE REQUIREMENTS: 68–85°F. Optimum breeding temperatures range from 74 to 80°F, depending upon the size of the aquarium. The larger the aquarium the warmer the water.

SEX DIFFERENCES: Male has longer, more pointed dorsal fin.

COUNTS: Dorsal XVI,8; anal VIII,8; pectoral 12 or 13; scales 28.

This is one of the most fiery-colored cichlids known to aquarists, but the pleasing colors only partly offset the evil disposition. It will eat any fish small enough to get into its mouth and it will often at-tack fishes larger than itself, especially if they are placed in the aquarium after the fire-mouths have become accustomed to their surroundings.

Breeding is no problem once the male has selected a mate, but the hobbyist must expect to lose several females before a male has made a suitable selection. Once a pair have spawned it is best to keep them together for future breedings. Spawns are large and in true cichlid fashion. Plants are torn up and sand is spit in all directions prior to the actual spawning process. Fry are fairly good-sized by the time they are free-swimming and they may be counted upon to eat large amounts of freshly hatched brine shrimp, microworms, and sifted *Daphnia*.

This species should not be confused with *Cichlasoma meeki* Hildebrand from El Salvador, now renamed *C. guija* Hildebrand.

Zebra or Convict Cichlid / *Cichlasoma nigrofasciatum* (Günther)

[ni'-gro-fas'-see-a'-tum: *nigro* = black; *fasciatum* = banded]

Heros nigrofasciatus Günther, Trans. Zool. Soc. London, 6:452, pl. 74, fig. 2, 1869 (type locality, Lakes Amatitlán and Atitlán)

RANGE: Guatemala, El Salvador, Costa Ríca, Panama.

SIZE: 6 inches; breeds at 3 inches.

TEMPERAMENT: A predaceous species best kept alone or with larger cichlids.

TEMPERATURE REQUIREMENTS: 65–80°F. Optimum breeding temperature 75°F.

SEX DIFFERENCES: The female has more rounded fins than the male and also has more reddish color than her mate. This is extraordinary among cichlids.

COUNTS: Dorsal XVII,7 or 8; anal IX,6; pectoral 13 or 14; scales 29 or 30.

The young of the black-banded cichlid is very attractively striped. It is usually sold under the name of the zebra or the convict cichlid. Some dealers have even named this fish, erroneously, the Congo cichlid.

This fish breeds like other cichlids, laying eggs on either a flat rock, a piece of slate, or the bottom of the aquarium. Pairs should be given an aquarium in which there is plenty of rock'work. They seem to prefer to hide among such rock formations as imitation caves, flowerpots lying on their sides, or a piece of slate slanted against the side of the aquarium. This fish does not have much liking for vegetation and will unceremoniously tear apart whatever aquascaping there is. This destruction does not stop with the plants but it will attack all smaller fishes; if it were in a breeding mood, it would even attack larger fishes.

The female, the more colorful of the pair, will usually be the aggressor and will also assume most of the responsibility for care of the spawn. Successful breeders prefer to use a male that is larger than the female, thus giving him a slight advantage over the more pugnacious female. Spawns are usually large and the fry need infusoria for the first week after hatching.

Banded Cichlid / *Cichlasoma severum* (Heckel)

[sev-er′-um: *severum* = stern or serious]

Heros severus Heckel, Ann. Wien. Mus. Naturges., 2:362, 1840 (type locality, Marabitanas in Rio Negro)

RANGE: Guianas; Rio Negro and Amazon Basins.

SIZE: 6 inches; breeds at 5 inches.

TEMPERAMENT: A predaceous fish not to be kept with small fishes.

TEMPERATURE REQUIREMENTS: 72–85°F. Optimum about 80°F.

SEX DIFFERENCES: Male has longer, more pointed anal and dorsal fins and shows rows of brownish-red dots on his body and in the fins.

COUNTS: Dorsal XVI,13; anal VII,12; pectoral 14; scales 30.

Breeding of this species is typically cichlid-like, though getting the fish to spawn is very difficult. The great scarcity of this fish is a hint of its spawning habits.

Many breeders have tried to get it to spawn, but with no commercial success. Spawns are small and weak and the parents are known to go after their fry. Pool spawning is being attempted in Florida and is partially successful but there is no hope, at present, of fulfilling the great demand for the fish.

The really important part in the breeding attempt is in preparing the fish themselves for the spawning process. They require bulk servings of live food; sandworms, earthworms, and any type of small fish will readily be taken. They should have a well-rounded appearance prior to being placed together for spawning.

The banded cichlid is so named for the bar across the rear of the body. The light green color is punctuated with rows of brownish-red dots in the male and some faint barring in the female.

Cichlasoma spectabile (Steindachner)

[spek-tab'-ill-ee: *spectabile* = remarkable]

Acara (*Petenia*) *spectabilis* Steindachner, Sitzb. Akad. Wiss. Wien, 71:96, pl. 4, 1875 (type locality, Amazon River at Gurupí and Óbidos)

RANGE: Amazon Basin.

SIZE: 8 inches; breeds at 6 inches.

TEMPERAMENT: A predaceous species best kept alone or with large fishes.

TEMPERATURE REQUIREMENTS: 70–85°F. Optimum breeding temperature 75°F.

SEX DIFFERENCES: Male has long, pointed dorsal and anal fin.

COUNTS: Dorsal XV,12; anal VI,9; pectoral 15; scales 30.

This species breeds in a typically cichlid-like manner, but it is hard to induce to spawn.

The over-all color is plain gray brown, with a large round dot or spot on the caudal peduncle and another similar spot slightly above the lateral line in the center of the side. The fins are reddish at times and the spot on the caudal peduncle may be ringed.

This species has been seen less often lately, probably because it has been replaced by more colorful and less vicious species.

Cichlasoma tetracanthus (Cuvier and Valenciennes)

[tet'-ra-can'-thus: *tetra* = four; *canthus* = spine]

Centrarchus tetracanthus Cuvier and Valenciennes, Histoire naturelle des poissons, 7:460, 1831 (type locality, Havana)

RANGE: Cuba, Santo Domingo.

SIZE: 7 inches; breeds at 5 inches.

TEMPERAMENT: A predaceous species not to be kept with fishes smaller than itself.

TEMPERATURE REQUIREMENTS: 70–85°F. Optimum breeding temperature 74°F.

SEX DIFFERENCES: Male has longer, more pointed dorsal fin.

COUNTS: Dorsal XV,10; anal IV,7 or 8; pectoral 14 or 15; scales 29 to 32.

This species must be considered as destructive, vicious individuals that will eagerly tear all the plants out of their rootings and then, further, continue to denude plant stalks. It may spit sand in all directions when it is preparing a spawning site and no fish, regardless of size, is absolutely safe when a pair starts to get "family ideas."

The female of this cichlid is the aggressor when it comes to spawning. She is the one that nudges the male and, if he does not seem too interested, will even start to tear his fins. Sometimes a female in her overanxiety will even cause sufficient harm to kill a male.

This fish requires copious amounts of bulk live foods; earthworms, sandworms, and the like are very greedily taken. It has also been known to go after all sorts of prepared foods and bits of meat. Dead fishes are a welcome change in the diet.

Fry are large enough after becoming free-swimming to take freshly hatched brine shrimp and sifted *Daphnia*.

The over-all color of this fish is a light brown with a mosaic of darker brown and black laid all over its body. Even the membranes of the fins are attractively colored.

Cichlasoma urophthalmus (Günther)

[your'-off-thal'-mus: *ur* = tail; *ophthalmus* = eye]

Heros urophthalmus Günther, Catalogue of the Fishes in the British Museum, vol. 4, p. 291, 1862 (type locality, Lake Petén, Guatemala)

RANGE: Central America.

SIZE: 7 inches; breeds at 6 inches.

TEMPERAMENT: A predaceous species best kept by itself.

TEMPERATURE REQUIREMENTS: 70–85°F. Optimum breeding temperature 75°F.

SEX DIFFERENCES: Male has longer, more pointed dorsal fin.

COUNTS: Dorsal XVI or XVII,9 to 12; anal V or VI,7 to 9; pectoral 13 to 16; scales 28.

Although a popular fish at one time, this is another of the "disappearing" cichlids because it lacks brilliant coloration and has vicious habits which make it little desired as an aquarium fish.

The breeding habits are typically cichlid-like. This species is hardy and may be induced to spawn rather easily.

The over-all color is an olive yellow, with the sides overlaid with 7 or 8 vertical bars of dark brown to blackish. There is a large eyespot on the caudal peduncle which adds contrast to the body, but the dark red margin on the dorsal fin is by far the most attractive attribute manifested. The anal and tail fins have light margins.

GENUS *Crenicichla* Heckel

[Kren'-i-sick'-la: *cren* = notched or crenate; *cichla* = a kind of fish]

TWO-SPOT PIKE CICHLID / *Crenicichla dorsocellata* Haseman

[dors'-os-el-la'-ta: *dorso* = back; *ocellata* = eyelike spot]

Crenicichla dorsocellata Haseman, Ann. Carnegie Mus., 7(3,4):355, pl. 63, 1911 (type locality, Campos, Rio Paraíba; Santarém, Igarape de Irura)

RANGE: Amazon Basin.

SIZE: 6 inches; breeding size 5 inches.

TEMPERAMENT: A predaceous species that cannot be trusted with other fishes.

TEMPERATURE REQUIREMENTS: 70–85°F.

SEX DIFFERENCES: Female has slightly longer and more pointed dorsal and anal fins.

COUNTS: Dorsal XX to XXIII,10 to 13; anal III,8; scales 62 to 65.

This species breeds the same way as *Crenicichla lepidota*. It is one of the more common members of the family, second to *C. lepidota* in popularity. It is generally colored blue green, with the back darker. There are several dark bars on the sides but the two outstanding identification marks are the eyespots on the upper edge in the middle of the dorsal fin and the upper part of the caudal peduncle. The fins are highly colored.

C. notophthalmus Regan (*Ann. Mag. Nat. Hist.*, (8)11:502, 1913, type locality, Manaus, Amazon River) is a synonym of this species.

Pike Cichlid / *Crenicichla lepidota* Heckel

[lep′-i-do′-ta: *lepidota* = scaly]

Crenicichla lepidota Heckel, Zool. Abh. Ann. Wien. Mus., 2: 429, pl. 30, figs. 13–16*b*, 1840 (type locality, Rio Guaporé)

RANGE: Eastern Brazil to Rio São Francisco, Rio Grande do Sul, Rio Guaporé.

SIZE: 8 inches; breeds at 6 inches.

TEMPERAMENT: An active, predaceous species that will ingest whole fishes smaller than itself. Not to be trusted with other fishes.

TEMPERATURE REQUIREMENTS: 70–85°F. Optimum breeding temperature 75°F.

SEX DIFFERENCES: Female has longer and more pointed dorsal and anal fins.

COUNTS: Dorsal XVII or XVIII,13 or 14; anal III,8 to 10; scales 38 to 46.

It is indeed unfortunate that a species as beautiful as this one cannot be trusted with other fishes. The general color is a rich orange brown, darker on the back and lighter on the belly. Brilliant reds and oranges appear in various parts of the body, sometimes on the fins, nearly always on the tail, and not infrequently on the body.

The mouth of this fish is deceiving; it is quite capable of taking in fairly large-sized fish in a single gulp. It is best described as pikelike in every way.

The breeding habits are much like other cichlids. It has fairly large spawns on flat stones or on stiff-leafed plants. Parents should be removed from their spawn as soon as the eggs have hatched. They are extremely vicious immediately prior to spawning.

The pike cichlid enjoys a well-planted aquarium and does not injure the plants at all. The aquarium should be kept covered because this fish can jump and will often dive out of the aquarium after a fly or mosquito.

RING-TAILED PIKE CICHLID / *Crenicichla saxatilis* (Linnaeus)

[sax′-at-til′-is: *saxatilis* = found among rocks]

Sparus saxatilis Linnaeus, Systema naturae, ed. 10, p. 278, 1758 (type locality, Surinam)

RANGE: Trinidad, Venezuela to Rio Grande do Sul, Amazon Basin, Paraguay, Uruguay.

SIZE: 10 inches; breeds at 6 inches.

TEMPERAMENT: A vicious species not suitable in the community tank.

TEMPERATURE REQUIREMENTS: 70–85°F.

SEX DIFFERENCES: Male has shorter and more rounded anal and dorsal fins.

COUNTS: Dorsal XVII to XX,13 to 16; anal III,8 to 10; pectoral 16 or 17; scales 50 to 60; pores in lateral lines 22 to 26 + 9 to 12.

This species breeds like other members of the genus.

At least 22 other members of the genus could be mentioned, but for reasons of size, availability, and temperament only three species have become popular. This is the least attractive of the three members of this genus herein discussed.

It is almost all brown; only the telltale ocellate spots on the caudal peduncle and behind the head just below the lateral line are anywhere near outstanding.

GENUS *Etroplus* Cuvier and Valenciennes

[Ee-tro'-plus: *etroplus* = refers to the abdomen]

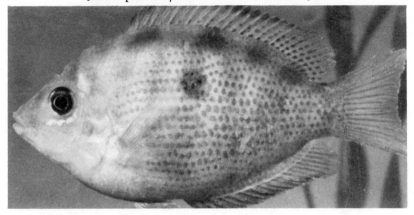

ORANGE CHROMIDE / *Etroplus maculatus* (Bloch)

[mack'-u-lay'-tus: *maculatus* = spotted]

Chaetodon maculatus Bloch, Natur-geschichte der ausländischen Fische, 9:244, pl. 427, 1795 (type locality, Malabar)

RANGE: Malabar, Madras, Ceylon.

SIZE: 3 inches; breeds at 3 inches.

TEMPERAMENT: A moderately peaceful cichlid that may be kept with slightly smaller fishes than itself in the community tank.

TEMPERATURE REQUIREMENTS: 72–85°F. Optimum breeding temperature 78°F.

SEX DIFFERENCES: See below.

COUNTS: Dorsal XVIII,8 to 10; anal XIII,7 or 8; pectoral 15 or 16; scales 36 or 37.

This cichlid is supposed to be one of the more difficult species to spawn, but when conditions are right it is hard to keep the pair from spawning. The main trouble seems to be the selection of a pair.

Sexing the orange chromide is very difficult and only by careful study of a group of fish is one able to select a pair. In the male look for a redder eye and more intense coloring; in the female look for heaviness, bulging sides when observed from above, and a slightly smaller size than the male.

This fish prefers to breed in hidden areas; several times pairs have dug deep tunnels under large rocks and spawned therein on the underside of rocks. It likes a heavily planted aquarium and will spawn on the underside of an inverted flowerpot. The fry are attached to the rock by a single strong filament which holds them fast until they are strong enough to be free-swimming. Parents look after their spawn and may be trusted unless they habitually devour their eggs.

Feed the fry infusoria, then small *Daphnia* and freshly hatched brine shrimp as they grow older.

GREEN CHROMIDE / *Etroplus suratensis* (Bloch)

[sur'-a-ten'-sis: named after the locality where collected]

Chaetodon suratensis Bloch, Naturgeschichte der ausländischen Fische, vol. 4, pl. 217, 1790 (type locality, Surat, Ceylon)

RANGE: Ceylon.

SIZE: 1 foot; breeding not observed.

TEMPERAMENT: This species should not be trusted with fishes smaller than half its size.

TEMPERATURE REQUIREMENTS: 72–85°F.

SEX DIFFERENCES: Not known.

COUNTS: Dorsal XVIII or XIX,14 or 15; anal XII or XIII,11 or 12; pectoral 17; scales 35 to 40.

Nothing is known about the breeding habits of this cichlid. It was included in this book because several hundred fish of this species have recently been imported. The specimens brought in were small, running about 2½ inches. The general color was green, whence the name "green chromide." There are 8 vertical bars on the sides, equally spaced from the gill cover to the caudal peduncle. Each scale located on the side of the body is punctuated with a fine pearly dot which adds beauty to the fish in the right light. There are many black dots on the undersides. All the fins have a gray color except the pectorals, which are mustard colored with a black base.

This species does well when kept in 25 per cent sea water as it is probably a brackish-water species. Specimens have been caught in both brackish and fresh water.

GENUS *Geophagus* Heckel

[Gee-off'-a-gus: *geo* = the earth or land; *phagus* = to eat]

Geophagus acuticeps Heckel

[a-cu'-ti-ceps: *acuti* = pointed; *ceps* = head]

Geophagus acuticeps Heckel, Ann. Wien. Mus. Naturges., 2:394, 1840 (type locality, Rio Negro)

RANGE: Rio Negro and Amazon Basin.

SIZE: 10 inches; breeding not observed.

TEMPERAMENT: Not suitable in the community aquarium except with fishes of its own size.

TEMPERATURE REQUIREMENTS: 72–85°F.

SEX DIFFERENCES: The male seems to have longer and more pointed anal, dorsal, and pelvic fins.

COUNTS: Dorsal XIII,11 or 12; anal III,7 or 8; pectoral 14 or 15; scales 30.

Not much is known about the breeding habits of this cichlid, although several authors claim that it is an egg layer and spawns like many other cichlids. There is doubt as to whether or not the fish is a mouthbreeder, as no author cites a case of having bred the fish himself or having seen the fish breed.

This fish looks very much like *Geophagus jurupari* except that the first rays on the pelvic fins are extremely long, especially in the male.

Feeding is no problem as it eats anything, including dog food straight from the can.

PEARL CICHLID / *Geophagus brasiliensis* (Quoy and Gaimard)

[bra'-zil-i-en'-sis: named after Brazil]

Chromis brasiliensis Quoy and Gaimard, Voyage autour du monde . . . *Uranie et la Physicienne* . . . 1817–1820, Zoologie, p. 286, 1824 (type locality, Rio Negro)

RANGE: Amazon and Orinoco Basins to Rio de La Plata Basin; Rio Grande do Sul; Uruguay.

SIZE: 10 inches; breeds at 4 inches.

TEMPERAMENT: Best kept with fishes of its own size in the community tank.

TEMPERATURE REQUIREMENTS: 72–85°F.

SEX DIFFERENCES: Male is said to be slightly larger than the female. However, a surer way to distinguish them is to observe the fish from the top and select the plumper fish for the female. There may be a slight difference in the pointedness of the fins.

COUNTS: Dorsal XII or XIII,11; anal III,8; pectoral 14 or 15; scales 30.

This species is one of the most popular members of the genus, with the possible exception of *Geophagus jurupari*. It breeds when quite small and may be dwarfed by keeping it in a small aquarium and not feeding it much.

As the fish gets older, regardless of its size, it acquires more of the mother-of-pearl spots that suggested its popular name "pearl cichlid." Most of these spots are metallic and resemble spangles. There is a large black spot located in the center of the body, the intensity of which varies with age, temperature, and condition of the fish. The darker the spot the happier the fish seems to be, except just before the fish dies, when the spot is brilliantly black and prominent.

Geophagus jurupari Heckel

[ju'-ru-par'-i: after a native name]

Geophagus jurupari Heckel, Ann. Wien. Mus. Naturges., 2:392, 1840 (type locality, mouth of Rio Negro in Amazon River)

RANGE: Guianas, Amazon Basin, to Paraguay.

SIZE: 10 inches; breeds at 5 inches.

TEMPERAMENT: This species may be kept with fishes not smaller than itself.

TEMPERATURE REQUIREMENTS: 72–85°F.

SEX DIFFERENCES: See below; look for slim males and heavy females. On some fish there does seem to be a difference in the pointedness of the fins.

COUNTS: Dorsal XV,10; anal III,7; pectoral 14 or 15; scales 29.

Odd stories have been told of the breeding habits of this fish, but the only possible conclusion is that the fish is a mouthbreeder. It has been successfully spawned in all types of aquaria—some small (6-gallon) and some large (50-gallon), some planted and some unplanted, some highly heated (82°F) and some comparatively cool (72°F). All in all, this gives the impression that the fish will spawn when it is ready and not before. Conditioning on fleshy fresh foods seems to be the best method of preparing the fish for spawning. Sexing a pair is very difficult and only when a female is well rounded can you tell her sex. Males are definitely sleeker, especially when viewed from above.

FAMILY CICHLIDAE

GENUS *Haplochromis* Hilgendorf

[Hap′-lo-chro′-mis: *haplo* = single; *chromis* = color]

MOFFAT'S MOUTHBREEDER / *Haplochromis moffati* (Castelnau)

[mof′-fat-eye: named in honor of the English missionary M. Moffat]

Chromys moffati Castelnau, Memoire sur les poissons de l'Africa australe, Paris, p. 16, 1861 (type locality, Kuruman, tributary of the Orange River)

RANGE: South Africa in upper tributaries of the Congo River.

SIZE: 4 inches; breeding at 3 inches.

TEMPERAMENT: Suitable in a community aquarium only with fish of same size.

TEMPERATURE REQUIREMENTS: 72–85°F. Best spawning temperature 80°F.

SEX DIFFERENCES: Male has red tip on his anal fin.

COUNTS: Dorsal XIII or XIV,9 to 11; anal III,8 to 10; pectoral 15; scales 26 to 31.

This mouthbreeder is not now a popular species. It is pretty, with a generally dark olive back, lighter on the sides and silver on the belly. A magnificent blue spot is found on the posterior tip of the gill cover. A thin horizontal line runs through the eye; faint barlike markings are manifested at different color stages.

When it is breeding the only bright markings are the mustard-colored dots that appear to pepper the upper part of the body, and the bluish dots that decorate the lower part of the body. Red and blue dots are to be noted in both the tail and dorsal fins, where the background color is an aqua shade. The anal fin is deep red with metallic blue dots, especially in the male, where an extra red tip is seen on the anal fin.

Condition the female thoroughly before attempting to spawn. The female will swim with her mate in circles about a small depression in the sand. Soon they will stop this sex play and spawn. The female takes the eggs into her mouth and incubates them, keeping her spawn and fry there until they are nearly ½ inch long. She does not eat during this period and should not be offered food. Remove the male after spawning.

Haplochromis philander (Weber) is a synonym of this species, according to Boulenger.

EGYPTIAN MOUTHBREEDER / *Haplochromis strigigena* (Pfeffer)

[stri'-gi-gee'-na: *strigigena* = striped]

Ctenochromis strigigena Pfeffer, Jahrb. Hamburg. Wiss. Anst., 10:155, pl. 2, figs. 5, 6, 8, 1893 (type locality, "Mbusini, Matomondo, Unguu")

RANGE: Nile Basin of Egypt.

SIZE: 3 inches; breeds at 2 inches.

TEMPERAMENT: Suitable in the community aquarium with fishes of its own size.

TEMPERATURE REQUIREMENTS: 72–85°F. Optimum breeding temperature 78°F.

SEX DIFFERENCES: The anal fin of the male is red-tipped.

COUNTS: Dorsal XIII to XV,8 to 10; anal III,6 to 8; pectoral 12; scales 25 to 29.

This mouthbreeder is quite popular because of its mild disposition, small size, and interesting breeding habits. When a pair is selected it should be placed in its own small aquarium (3½ to 5 gallons) and be fed well on meaty foods such as *Tubifex* and bits of fish and meat. Soon the pair will take on beautiful colors and the male will begin to fan a depression in

the sand. Once the depression has been dug the female will join the male in circling about the nest and soon spawning will take place. The female usually picks up the eggs in her mouth and incubates them. Interestingly enough, when a pair starts the encircling procedure and is moved from one tank to another, it will immediately resume love-making as though it had never been disturbed. The pair does not fan another depression but merely picks a natural site closely resembling that which it had previously constructed.

After spawning the male should be removed and the female left alone, unfed, with her spawn for the next 2 weeks. The fry will appear from 10 to 14 days after spawning and the female should be removed at that time and placed in an environment conducive to getting her in good condition again. The shrunken body of the mother fish after her 10 days without eating is quite noticeable. This species can live about 30 days without food other than whatever microscopic organisms exist in an aquarium.

Family CICHLIDAE

Genus *Hemichromis* Peters

[Hem'-i-chro'-mis: *hemi* = half; *chromis* = colored]

After James

Jewelfish / *Hemichromis bimaculatus* Gill

[bi-mack'-you-lay'-tus: *bi* = two; *maculatus* = spotted]

Hemichromis bimaculatus Gill, Proc. Acad. Nat. Sci. Philadelphia, p. 137, 1862 (type locality, "probably Liberia")

RANGE: Nile River in Africa to Niger and Congo.

SIZE: 4 inches; breeds at 3 inches.

TEMPERAMENT: Not suitable in the community aquarium.

TEMPERATURE REQUIREMENTS: 70–85°F.

SEX DIFFERENCES: Male is supposed to possess more and larger "jewel" spots on the gill plates, but colors vary from day to day so that this is not a true sexual difference.

COUNTS: Dorsal XIII to XV,9 to 13; anal III, 7 to 9; pectoral 14 or 15; scales 25 to 29.

The color plate clearly identifies the beautiful coloring this species is capable of manifesting during its breeding period. Normally it is not so intensely colored.

Breeding is similar to other cichlids, although the fish does prefer privacy and an overturned flowerpot seems to be the best spawning site. Most breeders prefer to remove the spawn from the parents; however, they are fairly trustworthy parents if not disturbed and if kept well-fed.

The spawns are usually about 300 eggs and the fry are small when first hatched. They require infusoria, followed by brine shrimp and *Daphnia* in its smallest sizes.

Spawners are dangerous to each other and it is sometimes difficult to obtain a pair. The male is especially nasty and may attack the female until she is dead. Otherwise they are fairly hardy and are extremely colorful.

Several scientists have used this fish as a laboratory animal and there is considerable scientific material available in the ichthyological literature. See especially the papers by Solberg and Brinley and by Aronson.

Banded Jewelfish / *Hemichromis fasciatus* Peters

[fas'-see-a'-tus: *fasciatus* = banded]

Hemichromis fasciatus Peters, Monatsb. Akad. Wiss. Berlin, p. 403, 1857 (type locality, Guinea, West Africa)

RANGE: West Africa from Senegal to Angola and Lake Ngami.

SIZE: 10 inches; breeds at 6 inches.

TEMPERAMENT: This species should not be kept with fishes smaller than itself.

TEMPERATURE REQUIREMENTS: 70–85°F.

SEX DIFFERENCES: Male has slightly more pointed dorsal and anal fins.

COUNTS: Dorsal XIII to XV,11 to 13; anal III,8 to 10; pectoral 15; scales 28 to 32.

This species breeds in the same manner as *Hemichromis bimaculatus*. Why this fish has become as popular as it has is open to speculation, for not only does it lack the beautiful color of the jewelfish but it is more vicious, grows much larger, and is extremely heavy in its eating habits. The best food for the larger fish is canned dog food, fed in small portions.

Its over-all color is a golden yellow, with a tendency toward olive yellow at times. There are about 6 dark vertical bars on the sides. During breeding time the fish does "dress up" a bit. Its nose becomes a wine-red color and the anal and caudal fins take on a reddish hue.

FAMILY CICHLIDAE

GENUS *Herichthys* Baird and Girard

[Hair-ik'-thees: *her* = a hero; *ichthys* = fish]

TEXAS CICHLID / *Herichthys cyanoguttatus* Baird and Girard

[si'-a-no'-gut-tay'-tus: *cyano* = dark blue; *guttatus* = spotted]

Herichthys cyanoguttatus Baird and Girard, Proc. Acad. Nat. Sci. Philadelphia, p. 25, 1854 (type locality, Rio Grande, Brownsville, Texas)

RANGE: Northeastern Mexico and into Texas.

SIZE: 10 inches; breeds at 6 inches.

TEMPERAMENT: A predaceous species only suitable in the community tank with fishes of its own size.

TEMPERATURE REQUIREMENTS: 65–85°F. Optimum breeding temperature 75°F.

SEX DIFFERENCES: Male has longer anal and dorsal fins.

COUNTS: Dorsal XVI or XVII,10 or 11; anal V or VI,9; pectoral 14 or 15; scales 29 or 30.

This fish breeds like the other cichlids. It is a large species which needs plenty of tank space. The spawns are fairly large and may run as high as 1,500 eggs. Parents should be removed after spawning as they are inclined to eat their spawn.

The grayish coloring with bluish pearl-like dots spread irregularly all over the body makes it easily recognizable.

The Texas cichlid is very interesting for certain studies as it is the most northern cichlid known. No other member of this large family is found as far north as Texas. For this reason it is fair to assume that this species may be able to acclimate itself to lower temperatures than other cichlids.

Genus *Nannacara* Regan

[Nan'-na-car'-a: *nann* = dwarf; *acara* = small]

Golden-eyed Dwarf Cichlid / *Nannacara anomala* Regan

[a-nom'-a-la: *anomala* = irregular]

Nannacara anomala Regan, Ann. Mag. Nat. Hist., (7)15:344, 1905 (type locality, Rio Essequibo, British Guiana)

RANGE: British Guiana.

SIZE: 2½ inches; male breeds at 2 inches, female at 2½ inches.

TEMPERAMENT: Suitable in the community tank only with fishes of its own size.

TEMPERATURE REQUIREMENTS: 72–85°F.

SEX DIFFERENCES: Male is more colorful and has a dark metallic-green color. His fins are also much longer and more pointed than the female's.

COUNTS: Dorsal XVI or XVII,7 or 8; anal III,7 or 8; pectoral 12 to 14; scales 23 or 24.

This species is fairly easy to breed if given the proper spawning environment in an undisturbed aquarium. The parents need a fairly heavily planted aquarium, as they are shy and like to spawn in hidden rock caves, under a cracked coconut shell or inside a flowerpot. The spawns are fairly small, averaging about 100 eggs, though at times they do run higher. Select smaller males for breeding if possible. Males are often inclined to kill females during the prespawning play, but in a large, well-planted aquarium the female has a better chance. Once the pair has spawned the female is again in danger and should be removed as soon as she has laid all her eggs.

The male is extremely beautiful with his brilliant metallic olive green. The long anal and dorsal fins make him look like a paradisefish, but in reality he is a cichlid. The female is not colored at all like the male although she may have a hint of the greenish color.

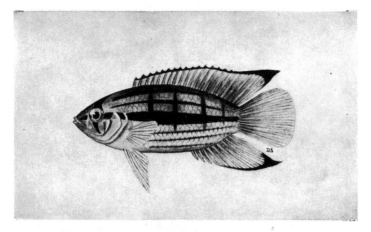

LATTICE DWARF CICHLID / *Nannacara taenia* Regan

[tee′-ni-a: *taenia* = striped]

Nannacara taenia Regan, Ann. Mag. Nat. Hist., (8)9:505, 1912 (type locality, Manaus, Amazon River)

RANGE: Manaus, Amazon Basin.

SIZE: 2 inches; female breeds at 1½ inches, male at 2 inches.

TEMPERAMENT: A fairly peaceful species that should be kept with fishes only of its own size.

TEMPERATURE REQUIREMENTS: 72–85°F.

SEX DIFFERENCES: Male is larger than female, has more color, and possesses longer, more pointed and flowing anal and dorsal fins.

COUNTS: Dorsal XVI,7; anal III,7; scales 24.

The breeding habits of the lattice dwarf are the same as for the golden-eyed dwarf.

There are 6 narrow lines parallel to a broader line running the entire length of the fish from the eye to the base of the caudal fin, 3 lines above this broader line and 3 below. There are times during sexual activity when the fish shows a pattern of vertical bars, giving the effect on the sides of a latticework, thus the popular name "lattice dwarf cichlid." The throat and belly of this fish may be dark at times, showing a brilliant velvety violet.

GENUS *Pelmatochromis* Steindachner

[Pel'-ma-to-chro'-mis: *pelmato* = a stalk; *chromis* = colored]

Pelmatochromis annectens (Boulenger)

[an-neck'-tens: *annectens* = connecting or joining]

Pelmatochromis annectens Boulenger, Ann. Mag. Nat. Hist., (8)12:485, 1913 (type locality, lower Niger River)

RANGE: West Africa in the lower Niger River.

SIZE: 4 inches; breeds at 3 inches.

TEMPERAMENT: Suitable in the community tank only with fishes of its own size.

TEMPERATURE REQUIREMENTS: 72–85°F. Breeding is best accomplished at 80°F.

SEX DIFFERENCES: Male has longer, more pointed dorsal, anal, and pelvic fins.

COUNTS: Dorsal XV,9 or 10; anal III,7 or 8; pectoral, about 14 or 15; scales 28 or 29.

Although other members of the genus have different breeding habits, this species and *Pelmatochromis subocellatus* breed the same way. A typical cichlid-like courtship between male and female is followed by a deliberate search for a spawning site. Both male and female will take turns in "scrubbing" the selected area with their mouths in order to remove all possible ex-

cess foreign matter. This species and *P. subocellatus* seem to prefer to spawn either in a rock cave of some sort or inside a tipped-over flowerpot. It prefers privacy and dense vegetation. It is very happy when the aquarium glass becomes covered with a dense growth of algae, which keeps disturbing shadows from falling onto the aquarium and frightening it.

Spawns are moderate in size, usually running close to 200. Fry hatch in a few days at 80°F, which is the optimum breeding temperature.

During its breeding period this fish has very bright colors. It shows blues and reds which are more vivid than in *Apistogramma ramirezi* (page 611). The male is a bit smaller than the female and is more colorful. This species is noted for the 3 dark horizontal stripes and 6 darker vertical bars that cross interestingly in a sort of patchwork on the sides. Both sexes show a distinct patch of white immediately above the vent in front of the anal fin.

The name of this species currently is *Thysia ansorgii*.

ARNOLD's CICHLID / *Pelmatochromis arnoldi* Boulenger

[are'-nold-eye: named in honor of the aquarist Johann Paul Arnold]

Pelmatochromis arnoldi Boulenger, Ann. Mag. Nat. Hist., (8)10:263, 1912 (type locality, lower Niger River)

RANGE: Lower Niger River, Africa.

SIZE: 4 inches; breeds at 3 inches.

TEMPERAMENT: Not suitable in the community aquarium with fishes smaller than itself.

TEMPERATURE REQUIREMENTS: 72–85°F.

SEX DIFFERENCES: Male has longer, more pointed anal and dorsal fins. Also has a deep-red color under the throat and belly.

COUNTS: Dorsal XV or XVI,10 or 11; anal III,8 or 9; pectoral about 14 or 15; scales 28.

There is no record of this species having been spawned, but there is considerable doubt that any serious attempt has been made.

This fish shows the beautiful colors of the popular fire-mouth cichlid, *Cichlasoma meeki* (page 612). Only in the male are the throat and belly brilliantly colored with fiery red. The fins are almost clear with a faint bluish tint. The unpaired fins are marked with small dots, while the sides show larger, darker spots which seem to mark the center of a series of 5 fainter vertical bars. Another dark spot is found on the posterior tip of the gill cover.

This species does not disturb plants.

The name of this species currently is *Thysia ansorgii*.

GÜNTHER'S CICHLID / *Pelmatochromis güntheri* (Sauvage)

[guen'-ther-eye: named in honor of the English ichthyologist Albert Günther]

Hemichromis güntheri Sauvage, Bull. soc. zool. France, p. 317, pl. 5, fig. 1, 1882 (type locality, Canina River)

RANGE: West Africa from the Gold Coast to Gabon.

SIZE: 6 inches; breeds at 4 inches.

TEMPERAMENT: Its predaceous nature makes it unsuitable with fishes smaller than itself.

TEMPERATURE REQUIREMENTS: 72–85°F. Optimum breeding temperature 80°F.

SEX DIFFERENCES: Male has longer, more pointed dorsal and anal fins. Also has the responsibility for the oral care of the young.

COUNTS: Dorsal XV to XVII, 9 to 12; anal III,7 or 8; pectoral 15; scales 28 to 31.

The breeding habits of this species are much in contrast with other members of the genus, for this fish is a mouthbreeder. Not only is it found in the same waters as the black-chinned mouthbreeder, *Tilapia macrocephala* (page 657), but the breeding habits are identical.

In coloration this species has the typical dull olive-green coloring of many cichlids without any of the scintillating blue or red. The only color appearing is a white or brassy band that runs along the top edge of the dorsal fin. This contrasts with the darker body colors and seems to be like the orange dorsal molly in some respects.

Though easily bred, this cichlid has never become popular.

The name of this species currently is *Chromidotilapia guentheri.*

Pelmatochromis kribensis Boulenger

[kri-ben'-sis: named after the river where collected]

Pelmatochromis kribensis Boulenger, Ann. Mag. Nat. Hist., (8)8:373, 1911 (type locality, Kribi River, southern Cameroons)

RANGE: Cameroons, West Africa.

SIZE: 3 inches; breeds at 2 inches.

TEMPERAMENT: A timid fish best kept in a well-planted aquarium.

TEMPERATURE REQUIREMENTS: 74–86°F.

SEX DIFFERENCES: Male is much more colorful than the female.

COUNTS: Dorsal XVI or XVII,8 or 9; anal III,6 or 7; scales 27 to 29 with 2 above and 9 below lateral line; lateral line pores 18 to 20 + 5 to 8.

Pairs may spawn when about 8 months old if kept in a heavily planted aquarium supplied with a few flat stones. They may be conditioned on dried or prepared foods, but they prefer *Tubifex* worms and *Daphnia*. The pair will dig under the stones and spawn on the underside. Most commercial breeders invert a flowerpot and tip it onto a stone, allowing just enough room for the fish to get inside. The pair will investigate this possible breeding area and then spend most of their time under the pot. A week or two later they will spawn therein. The parents should be removed immediately after their spawn hatches, if not sooner, as they will devour the free-swimming young.

Spawns number not more than 100 eggs and are not very hardy. The fry require infusoria immediately upon becoming free-swimming. A week or 10 days later, depending upon the size of the aquarium and condition of the spawn, they will be able to take the larger-particled live foods such as freshly hatched brine shrimp and finely sifted *Daphnia*.

EYESPOT CICHLID / *Pelmatochromis subocellatus* (Günther)

[sub'-os-sel-lay'-tus: *sub* = under or below; *ocellatus* = eyelike spot]

Hemichromis subocellatus Günther, Proc. Zool. Soc. London, p. 667, pl. 67, fig. C, 1871 (type locality, Gabon)

RANGE: Africa from Gabon to the lower Congo.

SIZE: 4 inches; breeds at 3 inches.

TEMPERAMENT: Suitable in the community aquarium with fishes of its own size.

TEMPERATURE REQUIREMENTS: 72–85°F. Optimum breeding temperature 80°F.

SEX DIFFERENCES: Male has an eyespot on the dorsal fin; female has an eyespot on the anal fin.

COUNTS: Dorsal XIV to XVI,8 to 10; anal III,6 to 8; scales 25 to 28.

This species spawns like *Pelmatochromis annectens*. Males may become vicious at times with members of the opposite sex and unless a careful check is kept upon their activities they are apt to kill a few females. This seems to be especially true during the winter months.

This fish shows a reddish-brown coloring at times, but generally when not in sexual activity it is a mustard color. The belly is yellowish most of the time with a faint red tinge. The sides show darker vertical bars and appear striped with a few indistinct dark marks. The tail fin is the most colorful of the fins, showing a brilliant blue; the other fins have less intense, though similar, coloring. The male has an attractive ocellus (eyespot) on the rear part of his dorsal fin. The female has a somewhat larger spot but it is on her anal fin instead.

The name of this species currently is *Pelvicachromis subocellatus*.

Pelmatochromis taeniatus Boulenger

[tea'-ni-a'-tus: *taeniatus* = striped]

Pelmatochromis taeniatus Boulenger, Proc. Zool. Soc. London, no. 1, p. 10, pl. 4, fig. 3, 1901 (type locality, Niger River Delta)

RANGE: Lower Niger River, West Africa.

SIZE: 3½ inches; breeds at 2 inches.

TEMPERAMENT: A timid fish best kept by itself.

TEMPERATURE REQUIREMENTS: 74–86°F.

SEX DIFFERENCES: Male is more colorful than the female.

COUNTS: Dorsal XVII or XVIIII,7 or 8; anal III,7; scales 28 or 29 with 2 above and 9 below lateral line; lateral line pores 19 to 21 + 7 to 9.

This species breeds the same as *Pelmatochromis kribensis*.

The two species look much alike except that, when in full breeding color, there is more red and orange in *kribensis* and more blue in *taeniatus*. Immature specimens of both species are so much alike that it is almost impossible to distinguish them.

The name of this species currently is *Pelvicachromis taeniatus*.

GENUS *Pterophyllum* Heckel

[Tare′-o-fill′-um: *ptero* = wing; *phyllum* = a leaf]

The famed German aquarist Ernst Ahl published and illustrated in 1928 in the *Zoologischer Anzeiger* a new species of angelfish, *Pterophyllum eime-kei*. He based this on five examples from the mouth of the Rio Negro in the Amazon. Ever since that time aquarists have been trying to find out whether they had *P. scalare* or *P. eimekei* in their tanks. Actually a third species, *P. altum*, is known to ichthyologists but has not been reported as a popular aquarium fish.

The three angelfishes may be distinguished by the number of fin rays and the number of oblique scale rows on the side of the body from the up-per edge of the opercular opening at the rear of the head to the base of the caudal fin. These obliquely vertical rows total 28 to 36 for *P. eimekei* and 38 to 40 for *P. scalare*.

Pellegrin, in his original 1903 description of *Pterophyllum altum*, gives the scales along the back as 47. Regan in 1905 for *P. altum*, based on two of Pellegrin's specimens, gives the number of scales on the back as 55 and those on the mid-sides as 41 to 47. Ahl in 1928 repeated Regan's counts for *P. altum*. One specimen examined indicates that the number 41 to 47 scales is correct for the side.

An examination of the tables indicates that *P. altum* always may be dis-tinguished by the high number of soft dorsal rays (about 28 or 29) and greater number of scales (41 to 47). These figures do not overlap with the other two species; therefore, *altum* may be identified by counting only the soft dorsal-fin rays. The other two species have 25 or fewer soft dorsal rays.

The next problem is which of the other two species represented in the tables should be assigned the name *P. eimekei*. All this decision can be based on are the counts and the figure presented by Ahl in 1928 when he named the species. His counts for *P. eimekei* agree beautifully with the counts made by the authors on the form of angelfish most abundantly available to aquar-ists. Thus we conclude that *eimekei* is a valid species.

The wide range and distribution of Ahl's counts for *P. scalare* indicates that he may have had a mixture of *eimekei* and *scalare*. The one character that helps to distinguish *eimekei* and *scalare*, as based on the specimens in the collections in the United States National Museum, involves counting with great care and accuracy the number of obliquely vertical scale rows from the upper edge of the opercular opening to the base of the caudal fin in a straight line just below the peduncular lateral line. For *eimekei* these rows vary from 28 to 36 and for *scalare* from 38 to 40. If more specimens of *sca-lare* were available there might be a small amount of overlapping of the scale counts for two species.

The color patterns of the two species are so much alike that one cannot with certainty distinguish *eimekei* from *scalare*.

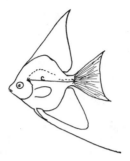

Pterophyllum. Line C: where to count the "vertical" scale rows.

Counts recorded for species of the angelfish, *Pterophyllum*

Number of fin rays: Spines represented by Roman numerals; soft rays by Arabic numbers.

DORSAL FIN

Species	XI	XII	XIII	21	22	23	24	25	26	27	28	29
P. altum°		X	.								X	X
P. altum‡		1										1
P. scalare†	X	X	X				X	X	X			
P. scalare‡	1	5						2	4			
P. eimekei†			X			X	X					
P. eimekei‡	1	23	18	5	11	8	3					

ANAL FIN

Species	V	VI	VII	22	23	24	25	26	27	28	29	30	31	32
P. altum°	X	X								X	X	X	X	X
P. altum‡		1											1	
P. scalare†	X	X	X				X	X	X	X	X			
P. scalare‡		6							1	4	1			
P. eimekei†		X					X	X						
P. eimekei‡		37	3	2	12	16	3	4	5					

Number of obliquely vertical scale rows from head in a straight line to base of caudal-fin rays.

Species	28	29	30	31	32	33	34	35	36	37	38	39	40	41	42	43	44	45	46	47
P. altum°														X	X	X	X	X	X	X
P. altum‡																				1
P. scalare†						X	X	X	X	X	X	X								
P. scalare‡													3	2	1					
P. eimekei†						X	X													
P. eimekei‡	1	2	1	4	14	4	8	6	2											

° Counts as recorded by Pellegrin in 1903.   † Counts recorded by Ahl in 1928.
‡ Authors' counts.

Pterophyllum eimekei Ahl

[eye-mek′-e-eye: named in honor of W. Eimeke of Hamburg]

Pterophyllum eimekei Ahl, Zool. Anz., 76:252, fig. 1, 1928 (type locality, Rio Negro in the Amazon Basin)

RANGE: Rio Negro and Amazon Basins.

SIZE: 5 inches; breeds at 3 inches.

TEMPERAMENT: This species is considered suitable for the community tank but it is a cichlid with traits that make it undesirable in aquaria containing small fishes.

TEMPERATURE REQUIREMENTS: 68–90°F.

SEX DIFFERENCES: See below.

COUNTS: Dorsal XII or XIII,21 to 25; anal VI or VII,22 to 27; pectoral 11 to 13; scales 29 to 36.

It could be said that the angelfish breeds like other cichlids, but so many spawning procedures and techniques are manifested by different pairs that it warrants a fuller treatment.

Procuring good breeding stock is of prime importance when dealing with angelfish. There are several ways one can obtain pairs. Buy a breeding pair which is guaranteed to be a mated pair; buy a spawn of small fish and bring them up to breeding size in a very large aquarium, hoping that a few will pair off; or purchase a dozen medium-size angelfish and

bring them to maturity in the same aquarium hoping that these fish will pair off.

To purchase a mated pair is usually prohibitively expensive. Not only is there the initial outlay of cash, but there is the gamble whether the pair will continue spawning under new conditions. Sometimes the change of water may not suit the pair, one of them may die, or the pair may have "spawned out." This is the least desirable way to obtain breeding stock, but if time is of the essence there is no other way.

The most desirable manner of obtaining breeding stock is by the group-pairing method. Purchase as large a group of smaller-than-breeding-size fish as you can safely raise to maturity in the tank space available. As the fish reach breeding size you will note that certain pairs will tend to separate themselves from the rest of the group. The two will seem to be fighting almost constantly, but should another fish try to attack one, the other will come to the rescue. There is good reason to believe that this pair will mate, so remove them to a 10- or 15-gallon aquarium, heavily planted with Amazon sword plants or giant *Sagittaria*, or, if you prefer to breed the fish commercially, then place a slate (tilted onto the side of the glass) in a bare

Black *Pterophyllum scalare.*

aquarium with them. The pair should spawn within a few weeks if they are brought to breeding condition by constant feedings of *Daphnia, Tubifex,* and small fishes. As other pairs manifest themselves they should also be separated.

If perchance the fish are brought to maturity in a very large aquarium, with no risk of overcrowding as the fish get larger, it may be possible to leave the entire batch of sexually matured fish together and merely remove the eggs from the aquarium as the fish spawn. This is not too desirable a method of commercially propagating the angelfish as many spawns may be lost owing to cannibalism. The accepted practice is to separate mated pairs and keep them in their own breeding tank.

Once a pair has spawned there are various techniques to follow: Either allow the parents to tend the fry until they are free-swimming, or to remove the eggs (or the parents) and raise the fry without the parents. Parent angelfish fulfill certain functions; if you intend to remove the parents then artificial means for fulfilling these functions of keeping the eggs clean

of bacteria and fungus and supplied with oxygen must be provided. The parent fish help keep the eggs clean by a process known as "fanning the spawn." This is accomplished by one of the breeders taking a position directly over the spawn and by a constant movement of its fins maintaining an unceasing circulation of water over the developing eggs. This not only keeps the eggs clear of bacteria (by keeping natural sediment from being deposited on the spawn) but also assures the spawn of a supply of freshly oxygenated water.

Developing eggs need oxygen as much as the free-swimming fry. The usual manner in which these parental functions are taken care of without the breeders is to place the eggs (which have been deposited, assumedly, either on the slate or on the leaf of a relatively stiff-leafed plant) in such a position that a fine stream of air bubbles may be directed over the top of them. This is accomplished by tilting the slate, eggs down, against the side of the hatching aquarium and placing the air releaser underneath it. Too much air will be detrimental to the fry as they start to hatch out. They remain attached to the slate by a rather delicate thread of sticky material which seems to come from the head, and a strong current of air bubbles might tear them loose and injure them. Some fry, however, always fall free onto the bottom of the aquarium; even these manage to come through.

In actual breeding the parents will cooperate in the thorough cleaning job that most cichlids go through prior to the deposition of their spawn. They seem to prefer a strip of slate about 12 inches long, 3 inches wide, and ½ inch thick, slanted at a 60-degree angle with the glass of the aquarium, upon which to place their spawn. There seems to be no true correlation with spawning and the amount of light, but they do like some sunshine.

A résumé of their likes and dislikes is as follows:

Light: Part of the aquarium should, if possible, receive some direct rays of sunlight each day; 12 hours of artificial light may be substituted for natural light. Though nothing definite is yet known, it is believed that the light cycle affects the spawning cycle.

Plants: Heavily planted aquaria are necessary if the angelfish are maintained in a busy area. They are "scary" fish, easily frightened by shadows. They are best kept in aquaria heavily vegetated with Amazon sword plants or other stiff, broad-leafed plants. If maintained in an aquarium without plants, be sure that it is placed high enough to be out of sight of passers-by.

Temperature: Between 68 and 90°F. Optimum breeding temperature 80°F.

Water: Must be clean, without discoloration. Slightly acid water from pH 6.6 to neutral (7.0) is best. Zero hardness.

Foods: Angelfish are carnivorous and should be fed mainly on a live-food diet. They will, however, eagerly take bits of dry food or mash. Baby angelfish should be fed rotifers or other infusoria of the same size until 10 days after they are free-swimming. At this time they will eagerly take newly hatched brine shrimp and sifted *Daphnia*.

Current ichthyological opinion holds that *Pterophyllum scalare* and *Pterophyllum eimekei* are synonymous.

Pterophyllum eimeki

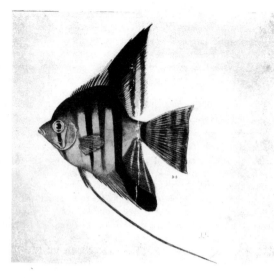

Pterophyllum scalare (Lichenstein)

[sca-lair'-e: *scalare* = ladderlike]

Zeus scalaris Lichenstein, Verzeichniss doubletten des Zoologischen Museums der Königlichen Universität zu Berlin, p. 114, 1823 (type locality, eastern Brazil)

RANGE: Guianas, Amazon, and Rio Negro.

SIZE: 6 inches; breeds at 3 inches.

TEMPERAMENT: Suitable in the community aquarium but it may eat small fishes.

TEMPERATURE REQUIREMENTS: 68–90°F.

SEX DIFFERENCES: See *P. eimekei* (page 651).

COUNTS: Dorsal XI or XII,24 or 25; anal VI,26 to 28; pectoral 11 to 13; scales 38 to 40.

See *P. eimekei* for discussion.

GENUS *Symphysodon* Heckel

[Sym-phi'-so-don: *sym* = together; *phys* = growth; *odon* = teeth]

DISCUS OR POMPADOURFISH / *Symphysodon discus* Heckel

[dis'-cus: *discus* = disk-shaped]

Symphysodon discus Heckel, Ann. Wien. Mus. Naturges., 2:333, pl. 30, figs. 21 and 22, 1840 (type locality, Rio Negro)

RANGE: Rio Negro and Amazon Basin.

SIZE: 9 inches; breeds at 4½ inches.

TEMPERAMENT: A peaceful species that may be kept in the community aquarium.

TEMPERATURE REQUIREMENTS: 70–85°F. Optimum breeding temperature 78°F.

SEX DIFFERENCES: Male shows more red in the belly region and the female is generally more golden colored. Majority of fish available are females.

COUNTS: Dorsal IX or X,30 or 31; anal VIII,30; pectoral 12 to 14; scales 57 to 62.

This lovely species breeds in the same manner as the angelfish. Considerable time has been spent by one of the authors observing a breeding pair. Time after time the spawn was eaten until finally it was decided to remove the slate from the aquarium and try to hatch the eggs without their parents. This method too, proved a failure. After a few years the pair finally were able to raise the fry from hatching to the free-swimming stage, then on to maturity. Several observations were made which seemed quite unusual; first, the parents took excellent care of the eggs until they hatched. They fanned them continually and were always picking away at seemingly invisible particles of sediment that became lodged on the spawn. Once the young hatched out and lost their yolk sacs the parents would take them into their mouths and hold them there for rather long periods of time (once more than 30 minutes). Sometimes they would swallow a batch; other times they would spit them out onto a leaf or back onto the slate, but always they kept the young for a period in their mouths. After spending a few days observing this behavior, it was noted that the parents only did this after they had eaten. Perhaps they were cleaning them like the African black-chinned mouthbreeder, *Tilapia macrocephala.* If the fry are removed from their parents prior to the sixth week they will not survive!

The best food for them is *Tubifex* worms, which they greedily eat. They will also take fairy shrimp, *Daphnia,* and adult brine shrimp. In shipping they lie flat on their sides. Do not let this bother you as they will right themselves as soon as they are removed from the can and have acclimated themselves to their new environment. Contrary to popular belief, the "worms" that seem to come out of their heads are not worms but protozoans. They may be controlled by treating the diseased fish with a mixture of 250 mg each of aureomycin and terramycin to 5 gallons of water.

GENUS *Tilapia* Smith

[Til-la′-pi-a: meaning of name not known]

BLACK-CHINNED MOUTHBREEDER / *Tilapia macrocephala* (Bleeker)

[mack′-row-seff′-a-la: *macro* = large; *cephala* = head]

Melanogenes macrocephala Bleeker, Nat. Verh. Holl. Maatsch. Wetens., 18(2):36, pl. 6, fig. 2, 1863 (type locality, Guinea)

RANGE: Gold Coast to Nigeria, Africa.

SIZE: 8 inches; breeds at 4 inches.

TEMPERAMENT: Not suitable in the community aquarium except when kept with fishes of its own size.

TEMPERATURE REQUIREMENTS: 68–35°F.

SEX DIFFERENCES: Female shows a pink blush through the operculum. Male seems to have slightly longer anal and dorsal fins.

COUNTS: Dorsal XV or XVI,10 to 12; anal III,7 to 9; pectoral 15; scales 27 to 30.

This species serves as a model for the breeding habits and techniques of many other types of cichlids. Much of this material is based on research at the Animal Behavior Department of the American Museum of Natural History in New York City. Lester Aronson, in charge of this department, probably knows more about this species than any other person. The authors are greatly appreciative of his generosity in supplying information to them.

Possibly the choice of a model was not wise, since this species has a habit which is far from general: the male is responsible for the oral incubation of the spawn. However, selection was made on the basis of the finer points in breeding techniques.

The black-chinned mouthbreeders are sexed and the sexes then separated. When a female shows signs of being heavy with eggs she is placed in an aquarium as large as possible, the optimum size being about 15 gallons (12 × 12 × 24 inches). The following day a male may be placed with her.

After much inquisitive circling of each other the two fish will suddenly face each other and, in a typical cichlid manner, "lock jaws," that is, they will meet lip to lip and then close their mouths upon each other's lips. As soon as a strong grip is made they will twist and turn each other for as long as a minute, testing each other's strength. Some observers say that if they are able to maintain this grip for a substantial period of time, the pair will immediately proceed with their spawning process, but this has not been ascertained. The locking of jaws may continue for a week or so until the next step is taken.

Once the fish have accepted each other as suitable mates (and there is usually not too much trouble if both are about the same size), the next step is the selection of a spawning site. If perchance there is a smooth rock lying about on the bottom of the aquarium, or even if there is a bit of slate showing through the sand, the pair will begin to clear away as much sand as possible from the selected site and gradually excavate a neat spawning pit or shelf upon which to place their spawn.

The actual spawning is interesting: the female will first deposit a few eggs in the depression, then the male will follow and fertilize them. After a number of deposits of this sort the male will pick up the eggs in his mouth and thus the oral incubation starts. (There have been some instances where the female has picked up the eggs in her mouth, but this is the exception rather than the rule.)

The female should be removed when this stage is reached and the male should be left in the aquarium with his precious cargo. Once the fry have hatched to the free-swimming stage he may be removed and the fry can fare pretty well for themselves. The function of the oral incubation has been the subject of much study. Observation has shown that unless the male is allowed to incubate the eggs in his mouth they will never hatch. The reason for this has been found to be that the eggs are very susceptible to attack by bacteria (with the fungus Saprolegnia as a secondary infection), which are capable of destroying the eggs. The male mouthbreeder is able to keep the eggs relatively free of bacteria and fungus by circulating water over the eggs in his mouth.

Laboratory experiments show that it is possible to hatch the eggs and raise the fry *without* the parent fish only by constantly sterilizing the eggs (every 4 to 6 hours) in a dilute formalin solution and by maintaining the eggs in sterile (boiled) water.

Once the fry are free-swimming they should be fed on either large protozoans, infusoria, or freshly hatched brine shrimp. After a few weeks they are able to take fine dry foods and larger crustaceans like *Daphnia* and rotifers.

The fry grow rapidly. They should be sorted according to size, to give them more tank room and keep the larger fish from being too competitive for food.

The name of this species currently is *Sarotherodon melanotheron*.

1. Preparing their nest.

2. The female lays the eggs in batches of about a dozen.

3. The male now fertilizes the eggs.

4. The male picks up the eggs in his mouth.

5. The male and the female in the nest after spawning is completed.

6. The male, his mouth bulging with eggs.

MOZAMBIQUE MOUTHBREEDER / *Tilapia mossambica* (Peters)

[mose'-sam-bek'-a: named after the locality in Africa where first found]

Chromis (*Tilapia*) *mossambicus* Peters, Monatsb. Berlin Akad., p. 681, 1852 (type locality, Mozambique)

RANGE: East Africa to Natal.

SIZE: 6 inches; breeds at 4 inches.

TEMPERAMENT: Not suitable in the community tank with fishes smaller than itself.

TEMPERATURE REQUIREMENTS: 70–85°F. Optimum breeding temperature 78°F.

SEX DIFFERENCES: Male shows much brighter orange tail than female.

COUNTS: Dorsal XV or XVI,10 or 11; anal III,9 or 10; pectoral 15; scales 30 to 33.

Breeding is the same as for *Tilapia macrocephala*.

The tail of the male fish is by far the outstanding color feature, displaying a magnificent wide orange band. Patches of white are at times visible against the dark sides when the fish is in excellent condition. The lips are thick and white, sometimes fooling one into thinking that the fish has a lip infection or fungus. These specimens are very hardy and require little in the way of care except volumes of food.

The female usually incubates the spawn; the male should be removed as soon after spawning as possible.

The name of this species currently is *Sarotherodon mossambicus*.

NATAL MOUTHBREEDER / *Tilapia natalensis* (Weber)

[nay'-tal-en'-sis: named after the locality, Natal]

Chromis natalensis Weber, Zool. Jahrb. Syst., 10:147, 1897 (type locality, Natal)

RANGE: East and South Africa.

SIZE: Over 1 foot long; breeds at a length a little shorter than 1 foot.

TEMPERAMENT: Not suitable in the community tank, as this species will ingest whole any fish small enough to be swallowed.

TEMPERATURE REQUIREMENTS: 72–85°F. Breeding is best accomplished at 78°F, according to one authority.

SEX DIFFERENCES: Male has slightly longer and more pointed dorsal and anal fins.

COUNTS: Dorsal XV to XVII,10 to 12; anal III,9 to 11; pectoral 14; scales 30 to 34.

Not much is known about the breeding habits of this species except that it is said to be a mouthbreeder.

This mustard-colored fish is fairly attractive but is not popular owing to its large size. The back is a dark yellowish or tan, the belly somewhat silvery. The upper lateral line is punctuated by a series of dark dots running above and below it. The tail fin is clear with an attractive black border, while the dorsal and anal fins have a red margin and several lighter spots.

The name of this species currently is *Sarotherodon mossambicus.*

NILE MOUTHBREEDER / *Tilapia nilotica* (Linnaeus)

[nil-o′-ti-ca: named after the Nile River]

Labrus niloticus Linnaeus, Systema naturae, ed. 12, 1:477, 1766 (type locality, Nile River, Egypt)

RANGE: Lake Galilee, the Jordan, southward in East Africa, the upper Congo, Lake Tanganyika, through the Chad Basin to Senegal and the Niger Basins.

SIZE: 1½ feet; breeds at 1 foot.

TEMPERAMENT: Not a good aquarium fish as it must be kept in no less than a 50-gallon tank if it is to be bred.

TEMPERATURE REQUIREMENTS: 72–85°F.

SEX DIFFERENCES: Male has slightly more pointed anal and dorsal fins.

COUNTS: Dorsal XVI or XVII,11 to 15; anal III,8 to 11; pectoral 15; scales 31 to 35.

Breeding is much like the black-chinned mouthbreeder, *Tilapia macrocephala*, with the female usually taking care of the eggs.

This fish is a food fish for many Africans and is important only for that reason. Many African students of ichthyology use it as a laboratory animal. There has been some attempt to rear it artificially, much as the Americans raise trout. The fish has a gray color with a metallic sheen.

The name of this species currently is *Sarotherodon niloticus.*

PEACOCK CICHLID / *Tilapia sparmanni* A. Smith

[spar'-man-eye: named in honor of A. Sparmann]

Tilapia sparmanni A. Smith, Illustrations of the Zoology of South Africa, pl. 5, 1845 (type locality, South Africa)

RANGE: Angola, Katanga, Lakes Mweru and Bangweulu, Zambezi to Orange Rivers and Natal.

SIZE: 8 inches; breeds at 5 inches.

TEMPERAMENT: Not suitable in the community tank except with fishes of its own size.

TEMPERATURE REQUIREMENTS: 70–85°F. Optimum breeding temperatures between 74 and 78°F.

SEX DIFFERENCES: Female has a more rounded body.

COUNTS: Dorsal XIII to XV,9 to 11; anal III,9 or 10; pectoral 15; scales 27 to 29.

This species breeds like other cichlids. It is not a mouthbreeder. Much use has been made of it in animal-behavior experiments.

It is gray colored with a metallic sheen. During breeding time it gets darker, and this merely tends to bring out the impressive metallic cast of the scales. About two-thirds of the way down the dorsal fin, right at its base, there is a distinctive ocellus (eyespot). The species is common in the New York metropolitan area because the Animal Behavior Department of the American Museum of Natural History breeds it in great numbers.

When a pair is kept together each seems to be extremely vicious, but when kept in large groups there is no great disturbance.

ZILLI'S CICHLID / *Tilapia zilli* (Gervais)

[zill'-eye: named in honor of an unknown Mr. Zilli]

Acerina zilli Gervais, Ann. Sci. Nat. Zool., (3)10:203, 1848 (type locality, Tuggur, Algeria)

RANGE: Israel, Egypt, Nile Basin, Lakes Rudolf and Gandjule, Chad Basin, Niger to Gold Coast and Liberia.

SIZE: 1 foot; breeds at 10 inches.

TEMPERAMENT: Not suitable in community tank with fishes smaller than itself.

TEMPERATURE REQUIREMENTS: 74–85°F. Optimum breeding temperature 78°F.

SEX DIFFERENCES: Male has slightly longer and more pointed fins and a more sleek appearance.

COUNTS: Dorsal XIV to XVI,10 to 13; anal III,7 to 10; pectoral 14 or 15; scales 28 to 33.

This *Tilapia* is not a mouthbreeder but propagates itself in the typical cichlid manner. Extraordinarily large spawns, running up to 5,000 eggs, may be placed on a flat stone or slate bottom by a 10-inch pair. Parents should be left with their spawn until the fry are free-swimming. This is usually about 4 days after the last of the eggs have been laid at 78°F.

This cichlid reminds one of *Astronotus ocellatus* (page 613). It too is a very large fish. It passes through some interesting color phases and is extremely attractive when small. It has a dark greenish-brown color. In the smaller specimens there are about half a dozen distinct dark vertical bars which are crossed by two less distinct horizontal stripes. Fins are irregularly colored but there is a definite spot on the base of the rear section of the dorsal fin. When sexually mature, at about 2½ years of age, the fish seems to darken considerably and looks nearly black when viewed from the top. Larger specimens are often mistaken for the popular "Jack Dempsey cichlid."

[El'-e-o'-tri-dee]

GENUS *Dormitator* Gill

[Dor'-mi-ta'-tor: *dormitator* = sleepy or sluggish]

BROAD-HEADED SLEEPER or GOBY / *Dormitator latifrons* (Richardson)

[lat'-i-frons: *lati* = broad; *frons* = forehead]

Eleotris latifrons Richardson, Voyage of the *Sulphur*, Fishes, p. 57, pl. 35, figs. 4, 5, 1844 (type locality, probably Pacific Coast of Central America)

RANGE: Pacific Coast of Central America, southern Mexico in marine and brackish waters.

SIZE: 10 inches; breeds at 4 inches.

TEMPERAMENT: Not suitable in the community aquarium as it will eat small fishes.

TEMPERATURE REQUIREMENTS: 68–85°F.

SEX DIFFERENCES: Male is more highly colored.

COUNTS: Dorsal VI to VIII-I,9 or 10; anal I,10; pectoral 14 to 16; pelvic I,5; scales 34 to 36.

This species is similar to *Dormitator maculatus* in color and in breeding habits. It should be maintained in 20 to 30 per cent sea water.

This goby has a group of about half a dozen brownish-red spots on the side. The fins are a greenish yellow and the dorsal and anal fins are marked with brownish-red spots.

SPOTTED GOBY; STRIPED SLEEPER / *Dormitator maculatus* (Bloch)

[mack'-you-lay'-tus: *maculatus* = spotted]

Sciaena maculata Bloch, Ichthyologie, ou histoire naturelle . . . poissons, pl. 299, fig. 2, 1785 (type locality, West Indies)

RANGE: Atlantic Coast of tropical America in marine and brackish waters.

SIZE: 10 inches; breeds at 4 inches.

TEMPERAMENT: Not a good community fish as it feeds on small live fishes.

TEMPERATURE REQUIREMENTS: 68–85°F.

SEX DIFFERENCES: Male has much more color.

COUNTS: Dorsal VI to VIII-I,9 or 10; anal I,10 or 11; pectoral 13 or 14; pelvic I,5; scales 34 to 36.

Reports indicate that this species cleans a stone and lays a small batch of eggs on the selected site. The eggs hatch in about 2 days. The fry need infusoria in great quantities. Not many of the young have been reported to survive. Parents should be removed immediately after spawning.

Its general color is grayish brown with a few high lights of blue in the anal fin and above the pectoral fins.

This species needs about 20 to 30 per cent sea water.

GENUS *Mogurnda* Gill

[Mo-gurn'-da: a native name in northern Australia]

PURPLE-STRIPED GUDGEON / *Mogurnda mogurnda* (Richardson)

Eleotris mogurnda Richardson, Voyage of the *Erebus* and *Terror*, Fish, p. 4, pl. 2, figs. 1, 2, 1844 (type locality, Port Essington, North Australia)

RANGE: North and central Australia in fresh water.

SIZE: 8 inches; breeds at 2 inches.

TEMPERAMENT: Not suitable as a community fish as it will tear the fins of small fishes.

TEMPERATURE REQUIREMENTS: 68–85°F.

SEX DIFFERENCES: Male is more colorful than the female.

COUNTS: Dorsal VIII-I,14; anal I,14; pectoral 16; pelvic I,5; scales about 55.

All that is necessary for the breeding of these delightful animals is to provide the basic essentials: A nicely planted aquarium, abundant meaty food like worms and *Daphnia*, and either pieces of rock or the glass of the aquarium. The female will work with a few males and clean off a spot on the rock or the glass. She will then spawn for hours with different males, placing about 100 eggs on the spawning site with sticky threads. One of the males will take charge during incubation of the eggs by moving them around with his pelvic fins. The female and all other males should be removed as soon as spawning is completed. After a little less than a week the eggs hatch and the fry start looking for food. They should be provided at once with infusoria and other small-particled foods. The male should be removed as soon as the fry are free-swimming.

GENUS *Oxyeleotris* Bleeker

[Ox'-i-e'-lee-o'-tris: *oxy* = sharp or quick; *eleotris* = a kind of fish]

MARBLED SLEEPER / *Oxyeleotris marmorata* (Bleeker)

[mar'-mor-a'-ta: *marmorata* = marbled]

Eleotris marmorata Bleeker, Nat. Tijdschr. Ned. Indie, 3:424, 1852 (type locality, Bandjermasin, Borneo)

RANGE: Borneo, Sumatra, Malaya, and Thailand.

SIZE: 1½ feet; breeding not observed.

TEMPERAMENT: Not suitable in the community tank.

TEMPERATURE REQUIREMENTS: 65–85°F.

SEX DIFFERENCES: Male is more colorful.

COUNTS: Dorsal VI-I,9 or 10; anal I,9 or 10; pectoral 17 or 18; pelvic I,5; scales 73 to 82.

This species has a voracious appetite and a deceptively large mouth. It can consume its weight in fish per day. When the owner runs out of live and dead fish, he can try bits of meat and dog food.

It is slow, always awaiting a victim by lying on the aquarium floor. It has little personality and is vicious. Males are highly colored and seem to be the only sex imported.

[Go-bi'-i-dee]

Genus *Brachygobius* Bleeker

[Brach'-i-go'-bi-us: *brachy* = short; *gobius* = a goby or kind of fish]

Doria's Bumblebeefish / *Brachygobius doriae* (Günther)

[dor'-i-ee: named in honor of the Italian zoologist G. Doria]

Gobius doriae Günther, Ann. Mag. Nat. Hist., (4)1:265, pl. 12, fig. A, 1868 (type locality, Sarawak)

RANGE: Borneo and possibly Malaya.

SIZE: 1½ inches; breeding not observed.

TEMPERAMENT: Suitable in the community tank because of its small size. It will eat small baby fishes.

TEMPERATURE REQUIREMENTS: 72–86°F.

SEX DIFFERENCES: Male is a bit more colorful.

COUNTS: Dorsal VI-I,7; anal I,7; pectoral 16; pelvic I,4; scales 27 to 30.

There is no doubt that this goby is the most popular aquarium fish among all gobies that have been introduced to aquarists. It is now imported in great quantities and more and more has been learned of its breeding habits.

Aside from normal variation, the following account gives the main points about its breeding habits:

1. After considerable conditioning on chopped earthworms and larger crustacea (adult brine shrimp) a pair may be placed together.

2. A large aquarium (12 gallons) is used for the breeding tank. It should contain an empty flowerpot and only 4 inches of water, just enough to cover the flowerpot.

3. The female enters the flowerpot and lays strings of eggs on its upper side, which necessitates an upside-down position. The male enters the pot and fertilizes the eggs.

4. About 2 drops of 5 per cent Methylene Blue may be added to the water to control fungus.

5. Eggs hatch in 5 days at 76°F while the male fans the eggs from his upside-down position. He does not bother the eggs or the young.

6. The fry should be fed infusoria and small-particled foods.

Brachygobius aggregatus.

Brachygobius xanthozonus (Bleeker), with 8 dark cross bars or black girdles and 50 scale rows along the side, has been badly confused with *B. doriae*, which has only 3 black bars or girdles and 27 to 30 scales. The color variety shown above with narrow black bars between the main broad black bars has been illustrated in aquarium books as *B. doriae,* with the true *doriae* being called *xanthozonus.*

The species illustrated on this page is *B. aggregatus* Herre (*Philippine Jour. Sci.,* 72 (4):361, pl. 4, 1940, type locality, Philippines). Counts: Dorsal VI-I,6; anal I,6; scales 22 to 26.

Genus *Periophthalmus* Bloch

[Pear'-i-off-thal'-mus: *peri* = around or in all directions; *ophthalmus* = eye, seeing in all directions]

Mudskipper / *Periophthalmus barbarus* (Linnaeus)

[bar-bar'-us: *barbarus* = strange]

Gobius barbarus Linnaeus, Systema naturae, ed. 12, p. 450, 1766 (no locality given)

RANGE: Tidal areas in fresh, nearly fresh, or brackish water from Japan to East Indies, India, South Pacific islands, East Africa, and Australia.

SIZE: 1 foot; breeding not observed.

TEMPERAMENT: Not suitable in the community tank because of its ecological needs.

TEMPERATURE REQUIREMENTS: 70–85°F.

SEX DIFFERENCES: Not known.

COUNTS: Dorsal X to XVII,12; anal 10 or 11; pectoral 13; scales 70 to 100.

This fish walks, jumps, skips, and sees in the air. The pectoral fins of this species are well-developed and have extraordinarily strong muscles at the base. These fins are used by the fish in locomotion on land. The methods of movement are in two distinct categories: walking and skipping. Reports indicate that it is capable of skipping (or jumping) as far as 20 feet. Two large eyes are located on the top of the head very close together. They are specially fitted on the end of a small extension which allows the fish to raise and lower the eyes at will. They are also capable of independent sight—one may be looking under water while the other is observing out of the water.

The fish lives normally in mudholes and has been observed to move about the complex root systems of mangrove swamps. A single pair when kept together will engage in fights. It requires a large aquarium (terrarium would be better) which has a base no less than 12 × 30 inches and contains only 2 inches of water in its deepest parts. There should be sand dunes and rocks for the fish to crawl upon to get out of the water. The entire aquarium should be covered to maintain as high a humidity as possible. Feed the fish bits of meat, worms, and other fish.

FAMILY **MASTACEMBELIDAE**

[Mas'-ta-sem-bel'-i-dee]

GENUS *Macrognathus* Lacepède

[Mak'-row-nath'-us: *macro* = large; *gnathus* = the jaws]

SPINY EEL / *Macrognathus aculeatus* (Bloch)

[a-kue'-lee-a'-tus: *aculeatus* = sharp-pointed]

Ophidium aculeatum Bloch, Ichthyologie, ou histoire naturelle . . . poissons, 5:60, pl. 159, fig. 2, 1788 (type locality, East Indies)

RANGE: India, Burma, Indochina, Malaya, Borneo, and Moluccas.

SIZE: 1 foot; breeding not observed.

TEMPERAMENT: It is capable of eating newborn live bearers, but otherwise is safe in the community tank.

TEMPERATURE REQUIREMENTS: 74–80°F.

SEX DIFFERENCES: Not known.

COUNTS: Dorsal XIV or XV,50 to 55; anal II,49 to 53; pectoral 18 or 19; pelvic absent; scales very small and numerous.

This fish has not been bred. Most of its time is spent buried in the sand with only the snout tip showing. The author lost several of these when they climbed up a plastic tube from the water and died on the top glass of the aquarium. Their climbing powers are fantastic. Otherwise the fish is hardy and will live a long time in either fresh or slightly brackish water. The chief foods are worms in any shape or form and bits of clam or crabmeat. It is nocturnal in habits and is seldom seen about the aquarium during the daylight hours.

[Ak'-i-ri'-dee]

GENUS *Achirus* Lacepède

[Ak'-i-rus: *achirus* = without hands]

SOLE / *Achirus fasciatus* Lacepède

[fas'-see-a'-tus: *fasciatus* = banded]

Achirus fasciatus Lacepède, Histoire naturelle des poissons, 4:659, 1803 (type locality, Charleston, South Carolina)

RANGE: Cape Cod to Texas, ascending into fresh water.

SIZE: 6 inches; breeding not known.

TEMPERAMENT: Suitable in the community aquarium when small but as it gets older it may nip fins.

TEMPERATURE REQUIREMENTS: 40–78°F.

SEX DIFFERENCES: No external difference is obvious.

COUNTS: Dorsal 50 to 56; anal 36 to 42; scales 66 to 75.

This marine fish enters brackish water at times. Some specimens are even found in the outlets of rivers where the water is nearly all fresh. These fish are the babies of the commercially valuable sole, a favorite food fish.

This sole is not well suited to the tropical aquarium and is not long-lived unless maintained in an unheated marine aquarium somewhat below room temperature.

In the larval stage it has normal eyes, one on each side of the head, but as it gets older the eyes rotate until finally both eyes are on one side of the head and the fish is blind on the other side. For this reason the sole is a bottom fish, keeping its blind side always flat on the bottom, awaiting the passing nearby of living food items. It is not the scavenger that many people believe and its peculiar habit of staying on the bottom or against the glass of the aquarium is not to clean off the algae as many dealers relate, but merely a natural environmental condition where its blind side is against a solid object. It prefers live foods and bits of clam, shrimp, lobster, and crabmeat.

The name of this species currently is *Trinectes maculatus*.

GLOSSARY

abdomen. Belly, the ventral side of the fish surrounding the cavity containing the digestive and reproductive organs.

abdominal. Pertaining to the belly; said of the pelvic fins of fishes when inserted behind pectorals.

abyssal fishes. Fishes living in the great depths of the ocean.

accessory caudal rays. Short procurrent rays on the upper or dorsal and lower or ventral rather than posterior edges of caudal-fin base.

accessory pelvic scale. An enlarged scale or fleshy appendage on upper or dorsal edge of base of pelvic fin.

acclimatization. The adaptation of fishes to a new environment or habitat or to different climatic conditions.

actinosts. A series of bones at the base of the rays of the paired fins.

acuminate. Tapering gradually to a point.

acute. Sharp, pointed.

adipose eyelid. The thickened or fleshy skin around the edge of the eye, some-times partly covering the eye except the pupil.

adipose fin. A fleshy finlike projection without rays, behind the rayed dorsal fin.

adnate. Adhering or grown together.

aestivate. See *estivate.*

agape. In a gaping state. Jaws open.

air bladder or *swim bladder.* A membranous sac filled with gas situated in the body cavity, ventral to the vertebral column and homologous with the lungs of higher vertebrates.

albino. Abnormal congenital deficiency of black pigmentation. Albinos have pink eyes because of lack of pigmentation.

alevin. Any young fish, especially referring to salmon and trout fry.

alimentary tract. The digestive tract or canal.

alveolus (pl. *alveoli*). A small cell or honeycomb-like cavity or air cell in lungs.

ammocoetes. The larval form of lampreys.

amphibious. Capable of living both on land and in water.

anadromous. Running up; ascending; said of fishes which migrate from the sea up rivers to spawn; in a broader sense, any fish running up rivers to spawn or going from deeper to shallow water for purpose of spawning.

anal. Pertaining to the anus or vent.

anal fin. The fin on the ventral median line behind the anus.

anal papilla. A protuberance in front of the genital pore and behind the vent in certain groups of fishes.

anchylosed. Grown firmly together.

animal pole. That end of the egg which contains the developing embryo.

annulus. A yearly mark formed by a zone of irregularities in the sculpturing on scales, corresponding to a period of slow growth.

anteroposterior axis. The lengthwise or horizontal axis.

antrorse. Turned forward.

anus. The external posterior opening of the intestine, the vent.

aquarium (pl. *aquaria*). A tank or other suitable container in which fishes and other aquatic organisms may be maintained.

artery. A blood vessel carrying blood away from the heart.

articular. The bone at the rear of the lower jaw that forms part of the hinge with the quadrate.

articulate. Jointed; said of the structure of soft fin rays.

assimilation. The transformation of digested nutriments into the fluids of an organism by a process of constructive metabolism.

atrophy. Nondevelopment. Diminution in size.

attenuate. Long and slender.

auditory. Referring to the ear or to hearing.

axila. The region just behind or under the pectoral-fin base.

backbone. Vertebral column.

bar. Vertical color mark on fishes.

barbel. An elongated fleshy projection, usually about the head.

basal. Pertaining to the base; at or near the base of a fin.

bathypelagic fishes. Fishes living above the abyssal fishes in the ocean.

bicolor. Two-colored.

bicuspid. Having two points, split into two parts.

binocular vision. Both eyes capable of focusing on a single point.

blastula. A hollow ball of cells, one of the early stages in embryological development.

bony fishes. Fishes having a hard calcified skeleton as contrasted with a cartilaginous one.

branchiae. Gills, the respiratory organs of fishes.

branchiocranium. The bony skeleton supporting the gill arches.

branchiostegals. The bony rays supporting the branchiostegal membrane, under the head of fishes, below the opercular bones, behind the lower jaw, and attached to the hyoid arch.

breast. An area with indefinite boundaries between the pelvic fins and the isthmus; sometimes called chest.

breeding tube. The genital papilla or the ovipositor.

bristle. A stiff hair or hairlike structure.

brood pouch. A saclike organ on the abdomen of male pipefishes and sea horses, in which the eggs are incubated and the young are carried until birth.

buccal. Pertaining to the mouth.

buccal incubation. Incubation of eggs in the mouth; oral incubation.

caducous. Falling off early or easily.

caecal. Of the form of a blind sac.

caecum (pl. *caeca*). An appendage in the form of a blind sac, connected with the alimentary canal, such as the pyloric caeca at the posterior end of the stomach or pylorus.

canines. In fishes, any distinctly enlarged conical teeth longer than others.

cardiform teeth. Sharp conical teeth arranged like the spikes on wool cards.

carinate. Keeled; having a ridge along the middle line.

carnivorous. Feeding or preying on living animals.

cartilage. Hard tissues, not calcified, that serve the purpose of bones in certain primitive fishes.

catadromous. Running down; said of fishes which migrate down rivers to spawn in the sea.

caudal. Pertaining to the tail.

caudal fin. The tail fin of fishes.

caudal peduncle. The tapering or slender portion of the body behind the base of the last ray of the anal fin. Its length is measured from the base of the last anal ray to the mid-base of the caudal fin. The least depth of caudal peduncle is taken as its slenderest part dorsoventrally.

cavernous. Containing cavities, whether empty or filled with mucous secretions.

centrum. The body of a vertebra.

cephalic fins. Fins on the head, as found in certain rays.

ceratobranchials. Certain bones in each gill arch or branchial arch.

cheek. The area on the side of the head of a fish below the eye.

chest. See *breast.*

chin. The region at the tip of the lower jaw where the rami of the dentary join.

chromatophores. Colored pigment cells.

chromosomes. Units of heredity in the nucleus of cells.

ciliated. Fringed with fine hairlike projections.

circuli. The more or less concentric growth marks in a fish scale.

cirrus (pl. *cirri*). Fringes; tendril-like flexible tufts of skin; hairlike.

claspers. Cartilaginous elongate organs attached to the pelvic fins of male sharks, rays, and skates; the myxopterygia.

cloaca. The common cavity into which the rectal, urinary, and genital ducts open.

coelomic cavity. The body cavity containing the internal organs.

coitus. Copulation, mating of male and female.

compressed. Flattened laterally or from side to side, as the angelfish.

conditioning breeders. Getting breeding-size fishes into physical and psychological condition for breeding. This is usually accomplished by heavy and persistent feedings of live foods and separation of the sexes.

copulation. Mating of male and female.

cornea. Outer covering of the eye.

crenulate. Scalloped, or with even rounded notches.

ctenoid. Rough or spiny-edged; said of cycloid-like scales having the posterior margin minutely spinous, pectinated, or fine-toothed.

cutis. The inner layer of the skin.

cycloid. Smooth-edged; said of scales with concentrically arranged striae, without any trace of minute spines.

cytoplasm. The contents of a cell.

deciduous. Temporary; falling off easily, said of the scales of certain fishes.

decurved. Curved downward or ventrally.

deep-sea fishes. Fishes living in the depths of the ocean, or any oceanic fishes.

demersal fishes. Fishes that lay eggs which are heavier than water and thus sink.

dentary. The anterior bone of the lower jaw or mandible, usually bearing teeth.

denticle. A little tooth.

dentition strong. Teeth very easily observed; highly and strongly developed teeth.

dentition weak. Teeth scarcely evident.

depressed. Flattened vertically, like the skates and rays.

depth. The vertical distance through the body at its deepest part along the dorsoventral axis, not including fins.

dermal. Pertaining to the skin.

dermis. The skin.

diaphanous. Translucent.

dioecious. Having the male and female organs borne by separate individuals.

disk (of ray or skate). The more or less depressed rounded body excluding tail, pelvic fins, and claspers.

disk (sucking disk of gobies). The cup- or saucer-shaped pelvic fins fused into a membranous disk.

distal. Remote from point of attachment.

dorsal. Pertaining to the back.

dorsal fin. The fin on the back or dorsal side, in front of the adipose fin if it is present.

ductus pneumaticus. A tube that connects the air bladder with the esophagus.

ectoparasite. A parasite living outside the body of the fish (host).

emarginate. Slightly forked or notched.

endoparasite. A parasite living inside the host.

endoskeleton. The skeleton proper; the inner bony framework.

epidermis. Outer layer of the skin.

epineural. Situated upon a neural arch, such as a spine of a vertebra.

erectile. Susceptible of being raised.

esophagus. The tube that connects the mouth with the stomach.

estivate. To pass the summer or dry season in a torpor or sleep.

excretion. Getting rid of or throwing off waste products by any organism.

exoskeleton. Hard bony parts on the exterior surfaces, such as scales, scutes, and bony plates.

exserted. Projecting beyond the general level, as fin rays beyond the membranes or beyond other rays.

eye. The diameter of the eye, called "eye" in descriptions, is measured across its fleshy horizontal diameter, since it is not always round. When the term orbit is used, this refers to the bony orbit. Most descriptions refer to the greatest diameter of the eye, and then the measurement may not be across its horizontal diameter.

eye in snout. A technique of ichthyological measurement—the diameter of the eye as stepped off into the length of the snout by means of proportional dividers.

falcate. Scythe-shaped; long, narrow, and curved.

falciform. Curved like a scythe.

family of fishes. A group of related genera and species of fishes.

fauna. The animals inhabiting any region, taken collectively.

feeler. See *barbel*.

fertilization. The union of the sperm and egg.

filamentous. Consisting of or bearing threadlike rays; usually applied to fins of fishes.

filiform. Threadlike, slender in structure.

fin height. The height of a fin, the length of its longest ray.

fin length. The length of a fin measured along its base, unless the length of the depressed fin is specified. The latter is measured from its origin to the most posterior point of the fin.

finlets. A series of specialized fin rays, usually separate from each other and occurring posterior to the main dorsal or anal fins.

fin-ray formula. In counting fin rays, each ray with a separate base is counted as one. In certain fishes the last ray may be split to the base, in which case it is counted as a single ray. In the formula XII,ii,15, capital Roman numbers represent spines, lower-case Roman numbers represent unbranched or simple soft rays, and Arabic numbers are branched soft rays. Two separated dorsal fins are represented by a dash "–" in the formula, for example XII–15. A comma indicates that all the elements are connected in a single fin.

fish. A vertebrate adapted for aquatic respiration by means of gills. When used in the plural, fish refers to two or more specimens of the same species.

fishes. The plural of fish used when referring to two or more kinds of fishes.

fontanel. An unossified space on top of the head, between the parietals, covered with a membrane.

foramen. A hole or opening.

forehead. Frontal curve of the head.

forficate. Deeply forked, furcate.

fossa (nasal). Groove in which the nostrils open, a shallow depression.

fossil fishes. Prehistoric fishes whose mineralized remains are preserved in rocks.

frenum. A small piece of skin binding the lip to the edge of the jaw.

frontal claspers. See *claspers*.

fulcrum (pl. *fulcra*). A spinelike scaly projection along the anterior rays of the fins of ganoid fishes.

fungus. A thallophytic plant, lacking chlorophyll, and deriving its nourishment from living tissues or nonliving organic compounds; some kinds are parasitic on fishes.

furcate. Forked.

fusiform. Spindle-shaped, tapering toward both ends but more abruptly forward.

gamete. A mature sexual reproductive cell.

ganoid. Covered with enamel, said of scales or plates.

gape. Opening of the mouth.

Gasserian ganglion. A large ganglion on the root of the fifth cranial nerve.

gastrula. The embryonic stage of development consisting of two layers enclosing a saclike central cavity with a pore at one end.

geniculate. Having kneelike bends, joints, or protuberances.

genus. One of the subdivisions of the family, which embraces one or more species.

gibbous. Sharply convex or rounded.

gill arches. The bony arches to which gill filaments are attached.

gill membranes. The skin or dermal membranes, supported by the branchiostegals, more or less restricting the gill opening in the region of the isthmus.

gill membranes free from the isthmus. The gill membranes not connected to the isthmus; a needle may pass between the isthmus and membranes when the latter are connected across the isthmus.

gill opening. The opening leading from the branchiae or gill filaments.

gill rakers. A series of bony appendages, variously arranged along the anterior and often the posterior edges of the gill arches. Those along the anterior edge of the first arch are counted unless otherwise specified. The number of rakers including all rudiments is counted above the angle, at the angle, and below the angle or bend of the arch. These counts are expressed in a formula, e.g., 10 + 1 + 25, which means 10 rakers above the angle, 1 raker at the angle, and 25 in the lower or ventral part of the arch.

gills. Highly vascular fleshy filaments used in aquatic respiration.

gill slit. The opening between any two gill arches. The "slit" behind the fourth gill arch may be porelike, absent, or very small. If porelike, it is a tiny round opening like the letter "o"; but if it is a small slit, it is a small elongate opening. This opening when tiny is located very close to the bony part of the arch and not in the loose membranous tissue.

glabrous. Smooth.

glossohyal. Pertaining to the hyoid arch and the tongue.

glottis. The opening into the tube (windpipe) that leads to the lung or air bladder.

gonads. Reproductive organs, testes and ovaries.

gonopodium. An external reproductive organ found in either male or female, modified from the anal fin in certain fishes.

graduated spines or rays. Progressively longer posteriorly; the third element is as much longer than the second as the second is longer than the first, etc.

granulated. Rough with small prominences.

guanin. A waste product of the blood with the power of reflecting light.

gular. Pertaining to the gula; in fishes, the region between the chin and the isthmus.

gular plate. A single hard plate or plates between the dentary bones of the lower jaw.

gullet. The esophagus.

head length. Usually called "head" in most descriptions. The length of the head is measured from the tip of the snout to the extreme hind margin of the fleshy portion of the opercle. It includes opercular spines if these project beyond the fleshy opercular membrane.

head width. Measured at the widest part.

height. Vertical diameter.

hemal arch. The arch between the hemal spines on the ventral side of caudal vertebrae for the passage of blood vessels.

hemal canal. The series of openings in the hemal arches as a whole.

hemal spine. The ventral spine of a caudal vertebra in fishes.

hermaphrodite. An individual that contains the reproductive or generative organs of both sexes.

hespid. Rough, with short stiff hairs or bristles.

heterocercal. Said of the tail of fishes when vertically unequal, the vertebral column being deflected dorsally into the upper lobe.

holotype. The specimen on which the description of a new species is based.

homocercal. Said of the tail of fishes when not externally unequal; the last vertebrae are fused into a more or less symmetrical plate, called the hypural plate.

horizontal. Along the anteroposterior axis or parallel to it.

humeral spine. A spine above the base of the pectoral fin, attached to the pectoral girdle and directed posteriorly.

hybrid. The offspring from crossing two different species.

hyoid apparatus. A series of bones supporting the tongue.

hyomandibular. A bone by which the posterior end of the suspensorium is articulated with the skull; the supporting element of the suspensorium, the mandible, the hyoid apparatus, and the opercular apparatus.

hypercoracoid. The upper of the two bones attached to the clavicle, indirectly bearing the pectoral fin.

hypobranchials. Bones of the branchial arches below the ceratobranchials.

hypurals. The modified platelike last few vertebrae supporting the caudal-fin rays.

ich. Ichthyophthirius, a protozoan parasite of fishes also called "white-spot disease."

ichthyology. The science of the study of fishes.

-id (suffix). Indicating membership in a family, thus percid, a member of the *Percidae.*

-idae (suffix). The family name always ends in *-idae,* as in Cyprinidae.

imbricate. Overlapping like shingles on a roof.

imperforate. Not pierced through.

-inae (suffix). The subfamily name always ends in *-inae,* as in *Cyprininae.*

inarticulate. Not jointed.

incisors. Teeth compressed to form a chisel-like cutting edge.

incubation. The process of development of embryos to the hatching period.

inferior pharyngeals. Synonymous with lower pharyngeals. Main bones of pharyngeal arch.

infraoral. Below the mouth. The teeth of the mouth or disk in lampreys below the oral opening.

infraorbitals. A chain of small bones bordering the eye and below it.

infundibulum. A hollow outgrowth from the floor of the forebrain.

inner ear. The auditory organ of vertebrates.

insertion of fin. A term applied to the point where the paired fins arise from the body.

interbranchial septum. The membrane separating the two gill filaments on a gill arch.

interhemal spines. Bony elements between the hemal spines supporting the anal fin.

intermaxillaries. The premaxillaries.

International Commission on Zoological Nomenclature. A group of men who form and interpret the rules of zoological nomenclature.

interneural spines. Bony elements, between the neural spines, supporting the dorsal-fin rays.

interopercle. Membrane bone between the preopercle and the branchiostegals, usually anterior to the subopercle when it is present.

interorbital space. The space between the eyes on the dorsal side of the head. The least width of the bony interorbital space is measured unless the fleshy interorbital space is indicated.

interspinous bones. The interneurals and interhemals.

intromittent organ. The gonopodium, a modified anal fin for reproduction.

iris. The curtain stretched across the aqueous chamber of the eye, in front of the lens, having a contractile aperture called the pupil.

isocercal. Said of the tail of fishes when the last vertebrae progressively become smaller and smaller and end in the median line of the caudal fin, the hypural plate being nearly obsolete.

isthmus. The region just anterior to the breast of a fish where the gill membranes converge. The fleshy interspace between gill openings.

jugular. Said of the pelvic fins when inserted in advance of the insertion of the pectoral fins.

keeled. Having a ridge along the mid-line.

lacustrine. Living in lakes.

lamellae. Platelike fleshy processes.

larva (pl. *larvae*). An immature form, which must undergo change of appearance or pass through a metamorphic stage to reach the adult state.

lateral. Pertaining to the side.

lateral line. A series of sensory tubes or pores opening to the exterior, sometimes through scales or a sensory canal along the sides of a fish. These may be single or multiple.

lateral line with an accessory branch. An extra branch runs off the main lateral line.

lateral line with an arch. The lateral line has a distinct elevation over the region of the pectoral fin in the form of an abrupt arch, not a gentle curve.

laterally. Sidewise.

length. This may refer to either the total length or the standard length, for which see under each item.

length of upper jaw. Often referred to as maxillaries. In descriptions it is measured from the tip of the snout to the posterior end of the maxillary.

leukocytes. The white blood corpuscles.

lingual. Pertaining to the tongue.

littoral. Pertaining to the habit of living on or near the shore.

luminescence. The "cold" light produced by various organisms and fishes.

lunate. Having the form of the new moon.

Malpighian body. The functional unit of the kidney, consisting of Bowman's capsule, the glomerulus, and the uriniferous tubule.

mandible. Anterior bone of lower jaw usually bearing teeth.

marbled. Variegated; partly clouded.

maxilla or *maxillary.* The hindmost bone of the upper jaw.

mesentery. A fold of the peritoneum that invests the intestine and supports it from the body wall.

metamorphosis. The rapid change in anatomical structure that transforms the larva or postlarva into the adult.

milt. The sperm of fishes.

molars. The grinding teeth; flat-topped teeth.

monogamous. Paired with but one mate.

mottled. Blotched; color spots running together.

mouth inferior. The mouth located ventrally and a little behind the tip of the projecting snout.

mouth oblique. The mouth lying at an angle to the horizontal axis of the body.

mouth ventral. The mouth located notably on the ventral side of the head.

muciferous. Producing or containing mucus.

mucus. A viscid or slimy substance secreted by the mucous glands.

myomere. The muscular part of a body segment.

myotomes. Muscle segments.

myxopterygia. See *claspers.*

nape. Posterodorsal edge of head.

nares. Nostrils, anterior and posterior openings.

nearctic region. North America and Greenland.

neotropical region. Tropical South America and adjoining islands.

neural arch. The dorsal arch of a vertebra for the passage of the spinal cord.

neural canal. The cavities formed by the neural arches as a whole.

neurocranium. The skeletal part of the skull surrounding the brain.

nictitating membrane. The third or inner eyelid found in certain sharks.

nuchal. Pertaining to nape.

nuptial tubercles. Bony excrescences usually on the head, sometimes on the paired fins of fishes, indicating sexual maturity.

obsolete. Faintly marked; scarcely evident.

obtuse. Blunt.

occiput. Dorsoposterior part of the head; the "cross line" separating the fleshy nape from the head.

ocellate. With eyelike spots.

ocellus. A roundish dark spot with pale or white border.

odontoid. Toothlike.

-oid (suffix). Like; as percoid, meaning perchlike.

oöspore. A fertilized oösphere or egglike spore.

for 7 days in a shallow, nonmetallic pan. Artificial aeration may hasten this aging.

second dorsal. The posterior of two fins, usually the soft-rayed dorsal fin of spiny-rayed fishes.

septum (pl. *septa*). A thin partition.

serrate. Notched or toothed like a saw.

sessile. Permanently attached.

setaceous. Bristly.

setiform. Bristlelike; like the bristles of a brush.

snout. The portion of the head in front of the eyes. The snout is measured from its most anterior tip to the anterior margin of the orbit.

soft dorsal. The part of the dorsal fin, sometimes all of it, composed of soft or articulated rays.

soft rays. Fin rays that are cross-striated or articulated, like a bamboo fish pole. Soft rays are paired.

spatulate. Shaped like a paddle or spatula.

spawning grass. Any medium in which fishes will spawn. Artificial grass is usually the Florida-grown Spanish moss. *Myriophyllum, Cabomba, Nitella,* and others are also called spawning grass.

species. A classificatory group or biological unit subordinate to the genus, the members of which differ among themselves only in the most minor details of structure, color, physiology, and behavior; they are capable of producing fertile offspring like the parents indefinitely.

spine. A sharp projecting bony point; of fin rays, technically inarticulated, unpaired median rays, regardless of whether or not they are stiff and pungent.

spinous dorsal. Anterior part of the dorsal fin of spiny-rayed fishes; any dorsal fin composed of inarticulated rays.

spiny rays. Pungent or non-cross-striated fin rays.

spiracle. A small respiratory opening, usually on the dorsal part of the head of some sharks, skates, rays, and certain other fishes.

splanchnocranium. The skeletal supports around the mouth and pharynx.

standard length. The distance from the tip of the snout to the base of the caudal-fin rays.

stellate. Starlike; with radiating ridges.

striate. Striped or streaked.

subcaudal. Below the tail.

subopercle. First bone below the opercle.

suborbitals. Chain of small bones below the eye.

suborbital stay. One of the suborbital bones in certain fishes that extends across the cheek, to or toward the preopercle.

subulate. Awl-shaped.

sucking disk. One or both paired fins modified into a saucer-shaped clinging organ, as found in gobies.

superpharyngeals. Upper pharyngeals; sometimes a synonym of pharyngobranchials.

supplemental maxillary. A small bone or bones lying along the upper edge of the maxillary in some fishes.

supraoral teeth. Teeth on the supraoral plate of lampreys.

supraorbital. Above the eye. In reference to a cirrus, it may occur on the eye or on the interorbital space.

suspensorium. The skeletal supports for the lower jaw.

suture. Line of union of two bones.

swim bladder. See *air bladder.*

symphysis. Point of junction of the two rami of the jaw; tip of the chin.

syncranium. The skull.

synonymy. Scientific names applied to the same species or genus, other than the valid name.

tactile. That which pertains to the sense of touch.

tail. Caudal fin of fishes. The part of the body behind the body cavity.

teeth bifid or *bicuspid.* With two projections.

teeth multicuspid. With many projections.

teeth trifid. With three projections.

temperament. How one fish gets along with other fishes, either of the same species or totally unrelated.

terete. Cylindrical and tapering.

terminal. At the end.

tessellated. Marked with little checks or squares, like mosaic work.

testes. Male generative or reproductive glands.

thoracic. Pertaining to the thorax or chest. Pelvic fins are thoracic when attached immediately below or a little behind the pectoral-fin base.

total length. The distance from the most anterior point of a fish to the tip of its tail.

transverse. Crosswise.

trenchant. Compressed to a sharp edge.

truncate. Abrupt, as if cut off squarely.

tubercle. A small excrescence like a pimple or a tiny blunt spine.

type. See *holotype* and *paratype.*

type locality. The locality or localities from which the holotype and paratypes were collected.

ultimate. Last or farthest.

unicolor. Of a single color or shade.

urostyle. The rudimentary or embryonic rear tip of the vertebral column that occurs on the dorsal edge of the hypural plate.

utriculus. A small sac of the internal ear.

vas deferens. The ducts by which sperm is conveyed to the seminal vesicles.

vein. A tubular vessel that carries blood to the heart.

vent. The external posterior opening of the alimentary canal; the anus.

ventral fins. This term, when applied to fishes, is the same as pelvic fins. In comparative anatomy the term "ventral fin" refers to the anal fin of fishes; be-cause of this confusion, modern ichthy-ologists do not use the term.

ventral plates. The row of plates along the belly of certain fishes between breast and vent.

vertebra (pl. *vertebrae*). One of the bones forming the backbone of vertebrates.

vertebrae, abdominal. Anterior vertebrae occurring dorsal to the body cavity, to which the ribs are attached. These ver-tebrae lack the hemal arch and hemal spines on their ventral sides.

vertebrae, caudal. Posterior vertebrae that possess the hemal arch and hemal spines on their ventral sides.

vertical fins. Fins along the median line of the body—the dorsal, anal, and caudal fins.

vertically. Up and down dorsiventrally.

vestigial. Rudimentary.

villiform. Said of the teeth of fishes when slender and crowded into velvety bands or compact patches.

viscous. Slimy.

vitelline membrane. The outer membrane of an egg.

viviparous. Bringing forth living young. The mother contributes food toward the development of the embryos.

vomer. In fishes, the bone lying immedi-ately behind the premaxillaries at the median front part of the roof of the mouth. This bone usually bears teeth.

Weberian ossicles. A chain of small bones developed in connection with the modi-fied anterior four vertebrae connecting the air bladder with the ear in the or-der Ostariophysi.

width. The width of a fish, taken at the widest part of the body.

zoogeography. The science of the distribu-tion of animals on the surface of the earth.

SELECTED REFERENCES

BOOKS

Arnold, Johann Paul, and Ernst Ahl: *Fremdländische Süsswasserfische,* Gustav Wenzel & Sohn, Braunschweig, Germany, 1936. (Out of print.)

Axelrod, Herbert R.: *Aquarium Plants,* T. F. H. Publications, Inc., Jersey City, N.J., 1954.

———: *Diseases of Tropical Fishes,* T. F. H. Publications, Inc., Jersey City, N.J., 1954.

———: *Goldfish as Pets,* T. F. H. Publications, Inc., Jersey City, N.J., 1954.

———: *Marine Fishes as Pets,* T. F. H. Publications, Inc., Jersey City, N.J., 1955.

———: *Tropical Fish as a Hobby,* McGraw-Hill Book Company, Inc., New York, 1952.

———: *Tropical Fish as Pets,* T. F. H. Publications, Inc., Jersey City, N.J., 1953.

———: *Tropical Fish Guide,* T. F. H. Publications, Inc., Jersey City, N.J., 1952.

———, W. Vorderwinkler, and G. J. M. Timmerman: *Color Guide to Tropical Fish,* Sterling, New York, 1955.

Bade, E.: *Das süsswasser Aquarium,* Pfenningstorf, Berlin, 1923.

Baerends, G. P., and J. M. Baerends-van Roon: *An Introduction to the Study of the Ethology of Cichlid Fishes,* E. J. Brill, Leiden, Netherlands, 1950.

Bateman, Gregory C.: *Freshwater Aquaria,* Bazaar Exchange and Mart, London, 1937.

Besnard, W.: *Capture et acclimatation des poissons exotiques,* Payot, Paris, 1938.

Boulenger, E. G.: *Keep an Aquarium,* Ward Lock, London, 1946.

Brünner, G.: *Wasserpflanzen,* Gustav Wenzel & Sohn, Braunschweig, Germany, 1952.

Coates, Christopher W.: *Tropical Fishes as Pets,* rev. ed., Liveright Publishing Corporation, New York, 1950.

Curtis, Brian: *The Life Story of the Fish,* Harcourt, Brace and Company, Inc., New York, 1949.

Deraniyagala, P. E. P.: *A Colored Atlas of Some Vertebrates from Ceylon,* vol. 1, *Fishes,* National Museum of Ceylon, 1952.

Dutta, Reginald: *The Right Way to Keep Pet Fish,* Right Way Books, A. G. Elliot, Kingswood, England, 1951.

Elwin, M. G.: *First Steps in Aquarium Keeping,* Water Life Series No. 1, Poultry World Ltd., London, 1946.

———: *Tropical Fishes,* Water Life Series No. 9, Poultry World Ltd., London, 1947.

Evans, Anthony: *Aquariums,* Dover Publications, New York, 1952.

Farris, Edmond J., and Myron Gordon: *The Care and Breeding of Laboratory Animals,* John Wiley & Sons, Inc., New York, 1950.

Fraser-Brunner, A.: *Aquarium Technique for the Beginner,* Buckley Press, Brentford, England, 1947.

———: *Cussons Book of Tropical Fishes,* Cussons, Manchester, England, 1950.

———: *The Guppy,* Buckley Press, Brentford, England, 1946.

Harman, Ian: *Tropical Aquariums,* Sidgwick & Jackson, Ltd., London, 1949.

Hems, Jack: *Tropical Fish-keeping,* Cage Birds and Aquaria World, London, 1935.

Hervey, G. F., and Jack Hems: *Freshwater Tropical Aquarium Fishes,* Batchworth Press, London, 1952.

Hodge, A. E.: *Tropical Aquarium-fishes,* Witherby, London, 1927.

Hoedeman, J. J.: *De Aquarium aan het Woord,* Uitgeverij De Regenboog, Amsterdam, 1953.

———: *Encyclopaedie voor de Aquariumhouder* (in Dutch), Uitgeverij De Regenboog, Amsterdam, 1954.

———: *Encyclopedia of Water Life* (published in English, 1 vol. only; in Dutch, 4 vols.), Uitgeverij De Regenboog, Amsterdam, 1948–1954.

Holly, Meinken, and Rachow: *Die Aquarienfische in Wort und Bild*, Alfred Kernen Verlag, Stuttgart, Germany, 1932–1954.

Innes, W. T.: *Exotic Aquarium Fishes*, Innes Publications, Philadelphia, 1953.

Knowles, Francis G. W.: *Freshwater and Salt-water Aquaria*, Harrap & Co., Ltd., Toronto, 1953.

Kramer, Kurt, and Hugo Weise: *Aquarienkunde*, Gustav Wenzel & Sohn, Braunschweig, Germany, 1943.

Ladiges, Werner: *Der Fisch in der Landschaft*, Gustav Wenzel & Sohn, Braunschweig, Germany, 1953.

———: *Durch Dschungel und Urwald*, Gustav Wenzel & Sohn, Braunschweig, Germany, 1954.

———: *Tropical Fishes*, Hamburg Aquarium, Hamburg, 1934.

———: *Zierfisch Bilderbuch*, Gustav Wenzel & Sohn, Braunschweig, 1949.

Lederer, Norbert: *Tropical Fish and Their Care*, Alfred A. Knopf, Inc., New York, 1934.

Mann, Lucille Q.: *Tropical Fish*, Sentinel Books, New York, 1944.

Mellen, Ida M., and Robert J. Lanier: *1001 Questions Answered about Your Aquarium*, Harrap, London, 1936.

Morgan, Alfred: *Tropical Fishes and Home Aquaria*, Charles Scribner's Sons, New York, 1947.

Norman, J. R.: *A History of Fishes*, A. A. Wyn, Inc., New York, 1951.

Peters, C. H.: *Life and Love in the Aquarium*, Empire Tropical Fish Import Co., New York, 1934.

Portielje, A. F. J.: *Mijn Aquarium*, Verkade, Zaandam, Netherlands, 1925.

Rachow, Arthur: *Tropical Aquariafisch Catalogue*, Aquarienfisch Import and Export, Wandsbeck, 1927.

Schreitmüller, Wilhelm: *Zierfische Ihre Pflege und Zucht*, Müller, Frankfurt-am-Main, 1931.

Schultz, Leonard P., with Edith Stern: *The Ways of Fishes*, D. Van Nostrand Company, Inc., New York, 1948.

Spinks, R. J.: *Introducing Tropical Fish*, U-needa Products, London, 1948.

Stoye, Frederick H.: *Tropical Fishes for the Home*, Stoye, Sayville, N.Y., 1948.

Thompson, Carl E.: *Tropical Fish Culture for the Beginner*, Thompson, New York, 1932.

Tusche, Hans, and J. Nachstedt: *Züchterkniffe*, Kernen, Stuttgart, 1953.

Watson, F. Austin: *Fishponds and Home Aquariums*, Collingridge, London, 1948.

———: *Tropical Fishkeeping for Beginners*, Bird Fancy and Aquaria News, London, 1933.

Wells, A. Laurence: *Live Foods for Aquarium Fishes*, Water Life Series No. 4, Poultry World Ltd., London, 1948.

———: *Tropical Aquariums, Plants and Fishes*, Warne, London, 1937.

Whitney, Leon F.: *All about Guppies*, Practical Science, Orange, Conn., 1952.

INDEX

All tropical fishes in this book are indexed and cross-indexed by the correct generic, specific, and popular names. Incorrect names, which have become familiar through usage, are also indexed, followed by the correct scientific name in parentheses. Boldface numbers indicate the pages on which the fishes are illustrated and described in detail.